Fishing Forays

Artist: **Roger Desoutter**   *SEPTEMBER EVENING*   Courtesy of: **Rosenstiels'**

Front Cover: Artist: **Robert Turnbull**   *FISHING THE TYNE, WYLAM*   Courtesy of: **The Artist**

Back Cover: Artist: **Robert Turnbull**   *THE TWEED AT COLDSTREAM*   Courtesy of: **The Artist**

KENSINGTON WEST PRODUCTIONS
LONDON
ENGLAND

ACKNOWLEDGEMENTS

Fishing Forays owes its metamorphosis from a good idea into this, our first edition, to a great number of extremely helpful individuals.

Foremost, we would like to thank all those who kindly agreed to their names being published as contacts for fishing throughout the British Isles and Ireland. Some rely on visiting fishermen as a source of income but others kindly gave permission merely to further the enjoyment of others and for this we are very grateful.

The research for Fishing Forays has taken over two years to complete and as a result, we are able to feature over four hundred rivers, lakes, lochs, loughs and llyns. Throughout England and Wales we were generously assisted in our endeavour to provide accurate and up to date information by all manner of 'bodies', particularly the unswerving National Rivers Authority, the regional water boards and water companies. In Scotland, the sporting agencies played a significant role and were extremely forthcoming with their advice, none more so than Lachie Rattray and Simon Cadzow of Finlayson Hughes in Perth. From Ireland, we are indebted to the Central Fishery Board, in particular, Kevin Linnane and Chris Meehan on the Shannon Region; the Irish Tourist Board; Foyle Fisheries Commission; Bann Systems Ltd and the Ministry of Agriculture (N.I.).

Throughout our forays we received invaluable assistance from numerous fishing clubs, sporting agents, estate owners, managers and keepers, tackleists, hoteliers, in particular Anne Voss Bark, and publicans. As you can imagine, we have met some extraordinary people!

A special mention must also be made for Rosemary Coates whose wonderful hand drawn maps and illustrations grace this book. We would also like to thank Robert Turnbull for the cover pictures together with Rosenstiel's and all the other artists and photographers who kindly lent us their work for use as illustrations within Fishing Forays.

KENSINGTON WEST PRODUCTIONS
338, Old York Road, Wandsworth, London SW18 1SS
Tel: 081-877 9394 Fax: 081-870 4270

Editors
David Birley and Tom Lawrence

Consultant Editors
**Janet Blair, Tom Hawthorn, Nova Jayne Heath, Lizzie Lawrence,
David MacLaren, Jason McCreight, Mathew Rowlands, Julian West**

Hotel Editors
Giles Appleton, Sally Conner, Jacqui Hawthorn

Cartography
Rosemary Coates

Typesetting
Wandsworth Typesetting Ltd., 205a St Johns Hill, London SW11

Origination
Trinity Graphics Ltd (Hong Kong)

Printing
Cronion S.A. (Spain)

FOREWORD

Commending a book like this to anglers, and to those who would like to be, is a pleasant duty. Some people think that the weeks of the Director of the Salmon & Trout Association must be pleasantly spent travelling from one stretch of river, teeming with fish, to another, choosing which of the many free-rising trout should have the privilege of being tempted by his fly, or that he is forever up to his waist in a Scottish river attached to a sea-liced salmon, the result of an elegant Spey cast, a deft mend and the controlled tightening of the hook firmly into the scissors of the jaw of this fish. Thus, it is thought, that not only do I have an enviable sinecure but also that I can advise on where to fish, where to stay and give an expert opinion on the quality of each based on personal experience.

Alas, the truth is that the work of the Association means that I am as desk-bound and committee-room bound as any other manager as I liaise with conservation and angling bodies, with Parliamentarians, with opinion formers and deal with the many queries which come from our Branches and members throughout the UK. My fishing is limited to odd days here and there,

thus I am no fount of knowledge. Hence my unqualified welcome to this splendid publication to which I can refer enquiries. If it were only that, 'Fishing Forays' would be a best buy, but it is more. The authors take us on a guided tour of nearly 400 rivers, lochs, reservoirs and lakes. Some of the important conservation issues which they meet on the way are summarised and commented on. We are introduced to fishing hotels and meet the people who run them. We get a flavour of the pleasures to come as we browse, the pictures conjuring up dreams of the tranquility and the spectacular scenery, the prose filling us with hope that the chosen stretch of river will be in good order for our visit.

I hope that readers will obtain the same pleasure and benefit from the book as I have. I hope, too, that they will, on their fishing forays, bear in mind the need for conservation and restraint and subscribe to the dictum that there is more to fishing than catching fish. This principle guided us in the writing and production of the Game Angling Code which is reproduced at the end of this book and which I also commend.

James Ferguson,
Director, Salmon & Trout Association.

 Artist: **W.D. Sadler** *A PEGGED DOWN FISHING MATCH* *Courtesy of:* **Rosenstiels'**

CONTENTS

Artist: **Wendy Reeves**   *FISHERMAN'S PARADISE*   *Courtesy of:* **Rosenstiels'**

CONTENTS

Artist: **John Oldfield**   **McFADGEON'S POOL, RIVER AWE**   *Courtesy of:* **The Artist**

FISHING FORAYS

INTRODUCTION

The sport of game fishing is supported by a plethora of books which describe in detail the attractions and infinite variety of views that surround the art of fishing. They cover tackle, techniques, particular rivers and even memoirs of great fishermen. Few, if any, actually give information on how to arrange a fishing break or indeed how to gain access to the rivers and water systems of Britain. As a result, we wondered whether a guide to the many fishing opportunities available in Britain and Ireland would appeal. We decided to 'test the water' and ask around. The response we received was staggering. The support for such a title was universal and we found a huge gap in the market for the many fishing enthusiasts who not only enjoy a quality book but who also wish to fish new waters.

This wonderful encouragement fired our own belief in the book and as we found yet more opportunities for reasonably priced fishing so our excitement grew. The result of two years work will hopefully give you, the reader, similar satisfaction. In possession of the first edition, you will no doubt have your own observations, comments and criticisms. We would be delighted to hear them so please do write to offer your advice as future editions can only benefit from such contributions.

The book does not pretend to be 'a bible' for the sport of game fishing in Britain and Ireland. What it does seek to do is to provide a range of up to date contacts which will enable you to gain access to the waters. As you can imagine, the fishing ranges dramatically in price, quality and variety. Prices have been included throughout the book to provide readers with a simple yardstick and all prices quoted were accurate at the time of going to print. There is, however, something here to meet everyone's budget whether you wish to fish the Tweed, a remote lough in Southern Ireland or the local lake.

Fishing and access differs enormously from region to region which is one of the more delightful facets of the sport. The differences will become apparent throughout Fishing Forays; whether they are geographical, historical, commercial or legislative. Compare Scotland's hundreds of natural highland lochs with the numerous commercial lakes of England. One created by nature, the other by market forces. You 'pay your money and take your choice' and, in some cases, you will pay a lot of money.

Artist: **John Trickett** **DEDICATION** *Courtesy of:* **Sally Mitchell Fine Arts**

FISHING FORAYS

We have endeavoured to give details for all areas covered in the book but as you would expect we are unable to comment fully on the existing state of some fisheries as rainfall levels vary dramatically from month to month and season to season. Nets are being bought off a number of rivers which will naturally benefit the rod angler but, by the same token, 'drifting' is still with us and consequently, runs of our migratory fish are being badly affected. In some areas, sea-trout fishing has declined badly and in others salmon fishing is clearly improving - we have endeavoured to point the way. As you can imagine, much of your success is in your own hands and, as ever, new waters should be investigated carefully before any excursion is planned. What we can say is that there are numerous good opportunities available with wonderful places to stay nearby.

The N.R.A. is a worthy organisation with some excellent individuals but limited power. They, along with various regional water companies are by and large doing a good job in maintaining and improving waters. Also, it is good to hear of the long overdue change of attitude from the Forestry Commission with regard to their future planting policy.

It is equally satisfying to report the unequivocal welcome for Fishing Forays we have received from hoteliers. Some have their own waters which naturally differ in standard, others have local contacts and some have no fishing at all but are still thoroughly recommended and will delight non-fishing partners or friends! Once again, prices vary but there is something here for everyone. Luxurious manor houses contrast with cosy bed and breakfasts and friendly inns - all have a tremendous individual appeal. Whether you are planning the trip of a life time or a quiet weekend away from it all, we know you will find a number of good establishments from which to choose.

In order to add to the overall quality of the book we have included a number of fishing scenes which will hopefully inspire the spirit for pastures new. We have also included maps to illustrate our selected areas. Naturally road maps are essential, but we hope that they at least shed some light on your expedition. After much consideration we have not included more detailed plans of featured waters, however, it is likely that these will be added in future editions. Indeed it is a sincere hope that following editions will build on the strengths of this our first of the title Fishing Forays. As a premier publication is will be of greater value than its ensuing editions we are grateful to you for purchasing it and we hope it brings you happiness on and off the water.

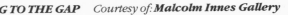

Artist: **G.D. Armour**   *SALMON FISHING – COMING TO THE GAP*   *Courtesy of:* **Malcolm Innes Gallery**

Fishing in the South   (Albury Estate)

THE SALMON & TROUT ASSOCIATION

Patron: H. M. Queen Elizabeth the Queen Mother

President: Lord Home of the Hirsel, KT, PC, DL

Chairman: T.A.F.Barnes, OBE

Director: James Ferguson

Founded in 1903, the Salmon and Trout Association has always been dedicated to the fight to safeguard and improve salmon and trout stocks and fisheries. It serves the interests of game anglers and all those, tackle dealers, hotel keepers and others, whose livelihoods depend on them.

The Association operates through an elected Council and three specialist committees dealing with the specific problems of migratory fish, stillwaters and conservation and water resources. The Association has fifty branches in the United Kingdom which serve as the ears, eyes and voice of the Association in local matters, as well as organising fishing and social events for their members. Every member of the Association is allocated to a branch of their choice.

As the recognised UK body representing the interests of game anglers, the Association keeps in close touch with the various Ministries of Government and with the National Rivers Authority. At Regional level, some seventy Association members sit on Rivers and Fisheries Advisory Committees. We have substantial lobbies in both Houses of Parliament. It is through these means, as well as through the media, that the Association expresses the views of game anglers and protects our sport against other hostile or conflicting interests.

As the threats to game fisheries increase, the need for action by the Association is correspondingly more urgent. Demand for water increases inexorably, especially in areas of high population and relatively low rainfall. The cheapest and easiest way of getting it is to tap the pure headwaters of our streams directly, or by boreholes, and to replace this spring water with treated effluents. This process can destroy rivers, replace natural weed with algae and drive away fish populations forever as it has done on many undefended rivers. The Association monitors proposed abstractions and, in cases of national significance, has participated at public enquiries and thereby helped to save some of our finest rivers from destruction.

The increasing catches of salmon by high seas netting, by coastal, drift and estuarial netting and the use of synthetic fibre monofilament in nets threaten the stocks of migratory fish. The Assocation is actively campaigning for a ban on the use of monfilament nets, the control of netting to ensure adequate spawning escapement and an end to high seas netting enforced by effective policing.

The incidence of illegal netting and poaching in many forms throughout the country is a threat both to fish and fisheries. The Assocation is actively pressing for more effective and punitive legislation against poachers and for proper control of the commercial outlets for salmon and sea trout.

Among the benefits of membership are a free copy of the Assocation's magazine, 'Salmon and Trout', at present published in March and October; social and piscatorial functions organised by branches; advice on fishery problems and junior fly fishing courses. But above all, membership of the Assocation means playing a part in helping to preserve game fish and fishing.

Direct all enquiries to the Association at: Fishmonger's Hall, London Bridge, London. Tel: 071 283 5838

Welsh Waters   (The Griffin Inn)

HIGHLANDS
AND ISLANDS

Artist: John Trickett   FISHING THE LOCH

OUTER HEBRIDES

ISLE OF LEWIS

HARRIS

LEVERBURGH

NORTH UIST

LOCHMADDY

BENBECULA

SOUTH UIST

LOCHBOISDALE

THE MINCH

LITTLE MINCH

DUNVEGAN ISLE OF SKYE PORTREE

INNER SOUND

LOCH TORR

KYLE OF LOCHALSH

KYLE AKIN

KEN -SIG

SOUND OF SLEAT

AIRD OF SLEAT

MALLAIG

L. MORAR

AILPORT

L. SHIEL

TOBERMORY DRIMIN

L. ARIENAS

SOUND OF MULL

LAUNE

SALEN

ISLE OF MULL

BUNESSAN

CAPE
WRATH
DURNESS
DUNNET HEAD
ST JOHN'S
LOCH
JOHN O'GROATS
A838
A838
DONARD
A838
THURSO
A9
L. HEILEN
L. HOPE
A836
MELVICH
L. CALDER
L. WATTEN
BOES
BETTYHILL
CRAGIE
WICK
A838
L. LOYAL
HALLADALE
A882
ARKLE
L. MEADIE
L. DRUIM
A'CHLIABHAIN
FORSINARD
L.
MORE
WICK
L. STACK
A894
L. NAVER
THURSO
A9
L. MEMARLIGG
L. MORE
ALTNAHARRA
L. NAN
CLAR
BADAN
MOCK
AN
RUATHAIR
A9
KYLE OF
STROME
MERKLAND
A836
LYBSTER
L. CHOIRE
L. RIMSDALE
BERRIEDALE
LATHERON
BRAEMORE
A838
L. ASSYNT
A837
L. RIMSDALE
BRORA
HELMSDALE
BERRIEDALE
SIONASCAIG
A838
BLACKWATER
L. BRORA
HELMSDALE
LOCH SHIN
AILSH
DALREAVOCH
BRORA
CASSLEY
OYKEL
A839
LAIRG
FLEET
GOLSPIE
ACHAL
A837
INVER
CARRON
A836
BONAR
BRIDGE
A9
DORNOCH
ULLAPOOL
CARRON
DORNOCH FIRTH
BRAEMORE
A835
L. MORIE
A836
L. VAICH
L. GLASS
LOCH FANNICH
BLACK
WATER
CROMARTY
A832
GARVE
DINGWALL
A832
CROMARTY
A890
L. MEIG
A835
COMON
MOIG
FARRAR
BEAULY
A9
MORAY FIRTH
NAIRN
MONAR
A831
A862
A96
INVERNESS
L. MULLARDOCH
GLASS
BEAULY
A82
NAIRN
A831
A9
L. AFFRIC
L. MEIKLIE
L. DUNTELCHAIG
AFFRIC
L. RUTHVEN
MORISTON
A887
LOCH NESS
A887
OICH
CLUANIE
FORT AUGUSTUS
L. LOYNE
ABINVER
GARRY
GMDOAN
L. GARRY
L. OICH
ROY
L. LOCHY
A82
SPEAN BRIDGE
ROY BRIDGE
FORT WILLIAM
NEVIS
A82

SHETLAND
ISLANDS
A968
A971
LERWICK
A970

ORKNEY
ISLANDS
L. SWANNAY
A966
O'
HARRY
STROMNESS
A964
KIRKWALL
PALO

SCOTLAND

When you are next stuck in one of those ridiculous motorway traffic jams spare some time to reflect on a Scottish fishing trip. As the motorway cones grow nearer and some wretched truck sprays you with dirt and grit, reflect on the highlands where the only traffic problems are likely to be caused by sheep straying carelessly into the road as if to monitor your speed. Unlike motorways which supposedly run in manmade straightened lines the country lines of Scotland are fashioned by nature. This, however, has many advantages for you will be ushered around the mazes of gracious lochs or follow the path of a bubbling stream.

As you finally reach the one lane of motorway that is open consider the single track that you will find in the highlands. Passing spots are regular but there is so little traffic they seem almost superfluous to your journey. Here time is not of the essence, as you inspect the rustic lanes for sheep or deer consider your motorway jam it might as well be a million miles away!

Among Scotland's rivers are some of the 'greats' and for those not lucky enough to fish one of the big name rivers there are plenty of alternatives. A small spate river fished in the right conditions will afford much better sport than a poor beat on a famous river. The fish may not run so big but it's better to catch an eight pounder than return from a big sluggish pool empty handed and, believe you me, their eight pounders will give you a hell of a fight.

Also consider the lochs which come in all sizes from the big, like Loch Shin to the thousands of smaller hill lochs or lochans that can be found only on the largest scale maps. They're there though make not mistake lying behind crags in hidden glens waiting for your casts. Remember your traffic jam once more and reflect that while you were surrounded by an angry throng - you may be the only person for miles in this wonderfully private land.

Many hotels can arrange a days fishing on these lochs, so if conditions on the river are against you there is no need to leave your rod in the tackle room while waiting for a change in the water. These small lochs will often be off the beaten track and require quite a walk but the scenery and surroundings will more than compensate for the effort. The trout are not big but a fish weighing over a pound is often one to remember. They are beautifully marked, wild and make wonderful eating.

The rivers of legend are here to behold, they are not impossible to fish and a holiday here is one to remember. Whether you are fighting a salmon on the Findhorn or a brown trout on an uncharted loch we wish you good cheer and good health. This is a land of fishing lore, let the game commence.

MELVICH HOTEL

The Melvich Hotel is an old fishing hotel dating from Victorian times, pleasantly situated at the mouth of the River Halladale, one of the best salmon fishing rivers in the Northern Highlands and overlooking the Pentland Firth and Orkney Islands. The rivers Thurso, Forss and Naver are nearby. Salmon fishing on all these rivers can be arranged privately - but book well in advance! There are many hill lochs in the area which have good brown trout fishing, some of which belong to the Hotel - fishing to residents is free. There is plenty of sea trout fishing in the river estuaries and sea-angling parties can be arranged. We can also put you in touch with angling instructors, with a knowledge of local conditions, at a moderate price.

The Hotel has 14 bedrooms which are part of a modern extension, all with private facilites, central heating, electric blankets, tea-making facilities and colour television. A laundry and ironing service is also available. From the bedrooms, lounge bar, dining room and large garden there are superb views of the Halladale Estuary over the Pentland Firth, and the Orkneys can be seen on a sunny day. There are always cosy peat fires around which to sit and chat about the latest catch and enjoy our wide range of malt whiskies and wines. Local seafood, salmon and venison are specialities of our Highland cuisine. Other amenities include: golf at Reay Club (18 holes) five miles away - special terms for residents of the hotel. Grouse and rough shooting, deer stalking, bird watching, hill walking and access to some of the most beautiful sandy beaches in Scotland.

AA RAC ** Scottish Tourist Board *** Commended
Les Routiers - Commended
Melvich Hotel
Melvich by Thurso
Sutherland KW14 7YJ
Tel: (06413) 206

HIGHLANDS AND ISLANDS

HALLADALE TO WICK

When you finally arrive in John O'Groats you will invariably have crossed many miles of moorland and, surprisingly, in the latter stage of your journey, cultivated land. Crops have been grown here since Viking times when Northern Scotland was a base for raids on unsuspecting communities elsewhere in the country.

A much bigger contrast is the nuclear power station at Dounreay where space-age technology contrasts oddly with the tranquility of the surrounding moorland. What would those Vikings have made of this peculiar edifice?

Caithness is the most northerly county in Britain and has recently been a centre of controversy between conservationists and commercial tree-planters. The point at issue has been the fate of the Flow country, a vast tract of magnificent moorland stretching from Ben Loyal in Sutherland to the Caithness coast. The Highland Regional Council has designated some areas unsuitable for planting, but even so over 100,000 acres have been lost. This land has been planted with foreign species of conifer and the planting is due in the main to advantageous tax concessions. One cannot help wondering whether any of the investors took the trouble to see this unique habitat which had lain undisturbed for 7000 years before the forestation took place.

Getting to Caithness from northern parts is much easier now that the A9 has been improved and further time can be saved by using the new bridge over Dornoch Firth. Previously one had to journey via Bonar Bridge giving the opportunity to make a small detour to the Shin Falls, a sight which cannot fail to gladden an angler's heart and for those of you with time on your hands this route should still be considered. Travelling on main roads is undoubtedly quicker but turning off at Helmsdale on to the Melvich road will afford a fisherman's treat for the road follows the Helmsdale and after Forsinard you journey into Strath Halladale. Already the office seems a distant memory and the heart pounds, not from pressure of work, but from exhilaration.

The **Halladale** is a comparatively little known river that deserves wider recognition. Ownership of the water has recently changed hands and it is now owned by the Bulmer family of cider fame who are keen fishermen, and run the river through the Halladale Partnership. Although some twenty miles in length, there are no lochs in the system and it is very much a spate river. As a result Halladale rods look for rain and the sport which almost inevitably follows. At Forsinard it is a tumbling stream but for much of its journey it appears sluggish and uninspiring. This, however, is the deceptive face of the river and do not let this put you off, there is fishing of the finest quality to be found. It is a fly-only river and the season runs from January 12th to September 30th with the best time traditionally being from June to September. Weekly rates vary from £132 to £660 plus VAT, day permits are restricted to locals (to discourage poaching!). The river is let through an agent, Mrs J. Atkinson, 8 Sinclair Street, Thurso (0847) 63291. The Forsinard Hotel (0641) 7221 has one of the upper beats and a popular fishing lodge which sleeps fourteen.

As the Halladale flows through peat country it is heavily stained when in spate and virtually unfishable. But rest assured the next day it will fall and begin to clear when such patterns as the Garry Dog and Yellow and Orange may prove successful. The pools are of a size that can be easily covered and favourites include Bridge, Macbeth, Munroe's, Run Out and Ashill. Being generally slow moving and a fly only river it is sometimes necessary to gently handline to give your fly a touch of life. The average size is about 7lb, though fish of 14lb and 15lb are caught; the best fish in the 1990 season being 16lb. Assuming the rain Gods are kind, the numbers can be excellent. Sea-trout may be caught in the estuary but there is not much of a run up into the river.

Apart from the all important hip flask, insect repellent is a must to combat the midges! The Melvich Hotel (06413) 206 is a good place to stay and has delightful views over the river's estuary. The proprietors can arrange salmon fishing for you if given enough advance warning and also provide trout fishing on their three lochs, with arrangements possible on several others.

Many keen fisherman are delighted to pass on learned local opinion and the newcomer to the area should always endeavour to pick the brains of seasoned locals. It might cost a dram or two but it may well be worth it. There's an old racing saying which runs 'never back an Irish tip at Cheltenham'. The reason is simple, if its going to trot up, you'll be the last to be told! Fishing folk have a different attitude and it is often based on the theory that if you have nothing to say it is because you have nothing to tell and if you've nothing to tell you're not worth talking to! 'Forss' is an old Norse word for a waterfall but despite its fairly extensive headwaters and tributaries the only part of the River **Forss** of real interest to the fishermen is a fairly short section flowing out of Loch Shurrery. Favoured flies include the Munro Killer and fish average at around the 8lb mark, the record for the 1990 season was however 22lb. The river is fly-only and it fishes best in the Spring and from July to September. This is a time share river but it is sometimes possible to get on it through Salar Management Services Ltd (0667) 55355. The cost varies between £200 and £350 per week and £20 to £50 a day depending on the time of season. If you do get a day's fishing, Falls Pool is likely to be the most productive even in low water. The locals assure me of this!

The **Thurso** is probably the most renowned river in the area. It used to be regarded as one of the best Spring rivers producing bright silver ingots of fresh run fish. However, in common with many other rivers including the mighty Spey, spring runs are nothing like they used to be and the best sport is often autumnal. Although netting still takes place, the nets and estuary are owned by Thurso Fisheries. The boats are manned by ghillies with the result that the rod fisherman's sport is borne very much in mind. The dam and sluice gates at Loch More, allow reasonable water levels to further the fisherman's enjoyment.

Although there may be salmon in the Thurso in January and February the season doesn't really get under way until March when surprisingly it is the upper beats near Loch More that can prove most productive. At this time of the year two inch tubes in patterns such as the Munro Killer or Yellow and Black can prove effective or you may care to try a long winged fly such as the Tadpole or Collie Dog. June can be a difficult month on the river if the weather is hot, but you can always try your luck on Loch More which fishes surprisingly well in such conditions. Late July, August and September are the best time - if there is rain! - and old favourites like the Stoats Tail, Hairy Mary and Garry can all work well.

In all its twenty-five mile journey from Loch More to the sea the river only falls some 300 feet, with the consequent result that there are quite a few slow moving pools. In such conditions it is worth trying 'backing-up'. The technique of this is to start at the bottom of a pool, rather than the top, and cast a long line straight out. Allow a few seconds for the fly to sink to the required depth then draw in a few yards of line to set the fly on its way. Then take a few paces upstream which will keep the fly on the move and work your way up the pool in a similar fashion. I know this sounds illogical and is against all tradition, but it works. The locals promised it would and it did!

The whole river is owned by Thurso Fisheries Ltd which belongs to Lord Thurso and prices vary between £365 and £678 a week and £27 to £61 a day according to the time of the season. Bookings are taken through the company secretary's office (0847) 63134. The fish average about 9lb but there is a chance of a 20lb fish. It is a lovely river to fish and divided into 14 rotating beats. As the whole river is under the control of one riparian owner, it is probably the only river in the British Isles where you can fish its entirety within a fortnight! Rods move

downstream two beats a day until the prolific Beat 2 (below is Beat 1 - the town beat). The Ulbster Arms (0847) 83206 is the place to stay here. This comfortable, well appointed hotel can also offer excellent trout fishing. It has ten hill lochs (seven with boats) and can also arrange fishing on Lochs Watten, St John's and Calder. It is particularly suitable for a family holiday not only because of the scenery and solitude but also because their lochs have difficult fishing for the experienced rod and easier water for novices and children.

To the east is the River **Wick** where fishing is managed by the Wick Angling Association. This river offers very affordable salmon fishing at either £25 a week or £8 a day. Permits can be obtained from the Hugo Ross tackle shop in Wick (0955) 4200 which can also offer boat fishing on Loch Watten and Loch Hempriggs if required. The average catch on the river is 250 - 300 salmon a season with the average being 9lb, though a fish of over 22lb was caught in 1979. It is a spate river and somewhat sluggish in character; some nine miles long, it can all but disappear in times of drought.

There is little sea-trout fishing in the rivers we have discussed but a few miles north of Wick there is the classic water of the **Wester** System (a loch and river). The river is only half a mile long so sea-trout have easy access to the loch and can provide

ULBSTER ARMS HOTEL

Anglers are beginning to re-discover the delights of brown trout fishing on the remote hill lochs of the northern Highlands. Apart from the natural beauty of their setting and the peace which surrounds them, they provide both fish and fishing of a quality far higher than many people today realise. Examples of the best of them are the hill lochs managed by Thurso Fisheries Limited for the Ulbster Arms Hotel, which has boats on these lochs and can arrange permits for others in the area.

The Hotel is the centre for fishing the River Thurso, one of Scotland's finest fly only salmon rivers, having both a Spring and Autumn run.

As well as fishing, many other outdoor pursuits can be undertaken using the hotel as a base; Birdwatching, Photography, Rambling, Painting and Geology, to name but a few, can all provide the visitor with the relaxation or stimulus that is desired.

The Hotel also arranges shooting and stalking over a wide variety of moors.

Caithness is renowned for its resident and visiting sea birds and waders, and fully equipped boats can be chartered for Sea Angling and Rock Pigeon Shooting in the Pentland Firth. There are also many sites of archaeological interest in the area and exploring the castles, cairns, standing stones and old buildings can fill fascinating hours.

Ulbster Arms Hotel
Halkirk
Caithness KW12 6XY
Tel: (084783) 206

tremendous sport in the autumn. As we know these wonderfully shy, hard fighting fish give a very good account of themselves, especially here where the average is 1lb 8oz and most seasons produce a memorable fish of over 5lb. One chap in 1991 had eleven sea-trout to his name at the end of the day, all over 1¼ lb, helped perhaps due to the salmon and sea-trout restocking programme. Daily permits are available from Auchorn Farm, Lyth (0955) 83208 for £5 per day in 1991 (boats available).

Caithness is also famous for its lochs and the genuinely wild brown trout they produce. The angler who is accustomed to fishing the stillwater stocked lakes in the south where anglers moan if the stocking size is under one and a half pounds and fish of 5-10 lb are not regularly caught, may wonder why people rave about loch fishing for wild brownies when a fish of one pound is often considered a good fish. All I would say is, try it and you will be converted! These trout come greedily to the fly and having taken it, set off at a furious pace giving the fisherman a memorable tussle.

Loch Watten is one of the finest brown trout fisheries in the whole of Scotland. £7 buys you a day ticket with a boat and there is no bag limit. The fish average 1lb but run to over 2lb. It is some 3 miles long by up to three quarters of a mile wide and can often be windy, so an outboard motor is essential unless you are either a fitness freak or a rowing blue. The fish are of excellent quality, a challenge to catch and a delight to hook. Both boat and bank permits are available from D. Gunn, Esq. (0955) 82217. The best fishing is in May, June and September.

Another renowned Caithness Loch is **Loch St John's** near Dunnet Head. Much work has recently been done to improve the quality of fishing on this loch. A day here with a boat will cost £5 and there are significant mayfly and cranefly hatches. Please contact the Northern Sands Hotel (0847) 85270 if you require more details. The **Dunnet Head Lochs** are the most northerly lochs in Britain. In fact Dunnet Head is the most northerly point of Britain and not John O'Groats as popularly thought, just look at a map. You can win many a pint at a bar armed with this little known fact! They are stocked on a regular basis and the fish average around the 2lb mark. These lochs are also a delight for the naturalist for there are several pairs of red throated divers and fishermen are expressly asked not to disturb them. Permits are available from The Dunnet Head Tearoom between 12.00 noon and 9.00pm (0847) 85774, packed lunches (including vegetarian) are also available. The most fickle loch in the area is **Loch Heilen.** On these 170 acres of windswept shallow water one may never see a fish all day but of course they are there and run up to 8lb and anything less than 2lb should be returned. It is the type of water that can either reduce one to tears or provide a real red letter day. Please contact H. Pottinger, Esq. (0847) 82210 for further details. **Loch Calder** is unusual for two reasons, firstly, it is the only loch in the area which is fishable on a Sunday and, secondly, because it is the only Caithness loch not restricted to fly-only. However, one or two of the riparian owners are looking to make changes so check with Harpers Fly Fishing Services (0847) 63179 before arriving with spinners on a Sunday! Other lochs in the area worth noting are Stemster, Airig, Lethaigd, Garbh, Caol and Ruathair and of course there are the hundreds of hill lochs which can often provide a memorable day.

FISHING FAYRE

The Highlands of Scotland are some of the most remote and delightfully unspoilt regions of Britain. The accommodation to be found is generally fairly matter of fact but the fishing is outstanding. The Melvich Hotel (06413) 206 is a comfortable country hotel which is situated at the mouth of the river Halladale. It enjoys magnificent sea views over the Pentland Firth to the Orkneys and makes a good centre for all manner of country pursuits notably salmon and trout fishing. The Melvich also boasts a range of over 100 malt whiskies and some splendid Highland cooking.

The Forsinard (0641) 7221 is another great favourite for those fishing the Halladale. The lodge here is particularly good for parties. The hotel's loch fishing is really first class and the variety of waters that the visitor has available adds even greater appeal. The hotel is set up as a sporting establishment and in that, it succeeds bountifully. It is also a friendly, hospitable place to pass away the time before your next foray on waters new.

Halkirk is home to the Ulbster Arms (0847) 83206 a celebrated sporting hotel with particularly high standards. Good food and abundant friendliness makes this a great fishing favourite. The hotel itself stands on the banks of the Thurso which will captivate the hearts of all fine fisherman. Imagine yourself - glass in hand, the memories of the day sift through your mind and the promise of more fine fishing tomorrow - marvellous!

Loch Watten, a superb fishing loch is extremely convenient for the Mount Pleasant House (0955) 82372. There are numerous other lochs in the area and this small modern hotel is a good base from which to fish them. The hotel is also convenient for Wick airport which is a useful communication point for those fisherman who are seeking to reduce the journey time, which is a long one by car.

This is wild and excellent fishing indeed, make no mistake, though the welcome at these hotels will be genuine and while many faces return year on year, new faces add to the character as much as old ones.

There are many delights to be found in Scotland and not all of them are found in the fast flowing waters of its rivers or the more quiet lochs or hillocks that grace the countryside. Mind you, many of them are fairly near by. Scotland's hotels are often close to water and many of them are riparian owners or have access to lochs or rivers that run nearby. Failing this, the hotelier, as a community figure, will often know someone who knows someone else, or will be able to help! Those hotels that do not have their own water often enjoy spectacular settings or boast first class facilities or restaurants. Fishing hotels may sometimes be more modestly equipped but as long as the beds are comfy and the bar full, many of us will be more than happy. There are a growing number of self catering lodges to be found in Scotland and many fishermen will have been travelling to more established dwellings for years! They will not need advice on their own patch but will hopefully find other points of interest to enjoy while journeying or as a diversion to try a new water. There will be hotels that are modestly priced, there will be some that are somewhat expensive but all should serve you well on your excursions through Scotland.

FORSINARD HOTEL

Salmon Fishing....

The Hotel has two salmon rivers for guests to fish, the River Halladale and the River Strathy. The Halladale rises on the north slopes of the Helmsdale watershed and empties into the sea at Melvich bay, with good salmon fishing from mid April to September.

The hotel beat starts at Forsinain Bridge and flows north for 2 1\2 miles to the junction with the river dyke. There are nine named pools. Best catch 6 Salmon and 1 Seatrout on a July spate.

The river Strathy rises on the Creag Anh-Lolaire Hills and flows north to Strathy Bay, this is a spate river and can give good summer sport. All Salmon fishing is by Fly only.

Trout Lochs....

The Hotel has 5 lochs exclusively for guests and 24 lochs open to non hotel guests, Loch Sletill is quoted as one of the best lochs in the north of Scotland. It lies to the east of the Hotel, 4 miles off the A897 road. There is a 3 mile drive on forestry roads and a 10 minute walk. Sletill is remote, beautiful and full of excellent trout. The average weight of 12oz and catches of 12 trout are common and fish of over 2lb are produced each season. All fishing is by boat and bank.

Loch Garbh, Loch Talaheel, Loch Leir, Loch Caise, The Cross Lochs, and Slethill are reserved for Hotel guests only.

Best Flies

Ke-He Black Pennell, Soldier Palmer, Worm fly, Greenwells, and Dapping Flys.

Loch An-Ruathair - This Loch is on the Achentoul Estate, and lies on the side of the A897 road 4 miles from the Hotel. Day permits are available to non guests. Worms and spinners can be used on Loch An-Rauthair ONLY. There is a fishing tackle and gift shop in the Hotel.

Forsinard Hotel
Forsinard
Sutherland KW13 6YT
Tel: (06417) 221 Fax: (06417) 259

HIGHLANDS AND ISLANDS

THE NAVER TO CAPE WRATH

Our ancestors knew a thing or two when it came to place names. Some were titled in optimistic anticipation like the Cape of Good Hope while others were functional descriptions. Visiting Cape Wrath it is easy to understand how it got its name. For the sea appears to be in a perpetual state of torment with each crashing breaker succeeded by another of equal ferocity.

Living off the land has never been easy in the Highlands, and a crofter's life is notoriously a tough one. But living is certainly easier than it used to be; if you fish Loch Naver think of the 2000 crofters who were evicted and exiled overseas by the Duchess of Sutherland in the 19th century to make way for sheep farming. However, the Scots are a canny race and somewhat levelled the score by erecting the statue of her husband so that he overlooked the sea rather than his estates. The Duchess was allegedly distraught on hearing the explanation that he now watched all his workers at sea. It was explained to the distraught Duchess that this was because he had sent so many of his tenants to sea. The countryside is still sparsely populated and roads are few and far between as a result. It is an area of great natural beauty and of course there is fishing - some of the finest in the kingdom!

The Naver is probably the best salmon stream in the far north, and it is privately owned by 4 estates making up the River Naver District Salmon Fishery Board. Only as a guest of one of the owners can one cast a fly on this fine water. Those lucky enough to do so will find the six beats have 50 named pools divided between them. However, all is far from lost as the Bettyhill Angling Club has the right to fish for salmon and sea trout for a mile or so above Naver bridge. There are three mainpools and three permits a day are available at a cost of £7 from Victor Stevens (0641) 6200, the River Manager. Below the bridge the fishing is free. June to August is a good time for the grilse run.

Journey west of the Naver and you will soon reach the River **Borgie**. This beautiful and well managed river covers some seven miles in its journey from Loch Slaim to the sea. They have their own hatchery and each year the river is stocked with salmon fry which augurs well for future anglers. Like so many in the area it is essentially a spate river, but the sluice gates at the loch help to maintain reasonable water levels. Four beats with two rods per beat are available from Mather Jamie (0509) 233433 at a cost of between £200 and £400 per rod a week. There is also one and a half miles of permit water on which tickets are obtainable from David Crichton (0641) 2231, the water bailiff. Good management has much improved the fishing over the past few years and the salmon are in great condition in May when Waddingtons are particularly effective. For the grilse run in June and August it is onto doubles and in September it's the faithful Waddingtons again.

Travelling further west we come to Strath Dionard and Cape Wrath, or the Parth as it is known locally. A quick glance at the road atlas will show you why this area is so special. The A838 is the only road in the area, you are alone! Those prepared to explore the remote hill lochs will be particularly well rewarded, for you will return with a heavy basket of breakfast sized trout and your fishing may well have been accompanied by the piping of greenshanks. This is an area for the true fisherman but ghillies are available to help the newcomer.

A distance of twelve miles separates the **Dionard** from its source in the loch of the same name, to the sea at the Kyle of Durness. Fishing on the lower water is held jointly by E.G. Fishings (0387) 54424 and The Cape Wrath Hotel (0971) 81274 while the fishing above Rhigolter Bridge is owned by the Gaulin Estate (0971) 82282. E.G. Fishings allow 4 rods on their water and a week will cost £265. Cape Wrath Hotel has 5 beats with 2 rods per beat at £300 a week. Gaulin Estate can offer 5 beats and fishing on the loch on a rotation basis at a cost of £60 a day for 2 rods.

Recent years have seen several improvements including a stocking programme. Like many rivers, fishing on the Dionard has been variable with 280 fish caught in 1989 and 80 in 1990, though seven fish have been caught in a day. The average weight is around 7lb, however each season produces a fair amount of heavier fish with the odd one over 20lb. Falls Pool is probably the best and also one of the prettiest pools in the north.

If conditions on the river are against you, do try the limestone lochs at **Durness**. These waters are famous for their land locked sea-trout. The fish feed off freshwater shrimp and are pink-fleshed and make superb eating. They can also be extremely big! **Loch Larlish** which is the smallest produced a whopper of fourteen and a half pounds in 1990. Local opinion is divided on whether the fish are brownies or sea-trout but if you are lucky enough to catch a fish like that, does terminology matter! **Loch Borralie** which is the deepest also holds Arctic char. The fish in these lochs average just under 3lb and anything under 1lb should be returned. It is important to remember that being limestone the waters are crystal clear and so casting errors must be avoided. The Cape Wrath Hotel will be able to assist you in fishing these lochs

The other river of note in this area is the Laxford but as this is the private property of the Duke of Westminster, let us explore the lochs.

Loch Hope is probably the best sea-trout fishery in the far north. It lies close to the Borgie and its six miles are divided into five beats. The Altnaharra Hotel (0549) 81222, a renowned fishing hotel, is the place to stay here; it can also offer fishing on eight other lochs and the River Mudale. Permits for this loch also available from I. MacDonald at the Keepers House (0847) 56272.

Outboard motors are not allowed on Loch Hope which has a reputation for being windy so it is advisable to have a ghillie, both for his expert advice and to avoid having aching shoulders at the end of the day! The sea-trout run to 7lb and there are some huge brownies with one of 7lb 13oz being recorded recently. Dapping is a favourite and very successful method on this loch. Some people frown at dapping, but it is not as easy as it may appear especially if the wind is up.

For the uninitiated 'Dapping' is a method which entails eliciting the help of the wind to blow your fly around. For this method you will require a floss-silk dapping line. Experts have it that the more blustery and dull the day, the more the fish are likely to take. If they spot the fly above them they will race towards it and come leaping out of the water often to three or more feet and will perhaps take it while the fly floats in the air or when it touches the surface. To see the fish rocketing from the depths is a memorable sight wich will cheer many a fireside memory. One further point, if having tempted your prey you lift the dap at the last moment there's a good chance he may take the traditional wet flies being used by your fellow rod.

In 1874 Francis Francis wrote 'The Laxford is by no means a large or heavy river and Loch Stack is quite a small sheet of water compared with many of its neighbours and the stream is a short one, but the crowds of sea-trout and salmon that constantly swarm up it are prodigious'. Fishing is not what it was, but that applies to every water and **Loch Stack** is the best in the area. As recently as the 1970's two rods accounted for 50lb of fish in a day. It is well stocked every year and the best fish last year was a six pounder. Five boats are available and there is no bag limit though fish under 1 lb should be returned. Most fish are taken close to the shore for the loch has many bays and corners where the fish lie. You might care to try Wilsons Bay, North Bay or the bays where the feeder streams enter. July and August are the best times for sea-trout and because of the fame of this loch advance booking is a must. The cost for 2 rods including a boat at this time of year is £38 falling to £30 in September.

Just the other side of Ben Screavie is the more modest water of **Loch More.** Here a boat for 2 rods will cost you £25 if you fish at the Kinloch end or £15 for the Smiddy end. Like Stack this is a fly only water and is stocked every year. Similarly there is no bag limit and fish under 1lb should be returned. Sea-trout average one and three quarter pounds amd salmon are due back in around 3 years time. August is the best time for sea-trout.

Both Loch Stack and More are owned by Reay Forest Estates (0971) 8422 and permits are available from them or the Scourie Hotel (0971) 2396. This comfortable and well appointed hotel was originally built as a coaching inn by the second Duke of Sutherland. Guests can enjoy fishing in the many hill lochs, 250 of which abound in the hotel's 25,000 acres. The hotel can also offer salmon and sea-trout fishing on waters such as the Lower and Upper Duart and Badna Bay. Perhaps travellers of the turf may be interested to note that here you can see the peaks of the original Foinaven and Arkle! The legendary chaser was owned by the Duchess of Westminster. As you look around you do remember that Arkle as a racehorse was never bettered nor will be. The name and the place are singularly appropriate.

Another good water in the area is **Loch Loyal**, managed by Tongue & District A.C. This loch is famous for its wild brownies and there are also sea-trout and some salmon to be found. This is a fly only and no bag limit water but fish under 9 inches should be returned. The season runs from mid-March to the end of October. The cost is £3 a day or £12 a week and boats with outboard motors are available at £10 a day. Permits are available from the Ben Loyal Hotel at Tongue (084755) 216 which also has fishing on 14 hill lochs and the Kyle of Tongue where a sea-trout of 4lb 14oz was caught in 1991.

Sutherland has been described as 'the half pound county' for the lochs and lochans abound with fish of this size. While it is only natural to want to catch a good fish these trout offer memorable tussles especially if you use very light tackle. Other lochs especially worth trying in the area include Meadie, Mor, Caol and Modsarie.

FISHING FAYRE

There are many explanations for people becoming hooked on fishing but there are few so compelling that bring out the optimism in man. Every cast is full of hope and even bad days are soon forgotten. Whether you have had a fishless week for salmon or you are 'gone with the wind' dapping for trout you should always remember that 'tomorrow is another day!'

The Altnaharra Hotel (054981) 222 is a renowned fishing venue which has recently seen some excellent improvements in its facilities, done without jeopardizing the charm of this former coaching inn. There are numerous outdoor pursuits that can be arranged from the hotel but the memorabilia on the walls leave the fisherman in little doubt that this is a real home from home. The whole atmosphere is one of peace, tranquility and the great outdoors. Two annexed cottages are well equipped for slightly larger groups or families and add to the twenty or so comfortable bedrooms.

There are numerous opportunities for enjoying some of the wildest and most beautiful landscapes in Britain and should you be venturing to the rugged delights of Cape Wrath then we suggest you visit Kinlochbervie en route. Here the Kinlochbervie Hotel (0971) 82275 is a companionably remote place at which to take stock. The hotel stands on an isolated hillside overlooking the sea and the bustling lounge bar is an excellent place to consider plans for the rest of your trip. The hotel does not proclaim to be a fishing hotel but it is worth a visit just the same, not least for its excellent restaurant where the smoked salmon from the hotel smokery is an absolute must. Lobster and game are also excellent and if you fancy a break from the fishing this is certainly one for the shortlist.

Even further north we come upon Cape Wrath - a wild, remote but captivating part of Britain. Here the Cape Wrath Hotel (097181) 274 offers some super fishing and provides a splendid welcome to all fishermen and many others beside. It is easy to understand how so many people in high pressure business love to fish. The reasons are simple. Firstly, fishing like golf is a great leveller, you might be able to buy the water but that does not guarantee you the fish. Secondly, fishing provides a thorough and undivided escape, a visit to the welcoming Cape Wrath Hotel will allow thorough relaxation far removed from the seemingly nonsensical pace of the 20th century.

Somewhat further round this marvellous coast we arrive at Tongue. Here the Ben Loyal (084755) 216 is a small but extremely friendly hotel. Good value lunches can be found here and some thirteen bedrooms are similarly kind to the pocket, the fishing that the hotel is able to arrange is of course a welcome bonus. There is superb Loch fishing in this area and this is accompanied with all the delights that such wild and unspoilt scenery bring with it. The weather, however, is sometimes cruel and as you trek wearily via Loch Loyal, Loch More and Loch Stack some warm respite is most definitely in order. Fear not, for Scourie has two obvious options in which to escape the storms. The Scourie Hotel (0971) 2396 is our first consideration. Some 25,000 acres of land are at the disposal of guests and this includes some splendid game fishing. The hotel itself is a welcome, unpretentious establishment with cosy bars, tartan carpets and comfortable bedrooms - the ideal place to stay when fishing in the region, a splendid bar is perhaps worth noting! Eddrachilles Hotel (0971) 2080, an 11th century house set in its own 300 acre estate is also one for the notebook. It enjoys wonderous views across Badcall Bay and its islands and is also a paradise for naturalists as opposed to naturists! Seals and dolphins and a multitude of birds are a delight to behold. The bedrooms are fairly small but cosy enough and the restaurant is good, the views, however, are breathtaking and are really worth a trip, fishing or nae!

This is a marvellous place to enjoy the very best of Britain's landscape, yes, it's remote but that's half its charm. The other half is its wildlife and fishing. Fishing records which run back over a century can be seen at Altnaharra and this sets the scene for the unspoilt fascination of the area. It is without question a paradise for the fisherman and the hoteliers know this. As a result they are thoroughly looked after and a visit is to be highly recommended for those who have not yet discovered its beauties.

CAPE WRATH HOTEL

Situated in one of the last truly unspoiled counties of Scotland, the Cape Wrath Hotel stands on a peninsula of the beautiful Kyle of Durness. You will marvel at the sheer beauty of the scenery surrounding the hotel, heather clad moorland alive with wild life, picturesque lochs and rivers teeming with fish, and the rugged grandeur of the mountains rising from the glens originally gouged out by the ice-age and little changed since.

The Cape Wrath hotel offers full facilities to all guests, including two well stocked bars, and two comfortable lounges.

The hotel prides itself on the high standard of cuisine in the fine restaurant. There is also a better than average cellar from which to choose the most appropriate wines to complement the delicious food.

For the game fisherman this region is a dream come true. Salmon fishing is available on three rivers, the Grudie, the Dall and a two mile stretch on one of Scotland's finest Salmon rivers, the Dionard. Last year an average of 50 Salmon per month, weighing between 8 and 10 lbs, were caught and landed on these rivers.

Brown trout renowned for their size and fighting characteristics are found in any of the four well stocked limestone Lochs, just fifteen minute walk from the hotel. The record brown trout caught some years ago weighed in at an amazing 14.5 lbs, this may be difficult to beat, but trout weighing 4/5 lbs are regularly caught on these waters and some 30 other Lochs on the estate. Sea Trout fishing is also available on the Kyle of Durness.

Throughout the year 'Walk up' shooting is available to hotel guests over some 40,000 acres of mountains and moorland, the natural habitat of Highland game including the famous Red Grouse.

For those interested in antiquities and archaeology there are many fine examples of ancient civilisations and early churches to explore locally. Whilst for those tired of hunting, shooting, fishing and walking, miles of sandy beaches, nestling between out crops of harsh unyielding rocks, provide a restful haven.

Cape Wrath Hotel
Durness
Sutherland IV27 4SW
Tel: (097181) 274

HIGHLANDS AND ISLANDS

HELMSDALE COUNTRY

The **Helmsdale** is one of the most famous salmon rivers in Scotland. It is easy to see why for it produces the best fishing in Sutherland and, for that matter, the whole of the north of Scotland. As if that wasn't enough, it is hard to imagine a more idyllic setting than the Strath of Kildonan. Although we all know of its reputation, facts are more difficult to ascertain. This is primarily due to the secrecy of those who fish this river and it has been said that you 'might' get on it if you were related to God! So what's all the fuss about? Although catch figures are seldom reported, a few years ago Beat 4 produced 31 fish in a day with a best week of 94 and a season's total of 599.

The river is owned by six estates which jointly make up the Helmsdale River Board. It is divided into 12 beats, the dividing point being the Kildonan falls. The beats rotate on a daily basis and there are two rods per beat. The season is from January 11th to September 30th but fish are unlikely to ascend the falls until the water rises to an acceptable level which is usually around the end of March. However, the quality of the Helmsdale is outstanding and there is a good chance of landing a salmon on the opening day. At the start of the season the pools may be frozen over and you and your ghillie may have to break the ice to clear a pool and this may well stir up the fish which may take a big tube fly such as a Willie Gunn, Garry Dog or Black and Yellow on a sinking line.

April and May are traditionally the best months and a Stoat's Tail may prove effective during this period. The grilse run is from June to August. A popular technique for fishing the broken headstreams of pools in low water conditions is dibbling. This is fishing with a dropper which should be longer than normal - say about 7 inches and tied about six feet above the point fly. The dropper dibbles across the surface cutting a wake in its path. Favoured flies for dibbling are such patterns as the Garry, Shrimp Fly and Elver Fly.

Those lucky enough to fish this first class river will always want to return, but because it is so good it is very, very difficult to get on. However, do not despair for the Garvault Hotel (0431) 3224 can sometimes get you a rod on one of the private beats and the Roxton Sporting Agency Ltd. in Hungerford lets beats (0488) 683222. Much more generally accessible is the 'Association Water' which comprises the lower mile of the Helmsdale. In 1991 prices ranged from £58.75 to £70.50 a week and £10.58 to £14.10 a day according to the time of year. Day tickets are for twenty-four hours so you can fish all night for sea-trout, these can be obtained from A. Sangster, Esq. (0431) 2343. It is worth mentioning that in the summer time there is almost constant daylight while in the winter months the evenings come very early.

Travelling north from Helmsdale we come to the and the **Berriedale Water** and the Langwell, though the latter only produces a handful of fish per season. The Berriedale, owned by the Langwell Estate, however, produces over 50 fish a year with an average weight of around the 8lb mark. This wild natural river is divided into 3 beats which rotate on a daily basis and whose two rods can fish 40 named pools. Access to some parts, particularly the middle beat, can be awkward, so elderly gentlemen should go carefully. In fact there is a somewhat gruelling story that tells of a spritely octagenarian breaking a somewhat spindley leg whilst endeavouring to fish the water. He

was not rescued for 24 hours but the resourceful chap managed to land a 6lb fish shortly before dawn and his subsequent rescue. There may be an element of exaggeration here but do beware at all times! The cost is £100 per rod a week and permits are available from the estate office (0593) 5237. A good place to stay is the Navidale House Hotel (0431) 2258 in Helmsdale which can also arrange trout fishing on at least five lochs.

South of the Helmsdale lies the **Brora**. This fine river has good early runs and February, which is when the season starts, can produce upwards of a hundred fish. The river is of two parts, the Upper and the Lower which are divided by Loch Brora. The Blackwater which joins the Upper Brora at Balnacoil can also provide good sport and the average over the last five years is 32 salmon. As a spring river the best time is February to May, though providing there is enough rain to provide reasonable water levels, salmon and grilse fishing in June and July can be first class. It is also fine sea-trout water.

Conservation is a topic which is often discussed at length, but alas all too little is actually done as a result of the hot air. How refreshing it is therefore to find a river whose management are proving that actions speak louder than words. As a result the fishing is improving which will surely be to the benefit of all. The season on the Blackwater closes early, on September 1st, to allow the fish a chance to get to the upper reaches for spawning. On the Brora all sea-trout caught before May should be returned and no hen fish may be killed on any beat after September 15th. On most waters spring fishing calls for fishing deep with a sinking line but on the Brora the fish will often take a big fly such as a Collie Dog or Tadpole fished close to the surface on a floating line. This defies tradition and convention but it can work extremely well; however, the traditional methods should also prove effective. If you are after sea-trout on Loch Brora you will find that Kenny's Killer more than justifies its name. A team of wet flies of such tried and trusted favourites as Black Pennell, Dunkeld and Peter Ross will stand you in good stead.

The Brora is certainly accessible to visitors and anyone booking well in advance should be able to get on this water. Ownership of the river is held by Sutherland Estates (0408) 633268, Gordon Bush Estates and Cadogan Estates. Gordon Bush Estates let the Upper Brora through the Roxton Sporting Agency (0488) 683222. They also let Balnacoil Lodge which sleeps 12 and overlooks the river. Cadogan Estates bought the north bank of the Lower Brora in 1990 and their letting is handled by Finlayson Hughes of Perth (0738) 30926. Sutherland Estates (which includes the Blackwater) let their fishing with their three sporting lodges which can take parties up to 14. Prices range from about £550 to around £800 for four rods for six days and beats alternate with the Cadogan Estate water to provide variety. Sutherland Estates can also arrange stalking and grouse shooting so there is always a chance of a McNab! Day tickets on the tidal water are available from Rob Wilson's tackle shop (0408) 21373.

The **Fleet** runs close by but is overshadowed by its famous neighbour. The nine miles of this lesser known river which flows into the tidal waters of Loch Fleet can fish well depending on the water levels. However, if the river is low and good water is hard to find, good fishing can be had in the loch. This is also good sea-trout water and small flies of traditional patterns such as the Dunkeld and Zulu are effective. The river is

privately owned, but fishing can occasionally be obtained through Bell Ingram in Bonar Bridge (0863) 2683. Rogart Angling Club also have a long term agreement with the Morvich Estate to fish for two days a week on a small section of the Lower Fleet which includes Polsons Pool and Davoch Beat. From May to October every day is split into three sessions which cost £10 each. Permits are obtainable from the Post Office Stores at Rogart (0408) 4200.

Lochs in the area include **Badanloch**, **Rimsdale** and **Nan Clar** to name but three. The Garvault Hotel near Kinbrace (0431) 3224 which is on the road from Helmsdale to Melvich has fishing on ten lochs and can arrange fishing on over twenty others. The best fish from the hotel's lochs was an eight and a half pounder two years ago and last year produced a five pounder. A short distance away at Forsinard one finds the Forsinard Hotel (0641) 7221 which has exclusive fishing on 6 lochs and can arrange fishing on a further 14. These lochs are full of wild brownies which average three quarters of a pound and anything over 2lb is a good fish. Because they are little known and off the beaten track these lochs offer tremendous sport as well as solitude. Now that there are so many trout waters in the south few people go to Scotland for a trout fishing holiday. However, when was the last time - if ever! - you caught over 60 fish in a day? As Tony Henderson of the Gervault Hotel will tell you, it is perfectly possible on the lochs in this beautiful and unspoilt area.

FISHING FAYRE

Another desirable area of unspoilt moorland, mountain and shoreline. All manner of rivers thread their way through this remote area and the fishing needless to say is wild and wonderful. It is also fairly tricky to get on the regions principal water, the Helmsdale. However, there are possibilities and there are also numerous hill lochs which produce some excellent game fishing with brown trout fighting as if they were three times their size. After all, this you will no doubt seek the comfort of a relaxing chair, a pleasant bar and accommodation. I hope the following ideas are of interest.

In Helmsdale itself we find a former shooting lodge which is set amidst woodlands and splendid gardens, the Navidale House (04312) 258. The hotel is not a renowned fishing hotel but its open fires, tremendous view over the Moray Firth and pleasant bedrooms make it a good base from which to explore the numerous lochs in the area. The hotel is delighted to help you arrange any such fishing jaunts.

The Garvault Hotel (0431) 3224 is wonderfully placed to organise magnificent loch fishing and the hotel also boasts an idyllic setting which should appeal to the nomadic angler. The Forsinard Hotel (0641) 7221 is another hotel which champions the cause of the fisherman and the hotel is a wonderful place from which to enjoy loch fishing. A number of the sporting agencies have lodges for rental for parties but the Forsinard is a splendid alternative. The bedrooms and bar are both comfortable which is just as well as many fishermen may only seek the solace of these chambers. This is a completely unspoilt hotel and if you are seeking good value and good hospitality you won't go far wrong here.

A quick word now for the visting angler who may well have the old golf bag in the boot of the car - wise move. Brora, Golspie and the celebrated Dornoch links make a handsome trio. A fine hotel to stay in Golspie is the Sutherland Arms (040863) 3234, while in Brora The Royal Marine (0408) 21252 and The Links (0408) 21225 are well worth a visit, the former boasts particularly wide ranging leisure facilities. In Dornoch itself, The Royal Golf (0862) 810283 and the delightful Dornoch Castle (0862) 810216 should also be shortlisted.

The thought of combining a golfing tour with a fishing trip positively lifts the heart. It is surely time to crank up the motor, pack the bags and family and make haste. When you arrive you will love it and when you depart you will crave more of that precious commodity, time.

Success   (Forsinard Hotel)

HIGHLANDS AND ISLANDS

THE SHINS TO THE ULLAPOOL

Holidays are short but memories are long! The memory of a fishing holiday in the Highlands will long outlast that of the two weeks spent in the likes of France, Spain or Italy. This is because the sport can be, and often is, outstanding. What is more, the setting will invariably be delightful. There is also the fun of sharing the triumphs and disasters with friends, companions or even total strangers after you've had a particularly memorable day! No true countryman can fail to be entranced by this part of the world for there is such variety. There are the fast angry torrents of a river in spate early in the season, the slow majestic flow of a big river in high summer, vast lochs surrounded by moorland and the lochans in the hills. Each has its own special environment and enchantment. Living in London surrounded by streets of similar houses one feels it's a far cry from the Highlands, but as I write I look up and see a splendid watercolour. It was painted towards the end of the last century by John MacWhirter who was considered rather sentimental until Victorian watercolours became fashionable, and the subject of this painting is a loch. Purple heather coated hills are in the distance, and the loch dominates the foreground. The shore is particularly prominent and it has a boat tied to a silver birch. This painting never fails to fill the imagination and as dreams turn to memories I fondly remember some wonderful days spent in the Highlands in a very similar boat in equally breathtaking scenery.

Before the advent of the new bridge over the Dornoch Firth anyone fishing the Helmsdale or more northerly rivers had to make the long detour via Bonar Bridge. However, this afforded the chance to see the Carron, Shin, Oykel and Cassley; there must be few places where one can see four such notable rivers within such a small area. Sadly, these rivers have all been affected by hydro-electric dams. No fisherman can but shake his head in sorrow at the ugly dam at the east end of Loch Shin which has reduced the river to a shadow of its former self.

When Andrew Young had the fishing of the River **Shin** in the 19th century the cost was £12 a month and in 1849 Major Cumming caught twenty-two salmon in ten hours. His fellow rod, Mr Fitzgibbon, the fishing correspondent of Bell's Life, took fifty-two fish in fifty-five hours! It is worth remembering that these prodigious feats were done with the heavy tackle then in use. Anyone who has spent a day casting with a big split cane salmon rod can imagine how their shoulders must have ached at the end of the day - but oh, how pleasurably! Paradise Pool is justly famous for producing big fish. Sadly, this pool was washed away in the torrential rains of 1988 but the damage was quickly repaired. Just north of Invershin are the Shin Falls. This is one of the few falls which are easily accessible to man and motor and as a result they are a popular tourist attraction complete with roadside cafe. The sight of a salmon leaping is one of the wonders of nature and when they are running here you will see hundreds of them. One can but watch in awe at the strength and bravery of the fish as they try to leap the falls. Often they will hit a rock and fall into the pool below, but driven by some primaeval instinct they will keep on trying until at last they lie spent and exhausted in the pool above.

A few miles further on the A836 is the town of Lairg. Here the Sutherland Arms Hotel (0549) 2291 will provide a comfortable pillow and has fishing books going back to 1861, and what fascinating reading they make. This hotel has a lease on the River Shin and can also arrange fishing on Loch Shin and Loch Craggie. **Loch Shin** is the largest loch in Sutherland and being some twenty miles long, it is possible to get marked weather differences at either end. Due to the hydro-electric power sluices there are few salmon but it is good trouting water and there are Arctic char at the western end. There can be a very large mayfly hatch which will naturally produce superb fishing. Permits may be obtained from R. Ross in Lairg (0549) 2239 which is the only tackle shop for miles around. A day's bank fishing costs £3 and boats with outboard motors are available at £20 a day. The Overscaig Hotel (0549) 83203 on the north side of the loch offers guests free fishing on this water and also has fishing on other lochs including Loch Merkland.

There are three lochs in Sutherland called **Craggie**, meaning 'big stones' or 'rocky'. The one we are referring to here is situated three miles north-east of Lairg and factored by the Sutherland Arms Hotel. Here you will find some of the best trout water in Scotland. The average weight is just under the pound and the best fish for 1990 was three and a half pounds, but there are some very big fish. Fishermen should note that there is no bank fishing whatsoever and a day for two rods, including a boat, costs £24 with a bag limit of 10 fish per boat. If your fellow rod gets more than his fair share then one feels justified in feeling a trifle peeved .... but such is life!

From its source in Loch Ailsh to Dornoch Falls, the course of the River **Oykel** covers some thirty-five miles and varies in character from tumbling rapids to gentle pools. It has long been famous as a prolific salmon water and is, as a result, hard to get on. George Ross (0549) 84259 is the fishing manager of the Lower Oykel fishings and people in their 40's write to him hoping to get on when they retire! His wife, Irene ties superb flies which are sold all over the world and if you can cast them on the river then you are indeed a fortunate fellow. The Lower Oykel runs from Oykel Falls to the Kyle of Sutherland. These seven miles are divided into four beats and here you will find such famous pools as George, Blue, Junction and Langwell.

The Upper Oykel is from Oykel Falls to Eileag Burn and is also very difficult to get on. There is a long waiting list and the expression 'dead man's shoes' comes speedily to mind. The splendid Oykel Bridge Hotel (0549) 84218 handles the lets and may be able to help you. These four miles are divided into three beats which rotate at 6pm. There are three rods per beat and the cost is approximately £400 per beat. Salmon run, on average, at about the 10lb mark and it is also good sea-trout water.

Slightly more accessible is the stretch from Eileag Burn to Loch Ailsh. This water is let through the Inver Lodge Hotel (0571) 4496 and is kept exclusively for hotel guests. These three miles are divided into two beats with two rods per beat and the costs vary between £18 and £48 a day. The best time is from July to September when it is not uncommon for two rods to account for a dozen salmon in a day. The average weight is 6lb and the best fish recorded in 1990 tipped the scales at eighteen and a half pounds. Among the notable pools are Lorna's Corner, Edmund's Pool, Keepers Pool and the Laird's Run. Advance booking is essential. The hotel also has three beats on the River Kirkaig available at between £18 to £48 per day, per rod. Furthermore, guests can take advantage of free fishing on Loch Ailsh and trout fishing on several other lochs. Trout fishing for non-residents is available at £17 a day including a boat.

HIGHLANDS AND ISLANDS

The principal tributary of the Oykel is the **Cassley**. This is a superb spate river which, given good water levels, provides excellent salmon fishing, and June often sees a great grilse run. The upper reaches of this river down to Duchally are owned by the Balnagowan Estate (0862) 842243 which belongs to Mr Fayed of Harrods fame. This water can fish well from July onwards and is often fished by stalkers staying at the estate lodges when they want a break from the hills. From Duchally to within a stone's throw of March Cottage, the north bank becomes the Glencassley fishings while the south bank is the Upper Cassley fishings which are let through Bell Ingram of Perth (0738) 21121, per rod per week, at a cost varying from £55 in May to £200 in September. The Upper Cassley beats comprise some seven miles with 37 pools, while rods on the Glencassley beats enjoy five miles and 23 pools. From March Cottage to the Achness Falls is the Glenrossal beat and below these falls is the Rosehall beat. The cost of a rod on the Glenrossal beat varies between £125 and £70 a week and on the Rosehall beat from £550 to £1050 per week but that is for three rods and also includes the services of a ghillie. The Achness Hotel at Rosehall (0549) 84239 can arrange the fishing for you, but there is a waiting list.

Driving to Bonar Bridge the River **Carron** is the first river one sees. Its character has been somewhat changed by the hydro-electric dam at its source, but this has had one beneficial effect for the water level falls very quickly during a spate. This is a first class salmon river with about ten miles of fishing belonging to nine owners. Three falls make natural divisions of this river. The lower part is from the Firth to Gledfield Falls. The best time to fish here is considered to be March and April for fish will stay below the falls until the water temperature rises above 38 degrees fahrenheit. The middle section is up to Morell Falls which fishes well in April and May. When the water temperature is above 42 degrees fahrenheit the upper reaches up to Glencarvie Falls will provide good sport from May to September. Prices vary according to beat and season and range from £150 for two rods to £4500 for four rods, including a comfortable lodge which sleeps eleven.

Some beats do become available but the best ones are very hard to get on; Finlayson Hughes of Perth (0738) 30926 may be able to help you. As on so many rivers, September sees some fine runs; however, spring is more likely to produce big fish and the best fish for 1990 was a 24lb beauty taken in April from the Cornhill beat.

Just north of Invershin is the turning for the A837. The road follows the course of the Oykel and is for many the nearest one will get to this famous river! Continuing on this road will Inchnadamph and **Loch Assynt**. The loch is some seven miles long and is good trout water. The average weight may be around half a pound, but eight and nine pounders are not uncommon. Here you will often find Willie Morrison who, with 70 years experience behind him, knows the moods of the loch well. The Inchnadamph Hotel (0571) 2202, of which Willie is proprietor, has five boats for the use of the guests and a days fishing with an outboard motor costs £16. The Assynt Angling Club has fishing on 34 lochs and further details can be obtained from the Tourist Information Office (0571) 4330.

The **Inver** is a short river whose six miles separate Loch Assynt from Inver Bay. It is here that in 1870, Dr. Almond caught the monster 27lb 4oz brown trout that remains the largest fish taken

from this river. It is divided into three beats with the top and bottom beat being owned by the Ben More Estate while the middle beat belongs to the Bradford family. The top beat is let through the Inver Lodge Hotel (0571) 4496 at a cost of between £18-£48 per rod, per day according to season. The beat is roughly a mile long and in a good season can produce upwards of a hundred salmon as there are several good pools, including the noted Black Pool.

The Inver Lodge Hotel may also be able to arrange fishing for you on the **Kirkaig** which lies just south of the Inver and is on the boundary between Sutherland and Ross-shire. The salmon, as the Romans knew when they christened him, is a great leaper, but no fish could ascend the fifty foot Falls of Kirkaig so, although the catchment area of the river may be eighty square miles, it is only the two miles down from the falls that hold fish. The river is divided into three beats and only the lower beat will suit those of advanced years. The middle beat requires some agility, and on the upper beat, where the river becomes a raging torrent as it flows through the gorge, it is more advisable to wear climbing boots than waders!

The A837 ends just south of Lochinver but those with a sense of adventure will follow the 'secondary' road to Inverpolly and **Lochs Sionascaig and Oscaig** (try saying these after a few 'wee ones'!). This is the heart of the Inverpolly Nature Reserve and the unspoilt landscape of Wester Ross is one of the finest imaginable. Loch Sionascaig is some three and a half miles in width and set against the backdrop of Cul Mor, Cul Beag and Stac Polly which all rise above 2000 feet. The loch has many bays with half pounders lying in wait. It also boasts scattered islands which are forbidden territory to anglers; teeming with wildlife they are a further attraction to a marvellous setting.

This is one of the few places left where, if you are lucky, you may see the majestic Osprey. Rival he may be but there are no finer 'anglers' than these magnificent birds. The loch is as deep as 200 feet in places and these murky depths are the haunt of large ferox trout; one of 16lb 14oz was caught in 1989. Permits for this water may be purchased from the Inverpolly Estate Office (0854) 82452. The Garvie, which has a heritage as a sea-trout water, flows out of Loch Oscaig. The Summer Isles Hotel (0854) 82282 can arrange permits for you to fish this loch which also offers good grilse fishing in high summer. A glance at the map will show you that this area is peppered with lochs and lochans nearly all of which will provide a good days sport.

A journey around the shore of Loch Lurgainn which lies in the shadow of Cul Beag will bring you back on to the A835 and a short distance south lies Ullapool. Apart from being able to take the ferry to the fishing delights of Lewis and Harris from here there is also the River **Ullapool**. Permits may be obtained either from the Highland Coastal Trading Company (0854) 612373 or Loch Broom hardware shop (0854) 612356. The river which fishes well in high summer is divided into three beats. A day on the lower beat costs £5 while the cost for the upper beat is £15. Salmon on this river average around the 6lb mark and sea-trout, which can also be taken on Loch Achall and in the estuary, almost 2lb.

I sincerely hope that you have fond memories of this wonderful region of Scotland when you return from your fishing trip.

HIGHLANDS AND ISLANDS

FISHING FAYRE

Loch Shin points northwards like a accusing finger and leaves a tear on the map for all to witness. There are many smaller abrasions and these waters offer celebrated game fishing on river, loch and stream.

Bonar Bridge is the southern most point of our area and here there are two hotels which merit some consideration. The Caledonian Hotel (08632) 214 has much to offer the visitor. Its most marvellous asset is perhaps its location, enjoying breathtaking views over the Kyle of Sutherland and the distant Ross-shire Hills. A pleasant atmosphere pervades this hotel which can also arrange fishing. The aptly named Bridge Hotel (08632) 204 is an old fashioned hotel which is a delightful port of call to those heading north on the A9. Bar and restaurant meals are wholesome and varied and there is some good accommodation should you wish to break your journey at this most pleasing spot.

Due north of Bonar Bridge, through marvellous scenery, we come to Lairg which nestles alongside Loch Shin. There are relatively few hotels to be found in this glorious vicinity but do not be put off for The Sutherland Arms (0549) 2291 is a fine exception to this rule, splendidly situated in the centre of the village, proudly overlooking Loch Shin. This is an renowned fishing hotel and thoroughly recommended. Its facilities are good, and lunches and dinner are worth a detour should you only be passing through the area. If you are merely travelling by, then perchance you are visiting Inchnadamph and the Inchnadamph Hotel (05712) 202 which is something of an 'anglers retreat'. Make no mistake this is not a luxurious hotel but its reputation amongst fishermen is celebrated. It stands at the head of Loch Assynt in the midst of some of Scotland's most joyous scenery surrounded by rugged mountainside. This is another haven for lovers of wildlife with the bird reserve at Hanoa and nearby seal colonies, two particularly splendid examples. The fishing for salmon and brown trout is renowned and good lunches and dinners can also be enjoyed. Imagine the fishermans' tales that have been exchanged here. This is not only a traditional, unspoiled and welcoming hotel for fishermen, it is something of a paradise.

Heading relentlessly westwards through magnificent landscapes one arrives at Lochinver and the Inver Lodge Hotel (05714) 496 which can also arrange salmon and trout fishing. The hotel is a modern edifice standing proudly amidst heather gardens and lawns. Many rooms enjoy splendid views over Lochinver Bay to the distant Hebrides. There is no question that this is a very comfortable hotel and the resident's lounge is particularly relaxing. The bedrooms are extremely well equipped and the restaurant is also highly considered. This is a hotel in which to pamper yourself in a sauna or solarium after fishing - after some days this will be an exhilarating thought!

Someway south of Lochinver one finds one of those delightful out of the way hotels, in this case, at Achiltibuie, the Summer Isles Hotel (085482) 282. There are country walks, good fishing and bird watching available but if you really want to escape and do nothing, well that's just fine. The restaurant is noted for two reasons: firstly its celebrated dinner meals and secondly the view. On a clear day they are simply breathtaking. There can be very few finer places to end a day having enjoyed some first class fishing.

Some of the great delights of Scotland are the variety of the scenery, the hotel accommodation and its overall peace. One highly individual place to pass a few hours in is the Ceilidh Place, Ullapool (0854) 612103. There are many reasons for visiting, not least, but not solely, the fishing. A coffee shop blends with a book shop which in turn revolves around something of a thespian's paradise. There are also tremendous views of loch and hill and bedrooms are characterful and cheery. This is a marvellous place to stay. If perchance you enjoy good cooking we have a directive for you. Venture to the Altnaharrie Inn (085483) 230. A boat crossing is required to reach the inn and this cocktail of sea breezes will prepare you for some of the most distinguished cooking in Scotland. The no choice five course dinners are legendary; game, seafood, and superb cheese and puddings will leave you somewhat lighter of pocket but infinitely satisfied. For those wishing to stay over, seven charming bedrooms are at your disposal. As with so many of the best hotels and restaurants it is essential to book well in advance.

Having been on an impressive diversion it is now necessary to concentrate the mind on the job in hand, game fishing. The Oykel Bridge Hotel (0549) 84218 is a legendary angling hotel. It is booked years in advance and boasts celebrated fishing. Due to its popularity it is well versed in the needs of the fisherman and your stay here will be memorable, especially if you enjoy a tight line or two.

A less celebrated but a worthy fishing hotel can be located at Rosehall. The Achness (054984) 239 is a popular haunt amongst the fishing fraternity and its bedrooms are comfortable. Cooking is also homely but the fishing is foremost and that's no bad thing, surely.

*Artist: **Clive Madgwick***
THAT ELUSIVE TROUT
*Courtesy of: **Rosenstiels'***

HIGHLANDS AND ISLANDS

LOCH MAREE TO CROMARTY FIRTH

No description of the joys of fishing in Scotland would be complete without a word about the ghillie. These gentlemen have always seemed to me to be a highland version of P.G. Wodehouse's creation Jeeves, for they are the sporting gentleman's personal gentleman! Like Jeeves they are always impeccably dressed for the occasion and know a great deal more than their masters! Alas, the pattern of social changes has made them a declining race but like the salmon there are still some 'gooduns' to be found. A good ghillie is worth his weight in gold for no matter how often you may have fished a piece of water there is always something new to learn and if you haven't fished the water before the ghillie is an essential advisor and companion. They know if there are fish in a pool, where the lies are and what fly is likely to do the trick; as if that wasn't enough they will also row for you. You can read all you like in books but there is nothing to beat the experience of the man on the spot who knows every mood of the water. They are men of many talents for they are often first class naturalists and can, if you are lucky, tie exactly the right fly for the particular state of the water. They are a fund of local lore and knowledge and if conditions should be against you, I know of no better way of passing the time than to offer the hip flask round and listen to the advice and stories of these gentlemen. (Mind you keep an eye on your hip flask!).

Coming south from Ullapool, the road follows the shore of Loch Broom. If you take the A382 coastal road you pass through the Dundonnell Forest. After skirting Little Loch Broom this road will bring you to Gruinard Bay where the Gruinard and Little Gruinard end their journies. These rivers are certainly more accessible today than they were in Victorian times; an old fishing guide suggests taking the train to Achnasheen 'which is only 50 miles or so away and from there a coach service often runs for most of the rest of the way'. There is no mention of the frequency of the service or how fishermen were to finally reach their destination! However, in those halcyon days there wasn't the pressure of modern office life and if one's holiday overran by a week or two it didn't matter. These are both spate rivers and while the salmon runs may not be what they were, there has been very good sea-trout fishing from July to September. In Gruinard Bay it was possible to see shoals of sea-trout gathering before swimming up their rivers. The Gruinard drains Loch na Sealga which is famous for the fighting qualities of its brownies. There are salmon here too and that tug on your line could be the start of a memorable fight as anyone who has caught a salmon on a trout rod will know! The Boat Pool is a favourite on the Little Gruinard where salmon average around 6lb and like its big sister has good sea-trout water as does Loch Fionn. Trout here average half a pound although there are some bigger ferox. This loch is surrounded by mountains which funnel the wind down so rowing can be fairly strenuous especially at the end of the day when a long pull may be required.

Leaving Gruinard, the road meanders alongside Loch Ewe and then on to Poolewe. Do take a minute to stop and take deep breaths of the fresh Atlantic air - it's marvellously bracing and you also have the pleasure of a glorious Hebredean view if the weather's fair. The River Ewe drains Loch Maree and is one of the most celebrated examples of the long loch and short river systems. At just over a mile long the river is one of the shortest in Scotland. Fairly sluggish to begin with, the Ewe narrows producing many fine holding pools such as Hen, Manse and Tee Pools separated by white-water rapids. This river was first made famous by Sir Humphrey Davy who thought nothing of catching twenty or more salmon a day. However, times have changed as they also have on **Loch Maree**. This is one of the most famous sea-trout fisheries in the world which in 1935 produced a record fish of 21lb. Up to the late 1960's double figure fish were not unusual but then came UDN which pretty well wiped out these big sea-trout and catches declined. In recent years it has had other problems, escapee farm salmon are a threat to the native stocks, the netting of sandeels which are the staple diet of sea-trout not to mention seals. Indeed grey seals have often been sighted in the river and even at the head of the loch.

Loch Meig   (East Lodge Hotel)

HIGHLANDS AND ISLANDS

However, things are looking up for this famous water. In 1988, Frank Buckley took over as fisheries consultant and his tireless efforts have brought about many improvements. By involving the Duke of Edinburgh Award Scheme and other volunteers a hatchery has been built and the spawning grounds in the feeder burns which had been choked are now cleared.

Dedicated work like this brings results and 1990 saw a best salmon of 22lb, a sea-trout of six and a half pounds and a brownie of four and a half pounds with 15 fish being caught in a day by one boat. Given another couple of good seasons, the loch may even be restored to its former glory as the best salmon and sea-trout loch in the country. Dapping is the favoured technique on these 14 miles of water which are over 300 feet deep in places, though trolling is permitted up to the end of June. The Loch Maree Hotel (044584) 288 has the fishing rights on about two thirds of the loch and its water is divided into ten beats. Boats are available and the cost for a days fishing for two rods including a boat is £10 from February until the end of June, rising to £36 for July and August and £20 from then until the close of the season in October.

Between Loch Maree and Loch Carron is an area of unspoilt countryside which has many good lochs such as Loch Damph, Lundie and Bad an Sgalaig. Roads are few and far between but those prepared to walk for their sport will have a memorable day. There are also some very good small spate rivers such as the Balgy, Torridon and Badachro. Fishing these rivers is a real delight and emphasises the overall high standard and availability of fishing in Scotland.

Taking the A835 across country from the Braemore Forest will bring you to **Loch Glascarnoch** where the fishing is free! This three and a half mile long water is owned by the Hydro-Electricity Board. If you are thinking that any fishing which is free must be of poor quality, then reconsider, as members of the Inverness Angling Club, who fish the water regularly, will confirm. South of here and below Fannich Forest is the fine water of Loch Fannich which is part of the River Conon system.

For many years, not only the River **Conon** but also its tributaries and lochs have been 'dammed' for hydro-electricity and this has naturally, or should I say unnaturally, affected water levels. Two of the dams have salmon counters which show a consistently good average number of fish. The system is also a notable brown trout water, for it was from Loch Garve at the top of the Blackwater that a monster of 26lb was caught in 1892. Frasers Newsagents at Strathpeffer (0997) 21346 issue permits for the four beats on the Upper Conon which is owned by Loch Achonachie Angling Club, at a cost of between £5 and £15 per day, according to season, and spinning is allowed when the water is up. Permits for fishing this part of the river are also available from the East Lodge Hotel at Strathconon (0997) 7222. This hotel can also issue permits for the Blackwater and sometimes arrange for guests to fish the Brora, Glass and Beauly. In 1991 it negotiated 8 miles of salmon fishing on the River **Meig** for guests and expects to be able to continue this in 1992.

The Fairburn Estate own part of the Middle Conon and lets are available from the Estate Office (0997) 3273. Some of this section is time shared during the summer and autumn but from

EAST LODGE HOTEL

A well appointed country hotel overlooking the River Meig, on which trout fishing can be arranged for hotel guests. Salmon fishing is available on The Blackwater.

East Lodge Hotel, a former shooting lodge, has been luxuriously furnished for your comfort and relaxation. All the rooms have private bathrooms, colour television and direct dial telephone.

After a leisurely meal, prepared from the finest local produce, relax in one of the lounges.

Ideal walking country for any none fishing members of the party.

Red deer stalking sometimes available.

For full details contact:

East Lodge Hotel
Strathconon
Muir of Ord
Ross-shire IV6 7QQ
Tel: (099) 77 222
Fax: (099) 77 243

HIGHLANDS AND ISLANDS

January to the end of June lets can be obtained from either Savills in Brechin (0356) 22187 or the Coul House Hotel, Contin (0997) 21487 at a cost of between £50 and £400 excluding VAT per rod per week according to season. If this is too expensive, Seaforth Highland Estate (0349) 61150 can offer you trout fishing at £3.50 a day or £12 a week and also lets out several holiday cottages.

The Lower Conon may not be the same quality of fishing but it is more affordable. It is managed by Dingwall Angling Club and the cost is a modest £7 or £10 a day depending on the time of season. Permits may be obtained from the Sports and Model shop in Tulloch Street, Dingwall (0349) 62346. These permits also cover Lochs Achanalt, Chuillin and Luichart.

Between Dingwall and Alness is the River **Glass**. This river is not to be confused with the water of the same name which is part of the Beauly system. It is totally different in character, quality of fishing and price. The river rises in several hill lochs under the shadow of Ben Wyvis before flowing into **Loch Glass**. This part of the river and downstream to the gorge is privately owned by the Wyvis Estate. Black Rock Gorge is over a mile long and is an awesome spectacle for there is a sheer drop of up to 200 feet and in some places it is only 6 feet wide. If standing on one of the footbridges looking at the raging torrent far below doesn't make your head spin, the smell of the wild garlic will! This grows so profusely that it is harvested twice a year by the cheese factory in Tain. From the gorge to Cromarty Firth the river is known as the 'Allt graad' and this three quarter mile stretch is divided into three beats. Permits may be had for £7 a day or £25 a season from Alcocks Newsagents in Evanton High Street (0349) 830672. The river is stocked on an annual basis and is the type of water that offers the chance of an occasional salmon or sea-trout at a very modest cost.

A few miles north of the Glass lies the well known **Alness** (or Averon, as it is sometimes known). This used to be prolific sea-trout water but like so many rivers it has seen a decline in recent years, but the salmon fishing has improved and now averages 400-600 fish a year. The best year in recent times was 1985 when over 800 fish were caught. Conifer plantations have encroached on the banks of this river and its main tributary, the **Blackwater**, and have led to flash floods which have done some damage to the spawning grounds. However, improvements are in hand and the river is stocked every year. Sea-trout average one and a half pounds and salmon 8-10lb though September usually sees some better fish of up to 20lb. The river which is largely owned by Novar Estates (0349) 830208 drains **Loch Morie**. This is good brown trout water and also offers the chance of char and ferox which run well into double figures; the best for 1990 being 15lb 4oz. A days fishing costs £15 for two rods including a boat. Water from the loch to Strath Rusdale is also owned by Novar Estates. From there to the Ardross Castle boundary is Alness Angling Club Water (secretary Brian Poe (0349) 883963) and there are three beats. Alness A. C. permits can also be obtained from Pattersons Ironmongers in Alness High Street, (0349) 882286. The castle water which extends to Dalreoch Burn is private and retained for family and friends. So if you're a friend of the family good fishing, if not either get acquainted or find pastures new! Below the burn, Novar Estates have four beats. After this the Alness Angling Club water continues all the way to Cromarty Firth. The cost of the Novar Estates water ranges from £12 to £35 per day per rod,

weekly lets are sometimes available and trout fishing on their three top beats below the loch cost £3 per day. The Alness Angling Club water costs between £15 and £50 per rod per week according to season. The Coul House Hotel at Contin (0997) 21487 can also arrange for guests to fish the Novar Estates water. Needless to say the advice is, as usual, to book as far in advance as possible.

Before we move on to other areas of the country we should perhaps consider our worthy friend the ghillie. The above is derived from the gaelic and literally means 'Lad' or 'Servant'. References to the word are made in the works of Spencer, Smollett and Scott and today this 'caddie' or 'butler' can be an invaluable aid to your fishing holidays. Some people may be too proud to ask for their advice but they will really be poorer without it. Fishing, like life, is about experience and knowledge. The ghillie may not provide all the answers but he'll certainly come up with some of the solutions.

FISHING FAYRE

South of Ullapool we can find some rare loch and river fishing. As we venture further south hotels tend to be thicker on the ground but the countryside remains unspoilt and the fisherman can still find peace. The coast here is amongst the most striking and beautiful in Britain and from sea lochs and coves flow some excellent rivers. I feel a few discoveries are in order.

Those of you travelling this far should consider the Dundonnel Hotel (085483) 234 which enjoys splendid views down Little Loch Broom. The hotel is shielded by the An Teallach mountains and has an impressive location and also offers attractive accommodation. In Aultbea the Aultbea Hotel (044582) is another which boasts a splendid view, on this occasion, over Loch Ewe. This water is also cross examined by the Pool House (044586) 272 which sits at the head of the water - once again this is an ideal hotel for fishermen touring this delightful spot and especially good for those with an eye towards Gruinard Bay. One of the most intrusive waterways into this area of the Scottish Highlands is that carved by Loch Maree. It is hoped that this Loch is on the way back and one of the first people who will know are the proprietors of the Loch Maree Hotel (044584) 288 which is certainly a must for those of you wishing to fish once celebrated waters. The hotel itself is a purpose built fishing hotel situated on the bank of the loch. It dates from pre-Victorian times but recent refurbishment has kept the hotel's standard high while retaining character - this is a fine place to stay. At Kinlochewe we find another unspoilt hotel, The Kinlochewe (044584) 253, which offers a cheery welcome, tasty homely cooking and good accommodation.

Gairloch is perhaps better known as part of the future King's poetry but it has other claims to fame, one of which is the Old Inn (0445) 2006 which has a splendid situation overlooking the harbour. This is a fine place to escape and another point from which to plan a fishing foray or two! Another equally splendid hotel is the Creag Mor Hotel, Charles Town (0445) 2068. The hotel is happy to organise fishing for guests and the restaurant specialises in seafoods, salmon, trout, Highland beef and venison - lesser nourishment is available throughout the day.

Torridon sits proudly betwixt the river and Loch of that name. The Loch Torridon Hotel (044587) 242 is a former hunting lodge which stands at the head of the Loch. As the word lodge implies this is a house of log fires, cosy lounges and splendid malts in stock - a fisherman's paradise. The hotel offers Loch and river fishing for salmon and trout and is a fine place to go if you love good fishing and a good time. Another beautifully situated hotel is found in Shieldaig, The Tiegh An Eilean (05205) 251 a small family run hotel, it is delightfully peaceful and ideal for a relaxing visit.

Loch Carron is yet another of the celebrated sea lochs of Western Scotland. The Loch Carron (05202) 226 is a beautifully situated hotel which lies on the shores of the Loch. This may not be a fisherman's paradise but its remote setting makes it an ideal point from which to explore the coastal highlands.

From west coast to east our journey now takes a turn to the fishes of Scotland's North Sea coast. The Conon is a first rate water and it is well served by hotels. In Contin the excellent Coul House Hotel (0997) 21487 is justly proud of its water which include celebrated beats on the Conon and some Loch fishing. The country mansion enjoys a wonderful setting with fine views toward mountain and over forest. The accommoda-

tion is first class, the food follows in a similar vein and for fine fishing in style this hotel is a fine catch. A hotel which boasts a first class Highland welcome is the East Lodge Hotel, Strathconon (0997) 7222, yet another to consider before making your plans. A similar commendation can be made of the remotely placed Inchbae Lodge (09975) 269 which is a comfortable place to stay. Bedrooms are finished in pine and the hotel can arrange fishing trips should you so wish.

There are all manner of less celebrated hotels, bed and breakfast and inns that you might wish to consider and the same can be said of the fishing in this area of Scotland. Aside from the noted rivers and lochs there is an abundance of small rivers, hill lochs and streams. It should be emphasised, however, that many of the favoured hotels are booked up many years in advance and planning for the complete angling tour should be made months and is some cases years in advance. They say half the fun of a holiday is in the planning - we hope that the above information assists you in your quest for salmon, trout and seatrout.

River Meig   (East Lodge Hotel)

LOCH MAREE HOTEL

Loch Maree Hotel was built in 1872 and has catered for fishermen ever since. It has been completely refurbished under the supervision of the new management. Mr Wilson and Mr Vincent have updated all the amenities to modern standards whilst maintaining the style of the original building.

The hotel is very comfortable with 22 double and twin bedded rooms, each with en suite facilities. The location of the hotel means that it can take advantage of the local produce, so the food is not only fresh but also of an exceptionally high standard.

For the fisherman the hotel excels; there is plenty of room for storage in the boat house with proper drying and boot room facilities. The hotel also boasts a small tackle shop, so it is very much self-contained. The guests of the hotel also enjoy preferential access to the fishing, although occasionally it can be arranged for non residents.

For the fisherman who enjoys his scenery as much as he enjoys his fishing, Loch Maree is legendary, offering the perfect combination, marvellous sea trout fishing in some of the best surroundings the Wester Islands can offer.

The sea trout fishing has been excellent for generations of fishermen and although current catches have been slightly down,

an active restocking programme will ensure Loch Maree remains one of the best locations for sea trout fishing in the British Isles.

The first sea trout of the year enter the loch in mid June through the River Ewe, with the main runs being in July and August. Although the fishing tapers off towards the end of September, this is often when the largest fish are taken.

The guests of the hotel have eight boats at their disposal, each with a ghillie assigned to assist the fisherman in locating the best fishing available that particular day.

There are ten beats, which are operated on a rotational basis, allowing each fisherman to fish the best spots at least once during his stay.

They all have names which will be known to the avid sea trout fisherman: the Grudie, Weedy Bay, Ash Island, Pig's Bay and Fool's Rock, Hotel, North Shore, Steamer Channel, Back of Islands, Isle of Maree and Coree.

If you enjoy dapping, then this style of fishing was developed here in the 1930's, offers an interesting alternative for the fly fisherman and hopefully will prove successful.

Loch Maree Hotel
Near Kinlochewe
Achnasheen
Wester Ross IV22 2HL
Tel: (044 584) 288
Fax: (044 584) 241

RIVER BEAULY FISHING

The River Beauly, one of Scotland's foremost salmon rivers recently purchased by The River Beauly Fishings Company Limited, enjoys the highly prized distinction of being one of the only remaining major salmon rivers in either England or Scotland to be in single ownership from top to bottom. The benefit of total management control is therefore possible and allows long term planning and investment for both restoration and improvement of the river.

The River Beauly is a **FLY ONLY** river and comprises 11 miles of double bank between the junction of the River Farrar and Glass and the Lovat Bridge. It is said to hold the catch record for one rod on any British river with 216 salmon and grilse taken in only 4 days in July 1896.

The River Beauly is divided into 3 sections:-
1) Two rotating (3 rod) beats on the Upper Beauly: The Eskadale and Aigas beat each with its own Ghillie.
2) The Dam/Ferry beat (3 rods) with its own Ghillies and boats.
3) Three rotating (5 rod) beats on the Lower Beauly, the Falls, Home and Downie beats. Each with its own Ghillie and boats.

The ten year average of the Lower Beauly is 537, this figure was however, comfortably exceeded in 1990 with a total of 803, in what was generally considered a poor fishing season in Scotland.

THE CRUIVES LODGE

The Cruives Lodge offers luxury accommodation for visitors coming to fish the River Beauly. The Lodge, set in breathtaking countryside across the river from Beaufort Castle and overlooking the ancient cruives (weirs), is within easy walking distance of pools on two of the beats as well as one of the principal fishing huts.

The Lodge has accommodation on two floors and comprises six double bedrooms with private bathrooms as well as a large comfortable drawing room and dining room, drying room, rod room and a modern kitchen.

The Lodge is available for parties of five to twelve people from Sunday to Sunday. The facilities within the Lodge offer accommodation for guests' accompanying staff, and arrangements can also be made to provide the services of a chef to meet with the guests' requirements.

Full details of the above fishings are available from:

Mr P Spence
The River Beauly Fishings Company Limited
The Kiln House
Kiln House Yard
Royston
Herts SG85AY

HIGHLANDS AND ISLANDS

BEAULY TO TORRIDON

Many of us remember Lord Baden Powell's motto 'Be Prepared' and this is particularly appropriate when fishing in the Highlands. Assuming we have secured a week or two away from the office and more importantly managed to book some fishing, the car is packed with rods, fly boxes, landing nets, creel and other angling impedimenta. Some hours and miles later we arrive at our destination. The hotel may be in a small village or in an isolated solitary situation and is frequently a long way from any town. Of course this has its advantages but is something of a bore if you happen to have forgotten to pack something! On the first day the rod is put up and the fly tied. The water level is just right, one fishes down the pool but there is no tug. The fly is changed but still no luck. What's the problem? On the next beat they are having rare sport. Over a dram in the evening a fellow fisherman commiserates on our lack of luck. The talk turns to flies and we find that the best fly for the water is left at home - marvellous! Fear not, one can be found in the 'local' tackle shop, which is perhaps twenty or more miles away and so a morning or afternoons fishing is wasted. Hotels and river owners want their guests to catch fish and are only too pleased to give advice on flies. However, it never ceases to surprise them how many guests either never ask or wait until they have arrived to find out which are the favoured flies. A phone call before you go could make it a much more successful holiday. It is well worth checking all your tackle and making sure you have plenty of spare casts before leaving home, so be prepared and check before you go. If this story sounds somewhat patronising - please forgive me I am only reciting a lesson learnt from my own bitter experience!

The **Beauly** is a superb salmon river and as a result it is very, very hard to get on! One may think that the desire to own salmon fishing stems from recent times but the Beauly has always been a prized water. After the estate had been forfeited following the Jacobite uprising of 1715, Lord Lovat asked his friend, the Duke of Gordon, to present a petition to the King.

The request was that 'one lea rig behind the castle' might be given to him and his heirs in perpetuity. Amused by such eccentricity, King George I granted the request only to find that 'lea rig' meant the river! A century and a half later the Master of Lovat recorded the memorable feat of taking 156 fish in five days. That is an average of 31 fish a day and was achieved using a 25' rod!

The Beauly is still a prolific salmon river and an average of 7000 fish a year are counted at the two dams. Catches of 40 fish in a day are not uncommon so it is not surprising that when Lovat Estates put seven beats on the market in 1990 the asking price was over £10 million. The purchaser, Landmatch PLC, formed The River Beauly Fishing Company (0763) 241181 to manage the now syndicated river. All the management are keen fishermen and the managing director is William Midwood whose family used to own the Naver. The company is undertaking a variety of conservation measures and its stocking policy gives us great hope for future years; it also has a first class consultant in William Shearer, the leading salmon biologist. In 1990 the Falls, Home and Downie beats twice produced over a hundred fish in a week. Favoured pools on these beats include Glide, Castle, Charlies and Greenbank. As with most time-shared fishing, it is possible for outsiders to get the odd week and further details may be had from the company. However, you don't have to be a millionaire to fish this famous river! A days permit from Morrisons (0463) 782213 in Beauly's West End will enable you to fish the tidal water from below Lovat Bridge to Wester Lovat Farm at a cost of £8 a week or for £3.50 a day you can also fish the North and South Estuary where spinning is allowed.

The Beauly has a vast catchment area extending to beyond the Great Glen in the North West Highlands and the whole system has been harnessed for hydro-electric power so there are many dams and power stations. I am not sure if there is a collective noun for dams but I know many fishermen who have seen the character of rivers changed beyond recognition would term it a damnation of dams! However, they do have their uses and

The River Beauly   (River Beauly Fishing Co)

can help to maintain reasonable water levels making a river fishable for longer periods. This appears to be a river of many names; flowing out of Loch Beinn a' Mheadhoin the River **Affric** combines with the **Cannich** to form the **River Glass**; which in turn is joined by the Farrar below Struy. At the confluence of these two streams the Beauly is born.

All the tributaries are marvellous salmon streams with the sole exception of the Cannich because the falls are unsurmountable. Fishing of this quality is understandably hard to come by, however, Lovat Estates (0463) 782205 have six beats on the River Glass and season tickets per rod vary from £1000 + VAT for May up to August 24th after which the cost is £1500 up to the end of the season on October 15th. L.A.H.Mure, Esq., (0456) 5251 has two miles of the Glass which are divided into three, two rod beats, however, as one would expect he is pretty booked up. F. Spencer-Nairn, Esq., (0463) 76285 may be able to help with fishing on the Farrar and also lets cottages.

The Glen Affric Hotel (0456) 5214 issues permits for you to fish the fine trout waters of **Lochs Monar** and **Mullardoch** where good bags of 20 fish or more are possible in the right conditions. The cost of £17 a day includes a boat with a maximum of four rods. The hotel also has a fly casting school so this could be the chance to brush up your technique. It always surprises me that many first class shots will go to a shooting school before the start of the season to get their eye in again yet once a fisherman thinks - and I repeat thinks! - he has mastered the art of casting he rarely bothers to seek expert guidance again. I know that at the start of every season my casting is pretty rough and it always requires a few days practice before the fly is landing where I want it to. Time at a casting school is never wasted for one can always improve one's technique and learn new tactics.

If you feel the cost of fishing the Beauly is a little pricey fear not for you can have a memorable holiday on the west coast by staying at the Loch Torridon Hotel (0445) 87242 and fishing **Loch Damh**, which is Gaelic for 'stag'. A reminder, if any were needed, of the abundant game that you find in so much of Highland Scotland. Iain Fraser of the hotel is a very keen fisherman and describes the loch as a miniature Loch Ness. It is essential to have a ghillie as the loch has an uneven bottom and there are many underwater obstructions. At four and a half miles long by a mile wide, it is not a particularly large water yet it is surprising how the markings of the trout vary in the different parts of the loch, with some having an almost golden appearance. The hotel has three boats. If you wish to hire one with an outboard motor this costs £18 per day and there is an extra charge of £7 for an extra rod. Tigh An Eilean Hotel (05205) 251 also has a boat on this loch. Damph is also a good sea-trout water and there are salmon - Iain Fraser is one of the few who knows where they can be caught but he won't tell a soul. Over the years many fishermen have tried to loosen his tongue with a dram or two, but to no avail. If you are thinking of trying to pry the secret out of him, forget it, with his practice he can drink anyone under the table! Perhaps there are no salmon and he just mentions them to get a free drink! Iain will also point you in the right direction of other lochs and lochans which may not appear in any fishing guide, but are excellent trout waters. The hotel also owns the River **Torridon**. A day on this river is available to guests at a cost of £8.50 a day.

This is a flash spate river and can be quite reasonable fishing. However, take a leaf out of Lord Baden Powell's book and

telephone Iain Fraser and his colleagues in advance. They will be delighted to pass on up-to-date fishing information but not perhaps the salmon lies of Loch Damh!

FISHING FAYRE

There are all manner of good reasons for going fishing, some less obvious than to catch a fish! If you happen to be heading for Scotland then the chances are, that given sufficient planning and luck, a fish will be landed. It might not be a very big one but what's size between friends. It is certainly true to say that good salmon fishing is fairly pricey but it is not fair to say that all fishing is over expensive. Hotel waters are often the answer and a number of hotels warrant closer inspection in this slice of Scotland that has huge appeal.

Our first suggested port of call is the Cozac Lodge (04565) 263, formerly an Edwardian Shooting Lodge which has since been transformed into a delightfully secluded hotel. The location is breathtaking. It is situated beside Loch Sealbhanach, halfway up Glen Cannich where wildlife is abundant. This is a really wonderful place to stay if you are someone who delights in the natural beauty of the British Isles. The hotel is run in a particularly friendly informal manner and fine food and wines add further good reason for passing through this way.

Someway north of here we find Struy where the Cnoc House (046376) 264 is also to be recommended. It is not grand but the food is fresh and wholesome and the bedrooms are extremely comfortable - another for the shortlist when fishing in the area.

The Kyle of Lochalsh is an important port of call for the fisherman, not least because it houses the ferry terminal to Skye. Those of you seeking to venture Skyewards should certainly consider the Lochalsh Hotel (0599) 4202. Bedrooms and bathrooms are all of a high standard and a 24 hour lounge service is an obvious benefit for people who are unable to time their journey to the second. The hotel can arrange fishing and the restaurant is growing in stature with seafood a particular speciality. The marvellously named, but distinctly unscottish sounding, Plockton is another that needs consideration. Here the Haven Hotel (059984) 223 is good value and thoroughly welcoming. Local produce is used to good advantage and the restaurant is very popular. The village is another great attraction as it has a really leisurely feeling and this good value hotel is a real favourite.

Someway south of the Kyle of Lochalsh one finds another friendly and comfortable hotel, the Glenelg Inn (059982) 273 which overlooks the sound of Sleat to the Isle of Skye. The dinner menu here is extremely well thought of and fresh produce, particularly the abundant seafood, can be enjoyed. Bedrooms are comfortable and, make no mistake, this is a hotel to consider when travelling through or staying in the area. They can also organise some particularly good brown trout fishing on a number of hill lochs.

It matters little whether you are passing through Sgurr Na Lapaich or heading forth on the Road to the Isles, this is an area of infinite beauty, some first class fishing and a number of fine hotels. Those of you lucky enough to know it well will recognise your good fortune in staying in its countryside and enjoying its fishing.

LOCH TORRIDON HOTEL

This elegant country house was built over a hundred years ago by the First Earl of Lovelace. It was originally called the Ben Damph Mansion House and has been home to five generations of Lovelaces - and today the family is always ready to extend a warm welcome. The hotel stands in wooded grounds, close to the loch.

If you enjoy fishing - the world is your oyster! There are salmon, sea trout and brown trout in the rivers and hill lochs around Wester Ross. The hotel can arrange fishing on the River Torridon, Loch an Iascaigh, Loch Damph and various hill lochs. All fishing is fly only, with the exception of Loch Damph, where trolling with lure is permitted. Fly casting instruction is available at the hotel as is the hire of rods, reels and fishing tackle. The Loch Torridon can also organise sea angling parties with local fishermen - weather permitting!

For those golfers among you the Gairloch Golf Club is worth a visit, with its magnificent views across to Isle of Skye. Or if you would prefer the hotel can arrange red deer stag and hind stalking at a neighbouring estate.

All around the majestic mountains keep guard, challenging hill walkers to some of the most spectacular routes in Britain. There are also gentler pleasures nearby - you can explore one of the National Trust for Scotlands nature trails, even make the acquaintance of hand reared deer.

The restaurant offers an extensive menu, using the best of local produce carefully selected and imaginatively prepared, complemented by an excellent wine cellar. Relax after a day in the fresh air in the drawing room, or have a nightcap in the cocktail bar.

Loch Torridon Hotel
Torridon
Wester Ross IV22 2EY
Tel: (044 587) 242

THE CNOC HOTEL

'Cnoc' is Gaelic for 'little hill'. 'Hotel' is French for 'hospitable place'. 'Cnoc Hotel' is all that is best in Highland Country Hotels.

Deep in Strathglass, close to Strathfarrar and Glen Affric, we are perfectly placed for guests fishing on the Beauly, Farrar or Glass; among the greatest of Scottish salmon and trout rivers, and we can organise your complete fishing holiday on any of these, or on many of the lochs in the region.

Great too is the local walking, climbing, mountain biking and stalking, and as we are surrounded by some fine golf courses, most sports are readily available. We can arrange these, sailing, clay pigeon or photography holidays to suit individual plans.

Good outside and good inside, our eight bedrooms are all you would expect from a 4 crown and Les Routiers recommended hotel. All en-suite, with hairdryers, self dial telephones and full hospitality units, and what a view!

Very comfortable public rooms, warm hospitality, an excellent choice of blended and malt whisky, a fine wine list, and delicious food, naturally with a strong Highland emphasis from our a la carte menu, which is changed daily, all make a memorable contribution to your stay.

To top it off, relax in our spa bath, sauna and tanning units, and your holiday will be as good a holiday as anywhere in the world.......Only better.

The Cnoc Hotel
Struy
Invernesshire IV4 7JU
Tel/Fax (046376) 264

HIGHLANDS AND ISLANDS

THE GREAT GLEN

'When am I going to catch a salmon?'is a question we have all asked ourselves, especially after a blank day or worse still a blank week. The problem is that salmon fishing is a very inexact art for no-one knows what makes a salmon take. Trout, by way of contrast are somewhat easier to assess, for if a fish is rising and you can match the hatch there is a fair chance of catching him. As we know salmon do not feed when they swim up a river, as a result it is extremely difficult to predict 'taking times' but it would seem that early morning, around lunchtime and evening are the optimum times. This is the same pattern as trout and we all look forward to the evening rise and will often stay out until the light goes.

So why not the same with salmon? Part of the problem is that understandably, ghillies go home for their tea at around 5.30pm! After a day on the river the thought of a bath, a dram and some good eating is a very appealing prospect - after all, this is meant to be a holiday! But if you want to catch a fish, I strongly urge you to fish on. It is surely no coincidence that many big fish, including Miss Ballantine's, were taken 'late' on in the day.

The other thing is to persevere through thick and thin, rain or shine. I know of a young lady who, while spring fishing, decided to seek the warmth and comfort of the fishing hut - the sleet was coming down the valley in horizontal sheets driven by a bitterly cold wind - who would really blame her for seeking shelter? However, it wasn't long before the ghillie found her and with an admonishing wag of his finger told her 'ye'll nae catch a fushie sitting thar, modom!' A few casts later she thought for a moment her hook had snagged the bottom but a while later an 18lb fish lay on the bank! My father-in-law went fishing for four years and each year he drew a blank which he bore with his usual good humour and fortitude. On the fifth year he had three fish totalling over 41lb in 51 minutes! While this illustrates the value of perseverance it also shows what a fickle business salmon fishing is.

The **Ness** System is the largest catchment area in the Highlands and at 25 miles long the loch is monster sized! However, the river is only about six miles long. It used to be regarded as the queen of Scottish rivers due to very productive yields and its great width. A fish that inhabits wide open waters will give a much better fight than his cousin in a small river who has less water to manoeuvre in. Steam navigation and the Caledonian Canal were thought to be the culprits for the decrease in salmon and the value of the fishing fell from £1100 p.a. - a considerable sum in Victorian times, to a quarter of that amount. This queen may have lost her crown, but the Ness is still a respectable salmon river.

As with so many other rivers the spring runs are a mere shade of times gone by but this has been more than compensated for by the increase in the summer runs of salmon and grilse. The Ness is a wide river and early season spinners will use a 10 foot rod and when the fly comes into its own from June onwards you will need a carbon rod of 15 foot or more. At the end of a day's fishing with such a rod you will be more than ready for a bath and a large dram or two! Inverness Angling Club has three miles of both banks where fly, worm and spinning are allowed. The cost of a day's fishing is £8 and permits can be obtained from J. Graham & Co., the tackle dealer (0463) 233178. Above the club water is Ness-side where lets are handled by

Angus Mackenzie & Co., (0463) 235353. These beats have produced some good fish with a lady taking a 24½ pounder in 1990 and in 1989 a gentleman of the cloth had a 25 pounder. Next is the mile or so of Ness Castle water where the agent is Mr R. M. Robertson (0542) 22411. Beyond this is the time-shared Laggan water which is run by Prime Salmon Fishings Ltd., (031-449) 3973. Finally, there is the Dochfour Estate beats and further details may be had from the Estate Office (0463) 86218.

Due to its size, fishing from a boat on **Loch Ness** can prove hazardous if there is a wind whipping up white horses. The golden rule is 'if in doubt, don't go out'. While the fly works well for sea-trout, trolling with two spinning rods is the favoured method for salmon which can run up to 30lb. The fishing is privately owned but hotels such as Inchnacardoch Lodge Hotel (0320) 6258 and Whitebridge Hotel (0456) 3226 may be able to help. The Glenmoriston Estate whose Head Keeper, Mr Alastair Mackintosh, also has two boats on the loch; including outboards they cost £60 a day for two rods. In 1990 these boats accounted for 69 salmon.

Glenmoriston Estates (0320) 51219 can also offer good trout fishing on twenty one hill lochs and 20 miles of salmon fishing on the River **Moriston**. The cost of a days fishing varies between £20 and £40 according to season. Mr. Macintosh's own pattern the 'Wee Tosh' is particularly successful but old favourites like the Hairy Mary and Stoats Tail work well. Seven miles of the headwaters of this river are owned by the Cluanie Inn (0320) 40238 and offer the occasional salmon at a cost of only 'a few pounds a day'. One should not expect top class fishing but for a modest sum you are at least in the running for a catch. Permits for Loch Cluanie may be had from Cluanie Lodge (0320) 40262 at a cost of £10 per day for a two rod boat. Outboards are extra and bring your own fuel! A boat and a day's fishing on the delightful **Loch Ruthven** can be had for £10 from R.Humfrey, Esq., (0808) 3283. These 375 acres produce good fighting brownies averaging around the pound mark which are often taken on the local favourite fly, the Badger.

The River **Enrick** rises in **Loch nan Eun** and flows alongside the A831 on its course through **Loch Meiklie** to enter Loch Ness at Urquhart Bay. The fishing is unexceptional but the scenery is gorgeous. Permission for the Enrick can be obtained from Mr. R. Sorenson at Kilmartin Hall (0456) 4269. Mrs Elizabeth Taylor (0456) 4275, Kilmartin House, may not have any Oscars on her mantlepiece but she does issue permits to fish Loch Meiklie at £6 a day (0900 - 1530 hours) including a boat. This super little fly-only loch has beautifully marked pink fleshed trout which average 1lb and any under 12 inches should be returned.

Loch Quoich covers some 4000 acres and is the kind of water where an outboard is essential. As with any water of this size weather conditions are an important factor but on the right day the fishing can be excellent and may be had for £3 a day for bank fishing or £18 for a boat with an outboard. The Gearr Garry drains this loch and flows through **Lochs Poulay, Inchlaggan and Garry**. Tomdoun Hotel (0809) 2218 can arrange for you to fish all the waters and also has three and a half miles of salmon fishing on the north bank of the River **Garry** which is free to hotel guests. Fishing the south bank is through Garry Gualach Ltd (0809) 2230 who run sporting holidays and can arrange shooting and stalking for you, should you wish to swap rod for rifle. A nymph fished on a sinking tip may well prove to be the downfall of a big 4lb plus Arctic char on Loch Garry which is also excellent trout water. Mr J.Morgan at Ardochy Lodge (0809) 2232 has rights for salmon and trout fishing but as he says, 'the loch is large and the salmon are few'. R.B.Scott Esq., at the Invergarry Post Office (0809) 3201 can arrange for you to fish the Garry between Loch Garry and **Loch Oich** at a cost of £37 a day. The price also includes salmon fishing on Loch Oich where trout fishing may be had from Glengarry Castle Hotel (0809) 3254 for £8 a day. The River **Oich** flows alongside the Caledonian Canal to join Loch Ness at Fort Augustus and a day's salmon fishing costs £12, while £2 is the cost of a days trouting from Miss J. Elice at Aberchalder Estate (0320) 6230.

Inexpensive salmon fishing can also be had on the River **Shiel**. £10 is the price for a day; contact Mrs Campbell (0599) 81282. A few miles west is Glenelg which is just across the water from Skye. Here you will find the lovely Glenelg Inn which arranges marvellous ceilidhs and a very original form of pub crawl, using inflatable dinghies! Before anyone writes to say that the Shiel cannot be so cheap I would point out that this is the one that flows into Loch Duich.

The other River **Shiel** (40 miles south) that drains the Loch of the same name is a totally different kettle of fish! This is another example of the long loch and short river system. These rivers can produce those great days we all dream of. The river is only three miles long, by comparison, the loch is some eighteen miles in length and for its size it is one of the narrowest in Scotland. Although there can be excellent summer runs of salmon and grilse, the river is probably best known for its sea-trout fishing. Unless there is a breeze to stir the water, which is fairly slow, night fishing is likely to prove the most productive method. Catches may not be what they were thirty years ago, yet the loch still ranks among the best sea-trout waters. An old advertisement for the Shiel Hotel offers fishing for five shillings a day! Alas, today it is one of those rivers that is almost impossible to get on unless you are prepared to wait fifteen or twenty years before fishing such pools as Garrison, Grassy Point and Parapet. Still, if you are looking for a long term plan then this is a tremendous water. Write to: R.S. - L.S.D.F.B., c/o C. Kennedy Esq, Robertson Neilson & Co., 95 Bothwell Street, Glasgow, G2 7JH.

Loch Shiel is much more accessible and what is more it must also be one of the prettiest in Scotland. The Jacobite uprising of 1745 began here for it was on the shores of Loch Shiel that Bonnie Prince Charlie raised his flag. This used to be very good sea-trout water but like so many others has seen a decline in numbers caught in recent years. Being a large loch, salmon are usually trolled for and make sure you tackle up, as 20 pounders are not uncommon and the best fish in recent years was a 42 pounder. There are many sand and gravel bays which provide excellent spawning grounds and a good spot for a picnic lunch while admiring the soaring mountains that surround you. It is also good trout water with an average of three quarters of a pound, and two pounders are not uncommon here. The Stage House Inn (0397) 83246 and the Glenfinnan House Hotel (0397) 83235 at the eastern end and Loch Shiel Hotel (0967) 85224 and Clanranald Hotel (0967) 85662 at the western end, all have boats and can offer a days fishing at around £15. Guests of E.Macaulay of Dalilea Farm (0967) 85253 will find the price of their accommodation includes fishing and boats with outboards.

The A830, 'The Road to the Isles', (A830) can be found at the northern end of Loch Shiel and if you travel west on this road you will find two jewels, the River **Ailort** and **Loch Eilt**. Although river and loch are both relatively small, the latter used to have a marvellous reputation for sea-trout. In more recent times these have been reared in cages on the loch and when released have run up the river back into the loch. It will be interesting to see how this experiment progresses. A week's fishing which includes both the river and the loch costs £250 from Salar Management Services Ltd (0667) 55355.

As we continue westwards we come to **Loch Morar** which lies a few miles south of Mallaig. There is also a railway service to Mallaig which must be one of the prettiest train journeys one could wish for, not terribly practical for fishermen, but a marvellous journey - should the motor fail you. The loch is twelve and a half miles long and while there are salmon and sea-trout, it is mainly a trout water. Bank fishing is available at £2.50 a day or a boat with an outboard can be hired for £17.50. Permits may be had from Morar Motors, Loch Morar Adventure Centre, (0687) 2164 and the Morar Hotel (0687) 2346 which has three boats for guests and can also arrange fishing on several hill lochs.

Returning eastwards one finds Fort William where you can fish in the shadow of Ben Nevis, Britain's highest mountain. There is no better way to appreciate the grandeur of the mighty Ben than by fishing the River **Nevis** which skirts round it. Snow from the peaks above the glen help to maintain reasonable water levels for most of the season. It is essentially a spate river and thus it all depends on getting the right conditions. On its day it can produce terrific fishing, especially for sea-trout which average about a pound, while salmon are about the 6lb mark. A day's permit costs £5 from the Rod and Gun Shop (0397) 702656 in Fort William.

The Nevis joins the River **Lochy** just before it flows into Loch Linnhe. The Lochy is the largest and best salmon river in the area and so very hard to get on. It is largely owned by the River Lochy Association, a group of private owners, and the waiting list is long. Wading can be particularly dangerous as there is a power station at the western end of Loch Lochy and if it starts to generate, the water level can rise very quickly, so it is safest to fish the larger pools from a boat. Beat 7 which stretches from the tidal waters to a mile above Fort William is available from the Rod and Gun Shop (0397) 702656 at a cost of between £17 and £22 a day. This is good water which produces about 450 salmon a year, some of which exceed 28lb.

Heading north from Fort William on the A82 will bring you to Spean Bridge with its famous war memorial, for it was in this area that the brave Commandos did much of their training during the Second World War. In the days before fishing conservation was treated seriously, the headwaters and the feeder lochs of the River **Spean** were harnessed to provide power for the British Aluminium plant which would have wiped it out as a salmon river were it not for its main tributary the river Roy. As a result the best fishing is from Roybridge down to the Lochy. The Spean Bridge Hotel (0397) 81250 can offer guests fishing on the stretch between the old viaduct and Wade Bridge at a cost of £10 a day. The Rod and Gun shop may be able to help you get on other beats of this river and many other waters in the area. This is a good river where sea-trout average one and a half pounds and salmon 8lb; but it has a deserved reputation for

producing big fish - a 37 pounder was caught in 1976.

Is there a river that has not had its character changed and harmed by man? Well, yes! There are thankfully a few and one is the **Roy** which rises close to Loch Spey, the source of that great river from which it takes its name. How refreshing it is to find such a river that has been left to its own devices. The fish like it too - for nearly all salmon and sea-trout which run the Spean are heading for the Roy. It is very much a spate river and as there is no loch for it to drain, it can make for a very frustrating time if the weather is against you. Permits may be had from the Roy Bridge Hotel (0397) 81236 and Stronlossit Hotel (0397) 81253 at £15 a day. Mrs Irene Pryke (0449) 741481 lets three beats which rotate and can also offer self-catering accommodation. There are two rods on each beat and currently the cost is £12 per day per rod.

Fishing is free on **Loch Lochy** which is the most western loch in the Caledonian Canal system. It is almost solely a trout water but there are 5 pounders for those prepared to work at fishing this deep water. Boat moorings are controlled by the West Highland Estate Office (0397) 702433 who also issue permits for **Loch Arkaig** at £2 per day. Before the Caledonian Canal was built this loch abounded in salmon. An old game book records the following: 67 fish in a week, 289 fish in a month, 19 fish in a morning and one week only produced 37 fish beside which is written 'disappointing' - all these fish were to two rods. Personally I wouldn't mind some disappointing fishing like that!

In conclusion to this marvellous area let us reconsider our state of mind - Game fishing is a funny pre-occupation and it will never appeal to an impatient person. Some may say the fish are fickle, others conject that 'it's merely a bad year'. The fun, however, like all sport is in the taking part and no matter what the weather if you don't make the cast 'you'll nae catch the fushie'!

FISHING FAYRE

The coast of Western Scotland which runs from Knoydart through Moidart to Loch Linnhe continues the trend of the Highlands in that it offers remote, rugged scenery that is totally unspoilt. The Ness System dominates much of the landscape as it moves from the north southwards. Given the attraction of a certain beastie in Loch Ness, and many other more visable historic sights the area is popular with tourists and a number of good hotels can be found. We have listed a small number of them.

Some two miles east of Inverness we came across a prestigious house that was Bonnie Prince Charlie's during the fateful battle of Culloden, Culloden House (0467) 790461. Today the scene is somewhat more settled and the hotel boasts excellent standards of accommodation. Furthermore, exceptional dining can also be found here. Three miles west of the town we come upon Bunchrew House (0463) 234917 which is also steeped in history. The hotel dates from the 17th century and features some fine furnishings, open log fires and bedrooms which are extremely comfortable. Once again, the restaurant is to be noted for lovers of fine cuisine. Dunain Park (0463) 230512 is another delightful country house near to Loch Ness which offers a great deal. The Glen Mhor (0463) 234308 occupies a prime position opposite the River Ness. The hoteliers are happy to give advice on game and fishing opportunities, and provide a good stand-

ard of food and accommodation particularly in the 11 bedroom annexe on the river. Given the number of time share and Association waters in the area I hope these hotels will be able to cater for you. There are, however, many more in and around Inverness.

Some way south of Inverness and some nine miles from Fort Augustus the traveller will find Whitebridge. Here the Whitebridge Hotel (04563) 226 is a fine place to stay. The hoteliers are often able to sort out fishing for guests and the hotel is particularly good value. A more pricey but outstanding hotel is Knockie Lodge (04563) 276. This former hunting lodge proudly surveys Loch Nan Lann and boasts a delightful air of peace and calm. The drawing room offers peat and log fires and has superb views. Bedrooms are cosy and the set dinner is generally excellent. Some fishing can be organised from the hotel and this is definitely one for the shortcut.

Fort Augustus is a settlement at the southern tip of Loch Ness and a number of hotels are situated here. The Inchnacardoch Lodge (0320) 6258 is one such establishment. It's actually a converted hunting lodge which has the additional benefit of overlooking the huge and mysterious Loch Ness. Food is good here and standards of accommodation are also to be commended. The hotel is not an out and out fishing hotel but contacts through the hotel which may allow you some good sport. A similar comment can be made of another extremely welcoming Highland hotel, the Glenmoriston Arms (0320) 51206 in Invermoriston. One should always make a quick 'phone call to check the state of play, particularly at this popular hotel where the proprietors are generally keen to advise on the fishing, stalking and shooting opportunities that are available locally.

If a mansion should suit your fancy more than a lodge then pencil in the Glengarry Castle, Invergarry (08093) 254, a Victorian house which offers good value accommodation. The ruins of Invergarry Castle lie within the grounds and the food and hospitality are well above average. The Tomdoun Hotel (0809) 2218 should also be contacted when planning your fishing trip to this area. Good free fishing is available to guests in addition to some fine hospitality.

Those fishing the Roy should consult the Roy Bridge Hotel (0397) 81236 a 19th century coaching inn, the Stronlossit Hotel (0397) 81253 for permits and residential details and the Glenspean Lodge (0397) 81224 which has a lofty position some two miles east of Roy Bridge. The hoteliers are eager to please and will endeavour to help in the management of your sporting activities. Letterfinley Lodge (039781) 622 is another relaxing hotel to consult. Situated on the banks of Loch Lochy, it exudes Scottish charm. The scenery is gorgeous and the well packed bar particularly cosy. Game fishing is available and for a fishing break this hotel has much to commend it. In Spean Bridge itself, The Spean Bridge (039781) 250, which offers fishing on the Roy, is a more modern abode but also one to note.

Finally, we arrive at Fort William. There are all manner of hotels in this busy town which overlooks Loch Linnhe. Our two recommended hotels are situated north of the town in the shadows of Ben Nevis. The first thought is for those of you who can think of nothing better than spoiling yourself. Inverlochy Castle (0397) 702177 is a formidable establishment which positively exudes excellence. The grounds, gardens and views are wonderful and the interior offers all manner of style and excellence. Service is outstanding and the elegant restaurant is also first class. All manner of country pursuits can be enjoyed from this hotel, once a favourite haunt of Queen Victoria, including some game fishing. This is a hotel of excellence and for some, fishing can take a backseat. The other place of style is more a restaurant than a hotel, though seven stylish bedrooms are available, it is the Factor's House (0397) 705767. Game and fish are outstanding and once again we have a house of real quality - clearly an area to spoil yourself - on and off the water!

One final thought for those of you who seek to journey further westwards, perhaps to the remote hills of Moidart and its fine game fishing, is Arisaig. Arisaig House (06875) 622 should be your port of call. It has an enchanting setting and peace and relaxation are very much the order of the day. This is a hotel to escape to, perhaps for a day away from the fishing to spoil a loved one who is less keen on our marvellously captivating sport!

Loch Shiel is a wild and lovely place which attracts many fishermen. There are numerous hotels that we have mentioned that can organise your fishing and they all have their own merits. Please have brochures sent so you can pick the most appropriate for your own wishes, whatever your preference in travel and budget. This is always the best plan of attack. One thing is certain, however, you will be warmly received and find some good salmon and brown trout fishing - a splendid place to get away from it all. Further adventures can be had in the gorgeously unspoilt countryside here such as Knoydart and Loch Morar. Here the Morar Hotel (0687) 2346 is a really super place to stay, far from the 'madding' crowd.

ARDVOURLIE CASTLE

Despite its name, Ardvourlie Castle on the Isle of Harris in the Outer Hebrides was a hunting lodge built in 1863 by the Earl of Dunsmore which has recently been restored to its former glory. The Castle stands on on the shores of Loch Seaforth and nearby are the sandy beaches of the west coast and the rocky wilderness of South Harris. Otters and seals frequent the bay and golden eagles can be seen soaring over the hills. It is a wild and lonely place but extraordinarily beautiful.

The Castle itself is furnished in keeping with the period and the elegance of the house itself. The ceilings have elaborate cornices and the decorations are pure Victoriana, There are many antiques while some of the rooms still have gas and oil lamps and fire grates from the period and you have the option of an open fire in your room at night should you so wish.

The catering is generous and based on good, natural ingredients fresh from the surrounding countryside. Wherever possible, the chef uses local produce, including salmon, trout and island lamb. Scottish cheeses and Stormaway oatcakes are also on the menu. Recipes are based on a blend of traditional and imaginative and the cuisine here has featured in many good food guide books.

Ardvourlie Castle is an ideal base for exploring the mountains and lochs of North Harris on foot. The hotel will be very happy to arrange sea or freshwater fishing for you in the many lochs and the River Harris is renowned for salmon and trout fishing.

Naturalists will find a great deal to interest them, whether amongst the wild flowers of the machair or the birds of the sea and mountains. There are many places of historical interest too, Stornaway Castle, the Callanish Stones on Stornaway and the Isles of Skye Barra and North and South Uist are all easily accessible from the Castle and all are quite beautiful.

Ardvourlie Castle
Aird a Mhulaidh
Harris
Western Isles
Scotland
Tel: (0859) 2307

HIGHLANDS AND ISLANDS

THE ISLANDS

For those who want to really get away from it all there are the Islands, each of which has its own unique delights and pleasures for the visiting fisherman. With ferries and air flights, communications are much easier than they used to be. One of the joys of collecting old fishing books is reading about those days when gentlemen could devote their lives to sporting activities with no care for office life or the need to earn a living and what a marvellous time they had. In the early 19th century Colonel Jameson was invited to stay with a friend on Lewis to enjoy some fishing and stalking. It is not recorded how long the journey to Ullapool took but there are many complaints about the state of the roads and the standard of food available at coaching inns. At Ullapool the weather was against him and it was eight days before he could get across. The sport began in earnest and every day's entry for a period of five weeks records a good day with salmon, sea-trout, trout and stalking. The least successful day records two sea-trout of 1½ lb and 2lb and a fight with a 'hefty' salmon who broke him; whereas the best day produced 11 salmon, 4 sea-trout and 'some good trout'. Getting back to the mainland was a problem and he had to wait three days for the weather to improve. On his way back to Lancashire the axle of the coach broke. However, the local laird invited him to stay and so much did he enjoy the trout fishing, that it was two weeks before he made his departure. Those were the days!

Just across the Firth of Lorne is **Mull**, one of the most beautiful islands of the Inner Hebrides. Here you will find pine forests, wild moorlands, deserted beaches, mountains and the famous fossil tree preserved in the lava of Ben More millions of years ago. You are unlikely to find gold, but it is certainly there! A Spanish ship carrying a large quantity of gold to pay troops sank off Tobermory during the Spanish Armada, but despite many attempts no-one has yet found the wreck. From a fishing point of view there are good spate rivers for salmon and trout and several noted trout lochs.

The Aros is perhaps the best known river for it was here that in 1911 a 45lb salmon was taken on Ash Tree Pool after a six hour fight - the main run on this river, which is just under five miles long, is in July but this may be later if there is a hot dry summer. Salmon average 7lb and it is also noted for its sea-trout which usually tip the scales at around 1½ lb but run up to 3lb. Linndhu House Hotel (0688) 2425 have the middle beat of this river which is available to guests at a cost of £15 a day. They can also arrange fishing all over the island.

Nearby is Loch Frisa where salmon and sea-trout are often seen but seldom caught. It is, however, an excellent trout water and being quite dangerous by island standards is best fished from a boat. Do be careful if the wind is up for the loch can be quite bold. Permits are available from the Forestry Commission (0680) 300346 at £2 per day for bank fishing or £12 to include a boat: The Forestry Commission also issue permits for the River Lussa with its famous Pedlars Pool. This is very much a spate river and fish may take some time to ascend the waterfall at Tor Ness. Most of the bigger fish including a 34 pounder have been taken below the falls. Salmon and sea-trout are about the same

PORT ASKAIG HOTEL

Port Askaig Hotel is an ideal base for brown trout fishing in several nearby lochs on the Dunlossit Estate. Other lochs easily accessible withn 20 minutes' drive. Salmon and sea trout available on upper reaches of Laggan River.

This is an original Island Inn carefully modernised to a high standard offering a warm welcome and friendly hospitality. Bedrooms have colour TV and radio, some have private bathrooms. Menus feature the best of local and home garden produce.

Holiday package available including car ferry or air tickets.

STB Classification: 3 Crowns Commended.
AA, RAC, RSAC 2 Star. Ashley Courtenay Recommended.
Details and brochure from Mavis Spears.

Port Askaig Hotel
Islay of Islay
Argyll PA46 7RD
Tel: (049 684) 245
Fax: (049 684) 295

size as on Aros and it is widely regarded as one of the best rivers on the island.

Arguably the best fishing is to be had on the River Forsa. At ten miles long it is the longest river and has some 40 pools - double figure fish of up to 18lb are caught, though the average is around 8 lb. Like so many of these island spate rivers it rises and falls very quickly and is best fished when in spate. Another fine river is the two and a half mile long Ba which is privately owned. There is a big pool near its mouth at Killiechronan where you can often see salmon and sea-trout waiting to run - an invigorating sight. The River Coladoir has four miles of pools broken by gentle falls and offers good sea-trout fishing and the occasional salmon. Another fine sea-trout water is the River Bellart on which it is possible to catch a dozen in a day. But those will often be finnock (small sea-trout) and once you have caught enough for supper you are urged to return any further catches so as to conserve stocks for the future.

At the northern end of the island is Loch Torr which was purpose-built for fishing in 1899. This is a fly-only water which is stocked with rainbows and brownies and produces the occasional salmon and sea-trout. If trouting is more your thing then do try the three Mishnish lochs which lie between Dervaig and Tobermory or lochs Pellach, Meadhoin and Carnain an Amis.

Loch Ba, like the river of the same name, is let by Killiechronan Estates (0680) 300438. This loch fishes very well for salmon and especially sea-trout - double figure fish are not uncommon! Sguabain is Gaelic for 'windswept' and the loch certainly lives up to its name. Weed is a problem here so take care when playing your fish. At the southern end of the island on Ross of Mull is Loch Assapoll where salmon average 8lb and sea-trout 2lb. This is superb fishing and the loch is also famous for its brownies which run up to 7lb.

'Tackle and Books' in Tobermory (0688) 2336 can arrange for you to fish most waters as can many hotels like the lovely Western Isles Hotel (0688 2012) which is also in Tobermory.

Just south of Mull are the islands of Islay and Jura, names to conjure with for any lover of malt whisky. Most salmon fishing on **Islay** is privately owned, but not impossible to attain. Mrs Fraser at the Laggan Estate Office, Bowmore (049681) 248 handles weekly lets for the Laggan. The cost for a rod per week is in the region of £240 and fishing begins on the 1st of July with the salmon running to a reasonable average of 7¼ lb. This great little spate river does not really require wading as you can fish from the both banks. The Islay Estate has various four rod packages for the Rivers Sorn, Grey and the Laggan. In addition, fishing on many lochs, including Loch Gorm can be had, the latter is very shallow so watch out for rocks when boating. Salmon fishing averages at about £400 per 4 rods per week from Mr B. Wiles at the Headkeepers House, Bridgend (049681) 293. The Machrie Hotel (0496) 2310 in Port Ellen has great brown trout fishing on the Machrie Burn and is also a good centre for any holiday. The Port Askaig Hotel (0496) 84245 organises bookings for the Dunlossit Estate. They have six very good trout lochs with Ballygrant, Lossit and Allan providing the best fishing. Ballygrant was producing some good bags in early 1991 with two rods catching 72 and 90 fish in a day! Wet and dry flies both do well and bank fishing costs only £3 per day and £7 for a beat. Incidentally, you will not need your hiking boots, as these three gems are accessible from the road.

Walking boots of some description are something of a must for **Jura**. This wild and wonderful island has only one road which finishes at the cottage where George Orwell completed '1984'. Fishing on this island, famed for its stalking (Jura is gaelic for 'The Island of Deer') is predominently for brown trout. However, the River Lussa when in spate, can produce interesting salmon and sea-trout fishing. Contact Mr.C.Fletcher at the Ardlussa Estate in Ardlussa (0496) 82323.

Across from Kintyre we come upon the delightful isle of **Arran**, more renowned for breathtaking scenery than its game fishing and dominated by the 2868 foot high Goat Fell. However, the Machrie river can produce good sport, especially from dusk onwards and the salmon tend to average around the 6lb mark. Contact Mr J.T. Boscawen at the Strathtay Estate Office, Boltachan, By Aberfeldy, Perthshire (0887) 20496. Prices vary between £90 and £145 per rod per week. For the River Iorsa and its loch contact the Dougarie Estate Office (0770) 84259.

Separated from Mull by the Ardnamurchan Peninsular - the most westerly point of the mainland - is **Skye** and its romantic associations with Bonnie Prince Charlie and Flora Macdonald. Being relatively easy to get to, it is popular with tourists and likely to get much busier with the proposed new road bridge. Ullinish Lodge Hotel (0470) 72214 has the rights for the River Ose and the upper four miles of the River Snizort and fishing is available to guests at £7.50 a day. Fishing on the lower eight miles of the Snizort is available to guests of the Skeabost House Hotel (0470) 32202 at a cost of £10 per day. Both hotels can also arrange trout fishing on lochs as can the Misty Isle Hotel (0470) 22208 on the shore of Loch Dunvegan. This is run by experienced fishermen who can also arrange sea fishing. Permits for the Uig Angling Association water on the River Hinnisdale are available from the bar of the Ferry Inn (0470) 42242 at £15 a day. As one would expect these are spate streams and rain is the all important factor. Portree Angling Association can offer visitors a wide choice of loch and some river fishing and permits may be had from Jansport in Portree (0478) 2559 at a cost of between £1.50 and £5 a day.

Scots and fishermen consider that Lewis, Harris, North Uist, Benbecula and South Uist make up the **Western Isles**. If you have the opportunity to visit, do go, for they are a fisherman's paradise. There is outstanding salmon and sea-trout fishing and literally hundreds of trout lochs. The islands' remoteness ensures that you can enjoy your fishing in perfect tranquillity disturbed only by the sight of red deer on the hills or rare birds like the red necked phalarope. I strongly advise you to make sure your fly box is suitably filled before coming here as tackle shops are few and far between. The Stoats Tail is a popular choice for salmon while for sea-trout I would take traditional patterns such as the Peter Ross, the Mallard and Claret, Silver Invicta, some Zulu's, a Wickham's Fancy, a Goat's Toe and my old favourite, the Muddler Minnow.

Lewis has several hundred lochs full of hard fighting wild brownies which can go up to 6lb. The Grimersta is a great river by national as well as island standards, and one of the most prolific waters you could wish for - its 57 fish taken on the fly in one day is a record that will take some beating. The fishing is owned by a syndicate which was formed by Lord Leverhulme in 1922 and is managed by Grimersta Estates Office (0851) 72358. The river itself is only some two miles long above which is a chain of lochs culminating in Loch Langavat which at seven miles

HIGHLANDS AND ISLANDS

long is the longest on the islands. It is fly only water except for Langavat where spinning is also permitted. A favoured technique is to fish a very small fly on the point and something much larger like a Muddler Minnow tied on a size 6 as a dropper. There are four beats and such famous pools as Bridge, Battery, Captains and Sea Pool. While Autumn may be the best time, May and June can produce catches of up to 50 fish a week but are not so predictable.

There are 3 miles of the River Laxay above Loch Valtos and one mile below it. River fishing is mainly on the three main pools of the lower section which are appropriately named Top, Middle and Lower; the loch is divided into beats each with a boat and a ghillie. Sea-trout average 1½ lb and salmon 7lb though a 33 pounder was caught back in 1933. The Creed is another good river. Its five miles are divided into 3 single rod beats which rotate on a daily basis while its loch is fished by two boats. The river flows through Lady Lever's park with its magnificent rhododendrons and noted pools include Fall, Bond and Junction. A day's permit costs £6.20 and is available from the Stornoway Trust Estate Office (0851) 702002. The Blackwater fishes well especially on the lower section which has some good holding pools; it is aptly named for the river is rather peaty and you will probably find that a fly with some orange or yellow will work best. The Uig is very much a spate river but if you hit it in the right conditions it can be very good. It was near here that the famous 12th century Lewis chessmen were found. Scaliscro Estates (085175) 325 can offer salmon and sea-trout fishing on the Rivers Creed and Blackwater and six lochs including Langavat. It also offers trout fishing on nine other lochs. The trout fishing is superb, take for example Loch Fhreunadail where the trout average ½ lb and the best day's log was 55. The premier loch in my opinion is Loch Bruiche Breivat where they average ¾ lb and run to 4lb plus. The most successful day record here was 100 brownies and 2 Arctic char! Trout fishing on Lewis is superb but do be prepared to walk or hire an argocat to get you across country.

Harris is world famous for its tweeds and no visit would be complete without a visit to see how they are made. Guests of the North Harris Estate (085986) 200 can stay at Amhuinnsuidhe Castle which is the most westerly castle in the country and enjoy fishing on 8 large lochs where salmon range from 5-8 lb and sea-trout 1-5lb, though there are bigger fish as the records are 18¾ lb and 11lb. Other good fishing on Harris includes the Scarista and Horsacleit which is very much a spate stream. The Rodel Hotel at Leverburgh (08598) 2210 offers guests good salmon, sea-trout and brown trout fishing on a number of lochs. Ardvourlie Castle (0859) 2307 is a great place to stay if you are fishing in the area. Here, on the shores of Loch Seaforth you can see otters and, if you are lucky, golden eagles. The lunches are both sumptuous and scenic - it is not unknown for an eagle to time his 'fly past' as you are seated - a marvellous diversion wouldn't you agree! Fishing for guests can be arranged on the nearby Aline Estate which boasts some first class water.

Lochmaddy Hotel (0876) 3331 is the place to stay for fishing **North Uist** and **Benbecula** or if you wish to be independent from the hotel, the North Uist Estate Office (0876) 3329 will be able to help you. There are many first class trout lochs and the Skelter System offers salmon and sea-trout fishing. The Department of Agriculture (0870) 2346 issue permits for several good lochs at £4 a week or £8 a day including a boat. At the northern end of the island is Loch Nan Geireann; here, at low tide, there

is a tidal pool where you can see salmon and sea-trout leaping and splashing in the clear shallow water which is a sight that will delight any fisherman.

The Lochboisdale Hotel (0878) 4332 manages most of the fishing on **South Uist**, which has some of the best Hebridean fishing. Two pound trout are the norm rather than the exception when fishing Grogarry Loch which fishes well from the bank as well as from a boat. Other good lochs include Bornish, Kildonan and Stilligarry. Lochs Howmore, Ollay, Fada and Roag are known for their salmon and superb sea-trout, which run up to 8lb and are often over 4lb. It is also worth emphasising once more the scenic beauty of these islands, field glasses are almost as important as your hip flask.

Although **Orkney** is only six miles across the Pentland Firth from Caithness, it was part of the Viking Kingdom of Norway and Denmark until 1468. The islands are rich in history, something the locals are proud of. Here you can see the standing stones of Stenness, a small circle dating from the third millenium BC. Close by is Maes Howe, the finest chambered tomb in Western Europe built before 2700 BC. It houses the largest collection of runic inscriptions to be found in any one place in the world! Beneath the waters of Scapa Flow are the remains of the 72 German Naval vessels scuttled in 1919. It is also the only place where you will see a round hazard sign for otters crossing the road.

From a fishing point of view there is some of the best trout water in the world. At 2528 acres Loch Harray is the largest Orkney water and an average depth of 8 feet and rarely exceeding 14 feet it is perfect trout water. There are good hatches of midges, olives, sedges and later on daddy-longlegs while an abundant supply of freshwater shrimp helps to give the flesh a lovely pink colour. Although a 17 pounder was caught thirty years ago they average about ¾ lb. However, these fish will fight like nothing you have met before and many an experienced angler has been convinced that he must be into at least a two pounder from the way it has fought and has been surprised to find that when brought to the net it is only a 1lb fish. These fish are very surface active and fast risers so quick reactions are needed. The Merkister Hotel (0856) 77366 is an ideal place to stay as the manager, Angus MacDonald, is a local expert.

Loch Swannay may be only a quarter of the size of Harray but it is a favourite with the locals and produces fish of 2lb and more with amazing regularity. Good baskets in recent years have been 10 fish for 17½lb, 4 for 8¼ lb and 3 for 12½lb - need we say more! Loch Stennes is famous for the record 29lb fish taken at the turn of the century and today fish of between 5 and 7lb are caught quite often. This is the one loch where it is worth casting a fly over the weed beds as these make good cover for the trout avoiding the attention of seals who are present throughout the year. It also serves as a larder, for these trout are piscivorous - one fish's bulging stomach revealed a 12 inch eel, 15 spined stickleback, lugworm and coalfish, as well as more normal samples of diet like midge, snails and daddy-longlegs. Two other good lochs are Boardhouse and Hundland which often fishes well in bright conditions. There are also several other smaller waters. Good Orkney flies include Black Pennell, Zulu, Invicta, Soldier Palmer, Dunkeld, Alexandra and local favourites like the Loch Ordie. There are no rivers and the only lochs for sea-trout are Stennes and Kirbister, but sea-trout can be caught in the bays and shorelines of the coastline. All you

have to do to enjoy this magnificent fishing is to join the Orkney Trout Fishing Association. The cost is under £10 and further details may be had from the Secretary, M. Russell, Esq. (0856) 76586 or the Orkney Tourist Board (0856) 2856.

The **Shetland Islands** are closer to Norway than Scotland and for hundreds of years were allowed to run their own affairs without interference from the mainland. Then oil was discovered in the North Sea and the islands were 'developed'. However the trout are still there and there are hundreds of lochs with good fighting brownies of up to 8lb and more; an added bonus for fishermen is that there are no midges here. Favourite lochs include Tingwall which is regularly stocked with native-bred fish, Benston where the average is 1½ lb and Girlsta which produced the 12½ lb record for Shetland. The outer islands have good fishing too. **Whalsay** has three first class lochs including Huxter. **Unst** has Lochs Cliff and Snarravoe and good sea-trout fishing at Burra Firth and Dales Voe. **Yell** has sea-trout and brownies in Loch Papil. Even tiny **Fetlar** has three lochs and you may see a snowy owl. As on Orkney, salt water spinning in the Voes is the thing for sea-trout and a strip of mackerel belly on the treble may help. The same flies as suggested for Orkney should do the trick though you might care to add a Ke-He. All this fishing is available for £10 by joining the Shetland Anglers Association whose secretary is Mr A. Miller (0595) 3729. The Association publishes a particularly useful booklet which includes maps, hints on technique and specific information on over 100 lochs. Alternatively, the Shetland Isles Tourist Board (0595) 3434 will be able to help and advise you.

FISHING FAYRE

If you really want a 'get away from it all' type of holiday, you could not wish for anything more enjoyable than a fishing foray to the Islands. While some fishing is as expensive and hard to come by as on the mainland, there is a great variety of loch and river fishing at very affordable prices.

The Mainland of Scotland may have some celebrated salmon rivers, but if you are seeking brown trout fishing, then the Islands are the big brother of the Mainland. Perhaps this is because they are remote, perhaps there is another reason but as you ponder away, one thing is certain, you will not regret a trip to the distant Islands of the Highlands of Scotland.

Mull is a beautiful isle and the principle port of call is Tobermory. The Linndhu House Hotel (0688) 2425 has fishing all over the island including a beat on the Aros. Tobermory is the busiest part of the island and the Tobermory Hotel (0688) 2091 is a delightful place to stay. Lovers of wildlife will also wish to consider Ulva House (0688) 2044. The proprietor here is an authority on the island's wildlife and organises expeditions to take in the charming wilderness of the countryside and the animals that seek shelter within it.

To the south of the island, the fisherman who wishes to spoil himself will visit Tiroran House (06815) 232. This is a delightfully remote hotel surrounded by the most stunning scenery. The house is extremely comfortable and there is a deliberate homeliness in the welcome. Dinner here is something of a treat and a special excursion is thoroughly recommended.

Although Arran may not be the best island in terms of fishing it boasts some majestic scenery and for people wanting to re-

ally relax and enjoy a number of pursuits, golf, walking, riding, fishing etc it is a splendid place to head for. The Auchrannie Country House Hotel (0770) 2234, in Brodick and the Lagg Hotel, Kilmory (0770) 87255 are two hotels to consider.

The Isle of Skye beckons and many visit. The Ullinish Lodge Hotel (0470) 72214 is a distinguished fishing hotel and is an extremely welcoming place to stay as is the Skeabost House (0470) 32202. The latter has a splendid woodland setting with fine views over Loch Snizort. There are a number of fine leisure facilities including a nine hole golf course as well as some fine river fishing - as a result it is a great favourite with anglers. Another great favourite with visitors to the isle is the Three Chimneys (047081) 258, here we find Scottish cooking at its best. A visit is thoroughly recommended to this fine restaurant in Colbost, near Dunvegan.

Lewis is home to some remarkable fishing. It is wonderfully remote and accommodation is somewhat difficult to come by. In Stornaway, the island's major hotel can be found, the Cabarfeidh (0851) 702604. It's a fine hotel and a good base for exploring the islands and the many fishing opportunities available. North Uist is another treat for those of us who have to get away from it all. Lochmaddy Hotel (0876) 3331 is the place to escape to and the fishing from here can be excellent. South Uist also beckons the angler. The hotel which gives the finest welcome is the Lochboisdale Hotel, Lochboisdale (08784) 332. Fishing prints adorn the walls and while the hotel has no pretensions to luxury it is welcoming and a delight for the fisherman.

Orkney is a wonderful island to visit and if you have been stuck in a rut, fishing the same water for years or worse still only fished in a reservoir a few miles from home consider a trip to Orkney, its waters are celebrated throughout the world, Loch Harray is the major attraction and the place to visit is the Merkister Hotel (085677) 366. The proprietor knows his fishing and when you set eyes on the bar you will know your trip has been a 'goodun' when you commence fishing. There will be serious questions asked as to when you will return. Sadly, it may not be possible to make that second trip but not to make that first pilgrimage is a tragic omission for anyone who enjoys the thrill of trout fishing.

Shetland, Orkney and the islands are generally well served by their tourist boards and all manner of ideas for self catering and small guest house accommodation can be found by contacting their offices. In the north of the island, in Brae, is the scenic Busta House Hotel (080622) 506. It is a delightful little hotel in an 18th century country manor house and useful if you are journeying to the waters of this area or heading towards Yell or Unst. In Kerwick itself The Shetland Hotel (0595) 5515 is purpose built but comfortable for those of you who are seeking a port of call after your ferry journey.

There are all manner of out of the way, sometimes undiscovered, waters in the Islands of Scotland. They are remote, hotels are often matter of fact and self catering lodges are often the favoured form of accommodation. What is for sure, they provide a wonderful escape from the pace of the 1990's.

LOCHBOISDALE HOTEL

On the south-east of South Uist, the Lochboisdale hotel rests on a deeply indented sea loch of the same name. The town is a small but busy port with car ferry connections and a delightful day long procession of tiny fishing boats coming to and fro.

The hotel is small and family-run, overlooking the loch and boasting sweeping panoramic views across the minch to Canna and Rhum. Eleven of the very comfortable rooms have private ensuite facilities and prices include breakfast.

The prime importance of this charming hotel though is for the committed fisherman. For Brown trout, there are sixteen boats available on as many lochs, many of which are "machair" lochs, where the high alkalinity caused by the shell sand bed produces large and beautifully conditioned trout. For the fisherman who prefers Sea Trout and Salmon, there are ten boats on eight lochs, with the opportunity to hire a gillie and the guarantee of breath-taking scenery.

For a change from fishing, the stunning natural beauty of the surrounding countryside offers a variety of outdoor pursuits. For the bird-watcher it is a paradise, with the possibility of spotting a rare Corncrake or elusive Golden Eagle. There are miles of silver sandy beaches to comb and a walk through the hills when the heather blooms is an experience not to be missed.

The district is much associated with Bonnie Prince Charlie, and Flora MacDonald who sailed to Skye with him, was born at Milton, a few miles north. A little further to the north are the gaunt ruins of Ormaclete castle, seven years in construction, occupied for seven years and then burned to the ground way back in 1715. Just to the north of this, at Howmore, are the graves of the ancient chiefs of the Clanranald.

After a hard day's relaxation the dining room of the hotel welcomes you back with a wide-ranging menu of excellent food. Fresh local produce is a speciality, including lobster, fresh and smoked salmon, venison from the estate, Hebredian lamb and prime Scotch beef. Retire afterwards to the lounge bar, with peat burning fire, cedar wood panelling and a full range of malt whiskies. The public bar can offer a fascinating atmosphere as local islanders and trawler fishermen gather for live music and no doubt, a sampling of that whiskey. Ideal for angler and non-angler alike, Lochboisdale prides itself on offering a traditional Uist "Ceud Mile Failte" to all.

Lochboisdale Hotel
Isle of South Uist
Western Isles
Scotland PA81 5TH
Tel: (08784) 332
Fax: (08784) 367

THE GRAMPIANS

Artist Wendy Reeves HIGHLAND RIVER Courtesy of Rosenstiels'

47

THE GREAT

SPEAN BRIDGE

FORT WILLIAM

THE

NEVIS

LOCH LINNHE

L. LAIDON

L. BA

LOCH

OBAN

AWE

LOCHAN SHIRA

ARDLUI

LOCH AWE

INVERARAY

LOCH LOMOND

TYNE

ADD

CRINAN

ECK

KILLCHIAN AIR

LOCHGILPHEAD

ROTHESAY

JURA

DU

FEOLIN FERRY

LOCH FYNE

PORT ASKAIG

GOCK

BRIDGEND

TARBERT

FIRTH OF CLYDE

LARGS

ISLAY

LAGGAN

ISLE OF ARRAN

KINTYRE

CARRADALE

BRODICK

MACHRIE

SUSSA

MACHRIHANISH

CAMBELTOWN

PORT ELLEN

SOUTHEND

48

ALVIE ESTATE

Alvie House is an unspoilt Victorian/Edwardian Shooting Lodge situated in its own grounds on Alvie Estate (13,000) acres in Strathspey. It maintains a dual role of family home and place of gracious entertainment. Past owners include Lady Caernarvon, widow of the ill-fated discoverer of Tutenkamhun's tomb, who modernised the house in the late 1920s. The present Laird, Jamie Williamson and his family are resident all year round and retire to private quarters within the house to make room for their guests.

The house itself enjoys a secluded setting, overlooking a small trout loch, surrounded by pine woodland with views of the Cairngorm Mountains beyond.

Alvie House retains the traditional character of a Highland Shooting Lodge while still providing its guests with the modern facilities they require. Stags heads adorn the walls, there are large fire places, enormous baths and a full size billiard table.

The spacious bedrooms accommodate up to 14 guests on the first floor with additional comfortable accommodation on the second floor to cater for larger groups. Alvie House is available for groups only (6-20 persons) although special arrangements can be made to accommodate larger numbers in the estate cottages.

Sporting facilities on the Estate and in the surrounding country-side are almost endless; fishing, shooting, falconry, clay pigeon shooting, archery, stalking and tennis are all laid on either in the grounds or on the Estate. Nearby there are skiing and ice climbing on Cairngorm (heli-skiing can be arranged) during the season plus curling, skating and husky races. The area is also famous for its hill-walking and bird watching and there are six golf courses within a 20 mile radius of Alvie.

Alvie fishing is particularly varied; Brown Trout from Lochs Alvie and Beag, Brown Trout, Arctic Char, Salmon, Sea Trout and Pike from Loch Insh or Brown Trout, Sea Trout and Salmon from the Rivers Spey and Feshie. There is also a two acre loch stocked with Rainbow Trout for beginners or those less successful days on the river or loch.

The lawn in front of Alvie House leads down to Little Loch Bourne which is stocked with large Trout exclusively for the entertainment of the keen anglers amongst the house guests.

Alvie House
Alvie Estate
Kincraig
Kingussie
Inverness-shire PH21 1NE
Tel: (0540) 651255/249
Fax: (0540) 651380

THE GRAMPIANS

SPEYSIDE

At last the mighty river **Spey** famous throughout the world as one of our great salmon rivers. It drains over one thousand two hundred square miles and is one of the fastest flowing rivers in the British Isles. It is also a big-fish water with twenty pounders and bigger being caught regularly. Although it has produced salmon over 50lb the heaviest fish was apparently a pike of 146lb! This is recorded in Colonel Thornton's delightful 'Sporting Tour', but he does admit that he had this story on heresay. I can't help feeling that a few pounds had been added in the telling of the story perhaps over a bottle of Scotch or three.

Speyside is an intoxicating area if not for it's glorious river but as a result of the number of distilleries in the area. Driving down Strathspey you will see the source of many a famous whisky. There are numerous distilleries in the area and high street brands mix with lesser known labels making a veritable treat. The local tourist board have coined the area the 'Whisky Trail,' according to a local gossip it is impossible to lose ones way even though the route is badly sign posted 'Follow the bodies' he said! Perhaps the answer is to take an extended holiday so you can do justice to the unique malts of this area.

The Spey has a special place in my heart for it was here that I caught my first salmon, but two years earlier I made a finer catch. The first take was at a dinner party and she was an extremely pretty girl. As I was plucking up the courage to propose a second rendez-vous she informed me that her annual trip to Scotland would take up the next two weeks. On further investigation, I discovered that her family fished the Spey. As you will understand, I loved her even before I knew this - but I have to confess to some satisfying 'icing' being put on the 'matrimonial cake'. After eighteen months of 'playing', I finally landed my catch and soon after we were on the Spey! On my first visit there were six rods in the party and it was bitterly cold. After two quiet days, only salvaged by some fine whisky our spirits were low. On the third day we were fishing Dipple and hopes were high - but by lunchtime my enthusiasm was waning. All was quiet and then he struck! A wondrous feeling - and after a memorable tussle a seven pound salmon was my prize. That evening we served him up with hollandaise sauce - never had a fish tasted so good!

The Spey is some one hundred miles long from source to mouth. It's source is the small Loch Spey near the River Roy and not far from Loch Lochy. From the loch it is joined by small burns from Corrieyairack Forest. These burns present a problem for as they tumble down the steep slopes they wash away the soil from the forestry plantations and as a result the spates are much more pronounced. When in spate, the water is very coloured, in fact almost black. The Upper Spey has been harnessed for hydro power but at Blargie it is joined by the River Mashie and from here begins to take on its real character.

This is Jacobite country. As you look at Cluny Castle, which was rebuilt in the 19th century, spare a thought for Cluny Macpherson. This clan chief hid for eight years in Cluny's Cave in the hills above following the failure of the 1745 rebellion and had to suffer the ignominy of watching 'Butcher' Cumberland's troops razing his ancestral home to the ground. Also in the area are the ruins of Ruthven Barracks, scene of one of the few Jacobite successes, for it was here that the interestingly named Gordon of Glenbucket defeated the government troops. How different history might have been had Bonnie Prince Charlie not turned back at Derby and retreated north. Harried all the way, the retreat became a rout until the desperate last stand at Culloden. Alas, claymores were no match for muskets nor was the fierce but poorly organised clan loyalty very effective against the regimented discipline of the English army.

For over fifty years, the Scots and English sympathisers had lived in hope of seeing a restoration of the Stuarts. Their hopes had been raised when 'Dutch' William - William of Orange - died after a fall from his horse which stumbled on a mole hole and gave rise to the Jacobite toast 'To the little gentleman in black velvet'. After the failure of the 1715 rebellion they continued to drink to the health of the King across the water out of the beautifully engraved Jacobean glasses with their secret Stuart motifs. All these hopes died at Culloden; this was one of the bloodiest battles fought on our soil and the rapacity with which survivors were hounded down and the clan system destroyed put paid to the last aspirations of those who espoused the Stuart cause.

But enough of history, what of the fishing? The next feeder stream of any consequence is the Truim and then, at Newtonmore, the Spey is joined by the Calder while below Kingussie we find the junction with the Tromie. Sadly, both the Calder and Tromie have been dammed for hydro power. Just above Kincraig it flows through Loch Insh whose shallow waters contain those rapacious eaters of salmon parr, pike, but netting keeps their numbers down. In the church at Kincraig is St Eunans bell. This little masterpiece of Celtic bronze work was carried in front of funeral processions 1400 years ago. Below the loch are the junctions with the Feshie, another victim of afforestation, and the Druie.

After passing through small old villages it is quite a surprise to come to Aviemore with its clusters of chalets and big modern hotels which seem most incongruous in such a setting. On our way to Fochabers we have often watched skiers coming down the runs and thought that skiing and salmon fishing would make an unusual biathlon event! A couple of miles further on the A9 is the fork for the A95 and the quaintly named village Boat of Garten, so called because a ferry was the only means of crossing the river until the bridge was built.

The next tributaries to join the Spey are the Nethy and Dulnain, the latter, a first class salmon river. After this we journey on to Grantown-on-Spey. This is the seat of Clan Grant and the capital of Strathspey. Although a popular tourist resort, it is also well known to fishermen for it is here that Arthur Oglesby -who has probably forgotten more about salmon fishing than most of us will ever learn! - runs his excellent fishing courses.

From Grantown to the estuary is the best fishing on the Spey with a succession of big deep holding pools broken by stretches of white water rapids. These pools can be deceptively dangerous and the greatest possible care should be taken when wading. Due to the fact that the river is so fast, the slightest slip can produce tragic results. There are far too many fishing accidents and while it may be tempting to wade a little further so that one can cover more water it is simply just not worth the risk.

At Ballindalloch the Spey is joined by the **Avon**, known as the A'an by locals. To whisky drinkers the Avon is famous for its tributary the Livet, source of that lovely malt, Glenlivet. Because the Avon's source is in the granite and quartz slopes of the Cairngorms it is crystal clear and so demands a careful approach if the fish are not going to be alerted. The Ballindalloch beats are prime salmon fishing, especially Junction Pool which has also produced a notable 8lb brown trout. There are many famous names hereabouts, Upper Pitchroy, Lower Pitchroy, Phonas Water, Knockando, Laggan and Carron, Wester Elchies, Kinermony, Aberlour, Easter Elchies and Craigellachie. All are superb fishing but are expensive as well. In 1989 a mile of north bank fishing on Faster Elchies which had six named pools was put on the market at an asking price of £900,000!

At Craigellachie, you can watch salmon and sea-trout running the rapids to Bridge Pool by standing on Telford's bridge. A mile or so downstream, the Spey is joined by another stream whose name is well known to whisky drinkers for the Fiddich is the home of Glenfiddich. It was the steep wooded sides of this valley combined with the need to be able to cover the big pools that led to the development of Spey casting. This method keeps the line in front of you at all times and is worth learning as it can come in useful on many other rivers.

Some of the estuary nets have been bought off, and hence the fishing has improved. That's all very well you might say but how do I get to fish? Surprisingly, despite the Spey's reputation, fishing is possible if you know where to go. The best beats are expensive but are excellent and are 'impossible' to get on. However, various hotels, fishing clubs and estates offer days or weeks that can be taken up if you book early enough. The clubs often have various restrictions, for example, Aberlour Angling Club requires that visitors fishing their one mile stretch stay the night(s) prior to fishing, in one of the village's three hotels. They also have a bag limit of two fish per day - one above the bridge and the other below. Any further fish caught have to be handed over to Munro's Tackle Shop to be sold 'for the good of the club and the village'. This does not happen very often! The following is a list of contacts that will be able to help you to fish this majestic river: (For Badenoch A.A.) A. & L. Donald, Main Street, Newtonmore (0540) 3242; Speyside Sports, Grampian Road, Aviemore (0479) 810656 (new Abernathy A.A. stretch, £10 per day); Alvie Estate, Kincraig (0540) 4255 (three beats, £20 per day); Lynwilg Hotel, Aviemore (0479) 810209 (three miles and four lochs); Rothiemurchus Estate, by Aviemore (0479) 810703 (three beats, £12/£18 per day, plus two lochs); Craigard Hotel, Boat of Garten (0479) 83206 (Abernathy A.A. six and a quarter miles both banks at £15 per day); The Boat Hotel, Boat of Garten, (0479) 83258; Allen's, Boat of Garten (0479) 83372 (also Abernathy A.A.); Caledonian Angling do personalised packages from the simple to the luxurious (0479) 82363. Strathspey A.A. have a seven mile stretch with several permit issuers in Grantown; Mortimers (0479) 2684 (£40 for 6 days), Spey Valley Hotel (0479) 2942, Seafield Lodge Hotel (0479) 2152; Strathspey Estate, Grantown (0479) 2529 retain three beats for between £300 and £1000 per rod per week; Nethybridge Hotel, Nethybridge (0479) 82203; Blairfindy Lodge Hotel, Glenlivet (0807) 3376 let the Carron/ Laggan Beat for one week each year at £2500 + VAT for five rods (can also arrange rods on the Avon); R. & R. Urquhart (0309) 72216; Aberlour A.C. have outlets in the town, for example: J.A.J. Munro in the High Street, Aberlour Hotel (0340) 871287; Lour Hotel (0340) 871224, Dowans Hotel (0340) 871488; the favourite, Craigellachie Lodge (0340) 881224; Linc Holdings Ltd (0205) 79444; Orton Estate (0343) 88240.

The tributaries of the Spey are easier to get on and more affordable. Strathspey Angling Association has twelve miles of the River **Dulnain**. This is good salmon fishing and also offers sea-trout, grilse and brown trout. As one would expect it is fly-only except when the water is high, when spinning is allowed. Permits at a cost of £40 a day may be had from Mortimers in Grantown (0479 2684) but you have to be staying locally. The Gordon Arms Hotel at Tomintoul (0807) 4206 can offer guests two miles of fishing on the Avon at £18 a day. Also there is the Richmond Arms Hotel (0807) 4209 which can offer guests fishing on over six miles of this gin clear water at a cost of £100 a week. This hotel also has two and a half miles of the Livet. R.G. Heape, Esq. at the Ballindalloch Estate Office (0807) 2205 can offer fishing on six miles of the Avon. This water averages 166 salmon and 226 sea-trout a season. Permits to fish the long stretch of the Fiddich leased by Mortlach Angling Club may be had for £6 a day from TV Services in Dufftown (0340) 20527.

A few miles west, along the coast we find Lossiemouth and the River **Lossie**. This river is overshadowed by its famous sisters the Spey and the Findhon but is the type of water that offers the occasional salmon at a modest cost. It is also a good sea-trout water for, while salmon average around 150 per season, sea-trout catches in recent years have varied between 1179 and 3166. Summer is the time for sea-trout and autumn for salmon. As it flows through arable land the bed of the river is muddy and pools tend to be small and deep. The course of this river from its source in Seven Sisters Spring to the Moray Firth is some 34 miles. On its journey it skirts the town of Elgin. Here, you can see the ruins of the cathedral known as 'the Lantern of the North', but this term does not derive from evangelical fame, but the fact that it was repeatedly burnt to the ground! Permits to fish the upper waters may be had for £8 a season from Mr W. Macdonald, President of the Dallas Angling Association (0343) 89367 provided you are staying in the parish. Incidentally, salmon do get up this far if there has been enough water for them to ascend the rocks at Kellas.

Continuing west along the A96 brings you to Forres and the River **Findhorn**. This is top quality salmon fishing in beautiful surroundings. Many years ago the then Earl of Moray netted Sluie Pool and took over 1300 salmon in one night! An early demonstration of the detrimental effect of netting. The course of the river was much changed by the tremendous floods of 1829 when the river rose by over 50 foot in places causing widespread loss of life and livestock. It still rises very quickly when in spate and can rise by as much as two feet in ten minutes so do be careful. The river's source in the Monadhliath Mountains is some sixty miles from the Moray Firth. Apart from the occasional conifer plantation, the river is very open down to Dulsie Bridge. Below here, the river thunders for some twenty miles through a gorge with sheer sides over 200 feet high in places for twenty miles. The river relies on snow melt to maintain its level and this cold water usually stops fish running beyond the gorge before May. However spring fishing in the gorge can produce 20 and even 30 pound fish. July is the time for grilse and as one would expect September is the best time on the upper river. It is a hard river to get on and you may find yourself on a long waiting list, however the following may be able to help you. J. Mitchell, Tackle Shop at Forres (0309) 72936 has access to private beats on one and a half miles at a cost varying from £200 to £1000 per week. Cawdor Estates (0667) 7666 let some of their beats. Mr D. McConnell of Moray Estates Office (0309) 72269 has a waiting list but serious enquiries for

THE GRAMPIANS

the future will be considered. A. Laing Esq., of Logie Estates (0309) 6208 lets beats at a cost of £700 per week for 4 rods; there is a waiting list but I understand it is not too lengthy - R. & R. Urquhart (0309) 72216 let the Coulmony Beat at a cost of £50 per rod per day - Muckrach Lodge Hotel (0479) 85257 at Dulnain Bridge has 2¾ miles. This water holds four rods and the cost of a day's fishing is £30 a day and a ghillie is available.

A few miles to the west lies the River **Nairn**. This is an area rich in history for here you will find Clava with its Druidical remains, Jacobite ghosts on Culloden Moor and Cawdor Castle, immortalised in Shakespeare's 'Macbeth'. The source of the river is high in the mountains south of Loch Ness. Parts of the upper river suffer from salting but downstream there are many good deep holding pools, although the bankside bushes and trees can cause a few casting problems. However being a narrow river it is not too difficult to cover the water. May and June are the best months for sea-trout fishing which can be superb, while August and September are best for salmon. It is a productive river and though spring runs are not what they were, salmon are caught in March and April. S.Newbould Esq., of the Nairn District Salmon Fishery Board (0667) 53495 may be able to help you get a day on one of the private beats. Nairn Angling Association has eight miles of fishing upstream from the harbour. Permits for this water cost £8 a day or £25 a week and may be had from Pat Fraser, Radio TV & Sports Shop, Nairn (0667) 53038. Clava Lodge Holiday Homes (0463) 790228 have one and three quarter miles of the south bank which costs £4 per rod per day.

Should you not be lucky enough to get on one of these rivers, you might care to have a day's trouting on **Lochindorb**. The loch is about two miles long and bank fishing is free though you are advised to get permission from one of the local tackle shops. The cost of a boat is £12 a day or £4 for an evening. The wild brownies here average between ½ lb and ¾ lb and the water is at present overstocked so rods are asked to kill all fish caught. With a breeze from the south or west rippling the surface you will do well to fish a team of dark pattern flies - good baskets may result. Slightly better fish averaging around the 1lb mark can be caught on **Loch Morlich**. This is near Aviemore so don't expect good catches until the snow melts and the water warms up, May is the recommended month. At three quarters of a mile long, it fishes well from the bank and it is not worth hiring a boat -especially as the loch is also a watersports centre! Permits cost £2.90 a day or £10.75 a week and can be had from the Forestry Commission Warden (0479) 86271 and the Loch Morlich Watersports Centre (0479) 86221. The manager of the watersports centre is a keen fisherman himself and will gladly point you in the direction of other lochs he fishes.

Speyside makes for some of the most compelling fishing in Scotland. Prices can be high but there is fishing to be had. I will never forget that first Spey salmon and the sense of satisfaction it brought. You may not need to marry to fish the Spey but if you make a similarly splendid catch you are indeed fortunate - good hunting!

FISHING FAYRE

In order to benefit the whole community and not just the fishing, many waters are only available to people who actually stay in the area. There is no major problem here because there are some fine places to stay which will cover most requirements

and budgets. The local tourist office is always a good source of accommodation and many now operate a room booking service which is worth remembering if you happen to want to change plans at the last minute. The Spey however demands long term planning - it is after all one of the principal jewels in the crown of Scottish rivers. Having said that, occasional beats do become available at the last minute so it is worth phoning around prior to going off if you are looking for some new adventure.

This is an area of great beauty. The hills of Cromdale and the Cairngorms which so often crowd the horizon are sights to behold and there are a number of hotels which are equally pleasant. In Kingussie, The Columba house (0540) 661402 is a fine place in which to stay as is The Osprey (0540) 661510, idyllically situated in the heart of the Spey valley. People who enjoy fine food should make a special expedition to the unpretentious but extremely fine restaurant, The Cross (0540) 661166. The fixed price menu features delightful game and local produce and there are three bedrooms should you wish to stay after dinner - a marvellous idea.

Venturing forth, through the Monadhliath Mountains, we find further relief for those who have fought long and hard on the banks of the Spey. An enjoyable place to stay is The Boat, at Boat Of Garten (0479) 83258 which is a charmingly friendly establishment. A little north of here, we find Carrbridge. The Dalrachney Lodge (0479) 84252 is now a splendid country house hotel with a delightful lounge and dining room. The lodge is convenient for the River Dulnain and lies a short distance east of the village. A similar type of establishment which is also close to the River Dulnain is the Muckrach Lodge (0479) 85257. It is quiet and peaceful and the bar and lounge are focal points for this characterful hotel. One final Lodge to consider is the Auchendean Lodge (0479) 85347 which lies in the shadows of the Cairngorms. This is a stylish but extremely welcoming hotel where the restaurant is excellent and well worth a detour whether or not you choose to stay here.

Grantown-On-Spey is something of a landmark and is a busy spot with much to commend it. The Garth Hotel (0479) 2836 which stands close to the town centre in its own grounds is well worth considering. Firstly, because it is a congenial place to stay with fine facilities. Secondly, because fishing can be arranged on the Spey.

The Seafield Lodge Hotel (0479) 2152 is another hotel which fishermen should frequent. It hosts the Arthur Oglesby Fly Fishing Courses and the proprietor himself is a keen fisherman. The hotel is extremely welcoming and the bar a wonderfully comfortable place to enjoy a drink or two. Bedrooms are also comfortable and this is a first rate place to stay for those who wish to fish hard, play hard and sleep well. A more humble dwelling, but one which welcome fishermen is the Cran-Tara Guest House (0479) 2197 which offers good value food and accommodation and makes for a fine staging post for any assault on the Spey and the many lochs that surround Grantown. Finally, take a note of the Tyree House Hotel (0479) 2615 which welcomes fishermen and is a well run and welcoming establishment.

There are two further establishments to consider which lie a short distance from Grantown-On-Spey. Tulchan Lodge (0807) 5200 is one of the best fishing hotels in Scotland but it is expensive. It is supremely well cared for and was originally built as a hunting and fishing lodge, a role it continues to play. The lodge itself is delightful and the bar, bedrooms and dining room are all first class. If you happen to have a healthy bank account this is the place for you to part with some of your hard earned loot.

If you are seeking to fish the Avon then there are a number of hotels to consider. The Gordon Arms at Tomintoul (0807) 4206 is a fine choice, as is The Richmond Arms (0807) 4209. Both are friendly and welcome fishermen. Lovers of whisky will no doubt head for Glenlivet, famous for its isolated distillery. the Blairfindy Lodge (0807) 3376 is a functional and friendly place to stay. Blazing log fires in the hall and bars will help to lift any chill and once again the hotel can arrange fishing on a number of rivers, including the Avon.

Craigellachie (0340) 881204, situated 12 miles south of Elgin is a Victorian fishing hotel which has recently been impressively refurbished. This is a great favourite with fishermen so do book well in advance. The hotel has excellent connections and all manner of first class fishing can be arranged. In short, this is a tremendous hotel!

A similarly popular fisherman's haunt is the Gordon Arms Fochabers (0343) 820508. The hotel does not organise fishing itself but will put you in touch with Mr Connelly (0343) 820327 who can organise fishing for you. As a result, many fishing in this region stay at the former coaching inn. The bar here is a particularly popular haunt of the fishing fraternity.

Little Elgin is further off the beaten track but there is an hotel here which should not be overlooked - the mansion House

(0343) 548811. It has a garden setting beside the River Lossie. It is an impressive house which dates from the mid 19th century and has much to commend it. A fine wine list, distinguished cooking and some extremely comfortable bedrooms not to mention the fishing that can be organised locally, or on the Spey.

If you are fortunate enough to be fishing the River Findhorn, then the Ramnee in Forres (0309) 72410 should be considered. it is a well run, unpretentious hotel which boasts some good bedrooms and good food. In Nairn, there are a number of hotels to consider and an excellent golf course for lovers of the fairways. The Clifton Hotel (0667) 53119 is a splendid and refined place to stay, while the Golf View Hotel (0667) 52301 has obvious merits for the links man. The leisure facilities here are particularly good.

The Spey is a splendid 'old man' of a river. It is most definitely fishable and there are many who will help you organise your trip. There are several other fine waters and, all in all, this is an area which has much to commend it. Before we move on, one final thought. You have fished well and fought hard; you may have stayed at a number of hotels, you may on the other hand, have been coming here for years and frequented only your favourite haunts. Whatever the case, visit Drybridge and the Old Monastery Restaurant (0542) 32660. This delightful eating place has breathtaking views across Spey Bay and the food is quite outstanding.

As you stop and stare, imagine the activities of years gone by and the wonders of the salmon that will return to the bay and the legendary river. One may have your name on - unlikely, but give him a wave just the same!

MINMORE HOUSE HOTEL

Minmore House was originally the home of George Smith, the famous founder of Glenlivet whisky, and the memory of his trade is kept alive in the hotel with each of the ten individual rooms named after a local Speyside malt, not to mention the impressive range of single malt whiskies available and proudly displayed in the beautiful oak-panelled bar.

The Minmore is a family run hotel and the atmosphere is relaxed. Set in four acres of its own, the secluded gardens that surround it make it a haven of peace and quiet. Log fires and an abundance of fresh flowers add to the homeliness.

The food is highland and hearty, with five-course meals ranging from salmon to venison as well as local, organically grown vegetables.

The hotel is ideally placed for a wonderful array of pastimes, exploring, walking, birdwatching, horse-riding, and for those with an interest in the colourful Scottish heritage, a grand variety of castles, art galleries, local museums and crafts, and of course, the famous Whisky Trail are all at your disposal.

Within the hotel grounds, there is a hard tennis court, croquet lawn, an outdoor pool for those long summer days, and plenty of space and tranquility in which to totally relax.

Minmore House
Glenlivet
Banffshire
AB3 9DB
Scotland
Tel: (08073) 378

THE GRAMPIANS

THE DEVERON TO THE DON

One of the hazards of spring fishing is the weather! Ocean racing has been compared to standing under a freezing cold shower while tearing up £50 notes and the same could be said of spring fishing though hopefully the notes would be of a smaller denomination! While March can produce shirt sleeves weather it can be, and more often than not is, bitterly cold. Naturally January and February are even less hospitable. Yet being British we think nothing of the odd tempest and we are positively delighted to pay large sums of money for the pleasure of being frozen to the marrow! There is often a howling gale either blowing straight into one's face or down one's neck just to make casting that bit more challenging and to add to the pleasure there may be rain or sleet coming down the valley in almost horizontal sheets. Of course, there is always the chance of a fish, providing your hands are not too numb to play him. Naturally, warm clothing is essential on any trip and if you,ve already frozen to death in a Scottish downpour you won't need to be told to wrap up.

Quite a few rivers are frozen over in places at the start of the season which creates an additional problem. Let me try and illustrate the point. Two brothers were surprised to find on their first morning that their beat was almost completely frozen over and was more like a skating rink then a salmon stream. Some brisk work cleared enough for one of them to fish while the other sought warmth and comfort in the fishing hut. Much to his surprise and delight a fish was hooked and despite almost frost-bitten fingers was successfully played. However there remained the ticklish business of netting him, for there was quite a lot of ice by the bank so the other brother was summoned from his warm lair and asked to do the honours. Lying at full stretch in the snow he managed to get the net in a suitable position. The fish was played and brought over the net, but then disaster struck! The netman's cigarette had burnt through the cast and in the twinkling of an eye the fish was off with a treble in his mouth and trailing a few yards of cast. At first, the fisherman was too furious to speak but the language that ensued melted the ice for quite a distance!

The River **Ythan** (pronounced 'eye-than') is truly a peach of a river. It used to be famous for its pearl-mussels and it is said that the most prominent pearl in the crown of Scotland came from this river. It is also one of the best known sea-trout fisheries and catch figures more than justify its reputation. In addition, the Ythan is one of the few rivers where salmon are on the increase.

From its source in a spring-fed well in a schoolmaster's garden at Strathbogie, to the estuary at Newburgh, the Ythan flows through approximately 31 miles of rich agricultural land. Newburgh is less than fifteen miles north of Aberdeen airport which makes fishing in this area very accessible. The airport has daily services from Paris and Amsterdam so don't be surprised if some of your fellow rods are French, German or Swiss as they know this is some of the finest sea-trout fishing in Europe.

Such is the fame of the estuary fishing that the river itself tends to be overlooked, but those in the know are aware that there is good fishing to be had here at a reasonable cost. Fyvie Angling Association has three miles of the upper river where a day's fishing costs £6 and permits are available from the Vale Hotel, Fyvie (0651) 6376. The Buchan Hotel at Ellon (0358) 20208 has a mile which costs £10 a day and the Aberdeen and District Angling Association also has some water. Now that the nets have been bought off, this is the type of fishing which can only improve and if the salmon runs continue increasing it could be very good in a few years.

However, for most the Ythan means estuary fishing. This of course is tidal water and the dependence on rainfall is far less than further upstream. At high tide it is rather like a lake, at low tide it changes into a small river. Here you will watch in awe as sea-trout splash and crash about across the water; a sight which is sure to get the pulse racing! The water is fished from both bank and boat depending on the state of the tide. On an incoming tide, especially when half way up, most rods will prefer to fish from a boat while bank fishing is best on an ebbing tide. There are seventeen pools and fishing is by fly or spinner. Fly is the most popular method but it will often be presented on a spinning rod because of the need to cast a fairly long line and don't forget the abundant weed is much easier to remove when using spinning tackle. Popular flies for traditional fly fishing include Peter Ross, Dunkeld, Zulu, Golden Butcher and the special Ythan fly of Eddie Forbes, the fishery manager, who has done so much to improve things. Most spinners will use an Ythan Terror which is an imitation minnow of blue and silver with some feathers on the end. This water is owned by the Udny and Dudwick Estate and has recently been leased for a 21 year period on a timeshare basis which can if required include a cottage. Ythan Fisheries (0358) 689297 will be able to give you further information on this scheme and let you know if there is a spare day or week. Some may say statistics are boring, but this water has a record of 17lb and 10lb plus fish are regularly taken. There was of course the day in 1953 when two rods had 63 fish totalling 169lb in two and a half hours! The average is two pounds, but these silver tornados feel three times that weight and they fight like demons. Just to complete this paradise the area is a nature reserve and bird sanctuary with large colonies of eider duck.

While a lot of the Spey is somewhat difficult to get on, the **Deveron,** which is twenty miles or so east, is much more accessible to the visiting fisherman. The river is some sixty miles long, from its source at the foot of Hill of Three Stanes, to the coast at Banff and Macduff. Unusually for a river of this size there are no lochs in the system and as a spate river, rain can play an important part in the fisherman's luck. However, it is not that chancy, for in an average year it will produce at least 1000 salmon and a similar figure for sea-trout, while a good year will yield 2500 salmon and 3000 sea-trout. It is also a big fish water which produced a 56 pounder in 1920, but even this was eclipsed by Mrs Morrison's magnificent 61 pounder in 1924. The fish in recent years may be of more modest proportions but within the last five years there has been a 34 pounder and quite a few over 20lb while the average is around 10lb.

From its source the Deveron flows to Cabrach village after which it rushes through the gorge formed by the steep banks of Meikle Firbriggs and Daugh of Corinacy. It is then joined by Black Water and flows through Glenfiddich Lodge Beat, Lesmurdie and Beldorney which is let by Bell Ingram of Perth (0738) 21121. Then come the Edinglassie and Invermarkie beats and the Huntly Angling Association water. The path of the river is a delight and will bring a smile to your face. Salmon fishing on these upper beats is fairly dependent on water levels but there is very good trouting to be had. Brown trout of 3lb and more are often caught and there are a few rainbows which have escaped from the fish farms.

Just below Huntly, which is the start of the superb salmon fishing on the lower beats, the Deveron is joined by the **Bogie**. This tributary which rises near Rhynie village offers good fishing for the salmon and sea-trout on their way to the spawning grounds in the headwaters. Below are the Huntly Lodge, Castle Hotel, Corniehaugh (with its famous Still Pool) and Avochie beats which regularly produce salmon in the 15 to 20lb class. The Castle Hotel at Huntly (0466) 792696 has one and a half miles of double bank fishing on which hotel guests have priority and the cost varies between £40 and £150 a week. The Huntly Angling Association (0466) 792291 can offer fishing on six miles of both the Deveron and the Bogie at £10 a day or £30 a week. At Inverisla the river is joined by the Isla which attracts few spawning fish as upriver access is difficult. The next beats downstream are Woodsie, Coniecleugh, Rothiemay Castle, Upper Mayen, Mayen House, Redhill and Carronhaugh. The weir at Coniecleugh halts the passage of fish when water temperatures are low and several large fish have been taken here. Rothiemay has the well known Sunnybrae pool and both this beat and Mayen can be fished by guests of the Forbes Arms Hotel (0466) 81248 at a cost of between £10 and £20 a day according to season.

Continuing our piscatorial voyage downstream we come to the Glennie, Turtory, Ardmeallie, Church, Boat of Tutory, Marnoch Lodge and Euchrie beats. Noted pools here include Falconer's, Bridge and Islands. Downstream, there are beats such as Netherdale, Carnousie, Forglen, Mountblairy and Montcrofter. In 1987 Netherdale produced a superb sea-trout of 14lb and Mountblairy as well as yielding the 61lb salmon caught by Mrs Morrison in 1924, has also produced the best fish in recent years. Below Turriff the flow of the river is reduced due to abstraction for drinking water and some of the lower pools can silt up. However, the District Fishing Board is doing its best to clear them. Finally, the river flows into the sea between the towns of Banff and Macduff.

As one would expect with a river of this size there are a number of owners and the following may be able to help you. Jaytee Sports of Banff (0261) 25821 issues permits at a cost of £10 per day (Monday to Friday) for the Banff and Macduff Angling Association Water. Tickets for the Turriff Angling Association are available from Ian Masson Fishing Tackle (0888) 62428 at a weekly cost of between £50 and £80 while a day's ticket in the spring is £5; also in the spring the Association has 5 private beats where a day will cost between £6 and £8. The Drummuir Estate's (0542) 81225 water is usually booked well ahead but some spring lets are available and it may be possible to get a day, later on in the season; the cost of a day here for four rods varies between £215 and £345. Salar Management Services (0667) 55355 let the Avochie Beat and Scotia Sporting Services (0339) 886891 may be able to help with other beats. The County Hotel in Banff (0261) 25353 can arrange fishing for guests or if you prefer to take a cottage Mr G. Manson of Huntly (0466) 794251 may be able to help and also looks after eight beats of the middle stretch where the cost varies between £3 and £25 a day. The Montcoffer Fishings are handled by Savills in Edinburgh (031) 226 6961. Good trout flies are March Brown, Black Pennell, Grouse and Claret and Greenwell's Glory, while favourite salmon flies include the Black Doctor, Stoats Tail, Garry

Dog and Munro Killer.

The **Don** flows into the North Sea at Bridge of Don, just north of Aberdeen and the mouth of the Dee. Despite their proximity, the two rivers are very different in character for while the Dee is one of the great Highland spate streams, the Don wends its way at a leisurely pace through water meadows and good farmland rather like a southern chalk stream. It used to be said that 'A Mile o' Don's worth two of Dee unless it be for fish or tree', a reference to the plantations on the upper Dee. It is perhaps unfair to compare the fishing for few rivers can compete with the Dee and the Don is certainly among the finest salmon and trout streams of Europe, particularly now that the nets have been bought off. It is also one of the few rivers which still has a good spring run.

This is another area that is rich in history and you will tread the same roads as that pioneer of Highland roads, General Wade, and Montrose the brilliant but ill-fated supporter of Charles I, Monymusk House used to have a relic of St Columba that was carried in front of the Scottish Army at the Battle of Bannockburn in 1314. The spectacular ruins of Kildrummy Castle, a victim of the 1715 Jacobite Rising bear mute witness to the capture of Robert the Bruce's brother in 1306, while Pictish cairns are evidence of an older civilisation.

There are some 63 beats on this river whose source is Well of Don on Little Geal Charn in the far off Grampian Mountains. Its head-waters are fast flowing but below Inchmore its progress starts to become more sedate. In this beautiful moorland setting you can hear the cry of the golden plover and watch pied wagtails darting to and fro. At Cock Bridge, the Don is crossed by the A939 which can often be blocked by snow in winter and here it sheds the Highland burn character of its infancy and becomes a more mature river. The Colquhonnie Hotel at Strathdon (0975) 651210 has seven beats on which a day's salmon fishing can be had for £15 a day and a day's trouting, £7 per day.

An added attraction of the Don is that it is one of the best trout streams anyone could wish for. Trees may test our casting abilities but in the water beneath their leafy shade lie brown trout which are frequently over 2lb. There is also a hatchery at Stathcon which releases good stocks of fry each year into the headwaters to ensure good fishing for the future generations.

Near Candacraig House is the Pot of Poldullie, a pool favoured by trout fishermen. It can produce lovely 3lb plus brownies. Then it is on to Deskry and Glenbucket Castle. At Glenkindie we come upon the ruins of Towie Castle and the far from ruined Glenkindie Arms (0975) 641288. The hotel beat costs £8 a day for salmon fishing or £5 for trout. Downstream are the Kildrummy Fishings; managed by Mr T. Hillary (0975) 571208 this is one of the best upper Don salmon beats.

At Bridge of Alford the river opens out and becomes a lady of more majestic and some would say stout proportions. Permits for these stretches may be had for £8 or £4 a day depending on whether salmon or trout is the quarry. Contact the Warden's office of the Grampian District Council (0975) 562107 for further details. W. R. Murray of 27 Main Street (0975) 562366 also handle booking for the Moonhaugh House beat which holds three rods. Here as ever advance booking is recommended. Just below are the Forbes Castle and Monymusk waters. It is no

coincidence that Forbes was once known as Putachie, which is gaelic for trout, as many consider these waters with the famous Dam Pool, to be the best trout fishing in Scotland. Forbes Estate Office (0975) 562524 has five beats where trout fishing may be had for £5 a day and a week's salmon fishing costs between £65 and £100 plus VAT. The Grant Arms Hotel at Monymusk (0467) 7226 offers salmon and trout fishing on the Monymusk Estate water at £21 a day or £90 a week. The hotel is run by Colin Hart, a great fisherman, and its water includes the well known Paradise Wood.

It's downstream again to Kemnay where a day's ticket costs £8 and can be had from Mr Foote (0467) 42228. Mr J.J. Watson (0467) 20321 issues permits for the Inverurie Angling Association water at £8 a day or £23 for a week's salmon fishing and £4 for a day's trout fishing - he can also arrange for you to fish the Manor beat at a cost of £10 a day. An unusual feature here is that Sunday fishing is allowed. On the Kintore beat J.Copland (0467) 32201, the Kintore Arms Inn (0467) 32216, or Hillhead Caravan Club (0467) 32809 can arrange salmon fishing by the day at around £7 or £23 for a week with trouting available at £4 a day. The Aberdeen, tackle shop, J.Somers & Son issues permits for the town's Angling Association's 10 miles of water at £15 a day for salmon and £4 a day for trout.

Among others who may be able to help you are: Mr McIntosh (0975) 651302 who lets the Tornashean Water. The Banchory office of Strutt & Parker (0330) 24888 lets the Tillypronie Estate water where cottages are also available, while Mrs Petrie (0975) 571342 issues daily permits at £10 and the gamekeeper Mr Steven Sharpe can arrange for you to fish a good hill loch for £12 a day including a boat. The sporting agencies may also be able to help. Macsport Ltd in Aboyne (0975) 571377 have two miles where a day costs £15 plus VAT. Ian Black of Meadowland Sporting (0224) 724286 can also arrange fishing on the Dee and mixed sporting holidays. Scotia Sporting Agency (0339) 886891 have access to Don and Deveron beats where the cost ranges from £20 to £50 a day.

The lower river tends to suffer from pollution and poaching, but the latter wouldn't happen if the fish weren't there so don't be put off! Popular salmon flies for the Don are Munro Killer, Stoats Tail, Hairy Mary, Shrimp Fly, General Practitioner and Garry Dog while one of those big brownies may be tempted by a March Brown or Greenwell's Glory.

There are not many lochs in the area and the only one of any size is **Loch of Strathbeg** where a day's fishing can be had for £6 from the Post Office in Crimond (0346) 32229. Sadly, the quality of fishing here has deteriorated in recent years and fishermen who are more concerned with the day's catch are turning to some of the excellent stocked waters in the area. Crimongate Fishery (0346) 32203 is five miles south of Fraserburgh off the B9033, has a six acre lake well stocked with browns and rainbows in a lovely rural setting. If you are not lucky enough to fish the estuary water at Newburgh you can console yourself with a day on Ythan Valley Fisheries' 11 acre lake which is also stocked with rainbows and brownies and is only a few miles upstream at Ellon.

Naturally the weather in Britain is particularly fickle. This makes fishing even more uncertain. However, if you should be iced over, spare a thought for our two brothers and remember never smoke when landing a salmon lying down in the snow. It's bad for your health and it will play merry hell with your landing!

FISHING FAYRE

The burns, streams and rivers north of the Grampian Hills provide a positive feast of fishing opportunities. The scene north of the Dee is remote, generally unspoilt and peaceful. There are a fair number of good fishing hotels and so without further ado let us plan our assault on these splendid waters.

Aberdeen airport may conceivably be your first port of call and on the off-chance you wish to have a quick kip then the Skean Dhu Hotel (0224) 725252 is your best bet. There are numerous other good hotels in the city, but more of that when we come to the glories of the Dee.

Kildrummy is a tremendous place to start or conclude any fishing foray. Kildrummy Castle (0975) 571288 is a striking castellated mansion which is surrounded by superbly kept grounds. The picture is made still more complete when we consider the ruins of the 13th century castle which the hotel overlooks. There is an excellent blend of tradition with modern comforts, the striking fireplaces and impressive tapestries are a joy to behold. The bedrooms are also well equipped and the restaurant is extremely well thought of. The hotel can arrange fly fishing for salmon and trout on the Don, for residents and this really provides the icing on an extremely impressive gateau. Lovers of heritage might also wish to sample Pittodrie House (0467) 6444 which dates from 1675. It's a fine all round hotel and a delight in which to stay.

Should you wish to enjoy another extremely welcoming hotel then make a note of the Castle at Huntly (0466) 792696, formerly the family home of the Gordons. It's a great favourite with fishermen and is a charming traditional hotel in which to escape the traumas of the twentieth century. The fishing that can be arranged by the hotel is particularly impressive. The Forbes Arms (0466) 81248 also offers some good fishing and is a fine place in which to stay. The Calquhonnie Hotel (0975) 651210 serves the angler who searches for waters on the Don. The Grant Arms (0467) 7226 in Monymusk is another welcoming fishing place.

Somewhere East of Huntly we find the River Ythan; a spot to head for here is Newburgh and The Udny Arms Hotel (0358) 689444. The bedrooms are characterful and it's a pleasant location from which to explore neighbouring scenery. The same can be said of Meldrum House, Old Meldrum (0651) 22294 which provides a delightful country house atmosphere in a marvellous setting, the restaurant here is also good.

As you would imagine, there are all manner of activities available aside from fishing - golfing and walking are two obvious examples. The Deveron is a fine river and if you should be visiting Banff then The County (0261) 25353 is a charming Georgian house in which to stay. It has fine views up the Bay and can also arrange fishing for guests.

There are a fabulous array of fishing opportunities available in the Grampian region of Scotland and while certain beats await the shoes of deadmen, others are positively alive with opportunity. We wish you good sport, whether you are treading in the steps of phantoms or wading in the waters of the fit and well!

THE CASTLE HOTEL

The Castle Hotel is a magnificent eighteenth-century stone building, standing in its own grounds above the ruins of Huntly Castle, on the banks of the River Deveron. Sandston as it was originally known was built as a family home for the Dukes of Gordon.

The hotel was purchased in March 1990 by a very keen fishing and hotel family. The Castle beat is the hotel's own double-banked Salmon and Sea Trout fishing which has recently undergone an extensive improvement scheme and now offers a variety of attractive pools which are a delight to fish especially with a fly. The beat is let regularly to guests of the hotel. We can also arrange fishing on other private beats of the River Deveron.

Following a recent refurbishment programme all bedrooms now have en suite facilities. The newly decorated Dining Room and Bar with their open log fires lend themselves to the Country House Hotel atmosphere. We have improved our facilities for fieldsportsmen and women - a new Rod Room, Drying Room, Strong Room for guns, Fly Tying desk, an impressive list of Sporting Videos, availability of late night and early morning snacks and a delicious picnic menu.

As well as fishing we can also arrange Roe Deer and Red Deer Stalking, Grouse and Pheasant Shooting, Walked Up and Mixed Shooting.

Our aim is to ensure that all visiting sportsmen and women have both enjoyable and successful visits.

Situated on the main A96 between Aberdeen (45 minutes away) and Inverness the hotel is easily reached by road, rail and air.

The Castle Hotel
Huntly
Aberdeenshire AB54 4SH
Tel: (0466) 792696
Fax: (0466) 792641

Artist: **Ernest Briggs**   **TROUT FISHING**   *Courtesy of:* **Malcolm Innes Gallery**

FOVERAN HOUSE

The well that once watered the garrison of the medieval Foveran Castle still refreshes the guests of this now converted Georgian Mansion. Its name is derived from the Gaelic 'Fobhar', meaning 'Well', and the ancient traditions are continued in this historic house. The ancient castle is long gone, lost to the ravages of war and time, but the stones from its legendary Turin Tower were used in the foundations of the present house. During the past two hundred and fifty years the House and surrounding estate have been home to a number of prosperous merchants, several Lord-Provosts of Aberdeen and a Major-General, all have left their personal mark, leaving a long tradition to enhance this unique Scottish house.

Scotland has a long history of hospitality and Foveran is no exception. Open fires add warmth and a general feeling of welcome and well-being. The hotel has many fascinating aspects, not least of which is the McBey Lounge with its permanent exhibition of etchings by the local, and now world-famous, artist James McBey. Its relaxed and distinctly individual atmosphere is the perfect place to enjoy a pre-dinner drink, or a comforting nightcap. The restaurant itself is the setting for the delicious preparations of the chef, who applies his long experience to mouth-watering traditional dishes, such as prime Aberdeen Angus beef, succulent game, seafood, and crisp vegetables, all made with the choicest of local ingredients to ensure a full, fresh flavour.

The leisure facilities available in Scotland as a whole are quite astonishing, and the Foveran itself is no exception. For the fisherman it is ideal, being less than five minutes drive from the River Ythan, recognised as some of the finest trout and salmon fishing in the country. This stunning body of water also provides the opportunity for a variety of water sports, winsurfing and sailing in particular are popular. Golf is almost a way of life here and there are many local courses to choose from for the serious sportsman. Of course the scenery of Scotland is renowned throughout the world and there is no better way to explore than walking, nearby are the sand dunes and moorlands that form the important Sands of Forvie Nature Reserve - a paradise for walkers and naturalists alike. Without even leaving the grounds of the hotel you can try your hand at clay pigeon shooting, with expert tutition available, and if the urge for the more demanding challenge of game shooting and stalking begins to grow, the hotel can easily arrange it a little further afield. Most of all for those interested in the country's great heritage, this is an ideal base from which to explore the famous Whisky, Fishing and Castle Trails.

At the end of a long day there can be nothing better than slipping into one of the deliciously comfortable beds in one of the individually furnished rooms. All, naturally, have private facilities.

There can be no doubt that the tradition and hospitality that form the backbone of Scotland and Foveran House will not fail to please.

Foveran House Hotel
Newburgh
Aberdeenshire AB4 0AP
Tel: (035 86) 89398
Fax: (035 86) 89398 Ext. 200

THE BIRSE LODGE HOTEL

A short journey down the road from Balmoral Castle a royal welcome of another sort awaits guests at The Birse Lodge Hotel. Jackie and Duncan Mackinnon have converted this former dower house into one of Scotland's finest rural hotels and their "family" of staff will ensure that your visit is a memorable one.

The Birse Lodge Hotel has lost none of its original charm and still smacks strongly of Scotland. The emphasis on traditional values is best illustrated by the chef's wide selection of national dishes, ranging from finest Scotch beef and Grampian venison to steaks from the magnificent Deeside salmon. Furthermore he will arrange a delicious picnic in a hamper for you to take with you on your day out. Log fires and impressive stone walls complete the homely atmosphere, while the colourful gardens guarantee that the immediate surroundings are equally inviting.

Balmoral Castle makes for an enchanting day out, while the town of Aboyne with its shops selling tweeds, sheepskins,

Edinburgh Crystal and Caithness Glass is a must for souvenirs and gifts. The Birse Lodge Hotel, however, is also your starting point for an escape into some of Scotland's most beautiful countryside. Explore it on horseback or foot, by car or canoe and keep an eye out for such local inhabitants as goshawks, ospreys, golden eagles and red deer, all of which have been spotted in the area.

Above all, The Birse Lodge Hotel should be considered a sportsman's mecca. Situated only a short cast from the Dee and surrounded by woodland that boasts some of Europe's finest hunting, the Lodge will not only arrange your fishing, but also provide kennels and care for your dog, who is no less welcome a visitor than yourself.

The hotel is easily accessible with regular flights and trains to Aberdeen airport and station. From there take the coach to Aboyne or enjoy the drive yourself along the Perth/Braemar/Aberdeen road (the A93).

The Birse Lodge Hotel
Charleston Road
Aboyne
Royal Deeside
AB3 5EL
Tel: (03398) 86253

THE GRAMPIANS

ROYAL DEESIDE

The River **Dee** is one of our best known rivers both for its superb fishing and its royal associations. In the earlier part of the 19th century, few people visited Scotland and before the age of the railway or reasonable road surfaces, large areas were inaccessible. However, Queen Victoria's purchase of the Balmoral Estate was largely responsible for changing public attitude and the novels of Sir Walter Scott, with their talk of daring deeds and descriptions of magnificent scenery that awaited the visitor, added the romantic flavour that the Victorians enjoyed so much.

Osborne on the Isle of Wight may have been a popular holiday resort for the royal family but it was Balmoral that held the special place in Victoria's heart. 'It seems like a dream' wrote the Queen 'to be here in our dear highland home again. Every year my heart becomes more fixed in this Paradise'. Away from the cases of government and the formality of Court life the royal couple were able to relax and enjoy, as far as possible, the simple way of life of the highlands. Their enthusiasm for Scotland was soon followed by the nation and tartan patterns became the rage. Queen Victoria even wrote a book about their times in Scotland and was much flattered when Disraeli, who was a celebrated novelist, as well as a politician, addressed her as 'we authors, Ma'am'. Edward VII's prowess as a shot is well attested, but his father was an even finer gun, especially on the hills. On one occasion he killed six deer with his 'three double rifles, firing the six shots in succession.' Five of the deer dropped in their tracks and the sixth ran only a short distance — a fine sporting achievement which is unlikely to be equalled. The Scots respected and genuinely liked Prince Albert, both as a fair landlord and as a man and there are many memorials in the area erected by the tenantry.

From the wells of Dee some 4000 feet above sea level in the Cairngorms to the sea at Aberdeen the course of the Dee is some 85 miles long. As with the Spey, snow melting at its source helps to give and maintain good Spring and early Summer water levels. This is one river that does not suffer from being hydrolysed and there are no natural or artificial obstructions until we reach the Linns above Braemar. The fishing is even better now that the Atlantic Salmon Conservancy Trust has bought out the netting stations at the mouth. As a result several beats have broken all past records and the sea-trout catch has trebled in three years - There are over fifty miles of first class salmon fishing on this exceptionally clear water which still has a good spring run. This of course is excellent news for fish and fishermen but what of the more distant predators. Today, catches in all our waters are vastly affected by deep sea netting. This is particularly commonplace in the migratory routes near the Faroes, Greenland and the like. It is a desperate situation and little seems to be being done but life goes on and in our simple way, rod in hand, let us return for a mornings fishing.

The Dee tumbles down from its lofty birthplace through Glen Dee. We find Chest of Dee where the river crashes down a steep staircase of broken rocks and pools. After a heavy rain or snow melt you can hear the river's angry roar for some distance. Then on to White Bridge where salmon rest after their fight through the Linn of Dee. There is a path from the road to the Linn and you can watch salmon as they leap or lie in the pools gathering strength for their continuing journey. Below the Linn, the Dee widens into a broad crystal fed stream with Scots pine adorning its banks. Nearby is Mar Lodge built by

Queen Victoria for her eldest daughter, Princess Louise and her husband the Duke of Fife. Braemar Castle is another interesting edifice. It was burnt to the ground twice in under thirty years. Firstly, in 1689 as a result of the Earl of Mar's failure to support the Jacobite cause and then in 1716 by the Duke of Argyll's forces because the Earl had led the Jacobite troops at the battle of Sheriffmuir. The Earl was known as 'Bobbing Johnnie' for his habit of changing sides, but he always seemed to end up on the losing side. At Invercauld Robert Louis Stevenson wrote most of 'Treasure Island', a book, which despite the passage of time, still delights each new generation. Nearby, Queen Victoria leased Gordon House until she bought it in 1848 and employed the services of the local architect in Aberdeen. After some rebuilding and enlarging, the house was renamed Balmoral.

Ballater is a favourite place for visiting fisherman for nearby are such famous beats as Birkhall, Monaltrie, Glenmuick and Abergeldie. At 'Countrywear' in Bridge Street (03397) 55453 you can see the cast of the famous 42 pound fish caught by Arthur Wood in 1926. As well as inventing the greased line method of fishing, this great sportsman 'grassed' 3,490 salmon from the Cairnton Fishing's beat between 1913 and 1934. Countrywear also issue permits for the Mar Estate Water. This beat which is some six and a half miles long holds 4 rods and costs £20 per rod per day. They can also arrange for you to fish the Glebe Pool beat for £15 a day.

Between Ballater and Aboyne the Dee is joined by three tributaries - The Gairn, the Muick and the Water of Tanar. The banks and surrounding hills are thick with Scots pine, birch, alder, willow and oak. Timber used to be a major Deeside industry with logs being floated down river to the Aberdeen mills which must have played havoc with the fishing. Below Aboyne the river loses the impetuosity of its highland youth and flows gently through fertile farmland. Around Banchory where the Dee is joined by the Feugh are such well known beats as Cairnton, Woodend, Commonty, Blackhall, Crathie, Invery, Park and Drum. Banchory is the centre for fishing the lower Dee and here you will find the Invery House Hotel (0330) 24782 which can arrange for guests to fish the Commonty beat at a cost of between £350 and £520 plus VAT per week which includes a ghillie. In 1991 an Austrian doctor staying at the hotel had two 20 pounders, and one of 26lb. The hotel also has sea-trout fishing on the **Feugh** which flows through its grounds. The Banchory Lodge Hotel (0330) 22625 has a three quarters of a mile of double bank fishing for guests at the same price as Invery House which similarly includes the services of a ghillie.

Between 8,000 and 13,000 salmon are caught every season on this superb river where the average fish weighs 8lb. An unusual feature is that all but six of the forty five beats are single bank and it is one of the very few rivers where spring fishing is still the best. Although spinning may be permitted most rods will prefer the fly and a Blue Charm, Logie, General Practitioner or Jeannie may do the trick. As one would expect with fishing of this quality, it is not an easy river to get on, however the sporting agencies may be able to help you. Scotia Sporting Agency (0339) 886891 has access to various beats where the cost ranges between £250 and £1000 per week. Meadowhead Sporting (0224) 724286 and Macsport of Aboyne (0975) 571377 may also be able to help. Glen Tanar Sport and Leisure (0339) 886451 normally let their water on a weekly or fortnightly basis but day permits are available in August and they also have a

THE GRAMPIANS

well stocked 10 acre loch. If your ambition is to have your own fishing then time shares on the Ardoe and Myrtle beats are for sale through Savills Edinburgh office (031) 226 6961.

Some forty miles South of Aberdeen on the A92 we find the town of Montrose and the North and South Esk. The **North Esk** is a fine spate river which now that some netting has been suspended is likely to improve. Actually, so far only two netting stations have been suspended and those only temporarily, however, it is hoped that this will become permanent and other nets will follow. The sources of the river are the waters Mark and Lee, two streams which come tumbling down the Grampian Mountains to join forces at Invermark and form the North Esk. It then flows through the beautiful heather and rowan landscape of Glen Esk and here you will find beats such as Invermark and Millden. The Dalhousie Estate Office (0356) 24566 lets the Millden Fisheries beat where the weekly cost for three rods ranges from £75 to £600 and day tickets are sometimes available. The estate also lets well appointed cottages which can sleep up to six.

Downstream lies Craigoshina and then it is on to Burn Loups and the Gannochy Estate (0356) 47331 water. This is usually let by the week but days are sometimes available. After Loups the river flows through fine farmland in the succession of long holding pools. The North Esk District Fishery Board has done a great deal to improve the river and Burn Loups is now the only obstacle fish face in the course of their run. The entrance to Glen Esk is guarded by Edzell Castle with its beautiful gardens of rambling roses and orderly box hedges. **West Water**, which, with its good spawning grounds is an important feeder, joining the Esk at the famous Junction Pool which has produced many fine catches of loch salmon and sea trout.

There are many well known beats such as Arnhall, Strachthro, Pert, Gallery, Morphie and Craigo to name but a few. However, this productive river which can often produce a fish on opening day is very popular and you may have to join the queue before casting a Blue Charm or Thunder and Lightening on this water. However, Mr G. Luke (0674) 73535 the secretary of the Montrose Angling Association may be able to sell you a permit at a cost of between £15 and £25 (according to the season) to fish their eleven and a half miles on a Thursday, Friday or Saturday providing you can prove you are a whisky drinker and not a lager lout! Scotia Sporting Agency may be able to help with several beats while Joseph Johnston and Sons (0674) 72666 issue both daily permits and weekly lets. The Morphie Fishings have recently been time shared and a few units are still available from Savills (031)-226 6961. The North Esk is very much a spate river and as one would expect spring and autumn tend to be the best times. However, the summer months can see good runs of grilse and sea-trout depending on the water level. Sea-trout average around 2lb and salmon 9lb though 20 pounders are caught every season.

The **South Esk** is also a spate river and as there are no feeder lochs in the system, the headwaters are of little interest to the fisherman. But it is a totally different matter after the White Water joins the river at the head of Glen Clova where some fine sport can be enjoyed. The Clova hotel (0575) 5222 has three miles of double bank fishing which holds 8 rods. Spinning and bait as well as fly are permitted on this water which costs £12 a day. Downstream from the glen there are some good holding pools and the river broadens out when it meets the Prosen

Water just beyond Cortachy Castle. From here, down to the Montrose basin is very good fishing particularly for sea-trout which average 21/2 lb but most seasons produce a six pounder. Famous beats include Careston, Finavon, Kinnaird and House of Dun. One of the best stretches is the Finavon Castle Water. There are two miles of double bank fishing and two and a half miles of single bank divided into three beats, Castle, Indies and Balgarrock Meadows which share more than 30 pools and lies between them. The manager is Miss Dawn Darling (0307) 85344 and prices for these outstanding beats may be had on application. Mr H. Burness (0575) 73456 is the secretary of Kirriemuir Angling Club which has seven miles of double bank fishing where a Dunkeld or Blue Charm may produce the magic tug. Permits are also available from Dykehead Post Office which is beyond Cortachy Castle on the B955. Spinning is also permitted and locals use a Toby, Devon or Mepps. The cost here is £50 a week or £10 a day but no day tickets are issued on a Saturday.

There are very few lochs that rank with those north of the Great Glen but the trout fisherman is well catered for as there are several stocked lakes and lochs for those who like their trouting and don't share the purist attitude that rivers and brownies are the only true form of trout fishing! The only loch of any size is Loch Muick but I would be surprised if I met anyone who had fished this water, as it is on the Balmoral Estate, and the only way you'll fish it, is as a guest or sneaking past whichever highland regiment is on guard duties at the time.

However, there are two fine hill lochs, **Loch Nan Eun** and **Loch Bainnie** on which a day's fishing will be rewarded by a bag of up to a dozen hard fighting wild browns. Good flies for these lochs are Black Pennell, Soldier Palmer and Peter Ross tied on a size 12 or 14. Before you set out it is advisable to check that you have everything you are likely to need, for these lochs take some getting to! Bainnie is a fairly level two and a half mile walk from the A93 just south of Braemar. The walk to Nan Eun is also fairly level, but it is nine miles! So it could be an idea to hire a 4-wheel drive vehicle even though the last two miles are still on foot, but well worth it, especially if you like peace and quiet (and a good walk!). The effort is well worthwhile for the trout are genuinely wild and there are majestic Grampian peaks all round. Permits may be had from either the Invercauld Estate Office (0339) 741224 or the game keeper, Mr R. Hepburn (0250) 85206. The season for this fly only water is March 12th to August 11th and the cost is £5 a day or £25 for the season.

The Royals' love of Deeside and Balmoral is still intense and who could disagree. This is a delightful area and fishing can be tremendous. There have been many tussles with fighting fish but there are few more celebrated lovers of the sport than the Queen Mother. As this amazing Lady reaches her 93rd year we should perhaps note that there are many attractions to this sporting life and one of them is, even if you don't live to a ripe old age, you will certainly enjoy some of its beauty!

FISHING FAYRE

While Parliament considers the taxing problem of taxing the Queen, Balmoral's future is in doubt. Well, this is how the story goes. I somehow doubt it, such is the love of the family for Balmoral. Especially the love shown to it by its most senior and gracious member. The Queen Mother's love of the the Dee is celebrated and it is fitting that this lady should grace these royal waters. Of course, the river and the salmon care not a jot for pomp or ceremony but it is surely fair to say that the Dee is a queen amongst rivers. As a result of this lofty position in the realm of river fishing, the Dee is often difficult - sometimes impossible and at other times and in other places, a little tricky to get on. Let us hope that the following lines reflect some of the opportunities available in this marvellous part of Scotland.

I must say that if Balmoral did go under the hammer, God forbid, then the lucky purchaser would be really tempted to turn this castle into the sporting hotel of Scotland. Given that this eventuality is unlikely, let us suggest more appropriate accommodation. The Maryculter House (0224) 732124 enjoys the most marvellous setting on the south bank of the River Dee. The hotel does not have its own fishing but can arrange fishing for about £20 a day. The hotel itself is fascinating and parts of the original building remain. In the bar an exposed stone wall towers up three storeys to reveal a splendid vaulted ceiling. The bedrooms are extremely well equipped and the principle restaurant here is well thought of.

Moving westwards down the A93 we come to the home of the celebrated fishing waters of the Dee, but we should not stop here, for there are some of the most wonderful fishing hotels imaginable in a very small radius. You have to persevere, however, because the fishing is extremely popular and people book year after year. Let me mention a few hotels which are particularly excellent. Banchory Lodge (0330) 22625 is a charming Georgian house on the banks of the River Dee. The hotel owns both banks and can, naturally enough, arrange fishing. People, however, book year after year and it is extremely difficult to get in but it isn't impossible, so do try. The proprietors are wonderfully welcoming and the hotel is a delight on antiques, paintings and flowers. The dining room is also first class and if you are lucky enough to stay there and fish, then you will be an extremely happy chappy - and the very best of luck to you.

Raemoir House (0330) 24884 is another delightful hotel. It is run by Kit Javin and family and they are a charming team. The hotel is magnificently set in 3500 acres but does not actually front the river. The house itself is delightfully preserved and you can not fail to be charmed by its many delights. The bar is particularly inviting and the counter is made from a Tudor four-poster bed. The bedrooms are also splendid. So what of the fishing? Well, the family are deeply immersed in the community and boats are often available on the sea. Naturally, the prices vary hugely but if you love your fishing, fine hotels and perhaps more than anything else genuine service and welcome, then contact Raemoir House - it is something of a delight.

Invery House (0330) 24782 at Bridge of Feugh is another glorious hotel in which to stay. In order to reach the house you must drive through a half mile canopy of silver birch and beech trees alongside the River Feugh. The hotel is delightfully peaceful and also has rights on the River Dee. Sir Walter Scott was a frequent visitor to the house and marvellous bedrooms are named in his memory. This is a first class hotel and the restaurant is similarly distinguished. It is expensive but if you do have a love of fishing and the good life, then there are few finer places to visit.

Aboyne is another place to note and here we come upon Birse Lodge (03398) 86253 another friendly and well run hotel. The former dower house which is set in its own gardens is close to the River Dee. The hotel does not have its own water but the management have a number of contacts in the village who can often help in arranging fishing. A similar situation occurs at Craigendarroch (0339) 755858 who use the services of a local expert. Fishing can be arranged on a number of rivers including the Dee and the approximate charge is £40 for a half day. This is a fine hotel to take non-fishing friends too, as it has an excellent Country Club - it is also part of a substantial time share complex. The hotel is particularly plush and the restaurant has an extremely good reputation.

Arranged fishing can also be made through Tullich Lodge (0339) 755406 who work closely with Cliff Jeffries at Countrywear, Ballater. The hotel enjoys splendid views of the Dee valley and is set amidst acres of pleasant woodland and garden. This is a very smart but informal country house hotel which offers some first class accommodation. It also provides outstanding dinners in the contrastingly formal dining room. Other fine accommodation can be found at Darroch Learg (0339) 755443 which also offers inspired views over the River Dee. Monaltrie (0339) 735417 is another fine hotel and several of the bedrooms overlook the Dee. An inspired view for the angler to look out onto as dawn comes. Fishing can be arranged on local waters although the hotel does not have its own beat.

Braemar, home of the highland gathering, has a hotel of some distinction which also, by virtue of local contacts can arrange fishing on the Dee. The Braemar Lodge (0339) 741627 has been well converted and apart from the fishing contacts the expertise in the catering department is also worthy of note. This granite built lodge is a fine place to stay and a visit is positively encouraged.

Moving away from the Dee we journey to other celebrated waters, those of the princely South Esk. The Clova Hotel (0575) 5222 is a splendid fishing hotel and is thoroughly welcoming. The situation is delightful and while the fish can not be guaranteed a really good trip can be!

It has to be said finding fishing on the South Esk is difficult but there are possibilities. The Panmure Arms (0356) 4420 has no water of its own but if you were to book a year or so in advance you may find a week or two could be arranged. Whatever the case make sure you visit for dinner - it is justly popular for miles around and the watering hole of many a fisherman. Naturally, many of the estates have lodges which can be let and many of these are taken by syndicates or timeshare owners. Many of these visitors come back year after year and many people will stay with friends or more often than not stay in self-catering accommodation. The local tourist boards are a wealth of knowledge on this type of accommodation and they are also able to provide lists of Bed and Breakfasts. As a result a quick telephone call should always be made before you finalise your plans if you seek this type of establishment.

Fishing in these regal waters is always going to be hit and miss and naturally the time of year, the prestige of the beat will be calculated when a price is charged. There are some people who endeavour to paint a flowery picture of all fishing in Scotland, which is patently not the case. There are, however, a number of hoteliers who are genuinely keen to help and we trust that the above are in that merry band.

POTARCH HOTEL

There has been an inn at Potarch since 1740 when the nearest crossing of the famous River Dee was a ford, half a mile south at Inchbrae. The route was used by the infamous General Wade, commander-in-chief in Scotland, to march government troops deep into the Highlands.

Crossing the Dee today is a little easier, though not without its natural charm. Just over the bridge on the south side and nestling in the heart of beautiful Deeside, is the Potarch Hotel. A traditionally cosy and welcoming place, popular with locals and visitors alike. The lounge is warm and friendly, offering an ideal atmosphere in which to relax, muse over the menu, and perhaps sample one of the wide range of whiskies available, some of them quite rare. The dining-room itself is cheerfully decorated, ideal for a small romantic dinner or perhaps a private function, wedding receptions and the like are easily catered for. The predominantly traditional cuisine relies heavily on fresh, local fare - the salmon, game and beef for which Deeside is so justly famous. Retiring afterwards to one of the seven comfortable bedrooms is the perfect end to a day in the Highlands. All the rooms have colour television and tea/coffee making facilities and ensuite bathrooms are available.

The splendour of Scottish Deeside naturally makes a wide range of pursuits easily available. Close by are ski slopes, golf courses, gliding strip and hills. For the tourist of course there is a rather bewildering choice on array - spectacular scenery with its wealth of wild life, some quite rare, the fascinating castles that dominate the hillsides and stand testimony to the country's past. The famous Highland Games are staged annually in most of the surrounding villages, and not forgetting of course, the famous whisky trail which is nearby.

For the fisherman, the area is well-known for its proximity to the Dee's prolific salmon fishing, attracting serious anglers from miles away.

The peace and natural splendour of the area that attracted Queen Victoria and her Prince Consort, choosing Deeside as a favourite retreat, still remains to be experienced and enjoyed from the doorway of the Potarch hotel.

Potarch Hotel
Royal Deeside
Kincardineshire AB3 4BD
Tel: (03398) 84339

MURRAYSHALL COUNTRY HOUSE HOTEL

The Murrayshall Country House Hotel and Golf Course is only 4 miles from Perth, set in 300 acres of parkland. Deer stroll the wooded hillside, pheasants and peacocks call from the greens. The natural beauty and splashes of colour in the garden are complemented by the mellow stone of the main house with its crow stepped gables.

The hotel, completely refurbished, is elegantly furnished in a traditional style but with the use of the wonderful fabric designs available today. The bedrooms all have en suite facilities, self dial telephone and colour television.

The aptly named Old Masters Restaurant has walls hung with Dutch Masters and table settings befitting the artistry of master chef, Bruce Sangster. The restaurant has received various culinary accolades and Bruce Sangster held the 'Scottish Chef Of The Year' title for 1989/90. Vegetables and herbs from the hotel's walled garden and an abundance of local produce form the basis of the menus which have a Scottish flavour with a hint of modern French cuisine. A well balanced wine list is complemented by the finest of rare malt whiskies.

The 6420 yard, 18 hole, par 73 course is interspersed with magnificent specimen trees lining the fairways, water hazards and white sanded bunkers to offer a challenge to all golfers. Buggies and sets of clubs are available for hire. Neil Mackintosh, our resident professional, is pleased to give tuition, from half an hour to a week's course. Perth is ideally situated for Scotland's courses. Golfers can relax in the newly refurbished club house which overlooks the course and provides informal dining.

Other sporting activities include tennis, croquet and bowls. However, situated only a few miles from the famous Salmon Waters of the River Tay, even closer to Perth Race Course, Murrayshall is uniquely placed to make it an attractive venue for whatever might bring you to this area of Scotland.

Private dining and conference facilities are available in both the hotel and club house. Conference organisers, requiring the best of service and attention for their senior delegates, will find Murrayshall the ideal conference haven.

Murrayshall is one of three group golf courses, the other two are Westerwood and Fernfell. Westerwood Golf Course was designed by Seve Ballesteros and Dave Thomas and is located at Cumbernauld, near Glasgow. The 47 bedroomed Hotel and Country Club opened in April 1991. Fernfell Golf and Country Club is located just out of Cranleigh, 8 miles from Guildford in Surrey. Corporate golf packages are offered at all three courses with the opportunity to place your company name and logo on a tee and to reserve the course for your company golf day. Golf Societies and Green Fee Payers are welcome.

Murrayshall Country House Hotel and Golf Course
Scone
Perthshire PH2 7PH
Tel: (0738) 51171
Fax: (0738) 52595

ROSETTE OF SMOKED SALMON AND QUAILS EGGS WITH SHALLOT BUTTER SAUCE

SERVES 4

INGREDIENTS

12oz (350g) Smoked Salmon (thinly sliced)

14 Quails Eggs

Sprig of Chervil

1 Medium Shallot

4oz (115ml) Dry White Wwine

1 Lemon

2oz (50g) Double Cream

4oz (115g) Best Quality Unsalted Butter

Pinch of Cayenne Pepper.

METHOD

Place the quails eggs in boiling salted water for 3½ minutes, then immerse immediately in cold water. Shell the eggs starting at the pointed end and set aside in warm salted water.

FOR THE SAUCE

Peel and chop the shallot as finely as possible, cover with the wine and place over a medium heat to reduce. Reduce by two thirds, then add the cream and return to the heat. Reduce this by one third then add the butter in small lumps and shake into the sauce. Season and add the lemon juice to taste.

TO SERVE

Dress the slices of smoked salmon on warm plates forming a rose like shape. Place one quails egg in the center of each plate surrounded by five half eggs. Place each plate under the grill for a few seconds to warm (the salmon should be served warm not hot) and coat with a little of the sauce. Decorate with sprigs of fresh chervil.

A FAVOURITE OF THE KINNARD ESTATE

KINNAIRD ESTATE

Mrs Constance Ward invites you to Kinnaird, a splendid country house dating in part from 1770, set in its own estate with lovely views over the Tay valley. With glorious gardens, open fires, a genuinely warm welcome and bedrooms of great charm and comfort, Kinnaird is a delightful spot for a relaxing break and is ideally situated for visiting the many beauty spots and places of interest in Perthshire.

Kinnaird owns over 2.5 miles of high quality fishing on the Tay and employs two full time ghillies. The Lower Kinnaird Beat is renowned for its fishing in September and October and consists of seven attractive pools, while the Upper Kinnaird Beat is a spring beat with an increasing annual catch. The three hill lochs provide fishing for brown trout and pike amongst some of Perthshire's most scenic surroudings.

In addition the estate offers a variety of other sporting activities including superb pheasant shooting for groups of eight guns, duck flighting and roe stalking.

Less taxing perhaps are the lovely walks that are available, from a gentle stroll around the garden to longer walks on the hill and moor. Two outdoor tennis courts and a croquet lawn provide entertainment for summer afternoons, although should the weather prove inclement, the cedar panelled sitting room provides a selection of amusements including bridge, backgammon, billiards or simply good conversation.

The award-winning restaurant, directed by Chef John Webber, offers modern cuisine of the highest standard. There is an extensive and detailed wine list partnered with a comprehensive selection of Malt Whiskey. Both dining rooms enjoy magnificent views, while the former drawing room features exquisite painted panels of figures and landscapes. These superb surroundings provide a stunning setting for a menu of carefully chosen dishes, imaginatively prepared and beautifully presented. In addition to table reservations, private luncheons, dinners and meetings may be reserved. Lunch and dinner are always available for both resident and non-resident guests and booking is appreciated.

For more information on fishing and hotel reservation please telephone (0796) 482440.

Kinnaird
Kinnaird Estate
By Dunkeld
Perthshire PH8 0LB
Tel: (0796) 482440
Fax: (0796) 482289

DUNKELD HOUSE HOTEL

A breathtaking location on the banks of the River Tay, 280 acres of grounds and a superb hotel offering a warm welcome to experienced anglers and novices alike.

Two miles of salmon fishing water offering the opportunity to fish from the bank or boat. Spinning and fly fishing available. Experienced ghillies who specialise in giving help and advice, not to mention catching fish!

Excellent trout fishing also available on our fishing beat or on a local loch. Make a day of it!

For an opportunity to catch a truly magnificent fish take advantage of our special 'Fishing Forays Package for 1992'.

A 3 day break to include 2 day's salmon fishing on the River Tay. From 1 May 1992 to August 1992. £240.00 per person to include dinner, bed and breakfast and all the fun that a 'Fishing foray' promises!

For more information or to make a booking please contact us on the number below:-

Dunkeld House Hotel
Dunkeld
Perthshire PH8 0HX
Tel: (03502) 771
Fax: (03502) 8924

THE GRAMPIANS

THE TAY AND ITS TRIBUTARIES

The North Atlantic Salmon Conservation Organisation reported that in 1990, 145,000 salmon were caught in Scotland, which was nearly a 50% fall from the previous year's figure of 280,000. Due to the growing popularity of salmon fishing it is becoming increasingly expensive and fishermen are understandably up in arms about the declining numbers. While catches will obviously vary from year to year there has got to be a reason for such a catastrophic decline. Despite the huge amount of research, all too little is known about the salmon's life at sea. It is, of course, a commonly known fact that they return to the rivers of their birth to spawn, and this is where netting comes in. Stake nets are bad enough and it is encouraging to see how many of these are now being bought off, but personally I can't help feeling that the villain of the piece is the drift net industry. Huge nets 600 yards long trap the fish on their return to spawning grounds. Mr Andrew Tennant, Scottish council member of the Salmon and Trout Association, has reported that 'The Northumberland and Yorkshire drift-net fishing took over 50,000 salmon and grilse in 1990 and we estimate that at least 75% of these fish were of Scottish origin.' Smoked salmon is popular all over the world and the demand for it has got to be satisfied but surely this is too high a price to pay. In terms of economics the North East coast drift net fishery employs just under 500 people while fishing in Scotland supports 5000 jobs and is valued at £50 million a year. Haven't salmon enough problems with trying to evade predators like seals and our flies and lures as well as ascending falls and other obstacles on their way to their spawning grounds? Similarly with up to £320,000 being asked for a week's timeshare on the Tay, isn't the fisherman entitled to expect a reasonable level of fish in the river? Something has got to be done and I urge you to support the associations which are trying to change this lamentable situation.

To see what the Tay can produce you only have to walk to Hardys in Pall Mall for there in a case is a cast of THE fish. At 6.15 pm on October 7th 1922 Miss G.W.Ballantine spinning bait - a dace - was taken in Boat Pool on the Glendevine Water. Nearly two hours later, 8.05 pm to be exact, it was landed. In 1820 the Earl of Howe is said to have landed a fish of 69¾ lb on the Tweed but this is somewhat legendary and at 64lb Miss Ballantine's fish holds the official record. In April of the same year Major Baker Carr took seventeen fish in a day which varied in weight from 9lb to 30lb. Back in Victorian times the Duke of Atholl regularly used to take six or seven salmon before breakfast. But perhaps this is not surprising considering the catch records of the time. Take 1843 for example, when returns show that 35,126 salmon and 43,617 grilse were killed and the river wasn't fished anything like as hard as it is nowadays. What a river!

Perth was formerly the capital of Scotland and was fortified by the Romans who were so struck by the mighty Tay that they compared it to the Tiber. But as Sir Walter Scott wrote in The Fair Maid of Perth:

'Behold the Tiber' the vain Roman cried,
Viewing the ample Tay from Baiglies side;
But where's the Scot that would the vaunt repay,
And hail the puny Tiber as the Tay?'

The **Tay** drains more than two thousand two hundred square miles of country and carries the largest volume of fresh water in the British Isles. It begins its 114 miles in the hills near Tyndrum on the west coast. Two feeder streams, the Dochart and Lochay, merge to become Fillan Water. This then tumbles past Crianlarich and on into Loch Dochart where on an island, the ruins of Dochart Castle still keep watch over the narrow pass into the glen. It is joined by the wild waters of Benmore Burn as it threads its way though boggy ground and on to Loch Iubhair. Then it is on to the falls of Dochart at Killin which is on the western shore of Loch Tay. Salmon rarely ascend the falls until the temperature is right which is usually in May. Loch Tay is some 14 miles long by ¾ of a mile wide and is over 450 foot deep in places. Trout average ¾lb but 3 and 4 pounders are taken regularly while big ferox lurk in its murky depths. The shallow areas of the east and west ends are probably the best fishing and as on all big lochs a ghillie is an indispensable asset. Trolling is likely to be the most successful method especially in the spring when the average fish is a hefty 17lb. Above the western shore are the ruins of Finlarig Castle, seat of 'Black Duncan' the Earl of Orchy. The well preserved dungeons and beheading pit are ample evidence that he lived up to his nickname. Overlooking the northern shore is the 3984 foot lofty eminence of Ben Lawers. From the summit of this mountain, on a clear day you can see both east and west coasts. Its slopes are covered with rare mosses and lichens such as mossy cyphel, Alpine forget-me-not and campion.

The Ardeonaig Hotel (0567) 2400 is the only hotel on the south side of the loch and is halfway along the shoreline, yards from the ancient ruins of Mains Castle. It is the ideal place for a fishing holiday as with one of the hotel's five 4 rod boats you can cover both the east and west ends of the loch. Also if you feel like a break from fishing you can always try the hotel's 9 hole golf course. Other fishing hotels are Clachgaig Hotel (0567) 2270 which has three boats and Croft-na-Caber (0887) 5236 which also has a water sports centre. Permits for a day's trouting can be had for £2 from the Kenmore Post Office (0887) 3200. The Kenmore Hotel (0887) 3205 has three boats for loch fishing and two miles of river fishing which is available to guests at £15 a day and non-residents at £20.50 a day. On January the 15th, which is the first day of the season, fishermen are piped down to the water and a bottle of whisky is cracked over the bows of one of the hotel's boats. Most rods will troll using Rapallas, Kynochs or Tobies. This method may not suit the purist, but on the other hand it does catch fish! Now that the downstream nets have been bought off and the Lochay has been improved, catches on the loch should improve in a few years time.

A short distance downstream from Kenmore is the junction with the River **Lyon** which is one of the biggest of the Tay's tributaries. Like the Lochay this river has been 'hydroised' and the dam at the eastern end of Loch Lyon prevents fish from reaching the loch and spawning the headwaters. The hydro scheme has, however, created some good deep holding pools and fish now spawn in the river's tributaries and its lower reaches and the best fishing is on the lower seven miles down to the junction with the Tay.

Much work has been done to improve the Lyon in recent years. Spawning grounds have been improved and it is being stocked with fry. It is a superb river to fish with large deep holding pools, cascading falls and white water runs. There are some particularly attractive pools on the Fortinglass water and here in the churchyard you can see the oldest tree in Europe, a 3000 year old yew. Although the back end of the season is likely to

THE GRAMPIANS

be best, the Lyon also produces good springers. The Coshieville Hotel (0887) 3319 has the first one and a half miles of water above the junction. This water has 6 pools and takes 4 rods and a boat is available for fishing Castle Pool. A day's trouting costs £5 while salmon fishing varies between £10 and £15. Two and a half pound trout are not uncommon here and September 1990 saw the best salmon of the season, a lovely fourteen pounder. The Post Office House (0887) 6221 at Bridge of Balgie issues daily permits for fishing some of the upstream beats.

Between the junction with the Lyon and Aberfeldy are the Tay's Farleyer and Bolfracks beats. It was from here that the Black Watch began its road to fame and glory in 1740. Until that date it had primarily been used to keep the peace between feuding Highlanders. However, war with Spain had broken out and troops were needed. It was decided that the regiment should be force marched to London and rumour spread that they were destined for the West Indies. Travelling south of the border was a big enough wrench for men who had never left their homeland before, but the West Indies with their fevers which decimated regiments was the worst possible destination (my how things change!). Some of the men deserted but those that were captured were shot in the Tower of London. However the regiment was sent to Europe and at Fontenoy, where opposing officers dropped handkerchiefs to signal that fighting could commence, received its first battle honour.

At Aberfeldy where the Urlar Burn joins the Tay is the Farleyer House Hotel (0887) 20332 which can usually arrange fishing for guests although it can be expensive. The Weem Hotel at Weem (0887) 20381 has privileged access to 1½ miles of good water for guests. If you think that all fishing on the Tay is expensive Mr and Mrs J.Garbutt of Grandtully (0796) 82207 have a pleasant surprise for you. They have a mile of single bank fishing below the Kinnaird beat where the cost of a day varies between £6 and £12. Now you may think that at this price the fishing can't be very good and your landing net is more likely to be used if you try one of the more expensive beats at say £40 a day. If you do, you are missing a great opportunity, for a 25 pounder was recently caught on this water where the average weight is around 10lb.

As one might expect with such a big river, many of its tributaries are fine salmon rivers in their own right and one such is the **Tummel** which joins the Tay at Logierait. Although its character has been effected by the hydro dam at Faskally this is good fly water and April sees some fantastic rises of trout to hatching olives. To whet your appetite there is a fish pass with a viewing gallery at Pitlochry. The Angling Club here has the fishing of the right bank and those hoping to fish are asked to write to the Secretary. Alternatively, you could try the Atholl Estate Office (0796) 81355 which has fishing on the Tummel, Garry and Tilt or stay at the East Haugh House Hotel (0796) 3121 which has leasing arrangements on various beats of the same three rivers and also the Shee.

Much of the Tay has wooded banks which together with it being so wide make it much more practicable to fish it from a boat. While it may be tempting for the bank fisherman to wade so as to cover that little bit extra water (which is sure to hold a fish), wading can be extremely dangerous as this is a fast flowing river and the pools can be very deep. The conifers surrounding Dunkeld House are thought to be more than two hundred years old and particularly stricking. The town in

medieval times was the religious centre of Scotland and you can see the tomb of Robert II in the cathedral. To most fishermen, Dunkeld is synonymous with the fly of the same name. This brightly coloured little temptress has proved the undoing of many a fat trout and one that has brought me a great deal of luck. Here the river is joined by the Braan whose Black Linn falls are impassable to salmon. Just below the town are the Birnam Woods of Macbeth fame while downstream is Glendelvine where Miss Ballantine caught her fish. Now that some of the nets have been bought off, Dunkeld is seeing much better runs of sea-trout.

A good place to stay is the Stakis Dunkeld House Hotel (0350) 2771 which has two miles of double bank fishing. The hotel is in the middle of its four beats which hold twelve rods and the services of two ghillies are available. Hotel guests understandably have priority but bookings from non-residents are welcome. Mr M.C. Smith (0350) 2593 lets the Dalguise Salmon Fishings, which are 1½ miles of double bank at between £20 and £35 a day according to season. Not far downstream is the Kinloch House Hotel (0250) 84237 which can arrange spring and summer fishing for guests on three beats where the cost ranges from £60 to £100 a day.

Below Glendelvine are Kercock and Meikleour after which the Tay is joined by the Isla at Islamouth. This is superb fishing but very expensive! The Tower of Lethendy fishings at Meikleour have recently been timeshared on 99 year leases with a top price of £350,000 and that's just for one week. Both the **Isla** and its tributary the **Ericht** which has good spawning beds have a justly deserved reputation for producing excellent fishing. Richmond & Co. (0382) 201964 manage the Gauldry beat on the Isla where a week for 4 rods costs between £200 and £500. This water got off to a very good start in 1991 and was more productive than some of the major Tay beats. Also on the Isla, Mrs Henderson (0828) 7226 can arrange for you to fish about 1¼ miles of single bank which has four named pools at between £15 and £25 per rod per day. Spinning tends to be best on the slack water here, but there are some nice runs which take the fly well. On the Ericht the Bridge of Cally Hotel (0250) 86231 water costs between £15 and £25 a day or you can try Finlayson Hughes (0738) 30926 who let the Craighall Rattray beat where you can enjoy such pools as Witches, Cauldron and Pipers Cave.

There is a tradition of spinning on the Tay partly because of its size and also because it is an early spring river and spun baits allow you to get down better and fish the Tay water. But where streams and pools can be covered by fly it is well worth a try. Beats such as Islamouth and Benchil have excellent fly water. However, you will need a big rod for although a 15 footer may cover some of the upper beats an 18 or 20 footer will be needed for the bigger pools. On the big pools another alternative to spinning is 'herling'. This involves trailing three lures on set lengths of line from a boat. With this method the boatman does all the work and the fisherman just has to wait until the rod bends and the reel plays its merry tune. This may seem boring but Miss Ballantine to name but one found it rather effective!

The lower beats are superb and very difficult to get on especially at the best times, unless you are lucky enough to be invited as a guest or happen to be a millionaire. The Tayside Hotel at Stanley (0738) 828249 has access to time-shared beats from May to July where a day can be had for between £12.50

70

THE GRAMPIANS

and £20. Perth District Council (0738) 439911 owns some fishing and if you can prove you are a resident of this fair city you can purchase a permit for £5 for five years. If you can prove you live within fifteen miles of the city you are eligible to join the Perth and District Angling Club. Applications for membership can be had from the local tackle shops and the fishing on the club's water can be excellent and is great value compared to the expensive adjoining beats.

If condition are favourable, just west of Pitlochry, there is excellent loch fishing to be had on lochs **Tummel**, **Rannoch** and **Dunalastaire** Water, where you will find the Dunalastaire Hotel (0882) 2303. The eastern end of Rannoch is guarded by Schiehallion 'The Fairy Hill of the Caledonians'. However, it is fat trout and not fairies that you will find here where the murky depths, more than 300 foot in places, are the haunts of some very big ferox -seven pounders are not uncommon. Much of the loch's banks are crowded with conifers and the shallower margins of the western shore are the best fishing areas. A day here with such flies as Greenwells Glory, March Brown or Blue Zulu should produce a good basket of ¾ lb brownies, while for the big ferox trolling is the best method. The loch is fed by the outflow from Loch Laidon which lies some six miles to the west and where a days fishing its attractive bays can produce twenty or more large bags of lively trout of between ½ and ¾ lb. Loch Rannoch Hotel (0882) 2201 is a good place to stay for fishing these lochs or exploring Rannoch Moor, whose waterlogged peat with its tufts of cotton grass and coarse sedges is alive with the calls of snipe, curlew and grouse. Permits for Loch Tummel are obtained from the Pitlochry Tourist Information Centre (0796) 2215.

The Tay is a colussus among the waters of the world. It may have reported decreasing catches and this is a worrying sign, but it is still a symbol of strength, power and beauty. Scotland is a land rich in scenic wonders and there are few more compelling sights than the waters of the Tay and her tributaries. There may be finer waters in Canada, Scandinavia or even Scotland but few if any have the stature of the Tay - a symbol of Scotland and salmon.

FISHING FAYRE

The Tay is one of Britain's legendary rivers - it is a water that excites all fishermen but by the same token it is a water that many feel is almost untouchable. Sacred, shall we say? Well, while locals may have it as something of a Ganges, it is by no means unfishable. Indeed, there are some excellent hotel waters and several other hotels have good contacts who can often arrange fishing on the Tay or her tributaries. Prices vary considerably as does the quality of the beats available but if you look hard enough, good fishing can be found.

Perthshire is a delightful part of Britain and boasts a large number of really outstanding hotels, self-catering accommodation and all manner of places in which to stay. A particularly peaceful place and a fine fishing hotel can be found on the south shore of Loch Tay at Ardeonaig. The Ardeonaig (0567) 2400 is extremely relaxing and an ideal choice for peace and quiet. It has significant charm and is a splendid place for those fishing in the area.

Kenmore is a charming village at the foot of Loch Tay. The Kenmore Hotel (0887) 3205 is an idyllic 16th century hotel

which has a beautiful position beside the River Tay. There are some fine bedrooms here and a pleasant dining room and bar. The hotel organises fishing for its guests and makes a delightful place in which to stay. Splendid loch fishing can also be organised on Loch Tay through the Croft-na-Caber Hotel (0887) 5236. It is a really friendly hotel which offers good bar meals and a selection of self catering accommodation if you prefer. The Fortingall Hotel (0887) 3367 is another popular haunt where fishing is a plus. Good value accommodation is an additional reason for including it in your 'Tayward' plans. Loch and river fishing can also be arranged through a number of hotels centred in Aberfeldy.

The first is the Weem hotel (0887) 20381 a characterful and comfortable hotel which offers good value accommodation. Those of you who have a somewhat bigger budget should consider Farleyer House (0887) 20332 which is located just outside Aberfeldy. The hotel is extremely elegant and its bedrooms are of an excellent quality. The restaurant here is outstanding and one to note if you are passing through the area or staying in self-catering premises. The Coshieville Hotel (0887) 3319 is located at the entrance to Glen Lyon which many feel is one of the most beautiful glens in Scotland. The hotel has two beats on the Lyon and is extremely keen to welcome lovers of the sport. Another unpretentious hotel which offers fine cooking is located at Killiecrankie. The Killiecrankie Hotel (0796) 3220 which stands close to the celebrated pass is a friendly place to stay and worth a detour. All around is majestic scenery with forest, loch, hills and river forever in your focus. The fishing is grand but merely being in Perthshire has much to commend it. Midway between Dunkeld and Kenmore one finds the Grandtully Hotel (0887) 4207. The hotel has some impressive fishing and this really is a first class hotel for the person who is keen to fish the Tay. Good food and fishing facilities are further plus points. A hotel with outstanding sporting facilities can be found at Dunkeld. The Stakis Dunkeld House (0350) 2771 is a first class hotel in which to stay. The house dates from the turn of the century when it was built by the 7th Duke of Atholl. The leisure complex is a more recent addition but will surely please anglers who have had a hard day on the Tay. Or perhaps the 'other half' who may not have a fancy for flies or streams! Bedrooms are comfortable and the bars are well stocked. What more could we ask for?

Well, one can ask, but it is often difficult to actually find fishing on the River Tay. The Ballathie House Hotel (0250) 83268 is a splendid Baronial-style mansion in a near perfect situation overlooking the Tay. The standard of the hotel is excellent with a fine restaurant and elegant bedrooms. Fishing is also available and if you give plenty of notice you might be lucky enough to get on. It is a relief therefore to be able to add to the list of possibilities an absolute pearl of a hotel and restaurant. Kinnaird House (0796) 82440 is situated on the Kinnaird Estate and is surely one of the most appealing hotels in Britain for the fisherman. It is pure paradise. Here, he can go back in time and reminisce of the great house parties of former years. The fishing is first class, the food is marvellous and the hotel is splendid. If you only had one more fishing weekend this would have to be on that sacred shortlist.

A little way south in Stanley itself, we come upon The Tayside Hotel, (0738) 828249, which is another popular centre for fishing parties. The hotel provides a warm welcome and practical rather than plush accommodation. The hotel is excellent value and should certainly be on the shorlist when heading towards the Tay. Lovers of fine food should also try and visit Murrayshall Country House Hotel (0738) 51171, a superb restaurant can be found here together with a championship golf course and really outstanding hotel.

Returning northwards in search of more fine fishing and fodder, we might chance upon Alyth, and more fortuitously still, the Lands of Loyal Hotel (0828) 33151 a Victorian mansion which will not fail to impress. The Bridge of Cally Hotel (0250) 86231 is a friendly hotel which offers comfortable bedrooms and a pleasant restaurant which merits consideration.

There are an abundance of trout lochs and small streams that will appeal to the less demanding fisherman and a hotel which is somewhat different to the more traditional Scottish hotel is the Log Cabin Hotel (0250) 81288 which is made wholly of Norwegian Pine. The restaurant here is extremely good and offers the best of Scottish fayre. All manner of country pursuits can be enjoyed from the hotel, not least trout fishing in the hotel's own loch. Elsewhere the fisherman might wish to visit Aldchlappie (0250) 81224 which resides beside the River Ardle and is thoroughly welcoming. The Malt Room bar has a fascinating range of malt whiskies to sample after a day or two on the river. Fishing can be arranged on the Dulmunzie House Estate, Spittal of Glenshee. The hotel (0250) 85224 is tremendously welcoming where all manner of leisure pursuits can be enjoyed to the full. It is a grand but delightfully informal hotel in which to stay and one which merits a detour. There are a number of good hotels in Blairgowrie, but one of the most appealing while on a fishing tour is lovely Kinloch House (0250) 84237. Splendid furniture graces the impressive interior of this former Scottish country house and a number of Scottish dishes which are prepared here are excellent. The hotel can arrange a number of leisure pursuits including fishing and is therefore still more appealing.

The Tummel is one of the Tay's most splendid tributaries and a brace of hotels should be mentioned for those who are going to fish the waters. The Green Park Hotel, Pitlochry (0796) 3248 is the only hotel on Loch Faskally. The gardens reach down to the water and make for a splendid view. Fishing can be arranged from the hotel and once again Scottish dishes are the source of some fine cooking. Lovers of hotels with waterside settings may also like to consider the Hotel Port-an-Eilean (0882) 4233 on the shores of Loch Tummel. The former shooting lodge which dates from 1865 enjoys a delightful lochside setting and is bordered on both flanks by glorious woodland. The emphasis here is most definitely on quiet relaxation, fishing and good food. If you are looking for tranquillity amidst breathtaking scenery, this fits the bill. The Bunrannoch Hotel (0882) 2267 is an unpretentious friendly village inn on the banks of the River Tummel and can offer both loch and river fishing. The bedrooms are cosy, the fire warms and crackles and good bar meals complete a wholesome picture.

If the Dee is the Queen of Rivers, the Tay may be considered King of Scotland's rivers. Many might argue with this conjecture but for those who fish the Tay and its tributaries or small Perthshire burns, which house some marvellously wild brown trout, then Perthshire is a magnificent place. Driving through the area alone lights the spirit and when the times are tight there are few finer places to go.

River Tay   (Kinnaird House)

THE ARDEONAIG HOTEL

A charming old coaching inn, dating back to the beginning of the seventeenth century, the Ardeonaig hotel rests in twenty private acres midway between Kenmore, at the start of the River Tay, and Killin, where the rivers Dochart and Lochay enter the Loch; the one silently and the other in a spectacular rush over a mile of jagged rocks.

For the serious fisherman, the Ardeonaig is ideal, surrounded as it is by such a wide variety of waters. Loch Tay is famed for its large salmon, ready to provide the sportsman with a decent competition. Trout is also available in the Loch and the hotel itself has four boats in its own private harbour, available to fish fourteen miles of the Loch. For a change, other types of fishing can be arranged on the Rivers Tay, Dochart, and Lyon, and several beautiful mountain lochs.

If golfing is more your bag, then the hotel is equally well-placed. Many of Scotland's finest and most famous courses are just a short drive away, including St Andrews and Gleneagles. The 18-hole Taymouth Castle Course is a mere eight miles away, and the hotel itself has a 9-hole course of its own.

For those accompanying their sporting partners with a little less enthusiasm for the noble sports, the surrounding area provides a wonderful array of pastimes. Walking is the perfect way to explore the stunning raw beauty, nearby is Ben Lawers with its National Trust Centre. Historic sites abound, Blair castle, Scone Palace and Balmoral to name but a few. All types of water-sports can be arranged locally, from windsurfing to jet-skiing, and guests can launch their own boats from the hotel harbour. Riding and skiing are available locally, including the relevant tuition if required. With superb packed lunches happily provided, there is never a need to go hungry in all this wonderful fresh air.

All of the hotel's bedrooms have ensuite facilities, telephone, television, 24-hour service and a "Through the Night" menu, well-used to the needs of well-exercised guests. The restaurant itself provides an excellent menu, including the regular appearance of fresh seafood and local game, all complemented by an extensive collection of superb wines. All in all the ideal place for that perfectly peaceful break.

The Ardeonaig Hotel
South Loch Hotel
Killin
Perthshire
Tel: (0572) 400

THE LANDS OF LOYAL HOTEL

Set on a hillside overlooking the Vale of Strathmore to the Sidlaw Hills beyond, are 10 acres of tiered and rambling gardens, at the heart of which lies the 'Lands of Loyal'.

This impressive Victorian mansion was built in the 1830s, commissioned by Sir William Ogilvy, who on his return from Waterloo, chose Loyal Hill as the site for this magnificent home.

The Lands of Loyal was subsequently owned by a succession of families until being converted into a Hotel in 1945.

It has since been very prominent in the area, holding fond memories for the oldest generations. It is also regarded as a second home to country sportsmen who have remained loyal for many years.

More recently, an extensive refurbishment programme, carried out in the public rooms, has further enhanced the unique atmosphere of this much respected country house hotel.

A highly acclaimed restaurant in its own right, our style of cuisine is traditional and imaginative, making full use of local fish and game.

An extensive wine list, featuring several wines and madeiras, some over 150 years old, is available to complement your meal.

The Lands of Loyal makes an excellent base for touring. Perth, Dundee, Glamis Castle. Scone Palace and Glenshee ski resort are all within a half hour's drive.

Highland destinations such as Royal Deeside, Aviemore, Speyside and Aberdeen are typical day excursions.

For the country sportsman, fishing and shooting are available with salmon and sea/brown trout in loch and river; pheasant and grouse on hill and low ground as well as wild fowling and deer stalking as the seasons permit.

The immediate area encompasses many golf clubs including the championship Rosemount course and directly in front of the hotel, the very popular Alyth course. World famous St Andrews, Carnoustie and Gleneagles are within 45 minutes drive. Golf can be arranged by the hotel.

All rooms have private facilities with shower or bath, colour/satellite TV, direct-dial telephone and tea/coffee facilities.

Dining arrangements are as flexible as possible to suit our guests. A choice of menus offering a full table d'hote dinner or a lighter supper style meal is available throughout the evening.

Karl-Peter & Patricia Howell
The Lands of Loyal Hotel
Alyth
Perthshire
Scotland
PH11 8JQ
Tel: (08283) 3151
Fax: (08283) 3313

MOOR OF RANNOCH HOTEL

This small fishing hotel is situated amidst some of Scotland's most breathtaking scenery 1,000 feet above sea level, on the edge of the renown Rannoch Moor.

It can be approached by rail on the West Highland line or by the Road to the Isles from Kinloch Rannoch and Pitlochry.

Our food is of the highest standard, with traditional game and fish dishes featuring frequently on the menu, complemented by fine wines.

The hotel is fully licensed, the bar specialising in Malt Whiskies from all over Scotland.

Within easy walking distance from the hotel, are dozens of small lochs with unpronounceable gaelic names, each teeming with wild brown trout where the fisherman can spend the day in total solitude with only the Red Deer, Grouse and Golden Eagles for company, and return to the warmth of the hotel in the evening, after a relaxing and successful day's fishing.

The hotel also has the fishing rights on nearby Loch Laidon, where both bank and boat fishing are available. Bags of wild brown trout for the day often reach three figures. Loch Laidon and the river Gaun are also famous for their huge Ferox Brown Trout, weighing up to 16 lb.

The area is also ideal for shooting, deerstalking, birdwatching or simply a peaceful highland holiday amidst beautiful scenery. The hotel can cater for all your fishing needs; tackle, boats, packed lunches, and of course local knowledge and experience.

For a fishing holiday away from it all, the Moor at Rannoch Hotel could be the oasis in the highlands you have been looking for.

Moor of Rannoch Hotel
Rannoch Station
Perthshire PH17 2QA
Tel: (08823) 238

KENMORE HOTEL AND RIVER TAY FISHING

'Tight Lines' - Each year the Kenmore Hotel opens the River Tay Salmon Fishing Season on January 15th - Sunday excepted - with the now familiar toast. Gathered from near and far the hardy Anglers don their apparel and gather in the Village Square at Kenmore. After an opening speech of welcome and a few courage building drams they march with the Piper round to the river where a further ceremony takes place - the launching of the first boat.

Set amid the splendour of Perthshire, the mighty River Tay meanders through the unspoilt tranquility of the Taymouth Estate. On either bank for two miles down stream the Kenmore Hotel has its own private pools, The Dairy, The Ladies, Chinese, Castle and Battery are names synonymous of times when the Campbells of Breadalbane ruled these lands - now used by the modern days angler who can imagine its former glory.

There is also fishing on Loch Tay for those who prefer. Take one of the hotel boats and motor up into the Loch for fly fishing or harling.

The Kenmore Hotel, Scotland's oldest Inn, built in 1572, offers the Fisherman all the modern comfort when not on the river. All 38 bedrooms have en-suite facilities, direct dial telephone, tea, coffee making facilities and colour television. Our restaurant offers local produce as well as European fayre and our cellar is stocked to complement our cuisine. Spring fishing at Kenmore produces not only the hardy Angler but the strongest and cleanest of Salmon. Sea-lice fish are common in our beat, giving the angler a fight before the priest whilst in September and October the fish are not so sprightly but still command the full attention of the angler.

The Kenmore Hotel
Kenmore
Perthshire PH15 2NU
Tel: (08873) 205
Fax: (08873) 262

CULCREUCH CASTLE

Culcreuch Castle, the home of the Barons of Culcreuch since 1699 and before this the ancestral fortalice of the Galbraiths and indeed Clan Castle of the Galbraith chiefs for over three centuries (1320 to 1630), has now been restored and converted by its present owners into a most comfortable family-run country house hotel, intimately blending the elegance of bygone days with modern comforts and personal service in an atmosphere of friendly informal hospitality. The eight individually decorated and furnished bedrooms all have en suite facilities, colour television and tea and coffee making facilities. Most command uninterrupted and quite unsurpassed views over the 1600 acre parkland grounds, described by the National Trust for Scotland as a 'gem of outstanding beauty', and beyond a kaleidoscope of spectacular scenery of hills, moorlands, lochs, burns and woods comprising the Endrick valley and the Campsie Fells above.

All the public rooms are decorated in period style and furnished with antiques giving the aura and grace of a bygone age. Log fires create warmth and intimacy and the candlelit evening meals in the panelled dining room make for most romantic occasions, well complemented by freshly prepared local produce and a carefully selected wine cellar.

The Loch Lomond, Stirling & Trossachs area offers the visitor a wide and varied range of country activities, including golf, fishing, shooting, water sports, nature study and bird watching, historical research, or simply walking and exploring in stunningly beautiful countryside.

With over 40 golf courses within a 25 mile radius of the Castle, Culcreuch is a golfer's paradise. A special Golfing Brochure is available on request which gives details of the packages available at a large number of these venues.

Culcreuch is best known, however, for its extensive fishing packages, covering a wide area of the Loch Lomond area including fishing on Loch Lomond itself. The angling season is as follows: Salmon and Sea Trout: 11th February to 31st October, Brown Trout: 15th March to 6th October (Sunday Fishing is strictly prohibited)

Packages are available on the following waters. Salmon and Sea Trout - Loch Lomond, River Leven, River Fruin, Luss Water (except Arden Estate Water), The Gareloch (part) and the River Endrick (major part, - The River Endrick flows through the Culcreuch Estate). Full details, including maps of each water showing pools and other important information, are available in our Fishing Brochure available on request.

Whether for either business or pleasure, Culcreuch is a most convenient, centrally positioned base for visiting Edinburgh (55 minutes by motorway), Glasgow (35 minutes) and Stirling (25 minutes). For business clients there is no comparable venue for entertaining and the Castle specialises in offering its unique facilities for small meetings.

From Autumn to Spring, reduced terms for off-season breaks are offered, together with House Parties over the Christmas and New Year Holidays; and during these cooler months the log fires offer a cheerful welcome on your return from a day out in the Trossachs.

The location of Culcreuch is rural but not isolated, and with the fresh air of the countryside, the space, grace, comfort, good wholesome food and that unique warmth of friendship and hospitality offered from a family run home from home, a stay here is most conducive to shedding the cares and pressures of modern day life and utterly relaxing. We look forward to your company. — The Haslam Family

Culcreuch Castle
Fintry
Stirlingshire G63 0LW
Tel: (036 086) 228
Fax: (0532) 390093
Telex: 557299

THE GRAMPIANS

LOCH LOMOND TO LOCH LEVEN

What's the attraction of loch fishing? A few years ago I was fishing a stillwater in England. I had woken at five and the cloudy sky and light wind seemed good omens and so after a fortifying breakfast I set off. I arrived at the fishery around 6.30 which was half an hour before fishing was permitted. Personally I like to get on a stillwater as early as possible for several reasons. Firstly it is often a good time and secondly it is less likely to be crowded; one of the things I enjoy about fishing is getting away from the hustle and bustle of town life and being able to enjoy the quiet and peace of the countryside. Standing in a line of fellow anglers fishing some 'hot spot' is not my idea of fun. Also getting down to the water early gives you the opportunity to have a walk round and see what is happening and plan one's tactics accordingly. On this particular occasion my early start was rewarded by three nice rainbows and to spin out my four fish ticket I decided to rest the water. It wasn't long before the clouds rolled away and it was another baking hot summer's day. As the day warmed up the fishing turned dour so I decided to take an early lunch in the local pub. I was sitting at the bar with a thirst quenching pint of bitter when another rod came in wearing a jacket festooned with a multitude of flies of all sizes and colours. Some fishermen are great talkers and this one whom I had secretly named 'Trout Jacket' was one of them. He asked me how I had got on and what I had taken them on. He had had no luck as yet and was wondering about trying another fishery nearby. The conversation turned to other fisheries and I mentioned I hoped to be going up to Scotland to fish a loch or two. This aroused Trout Jacket's curiosity, for he had only fished within a thirty mile radius of his home and he proceeded to ply me with questions. 'Was the fishing good', which I answered 'could be great'. 'Were there big trout?' My reply of 'sometimes, but usually they are between ½ and ¾ lb and a two pounder is a prized catch' received a derisory snort and the tale of how he had caught a seven pound rainbow a season or two ago. 'Were lochs easy to get to and were there good pubs nearby?' I answered with a polite 'no' without revealing that many a loch requires a tramp across the moor to get to it. Trout Jacket shrugged his shoulders and said he couldn't see the point in going all that way when there were so many well stocked waters close at hand. It's just as well we don't all like the same things!

Don't misunderstand me, I have had many happy days on stocked water and enjoyed some good tussles with rainbows. However loch fishing is completely different. The fish may be small but they are wild and I would rather have one of these hard fighting half pounders than quite a few one pound 'stockies' which often have little or no flavour to their flesh.

Having described one of the joys of loch fishing as being able to enjoy the quiet and solitude of the country you may think it inappropriate to discuss **Loch Lomond** for it is only a short distance from Glasgow and there is a main road along the whole of the western shoreline. It is also a major tourist attraction as so many people have heard of it's 'bonnie bonnie banks.' However, Lomond is a big water covering some 27 square miles and this combined with its many small wooded islands ensure there is ample room for both tourist and fisherman.

One of the fascinating things about Lomond is the difference in character between its north and south ends. This is principally because it is a product of the Ice Age. There is a geo-

graphical fault line running from Arden to Balmaha and the loch differs dramatically below the village of Luss. Above this point it is narrow, steep-banked and as deep as 450 feet in parts. South of Luss the loch broadens out and gets progressively shallower as you near Balloch at the southern end. This is important from a fishing point of view for while 20 foot of water may suit sea-trout, salmon prefer much shallower water, a depth of between five and eight foot. The great banks of silt and sand such as Pilot Bank above Ross are the product of glacial deposits left after the Ice Age.

As it is such a vast expanse of water, bank fishing is pretty unproductive and the only really practical way to fish it is from a boat drifting gently between the islands. In medieval times mainlanders used the islands as a sanctuary for themselves and their livestock. This however, was no guarantee of safety from the marauding Norsemen. In 1263 King Haakon sailed his galleys up Loch Long and then carried them overland to Lomond - no mean feat! Here they were relaunched and he systematically plundered and laid waste to the islands. Several centuries later the islands were used to house drunkards and lunatics, but all is quiet now except for the piping of birds.

The most likely way of catching a salmon is to troll. This involves using three rods with two carrying lures some 25 yards behind the boat and a short stiff rod, usually called a poker, fishing some ten yards nearer in. The start of the season will see natural baits such as the golden Sprat and at the beginning of June, artificials like Rapallas and the Kynoch Killer are favoured. This method calls for some smart action when you get a take. The first thing to do is to head for deeper water, then wind in the spare lures and start playing your fish, but you have to be quick about it.

May sees the beginning of the fly season when a team of traditional flies such as Black Pennell, Peter Ross and Dunkeld will be used, for this is also good sea-trout water. Among the local favourites are the Turkey and Gold and the Burton. Dapping is also a popular technique but because Lomond is so big and regularly fished by the locals, you will find that everyone has their own method and their own favourite fly. Among the islands, Inch Moan and Inch Fad are popular but the best advice on a 'likely' place will come from those who hire out the boats as they will know what's been happening. Macfarlane & Sons of Balmaha (0360) 87214 hire out boats at £10 a day or £20 to include an outboard. The 13th April 1991 was a lucky day for one of these boats which took a lovely 27 pounder from the 'Stables', near Ross Priory. They also issue permits as do R.A. Clement & Co of Glasgow (041)-221 0068 on behalf of the Loch Lomond Angling Improvement Association. The cost of a day's ticket is £8.68, a week is £25.54, while a season ticket which also covers the River Endrick costs £102.18 and there is a £25.54 joining fee. These permits cover salmon and trout; 8 to 12 oz is the average for trout which will be found all along the shores, though the northern end is likely to be more productive.

The source of the River **Endrick** is in west Stirlingshire and flows into the loch near Balmaha. The upper part of the river is not worth fishing for although the salmon is a mighty leaper no fish can ascend the 90 foot Loup o'Fintry falls. Below the falls there are some good pools but downstream there are more falls, the Pot of Gartness, and salmon need the right level of water to ascend them. Below the Pot is the meeting with the Blane which is the main tributary and the junction pool known as the Meetings of Lynn is a favourite spot. Below Drymen the river flows through rich pasture and woodland and can be a bit sluggish. It really requires a good spate to provide exciting fishing; but then pools such as Oak Tree and Coolies Linn can produce salmon of around 10lb and sea-trout which average around 2½ lb. It takes the right conditions to get fish into the river and many find that trolling on the loch by the mouth of the river can produce excellent results.

Despite the mass of water in the loch, the **Leven** which connects it to the Clyde is relatively slow moving due to the barrage at Balloch. As is to be expected from being so near a big city, the river is heavily fished. This is also because it can be very good as Mr S.Burgoyne will tell you, for in July 1989 he caught a magnificent sea-trout of 22lb 8oz. This river is also controlled by the Loch Lomond Angling Improvement Association and day tickets can be had for £12.77 while £51.09 is the cost of a season's ticket.

Heading north over the Forth brings you to the start of the M90 and in a short while you are alongside **Loch Leven**. This water is world famous and many international fishing competitions are held here. Its reputation derives from the superb hard fighting qualities of its brownies which have been used to stock waters all over the world. It is fair to say that in recent years catches have fallen and also that the trout seem to feed off the bottom. A perplexing change and one which will surely keep the experts busy for some time. As a result of these developments many rods are now using sinking lines, but as most of the loch is shallow you don't have to go down too far. Despite such problems this is still one of the great trout waters and you will find that traditional small double-hook flies such as March Brown, Dunkeld, Invicta, Black Pennel and Soldier Palmer can be effective. One of the attractions of the loch is the size of the trout, for they average around 1¼ lb and three pounders are taken regularly. The best fish in recent years has been 6lb 6oz. It should also be noted that boats are essential on this water. Permits can be had from Loch Leven Fisheries at The Pier (0577) 63407 where you can also hire boats and it is a good idea to book in advance. The day is divided into three sessions; dawn - which can be 2.30 am! -to 9 am which costs £24.50, 10 am to 6 pm. at £20.50 and 6.30 pm to 11.30 pm for £27.50. The Loch is not only a tremendous water it is also a most beautiful one. Imagine the scene as the sun comes up - you have fished hard and had good results - the occasional joke has rudely disrupted the lapping of the water on your boat. This is what life is about, do you remember your holiday with your head buried in the sand in Southern Spain? Well make no mistake - to enjoy a dawn on Loch Leven is a memory you will never forget.

Continuing still further north on the M90 towards Perth brings you to Bridge of Earn. It is a mistake to regard the River **Earn** as a tributary of the Tay for it flows into the Firth below the tide. This is however, not a bad salmon river and some say better than the Tay for sea-trout which average 2lb and can be over 7lb. The Earn flows out of Loch Earn which is a good watersports centre. There is trout fishing on the loch and permits may be had from either St Fillans and Loch Earn Head Post Offices or J.R.Mills & Co of St Fillans (0764) 85217 who can also hire you a boat. The cost of a day's fishing on the loch is only £2 but that reflects the quality of the fishing. The lower river tends to be slow and sluggish but upstream from Kinkell Bridge at Strathallan it is a pleasing streamy river with some good pools. The Earn Angling Improvement Association has been

doing sterling work to improve fishing here. The river is now being stocked with native fish and all but two of the nets have been bought off. The fact that two miles were recently sold for £570,000 will give you some idea of the quality of the fishing. A day on the Lawers Estate Co. Ltd. (0764) 70050 water costs £50 and season tickets are available. This beat is a little awkward to reach but well worth the effort. Rather more affordable is the Crieff Angling Club's water which costs £8 a day for salmon or £3 for trout - which can be excellent. Permits from Mr J.Boyd's newsagent shop in Crieff (0764) 3871 and it is advisable to book ahead for week-ends as Sunday fishing is allowed.

'Fly fishing on the River **Forth**? You must be joking!' would be the natural reaction of many a southerner brought up on images of factories discharging waste into the river. The ill informed might argue that there was no point in going and that you might just as well try a day's salmon fishing on the Thames as the result would be the same. How wrong can you be! In 1988 over 1000 salmon and grilse were taken from the Town Water at Stirling alone. The Scots really care about their fishing and a tremendous amount of work has gone into improving the rivers. The Forth is one of the great success stories and the river and its tributaries, the Teith, Allan and Devon, also have good runs of sea-trout. The good news story continues for the spring run is actually increasing; opening day, February 1st 1991, produced a 25 pounder at Callander and April has seen several fish of around 30lb. A day's permit for the Forth costs £22 and a season's ticket is £63.30 which strikes me as being good value for money. They may be had from Mr D. Crockart (0786) 73443 who can also arrange a day for you on the Blue Bank Fishings on the **Teith** where the cost varies between £10 and £25 a day. James Bayne of Callander (0877) 30218 also issues permits for the Teith and the 'Town Water' at a cost of £12 a day. The **Devon** still suffers from some pollution, but this is reflected in the cost of £3 a day or £10 for a season and it can fish well in the Autumn. The **Allan**, where a day costs between £10 and £25 is beginning to be very good for sea-trout and the numbers of grilse are increasing.

There are a number of stocked fisheries in the area but if you fancy a change from rainbows what about American book trout? Unless you have fished in the States, which has some great trouting areas like Montana, you may not have come across these fish before, but of all the stocked varieties they are the ones most likely to put up a memorable fight. There are two fisheries in the area which are stocked with them: Mill Dam and Loch Monzievaird and permits can be had for them from Kettles in Dunkeld (0350) 2556 and Mr Groot of Crieff (0764) 3963.

These wilds of Scotland differ vastly from the southern lakes. The fish are smaller, the access is somewhat tricky in places and even the bar is often further away - but make no mistake the sport is worth it, for when you hook a wild brownie and if you are well prepared, having a drink to celebrate would never be a problem!

FISHING FAYRE

Aside from the celebrated lochs of Lomond and Leven, there are a number of excellent rivers which run through this region. Hotels in the Kingdom of Fife are a touch thin on the ground (golf courses hold centre stage here), but south Perthshire has a whole multitude of self-catering and hotel accommodation to whet the appetite.

THE GRAMPIANS

Dunblane should be our first port of call as it sits happily midway between Loch Leven and Loch Lomond and is therefore a fine place from which to take in the entire scene. It is also home to Cromlix House (0786) 822125 where a charming mix of Edwardian and Victorian architecture make up one of Britain's most celebrated country house hotels. The library, conservatory, chapel and an abundance of fine paintings and antiques are delightful. The house sits in a 5000 acre estate, and needless to say fishing can be organized through the hotel. The restaurant is also first class and if you are celebrating your first salmon (or 100th, for that matter) or even if you've caught nothing for years, do make a point of dining here, it's positively exquisite.

Another hotel which merits considerable attention and a fairly huge bank balance is the delightful Gleneagles Hotel (0764) 62231 where leisure facilities are simply unrivalled. This is the place at which to spoil yourself to the extreme. Leisure centres, three championship golf-courses, riding, tennis, shooting and just about everything else you care to think of. But what of the fishing? Well, fear not, the hotel does not let you down here. It has two boats on the Tay and fishing ranges radically in prices with the season. Rods can be reserved but the boats do get very booked up. The hotel offers two day salmon fishing packages and these should be considered if you are one who loves to stay in the very best hotel accommodation. Gleneagles is first class in every way - to stay there is a magnificent experience.

Comrie lies close to the River Earn and the Royal (0764) 70200 is a traditional hotel with comfortable bedrooms and fishing can be arranged. Lochearnhead (0567) 3229 is another small hotel which is pleasantly situated on the shores of Loch Earn. Fishing is not organised through the hotel but arrangements are relatively easy to make.

Loch Leven is a superb trout loch and those seeking to fish its waters will often stay at the Green Hotel (0577) 63467, an old coaching inn which now boasts a number of more contemporary facilities. The hotel has private fishing on the loch and also arranges trout fishing on other lochs nearby. The hotel is also able to arrange salmon and sea-trout fishing on the Rivers Tay and Earn.

Returning from loch to river we come to Lavander and the River Teith. The Roman Lamp Hotel (0877) 30003 is a delightful establishment. It dates from 1625 and offers excellent accommodation, a first class restaurant and twenty acres of superb grounds. The River Teith runs through the property and guests are free to fish in these good trout waters. Salmon fishing is not so hot here, but the hotel can arrange other waters should guests so require.

Loch Lomond is a majestic piece of water and also has much to attract the visitor. There are, however, surprisingly few good hotels in the region and it is therefore a case of either remaining east of the Loch or staying in some of the many self-catering establishments that are available. However, people should know the Inverbeg Inn, Luss (0436) 86678, an attractive inn which stands close to the banks of the Loch. It has no illusions of grandeur but is comfortable and well located.

From Gleneagles to a small tent in a wooded valley, Scotland caters to all sorts. You don't have to be a millionaire to fish in Scotland. Loch and small river fishing are both easy to find and good value sport. If on the other hand, you are staying at Gleneagles you are thoroughly fortunate, probably American and will have a splendid time - which will be made even finer if you take a fish from the Tay.

THE GLENDARUEL HOTEL

In 1110 AD, Meckau, son of Magnus Barefoot, King of Norway, met the Scots on the banks of the river that flows through this glen. The fighting Scots won the ensuing battle and the bodies of their slaughtered enemies were thrown into the water, turning it red with blood. The river passed into history as 'Ruail' and the Glen as 'Glen-da-ruail', the 'Glen of red blood'. Over the years the name became anglicised to the modern Glendaruel.

Despite its violent beginnings, the river now provides a somewhat more pleasing pastime - fishing. The hotel offers private salmon and trout fishing to its guests on the Ruel, which flows directly behind it.. In addition there are arrangements with local angling clubs to fish many other waters including the hiring of boats to fish larger lochs and sea.

The hotel itself is small, friendly and family-run. It offers the best in Scottish hospitality with delicious home-cooking. Naturally the private rooms offer the usual range of modern facilities, including colour TV, and most have ensuite bathrooms.

For a fascinating break from fishing, the surrounding area offers a wealth of open opportunities. Deer stalking is available, as is golf on three courses. Hillwalking provides a rare opportunity to experience first-hand the splendour of the Highland countryside and the possibility of seeing some of the roaming wildlife, including red and roe deer, buzzards and golden eagles. All of this, and not to mention the wealth of history that surrounds the local area.

The Glendaruel Hotel
Clachan of Glendaruel
Argyll PA22 3AA
Tel: (036982) 274
Fax: (036982) 317

THE PORTSONACHAN HOTEL

Portsonachan, the Gaelic for 'Port of Peace', is situated on the southern shore of Loch Awe, Argyll.

At twenty-seven miles long, Loch Awe is the longest fresh water loch in Scotland and has fish to suit most anglers - salmon, brown and rainbow trout, pike, perch and char. The fishing on the loch is free and permits can be obtained for fishing on the River Awe and in the rivers that feed the loch, such as the Orchy. There are also many hill lochs that can be fished by permit.

The Portsonachan Hotel stands over the ferry jetty that was the south end of the ferry link between Taychreggan and Portsonachan, an essential link in one of the drovers' routes to the isles. In 1773 Dr Samuel Johnson and James Boswell stayed in the drovers' inn on the site of the present hotel.

The hotel, with thirteen en suite bedrooms, has cosy bars that are well stocked with malt and blended whisky from distiller-

ies in the Highlands, Islands, and Lowlands. Table d'hote and a la carte meals are served in the dining room overlooking the loch. The mountain Ben Cruachan towers over the north shore, with the famous dam that serves the hydro-electric generating station at its base. The generating station, built inside the mountain, has earned it the name of the 'hollow mountain'.

The area around Portsonachan is one of outstanding beauty and ever-changing moods. Many gardens are open to visitors and excel in spring and early summer with shows of azaleas and rhododendrons. With so much to see, the non-angler need never be bored.

Within easy reach is Oban, offering access to the islands, and Inveraray, the seat of the Clan Campbell. The area is also full of wild life - deer, badgers, wild cats, otters, and birds of prey, such as eagles, ospreys and falcons. When out fishing, one may even be fortunate enough to spot deer swimming powerfully over the loch.

The Portsonachan Hotel
South Lochaweside
Near Dalmally
Argyll PA33 1BL
Tel: (086 63) 224/328
Fax: (086 63) 346

THE GRAMPIANS

OBAN TO KINTYRE

Although this area is within easy driving distance of Glasgow and its neighbouring towns, it's a region of outstanding natural beauty. However, parts of it have suffered from the demands of 20th century man. Over 50% of Argyll is down to forestry - why, oh why, and how did we let it happen? Of course it is understandable that any landowner wishes to maximise the return from his holdings but surely afforestation on this scale here and also in many other parts of Scotland was ill conceived. Tax concessions have played a great part in these schemes but what is their purpose? No doubt the mandarins of Whitehall looked at the balance of trade in timber and decided we should try and become more self sufficient. A glance at the map indicated sparsely populated areas of Scotland and the decision was made.

Now that everyone is much more conservation minded there is quite rightly an international outcry over what is happening to the Amazon rain forest and it may seem strange to criticise those who are planting trees. However, what is occurring in Scotland is unnatural and damaging the countryside, its wild life and fishing. Areas of unique flora and fauna which lay undisturbed for thousands of years have been ploughed up and lost. The new 'forests' are often surrounded by high wire fences to prevent deer entering and are planted with Scandinavian varieties. The only reason for this is that they grow quicker than indigenous varieties and so the financial harvest can be reaped sooner. Many a river or tributary has suffocating new plantations on its banks and what's the result? Flash floods which can destroy spawning beds and alter pools out of all recognition. If this work is to continue, isn't it time for a more balanced approach where the existing environment and other interests are taken into account?

The other problem, and one which has affected so many rivers is dams, or as fishermen would say, 'those damned dams'. Hydro schemes have altered the character of many rivers seemingly without any regard or planning for the future. In fairness, it may be admitted that many of these schemes came into being before fishing became so popular and valuable. It is fair to say that they are a relatively inexpensive way of providing electricity for some remote areas. Also, it must be said that they have lessened the danger of flooding on some rivers but in general, from a fishing perspective, they have done far more harm than good. Added to which they don't exactly blend in with the landscape! The rivers and lochs are a unique environment and surely it is time we took greater steps to preserve them for future generations.

The River **Awe** is yet another river that has been affected, in this case by a 60 foot barrage. Before this development, the river truly justified its name with its roaring stream of fast flowing pools and deep rocky runs. It also used to produce fish of awesome proportions. In 1921 Major Huntington had a 57 pounder while four years later, his wife had one of 51lb. There are a number of other 50lb plus fish recorded, still more 40 pounders and a great many of 30 or more while 20 pounders were a weekly, if not daily, occurrence.

While it may no longer be a glass case river it is still very, very good and a day or if you are lucky a week on one of its seven beats will be a treasured memory. As it drains, Loch Awe is half river, half estuary after which it tumbles down the Pass of Brander

before assuming a more gentle pace with banks decked with silver birch and oak, flowing through rich meadows to join the salt water of Loch Etive. Over 3000 fish a year are counted through the barrage and further good news is that UDN which has plagued the river for more than twenty years is on the decline. Bell Ingram (0738) 21121 can arrange for you to fish the Barrage Beat at a cost of between £210 and £240 per week. Mr Campbell-Preston of Inverawe Fisheries (086602) 446 may also be able to help you cast a fly on the illustrious river. The cost per rod is £25 a day or £125 a week and three charming cottages are available for letting. As one would expect with a river of this quality, it is a fly only water where the early season will see large tues fished on a sinking line, as the water warms up rods will change to an intermediate floating or sink tip depending on their preference. Flies tend to be fairly small, and black is the favourite colour, so a size 10 Stoats Tail, for example, would be a popular choice.

Loch Awe is a long thin ribbon of a loch which has become very popular for in addition to salmon, sea trout and brown trout, its waters also hold ferox of monster proportions, perch, char, pike and escapee rainbows from a fish farm. I cannot help thinking that in some cases not enough thought has been given to the operation of fish farms. Escapees can cause havoc with stocks of fly and small as they have been here this results in some big fish. One rod took 19 rainbows in a day with five of them over 7lb. 1988 saw several double figure fish with a best of 14lb while two years earlier a massive rainbow of 21lb 4oz was taken by Mr Graham. The ferox are rather more elusive but they are huge. One was washed up on the shore with a partially eaten belly which still weighed in at over 21lb. Then there is the monster 37lb 8oz fish of Mr W. Muir which was caught in 1866. Trout fishing is good and at present free, though the riparian owners have applied for a protection order so that it can be properly managed and stocks conserved. Sea-trout fishing is not what it used to be, but this is a common tale of woe on west coast waters. Most salmon are taken from the northern end and fishing round the islands is likely to be most profitable. Because trouting is free, it is sad to say that there are quite a few who don't bother to obtain a salmon permit. This is not fair on those who do or the riparian owners and anyone fishing with a suspicious looking 'trout' rod should be reported.

A day's ticket only costs £20 and that includes a boat with an outboard. Tickets can be got from the Ardbrecknish House at Dalmally (08663) 223. The loch can be dangerous water for it is nearly three hundred foot deep in places and the wind can whip down it, so always wear a life-jacket. Although it is very popular it is still easy to find a quiet, secluded spot as the loch is some 25 miles long. It is an attractive setting with its wooded shores and islands such as Fraoch Eilean where you can see the ruined castle of Lorne, a delightful sight. Fishing in its compass is tremendous.

The reason why most salmon are taken from the northern end is that they are bound for the spawning grounds of the River **Orchy**. This river drains Loch Tulla and its ten mile journey takes it through Glen Orchy which with its famous Iron Bridge Falls must be one of the prettiest glens you could wish to find. The barrage on the Awe has affected this river as salmon which used to enter the river in March and April will not be seen in any number until the beginning of June and July through to September. As a result, these are now the best months. Salmon tend to be held back by the falls until the June spates and pools below the falls such as Pulpit and Gut can be particularly rewarding. Those wishing to fish the upper river may care to stay at the Bridge of Orchy Hotel (08384) 208 which has a beat reserved for hotel guests. Some of the best fishing is the Craig Beat which has recently been time shared. There are 21 named pools on these two miles and the five year average is 90 fish. The owner of the Upper Craig Beat is Mr L. Campbell (08383) 282 and day tickets are available at a cost of between £12 and £22. Croggan Crafts (08382) 201, the tackle and country clothing shop in Dalmally, has daily permits for five privately owned beats and others where the cost ranges between £14 and £25 a day. Carraig Thura Hotel (0838) 2210 can offer guests fishing on its own water. The Dalmally Beat is owned by West Highlands Estates of Oban (0631) 63617. Their chalets which sleep 4 cost between £150 and £180 a week and the fishing costs between £70 and £120 per rod a week according to the season. Spinning is probably the best method of fishing the rocky gorges near the falls, but much of the river deserves to be fly only water especially as the fly works so well.

South east of Loch Awe are the salt waters of Loch Fyne and its spate rivers. Argyll Estates (0499) 2203 can arrange fishing for you on the Rivers **Shira, Aray** and **Dubh Loch** at a cost of between £550.95 and £700 per week, which includes self-catering accommodation in a lodge and fishing for four rods. The Aray is a good salmon and sea-trout water and provides an attractive setting on its lower reaches where it flows through the park surrounding Inverarary Castle. The ornamental gardens and ornate bridges here are in marked contrast to the heavily wooded upper beats. The afforestation causes rapid changes in water levels and the ability to spey cast will ensure that you don't lose too many flies in the trees. The river suffers further from netting at its mouth but the lower pools are worth fishing. Both the Shira and the Fyne are victims of hydro schemes but offer good sport. Fishing on the Fyne was owned by Lord Glenkinglas but has now been divided between his sons. The four beats are owned by Ardinglas Estate (0499) 6261 and Cairndew Estate (0499) 6284. The season starts at the end of June and extends until the first week in October. A week's fishing for two rods costs £630 plus VAT and though it is a popular river those who communicate well in advance may be lucky. Loch Shira is really a bay of Loch Fyne while just above it is Dubh Loch in whose tidal waters you may also find grey mullet. Salmon usually rest in Dubh in July and August before running the river in September. On the western shore of Loch Fyne is **Douglas Water**. This little river is twelve miles long but impassable falls three miles upstream from the Loch confine fishing to the lower river. There you will find ten good pools with Roman Bridge Pool probably being the best. Permits can be had from Argyll Caravan Park (0499) 2285.

On the opposite shore is Strachur and taking the A815 south brings you to **Loch Eck** and its river the **Eachaig** which connects it to Holy Loch with its naval bases. The Eachaig may be under five miles long but there are forty pools divided between three beats. Although famous for both the number and size of its sea-trout — 1989 saw a 15lb 8oz fish taken on Ashtree Pool — it is also good salmon water. Further details may be had from Salar Management Services Ltd. (0667) 55355. The Loch is a narrow water some six miles long and up to 140 foot deep which is largely surrounded by forestry. As well as salmon, sea-trout and brown trout, its waters hold some powan, a rare relation of the grayling, and I am sure some ferox must stalk its depths. Permits can be had from the Whistlefield Inn (0369 86)

440 where a day including the use of one of the hotel's five boats with an outboard which can hold up to six rods costs £17. Fly works well at the northern end where the Cur flows in but trolling will produce good results in all parts. Talking of good results the best salmon and sea-trout for the 1990 season were 19lb 6oz and 8lb 1oz respectively. It is also very good trout water as the average weight of 2lb proves.

Purdies, the tackle shop in Dunoon (0369) 3232, issue permits for the Dunoon and District Angling Club who have fishing rights on several small rivers and lochs in the area. In the way of clubs, the Oban and Lorn Angling Club have 23 lochs, most of which are easy to get to though a few involve a cross country hike. Anglers Corner (0631) 66374 will issue you a permit if you pretend you live within twenty five miles of Oban! - the first year including joining fees costs £22; Southerners will have to brush up on the accent! Lochgilphead and District Angling Club has the fishing of several lochs and rivers and permits for these are available from The Sports Shop (0546) 2390.

The A83 runs south of Lochgilphead into Kintyre. There may be an airport at Campbeltown but the long detour which involves driving round the head of Loch Fyne ensures that the visitor will be able to enjoy the peninsular's lochs and little rivers in perfect peace. Having said that, because of its remoteness, there is a certain free and easy approach to fishing on some rivers. This especially applies the further south you go and it has been suggested that those wishing to fish the **Breackerie** or **Connie Glen Water** which lie at the southern tip could be well advised to ask the local poachers in case they interfere with their poaching operations! A similar spirit exists on **Machrihanish Water** where if the river is right and fish are running, all the locals will get out their worming rods. The **Lussa** flows from its Loch through a pretty glen to enter the Sea at Peninver. Even here there is no escape from hydro schemes and the erection of a dam with no compensating flow on the Loch has severely altered the character of the river and the best fishing is on the bottom beats. The river still manages to produce around 400 salmon a season and it is also good sea-trout water. At £8 a day or £80 a season it must be some of the least expensive salmon fishing available. Permits for the Lussa which produced a best fish of 14lb in 1990 may be had from Inland Fisheries of Peninver (0586) 52774. Even less expensive are the waters of the Kintyre Fish Protection Angling Club and Carradale Angling Club where a day's permit from A. P. MacGrory of Campbeltown costs only £1.50! Both the Carradale and Claonaig are spate rivers and it is a matter of hitting them at the right time.

Perhaps the best river in the Kintyre district is the **Add**. Several tumbling burns continue to form this river and in the upper reaches there are steep rocky pools, but the river becomes more sedate as it nears the Crinan Canal and the flow fades away, in fact the last two miles of the river are tidal. This is another river which has suffered from both a hydro scheme and afforestation which give it a Jekyll and Hyde character as one day there will be a flash spate while another day it may be almost dead for there is little compensatory flow. The upper reaches are owned by David Bracey of Kirnan Hotel (054 684) 217 while the lower river is owned by Robert Malcolm, Esq., of Dunhrune Castle (05465) 283. The river is divided into three beats Minard, Kirnan and Poltalloch. Both Kirnan and especially Poltalloch fish well and although Mr Malcolm does not let his water on a regular basis, a day's fishing can be had for about £7.

THE GRAMPIANS

It is tragic to see areas of natural purple bonnie heather devastated by forest - the economic arguments are slowly being eroded by those of the conservationists. The fisherman must argue his corner loud and clear to prevent any further damage to this unique environment.

FISHING FAYRE

Now this, dear reader, is a splendid part of the British Isles. Lochs mix with expanses of mountains and hurry through hillsides. A number of gracious Scottish country houses have been converted to hotels and they provide some first class facilities for people travelling through this area. Yes, awesome dams and forests have not made fishing any easier but the scenery is still superb and the fishing can often be outstanding.

There are a number of staggeringly beautiful country house hotels south of Fort William and many proudly overlook Loch Linnhe. These are not by and large great fishing hotels but it is worth mentioning a brace just in case the waters are poor or you feel like a change of scenery. Certainly one thing these houses boast is some majestic situations. In Port Appin, Airds (063173) 236, is a delightful hotel in which to stay. The interior is wonderfully stylish but cosy and welcoming and the restaurant here is absolutely excellent. If you enjoy fine cuisine make a diversion - you will not be disappointed. Another hotel which offers first class cooking and a friendly house party atmosphere is Ardsheal House, Kentallen (063174) 227. Before you even arrive you will be in love with the place; as you approach you will pass countryside of outstanding beauty. This is an inspiring location in which to stay. Fishing can be put on hold for a short time!

Some six miles south of Oban, halfway along the shore of Loch Feochan, we find another distinguished country house hotel with more splendid views and another remarkable restaurant. The hotel offers an excellent array of malts and can organise all manner of sports including trout, salmon and sea fishing. Returning inland we come to the River Orchy. It is a wonderful sight which will delight all who love to fish and many who

don't. The nearby hotels may not be smart country house hotels but they are welcoming and for the majority of fishermen will be just what's required. The Bridge of Orchy (08384) 208 and the Carraig Thura (08382) 210 are two for consideration.

The Awe is a huge water and in places its depth is witnessed by dark, almost fearsome, waters. There are numerous opportunities for fishing and a fine place to stay is Portsonachan Hotel (08663) 224 which can arrange fishing and is a delightfully welcoming hotel in which to stay. Carraig Thura (08382) 210 offers free salmon fishing to guests and is another fine place to stay. The hotel exudes tranquility and the dining room, where game is strongly featured, overlooks the majestic loch.

Another superb scene is that which befalls you when you view Loch Fyne. There are several good hotels in this area and two to note are the Creggow Inn (036986) 279 and the Kilfinan Hotel (070082) 201; both are able to arrange game fishing for their guests and both offer good value accommodation. The restaurant at Kilfinan is particularly good. There are two fine hotels for people heading towards Dunoon. The Enmore Hotel (0369) 2230 is luxurious and delightful and Ardfillayne (0369) 2267 has a super setting and can arrange fishing on Loch Eck. Both have good restaurants which are worth making a detour for. For those intrepid explorers who are seeking the delights of Kintyre, a delightful expedition should perhaps shortlist The Stonefield Castle Hotel, Tarbert (0880) 820836 which enjoys a marvellous setting and some good food as well as a number of leisure facilities for the more active. For those heading further south, a number of hotels are well placed - The Royal (0586) 52017, which overlooks the harbour and the Seafield (0586) 54385 are two which will be particularly welcoming.

Finally, for those seeking to escape to the islands or Argyll, a number of waters and hotels should be considered on Islay. The Bridgend (04961) 212 is a long established fishing hotel while in Port Askaig, the Port Askaig Hotel (049684) 245 is extremely welcoming, good value and well equipped - a fine recommendation for those visiting and fishing this super part of Scotland.

Artist: **D.F. Dane** **EARLY MORNING** *Courtesy of:* **Rosenstiel's**

SOUTHERN UPLANDS

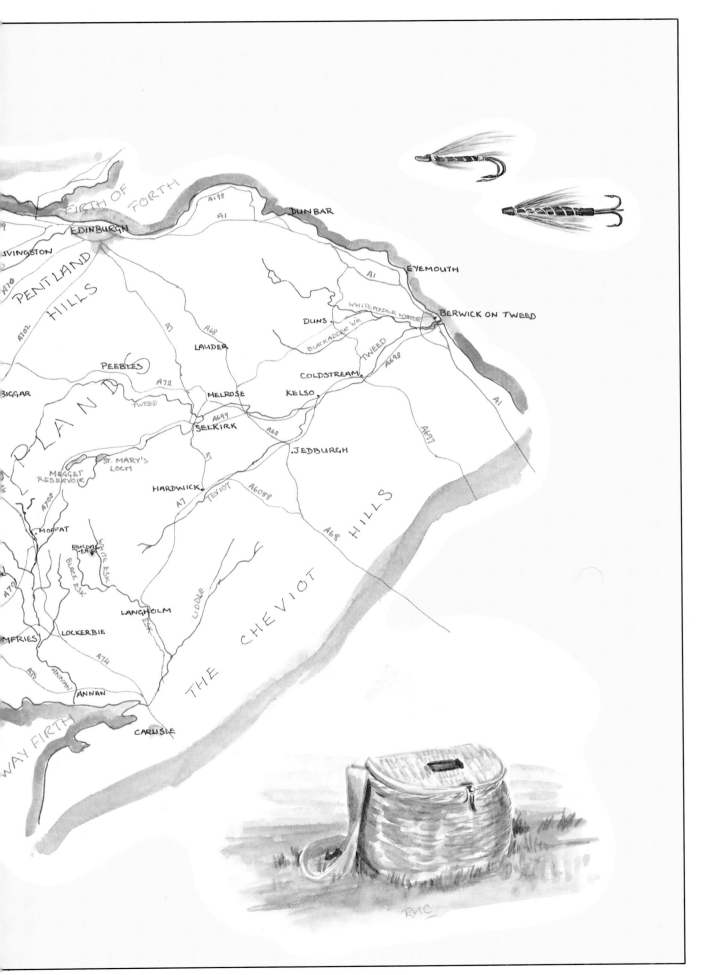

FIRTH OF FORTH

EDINBURGH

LIVINGSTON

PENTLAND HILLS

A70
A702

BIGGAR

PEEBLES

A72

TWEED

MELROSE

A699

SELKIRK

A68

ST. MARY'S LOCH

MEGGET RESERVOIR

A708

HARDWICK

A7

TEVIOT

A6088

MOFFAT

ESKDALE-MUIR

WHITE ESK

BLACK ESK

A70

LIDDLE

LANGHOLM

ESK

LOCKERBIE

DUMFRIES

A74

A75

A714

ANNAN

ANNAN

CARLISLE

SOLWAY FIRTH

A198

A1

DUNBAR

A1

EYEMOUTH

WHITEADDER WATER

BERWICK ON TWEED

DUNS

BLACKADDER WR.

LAUDER

A7

A68

TWEED

COLDSTREAM

A698

KELSO

A1

A697

JEDBURGH

A68 HILLS

THE CHEVIOT

RMC

85

SOUTHERN UPLANDS

IRVINE AND CLYDE

One of the pleasures of fishing is that it takes you to some beautiful parts of the country. You may think this an odd remark with which to preface this section which takes in Glasgow and its industrial heartland, but in Scotland you are never far away from the countryside. Glaswegians have the choice of a day's fishing on Loch Lomond or a round of golf at any number of championship golf courses which are nearby. Residents of as fair a city as Edinburgh may not wish to leave, but if they do want a day out they have the Pentland Hills on their doorstep and these instances are just some of the area's attractions.

Having lived for a long time - perhaps too long - in London, I yearn for such a wealth and variety of countryside. Of course there are some lovely places near our cities but even in this motorised age, the main problem is getting out to see them. Added to which having finally arrived at your destination you can be sure that quite a few others will have had the same ideas. Solace it seems is difficult to find. Indeed there are very few parts of England where you can find the peace and solitude that is so readily available in much of Scotland.

Roads in Scotland are few and far between compared with those South of the border and detours one has to make round Lochs and mountains merely add to the enjoyment of a drive. Of course the reason why there are fewer roads is that there are fewer people and in this type of environment man and nature can exist on a much more equitable footing. Apart from fishing, trips to Scotland have provided me with many magical moments that I will always treasure.

I remember going to stay with a school friend on the Ardnamurchan Peninsular some thirty years ago. It took three full days of driving to get there and the last thirty miles were on a single track road where the surface was pockmarked with holes and clumps of grass. Passing bays were few and far between, and never having been there before I began to wonder what our final destination was going to be like. The lodge was set in a hillside protected by trees. There were spectacular views with not another house in sight and for three weeks I had the time of my life. There was a marvellous old chap who beside helping in the house was also ghillie and stalker. I had my first day's stalking here and returned to the lodge tired but flushed with excitement. We fished several little hill lochs and I was lucky enough to catch a lovely pound and a half trout, which gave me a furious battle before relenting. However, the thing I most remember was when Ian, the ghillie, asked us if we would like to see something 'verra' unusual. Despite being told we would have to be up before dawn, our enthusiasm knew no bounds. We were woken at 3.00am and after a fortifying breakfast in the kitchen where the dogs blinked sleepily at us from the warmth of their baskets, we set off.

We walked up and down hillsides for well over an hour and I was beginning to wonder what lay in store when Ian motioned us to lie down. Slowly we crawled towards the sky line and looked around but there was nothing to see. Whispered words and gestures urged us to be quiet and wait. We kept as still as we could and soon I felt I knew every rock that was digging into me and began to wonder why we were here. Then Ian pointed and not far away two birds soared into the sky. They were the biggest birds I had ever seen which was not surprising as they were golden eagles. I shall never forget watching these

magnificent birds as they wheeled across a cloudless sky and seeing them silhouetted against the morning sun.

A more recent memory is of fishing a small highland spate river. All week the weather had been against us with one hot, dry day succeeding another. The water was down and sluggish and there seemed little sign of piscine life. I fished the pool carefully but to no avail. I retired some way from the bank and sat down to open the sandwich box which looked decidedly more promising than the fly box! As I looked at the pool there was a rustling in the bushes at the bottom of the far bank and an otter popped its head out. It paused to look round and sniff the air and then satisfied that all was well entered the pool. Shortly afterwards, three cubs appeared and entered the pool without any of the precautionary preliminaries of their parent. For some twenty minutes the otters played and frolicked in the pool diving and chasing each other like children playing tag. Their morning exercise over, they returned to the bank, shook themselves and disappeared into the bushes.

Despite the geographical size of this area there is little fishing of note. Similarly there are few lochs but none that can compete with the fame of their more northerly sisters. Also as one would expect in such an industrial area there are a great many reservoirs. There are some good trout fisheries and Drew Jamieson of the Lothian Regional Council in Edinburgh (031)-229 9292 (ext. 3849) is the best person to advise you on them.

There is of course the **Clyde** - to most sassenachs the Clyde conjures up images of shipyards and heavy industry or it did before the economic climate changed. So what do we expect now, a deserted and polluted wasteland? Wrong, wrong and thrice wrong! There is excellent fishing to be had here. There is some first class trout water and salmon and sea-trout are being re-introduced. This is clearly a river of the future and though the pre-industrial revolution glory days which saw salmon of over 40lb and sea-trout of 14lb may not return, it seems likely that good salmon and sea-trout fishing will be restored. Why? well purely and simply because something has been done about it. The Clyde River Purification Board has done much hard work as have the various clubs like the United Clyde Angling Protective Association. The work has included cleaning, restocking, creating and improving pools as well as buying out estuary nets. Conservation is not new here for the UCAPA was founded in 1887 and has always been at the forefront of fishing improvements. Many people associate the Clyde with Glasgow alone but the river is some 80 miles long. Its source is in the Lowther Hills not far from the Wells of Tweed and its upper reaches abound with half and three-quarter pound trout. On its way the river broadens out and so do the trout! Two pounders are regularly caught on some of the lower reaches such as Crawford, Hazelbank and Crossford. Permits for the Lamington and District may be had from Brydens Newsagents (and tackle shop) at Biggar (0899) 20069 for £4 a day. The average weight here is one pound and just to whet your appetite, May 1991 produced an eleven pounder! Downstream at Lanark a day on the District Angling Association's water also costs £4 and permits can be had from Eddie Wilson's watch repair shop at 58 Wellgate. Permits for the UCAPA water where the cost is £15 for a year may be had from tackle shops or the secretary, J. Quigley, Esq. of Wishaw (0698) 382479.

Perhaps the reason that the Clyde is not better known is that the Scots are a canny race and understandably believe in keeping a good thing to themselves! But take a tip, the Clyde offers very good trouting at present and judging by what's happening I am sure it will be a good salmon and sea-trout water in a few years time.

South East of Glasgow on the A736 is the Ayrshire coastal town of Irvine and it is here that the rivers **Garnock** and **Irvine** share a common estuary. A further attraction here is that if you fancy a change from fishing, the renowned golf courses of Prestwick and Troon are both a few miles away. Mind you there are many others and playing these Open courses is sometimes more difficult than finding good autumn fishing! The source of the Garnock is east of Largs and its course is some fifteen miles long which makes it one of the country's smallest salmon rivers. Despite much excellent work the river still suffers from pollution and there have been some tragic occurrences. That there are still a reasonable number of salmon says much for the resilience of this river's stock. All the same it can produce a memorable day and hopefully things will improve. A day on the Eglinton Angling Club water can be had for £5 a day from The Craft Shop at Kilwinning (0294) 58559.

The Irvine has a varied life in its twenty five mile journey to the sea. It flows through agricultural, industrial and urban areas. Hopefully pollution is a problem of the past for much work has been done by a local improvement association and the river now shows consistent good sport especially since the nets have been bought out. The lower reaches of the river were damaged in the 18th and 19th centuries by the erection of dams to provide power to drive a variety of mills. The mills are now disused but the dams are still intact and impale migrating fish at low water. The river is also well stocked with trout and a day's permit for the Dreghorn Angling Club's three miles of water costs £5 and is obtainable from Alysons's Flower Shop in Irvine (0294) 76716. This club also has fishing in the Annick Water. This is a delightful little trout stream where spider patterns such as a size 12 or 14 Black and Peacock or Black Spider do consistently well.

Those who like their loch fishing might care to try **Loch Thom**. The Loch lies north of the Garnock at the head of the Naddsdale Water and is a short distance south of Greenock. At just under 500 acres, this is not a big water, nor does it hold particularly large trout for the average weight is around the half pound mark. However, it does offer good fishing at a modest cost. A day costs £2 and a week £6, permits are available from Brian Peterson at The Fishing Shop in Greenock (0475) 888085. It is one of the waters that should be fished with very light tackle and skimming a moth imitation across the surface around dusk can make for some exciting moments.

FISHING FAYRE

Glasgow proclaimed some years ago that it was miles better and not without good reason. It has recently been the 'European City of Culture' and its businesses are becoming more diverse and multinational in their make up. Let us hope that England, when removing more of its satanic mills, ensures that it becomes once more a somewhat greener and as a result more pleasant land. It is tremendous to see the improvements that are taking place on the Clyde and it is similarly significant to note that Glasgow really is miles better than it was in the 70's. However, the fisherman on his hard earned hols is unlikely to wish to stay in the busy streets of Scotland's second city and

with that in mind we have listed a number of hotels that are good stop over points for those journeys north as well as a few ideas for those holidaying in Ayrshire and Argyllshire.

The Kirkhouse Inn in Strathblane (0360) 70621 is a pleasant house for a break from the wheel. It's popular locally and is more characterful than the towering city centre establishment of Glasgow. Gleddoch House (047554) 711 Langbank is another well appointed hotel overlooking the countryside north west of Glasgow. Bedrooms are comfortable and leisure facilities including golf and riding are welcome additions to the attributes of the hotel. So up to the city; there are a number of hotels from which to choose. Montgreenan Mansion (0294) 57733 is an impressive edifice of Georgian style, convenient for the Irvine. A similar description can be made of Chapeltoun House (0560) 82696 two miles out of Stewarton. It is small but extremely luxurious and ideal for those who enjoy country house style hotels. The Hospitality Inn at Irvine (0294) 74272 may lack a little of the charm of such houses but is comfortable and has some good facilities including a fine restaurant. In Troon, the Marine Highland (0292) 314444 is more popular with golfers than fishermen but it is a good hotel for those visiting the area especially if you happen to enjoy golf. Though you should remember that you have to be able to play well before being allowed the pleasure of playing the open championship links. West of Edinburgh one finds another hotel favoured by golfers, The Dalmahoy (031)-333 1845 It's a tremendously well equipped hotel and a superb place to break your journey as is Houstoun House (0506) 853831, a baronial house with splendid bedrooms and a fine restaurant and popular bar. A fine place to consider following an expedition into Scotland's northern climes and the fishing offered there.

Flies (Rosemary Coates)

SOUTHERN UPLANDS

THE AYR TO THE NITH

A question that is repeatedly asked is, why are ladies so successful at salmon fishing? Miss Ballantine is perhaps the most celebrated but through the years there has been no doubt that ladies consistently catch salmon and big ones at that. To rub salt in the wound, they will often succeed where men have failed. I have heard many stories of men who have returned disconsolate to the hut after trying a good pool without a sign of a fish. They have duly passed the rod to the wife, only to see it bent over within a few minutes and hear the excited cry of 'fish'!

A very experienced fishing friend of mine recounts with a wry smile the tale of how his wife decided to try her luck one day and duly went off eager and enthusiastic with the ghillie. After quite a while they had not returned so he went to the pool they were supposed to be fishing only to find five salmon laid out on the bank. Naturally, he thought this was going to be his lucky day too so he took over the rod and fished the pool carefully but didn't receive as much as an offer. On another occasion his wife landed seven fish in a morning and thinking, or rather hoping, she must be tired he offered to take over the rod. He fished tirelessly until dusk without so much as a touch. On a personal level, my wife's first fish was a lovely 19 pounder and I am still waiting to beat that! What is their secret? Is it because they are more careful and gentle in their ways, does some aura of their femininity get communicated to the fish in a mysterious way? Are they more thoughtful and cunning perhaps? My wife assures me that the secret lies in the pheremones of the superior sex!

The **Ayr** is the largest river in the county and has a wide catchment area. As a result its spates are less flashy and, like the Nith, take longer to get started and last longer. It is another river that has been a victim of the Industrial Revolution. A great deal of the pollution problem here comes from disused coal mines and on top of this there are several sewage and other discharges in the area. There are dams and weirs that used to power the now redundant mills and there is a fair amount of poaching - this, however, cannot be blamed on the Industrial Revolution! Despite all this it is still a good river and when these problems are resolved, it could be extremely good. On top of the problems created by man, the fish have had to contend with UDN which so devastated the spring stock that the early run has never really recovered. At present August, September and October are likely to be the best months and most locals will choose to spin or worm. A Yellow Belly Minnow or Zebra Toby can often prove successful for the spinner. There are parts of the river which take the fly well and favourites include the Brown Turkey, Blue Charm and Stinchar Stout.

The river is some thirty-nine miles long from its source on Wardlaw Hill to the popular seaside resort of Ayr. A wide and shallow river, it can be prone to flooding in its lower reaches. The best salmon and sea-trout fishing is from the weir at Catrine down to the estuary. Perhaps the most attractive stretch is from Failford to Stair. Salmon average around 6lb and sea-trout 1½lb. All the river fishes well for trout and it is stocked every year. The Sorn Inn at Sorn (0290) 51305 which is just up from Catrine has a small stretch. Linwood & Johnstone, the newsagents (0290) 50219 in Mauchline issue permits. The Failford Inn at Failford (0292) 541674 has two and a half miles and the cost here on a weekday is £5.

Just south of Ayr is the River **Doon**. This river drains Loch Doon and the A713 follows much of its course from Glen Ness to the sea. It is good to learn that salmon stocks are increasing here, but sea-trout are, alas, on the decline. It is a difficult river to get on as much of it is either privately owned or syndicated. However, the Skeldon Estate sometimes issue day tickets for their water, which has twelve named pools and it is worth contacting the Estate Manager (0292) 56656.

Bladnoch Fishing   (Richmond Hill Leisure)

SOUTHERN UPLANDS

Continuing our coastal drive south on the A77 will bring us to Ballantrae which some people will associate with Robert Louis Stevenson's famous novel of Jacobite times but to fisherman it is famous for being at the mouth of the **Stinchar**. In recent years the Doon has fished well but the Stinchar is the most productive river in Ayrshire. Unlike other rivers in the county, the river has not suffered from pollution for it lies well away from industrial areas and towns. As a result the water is remarkably clear and this well managed river with its fine holding pools is one of the best fly waters in south-west Scotland, indeed many would argue that it is a crime to fish it using any other method.

The source of the river is Loch Linfern in the Carrick Forest and in its twenty mile journey to the sea it is joined by its tributaries, the Duisk, Muck and Water of Tig. Loch Linfern is fairly small and as there are no reservoirs the river has spate characteristics. Afforestation, which covers much of its catchment area, has made the situation worse. Heavy rain in late Autumn can bring the river into flood but it does not take long to fine down to a good fishing level. Although there is no stocking programme and still some netting, salmon and sea-trout spawn throughout the length of the river and its tributaries. Very few salmon enter the river in the early months of the season and July with its good grilse run is really the start of the season. Summer sport is highly dependent on rain, but can produce some great days and this is also the time for sea-trout. As rain becomes more predictable with the approach of autumn the tempo increases, September and October are often the finest months.

Some of the best fishing is on the Duke of Wellington's Knockdolian Estate which can produce up to 700 fish a season. A popular fly here is the appropriately named Duke's Killer. On the first occasion that the Duke tried it he hooked four fish! As one might expect this is a difficult beat to get on, but if you are prepared to take a summer week while waiting for a back-end one, it may be worth contacting the Estate Office (0465) 88237. The Ballantrae Beat, which comprises one mile of double bank fishing upstream from the mouth and has both tidal and freshwater pools, is let at £1650 per week. This price includes fishing for four rods and a lodge. Vacancies are rare but it is still worth contacting R. Dalrymple, Esq. (0465) 83418. Some water round Colmonell is owned by the Church of Scotland and forms part of the Rev. Jones' glebe. The fishing here is handled by Mrs G. B. Shankland of Barnfoot Farm (0465) 88220 and a day costs around £10. The Dalreoch Estate has 1¾ miles of mainly double bank fishing where a daily permit costs between £15 and £28; it is available until the end of August after which it is let on a weekly basis at a cost of approximately £160 per rod per week. A self catering lodge is available. Permits can be obtained from the head keeper Mr D. Overend (0465) 88214.

Stinchar salmon average around 8lb and sea-trout 1½ lb. There are also some rainbows which have escaped from fish farms that run up to 3lb. It is not a large river and a single-handed 10 foot carbon should prove adequate for summer fishing and can also be used for sea-trout, while a double handed 14 footer will be required when the river swells with late autumn rain. The most popular and effective fly is the Stinchar Stoat which is much the same as a standard Stoats Tail except that the hackle is orange rather than black. Another popular fly here and on many other waters is the General Practitioner which was first tried by the late Colonel Esmond Drury.

Dumfries and Nithsdale is an area of much historical interest. Much of Robert Burns' work was written while he was working as an exciseman at a time when smuggling was a major local industry. His farm at Ellisland and house in Dumfries are now museums. Other buildings of note are the ruins of Sweetheart Abbey and Caerlaverock Castle which has a nature reserve, while at Sanquhar you can see Britain's oldest post office. Robert the Bruce murdered his rival John Comgh during the struggle for Scottish independence at Dumfries, and Arbigland is a popular spot with American tourists for it was here that John Paul Jones, the founder of the American navy, was born.

It is also an area of much piscatorial interest for here is the River **Nith**, Solway's crowning glory and one of the finest salmon and sea-trout rivers in Scotland. In 1988 over 4000 salmon, 1600 grilse and 4500 sea-trout were caught on the Nith and these figures would have been better still were it not for the activities of poachers. The average salmon was around 9lb, grilse about 5½ lb and sea-trout 2lb. The best months are September, October and November and the Burgh Water in Dumfries produces about 20 fish a day. This is also the time for big fish which can be up to 30lb. Though no fish today can compete with the reputed 67 pounder caught by Jock Wallace, the poacher, on the Barjarg water in 1812!

The Nith is born in Ayrshire, but its life at its source near Dalmellington is short lived as it enters Dumfriesshire at Kirkconnel and then flows on past the main centres of Sanquhar, Thornhill and Dumfries to join the Solway Firth. Above Sanquhar there are long stretches of sluggish canal-like water. The only white water to be found is in Drumlanrig Gorge but there are many excellent holding pools. Above Thornhill are seven miles of double bank fishing divided into 4 beats, all owned by the Duke of Buccleuch whose seat, Drumlanrig Castle, is nearby - quite a lot of fishing around Thornhill is controlled by the Mid-Nithsdale Angling Association. Lower beats include such famous names as Closeburn Castle, Friar's Carse, Portrack and Barjarg.

The river has many feeders and tributaries but the principal one is Cairn Water which joins the Nith below Lincluden College. The Cairn has some great fishing especially in the small pools between Moniavie and Dunscore. The pool below Cluden Rock acts as a temperature barrier to fish and, unfortunately, as a magnet to poachers. The Cairn has other attractions besides salmon for the Dumfries and Galloway Angling Association planted out 10,000 sea-trout fry in 1987 and the same year saw the introduction of 3500 brown trout some of whom are now up to 2½ lb. This is a water which needs the autumn rains as in a hot dry summer it can be very weedy and shrink to a mere trickle.

The outbreak of UDN in 1967 did tremendous damage to the spring stock and so spring runs are really a thing of the past but fishing below the caul in Dumfries at this time of the year can be productive. Flies that are well worth trying are Colonel's Wood, Castledykes and Slae Bushes.

As you will have guessed, it is a spate river and, with no feeder lochs in the system, results are heavily dependent on rainfall. But rain is a mixed blessing since Upper Nithsdale is the victim of large scale afforestation and after heavy rain the river can be very coloured and it can be two or three days before serious fishing can begin again. Initially, worm will be the most productive method, while the next day will be suitable for spinners and then you should revert to fly. Because of its character most rods equip themselves with fly, spinning and worming tackle. It is a medium sized river and thigh waders will enable you to cover most waters.

Popular flies include the Hairy Mary, Blue Charm, Shrimp Fly, Stoats Tail and of course that local favourite, the Brown Turkey. In high water a two inch Yellow Dog tube fly can prove deadly, but many will be spinning with a similar size or slightly larger Devon Minnow, in colours such as black and red, blue and pearl, green and yellow and brown and gold. In high water, sea-trout are also taken on a worm or a spinner such as a Mepps or small Toby, but in reasonable water levels fly is the most popular method. Two flies are normally fished on the leader as Nith sea-trout are often tempted by a bushy dropper such as a Black Pennell. Good patterns here are Blue and Silver, Wickham's Fancy, Greenwell's Glory and Peter Ross. Later on in the evening and before dawn a team of spider patterns often works particularly well.

The Nith is an exceptional river and well worth a lot of effort to get on. Those who may be able to help you are: The Mid-Nithsdale Angling Club where the cost is between £10 to £25 a day or £50 to £125 a week. Permits can be had from S & I Milligan of Thornhill (0848) 30555. The Killylong Estate (0387) 720415 has three-quarters of a mile of double bank fishing. Autumn fishing here is well booked with a waiting list, but summer sport is available. Nithsdale District Council (0387) 53166 charge £30 a day or £90 a week and visitors are only allowed to fish Monday to Friday. The Dumfries Office of Smiths Gore (0387) 63066 are the agents for the Blackwood beat. A week on the Buccleuch Estates (08486) 283 water costs between £120 to £800 plus VAT, but that is for two rods. They also plan to sell time shares on the middle and lower beats on 21 year leases and interested parties should write to the Estate Office for further details. Mr E. Tagg of The Blackaddie House Hotel at Sanquhar (0659) 50270 handles fishing on the Ryehill beat where the cost is between £15 and £35 a day and he can also arrange for you to fish the Upper Nithsdale Angling Club's water, two pools of which are right outside the hotel. There are no Lochs which really stand out in this area but there are many good small lochs and stocked fisheries. Enquire locally for what would suit you best.

Many novices consider the wild Highlands of Scotland to be the exclusive terrain of game fishing. How wrong can they be! The Nith is a marvellous river and although the autumn beats are both expensive and popular they are well worth trying for. What's more, if you just let the wife have a cast, you may have good results for, as we are constantly being told, they are charmed when it comes to catching fish!

FISHING FAYRE

Much of the water in Ayrshire and Dumfries and Galloway is club or estate water but hotels are often well-connected and able to introduce their guests to some good fishing.

In Alloway, the Burns Monument (0292) 42466 is a first class place to stay. The hotel is set at the very heart of Burns country. A thoroughly appealing hotel, its Alloway Lounge and landscaped gardens offer wonderful views over the river Doon on which fishing can be organised. All in all a splendid setting and a good place to stay when in Ayrshire.

Turnberry is a landmark better known to golfers than anglers. Its two celebrated championship courses are most impressive and the hotel itself is marvellously comfortable and well equipped. Leisure facilities are currently being developed which will shortly make it even more prestigious. A less grand but nevertheless thoroughly welcoming hotel can be found in Girvan, the Kings Arms (0465) 3322. Another clear cut golfing hotel which also acts as a fine base for those who represent the fraternity of fishermen.

There are numerous lochs and rivers in the area, many of which merit the attentions of serious fishermen. It does not take too long to reach the Borders of Scotland and it's a mere hour or so on and you're into Ayrshire. The journey time to get here is dramatically less than it is to more northerly outposts but the scenery is still superb and a visit should be made whenever possible! Kildonan (077082) 207, in Barrhill is a splendid example of a wonderful hotel that is beautifully hidden away and delightfully peaceful. The house, designed by Sir Edwin Lutyens, is charming and the leisure facilities here are excellent. This is definitely one to consider if you are travelling to the area. Furthermore, the hotel can arrange game fishing.

Some distance to the west, we come to the superb hotel, Knockinaam Lodge (077681) 471. There are few hotels which will give you such a friendly welcome and this Victorian Lodge, in a charming glen, is one of the most pleasurable places to have dinner in Britain. A trip is therefore thoroughly recommended.

Travelling around the coast we come to Port William. Here we find another wonderful hotel in which to stay, which also organises fishing. Corsemalzie House (098886) 254 is an absolute delight and its splendid scenery will surely inspire you to great things on river and loch. If not, well fear not - the bar is a welcoming place to forget the one that got away. In fact, later in the evening you'll have probably landed him three or four times! There are a number of fine hotels in and around Newton Stewart. Creebridge House (0671) 2121 is a popular haunt and, formerly a shooting lodge for the Earls of Galloway, is one for the notebook. Its well-equipped, offers enjoyable food and is an ideal port of call. Returning southwards to Gatehouse of Fleet, we find Cally Palace (0557) 814341, another pleasing place in which to stay.

There are all manner of unspoilt nooks and crannies in Southern Scotland and Culgruff House (055667) 230 is one such delight. The hotel proudly overlooks the village of Crossmichael and the Ken Valley. There are log fires which give a homely feel and the welcome is equally warm. Woodlea in Moniaive (08482) 209 is a superb hotel in which to unwind; there are good leisure facilities here and, once again, the focus is on relaxing. Our final thought for the day can be found at Sanquhar - here the Mennockfoot Lodge (0659) 50382 has a wonderfully serene location beside the Mennock water where it joins the River Nith. The hotel is not luxurious but is good value and has a pleasant atmosphere. When you are on holiday, what could be a better formula for success?

CREEBRIDGE HOUSE

Creebridge House, formerly residence to the Earls of Galloway has been transformed into an hotel that characterises the tradition of Scottish country house living at its best.

Situated in three acres of gardens and woodland, the hotel preserves a peaceful, relaxed atmosphere throughout its elegant restaurant and drawing room and its individually appointed bedrooms.

All seventeen bedrooms have private bathrooms and modern amenities. The gracious drawing room has a magnificent fireplace to welcome those who wish to study the menu or well-balanced wine list before dinner in the restaurant over looking the garden.

Many activities are open to our guests, namely, fishing, golf, shooting, walking, pony trekking and birdwatching.

For 1991 we will have even more fishing to offer and the option for you to mix days fishing on different stretches to make your holiday more eventful.

There's the River Bladroch - a two mile private beat with only four rods fishing a mile per pair where last year hotel guests averaged a salmon each with the average weight of 8.7lbs and the largest 11lbs.

Then there's four miles of the Minnoch river - a beautiful forestry stream easily accessed by road to the river bank with large, deep pools where fish - and often exciting wildlife such as Golden Eagles, buzzards and otters - are easily visible.

The Minnoch feeds into the River Cree - just two minutes walk from our hotel door - which has an excellent salmon catch record.

The pursuit of happiness is a very individual quest. At Creebridge House Hotel we think you will find it.

Creebridge House Hotel
Newton Stewart
Wigtownshire DG8 6NP
Tel: (0671) 2121

RICHMOND HILL LEISURE

'Game Fishing and Country Holidays for Family and Friends.'

Kirkland House - Kirkcowan - Newton Stewart - Galloway South West Scotland, D68 0HJ.

We welcome you to a relaxed 'away from it all' holiday in un-spoilt 'Bonnie Galloway' where you can share in the beauty of this fascinating area from your very own holiday home in the country.

Our self-catering accommodation is set in peaceful and secluded grounds and consists of the main house, two detached cottages in their own private courtyard at the rear of the house and no. 1 Coach-House in the tranquillity of Mochram Park nearby.

All accommodation is furnished and equipped to a very high standard and is suitable for family holidays, in comfort, at any time of the year. The large garden adjacent to the main house can be used for relaxation by house guests.

'Salar - Sail On'

The sight of a manicured - well cared for 'green'
Will never give me a pain in the 'spleen'
So much as 'whitewater' - agleam in the 'Beck
And the glimpse of a 'Clean Fish' breasting the 'neck'
(Chubby Reeve 1988).

Fishing.

We have three private beats, totalling 12 miles, for our guests on the River Bladnoch and its main tributary, the Tarff.

Seasons are:

Salmon 11 February to 31 October
Brown Trout 15 March to 30 September

The Bladnoch is unique in the Solway area in that it boasts a substantial run of Spring Salmon, beginning in February. Grilse run in large numbers from July onwards and Summer Salmon overlap into the Autumn runs. Fishing for wild Brown Trout is extremely good in the streamy water such as the Bladnoch stretch just below Barhoise Farm and the Tarff above the mill weir at Kirkcowan. There is a superb availability of Loch Trout Fishing for you should the Rivers not be in ply. Beats are rotated daily in order to give our Guests variety and the best opportunity of contacting fish.

'Whent' burn's up - gang up - when t' burn's doon - gang doon'.

The numbers of rods available allows us to give you that feeling of exclusivity, which we all like to enjoy when Game Fishing!

Full colour brochure available on request from:-
Richmond Hill Leisure
Glenalmond
Quarry Moor Lane
Ripon HG4 2SA
North Yorkshire
Tel: (0765) 600984

THE LAURIE ARMS HOTEL

The Laurie Arms is small and cosy and is the centre of attraction to the country sportsperson. It is full of character and atmosphere with open log fires and is decorated with sporting memorabilia including a 31lb salmon caught in 1909.

The hotel is renowned for its good food and value for money and is known as 'the place for a steak'. We also have local salmon, trout and venison on the menu and you can finish off your evening by trying one of more than 100 malt whiskies.

The hotel is 100 yards from the river Urr — a somewhat underestimated river which more often than not produces good runs of salmon and sea trout. We are situated on the Castle Douglas Angling Association Water, but tickets are also available for Dalbeattie Water. The river is stocked annually with brown trout to supplement the wild brownies. The season opens on

the 25th February and closes on the 30th November for salmon and sea trout. Brown trout from 1st April to 6th October.

Other rivers are within easy reach such as the Nith, Annan, Cree and Blandnoch. Several local lochs offer fly only fishing for brown and rainbow trout in some of the most beautiful scenery in the area. Once again you can arrange to visit them through the hotel. Galloway has always been renowned for its course fishing and an abundance of lochs are at hand.

American brook trout are also available in some lochs. We can provide guides and ghillies also to give first hand knowledge of the area and lochs. Our 4-wheel drive vehicle is an ideal way to see the area and access hidden lochs amidst some of Galloway's breathtaking scenery.

The Laurie Arms Hotel
Laurieston
Castle Douglas
Kirkcudbrightshire DG7 2PW
Tel: (0566) 66246

THE CROSS KEYS HOTEL

Explore the many prime fishing possibilities in the Scottish Borders from your base in Kelso - Game fishing in the Tweed, its tributaries and reservoirs plus seafishing off the nearby coast.

On one of our short breaks you may get 'the big one' but you'll definitely enjoy the fact that you 'got away'.

Relax afterwards in our welcoming family run hotel, guaranteed comfortable en-suite accommodation, good food and friendly service.

For further details contact:

M Becattelli
The Cross Keys Hotel
The Square
Kelso TD5 7HL
Tel: (0573) 23303
Fax: (0573) 25792

3 star AA and RAC, 4 Crown STB

WARMANBIE HOTEL

Warmanbie, a Georgian country house hotel set in 40 acres of secluded woodland grounds overlooking the river Annan, has been owned by the Duncan family since 1953 (converted into a hotel in 1983). Rod Duncan, who runs Warmanbie, still thinks of it as the family home and won't do anything that will spoil it. Here you can relax and unwind from the pressures of everyday life. Fishing is free on our private stretch (except 9/9 to 15/11 when there is a charge of £8.00 per day) and we've access to numerous other stretches. A ghillie is available. We have rods/tackle for sale/hire, a large freezer and drying facilities. Meal times are flexible to suit your fishing. Your bedroom will have a private bathroom, colour television, tea/coffee making facilities and direct dial telephone as well as many extra little touches. We are Scottish Tourist Board commended four crowns, and recommended by Egon Ronay. You'll enjoy our large steaks (using local beef) and fresh mussels or you can try one of our more creative dishes such as pork fillet in pastry with a mushroom, cointreau and orange stuffing or strips of raw beef with green peppercorn sauce. Our Scottish breakfasts are huge. How about porridge with Drambuie or a champagne breakfast with smoked salmon and scrambled eggs? You'll find wildfowling, golf, tennis, squash, curling and various water sports all nearby. Warmanbie is also an ideal base for beachcombing on the Solway coast and exploring the picturesque countryside of South West Scotland, the Borders and Lake District.

Warmanbie Hotel
Annan, F/F
Dumfriesshire DG12 5LL
Tel: (0461) 204015

SOUTHERN UPLANDS

THE ANNAN TO THE TWEED

One of the things that saddens me is the increasing number of accidents related to fishing. I suppose this is not really surprising as fishing is becoming increasingly popular, however, I cannot help thinking that a number could be prevented by common sense and a little forethought. Wading can be dangerous especially on some spate rivers where the water level can rise very quickly in a short space of time. Personally I always carry a wading stick and will always ask local advice as even shallow river beds can be deceptively dangerous. I cannot understand those who don't wear a life jacket while boat fishing on big lochs. They always restrict one's movement a little but big lochs, especially those where the wind is funnelled between mountain sides, can rapidly change character and become dangerous places.

Casting can be a tricky business and flies can get caught anywhere though of course one's face is the most vulnerable part. I have seen people hook themselves in the ear, nose and cheek all of which can be very painful. Eyes are particularly vulnerable and I never go out without a pair of glasses. There are some excellent makes of fishing glasses which can be very helpful, the polaroid lenses take the glare off the water and they often have little strong lenses below them to help you tie the fly and side lenses help to protect the corners of the eye. I know of one unfortunate fisherman who got a whiplash when trying to pull a fly from a tree and the fly became embedded in his eye. Instead of calling for help he tried to jiggle the fly out and despite excellent care in the local hospital he lost the use of his eye.

To continue on a somewhat lighter note let us recount a tale on that wooliest of creatures - the sheep. Two fishermen were sheltering in a hut during a snow storm when they noticed one of their rods moving across the doorway. Intrigued, they braved the elements and were surprised to see a sheep with part of a Yellow Belly showing from its mouth dragging the rod behind it. The rod was eventually recaptured but as we all know sheep can be tricky customers. Playing a salmon in a pool is much easier than playing a sheep in a field especially when the purpose is to release the animal. The more they tried the longer the length of line the sheep took out until after a hectic twenty minutes the animal was finally cornered and released. One of the rods was a surgeon and the other a GP which helped matters but it was the first time either had operated on a sheep!

A few miles east of the Nith is the **Annan** which is a good Salmon river and even better for sea-trout. Its source is on the slopes of the delightfully named Devil's Beef Tub from whence it flows to Moffat. This delightful little town is just off the main road that connects Carlisle and Glasgow and was one of the only two spa towns in Scotland. However, the only waters we are interested in are those that take the fly and the Beattock House Hotel (06833) 402) at Beattock, which is just below Moffat, issue permits for the Upper-Annandale Angling Association Water. Downsteam from Moffat the river is joined by Evan Water and Moffat Water. The tributaries are far bigger than the Annan at this stage of its journey and some would argue that the true source of the river is Loch Skeen which lies at the top of the Moffat Water just above the beautiful Grey Mare's Tail waterfall which you can see from the A708. This is a river that has many picturesque names and among its tributaries is the Water of Milk; others join it on its way to Annan and

the Solway Firth: Kinnel Water, Dryfe Water and Mein Water.

Beats on the Annan include the Annandale Estate, Halleaths with its deep slow moving pools, Royal Four Towns, Hoddom with its famous Goat's and Kirkyard Pools and Newbie which is now time shared. Permits for the Castlemilk water which includes the Royal Four Towns beat may be had from the Estate Office in Lockerbie (05765) 203. The cost of a day ranges between £8 and £20 plus VAT. Regular permit holders are given priority over visitors and no visitor permits are issued for Saturdays in October. Rather less expensive is the Hoddom and Kinmount Estates Water whose water-bailiff is Miss Marsh of Hoddom (05763) 488. The Warmanbie Hotel at Annan (0461) 204015 has a small stretch for hotel quests. Those wishing to fish the time shared Newbie beat are advised to contact the water-bailiff Mr Mick Aprile (0461) 202608.

It is a spate river and forestry drainage from its catchment area naturally leads to fast run-offs and coloured water. In normal conditions it can be on the sluggish side and gentle handlining is the way to make the fly swim. Due to its colour in spate, worming and spinning are popular methods but it is good to know that a number of beats have a fly only rule. The Annan used to have a good spring run but this has declined and springers are now usually taken below Milnbie. A wet summer can make for some exciting days, especially for sea-trout which average around 2lb though most seasons will produce better fish of over 6lb. For salmon, autumn is the best time when several 20lb plus fish will be recorded and the average is a high 12lb.

The **Border Esk** is aptly named, not only does it cross the border, part of it and its main tributary the Liddle, actually form the border between England and Scotland. Although its mouth and lower reaches are in England, the middle and upper reaches and principal tributaries are all in Scotland. The river is formed by the junction of the Black Esk and White Esk just below Castle O'er. After this it is joined by a number of tributaries, the main ones being Meggat Water, Ewes Water and the Wauchope before reaching the town of Langholm. From this point south the A7 runs alongside the river as it collects the Tarras Water and below Canonbie it is joined by the **Liddle** which has its source in Kielder Forest. This is a noted salmon and sea-trout water in its own right. At Longtown, road and river part company as the Esk heads for the Solway Firth and just north of Metalbridge it receives its final tributary the Lyne before spilling over the mud-flats of Rockcliff marsh.

There are some wild brown trout in the river's upper reaches and tributaries, but these parts can take some getting to, so be prepared for a little rock climbing, for people who love a little extra adventure this is, however, a marvellous way to start the day and when you are finally fishing you feel alone, satisfied and totally at ease. Salmon run the river but not in any great number, however, that may be different in a few years as fry have been planted out in the tributaries. Autumn is the best time and though they may average 10lb a superb twenty eight and a half pounder was caught in 1988. Popular flies are the Blue Charm and a Silver Doctor with the Garry Dog being the local favourite.

Afforestation on the upper reaches of the river and its tributaries can make for variable water levels with occasional flash floods. Much of the river between Langholm and Canonbie is tree-lined so the ability to spey cast will be a useful asset. Do be careful when wading for although some pools are easy to wade, others are deceptively deep, so do make a thorough reconaissance before going out at night.

Night fishing of course means sea-trout and this is the Esk's main claim to fame, indeed it is one of the great sea-trout waters. In most seasons, over 5000 of these shy warriors are taken with some topping the 8lb mark. Locals tend to use a double handed 12 foot rod, but a single handed 10 foot carbon will enable you to cover the water and being more sensitive will give you a better feel when the action begins. A floating line is the best for the dusk rise after which it may be advisable to change to a sink tip or intermediate. The favourite local fly is the Langholm Silver also known as the Whaup and Silver, however, these are hard to come by as the Whaup (Curlew) is a protected bird. Other popular flies are the Peter Ross and the Invicta, and a Black Pennell on the dropper can prove very effective.

There is something magical about night fishing. First there is the dusk rise with sea-trout plopping all over the pool then as night approaches things become quieter and the flat surface of the water is only rarely broken by the rings of the rising fish. After this there is the fun of stalking fish or casting over the likely lie you noticed earlier in the day. Then as day breaks it is time to head for home and proudly display the results of your night's work, at least, that's the theory! I would add that rods are particularly asked not to take too many herling - young sea-trout - so as to conserve stocks for the future.

The river is largely owned by Buccleuch Estates and most of it is controlled by the Esk and Liddle Fishery Association. Permits and further information may be had from the Secretary, Mr R. J. B. Hill (03873) 80428 or Mr George Graham, the Head River Watcher (03873) 71416. The Cross Keys Hotel at Canonbie (03873) 71205 also issues weekly permits.

The Wells of Tweed are a few miles north of Moffat and the Annan and it is here that the **Tweed** commences its illustrious journey to the sea at Berwick-Upon-Tweed. Its prominence is perhaps best summed up by the fact that it is the only river I know that has its own telephone line! In fact the aptly named Tweedline has three numbers, (0898) 666410 for fishing reports and prospects, (0898) 666411 for river levels which are updated daily and, most importantly from our point of view, (0898) 666412 which is the number for last minute rod vacancies.

Sparkling burns like Carr Water and Tweedhope Burn join the Tweed as it flows north to Tweedsmuir which was the childhood home of John Buchan. Salmon are rarely seen this far up but there is very good trouting and the Crook Inn at Tweedsmuir (08997) 272 has its own stretch which is free to residents. This hotel also issues permits for the Peebles Trout Fishing Association water which costs £5 a day or £14 a week. Talla and Fruid which once used to swell the infant river have now been dammed to provide water for Edinburgh.

After being joined by Biggar and Holms water, the rough moorland banks give way to a more noble setting of pastures and parklands. By Peebles the river is joined by the swirling peaty Manor Water and the Lyne, another reservoir victim. Just west of Peebles is Neidpath Castle whose walls bear the scars of Cromwell's artillery. Peebles with its famous 15th century

bridge is where salmon fishing really begins. Blackwood & Smith (0721) 20131 handle lets for the Peebleshire Salmon Fishing Association which is an association of fishing proprietors who allow fishing by permit. Below the town the river skirts Kailzie Gardens and the dense conifers of Cardrona Forest and here you will find such beats as Haystoun, Horsburgh Castle and Traquair. Traquair House, the home of Maxwell Stuart, is Scotland's oldest occupied home and legend says that The Bear Gates will never be opened until a Stuart sits on the English throne again. Innerleithen is famous for its textile manufacturing and just downstream at Walkerburn is the Scottish Textile Museum.

The Traquair Arms Hotel (0896) 830229 can offer good autumn fishing on four beats where the cost varies from £40 a day to £64. The Tweed Valley Hotel at Walkerburn (0896) 823070, have some private beats in beautiful surroundings where the cost of a day's fishing varies between £15 and £40. Many of their guests are regulars, but the properietor, Charles Miller, can sometimes arrange for his guests to fish other beats. The best fish taken recently by guests was a 32lb salmon and a sea-trout of 21lb which is not far off the national record. This hotel also has two miles of private trout fishing on the Tweed and two lochs, one with wild brownies and the other with stocked rainbows which can be fished for £5 a day.

Below Innerleithen the banks are again victims of conifer plantations and here are beats such as Caddonfoot, Sunderland, Thornilee, Elbibank and Peel as just north of Selkirk it is joined by the **Ettrick** which marks the beginning of the Middle Tweed. The Ettrick is a good salmon river in its own right and like its tributary the Yarrow is noted for its trout which go up to 3lb. Buccleuch Estates at Bowhill (0750) 20753 issue day tickets for their water on the Ettrick, Yarrow and Teviot at a cost of between £15 and £30 a day.

Ettrickshaws Hotel at Ettrick (0750) 52229 have two miles of single bank fishing on the Ettrick which is available to guests at between £15.00 and £20.00 a day. The water here is spate river and fishes well late in the season. At Selkirk there is a statue to that intrepid Victorian explorer, Mungo Park, who discovered the source of the River Niger in Africa.

Gala and Allan Water join the Tweed above Melrose where the heart of Robert the Bruce is reputed to be buried in the ruins of the Cistercian Abbey. A Roman fort stands guard over the town and river and from its lofty position on Eildon Hills would also have given a clear view of Dere Street, the main England to Scotland road in those days. On this stretch will be found such famous beats as Drygrange, Maxton, Merton, Rutherford, Gledswood, Bemersyde and Ravenswood.

From where the Leader Water joins the Tweed at Leaderfoot is what is widely regarded as the best salmon fishing in the world. In 1730 the Earl of Home caught a 69lb 12oz salmon and 1866 produced one of 57lb 8oz. Fish of such majestic proportions or anything like them have not been seen for many a year, a fact which may well be connected with the drift net industry. Nowadays most Tweed salmon are around 10lb or slightly better with the odd 30 pounder falling to some lucky rod occasionally. Nearby is the small town of St Boswells where Sir Walter Scott and Earl Haig of First World War and Poppy Day fame are buried. As one might expect water of this quality is extremely difficult and expensive to get on. However, if you are lucky

enough to be able to afford it you might care to buy one of the weeks on the Lower Floors beat which the Duke of Roxburghe is selling on a 30 year lease through Savills Edinburgh office (031) - 226 6961.

At Kelso we find the most famous pool on the river, Junction. This is where the Teviot joins the Tweed and despite the fact that a week here for five rods is over £17,000 it is booked for years in advance. The **Teviot** is another tributary that is a fine salmon river in its own right - it has such good pools as Ferry Stream, Lower and Quarry which have all produced fish of over 20lb. Mr Bill Wright of Hawick (0450) 85252 has his own beat for two rods on the Teviot and may be able to organise other fishing including the Tweed when available. Tweedside Tackle of Kelso (0573) 25306 can arrange days on various private beats subject to availability and also issue permits for the Kelso Angling Association Water.

There are some famous beats between Junction Pool and below Coldstream where the Tweed receives the Till. Among names to conjure with are Sprouston, Birgham, Carham, Wark,Cornhill and Lennel. From the junction with Eden Water the Tweed forms the boundary between England and Scotland. The Till is also a fine salmon and sea-trout water. Its headwaters are sparkling burns which tumble down the Cheviot Hills and it is only at Chillingham Castle with its famous wild white cattle that it becomes the Till. Many rods fortunate enough to fish the beats in this area stay at either the Ednam House Hotel (0573) 24168 or the Crown Hotel at Coldstream (0890) 2558. Coldstream has military connections other than the famous regiment of Guards which bears its name for just south of here is the site of Flodden Field. In 1513 James IV of Scotland was killed here and history took another peculiar twist - an eerie place for June.

From Till junction the Tweed progresses at a stately pace with deep pools, wide rapids and streaming round the many islands. It is here that you will find the famous Lady Kirk and Norham beats. Norham Castle was painted by Turner and Sir Walter Scott termed it the most dangerous place to be in England. A mile east of Paxton the border crosses the river which is now wholly in England and shortly after this it receives its last tributary the **Whiteadder**. The upper reaches of this river have been dammed and flooded to form a reservoir to provide water for Edinburgh, it is however good trout water and the Allanton Inn at Allanton (0890) 81260 issue permits for the Whiteadder Angling Club Waters which cost between £10 and £20 a season. Its tributary, the **Blackadder**, offers good sporting trouting and a season ticket may be had from the Cross Keys Hotel at Greenlaw (03616) 247 for £5. Below Whiteadder junction the Tweed is affected by tides which ebb and flow shifting sands and mud until the river enters the North Sea at Tweedmouth.

Trying to book fishing yourself on the Tweed can be a headache to say the least. There are many beats and good tributaries but there is also a lot of competition for them and, as you can imagine, many people return year after year. You could spend several days on the telephone and get nowhere, alternatively you could save a lot of time by ringing the sporting agents.

Ted Hunter of Anglers Choice in Melrose (0896) 823070 has access to some private beats. James Leeming of Kelso (0573) 7280 was formerly a land agent in the early eighties but soon moved towards becoming a fishing agent. He has access to

approximately 12 beats a year where the cost varies between £20 and £400 a day. I. Fraser Sports of Peebles (0721) 20979 was changing hands at the time of going to print and the name will be changed by the new owner Mr E. MacDonald. Apart from remaining an excellent tackle shop it will still issue trout permits. However, Mrs Lena Fraser will carry on her late husband's salmon fishing as Fraser's Salmon Fishing and Hire Ltd (0721) 22960. They have 2 beats which are let from £30 a day.

Like so many rivers the spring run is not what it used to be and most springers are taken below Kelso because fish will stay below the caul at Kelso until the water temperature has risen. Summer fishing can, as one would expect, be rather chancy. However, a wet autumn and its attendant spates will see thousands upon thousands of fish running the river. Autumn fish average around 10lb but 20 and 30 pounders are not too rare. This is a big river and you need to have as long a rod as you can comfortably handle and I would suggest either a 14 or 15 footer. Although some pools are very deep most fish are taken in fairly shallow water and a medium or intermediate sinking line should suffice. Popular flies include the Garry, Willie, Gun, Comet or patterns such as the Munro Killer, Hairy Mary and Stoat's Tail for summer fishing. The best advice is to go to one of the tackle shops like Angler's Choice in Melrose and find out the latest thoughts on flies, times and locations of recent catches.

For those who like their stillwater fishing, taking the A707 south from Selkirk will bring you to **Megget Reservoir** and **St Mary's Loch**. Megget covers some 640 acres, is 200 feet deep in places and for the statistician holds on average 13.5 thousand million gallons of drinking water! Tibby Shiels Inn (0750) 42231 issue permits which cost £2.50 a day for bank fishing and boats are available. There is a modest stocking programme every year and Arctic char are being introduced on a small scale as an experiment. This brown trout water is fly-only and traditional wet flies work well as do nymphs and dapping is becoming increasingly popular. As this is over 1000 feet above sea level it can be very cold so do not forget to take an extra sweater. Anglers Choice of Melrose (0869) 823070 issue permits for St Mary's Loch which costs £2 a day for fly fishers or £4 a day for spinners and those using bait. This price differential probably says quite a lot about the availability of this water. The large loch also holds perch and pike and there is a watersports centre. I understand spinning is popular and the trout averages a good 1lb but I must confess that the idea of trolling for trout with a spinner does not appeal to me. Perhaps that is because I am still dreaming of getting a week on the Tweed!

Although sometimes turning a dream into reality is somewhat difficult it is not impossible to find fishing on the Tweed. If at first you do not succeed, try, try again; it is a tremendous river and worthy of its stature among the waters of the world.

FISHING FAYRE

The Border country is perfect for a fishing expedition for many fishermen who live south of the border. The Borderers are a friendly bunch by and large (unless, of course, the Calcutta Cup has drifted south) and they also know a dram when they see one. Be warned, to get into a drinking session with one of those fine British beasties is a fate akin to death. In fact, the only cure to what can be the most ridiculous hangover is to get up early and embark upon a spot of fishing.

SOUTHERN UPLANDS

Beattock is a splendid place to start or end your tour. Rivers converge on the town from all sides and fishing is available through a number of fishing hotels. The Auchen Castle (06833) 407, situated about a mile north of the village, has a lovely situation surrounded by woodland. The hotel is not a fishing hotel as such, but if you are seeking to fish the Annan it is a fine place to stay. Another hotel which welcomes visitors and has some fishing of its own is the Beattock House (06833) 403. This is not a grand hotel but it's good value and friendly. In Moffat, the Moffat House Hotel (0683) 20039 is a well run hotel with good bar meals.

In Annan itself we find a hotel which is particularly popular with the fishing fraternity. The Warmanbie hotel (0461) 204015 is informally run and makes for an ideal base for your fishing foray. The Eskdale Hotel, (03873) 80357 Langholm is another unpretentious but thoroughly worthy and well equipped hotel for your sporting break. Fishing permits are available from the hotel and once again this is a good base from which to explore the Borders. Eskdalemuir is somewhat more hit and miss when it comes to fishing the Esk and when the water is low, well things will be tough, but when it's high, the fishing can be extremely good. The place to stay if you are in these parts is Hart Manor (03873) 73217 which enjoys a delightful setting and also boasts some excellent dining.

An inn which has no pretence of trying to organise fishing but should still be considered for your visit is the marvellous Riverside Inn (03873) 71295 in Canonbie. The river to which it borders is the Esk and the cuisine here is outstanding. There are also a small number of attractive bedrooms should you require overnight accommodation.

The Tweed is an illustrious water and as a result it is difficult to get on, but a number of hotels are able to help you in this respect. Other hotels are merely for your reference should you have secured water through friends or estate owners. The Cringletie House (07213) 233 in Peebles is a splendid place to unpack the old suitcase. Its turreted architecture adds to its beauty and the restaurant is also to be recommended. Tweedsmuir is another point to mark and an establishmenet of great character is the Crook Inn (08997) 272. The hotel is to be found in the upper reaches of the Tweed Valley and dates from the early 17th century. The hotel is thoroughly welcoming and a delightful location from which to enjoy an informal fishing holiday.

The Traquair Arms Hotel (0896) 830229 is a friendly fishing hotel which has much to commend it, not least four beats on the Tweed. The Tweed Valley Hotel (089687) 636 in Walkerburn is another fine hotel in which to stay and has great appeal to the sportsman. The sauna might appeal after a wet day's fishing before a fine dinner. Those people who are fishing the Ettrick will surely visit the splendid Ettrickshaws, Ettrickbridge (0750) 52229. This is a splendid place in which to stay with fireplaces, oak panelling and some very comfortable accommodation. The fishing here, assuming spate conditions, is first class and as you can imagine October does become extremely busy.

There are a number of super hotels in this delightful Border country and hopefully these ideas will whet the appetite. The Woodlands Country House Hotel (0869) 4722 in Galashiels is an impressive country house and the restaurant is well worth a visit. In Melrose, Burts Hotel (089682) 2285 is a splendid place for the game fisherman to stay. The hotel advises guests to consult Anglers Choice in Melrose for their fishing information. Indeed it is fair to say that a number of hotels who do not actually have rods themselves are eager to provide information on people who can help. Another friendly establishment which is in a similar position is the Buccleuch Arms (0835) 22243, St Boswells. Trout fishing on the Tweed can be organised fairly readily but when it comes to salmon fishing there is little available. But the hotel does have contacts so do call and you might be fortunate, whatever the situation the hotel is an extremely friendly and comfortable place to stay.

We now have something of a cautionary tale and we also have something on a superb hotel to tell you about. Sunlaws House Hotel (05735) 331 is situated just outside Kelso and is one of the most delightful hotels in which to stay. The bar exudes character, the bedrooms are cosy and the restaurant is outstanding. People staying here are able to fish the Teviot and the hotel has its own pond which is beautifully laid out and great fun to fish.

Now for the cautionary tale. Do not listen to people who say fishing is impossible to find. It is difficult but not impossible. Indeed, as I was researching into this area I came across two prime beats which had become available on the Tweed. The cost was high, but good quality in any sphere does not come cheaply. The point is that some fishing is available and for around £2500 I could have arranged for 4 rods on the Tweed. Yes, I would have had to stay at Sunlaws House but that is an added bonus. The moral here is if you don't ask, you can't possibly find out!

Another fine place to stay is the Cross Keys (0573) 23303, which has a delightful situation overlooking Kelso's cobbled square. This is a delightful old inn in which to stay. Our final thought of Kelso is the renowned fishing hotel Ednam House (0573) 24168. It has a wonderfully welcoming atmosphere and has a marvellous situation overlooking the River Tweed. The hotel has its own excellent fishing and is a simply marvellous place in which to stay.

Another welcoming establishment can be found four miles south east of Greenlaw. Purves Hall (089084) 558 has a delightfully rural and unspoilt setting and welcomes fishermen to it doors. A stay here is also to be recommended. Make no mistake, this is a splendid area in which to fish - the Highland and Islands will have to wait for next year!

CORSEMALZIE HOUSE HOTEL

Corsemalzie House Hotel, a secluded country mansion is set in the heart of the picturesque countryside of the Machars (moors) of Wigtownshire, away from the rigours of city life. Relax in a setting which is hard to beat, the only noise to upset the tranquillity are the cries of the whaup (curlew) and the babbling burn. The seasonal changes create a different backdrop for the hotel, making Corsemalzie a delight to stay at whatever time of year is your preference.

The gastronome will find Corsemalzie has a great deal to offer, with dishes created using only the finest ingredients carefully and enthusiastically supervised by the proprietor Mr Peter McDougall. Fresh and local produce is used whenever possible.

This attention to detail is carried throughout the hotel with Mr and Mrs McDougall ensuring that your stay will not only be memorable for the cuisine but also for the little things that make the difference between a good hotel and a great hotel.

If you can drag yourself away from this comfort, the surrounding area has much to offer, with riding pony trekking and walking, some superb golf on your doorstep, a whole host of 9 hole courses, with 18 hole courses at Portpatrick, Glenluce where the hotel pays half your geenfees, Stranraer and a little further afield at the famous Turnberry Links course. For the game sportsmen, shooting and fishing are here in an abundance, Mr McDougall will personally organise and assist you shooting for pheasant, grouse, partridge, duck geese, snipe woodcock, rabbits and hares in the hotel grounds and neighbouring estates amounting to some 8,000 acres.

Corsemalzie House Hotel
Port William
Newton Stewart
Wigtownshire
Scotland DG8 9RL
Tel: (098 886) 254
Fax: (098 886) 213

SUNLAWS HOUSE

Sunlaws House stands in the heart of Scotland's beautiful Border country, in 200 acres of gardens and mature parkland along the banks of the Teviot, three miles from the historic town of Kelso.There has been a house on the same site at Sunlaws for nearly 500 years and from its beginnings it has always been a Scottish family house – and that, to all intents and purposes, is how it will stay!

Sunlaws has a place in history, from the faint echoes of ancient strife when English armies of the 15th and 16th centuries came marauding through Roxburghshire and the Borders, to the Jacobite rebellion of 1745. Indeed Prince Charles Edward Stuart is reputed to have stayed on November 5th 1745 and to have planted a white rose bush in the grounds.

Sunlaws hope that their guests will find that in the intervening year there have been some welcome changes. Its owner, the Duke of Roxburghe, has carefully converted Sunlaws into the small, welcoming but unpretentious hotel of comfort and character that it is.

There are 22 bedrooms, which include the splendid Bowmont Suite and six delightful rooms in the stable courtyard, all furnished with care to His Graces' own taste and all with private bathroom or shower, colour television, radio and direct-dial telephone. Disabled guests too are provided with the amenities they need.

The spacious public rooms are furnished with the same care and elegance, which adds to the overall atmosphere of warmth and welcome with log fires burning in the main and inner hall, drawing room, library bar and dining room, throughout the winter and on cold summer evenings.

Flowers and plants, from the gardens and the conservatory, will be found all over the house; herbs too are grown for the kitchen and will be found in many of the traditional dishes that are prepared for the dining room. Not only is Sunlaws right in the heart of Scotland's beautiful Border Country, it is also the perfect centre for a host of holiday activities. Sporting and cultural interests are well served, too.

Salmon and trout fishing, and a complete range of shooting are available at the Hotel, with golf, horse-riding, racing and fox hunting all nearby.

Sunlaws is the perfect location for touring the Borders, with great country houses including Abbotsford, the home of Sir Walter Scott, and a number of abbeys and museums all within easy reach.

Sunlaws House Hotel
Kelso
Roxburghshire
Scotland
Tel: (05735) 331 Fax: (05735) 611

PURVES HALL HOTEL

Purves Hall is a fine country house built in 1908, with historic connections going back to the 1670's. It is set in 10 acres of wooded parkland, with superb views south to the Cheviot Hills. There are secluded gardens in which to relax, and walks through the woods or surrounding country lanes for those who enjoy walking. For family leisure activities, Purves Hall has a tennis court, heated outdoor swimming pool, croquet lawn, and putting green. Stables are available for those who wish to bring horses.

The resident proprietors, Wing Commander and Mrs B.D. Everett, and their staff personally prepare all meals and seek to ensure that your stay at Purves is comfortable and enjoyable. The Hall with its log fires is also centrally heated throughout. The en-suite bedrooms have full tea making facilities and colour TV's with video system and telephone. The Cheviot Restaurant offers a varied menu and fine wines. Coffee is served in the elegant main lounge adjoining the cocktail bar where a wide selection of liqueurs is available.

The area has many fine golf courses and good river fishing. Shooting can be arranged (in season) with sufficient advance notice. Bird watching on the East Coast at St Abb's and the Farne Islands. Chillingham Castle, home of the white wild cattle, who are descendants from prehistoric herds of the Great Caledonian Forests, all await the visitor in pursuit pleasure and relaxation.

Purves Hall is situated in the centre of the Scottish Borders Region and all its historic towns, castles and stately homes, most places of interest being less than one hours drive. Peebles, Selkirk, Melrose, Kelso, Jedburgh, Berwick, Duns, Coldstream and St Abb's are but a few well worth visiting. The East Coasts of Berwickshire and Northumberland can easily be reached through quiet country roads and Edinburgh is less than one hour away.

Purves Hall Hotel
Greenlaw
Berwickshire
Scotland TD10 6UJ
Tel: (089 084) 558

SCOTLAND : FURTHER FORAYS

DUMFRIESSHIRE, GALLOWAY & BORDERS

BALCARY BAY HOTEL,
Auchencairn, Nr. Castle Douglas, Tel: (055664) 217
Despite a rich history that was wrapped up with local smuggling practices, Balcary today concentrates on Scottish hospitality, modern facilities and traditional atmosphere. The presence of the Gulf Stream ensures a predominantly mild climate, enabling visitors to enjoy local golf and fishing.

COMLONGON CASTLE,
Clarencefield, Dumfries, Tel: (038) 787 283
Comlongon offers guests excellent hospitality in an awe-inspiring setting. Rooms are spacious and comfortable and fifty acres of grounds provide nature trails and woodland walks. Golf and fishing are also to be found nearby.

CORGEMALZIE HOUSE HOTEL,
Port William, Newton Stewart, Wigtownshire Tel: (098) 886254
This popular hotel is perfect for golfers, anglers and active tourists, with Culzean Castle not too far afield. Guests can obtain a 10% reduction on production of a copy of Fishing Forays.

COUL HOUSE HOTEL,
Contin, By Strathpeffer, Ross-shire, Tel: (0997) 21487
Situated in seven acres of gardens and grounds, Coul House offers fabulous forest and mountain views. Golfing, pony trekking and sailing holidays can be provided and salmon\trout fishing is available on the river Alness.

CREEBRIGE HOUSE HOTEL,
Newton Stewart, Wigtownshire, Tel: (0671) 2121
Built in 1760 and formerly owned by the Earl of Galloway, the hotel sits in three acres of gardens and woodlands and is now an eighteen bedroom Country House Hotel with accommodation of an extremely high standard. Excellent local fishing is on hand.

DUNRAVEN LODGE HOTEL,
Golf Road, Strathpeffer, Ross-shire, Tel: (0997) 21210
The Dunraven is superbly positioned to take advantage of both the East Coast amenities and the wild scenery of Wester Ross. The hotel is an ideal base for all sorts of activities , including golf, with many courses in close proximity.

EDNAM HOUSE HOTEL,
Kelso, Tel: (0573) 24168
Ednam House, built in 1761 is considered one of the finest Georgian mansions in Roxburghshire. Thirty two bedrooms are all beautifully furnished and many are populated by fishermen, attracted by the glories of the river Tweed.

HART MANOR HOTEL,
Eskdalemuir, By Langholm, Dumfriesshire, Tel: (0387) 373217
This friendly establishment is popular with touring holidaymakers. Fishing is available on the White Esk only three hundred yards from the hotel and Bowhill at Selkirk proves another local favourite.

HEATHERLIE HOUSE HOTEL,
Heatherlie Park, Selkirk, Tel: (0750) 21200
Heatherlie is a privately owned and managed mansion house of great character, set in secluded wooded grounds that offer interesting walks. The hotel is noted for its relaxed, friendly atmosphere, for its excellent food prepared by Mrs Fleming and for an extensive wine list.

HOEBRIDGE INN,
Gattonside, Melrose, Tel: (0896 82) 3082
This locally renowned restaurant comes highly recommended. Enjoy a freshly prepared meal of local game and fish, a vegetarian dish or one of our Italian specialities in a friendly informal atmosphere. Managed by Chef proprietor Carlo Campari and his wife Joy, the restaurant is only ten minutes from Melrose and Galashiels.

MENNOCKFOOT LODGE HOTEL,
Mennock, By Sanquar, Dumfriesshire, Tel: (0659) 50382
For golfers and anglers, Mennockfoot Lodge is a splendid retreat. Fishing is to be had in abundance within twenty yards of the hotel, whilst the golf courses of Sanquar, Thornhill and many others await the enthusiast.

MOFFAT FISHERY,
Hammerlands, Moffat, Dumfriesshire, Tel: (0683) 21068
This friendly and welcoming fishery offers a complete range of fishing services and features. Comprehensive fishing facilities are available for beginner and expert alike, together with a well-stocked fish farm and smokehouse.

MURRAY ARMS,
Gatehouse of Fleet, Tel: (05574) 207
A warm welcome and good food are guaranteed at this fine hotel. Most bedrooms are ensuite and all feature central heating, T.V., direct dial telephones and baby listening facility. As well as the splendours of the surrounding countryside, golf, fishing and tennis can be arranged.

SELKIRK ARMS HOTEL,
High Street, Kirkubright, Tel: (0557) 30402
Set in the pretty fishing town of Kirkubright, the hotel has sixteen bedrooms, all ensuite. A fine restaurant is justly proud of its dishes, made from fresh Galloway beef or locally caught fish, especially Dover Sole and Scallops. A generous low season discount is available to readers of this book.

SOLWAYSIDE HOUSE HOTEL,
Auchencairn, Castle Douglas, Tel: (055) 664 280
A comfortable, family run hotel offering good food and superb sea and country views. Amongst the many local attractions are Dundrennan Castle, Sweetheart Abbey and Threave Garden and Castle. Excellent local fishing is also available and the hotel provides freezing facilities and a drying room.

THE IMPERIAL HOTEL,
35 King Street, Castle Douglas, Southerness, Tel: (0556) 2086
The Imperial enjoys a central, convenient location and makes a perfect holiday base. Golfers are particularly well catered for with Castle Douglas and the acclaimed Southerness little more than a well struck drive away.

EAST BARCLOY,
Colvend, Dalbeattie, Dumfries, Tel: (055663) 424
Guests are assured of a warm welcome, fantastic cooking and comfortable rooms at this highly recommended farmhouse cottage. Mr and Mrs Beckitt make friendly and attentive hosts.

LOTHIAN

CRINLETIE HOUSE HOTEL,
Peebles, Tel: (0672 13) 244
Cringletie is an elegant and distinguished mansion, that exudes the genteel atmosphere of a country house. At only twenty miles from Edinburgh, there is no shortage of things to do and places to see.

JOHN DICKSON AND SON LTD,
21 Frederick Street, Edinburgh, Tel: 031-225 4218
John Dickson and Son is Scotland's premier tackle shop, set in the heart of the capital. It stocks all leading brands of British-made rods, reels and accessories with quality and service a top priority.

HOPE COTTAGE,
Stenton, By Dunbar, Tel: (03685) 293
Hope Cottage provides travellers with a comfortable resting place. Situated in a conservation village between the Lammermuir Hills and the sea, Hope Cottage is ideally situated for golf, fishing and racing.

SCOTLAND : FURTHER FORAYS

GEORGE C. JAMIESON,
Taxidermist, Crammond Tower, Kirk Crammond, Edinburgh, Tel: 031-336 1916
A full range of services are provided by this popular and highly recommended establishment. Expert advice is also offered by the friendly and highly qualified owner.

MALLARD HOTEL,
East Links Road, Gullane, East Lothian, Tel: (0620) 843288
One of the area's most popular hotels, the Mallard is a popular haunt for both locals and visitors. Many notable golf courses are within easy reach, in particular Gullane's three courses and Muirfield.

OPEN ARMS HOTEL,
Dirleton, East Lothian, Tel: (0620) 85 241
This is a splendid hotel that offers the highest standard of accommodation, in a quiet, intimate atmosphere. Golf, fishing, racing and other places of interest are all within easy reach.

POINT GARRY HOTEL,
20 West Bay Road, North Berwick, Tel: (0620) 2380
The attractive resort of North Berwick is the location for this popular hotel. The acclaimed West Course is literally a few yards away and there are plenty of alternative courses and places of interest.

SIBBET HOUSE,
26 Northumberland Street, Edinburgh, Tel: 031-556 1078
Sibbet House was built in 1809 and is generously furnished with antiques and draperies. An elegant, but comfortable family Georgian family home, Sibbet offers well-appointed guest rooms with private facilities.

STUART HOUSE,
12 East Claremont Street, Edinburgh, Tel: 031-557 9030
Stuart House is a lovely Georgian-style Town House located in the refined elegance of New Town, Edinburgh. All bedrooms are ensuite and also feature direct-dial telephone, colour television and tea/coffee hospitality tray.

WOODLANDS,
55 Barnton Avenue, Davidson Mains, Edinburgh, Tel: 031-336 1685
Edinburgh is renowned for the number and quality of its golf courses and this comfortable Bed & Breakfast overlooks the eleventh tee of one of its finest, Royal Burgess. The equally challenging Bruntsfield course is also within close proximity

STRATHCLYDE

ARDSHEAL HOUSE HOTEL,
Kentallen of Appin, Argyll, Tel: (063) 174 227
This historic Stewart Manor house, now a small country hotel, is set in nine hundred acres of the woods and meadows of the magnificent West Highlands. A shorefront location completes the idyllic picture.

ARDSHIEL HOTEL,
Kilkerren Road, Campbelltown, Tel: (0586) 52133
The spectacular links of Machrihanish are only three miles from this popular establishment. Anglers will find excellent sport at Lussa reservoir whilst Brodick Castle is one of several local places of historic interest.

ARGYLL ARMS HOTEL,
60 Main Street, Campbeltown, Tel: (0586) 53431
This town centre hotel is a popular meeting place amongst the local population and provides high-quality accommodation for visitors. A restaurant serves appetizing fare and snooker provides relaxing indoor relaxation.

BLACKWATERFOOT HOTEL,
Isle of Arran, Tel: (0770 86) 202,
A warm welcome is the order of the day at this friendly, family-run hotel in the glorious Isle of Arran. Good food is an additional bonus and can be sampled by readers at a reduced rate.

DRUIMNACROISH COUNTRY HOUSE HOTEL,
Druimnacroish, Isle of Mull, Argyll, Tel: (06884) 274
Druimnacroish is a small, exclusive Country House Hotel, situated in the beautiful Bellart Glen. A Scottish Country House atmosphere contributes to a uniquely personal service for guests. The hotel has its own stalking and can arrange fishing.

GLENFEOCHAN HOUSE,
Kilmore, Oban, Argyll, Tel: (063 177) 273
Glenfeochan House offers its guests fishing on the two and a half mile long River Nell and the Sea Loch Feochan. Salmon and Sea Trout run from May-July and September-October. The Glenfeochan Estate also contains a rich and varied wildlife population.

KIRKTON HOUSE,
Cardross, Dunbartonshire, Tel: (0389) 841 951
This comfortable guesthouse is within easy reach of the thriving city of Glasgow and its huge array of attractions. Pollok House and the fantastic Burrell collection will be of particular interest to many patrons.

MALIN COURT,
Turnberry, Ayrshire, Tel: (0655) 31457
There are few more inspiring sights in the world of golf than Turnberry and Malin Court has the good fortune to overlook the famous links. The quiet, ranch style building is extremely comfortably furnished.

MARINE HIGHLAND HOTEL,
Troon, Ayrshire, KA10 6HE, Tel: (0292) 314444
Only 45 minutes from Glasgow and five minutes from Prestwick Airport, the Marine Highland is one of Scotland's finest hotels. Seventy two immaculately furnished bedrooms are complemented by a fine range of cuisine and breathtaking views across to the Isle of Arran.

RICHMOND PRIVATE HOTEL,
38 Park Circus, Ayr, Tel: (0292) 265153
Situated in a quiet conservation area minutes from the town centre, this friendly, family-run guesthouse offers good food and comfortable, ensuite bedrooms. The racecourse and dozens of golf courses are within easy reach.

SAVOY PARK HOTEL,
16 Racecourse Road, Ayr, Tel: (0292) 266112
An elegant building and traditional furnishings are features of this comfortable, family run hotel. A high level of service and cuisine also ensures that guests return regularly, with the nearby racecourse a popular attraction.

SOUTH BEACH HOTEL,
South Beach, Troon, Tel: (0292) 312033
The popular seaside town of Troon is the setting for this well-established hotel. Rooms are nicely furnished and include two luxury penthouse suites. Local places of interest include Burns' Cottage and Blairquhan Castle.

ST NICHOLAS HOTEL,
41 Ayr Road, Prestwick, Tel: (0292) 79568
This well established hotel is within five miles of numerous well known golf courses. All bedrooms have colour TV, phones and en suite bathrooms. Meals are served from 1200-1400 and 1700-2100 hrs.

SCOTLAND : FURTHER FORAYS

FIFE

COTTAGE,
Blairburn, Culross, Tel: (0383) 880704
Centrally situated and convenient for Perth, Stirling, Glasgow and Edinburgh, this guesthouse is naturally popular with wayfarers travelling from and in various directions. A bedtime drink is one of many thoughtful extras.

DUNBOG,
Newburgh, Fife, KY14 6JF, Tel: (0337) 40455
Dunbog is a charming farm house situated in the gentle hills of Fife, close to the river Tay. Two comfortable twin bedrooms are both ensuite and evening meals can be arranged by appointment.

DYKES,
69 Pittenweem Road, Anstruther, Tel: (0333) 310537
Fishing, riding, golf, castles, stately homes and beaches should make a visit to this part of the world a pleasure for the most demanding tourist. All rooms here have modern facilities.

EARL DAVID HOTEL,
Coaltown of Wemyss, Fife, Tel: (0592) 54938
Friendly and efficient service is the priority at this family-run hotel. All rooms are ensuite and feature colour TV with satellite and video channels. Special packages including transport can be arranged for visiting golfers.

GREIGSTON FARM,
Peat Inn, Cupar, Tel: (033) 484284
This elderly stone house offers comfortable accommodation in an attractive environment-interior and exterior. Meals are most definitely edible, served by a friendly host.

MELANTEE,
Achintore Road, Fort William, Tel: (0397) 5329
For delightful accommodation, splendid countryside and exceptional service, Melantee scores high marks. Ben Nevis, Skye and the entire Highland Region are tantalisingly close.

RED HOUSE,
Freuchie, Falkland, Tel: (0337) 57555
The golfing kingdom of Fife is a golfers paradise and The Red House will spare no effort to ensure a memorable stay. However the delights of Fife are far from limited to golf and guests will find a multitude of things to do and see.

RESCOBIE HOTEL,
Rescobie Hotel, Leslie, Fife, Tel: (0592) 742143
Ten comfortable and well appointed bedrooms make this hotel a perennial favourite. Every effort will be made to accommodate conferences and receptions with an added bonus special 3 and 6 day sporting rates.

ROYAL HOTEL,
20 Rodger Street, Anstruther, Tel: (0333) 310581
The Royal attracts more than it's fare share of local and visiting trade. all are attracted, no doubt, by tastefully furnished bedrooms and a splendid restaurant. Special golfers rates are available.

SCORES HOTEL,
St Andrews, Fife, Tel: (0334) 72451
The Scores is a traditional, 3-star, independently owned hotel with magnificent views over St Andrews Bay and the Royal and Ancient Clubhouse. First-time visitors are always delighted to discover that the first tee of the Old Course is less than a hundred yards away.

THE SPENDRIFT,
Pittenweem Road, Anstruther, Fife, Tel: (0333) 310573
Escape to a little piece of paradise in the heart of Fife. All bedrooms have private facilities, colour TV, hospitality tray and sea views. Golf and fishing opportunities abound, together with a wealth of local attractions.

TAYSIDE AND CENTRAL

BHEINNE MHOR,
Perth Road, Birnam, Dunkeld, Tel: (03502) 779/from spring 1992 (0350) 727779
This charming, Victorian turreted house offers four comfortable guestrooms with modern amenities. Features include an attractive guest TV lounge and good home-cooking, together with a splendid setting in the heart of Perthshire.

CENTRAL HOTEL,
Church Street, Edzell, Tel: (03564) 218
Twenty comfortable and well appointed rooms are at the disposal of guests in this highly recommended establishment. Edzell golf course is nearby, and the challenges of St Andrews and Carnoustie are well within reach.

CLAYMORE HOTEL,
Atholl Road, Pitlochry, Tel: (0796) 2888
This superbly situated high class hotel is convenient for Pitlochry golf course and provides an ideal base for exploring the magnificent local countryside. Hospitality and cuisine are both superb.

CLUNIE GUESTHOUSE,
12 Pitcullen Crescent, Perth, Tel: (0738) 23625
This appealing guesthouse is conveniently situated for the many delights of the city of Perth. Seven comfortable bedrooms will ensure that guests depart refreshed and relaxed. Murrayshall restaurant and golf course are only minutes away

COLLEARN HOUSE HOTEL,
Auchterarder, Perthshire, Tel: (0764) 63553
Golf, fishing and heritage devotees will find this relaxing guesthouse a perfect location. Gleneagles, the rivers Earn and Tay and Scone Palace are all worthy of exploration. Special three-day stays are available.

COSHIEVILLE HOTEL,
By Aberfendy, Perthshire, Tel: (08873) 319
The Coshieville is a small country Inn with pleasant ensuite accommodation and a relaxed atmosphere. Traditional Scottish food is served by happy and attentive staff, guaranteeing guests an extremely agreeable stay.

FORTINGALL HOTEL,
By Aberfeldy, Perthshire, PH15 2NQ, Tel: (088) 73 367
Fortingall Hotel is a friendly family concern situated amongst some of Scotland's finest scenic and landscaped conservation areas. Accommodation is tastefully designed and leisure pursuits available include fishing and deer-stalking.

GALVELMORE HOUSE,
Gavelmore Street, Crieff, Perthshire, Tel: 0764 2277
This comfortable Georgian House is located close to the centre of picturesque Crieff, near to the challenging 18-hole golf course. Numerous other course, including Gleneagles are within reach and Perth also provides regular race meetings.

GRAIGOWER HOTEL,
134-136 Athull Road, Pitlochry, Perthshire, Tel: (0796) 2590
One of Scotland's prettiest and best-known towns, Pitlochry, is a never-changing joy for tourists, and the Craigower Hotel makes an extremely convenient headquarters. A discount for readers is available between November and January.

GUINACH HOUSE,
By the Birks, Aberfeldy, Tel: (0887) 20251
The agreeable combination of excellent accommodation and spectacular scenery can be discovered through a stay at this comfortable hotel. Golf, fishing and racing are all available in the vicinity and Scone Palace and Blair Castle are other notable attractions.

SCOTLAND : FURTHER FORAYS

IONA GUEST HOUSE,
2 Pitcullen Crescent, Perth, Tel: (0738) 27261
A warm welcome awaits at this popular guesthouse. Rooms, many of which are ensuite, feature colour TV, hospitality trays and central heating. A residents lounge is available all day, and excellent evening meals will satisfy every palate.

LETTER FARM,
Loch of Lowes, By Dunkeld, Perthshire, Tel: (03504) 254
Set in the heart of Perthshire's best fishing waters and ideally situated for several challenging golf courses, Scone Palace, Blair and Glamis Castles, Letter Farm offers quality accommodation in a tranquil location. Bird and wildlife enthusiasts will also find both in abundance.

MERRYBURN HOTEL,
Station road, Birnam, Dunkeld, Pethshire, Tel: (03502) 216
The historic and beautiful village of Dunkeld is a visitors paradise and the Merryburn Hotel is where many head. Well appointed rooms are complemented by personal attention and traditional Scottish food. Golf and fishing head the list of things to see and do.

THE NORTHERN HOTEL,
2-4 Clerk Street, Brechin, Scotland, DD9 6AE, Tel: (03562) 2156
This well-known and established hotel caters for the business and holiday traveller alike. Brechin is situated between Aberdeen and Dundee in the heart of golf-rich Angus and is also at the centre of some of the best fishing and shooting on the East Coast.

THE OLD BANK HOUSE,
Brown Street, Blairgowrie, Perthshire, Tel: (0250) 2902
Situated adjacent to Rosemount golf course, The Old Bank House has been tastefully converted, retaining the elegance of the Georgian era, whilst having a warm, relaxed atmosphere. The beautifully furnished bedrooms are all ensuite and the cuisine on offer is highly recommended.

TIGH-NA-CLOICH HOTEL,
Larchwood Road, Pitlochry, Tel: (0796) 2216 (changes 1992)
Hospitality, comfort, good food and beautiful views typify this small, highly-recommended Highland hotel. Bedrooms are thoughtfully and pleasantly furnished and the traditional Scottish dishes are prepared using the best of local produce.

GRAMPIAN AND HIGHLAND

ALTNAHARRA,
Altnaharra, By Lairg, Sutherland, Tel: (054) 981 222
Altnaharra is one of Scotland's best known fishing hotels. Sixteen comfortable bedrooms are all en-suite and have been refurbished to a very high standard. Open from March to November, excellent fishing is possible on local lochs and rivers.

ARISAIG HOUSE,
Beasdale, Arisaig, Inverness-shire, Tel: (068 75) 622
Arisaig House lies by the famous 'Road to the Isles' to the west of Fortwilliam. Built in 1864, the hotel offers elegant and high-standard accommodation amid beautiful gardens and spectacular scenery.

AUCHENDEAN LODGE,
Dulnain Bridge, Grantown-on-Spey, Morayshire, Tel: (047) 985 347
Situated high above the river Spey, eight comfortable bedrooms make this a perfect base for no less than ten golf courses within forty-five minutes drive. Auchendean Lodge also features log fires, award-winning food, forest and mountain views and excellent fishing.

BREADALBANE HOUSE HOTEL,
Breadalbane Crescent, Wick, Caithness, Tel: (0955) 3911
A wealth of local fishing is at the doorstep of residents of this popular hotel. All bedrooms are en-suite and have tea and coffee making facilities. Babies and disabled guests are also welcomed and private parking is available.

BRIDGE HOTEL,
Dunrobin Street, Helmsdale, Sutherland, Tel: (04312) 219
Only yards away from the river Helmsdale, this friendly hotel represent's a fisherman's dream. Loch and sea fishing are all available as part of inclusive packages and golfing enthusiasts are equally well catered for.

CALEDONIAN THISTLE HOTEL,
Union Terrace, Aberdeen, Tel: (0224) 640233
This excellent city-centre hotel offers elegant accommodation and modern facilities. Aberdeen is a thriving city with a wealth of attractions. Local golfers and anglers are also superbly catered for.

COPTHORNE,
The Coptho, 122 Huntly Street, Aberdeen, Tel: (0224) 630404
The Copthorne combines the facilities of a first-class international hotel with traditional Scottish hospitality. This elegant establishment, in association with Better Golf Scotland, can also offer the opportunity of sampling twelve local golf courses including the renowned Royal Aberdeen.

CORROUR HOUSE HOTEL,
Inverdruie, Aviemore, Inverness-shire, Tel: (0479) 810220
The many and varied attractions of Aviemore make this comfortable hotel perfect for a family holiday. A range of accommodation is available and discounts are available during the low season. There is naturally much to occupy keen golfers and fishers.

CRAIGELLACHIE HOTEL,
Craigellachie, Aberlour, Banffshire, Tel: (0340) 881204
A wealth of sporting and leisure opportunities await visitors to this splendid hotel. As well as a gym sauna and solarium, tennis, golf and fishing are all within easy reach. Nearby Balmoral is an additional attraction.

CRANNTARA GUESTHOUSE,
High Street, Grantown-on-Spey, Tel: (0479) 2197
This comfortable hotel offers friendly service and a wealth of local amenities. Golfers and fishermen are particularly well catered for with numerous local golf courses and trout/salmon fishing easily available. Excellent local produce is served in the Dining Room.

CULDUTHEL LODGE,
14 Culduthel Road, Inverness, Tel: (0463) 240089
Culduthel Lodge is a Georgian Mansion Hotel located in lively Inverness. All bedrooms are tastefully furnished and offer extensive views of the beautiful surroundings. Inverness golf club is within one mile and Royal Dornoch and Nairn are tantalisingly close.

CULLIGRAN COTTAGES
Culligran Estate, Glen Strathfarrar, Struy, Nr. Beauly, Inverness, Tel: (046) 376285
Here on the spectacular headwaters of the famous Beauly River, the best months for catching salmon are July/October and trout in April/July. Culligran offers comfortable accommodation to let — one cottage and four chalets for between £99 and £319 per week.

DELNASHAUGH INN,
Ballindalloch, Banffshire, Tel: (08072) 255
This recently renovated and refurbished Old Drovers Inn is ideally placed between the rivers Avon and Spey. The hotel is personally run by proprietors Mr and Mrs D.M. Odgen who will be pleased to advise on local fishing, shooting, golf and malt whisky trails.

SCOTLAND : FURTHER FORAYS

DUNAIN PARK HOTEL,
Dunain Park, Inverness, Tel: (0463) 230512
Twelve comfortable twin and double rooms in this elegant house are complemented by an award winning restaurant, indoor heated swimming pool, sauna and six acres of beautiful gardens. Excellent local fishing and golf are easy to find.

EIGHT ACRES HOTEL,
Sherrifmill, Elgin, Moray, Tel: (0343) 543077
This popular establishment is equipped to satisfy every holiday requirement. Weddings and conferences can also be arranged, with visitors able to enjoy the indoor pool, squash courts, sauna, gym and solarium.

GLENGARRY HOUSE HOTEL,
Invergarry, Inverness-shire, Tel: (08093) 254
A range of comfortable accommodation is available at this highly recommended hotel. All rooms are furnished to a high standard and offer relaxing comfort after a day's energetic tennis or fishing.

HAUGH HOTEL,
Cromdale, Morayshire, PH26 3LW, Tel: (0479) 2583
This comfortable roadside hotel on the banks of the river Spey is an ideal base for a Highland holiday. This is an area famous for its fishing, malt whiskies and many local places of interest. Four good golf courses are within a short drive.

HOTEL SEAFORTH,
Dundee Road, Arbroath, Tel: (0241) 722232
This is an extremely comfortable and welcoming hotel and is convenient for the wealth of golf courses that characterize this area. The Elliot course is virtually on the hotel doorstep and famous Carnoustie is a mere six miles away.

KILBRECK GUEST HOUSE,
410 Great Western Road, Aberdeen, Tel: (0224) 316115
Situated in a quiet, residential area in the west end of the city, Kilbreck offers comfort and service and is within easy reach of many places of interest such as Drum Castle, Crathes Castle, Fyvie Castle, Fraser Castle and Craigievar Castle.

KNOCKOMIE HOTEL,
Grantown Road, Forres, Moray, Tel: (0309) 73146
The challenging course at Forres is only a mile from this pleasant hotel, with the famous links at Lossiemouth not much further afield. Conferences and weddings can be catered for and readers benefit from a 10% discount between November and April.

LINKS HOTEL,
1 Seafield Street, Nairn, Tel: (0667) 53321
The Links Hotel is conveniently located midway between the challenging links of Nairn West and Nairn Dunbar with magnificent views of the Black Isle. Ten comfortable bedrooms are at the disposal of touring golfers and anybody also exploring the glorious Highlands of Scotland.

LOCH INSH WATERSPORTS AND SKIING CENTRE,
Loch Insh, Kincraig, Inverness-shire, Tel: (05404) 272
Part of the river Spey, Loch Insh offers boat fishing for salmon, trout, arctic char and pike between March and September. Two boats and four rods can be hired for £15 per day per rod. Outboard, tackle and parking are also available.

LOVAT ARMS HOTEL,
Beauly, Nr. Inverness, Tel: (0463) 782313
Good food and comfort are available in this elegant, 'A' listed building. All rooms are ensuite with telephone, T.V. and tea/coffee makers. The Capital of the Highlands, Inverness, is only ten miles distant. Local fishing is plentiful.

NETHER LOCHABER HOTEL,
Onich, Fort William, Inverness-shire, Tel: (085) 53235
This comfortable and cosy Highland inn is an ideal base from which to explore Lochaber, the Ardnamurchan Peninsula and Glencoe. Traditional home cooking goes hand in hand with homely service and accommodation.

POLMAILY HOUSE HOTEL,
Drumnadrochit, Inverness-shire, Tel: (045 62) 343
Polmaily House is a small, comfortable Country House Hotel situated on the slopes of Glen Urquhart. Great golf can be played at Dornoch and Nairn, fishing is available locally and Cawdor and Brodie are nearby stately homes.

ROSSLEA HOTEL,
Ferry Road, Rhu, Helensburgh, Dunbartonshire,
Tel: (0436) 820684
Full amenities and facilities are found at this highly recommended hotel. Conferences and weddings can be tailored to individual requirements, with local fishing and golf a bonus for the leisure enthusiast.

ROYAL HOTEL,
Fortrose, Tel: (0381) 20236
The Royal is the perfect loaction for a Highland golfing break with Fortrose, Rosemarkie and Nairn amongst others within easy reach. All rooms are well appointed and are complemented by good food and hospitality.

ROYAL HOTEL (CAITHNESS),
Trail Street, Thurso, Caithness, Tel: (0847) 63191/2
This is a large, 104 bedroom, family run hotel. All rooms have private facilities, T.V. and tea and coffee making facilities. Three golf courses-Thurso, Reay and Wick are within easy reach and discounts can be arranged.

SAPLINBRAE HOUSE HOTEL,
Mintlaw, Nr Peterhead, Aberdeenshire, Tel: (0771) 23515
Tourists and businessmen will find this hotel relaxing and comfortable. Renowned cuisine is served in the elegant restaurant, and trout fishing is available in a 30 acre lake close to the hotel.

ST ANNS HOUSE HOTEL,
37 Harrowden Road, Inverness, Tel: (0463) 236157
A first class, family run establishment enjoying a reputation for friendliness and good service. All rooms have central heating, facilities and colour T.V.'s. The town centre is only ten minutes walk away.

SUNNY BRAE GUESTHOUSE,
Marine Road, Nairn, Tel:(0667) 52309
This relaxing guesthouse is an ideal base for touring the North of Scotland, with golf at Nairn an additional attraction. Cawdor and Brodie are well worth an inspection. Clean, reasonably priced accommodation is provided.

THE STAGE HOUSE,
Glenfinnan, Inverness-shire, Tel: (0397) 83246
This beautiful old coaching inn dates back to 1658 and is situated in a picturesque glen at the head of Loch Shiel. The hotel owns fishing rights on Loch Shiel which is famous for salmon and sea trout.

WHITEBRIDGE HOTEL,
Whitebridge, Stratherrick, Inverness, Tel: (04563) 226
This is a welcoming, traditional fishing hotel situated amid the foothills of the Monadhliath mountains to the south of Loch Ness. The hotel is comfortable and has modern facilities throughout.

KNOCKINAAM LODGE

Knockinaam was built as a holiday house for Lady Hunter Blair in 1869 and enlarged in 1901. The house stands in a secluded enclave at the foot of a deep and thickly wooded glen, surrounded on three sides by sheltering cliffs and looking out to sea. A beautiful garden with wide lawns runs down to a private sandy beach where guests can enjoy magnificent views of the distant Irish coastline, the changing moods of sea and sky, and stupendous sunsets. Indeed, such is the timeless tranquility of this extraordinary place, that Sir Winston Churchill chose it during the Second World War for a secret meeting with General Eisenhower and their Chiefs of Staff.

The house was converted into a 'restaurant avec chambres' and quickly established a reputation for the finest cooking in the south of Scotland. This reputation has been assiduously maintained and today, you can sit in the attractive dining room with the sea breaking over the rocks at the end of the lawn and dine on the tender Galloway beef – surely the best in the world? – fresh lobsters, scallops, scampi and many other locally produced delicacies, including home grown vegetables. In cooler weather, log fires burn in the public rooms and there is full central heating throughout the house. Small business meetings can be accommodated during the autumn.

Knockinaam is an ideal base for exploring this little known and unspoiled corner of Scotland. Quaint villages, early Christian sites, ruined and still inhabited castles, standing stones dot an undulating green landscape, dissected by rough, dry stone walls and twisting single track roads. The unusually mild climate engendered by the Gulf Stream can support almost every species of tropical plant and there are many famous gardens within easy reach. There are two excellent golf courses close to the hotel, and world famous Turnberry is less than an hour's drive. Further inland, forests of spruce and larch lead into vast racts of wild country, easily accessible by car or on foot, where a wonderful variety of wild game abounds amongst lochs, rivers and tawny hills.

Knockinaam offers its visitors the chance to escape from the pressures of the outside world, to shed cares and restore neglected values. The passage of time has left the holiday house atmosphere intact, and those romantic qualities that Sir Winston Churchill appreciated, remain unchanged.

The resident owners, Marcel and Corina Frichot and their attentive young staff, look forward to welcoming you to this unique and unforgettable place.

Knockinaam Lodge Hotel
Portpatrick
Wigtownshire
Scotland DG9 9AD
Tel: (077681) 471   Fax: (077681) 435

ENGLAND'S NORTH

Artist Wendy Reeves   *FISHING THE RIVER*   Courtesy of Rose…

CHEVIOT HILLS

REDE   A68

KIELDER

N.TYNE

A69

S.TYNE   P E N N

SOLWAY FIRTH

CARLISLE

A596

DERWENT

EDEN

A6

PENRITH

A66

CONGRA
MOSS

EHEN

LAKE

A595

DISTRICT

CONISTON
WATER   WINDERMERE

KENT

LUNE

KIRBY
STEPHEN

BALD
BALE

W

TE

WHAR

SKIPFA

KENDAL

A6

IRISH SEA

MORECAMBE BAY

HODDER

RIBBLE

M6

BLACKPOOL   M55

CALDER

M6

M61

M6

LIVERPOOL

110

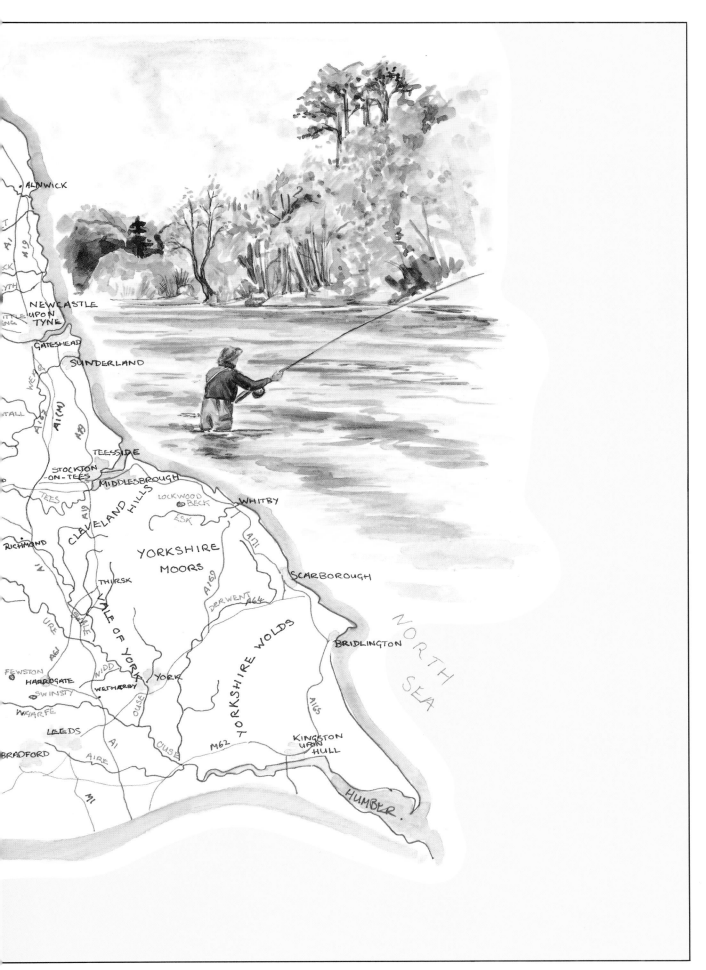

TUFTON ARMS HOTEL

The Tufton Arms stands at the heart of historic Appleby, the erstwhile county town of Westmorland, sheltered from the East by the Pennines and the West by the Lakeland Fells. Appleby enjoys a much drier and warmer climate than much of Cumbria.

The Tufton was bought by the Milsom family in 1989 and has been totally refurbished using a top designer to recapture the Victorian feel of the building.

The hotel has 19 individually furnished suites and bedrooms to suit all pockets, all fully en suite with direct dial telephone, television and tea and coffee making facilities.

In the Conservatory restaurant, Head Chef David Milsom serves an exciting A La Carte and a daily changing Table D'Hote menu using, wherever possible, fresh produce from the fertile Eden Valley. All this is complemented by an extensive Wine List ranging from honest country wine to mature and complex vintages.

The hotel specialises in fishing and shooting breaks, and can provide fishing on 24 miles of the main River Eden, some of the finest wild brown trout water in the British Isles; salmon fishing on various beats on the lower Eden; grouse and pheasant days can also be arranged. Appleby also boasts a spectacular 18 hole moorland golf course and makes an ideal centre for walking or touring the Lakes, Dales and Eden Valley.

AA/RAC ***, Egon Ronay, Johansens, Ackerman, RAC/ Consort Hotel of the Year 1990/91.

Tufton Arms Hotel
Market Square
Appleby-in-Westmorland
Cumbria CA16 6XA
Tel: (07683) 51593
Fax: (07683) 52761

ABBEY HOUSE HOTEL

This most impressive red sandstone building is a superb and slightly unusual example of the work of the eminent English architect, Sir Edwin Lutyens. It was completed in 1914 as a business guest house and, in its conversion to a graceful hotel of the very highest calibre, virtually all of the magnificently-proportioned rooms have adapted to their new role with minimal disturbance. There is an inherent grandeur and quiet dignity about the hotel equalled only by the fourteen acres of grounds comprising a beautifully balanced mixture of formal gardens and wooded copses. Beyond these lies a splendid vista of mature woodland and meadow interspersed with established walkways which lead to the ruins of nearby Furness Abbey. In less than half-an-hour's drive you are in the centre of the English Lake District with all the historic and picturesque places of interest in and around Grizedale Forest.

Barrow-in-Furness lies on a peninsula with a road bridge to the Isle of Walney, and some tiny isolated islands in and around sheltered bays; Sailing craft complete the coastal picture. Inland excursions bring you to the tarns, fells and pikes of the Cumbrian Mountains.

In less than 20 minutes you can reach the famous Duddon Valley with of course the 'River Duddon', which is one of the most exquisite and celebrated sea trout and salmon rivers in the entire Northern Counties. The members of the small favoured group who make up the Penny Parrock Angling Company welcome visitors to enjoy the pleasures of fishing here. The

Abbey House Hotel will only be too pleased to obtain day tickets for this memorable river.

Abbey House offers impeccable accommodation for business and holiday visitors alike, and the finest a la carte English and French cuisine of the Abbey Restaurant is available to residents and non-residents. Excellent conference and banqueting facilities can be provided. Special discounted rates to Fishing Parties from 4-40 persons.

Abbey House Hotel
Abbey Road
Barrow in Furness
Cumbria LA13 OPA
Tel: (0229) 838282
Fax: (0229) 820403

ENGLAND'S NORTH

The privatisation of British water may have raised the hackles of a number of Labour MP's but for many it is a welcome start to the 'freeing' of a national industry. Water is also a national commodity and it is therefore critical that conservation and capitalism form a happy bond. It is also clear that in addition to essential investment, Water Authorities act in a tough way with industries who abuse the environment in any way. A lobby for tougher punitive fines and perhaps more significantly, compensatory damages to the waters effected should become common practice.

For our purposes, Northern England will take in the superb lakeland scenery with its steep fells, tarns and delightful villages. We will travel south to Lancashire where a number of excellent fisheries can be found. Crossing the Pennines we struggle through the remote and rugged uplands to the contrasting areas of South and North Yorkshire. The dales and peaks of the White Rose County make for stunning countryside. Heading north again through moorlands we arrive in the vast expanse of Northumbria, the unspoiled and undeveloped hinterland contrasting with the cities of Durham, Sunderland and Newcastle-Upon-Tyne. From the Tyne to the Tweed we promise you an exciting and inspiring journey.

CUMBRIAN LAKES AND RIVERS

North West Water who control much of this area's waters are making commendable efforts to upgrade the waters in the region. Restricting netting on the Solway and banning the use of drift nets in the River Eden are just two examples of recent improvements. The hope is, clearly, to see increased runs of migratory fish and we wish them and the NRA all good fortune in this endeavour.

The Border Esk which in part marks the Anglo-Scottish border has been considered in our South Scotland section and, as a result, the first great river we should consider is the **Eden**. The river runs for some seventy miles; at its estuary and for its first 20 miles there is some fine salmon fishing but sadly, the sea-trout fishing could only be described as indifferent.

A few miles south of Carlisle we find a productive stretch under the control of Warwick Hall. The stretch has done quite well for salmon in recent years with May and June being particularly noteworthy months. As you can imagine, the fishing is extremely popular and you will have to be well organised if you wish to fish here. Indeed, a booking some 12 months in advance is probably the best advice I could give, although it is fair to say that the odd day ticket does become available at short notice. There are two people who will be able to help you here; Don Haughin at Keepers Cottage (0228) 60545 and Major Murphy (0228) 61918 at The Annexe. Both are situated at Warwick Hall itself. The Eden is particularly rich in natural food and another location where excellent cuisine can be found is in the Tufton Arms Hotel (0768) 351593. The performance of this stretch of the water is largely determined by water levels and given a good period of rainfall salmon run up to the Appleby area before the close of the season. Indeed, the spawning grounds are not usually reached until very late in the season. Appleby is one such spawning area but it is also good for brown trout. The remaining 50 miles of the river are dominated by some really excellent trouting. The Tufton Arms itself has good

The River Eden   (Cumbria Tourist Board)

access to some first class water on over 23 miles of river and salmon fishing can be arranged from here too. Fishing from the hotel costs in the order of £40 per day and you also have the option of fishing two picturesque tarns which are well stocked with rainbows. The salmon and sea-trout fishing, on estate water lower down the river, ranges from £15 to £50 depending on the season and the beat. The Tufton Arms can arrange tuition aimed at both the beginner and the more experienced fisherman who is seeking to brush up certain aspects of his technique. These courses are a delightful way of enjoying your fishing, combining practical guidance with some fishing on the glorious Eden. Should you also wish to do a little shooting that too can be organised for you. Finally, for the racing enthusiast, the Greystoke Estate is now a renowned training centre for racehorses. Despite the many sporting attractions, we must also emphasise the natural beauty of the Eden Valley which boasts a rugged charm and a wealth of wild life.

The Eden differs from many English rivers in that there are very few stretches retained for private use and a number of fishing clubs have access to good water. It may, therefore, be of help to indicate some useful contacts. The Upper Appleby fishings which are controlled by John Pape are well worth noting. This is a fine stretch for brown trout. It includes five miles of double and single bank, with a maximum of four rods at any one time. The brownies here are wild and furious and a battle royal often ensues to the delight of all lovers of the sport. Permits are £10 per day and are available from Mr Pape's shop; Appleby Shoe and Sports (0768) 352148. Mind you, you'll be lucky to snare the man himself as he's a passionate practitioner of the sport, runs some superb practical courses for small groups and is also

the local chiropodist!

While Appleby may be something of a centre point for those seeking to fish the Eden, Carlisle Angling Association have approximately seven miles of double bank fishing as well as some tidal waters. There are two principal points to note here, firstly, the value is excellent and, secondly, all legal methods are allowed. A permit for the season would cost in the order of £7 for brown trout and sea-trout. A day ticket for salmon fishing will cost £7 up until the end of August when weekly permits are available at £17. All the necessary permits can be obtained from the excellent tackle shop McHardy's (0228) 23988 in South Henry Street, Carlisle.

The Lazonby Estate, a little way north of Carlisle, has approximately four miles of single bank fishing which ranges from £10 to £25 per day. This comprises the lower and upper beats, both of which hold four rods. There is some good salmon fishing here. In 1990, a 29lb beauty was taken from the Hollingstown Pool on the lower beat. Bookings are taken in advance but you need to be quick off the mark to be successful. Please contact Mrs Boyd (0699) 2453 for further details. The Estate can also organise some delightful beck fishing and the moorland streams are also great fun, especially for the beginner. They also provide good sport in the middle of the summer when other fishing is less good. There is a lodge available for hire and guests here receive discounted rates on fishing. Those of you contemplating a move to the area should consider a seasonal rod which gives you one day's fishing per week at a cost of £300 for weekdays or £350 for weekends. Spinning is permitted on the Skye Foot beat. Lovers of shooting should note the facilities

Little Langdale Tarn   (Cumbria Tourist Board)

here - they are outstanding so get in touch if you wish to combine a bit of shooting and fishing. What a splendid thought.

Returning to a somewhat more tranquil scene, we should consider the Penrith Angler's water which is both varied and good. Some five different tickets are available here but perhaps the best value means of enjoying the fishing is to purchase a general weekly ticket. This costs in the region of £40 which covers two miles of fishing on the Eden and stretches of its tributaries, the Lowther, Eamont and Petteril. Contact the Gun and Tackle Shop in Penrith (0768) 62418 for further details. Incidentally, the proprietor Mr Rosling is an experienced fisherman himself and also a mine of local knowledge. If you buy a couple of permits here you will be making a solid investment as this will hopefully give you the opportunity to 'pick his brains' and receive some excellent advice.

The Eden stretches through some really unspoiled land and the Kirkby Stephen and District Anglers Association has some super fishing upstream, some four miles from its source. Here, you find broad grouse moors and beautiful, if somewhat remote open countryside. The Association's water is approximately twelve miles in length and provides a rich variety of fishing. Runs contrast with the many pools and the river itself changes tempo, flowing fast and free then slowing to a more sedate pace. The average weight of fish ranges from ½ to ¾ lb but fish weighing between 2lb and 3lb are not uncommon. There are some excellent lies to be found and trout and grayling fishing are both good at the confluence of the River Belah. Day tickets cost £15 per day and are available from Robinsons in Kirkby Stephen (0768) 371519.

The Eden is a marvellously scenic river yet there are many challenges to its depths. It is a real delight to those who class themselves in the true sportsmans league. The brownies are particularly tricky customers. They have been harried by mink, heron and other predators all their lives and have no intention of succumbing to your fly without putting up a good fight.

To the west is the River **Derwent,** a prime salmon water and one of Cumbria's most important river systems. It runs for some thirty miles and its source at Scafell lies amidst the most beautiful scenery. The river flows through the Borrowdale Valley passing into Derwentwater and Bassenthwaite Lake before it reaches the Irish Sea at Workington. Poaching used to be an enormous problem on this water but the water bailiffs and the NRA have now got the situation pretty well under control. The best months for sea-trout tend to be July and August.

1991 saw an excellent early start to the season with a 12lb fish being taken in early June. Salmon fishing seems to be at its best between July and October. The run may start in late June but this depends on the spring rains and the subsequent water levels. The average weight is in the 9lb region but usually a few fish are taken around the 24lb mark. In 1990, one rod successfully caught some 42 fish in two splendid September days. The brown trout fishing is good and the bigger fish tend to be lower down the river. A large section of the river is owned by the Leckonfield Estate. The fishing is handled by their subsidiary, Castle Fisheries (0900) 826320. The Estate issues a limited number of permits for salmon, sea-trout and brown trout and the chap to talk to is the redoubtable Stan Payne. He has put some twenty years of service into the Estate and knows the

Loweswater   (Cumbria Tourist Board)

ENGLAND'S NORTH

scene intimately. The fishing is normally let to the same people, however, at the time of enquiring some weeks were available. There are six rotating beats of two rods per beat, the cheapest day rod is in the order of £35 and a weekly rod for a renowned time of year (September) would cost £850. Ghillies are also available at a cost of £25 per day. The Derwent is essentially straight forward to fish and wading is no problem. The more successful flies tend to be Stoats Tail, Garry Dog and Shrimp Fly.

There is also some town water details of which can be obtained from the local tourist board (0900) 822634 in Cockermouth. The fishing is available on both banks and the right bank stretches from Derwent Bridge to Harris Mill Bridge and the left spans the water between High Sand Lane and Low Sand Lane and also from the junction of the River Cocker to the prominent N.W.E.B. pylon. The permit charge is £5 per day but you are required to stay within the boundaries, perhaps the best place to stay is the Trout Hotel (0900) 823591. The hotel have the fishing rights on the water behind them but acknowledge that the good beats are available through Castle Fisheries.

Keswick Anglers Association have a two and a half mile stretch which runs from Portinscale to High Stock Bridge in addition to water on the River **Greta** (a less significant salmon and sea trout river.) Day permits for salmon are £16 and £4 is the charge for trout. Weekly tickets range from £62.50 to £20 for salmon and trout respectively. This section of the river flows through farmland which is surrounded on all sides by the Cumbrian Hills. The river can be quite fast flowing in places with good pools allowing for some splendid wet fly fishing with traditional flies. Permits are available from Field and Stream in Main Street, Keswick (0768) 774396. There are a number of stretches where your charm is as important as your casting ability. Workington Anglers Association and Cockermouth Anglers Association are essentially private clubs requiring you to be guests of members. We recommend you scour the local pub for that elusive catch. The fortunate fisherman will find water on a three mile stretch which runs from Carmeadow Bridge to the sea. If the water is below the 2 feet 4 inches guage you must use a fly but if it rises to 3 feet or the water is dirty or coloured then a worm can be used.

Cockermouth and District Anglers Association allow members six guest days per year and they make use of a four mile stretch running through Cockermouth and wooded farmland. Cockermouth is the birthplace of two very different characters; the poet Wordsworth and the mutineer Fletcher Christian of The Bounty. A less renowned 'son' of the area is Mr D.W. Lothian who is a dab hand at fixing your clocks and also has a fair range of tackle (0900) 822006. The River **Cocker** is a significant tributary with good runs of salmon and sea-trout and some first class brown trout fishing. Tickets are available from the Gun Shop in Cockermouth (0900) 822058. The National Trust also have some water and information is available from Wordsworth House (0900) 824805. This is a super place to visit and although fishing is not the best in the world, there are some opportunities and in addition, there are a number of becks in the Derwent system which offer a certain amount of free fishing. Coldale and Newlands Becks which flow into Bassenthwaite Lake are super stretches as are the River Greta and Mosedale Beck. You should always seek permission but essentially fishing is free and accessible, set amidst beautiful scenery.

A little way north of the River Calder, we come to the River **Ehen** which drains Ennerdale Water through Cleator Moor, flowing into the Irish Sea between Seascale and Nethertown. Egremont Angling Association runs about seven miles of desirable bank fishing and also has fishing on Ennersdale Water. A £30 permit allows reasonable salmon and some fine trout fishing. Salmon tend to be best from June to August and permits are available from the Rod and Gun Shop in Egremont (0946) 820368.

The Scawfell Hotel (0946) 728400 has a stretch on the River **Irt** some two miles from the hotel. This includes three quarters of a mile of double bank fishing. Five rods are available and the cost is approximately £15 per day. The water is a lesser known river but the sea-trout and salmon fishing is not bad at all and in the summer months some splendid brown trout fishing can also be enjoyed.

The River **Kent** meanders steadily through from Kentmere Reservoir which is located north of Staveley. Its principal tributaries include the Gowan and Sprint. The river flows through some of the most beautiful countryside in Britain and is a delight to fish. Despite an unfortunate poisoning, the river still provides the game fisherman with some quality sport. The better salmon and sea-trout fishing generally takes place later in the season - from September - and it is fair to say that the river is generally more renowned as a brown trout fishery. There are a number of stretches that can be fished by the nomadic angler as well as some waters that become available, if you're lucky. There is a two to three mile stretch of private water owned by The Levens Hall Estate. The fishing is excellent here but there is a waiting list. What's more, only season tickets are issued. If you are interested, write to The Estate Office, Levens Hall, Kendal, Cumbria. Another private stretch of about one mile which offers some good value day permits (£3 - £5 per day) is found a short distance below Lower Levens Farm. Permits here are available from Olde Peat Cotes, Sampool Lane, Levens, Nr Kendal, Cumbria.

Burnside and District Angling Association has some four miles on the main river which also encompasses the confluence of the River Sprint. Permits can be purchased from either the Burnside Post Office (0539) 726114 or the local boozer, appropriately named the Jolly Angler's Inn (0539) 732552. Although this stretch is some 30 miles from the sea, some impressive 30lb catches have been recorded in the area! All legal methods of fishing are allowed but here's a tip for you; bright orange lures do particularly well.

Staveley is some eight miles from the Kent's source which flows from Kentmere Reservoir. Staveley Angler's Association has approximately four miles of fishing available and permits are obtainable from D. & H. Woof in the Main Street, Staveley (0539) 821253. The cost of the permit will be £5 for a day ticket and an extremely reasonable £40 for a weekly permit. This allows fishing for salmon, sea-trout and brown trout. The salmon run does not tend to peak until late August or early September. A 26lb salmon was recently caught but the cheeky blighter who caught it was not in possession of a rod or line! A fine freehouse in which to hear some good fishing tales is the Eagle and Child, Staveley (0539) 821320. The owner here is Lenny Sosnowsky, a keen fisherman of Russian descent. He has many a yarn, some good local knowledge and pulls a fine pint. Furthermore, he owns the stretch of river which fronts the inn and hosts the local Fly Dressers Guild. This celebrated fishing pub is situated at the confluence of the Rivers Kent and Gowan and is a splendid place to visit. Permits for about 20 nearby tarns of the Windermere and District Angler's Association are also available here.

The largest association on this fine river is the Kent Anglers with approximatelely 8 miles of fishing - five miles stretching downstream of Kendal and three miles upstream, with free town water in between. This is available to visiting fisherman for between £7 and £10 per day and £20 and £40 per week according to the time of season. Fly, spin and worm allowed, although most members prefer to fly as other methods catch to many young fish! Permits are readily available from either Kendal Sports (0539) 721554, 30 Stramongate, Kendal or Mr. V. Carlson at 64 Kirkland (0539) 724867. Kendal, home of the mint cake, is a lovely town on the edge of the Lake District from which to commence any outdoor pursuit. Interestingly this town has one of the few surviving snuff mills and the castle is famous for being the former home of Catherine Parr - the last of the wives of Henry VIII, who actually outlived him.

Closely stalking the direction of the Kent a few miles east is the River **Lune**. This is another river with a good reputation for sea-trout and salmon, running some forty five miles from its source in Ravenstonedale Common, about six miles south of Kirkby Stephen, to its mouth at Lancaster. This important river passes through some celebrated scenery and the angler has the double delight of some fine fishing with a wonderful backdrop.

The upper reaches offer some splendid trout fishing and the Tebay Fishing Club has twenty one miles of double bank fishing. Permits are available from the Cross Keys Inn (0587) 4240 which is handily located a mere quarter of a mile from junction 38 off the M6. The price for a weekly permit ranges from £25 to £50. Anglers staying in the area will be at a considerable advantage when it comes to securing permits. The Kirkby Lonsdale A.A. water near to Tebay and down to Kirkby is particularly well stocked with brownies. As the river becomes wider and deeper the fish become larger. Weekly tickets are available from the Tourist Information Centre in the Main Street (0524) 271437 next door but one to the Royal Hotel. Prices range from £35 to £50 per week.

There is also some good fishing for wild brown trout around Sedbergh. Lowis' in the Main Street issue weekly tickets. Although there are still nets in the estuary, there is some fine salmon fishing in the lower reaches of the river. Mrs Anne Curwen (0524) 770078 sells day tickets on behalf of the Lancaster and District Angler's Association. For salmon, sea-trout and brown trout, prices will vary depending on the day but are usually between £10 and £17. Visitors should note, however, that these permits are only issued on weekdays. This is not a major worry as there are all manner of other opportunities for fishing locally. The stretch covered by this water runs for one and a half miles and provides good fishing for salmon and sea-trout. Mrs Carwen also sells tickets for the NRA's Halton Fishery which cost £6 to £11 per night (8.00pm to 4.00am). Mr Shallis at the Halton Stores and Off Licence (handy for all night vigils) can also supply day permits for the Halton beats and day and night permits for the Skerton beats. This is excellent value fishing and sea-trout are, despite the ravages of UDN, well worth going for. The waters vary, with the upper beat sluggish in character, while below Forge Weir the river offers fast runs and a succession of rocky pools. If you are planning to fish at night it is critical to familiarise yourself with the nature of the river-

bed and locals advise chest waders for all but a few of the pools. The best fishing runs from late June through July although unusually, the lower reaches of the river have a run of fresh sea-trout until the close of the season in mid-October. The favoured salmon waters are the Halton beats at higher river levels, with two feet to three feet being the best for spinning, with fly and shrimp coming into their own when the water is down to one foot. However, the lower beat is fly-only but the Toby and Koster are fine in heavy waters. The Garry Dog is popular in the spring and autumn, while the Stoats Tail and Munro Killer are effective in the summer and early autumn. The Mallard and Claret used on the dropper is another first class way of maximising your chances with the sea-trout. Do book up well in advance and hope for a good spate as algae can be a problem.

Despite the excellence of the river systems in Cumbria, there are a number of excellent fisheries and reservoirs, not to mention the numerous tarns, becks and lakes. The border country is particularly well blessed and the countryside is delightfully unspoiled. Fell walking, riding, bird-watching and fishing are just some of the outdoor pursuits to be enjoyed. Border Game Fisheries Ltd are based in Longtown, Cumbria (0228) 791108 and have a number of fishing opportunities including day tickets for fishing on the Esk priced at £12 to £50, as well as a number of other excellent stretches on other northern rivers. The company also has 60 acres of land with two lakes of 10 and 15 acres which make up Oakbank Fisheries. There is also a preserved marshland with covered observation huts, grassland walks and nature woodlands. Oakbank Lake is restricted to fly fishing from the bank but Barn Lake offers some boats and has some limited fishing. The waters are regularly stocked with rainbow and some browns and a catch and release policy has resulted in fish up to 8lb. Some two miles from Hadrian's Wall, we find the New Mills Trout Farm. The Romans quarried stone from Quarry beck and this is where you will find this well run farm. The farm is essentially dealing with catering and restocking planning but also provides a pleasant excuse for some good fishing in picturesque surroundings. Finally, if you haven't caught anything in years, the Ford Pool is a place to lift the spirits.

Watendlath Fishery (07687) 77293 near Borrowdale is another for the shortlist. It is generally a late starter due to its location but is well stocked with fish as well as having wild browns. The water is open from Easter to the end of October from 8.00am to dusk and there is a limit of 12 rods per day so advance booking is essential. The scenery here is magnificent and outside July and August, the waters are often secluded so the fishing is very peaceful indeed. The water is fly only and barbless hooks are required. Boats are available at a charge of £11 per day and there is a bag limit here of four fish. Alternatively, a half-day ticket is priced at £9 with a bag limit of two fish.

Kentmere Tarn (0539) 821002 is situated on the floor of the Kentmere Valley, surrounded by hills creating a beautifully secluded spot. Deer and badgers lurk in the nearby woods and the wildfowl add further colour to the scene. The water covers a total of ten acres and is stocked with browns although wild ones and the odd indigenous salmon can be caught in these 20 feet depths. The season runs from mid March to the end of September and a charge of £10 a week is levied for the visiting angler (£5 per day). From the banks, anglers may fish with fly or bait and there is a boat for hire for fly fishing only. A similar

ENGLAND'S NORTH

summary can be applied to Pinfold lake at Raisbeck which once again is rich in flora and fauna. The lake itself is stocked with rainbow and is open all year. The water covers four acres and there is a four rod limit and a four fish limit too. The water may be fished by fly only and the four fish day ticket is priced at £14. This lake is particularly convenient for the M6 motorway which is only five minutes drive away, exit at junction 38. Despite the presence of this major road the area is unspoiled and peaceful. Tickets are obtainable from John Pape (07683) 52148 in the Market place at Appleby-In-Westmoreland.

Those of you keen to take the family on a sporting holiday should consider the Lake District - it offers some marvellous opportunities but do not expect a peaceful holiday if you go 'in season' as this is a very popular place for tourists. Bigland Hall Country Sports Ltd. (05395) 31361 offers clay pigeon shooting, archery, windsurfing, a riding centre and most importantly 16 acres of fishing away from the 'madding' crowd. The water is well stocked with rainbows, the record fish being 12lb. The number of rods is strictly controlled and you should endeavour to book well in advance. The day permit costs some £15 with an evening charge of £10.50. If you can't manage to pack your own then rod hire is £8 per day.

Esthwaite water is another for the short list. It lies amidst the more gentle hills of the southern lakeland and is unusual in that it is the only major Cumbrian lake commercially stocked with rainbows. The water is controlled by the Hawkshead Trout Farm (09666) 541 and is popular with locals and visitors. The scenery is once again superb and the fish, often tending to congregate at the end of the lake, are great fighters - this may

be due to the fact that the pike, for which this lake is renowned, are monstrously large. The browns, ever keen to avoid these freshwater sharks are both elusive and fight like tigers when hooked. Day tickets are priced at £8.50 and there is a bag limit of four fish. Weekly and season tickets are priced at £32 and £145 respectively. Those anglers may take two fish per visit. There are 12 boats for hire priced at £7 per day. You may fly fish, spin or use bait but no maggots are allowed. The fishery's record for a brown trout is 4lb 4oz and 11lb 8oz for a rainbow. The largest pike weighed in at 37lb!

Heading northwards, we arrive at Lamplugh and Cogra Moss (0900) 823638, a 41 acre lake which offers fly fishing for the resident brown trout and stocked rainbows. The water is open daily from sunrise to an hour after sunset and tickets are available from West Lothian in Cockermouth (0900) 822006. Cogra Moss enjoys a perfect setting amidst hills and forests. There are several island accessible to anglers, except one built by the RSPB for wild fowl, currently inhabited by nesting grebes. Season tickets are £75 with a limit of four fish per day while day tickets cost £8 with a similar catch restriction.

There are a whole host of delightful small tarns, in fact a number all share the same name which is very confusing! These are often remote and rugged waters but are a delight to fish. Burnmore tarn is a two mile walk from the isolated village of Bouth. The sport however can be marvellous not to mention idyllic! Then there are the vast waters of Coniston. Tickets for these waters are available from the Tourist Centre (05394) 41533. Salmon are far from abundant in the water but the brown trout are quite prolific as is the less common char, a landlocked

Janet's Foss, River Ribble   (N.R.A. Leeds)

ENGLAND'S NORTH

relative of the salmon. The char generally inhabits deeper sections of the lake which can be up to 180 feet in places. The popular way of fishing for these super game fish is to trail a small spinner from a light rod - great sport if you find the depth at which they are feeding.

Ullswater is another splendid large lake to fish. Trout here are generally free rising and drifts around Pooley Bridge and Howtown Bay can be especially productive. Night rises can also be excellent, given good weather on such an evening you will surely be a happy chappie. It is a majestic lake and a splendid scene against the craggy backdrop of Place Fell. Boats are available for hire from Glenridding in the south or Pooley Bridge at the northern end.

Windermere is also good for fishing but it gets horribly crowded in the summer. However, despite all the distractions, brown trout fishing can be good and fish up to 4lb are regularly caught. The lake is effectively divided into two by Belle Isle and the Lake's several large islands are noted spots, indeed boat fishing tends to be favoured, contact the Tourist Information Centre in Windermere for further details. This is an excellent lake and in the early morning and evening fishing can be memorable. Boats can be hired in Ambleside (05394) 33187 or Bowness on Windermere (09662) 3360.

LANCASTRIAN WATERS

The River **Ribble** probably deserves the prize as Lancashire's most prolific fresh water. However, Yorkshire, the county of the White Rose, should also receive some acclaim for the Ribble has its source in the North Riding on Cam Fell, some eight miles north of Settle. There can be no doubt, however, that the principle waters are in Red Rose country. The best returns for the game fisherman tend to be upstream of the rivers confluence with its two main tributaries the Hodder and the Calder. Few salmon or sea-trout journey beyond Settle and the water tends to be regarded as a good water at the back end of the season with salmon still swimming upstream in October.

The river is tied up with a number of fishing associations and some clubs have a guest day, however, only limited water is available to visitors. Some fishing is possible and the Ribble Valley Borough Council have two stretches above the bridge at Brungerley and at Edisford Bridge. Permits are available from Ken Varey (0200) 23267. Fishing costs £4 per day and £9 per week and there is a bag limit of three fish.

The Mitton Fishery which is controlled by the NRA is a fine stretch to note. Tickets are available from Mrs Haynes at Mitton Hall farm (0254) 86281. There are 10 permits available for salmon and sea-trout and prices vary between £6 to £11 per day. A brown trout permit will set you back some £3 but only four are available per day and there is a daily bag limit of six. The methods allowed tend to vary with the water level and fly only fishing is permitted when the level is below the mark stipulated on Mitton Bridge. Fly and spinning are possible when the river rises over the mark. However, from the marker post at Hodder Foot to, and including, the River Calder's confluence, spinning, fly and worm fishing can be carried out at all levels. The neighbouring stretch of water is owned by Townson Brothers (0200) 41542 who issue season tickets at £150. This section of the Ribble makes for a delightful scene and is an ideal spot for the fisherman. It runs through lush green pastures and the

neighbouring farmland has both dairy and sheep farming - in short a peaceful place to escape to. Great Mitton itself is a charming village with two friendly alehouses at which to celebrate or quench your thirst.

The Royal Oak, Settle (0729) 822561 is another splendid establishment. On this occasion, a former coaching inn dating from 1684. The hotel sells permits at £12 per day on the Settle Angler's Association stretch which is fly-only water and runs for approximately seven miles, five of which are double bank fishing.

The River **Hodder** is a large tributary of the Ribble. The river starts life on Burn Moor, flowing through Stocks Reservoir before joining the Ribble at Great Mitton. The river is largely preserved which is a pity as some great sport is to be found. There are however, some spots available, for instance, a one mile stretch on the Slaidburn Estate. Permits are available from The Jam Pot in Slaidburn (0200) 6225 and are priced at £7 and £20 for a day and week respectively. This is another delightful spot in which to fish surrounded by vast expanses of Lancashire moorland. The village pub, the Hark to Bounty is a fine place to whet your whistle. The Hodder Bridge Hotel (0254) 826216 is another hostelry to shortlist. It has a private 600 yard stretch and can organise good and inexpensive fishing on the Rivers Ribble and Hodder. The Inn at Whitewell (02008) 222 overlooks, and has the rights to approximately four miles of the Hodder. Costs vary significantly with the season. Day tickets range from £9 to £20. This is a beautiful part of Lancashire and the riverbank setting quite superb.

Bank House Fishery is situated in the picturesque Lune Valley at the edge of Caton Village, some two miles from the M6 (junction 34). This man-made water has been thoughtfully landscaped of late, with several secluded islands and a number of casting jetties. The water is well stocked with brown and rainbow trout and provides excellent fishing. Some 500 yards away we find a more illustrious water, the River Lune. Rods are limited here which adds to the feeling of seclusion. The record rainbow weighed in at 13lb - so you can see the inmates are very large. There is a bag limit of four fish per day and two fish for an evening or for a half rod. The season runs from March to the end of October and a day ticket is £16.50 and £10 for an evening or half rod. You are advised to book in advance and can do so by contacting Bank House (0524) 770412. Stocks Fishery (05242) 61305 is another well run fishery in Clitheroe. Should you need to contact them after the start of the season in March then try the Fishing Lodge (02006) 602. The fishery has a superb moorland setting in the Hodder Valley, close to the source of this celebrated river, as well as the trout, deer, rabbit and all manner of wildlife inhabit the environs. Bank fishing is permitted from 8.30am until an hour after sunset. Boat fishing is possible from 8.30am until sunset itself. The Lodge is located a mile off the Slaidburn to High Bentham Road. There are numerous charges here, but a day permit costs £10. Rowing boats and outboard motors can also be hired and tackle is available too. One of the delights of Stocks is the abundant wildlife and all visitors to the area are asked to tread with care! This is a well run fishery with an impressive catch rate.

The nearby Trout Fishery at Whalley (0254) 822211 is also worth noting. It is stocked with rainbows and has a number of wild browns. The fishery is open from the 15th March to the end of September for brownies and throughout the year for rainbows. Some 36 rods per day and fly fishing only is allowed with barbless hooks. There are some large fish here and a day ticket will cost some £14.50 with a limit of four fish. A five hour ticket is £6 cheaper and a father and son ticket good value at £11.50. There is a two fish limit here. There are three double boats available for hire at £6 per day and a single boat at £4. The fishery is situated amidst the shadows of Pendle Hill, witches and all, and the scenery is beautiful. The Pennine Trout Fishery (0706) 378325 is another extremely popular fishery with some monstrous fish lurking its 30 feet depths. There are two lakes with a total surface of five acres. It is close to Greater Manchester but despite this, bookings are generally only required for weekends or Bank Holidays. It is open 24 hours with night fishing by floodlight which should suit all insomniacs. There is little chance of nodding off either - the 11lb brown or 24lb rainbow which were taken here should have everyone on their toes. The Top Lake has 28 rods and the Bottom Lake 12. Four hours fishing costs £10.50 and eight hours £16. There is a two fish limit for the shorter stint and three for the eight hours. If you catch an additional fish you may keep it provided you fork out an extra £3.50. If it's an 11 pounder then that is good value!

Hurleston Hall (0704) 841026 is another fishery that merits attention. It is situated at Scarisbrick on the A570, Southport Road, a mile or so from Ormskirk. This is a place with a past and there are legends involving ghosts, civil war relics and tunnels for escaping prisoners. This is a haven for spooks and sportsmen alike and the rainbows range from 1lb 8oz to 15lb. The water is restricted to fly-only, barbless hooks (maximum size 8). A full day's fishing will cost £9, five and three hours are priced at £6 and £4 respectively. There are some good rates for juniors and rods can be hired for £3. All fish taken are costed at £1.70 per pound. Ironically, the water is known as the friendly fishery - one can only assume that the ghosties are similarly inclined!

Preston is well served by trout fisheries and Rawcliffe (0253) 700279 is one suggestion. The fishery lies some six miles from Blackpool and tickets are priced at £7 per half day or £4 for an evening. Barbless hooks are once again required and your prey will be rainbows or wild browns. The lake is small but well worth a peep. The Twin Lakes Trout Fishery (0772) 601093 at Croston is well worth a visit too. It comprises two six acre lakes and the North Lake is fly-only. Opening hours range from 8.00am to dusk until October and thereafter from 8.00am to 4.30pm. Tickets cost £15.30 per day with a four fish limit and five hours is a little over £9 with a two fish limit. The lake is stocked three times a week with rainbows. The fish are often in double figures in weight and the fishery record currently stands at 15lb 4oz. Tuition is available by arrangement along with rod hire. There are excellent facilities including a tackle shop and licenced bar - another good excuse for an afternoon's sport here.

THE DALES

The River **Aire** offers trout and grayling fishing in its upper reaches where it is a typical tumbling dales river. Heavy brown trout are recorded downstream of Gargrave and in the Skipton area. Keighley Angling Club has approximately 14 miles of fishing and day tickets are available from various tackle shops in the area for as little as £2 per day. Willis Walker in Keighley (0535) 602928 and K. Tackle (0756) 794451 handle the permits

for Skipton Angler's Association who have three miles of double bank fishing. Saltaire Angler's Association has a further two miles, again all double bank, and you should contact the Shipley Angling Centre (0274) 595726 for more information. It is fair to say that the Aire in its lower reaches is polluted, but the game fishing in its upper reaches is well worth sampling and, as you might imagine, the setting is somewhat more attractive in these remote parts too.

It would not be too outrageous to suggest that fishing in the north and west of Yorkshire is somewhat superior to that in the south of this large county. The River **Wharfe** is a delightful and extremely popular river. The water has numerous fishing opportunities and the game fisherman will find some fine trout fishing. This is generally in the upper reaches of the river and around Bolton Bridge, Burnsall and Grassington.

The Wharfe rises in Langstrothdale and in its upper reaches the water passes through dramatic upland country. It has fast rushing waterfalls combined with long slow glides and an abundance of tree lined banks. After Otley, it becomes an altogether more sedate water and thereafter coarse fish are increasingly prevalent. The season spans the months of April, through summer to September. Bradford City Angling Association has a two mile stretch near to the village of Buckden and day permits are available from the Buck Inn (075676) 227. The New Inn, Appletreewick (075672) 252 also has a number of permits for their short beat which spans a quarter of a mile.

Linton, Threshfield and Grassington Angling Club control two miles of water in the environs of the village of Linton. The Devonshire Arms Hotel (0756) 752525 issues day permits for this fly-only water which is restricted to members only on Sundays. Between Grassington and the village of Barden we find seven miles of single and double bank fishing. Day tickets are available from the Red Lion at Burnsall (0756) 72204. Fly fishing is permitted and there is a six fish limit. Brown trout costs £16 per day and grayling £8 per day. Another splendid location is on the Duke of Devonshire's Estate at Bolton Abbey (075671) 227. There are five miles of double bank fishing here and the charge is £10 per day with a bag limit of four fish. The average weight is 1lb but the best fish last year weighed in at 2½ lb. The river at this point is still fast flowing and strewn with rocks. The Estate have their own hatcheries and as a result the waters are well stocked. Tickets are also available from the splendid Devonshire Arms Hotel (075671) 441.

Should you be an angler who also enjoys a beverage or two then visit The Tennants Arms, Kilnsey (0756) 752301. The Keeper for the Kettlewell to Kilnsey stretch issues permits here between 9.00am and 10.00am and prices are in the order of £10 per day. Although the large conurbations of South Yorkshire are relatively close by, much of the river is isolated and tranquil and some fine sport can be anticipated.

Similar charm and scenery can be found on many stretches of the River **Nidd**, another tributary of the Ouse System. The river's source is on Great Whernside from where it flows to Nidderdale, past Pateley Bridge and Knaresborough. Most of the water is controlled by local angling associations but a number of day tickets can be found.

Great Whernside reveals bleak moorland, akin to that of the Bronte novels. The river initially feeds two reservoirs and its

ENGLAND'S NORTH

character is shallow and rocky in its infancy. As the river flows from Gouthwaite Reservoir, it takes on an enlarged character. Here, its steep banks are predominantly tree-lined and the scene is a real delight. Nidderdale Angling Club controls eight miles in the area of Pateley Bridge. Day tickets are available from the Royal Oak Hotel (0423) 780200 situated on the village green at Dacre, ten miles from Harrogate on the A59. Theakstones bitter is brewed in nearby Masham and adds further attraction to this delightful area.

The York and District Angler's Association waters are not as renowned as those one finds further upstream. Nevertheless, day tickets can be purchased from the tackleist P. H. & J. R. Smith, High Street Knaresborough (0423) 863322, which lies opposite the Little Elephant pub. The staff here are extremely helpful and will advise you on various good waters in the vicinity. Some of the best water is retained by the Harrogate Fly Fishers but sadly the water is restricted to members and their guests. Such is life! There is some fine fishing available, a number of outstanding real ales to sample and some really tremendous countryside which the trout, as you will perhaps find out, are far from happy to leave!

The River **Ure** holds some good trout and stretches for some forty five miles from Abbotside Common to its confluence with the Swale at Boroughbridge. Although trout are present throughout the water, they are more prolific in the reaches above Middleham where some 5lb brown trout are taken each year, a couple of 8lb fish have been reported, so be prepared!

Wensleydale Anglers Association has some four miles of dou-

ble bank fishing on the Ure and day tickets can be obtained from the Rose and Crown Hotel (0969) 50225 on Bainbridge village green. Permits cost £16 a day and £12 a week and fishing can also be enjoyed on the River **Bain,** this is a delightful little river that provides some fine fishing for browns and grayling. Palmer Flatts Hotel (0969) 663228 some five minutes down from the wild Aysgarth Falls has a small stretch which is free to guests and some £2 a day for non-residents. Further good fishing can be purchased from Lewis Country Wear in Hawes (0969) 667443 who represent the Hawes and High Abbotside Anglers Association. Dry and wet fly as well as worm fishing is allowed from 24th March to October lst.

The River **Swale** shares many characteristics with its near neighbour the Ure. It provides an ever changing scene with deep slow-moving bends and contrasting fast flowing runs. The water is renowned for chub and barbel but some good trout fishing can also be enjoyed in the upper reaches, particularly above Richmond. The Northallerton Angling Club have some five miles of single bank available for non-members below Morton Bridge on the Northallerton to Bedale Road. Permits cost £3 per day and a 4lb brown trout was taken here in June 1991. Permits are obtainable from 'Angling' (0609) 779140 in Northallerton. W. Metcalfe, Guns and Tackle, Richmond (0748) 822108 issues permits for the Richmond and District Angling Club for £12 a week and offers approximately eight to nine miles of double bank fishing between Maske Bridge and Brompton-on-Swale.

Despite its rural splendour and its many rivers, Yorkshire only lays claim to one salmon river, the **Esk**. As you can imagine, the

Artist: **D.F. Dane** *WAITING* *Courtesy of:* **Rosenstiels'**

ENGLAND'S NORTH

Yorkshire folk are proud of this particular water but they are not overly possessive and day tickets can be bought. In recent times, the river has suffered from low water and some have even written it off as a salmon and sea-trout river. This seems a trifle premature and invariably some good fish are landed particularly towards the end of the season.

The NRA have embarked upon a smolt re-introduction scheme which is producing good results and which augurs well for the future. As the environment continues to play havoc and the demands on the water supply become ever greater the situation on the Esk will be fascinating to watch.

The Esk rises on Westerdale Moor and runs into the sea at Whitby. There are fine stocks of brown trout in the many moorland beats which flow into the Esk. The river is largely controlled by the Esk Fishery Association but a number of very attractive stretches are accessible. The Egton Estate (0947) 85466 has a delightful one and a half mile stretch of double bank fishing which holds three rods. There are some fine holding pools and the brown trout are prolific here. Permits range from £9 to £15 per day to include salmon.

Woodlands Hall (0947) 811180 some four miles from Whitby has some superbly scenic waters in the Yorkshire National Park. Permits can be obtained from £10 to £15. Always phone in advance as only two rods per day are permitted. The water includes two salmon pools and three trout runs. John Hobbs will help you with your enquiries here and the nearby Mallyan Spout Hotel (0947) 86206 is one for the notebook.

The North Yorks Steam Railway which has a delightful journey through the Yorkshire woodlands from Grosmont to Pickering. This is a quaint intrusion into a relatively quiet untroubled world. Danby Angling Club has some seven miles of double bank fishing and the brown trout fishing here is good. Tickets are available at a cost of £5 from the Duke of Wellington (0287) 660351 which stands proudly in the middle of Danby.

Although much of the fishing is kept on a tight rein and is closely preserved, the Ruswarp Pleasure Boat Company in Ruswarp (0947) 604658 leases one and a half miles from the Esk Fishery Association from the weir at Ruswarp to Iburndale Beck. This allows some really good value fishing and the possibility that the salmon will return in ever increasing numbers in the years to come - fingers crossed anyway!

The Recreational Department of Yorkshire Water have created some fine fishing opportunities in well stocked reservoirs in the region. But beware, coin operated systems are used at many of the waters in the Yorkshire region so take plenty of change with you.

Not all the fisheries are run by the Authority and the Cleatham Fishery (0724) 855972 is one such example. Although the fishery is a mere four miles from the M18 it is surrounded by agricultural countryside and woodland. The water has a popular catch and release system but four fish can be taken for £10. Heading westwards, we arrive at Hepworth and Heathcote Trout Fishery (0274) 877498. This is a delightful two acre lake set amidst ten acres of woodland. It is stocked with rainbows, brown trout and Arctic char. There is an interesting policy as any fish over 4lb must be returned. The owner Mr Ted Heathcote-Walker believes that big fish are seldom eaten and often end up

in the bin! The policy, therefore, is to leave them and let others enjoy the challenge as they become increasingly weighty. There are several big fish in these waters, one of which was 24lb 8oz, however, it was not a record as it was not killed. Tuition is available and the first lesson is free - an excellent idea. Recently, a blind person learnt to fish here and caught a 12 pounder!

The Washburn Valley Fisheries are made up of four reservoirs including the excellent Fewston and Swinsty. Each water is in excess of 150 acres and all are regularly stocked with brown trout and rainbows. The season can run from mid March until the end of October and the fisheries are open daily from 7.30am. Children under the age of 15 may fish without a permit if accompanied by an experienced adult who does possess a permit. Fewston is easy to find, on the A59 road between Harrogate and Blubberhouses Moor. Fewston is restricted to fly-only fishing whilst Swinsty allows some bait fishing. The Authority is endeavouring to encourage all manner of recreation on the reservoirs but but this will not be allowed to detract from the fishing.

Another water which boasts a number of attractions is the Kilnsey Park Water (0756) 752150 which is set in the heart of the delightful Yorkshire dales. This is a relatively friendly introduction to fly fishing but the scenery is beautiful and there is a catch and return policy in operation at the lake. Tickets are available from the farm shop for a full or half day's fishing. The waters are regularly stocked by the adjoining trout farm which also supplies the shop. As you can see, this will appeal to the casual fisherman. Furthermore, the 'Daleslife' Visitor Centre has a unique aquarium of freshwater fish which are beautifully displayed and labelled. The Fly Fishing in Wharfedale Exhibition provides a visual account of the sport in the area.

Leighton Reservoir (0765) 689224 is another extremely popular fishery, situated on the edge of the windy Masham Moor. The water is controlled by Swainton Estate who have their own hatchery. Browns of 5lb and rainbows of 10lb are commonly caught. Season tickets are available and the fishery is open from late March to the end of November. A four fish day ticket will cost in the region of £8. There is a coin operated system here too so take plenty of change.

NORTHUMBRIA

The River **Tees** has a remote Pennine setting in Cumbria's Cross Fell. The brown trout is the prolific species of game fish to be found on the Tees and the best locations are generally in the upper reaches. The waters between Middleton in Teesdale and a short distance further downstream at Barnard Castle are particularly recommended. The grayling also revel in the faster flowing parts of the upper reaches and Barnard Castle is once again a popular location. Serious pollution in the industrialised areas of Middlesborough have restricted salmon and sea-trout runs but there is much work being done to try and redress the balance. It will take time, effort and money but let us hope that this once notable salmon river recovers some of its esteem.

The Raby Estate Office (0833) 40209 have some good brown trout fishing on nine miles of the river's north bank. The fee is £5.50 per day with a big limit of four. The Estate office is located opposite the Teesdale Hotel and tickets can also be obtained from the High Force Hotel (0833) 22264. The Teesdale Hotel (0833) 40264 should not be overlooked as they issue day tick-

ets for the Strathmore Estate who own the South Bank. The price of £5.50 is identical as Raby Estate. The upper reaches are set amidst some delightful scenery and High Force is a celebrated landmark. If there is a good head of water, the falls are truly spectacular and well worth a detour.

The River **Wear** rises on Burnhope Seat to the west of the county, amidst the delightful ragged fells where Cumbria borders Durham. It flows east, a distance of some 65 miles through Stanhope, Bishop Auckland and Durham before it spills into the North Sea at Sunderland. Some serious anti-pollution work and a gradual re-stocking programme have ensured the river's renaissance and the game angler can now enjoy some fine sea-trout fishing. The salmon runs could not be described as substantial but they are progressing which is tremendous to report.

Bishop Auckland and District Angling Club have approximately 20 miles available for day tickets which range from £5 to £20 depending on the season. The higher price is naturally charged in the later months when the salmon and sea-trout fishing comes into its own. Assuming a good level of rainfall, the river fishes well, particularly late in the season. Season tickets can be had from the Secretary, J. Winter (0388) 762538 and day tickets from Windrow Sports in Bishop Auckland (0388) 603759. The Club also have one mile on the River Browney which joins the Wear at Sunderland Bridge; this tributary offers good brown trout fishing.

The Upper Wear behaves more like a spate river and if there has been sufficient rainfall, sea-trout can be good at the back end of the season and salmon also come up to a mile or so below St John's Chapel, some 40 miles from the sea. The Upper Weardale Angling Club has some six miles of water here and permits can be obtained from the Post Office or the Golden Lion (0388) 537231 beside the cattle market. The sea-trout tend to be most prolific in September and October and dependent on summer rainfalls which sometimes arrive earlier. In other words, keep in tune with the summer weather!

Energetic work in re-stocking and the closure of several collieries, together with an improved attitude to pollution by a number of industries. The Wear has seen some great improvements but it is still shadowed by its more illustrious and much improved sister, the **Tyne**. This is a tremendous credit to the water companies and all involved but pollution incidents still occur and a recent spill resulted in tragic consequences. At the time of writing, the culprit had not been traced but it does go to show how tough a job it is keeping the water of Britain free from pollution.

The North Tyne flows out of the massive Kielder Water and joins the South Tyne near Hexham. Thereafter, the Tyne flows through Corbridge, Prudhoe and Newcastle before arriving at the North Sea at Tynemouth. The river journeys through some delightful Northumberland scenery and there are a number of fishing opportunities for the visiting angler. Falstone Fishing Club have a good two mile stretch of double bank fishing. Permits are available from the Black Cock Inn (0434) 240200. This charming 380 year old inn sits next to the church and is a fine spot if you happen to like real ale. A 7th century cross was discovered here in the 1950's so keep your eyes open for similar relics! Day tickets are £10 a day and £25 a week. The George at Chollerford (0434) 681611 also have water on the North

Tyne. The fishing here is excellent value for residents and the setting is absolutely enchanting. The Northumberland Angler's Federation has three good stretches of approximately five miles which is well stocked with brown trout. Salmon were making a good showing in 1991. The only ticket that is currently available is a 14 day permit which costs £35 and includes one and a half miles on the River Coquet. Permits are available from the Head Bailiff, Mr Bagnall at Thirston Mill, West Thirston (0670) 787663. There are a number of opportunities for fishing the Tyne with a premier beat eight miles east of Hexham which covers a three mile stretch which can be fished from both banks. There is some first class fishing here with some good salmon being taken in 1991. The best months for salmon are from February to May and September to October with sea-trout fishing from May onwards, although September is the best month where both fly and spinning is permitted. Mr A.F. Pollard of Reeltime Fishing Services (0661) 843799 will assist with enquiries. Season rods offer one manned day per week and occasional day rods.

The North and South Tynes are generally fast running rivers which favour dry fly trout fishing. Deep pools near Haltwhistle can be found and trout in the 5lb bracket are lurking - so be prepared! The North Tyne has a number of fine beats; some five miles north of Hexham; Chollerford; up river between Wark and Simonhorn; above Wark as well as various other beats. Salmon run from March onwards, with March, April and May being good months. September and October are also extremely good and are the two prime months for sea-trout which tend to run from June onwards. The beats are mainly let on a weekly basis and you should contact Mr Gaisford at J. M. Clarke and Partners on (0434) 602301 for all the details. The South Tyne has some quality association waters. The river requires good water and when in spate provides some fine fishing. The salmon run from May with August through to October being the favoured times. Sea-trout will run from June given good water but the best months are again September and October. Weekly permits are available and you are advised to contact Greggs Sports in Haltwhistle (0434) 320255 for further details. Finally, Haydon Bridge Angling Club offers visitors who are staying in the area weekly permits. Details can be obtained from the splendid Langley Castle Hotel (0434) 688888. If you are looking for good fishing in England, the Tyne provides a plethora of good opportunities.

The River **Rede** is a tributary of the Tyne that is well worth exploring and two excellent places from which to plan your attack are The Percy Arms (0830) 20261 and The Otterburn Tower (0830) 20620 - two extremely pleasant establishments in which to stay.

The delightful Northumbrian scenery reveals a number of other splendid rivers for the visiting angler. The River **Wansbeck** is tied up with private syndicates and Clubs but there is a two mile stretch below Morpeth at Wansbeck Riverside Park. It is owned by the council and has produced some good trout in recent years. Permits can be purchased from the Park Warden in Green Lane, Ashington (0670) 812323.

The River **Coquet** is a delightful water which rises in the wilds of the Cheviot Hills and flows through Rothbury and, after some 40 miles, enters the North Sea at Warkworth. This is a good game fishing river with salmon, sea-trout and brown trout all to be found. The Coquet is generally regarded as a late river with a good run of salmon and sea-trout well into October. The Northumberland Angling Federation lease waters from the Duke of Northumberland and this comprises some eleven miles of fishing which is spread along the river and includes a variety of waters. 1991 reports for the river looked good with salmon and brown trout prolific. If you are seeking advice or information on the Coquet contact The Sports Shop in Fawcett's Yard, Morpeth (0670) 514760. For visitor's tickets and salmon fishing contact Mr Bagnall at Thirston Mill, Felton (0670) 787663. The Whitton Farmhouse Hotel (0669) 20811, next to Whitton's Riding Stables, also issues 14 day trout permits for the NAF. The Angler's Arms Hotel (0665) 570655 at Weldon Bridge also has a small stretch which provides more fine brown trout fishing. Furthermore, in September and October, some great value salmon fishing can be had for £7.50 a day. The Angler's Arms is a classic coaching inn remotely situated beside the bridge where the A697 crosses the Coquet. It is a classic country pub and the nearest neighbours tend to be oyster catchers and goosanders.

Rothbury and Thropton Angling Club have three and a half miles of single bank fishing. Permits cost in the region of £8 per day and are available from the Thropton Village Shop (0669) 20412, beside the The Three Wheat Heads. Night fishing for sea-trout is also permitted here should you be keen on night fishing, or if you are an insomniac.

Murraysport in Alnwick (0665) 602462 handle a good private beat on the Coquet, The Weldon Water, which offers two miles of mainly double bank fishing and also has some fine pools. However, rods are limited to only two per day and day tickets cost £10 between February and August and £15 for the months of September and October.

The River **Aln** is comparatively short and flows into the sea at Alnmouth. The Aln Angler's Association, who control a seven mile stretch downstream from Denwick Bridge, is a working trust and all monies are reinvested into the upkeep of the river. This is fly water and includes some tidal waters where the sea-trout and salmon are most prolific. In 1989, a weighty 17lb sea-trout was caught and 4 to 9lb are regularly caught here. The Silver Doctor is the fly which locals recommend. Fish tend to run in February and March and September and October. The water also provides some fine brown trout sport and comes into its own in the late spring and summer months. There are only weekly or monthly tickets available and the weekly permit will set you back £20. There is no Sunday fishing for visitors. Permits can be obtained from R. L. Johnson (0665) 602135, beside the Hotspur Tower in Alnwick or from Murraysport (0665) 602462.

Lockwood Beck is one of several waters in the Durham and Cleveland area. It is pleasantly secluded, situated just north of the A171 Guisborough to Whitby Road. A total of five streams and three becks run into the reservoir and fishing takes place from boats as well as from the banks of the reservoir which is well stocked with brown and rainbow trout. The area is set amidst some beautiful woods and mallards, tufted ducks and great crested grebes are among a number of frequent visitors. Curlew and woodcock also abound in the wooded area beyond. The reservoir is limited to fly fishing and is managed by the Northumbrian Water Authority. Tickets are usually dispensed from a machine for both day and evening fishing.

One of the delights of reservoir fishing is that it often takes you to some wonderful places and Balderhead (0833) 40589 is no exception. This reservoir, which spans some 270 acres, is ten miles from Barnard Castle and situated on open, hilly moorland. Peregrine falcon will be your companions here, together with a variety of other wildlife. The day tickets are priced at £4 and there is no bag limit which is of great value. Should you not have a licence, an extra £1.25 is charged. Check before you plan your visit that the lake is not being used for watersports. For the up to date brochure of the various options available in the north east you should contact the Northumbrian Water Recreation Department (091)-383 2222.

Tunstall Reservoir (0388) 527293 lies in the valley of Waskerley Beck, three miles north of Wolsingham in Weardale. The water is surrounded by mature woodland and is well stocked with brown and rainbow trout. The woods are good shelter from the cold north winds. Boats are available too and day permits can be purchased here. Another fishery which enjoys a Wear Valley setting is the Witton Castle Water which is bounded by the more famous Wear. The water is managed by the Bishop Aukland Angling Club (0388) 762538. The fishery is stocked with rainbow trout between 2lb and 12lb and there are also a number of brown trout which should be returned if caught. The fishery operates a barbless hook rule. The facilities here are very good and the isolated location ensures a peaceful day out.

Kielder Water is surely the 'Big Daddy' of all Northumbrian waters. The reservoir enjoys a delightful setting and caters for all manner of leisure pursuits. Although sailors and water skiers run amok here, the water is massive and there is plenty of room for all. The fishing comes into its own in the evening and the Kielder's wild brown trout are prolific. The reservoir is surrounded by rolling hills and lies in the heart of the Border Forest Park. There are some 27 miles of bank fishing and boats are available for hire and can be reserved in advance by telephoning (0434) 250203. Kielder Water is a splendid place to get away from it all and if Paul Gasgoine can escape the press and adoring fans here then surely you must be able to find a little bit of peace and quiet too!

Our final though for this area are the Whittle Dene Reservoirs where a day's fishing will cost you £12 with a six fish limit. The water lies in close proximity to Hadrian's wall and other Roman remains, surrounded by woodland and farming - a real delight. Boats can be hired from around £6 per day and permits will cost £8.50. There are a total of four reservoirs here, all well stocked and providing yet another good reason for visiting this charming part of the country.

Although the rivers of Scotland enjoy greater esteem than those running through English territory, there are still a number of magnificent salmon waters in Northern England that are being cleaned up and, as a result, are providing many more opportunities for the visiting angler. The chalk streams of the south often preoccupy the attentions of people living in Southern England, but they should spare a thought for some of the superb sport in the Cumbrian tarns, the Daleside streams and the Northumbrian rivers. As most will agree, one thing the north is not short on is water - no drought here. In fact, Northumberland actually exports this precious commodity to the Middle East. Generally speaking, fishing waters are also fairly abundant and the fish provide some frantic tustles. For many the north is only industrial slag heaps and pit villages. What they fail to see is some of the most rugged and remote and the most beautiful scenery in the country. The Pennines, the Lakes, the deserted coastal areas and the wild moorlands all provide a haven for the fisherman. Fishing is here aplenty, and it is never dull.

FISHING FAYRE

Cumbria is renowned as one of the most scenic and popular of all England's counties. The lakes and the fells provide a stunning backdrop for the rivers which wind their way seaward. There are also hundereds of hotels in the area and all manner of pubs, inns and bed & breakfasts are scattered liberally throughout the region. The Tourist Boards are particularly helpful and will always point you in the right direction but these thoughts should be of some help too.

The Eden is a marvellous water to fish and in addition to the accommodation at the lodges of Estate waters, there are some splendid hotels nearby. The Crosby Lodge House Hotel (0228) 573618 at Crosby-On-Eden is a relaxing place in which to stay. Newby Grange (0228) 573645 is another excellent hotel. Brampton is a picturesque little village and Farlham Hall (06973) 234 has to be one of the most delightful hotels in the area. It has a superb seat and a restaurant of rare distinction. Tarn End (06977) 2340 is less grand but equally welcoming and the hotel enjoys a watery setting on the banks of Talkin Tarn. The restaurant serves a variety of excellent dishes and the bar snacks are to be recommended too. The Hayton Castle (0228) 70651 is

also well worth considering with good facilities and friendly atmosphere.

Some way upstream, at Temple Sowerby, we find the 17th century Temple Sowerby House (07683) 61578. More good cooking, log fires and ample character make this a local favourite. Appleby-In-Westmoreland also reveals some excellent hotels in this pleasant Cumbrian town. The Tufton Arms (07683) 51593 is an outstanding place to stay. The hotel has fishing rights and has recently been restored to provide both comfort and style for the discerning angler. The Royal Oak Inn (07683) 51463 dating back to the 18th century, offers good food and a traditional friendly atmosphere. In Kirkby Stephen's Market Place you will find the King's Arms (07683) 71378. This former coaching inn is a most enjoyable place to stay and ideally situated for exploring the upper reaches of the Eden.

The Derwent takes us through some delightful scenery from its source in Scafell through lakeland and sheep-filled valleys. Those of you wishing to visit the source should journey to Rosthwaite and the Scafell Hotel (059684) 208. This is a remote situation but the welcome here is warm and the scenery is needless to say wonderful. Journeying through Borrowdale and Derwent Water we arrive in Keswick. There are numerous hotels here; The Derwent Water Hotel (07687) 22538 has its own fishing and is continually being upgraded. The Grange (07687) 72500 also has a beautiful setting and is well recommended, while finally here we would recommend the stylish Brandholme Country House Hotel (07687) 74495 which boasts excellent cooking as well as all the comforts expected of a fine

River Eden   (Cumbria Tourist Board)

hotel. Turning our attention away briefly from the lakeside settings to Mungrisdale, we find the Mill (07687) 79659, a delightful unpretentious mill cottage bordered by a trout stream - a pleasant thought for an evening's entertainment. The Pheasant Inn (059681) 234 is another abode that exudes charm. This is an ideal base for a lakeland holiday and self-catering units are also available. The inn lies between Bassenthwaite Lake and Thornthwaite Forest in idyllic surroundings. Cockermouth also has its fair share of good hotels and The Trout (0900) 823591 in Crown Street is one to note. The gardens sweep down to the river bank providing a truly delightful setting for such a hotel.

Ullswater, Coniston and Windermere are huge stretches of water and for many they are the most celebrated waters. Although crowds flock here in high season there is some good fishing to be enjoyed at the beginning and end of the season. Coniston has a number of hotels to consider including the Coniston Sun (05394) 41248 which is a comfortable hotel enjoying a marvellous location. The Coniston Road, a little way outside Ambleside, reveals another distinguished place in which to stay; Rothay Manor (05394) 33605. The Wateredge in Waterhead (05394) 32332 is another establishment to note, originally two fishermen's cottages the hotel is situated on the shores of Lake Windermere. This a remarkably comfortable hotel where a day's fishing is followed by a first rate dinner. A little further field, someway west of Ambleside, the Skelwith Bridge (05394) 32115 is another welcoming inn which enjoys a picturesque lakeland situation and is highly recommended. Troutbeck provides another good value inn, The Mortal Man (05394) 33193 - an extremely pleasant place to stay.

Windermere itself has many good hotels, the biggest problem is choosing one to stay in. The excellent Miller Howe (09662) 2536 is quite outstanding and the proprietor, John Tovey's cuisine renowned. Lindeth Fell (09662) 3286 in Bowness is impressive too. Newly Bridge at the foot of the Lake has the Lakeside (05395) 31207, enjoying a pleasant setting and offering very comfortable accommodation. The Swan (05395) 31681 is also full of character and well worth considering, as is the Newby Bridge Hotel (05395) 31222 at the southern end of Lake Windermere.

Ullswater offers the Sharrow Bay (07684) 86301 - one of England's finest country house hotels. The cuisine here is superb. This is for the fisherman who really likes to spoil his other half! However, there are a number of hotels which will happily organise fishing for you such as the Old Church Hotel in Watermillock (07684) 86204 - a first class hotel. The Rampsbeck (07684) 86442 is another thoroughly charming country house with an excellent restaurant.

There are yet more superb hotels south of The Lakes in picturesque Cumbrian towns and villages. The Abbey House Hotel (0229) 838282 in Barrow-in-Furness is one such example. The Rivers Kent and Lune are worthy of attention and a number of hotels are well situated here. Witherslack reveals the Old Vicarage (044852) 381, a superb hotel and a delight to stay in. In Kendal itself there are several hotels from which to choose. The Riverside (0539) 724707 sits on the banks of the River Kent, whilst the Westmoreland (0539) 723852 also exudes much charm.

The Lune ends its journey in Lancaster but the upper reaches

flow through some delightful rugged countryside. In Ravenstonedale, The Black Swan (05873) 204 is worth a visit. Journeying south to Kirkby Lonsdale you will chance upon The Pheasant Inn (05242) 71230 and in the centre of the town is The Royal (05242) 71217 is another fine place to stay.

The Ribble and the Hodder offer some first class opportunities for some excellent fishing forays. The Blackmoor Country House Hotel in Thornley (0772) 783148 is extremely welcoming as is the Shireburn Arms (025486) 518 in Hurst Green. Both have their own unique and charming character.

The Hodder winds through some beautiful scenery and its course also brings to light some excellent hotels. The Inn and Whitewell is set on the River Hodder and is a quite outstanding inn. In Slaidburn, there are two establishments from which to choose. The Hodder Bridge (0254) 86216 is extremely welcoming and has some good fishing while the Hark To Bounty (02006) 246 is another delightful place to stay. Finally in this part of the country, the Royal Oak (07292) 2561 in Settle offers good food and comfortable accommodation in this peaceful village.

Like the rivers, many of the better hotels are to found in North Yorkshire. A large number of hotels in the southern half of the county cater for the businessman rather than the holiday maker or fisherman. There are, however, a number of hotels which have retained their character and should be shortlisted. The Ouse system, which plays such a significant role in the make up of Yorkshire's waterways, offers much good fishing although much is of the course variety and therefore outside the bounds of this book. Some of the Ouse's tributaries do provide good sport and the Aire has worthwhile trout fishing in its upper reaches. A little south of Skipton, we find the village of Kildwick and Kildwick Hall (0535) 632244. This is an excellent hotel and is held in high regard amongst Yorkshire folk. It is a fine building, extremely comfortable and enjoying marvellous views of Airedale. A short distance away we find Haworth, 'Bronte Country'. Amidst the moors and bleak uplands we find the sophisticated Rydings Hotel (0535) 45206 - a very friendly place to stay.

Wharfedale runs through some delightful scenery and on its banks some pleasant village pubs and small hotels can be found. Although the Wharfe is the dominant water there are a number of smaller streams and daleside waters which produce some good fishing too. The Black Inn in Buckden (075676) 227 is extremely pleasant as is The Racehorses (075676) 233 in Kettlewell, an 18th century inn of character with a lovely riverside setting. The Tennant Arms (0756) 752301 also enjoys a superb riverside setting and is well recommended. Threshfield and Grassington both reveal celebrated hostelries. The former, the Wilson Arms (0756) 752666 is a comfortable inn and the latter, The Black Horse, (0756) 752770 serves good bar food.

Burnsall enjoys spectacular views of the Wharfe and the Red Lion (075672) 204 sits in the middle of the village overlooking it. Both the food and accommodation are recommended here. One of the best spots from which to fish the Wharfe is from within the grounds of the outstanding Devonshire Arms (075671) 441, a country house hotel of distinction. The grounds here are superb and the restaurant and accommodation of a very high standard. There are a number of excellent eating establishments in the environs of the Wharfe and Ilkley produces The

Box Tree (0943) 816793, a restaurant renowned for its first class cuisine and charming atmosphere. People staying in the area should be happy at the Rombalds (0943) 603201, an extremely pleasant hotel.

Towards Otley, the game fishing tends to become less significant but those seeking accommodation should sample the delights of Chevin Lodge (0943) 467818, surrounded by pine trees. Alternatively, in Linton, Wood Hall (0937) 67271 is set in over 100 acres of park and woodland and is a superb place to stay.

The Nidd also reveals some excellent establishments in which to escape the stresses of the 20th century. The picturesque Yorke Arms (0423) 755243 in Ramsgill is a fine place to start ones journey and the restaurant has much appeal. The Yorkshire Dales are breathtakingly beautiful but on a bleak day the crackle of a log fire is a welcoming sight and there are plenty of those to be found in the many pubs dotted around this area. Throughout Nidderdale, there are many such good establishments but one which stands out is the Sportsman's Arms (0423) 711306, in Wath-in-Nidderdale. Here, the trout served in the restauarnt may well be from the local river always beautifully prepared. The bar here is also a very friendly place to enjoy a good Yorkshire pint. Those who seek a variety of sporting entertainment should consider Nidd Hall (0423) 771598, a magnificent country house. Another good hotel with excellent facilities but a less grand setting is the Dower House Hotel in Knaresborough (0423) 863302.

Anglers visiting the Ure should visit the Miller's House at Middleham (0969) 22630, an extremely well maintained hotel with comfortable rooms. Jervaulx Hall (0677) 60235 in Jervaulx, is a hotel with a warm welcome and a charming setting - a stylish place to stay. Similarly, the elegant Simonstone Hall in Hawes (09697) 255 is a very fine base to use whilst fishing a number of local rivers, including the Swale. There are many other good hotels too. In Kirkby Fleetham, Kirkby Fleetham Hall (0609) 748711 is an imposing hotel which once again offers style and comfort, together with an impressive restaurant. If you wish to stay within a budget then the Nags Head at Pickshill (0845) 567391 is well worth considering - good value accommodation is found here and the atmosphere and facilities are excellent.

Journeying north into the historic county of Durham we find more beautiful countryside bordering the Tees and the Wear. In Middleton-in-Teesdale, the Teesdale Hotel (0833) 40264 is a former coaching inn and a friendly place in which to stay. Another charming village inn to shortlist is the Rose and Crown (0833) 50213, beside the Church and overlooking the village green. It is a tremendous hotel to use as a base for exploring the surrounding countryside. The Jersey Farm Hotel, Barnard Castle (0833) 38223 is another informal and friendly place to stay. There are some delightfully rustic areas here and a charming old inn from which to explore further is the Morritt Arms Hotel (0833) 27232 - full of character. The Dickens Bar here will appeal to the more literary anglers!

The River Wear flows through some spectacular scenery, especially in its upper reaches and Weardale is quite beautiful. The City of Durham, dominated by the Norman cathedral and castle has many good hotels and the city itself is one of the north's most attractive. Just outside Durham, to the east, we find Hallgarth Manor (091)-372 1188, a first class hotel whilst Lumley

Castle (091)-389 1111 in Chester-Le-Street offers some excellent accommodation in the castle which dates back to the 13th century. Bishop Auckland is the setting for the Park Head Hotel (0388) 661727, another quite charming hotel.

The Tyne's rapid regeneration is quite something and naturally this area is becomuing more popular every year. There are numerous inns and hotels to consider in the area. The Northumbrian countryside is some of the most unspoiled and spectacular in the world despite its less glamorous image. The upper reaches of the Tyne consist of two tributaries; the South and North Tyne. The South Tyne rises in Cumbria and the Lovelady Shield Country House (0434) 381203 is a delightful hotel in which to stay. Those of you seeking a drink, or refuge from the weather, should consider the Milecastle Inn (0498) 20682, overlooking Hadrian's Wall. A Tyneside setting awaits those who choose to stay at The Anchor (0434) 684227 in Haydon Bridge. This former inn is very good value and enjoys a marvellous setting. The General Havelock is also very pleasant, serving good bar snacks. Langley Castle (0434) 688888 is an hotel of great character and a pleasant place to stay in this area.

More Tyneside charm, this time at Riverdale Hall (0434) 220254, Bellingham - a really excellent place to rest your bags when fishing the local waters. More modest but still vey comfortable accommodation can be found at Wark. Here, The Village Inn, Battlesteads (0660) 30209 is the place to earmark. Also, a really first rate hotel which offers a superb riverside setting, excellent cuisine and good value weekend breaks is The George at Chollerford (043481) 611. Corbridge is a quaint market town and here there are too many hotels to be recommended, but one in the very centre of the town is The Angel Inn (0434) 632119, a very friendly establishment. One final thought here is Laburnum House (0661) 852185 in Wylam. The restaurant is the focal point of this 18th century house which also has some pleasant bedrooms.

North of the Tyne, the Rivers Blyth, Wansbeck, Coquet and Aln are all near parallel veins running through some superb countryside in the 'upper body' of Northumberland. The fishing varies somewhat but the scenery is generally superb. There are a number of places to consider if you are fishing these waters. Linden Hall (0670) 51611 at Longhorsley is a beautiful country house hotel set in its own wooded estate and a fine focal point for exploring the surrounding countryside. Less grand, but with an equally splendid location is Coquet Vale (0669) 20305 at Rothbury which is comfortable and good value. The same summary can be applied to The Granby Inn (066570) 228 in Longframlington.

In Alnwick, The White Swan (0665) 602109 and The Hotspur (0665) 602924 are both welcome retreats. A short distance north of this market town, we find Wooler and The Tankerville Arms (0668) 81581 - a 17th century coaching inn of great charm.

Although the Tweed is covered in detail in our Scottish Section, no game fisherman will wish to overlook the Tillmouth Park (0890) 2255, full of fishing memorabilia. The hotel is set in extensive grounds, three miles north east of the village. Boats and ghillies are available and there are few finer hotels for a fishing break.

The prime salmon fishing might be in Scotland but the counties of Cumbria, Lancashire, Yorkshire and Northumbria provide some first class sporting opportunities.

ANGLERS' CO-OPERATIVE ASSOCIATION

The ACA is unique. It fights pollution actively - not just with words. Its whole, its only, function is to protect the waters you fish, not only for yourself but for your children and grandchildren. Over the years the ACA has achieved some remarkable successes. But it can't continue to do so without your help.

The key to the ACA's success, is that for centuries, the Common Law of this country has enabled private citizens to take legal action against anyone who causes pollution, but, until the ACA was formed in 1948, hardly anyone took this course of action - for the simple reason that, if the action was unsuccessful, it could cost the person who brought it thousands of pounds. The formation of the ACA provided a simple and effective answer to this problem. By contributing a small sum of money each, thousands of anglers shared - and minimised - the risk of losing an action against polluters. In fact, the ACA has lost only one case among the hundreds which it has fought - and that was on a technicality.

The ACA has teeth. And polluters know it. Often, a letter from the Association is enough to stop a would-be polluter in his tracks. The ACA has also recovered hundreds of thousands of pounds in damages to enable polluted fisheries to be cleaned up and restocked.

Continuous or Recurrent Pollution: Cases of chronic or continuous pollution should first be notified to the ACA by letter. The letter should state the name and address of the club or person who owns or leases the water affected, and the name and address of the suspected polluter, and if possible the nature of the polluting matter. In all such cases you should be careful to distinguish between what you yourself know or have

actually seen, and what you have been told by others. Eyewitnesses of the pollution should be asked to provide a written statement before memory fades. The ACA will then arrange for the investigation of the case by our experts, but you should not expect this to happen immediately, because there are many cases of this kind and the ACA's resources are limited.

National Rivers Authority: You should always notify your local NRA Office in the case of pollution (keep a record of their phone number handy), but please remember that any action taken by the Authority will be quite separate from the ACA. Even if the Authority decides to prosecute, the action will be quite separate from the ACA's, so in all cases make sure that water samples are taken for the ACA, so that there will be an analysis separate from the NRA's if possible.

If a fishery owner decides to make any sort of claim against the polluter through the ACA, he must do so without regard to anything the NRA does.

The ACA has more cases on its hands than ever before. The costs of handling those cases have risen dramatically. And the ACA relies solely on voluntary contributions. We receive no grants, no subsidies. Over fifteen thousand individuals and hundreds of clubs have already joined and given us their support, but it's a sobering thought that over four million people regularly go fishing in Great Britain. Think what we could do if only half of them joined the ACA. Please - join us in the fight against pollution. You get a lot out of fishing. Is £3 or £5 a year really too much to put back? Send for an enrolment form. Not at the end of the week. But now. Some day, you may need our help. Right now, we need yours.

Anglers' Co-operative Association
23 Castlegate
Grantham
Lincolnshire NG31 6SW
Tel: (0476) 61008

TILLMOUTH PARK HOTEL

Comment:

Spring runs on the Tweed are increasing and with the Tweed nets off, summer fishing offers an exciting new dimension. Latest catch records prove the point. Spring is up 48%, summer is up 112%, August is up 93%.

The Autumn fishing is superb, many heavy fish have been taken - best 43lbs by Lady Burnett. In 1990 there was one of 30lb with many over 25lb. The best September day saw 28 fish into the hotel, the best October day 14, the best November day 12. In 1990 rods staying at the hotel took 619 fish. The best individual rod daily take in 1990, 10 fish, best 19lb.

The hotel offers fine cuisine, classic bedrooms and a service to cover all angling requirements.

I rate it as one of Britain's top angling hotels.
Maynard Atkinson
Angling Correspondent to the leading sporting journals.

The Unique Tweed Fishing Package for Salmon, Sea Trout
with Ghillie
3 Star Hotel * Fishing * Boat * Ghillie

If you are considering fishing the Tweed, we are possibly the only place able to offer this package.

A traditional Country House Hotel, set in lovely grounds, with good fresh food, friendly service and five miles of the Tweed for you to have the experience of a lifetime.

Some of our senior fishers have been coming for 32 years. Perhaps you might like to join them.

You will be a most welcome guest.

Tillmouth Park Hotel
Cornhill-On-Tweed
Northumberland TD12 4UU
Tel: (0890) 2255

THE MIDDLE SHIRES

Artist: **Wendy Reeves**   **THE LAKE**   Courtesy of: **Rosenstiels'**

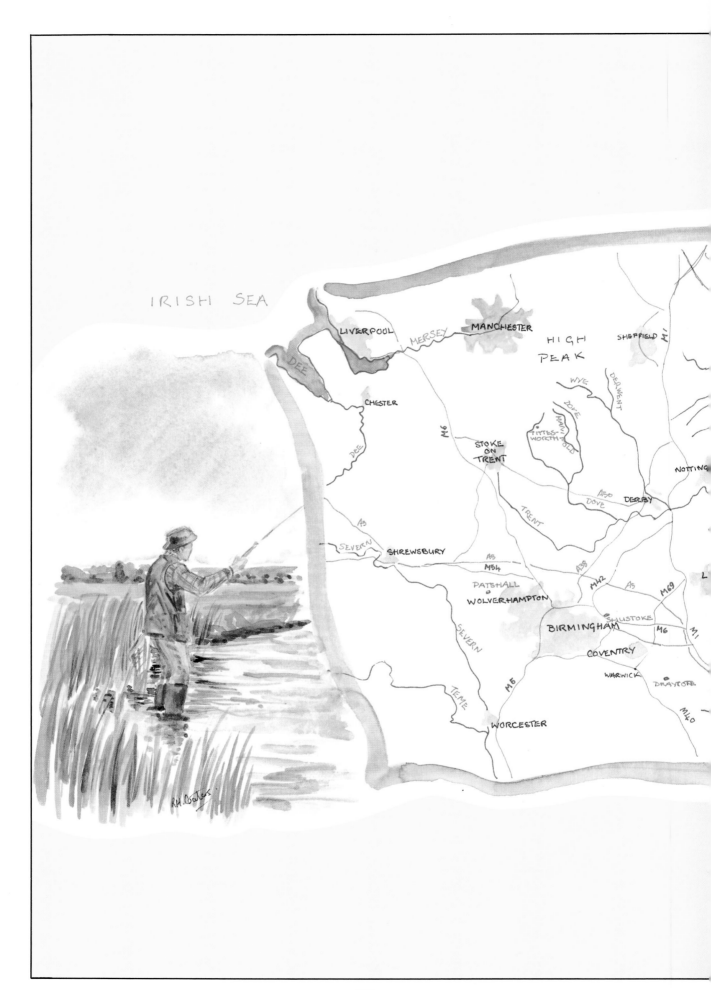

IRISH SEA

LIVERPOOL
MERSEY
MANCHESTER
HIGH PEAK
SHEFFIELD
DEE
CHESTER
WYE
DOVE
DERWENT
M6
TITTES-WORTH
MANIFOLD
STOKE ON TRENT
NOTTING
A50
DOVE
DERBY
DEE
TRENT
A5
SEVERN
SHREWSBURY
A5
M54
A38
M42
A5
M69
L
PATSHALL
WOLVERHAMPTON
SEVERN
SHUSTOKE
M6
M1
BIRMINGHAM
COVENTRY
TEME
WARWICK
DRAYCOTE
M6
WORCESTER
M40

RH Bates

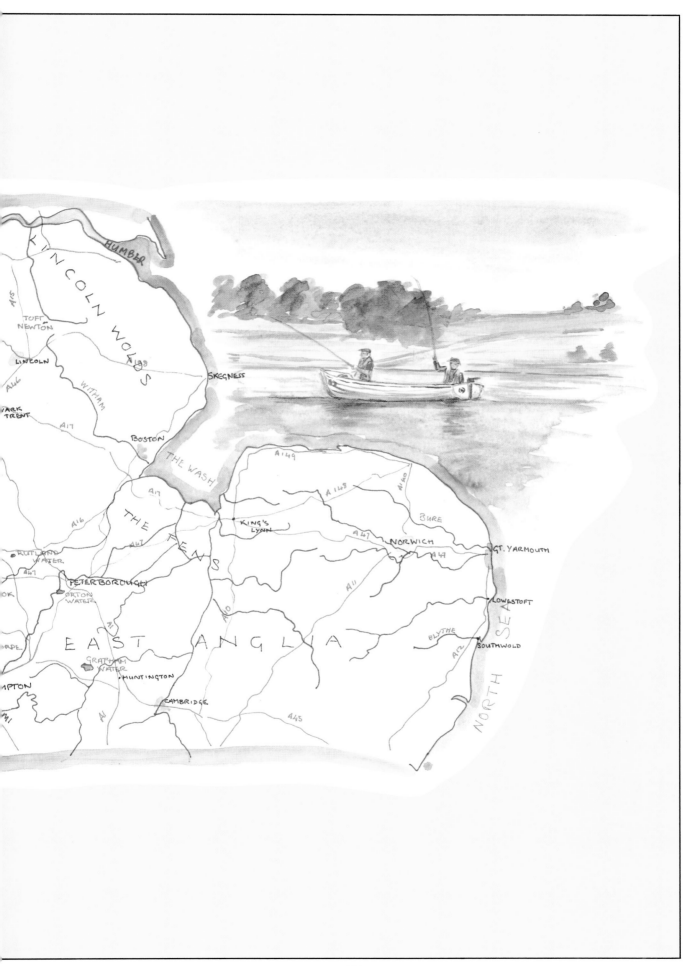

THE MIDDLE SHIRES

Stillwater game fishing owes a great deal of its popularity to Grafham Water, the reservoir that celebrated its 25th anniversary in 1991. Grafham was not the first reservoir to be opened to the public for trout fishing, that honour belongs to Blagdon, which set the precedent in Edwardian times. Fishing then, however, was the exclusive preserve of the landed gentry and their friends. After two world wars the social order had changed and so had the distribution of wealth and Grafham opened at the right time and in the right place. The 1960's saw a tremendous increase in car ownership and private motoring became affordable for all levels of society. The period was also the beginning of the leisure age when the number of working hours for most people was reduced and wages increased, thus a large part of the population had more time and more money to spend on hobbies and pastimes.

Grafham is situated in what used to be Huntingdonshire (why did we have to mess around with our old county system?) and is within easy motoring distance of huge centres of population which had a long tradition of coarse fishing. We are a curious nation and these coarse fishermen came to have a look at what was going on and, enjoying the fighting qualities of a trout and the fact that you could eat your catch, became converted to game fishing. Not content with merely participating they set about devising new tackle and tactics. It was a coarse fisherman who designed the world's first carbon-fibre fly rod, an invention which has changed all aspects of game fishing. Anyone who has compared days of wielding a big split cane salmon rod to a day with a carbon rod will appreciate the difference. Covering 1500 acres, Grafham is an enormous water and to fish stillwaters successfully, you have to be able to cover the water, so new types of line were developed that, when used with the new rods, would give much greater casting length. The other great area of change has been in flies. Unencumbered by the legacies of traditional fishing methods, the new generation set out to experiment on different ways of attracting fish and now you can not pick up a copy of a fishing magazine without seeing pages of new flies and how to tie them.

The initial ripple started by Grafham soon became a tidal wave and reservoirs up and down the country stocked their waters with trout and privately owned fisheries sprung up like mushrooms all over the place.

The popularity of stillwater game fishing has created problems. It has to be said that some stillwaters are awful and seem to have been created by landowners anxious to get on the bandwagon, who think all they have to do is to excavate some land, fill it with water and chuck in some trout without any thought of what makes a good fishery. Private fisheries are of course commercial ventures and the competition to attract customers, for that is what we are, has seen some strange developments. Stocking stillwaters with salmon is one of them. Somehow it does not seem right, to limit the perimeters of this amazing migratory fish. Added to which it can bring out the worst of human characteristics. I spoke to a fishery manager who no longer stocks his sizeable lake with salmon. He explained that as salmon cruise the shallows, they are often very visible to frustrated fishermen, who would cast over them with the sole intention of foul hooking them. One morning he found a fish washed up, with no less than nine hooks jutting out of its flanks like banderias in a bullfight. Another day he watched an angler scoop up a salmon from the shallows with a landing net and quickly hide it in the boot of his car. The angler was still

denying this fact even when the manager was searching the boot of his car. He then, apparently, produced an Oscar winning performance feigning surprise.

Some fisheries specialise in big fish, but where is the excitement in catching one of them when you know that there is nothing less than four pounds in the water? Surely the thrill is in fishing a water where the fish are of mixed sizes and catching a large fish is an uncommon event. There seems to be a competition going on as to which fishery can produce the biggest trout. Personally, I think some of these 'submarine' sized fish offer little sport as they can be very sluggish and at worst almost a dead weight that has to be hauled out and I would far rather have a good battle with a fighting fit four-pounder. There are fisheries which operate a catch and release system which is fine if rods know how to do it properly and it is up to the fishery manager to ensure that they do. I have seen fish kept out of the water for several minutes while the hook is literally torn out of their mouths and it is small wonder that such places see a number of fish floating belly up. On such waters I always fish with a barbless hook and release the fish in the water as soon as possible, or if there are any problems I will kill it. One of my main complaints is the number of rods that some fisheries admit. Of course their income depends on the number of tickets they sell, but I cannot believe there are many who enjoy standing in a line almost shoulder to shoulder in some hot spot or being crowded round and bombarded with questions while playing a fish.

Having said all that, I will now commit sacrilege and say that stillwater fishing at its best is certainly comparable to if not better than some of the big name river fishing that is available. A day on a famous trout stream can be ruinously expensive and the water will as often as not, be stocked probably with rainbows as well as brownies, with a few exceptions you have got to go to the lochs of Scotland (or the loughs of Ireland) for genuinely wild brown trout fishing. So what constitutes my ideal still water? Firstly, I go fishing for fun and to relax so it should be in pleasant surroundings. There should be a good amount of weed and bankside vegetation with woodland nearby but not so close as to make casting a problem. This will ensure a good range of fly life both in and on the water which will be gin clear as it is chalk stream fed. The water will be stocked with fish from one to five pounds and being clear, I will be able to stalk them. The level of stocking will be such that getting in a day's limit will be an achievement but on the other hand hopefully one will not return home empty handed. The number of rods will be strictly limited so that I will be free to try different places as I wish and feel that I am on my own. Finally, the other rods will be kindred spirits so that at the end of the day we can all go off and enjoy a drink and a chat in the excellent nearby pub!

One might not think of East Anglia as a game fishing area, but there are good still waters and trout streams to be enjoyed here. A short distance off the A12 near Thaxted in Suffolk is the village of Walpole, and Valley Fisheries (098684) 488 have a two and a half acre spring fed lake which is regularly stocked with brownies as well as rainbows; a day ticket here for five fish costs £18. Near Bury St. Edmunds there is the two lake Larkwood Fishery (0284) 728612, while on the Norfolk, Suffolk border off the A143 near Harleston is Mendham Mill Trout Fishery (0379) 852328. Mendham offers four acres of fishing in lakes as well as the River Waveney Mill race and is set in the

THE MIDDLE SHIRES

picturesque Waveney Valley. Locally tied flies and tuition are available and a four fish day ticket costs £10. The number of rods is limited to sixteen a day so advance booking is recommended.

Across the border in Norfolk is the Salmon and Trout Association's stillwater at Lenwade. This is a season ticket water only and you must be a member of the Association. Membership in 1991 cost £12 and can be obtained from Lt. Cdr. L. D. Temple-Richards (032878) 217. Normal membership of the STA is also required for a day ticket at Roosting Hills (0362) 860273, which is at Beetley near Dereham. Nearby are the four acre Whinburgh Trout Lakes (0362) 850201 and near King's Lynn are Narborough Trout Lakes (0760) 338005. These five lakes are well stocked and hold some big fish. North east of Aylesham, just off the B1354 are Bure Valley lake Fisheries (026387) 666. The fishery's three lakes total ten acres and it has a mile of the River **Bure**, salmon are being introduced in 1991 and the fishery has been featured on ITV's 'Go Fishing' programme. Downstream at Abbots Hall, Ingworth, members of the STA can enjoy a mile of double bank fishing on the Bure for £8 a day or £60 a season. There is however, a waiting list for season tickets. Fakenham Angling Club have two miles of the River **Wensum**. Day tickets are available from Dave's tackle Shop at No 1, Rear of Norwich Street, Fakenham (0328) 862543. This river does tend to get heavily weeded from mid-summer so it is proably best to inspect the river first. Close to Peterborough in Cambridgeshire, is the Orton Water Trout Fishery at Orton Waterville (0733) 239995. Boats are available on this twenty-five acre water which also holds brook trout and has produced a rainbow of 15lb 10oz and a brown of 7lb 4oz. It is set in the pretty Nene Country Park and is an ideal spot for a family day out as other attractions include steam trains, horse riding and bird watching. There is an 18 hole golf course very near by so watch out for sliced shots! A five-fish day ticket costs £10 and a father and son day is £12.50.

The county that once bore the name of Huntingdonshire has sadly disappeared from the maps, but of course there is still the former county town of Huntingdon and its name lives on in the legends of Robin Hood. From a fishing point of view its chief glory is **Grafham** which is now in Cambridgeshire. The county of Rutland has also disappeared from the maps, but the locals strive to keep the name alive and Rutland Water helps to preserve its fame. I cannot help thinking that if the name of this fishery had been changed to something like East Midlands Fishery, it would have lost part of its charm. I attempted to sing Grafham's praises at the beginning of this section, but the only way to find out what it is really like is to spend a day there. It is a veritable giant among stillwaters for it covers 1569 acres and holds 13,000 million gallons of water. Over the years it has mellowed and now blends in with the local landscape, this is largely due to the care and conservation policies of Anglian Water. It is an SSI and in recent years, has held nationally important numbers of wintering Great Crested Grebe, Tufted Duck and Coot, while late summer sees significant numbers of moulting Mute Swan. There is a wide variety of bank fishing and boats are available, details of costs etc. may be found from the fishery manager (0480) 810531. The world championships were held here in 1987 and the water has produced a 12lb 6oz brownie. Grafham is the sort of water that can always be relied on to produce good fish and the beginning of May 1991 saw a great bag of three brownies weighing 15lb 12oz, while a week later a magnificent brown of 10lb was recorded. An eight-fish day

ticket will set you back £10.

I suppose its original title of Empingham reservoir would have been preferable to East Midlands Fishery but thank goodness local pressure prevailed and it was called **Rutland Water**. I am sure the bells of Normanton Church, the well known local landmark, would have rung out in anger at any other name. Although comparatively new, the original detailed landscaping work of Dame Sylvia Crewe has insured that it now blends in perfectly with the local scenery. Grafham is huge but Rutland is a monster for it covers over 3000 acres which is roughly the same size as Lake Windermere. Peace and quiet are assured here for, although sailing is permitted, intrusive sports such as water-skiing and power boating are banned. An eight-fish day ticket costs £9.70 and boats are available, further details can be obtained from the fishing lodge (0780) 86770. Part of the western end is a nature reserve and one of the richest reservoir locations for wintering and passage wildfowl in Britain. It is particularly notable for its numbers of Mallard, Shoveler, Gadwell, Teal, Wigeon, Pochard, Tufted Duck and Goldeneye. Rutland co-hosted the 1987 world championship with Grafham and this is not surprising when you consider that over 50,000 anglers fish here every season and the total catch weight is over 50 tons. Both rainbows and browns of over 12lb have been caught as has an eight fish bag totalling 48lb, a record for any European reservoir. North from Kettering on the A6003 is Eyebrook Reservoir at Caldecott (0536) 770264. This 400 acre water is set in a natural valley and has very good weed growth with plenty of snacks; shrimp, sedge, midge and ceria. Not far away is the 50 acre Elinor Trout Fishery (08015) 786 at Aldwincle near Kettering. Boats are available although the bank fishing is excellent, and the price of a six day ticket is £9. A few miles north of Northampton are two more well known Anglian Water Reservoirs, Ravensthorpe and Pitsford. Built in 1886, Ravensthorpe is a very mature water and many would say the most attractive of the Northamptonshire reservoirs. Further details can be had from the fishing lodge (0604) 770875. Pitsford (0604) 781350 is a 750 acre water whose popularity has increased enormously in recent years due to Anglian Water's hard work in improving stocks and facilities. Unlike many reservoirs, Pitsford trout have a reputation for surface feeding and dry flies are usually very effective. A good range of courses are on offer here and at Grafham. If you prefer river fishing you might care to join the Kettering and District Fly Fishers Association, whose Secretary is Mrs J. Bozicek (0536) 521304, day tickets are available from B.P. Tackle, Mill Road, Kettering (0536) 81118. The cost of membership is £35 and that will allow you to fish the Association's stretch of the River **Ise**.

With so many good fisheries in such pleasant surroundings it is hard to remember that the Midlands used to be called 'The Black Country'. However, local industry has seen a lot of changes and coal is no longer king, added to which many authorities have done a great deal of conservation work. At Bishop's Itchington near Leamington Spa are the Bishop's Bowl Lakes (0926) 613344, which hosted the final of the Troutmasters competition a few years ago. The lakes cover 40 acres and are formed from old limestone quarries. The actual rocks are more than 170 million years old and contain a wealth of fossils. Quarrying in 1927 revealed the intact skeleton of a Plesiosaur, an aquatic reptile often thought to be the identity of the Loch Ness Monster. This skeleton, which is eighteen feet long, can be seen in the Natural History Museum in London. There are three lakes here; White Bishop Lake is designed to be a 'quick

BARNSDALE LODGE

Barnsdale Lodge is a substantial, beautiful and recently-restored 17th century farmhouse, set in the heart of the ancient county of Rutland amongst unspoiled countryside overlooking Rutland Water - one of the largest man-made lakes in Europe.

At Barnsdale Lodge, guests can enjoy the luxury and warmth of an English country house with all the charm and splendour of a bygone era.

The hosts, Robert Reid and the Hon. Thomas Noel, welcome guests to the gracious living of times gone by in the seventeen bedrooms, each furnished in Edwardian style and with private facilities. Guests can relax in style and comfort and enjoy the traditional English cuisine and fine wines in the dining rooms. Elevenses, buttery lunches, afternoon teas and suppers can be taken in the bar, drawing rooms, or on the terrace. There are three fully-equipped conference rooms and parties and wedding receptions are catered for in the Barn/Marquee which can accommodate up to 220 guests.

This haven of rural peace is only two miles from the tranquil market town of Oakham, and within easy reach of the historic town of Stamford and historic attractions such as Burghley House, Belvoir and Rockingham Castles, and cathedrals at Ely and Peterborough. Rutland Water is of great interest both to the sports enthusiast and to nature lovers. Guests can take a trip on 'The Rutland Belle', the Water's passenger cruiser, or take advantage of the dinghy sailing and wind-surfing available.

The keen fisherman will find himself in heaven - trout fishing is available from the shore or hire boats, and the 350 acre nature reserve offers the opportunity for birdwatching, guided tours and a nature trail.

Barnsdale Lodge provides all those traditional qualities of English service so often forgotten, together with a welcome second to none. The hotel is situated on the A606 Oakham to Stamford road.

Barnsdale Lodge
The Avenue
Rutland Water
Near Oakham
Rutland LE15 8AH
Tel: (0572) 724678
Fax: (0572) 724961

NORMANTON PARK HOTEL

The picturesque Normanton Park Hotel is situated on the south shore of Rutland water, one of the country's leading sports and leisure centres that offers canoeing, water-skiing, yachting and wind surfing. With such a wealth of facilities right on the doorstep, Normanton Park is a veritable water sportsman's paradise. The hotel itself is a Grade II listed, award-winning Georgian coach house which through imaginative and meticulous planning is able to offer visitors every conceivable luxury whilst retaining the character of the original architectural features.

Of particular repute is the elegant Peacock Room restaurant which, as well as serving the finest of traditional English menus-using fresh local produce, also affords quite magnificent views over the water shimmering and glistening just fifty yards distant. Fine cuisine is complemented by a wine list that offers something to satisfy every palate. Should a formal meal not be required, the stylish galleried coffee lounge serves snack meals, cream teas and speciality ice-creams all day long.

Set in the heart of the Midlands, Normanton Park is an ideal base for exploration not just the magnificent hotel gardens that house one of the oldest Cedar of Lebanon trees in the country but also the many and varied market towns of East Anglia, Cambridge and Calke Abbey.

The National Trust Properties of Belton House and Canons Ashby are also only a short drive away which will not disappoint. Cycling, horse-riding and birdwatching are also available locally. The hotel facilities leave absolutely nothing to chance and combine traditional elegance with modern comfort. En-suite bedrooms-single, double, triple and family are all furnished to a high and tasteful standard and are fitted with colour T.V., teletext, radio, direct dial telephone, hairdryers and tea and coffee making facilities.

Normanton Park is also specially equipped to welcome disabled guests; four specially converted rooms have wheelchair access, as do all public rooms on the ground floor. Ample car-parking is available on-site and eight rooms are directly accessible from the original courtyard, at ground level. Normanton Park Hotel is the perfect resting place for tourist and business persons alike. With a beautiful setting, ideal location and superb facilities nobody will fail to leave refreshed and relaxed by one of the Midland's most popular hotels.

Normanton Park Hotel
Normanton Park,
Rutland Water South Shore
Rutland,
Leicestershire LE15 8RP
Tel: (0780) 720315
Fax: (0780) 721086

catch' lake and is ideal for the less experienced. The five acre Mitre Pool holds bigger fish as does Bishop's Bowl which has a great mayfly hatch, and both lakes are designed to appeal to the more experienced rod. Four-fish day tickets cost £17 and casting instruction is available.

Less than two miles away at Harbury is Chesterton Mill Pool (0926) 613235. The fishery is set in 20 acres, surrounded by lovely unspoiled countryside and woodland. The watermill, like the windmill, was built in the 1630's by Sir Edward Pegto, then Sheriff of the county. The mill was used to grind corn right up to the 1950s when it fell into disuse. By 1976 the lake was so full of silt and overgrown with reeds that the water area was down to half an acre. Restoration work started in 1980 and the lake is now some four and a half acres and has just the right amount of weed and bankside vegetation to ensure good fly life. A five-fish ticket costs £16.50 and the water is stocked with browns and rainbows. Severn Trent's 600 acre Draycote Water (0788) 812018 is near Rugby and an eight fish day ticket costs £10.50. In 1991 the proposed stocking programme was 48,000 mixed browns and rainbows. The rainbows were mainly around one and a quarter pounds but there was a significant number of 4lb fish and some over 10lb. At Meriden, near Coventry, is Lord Guernsey's Packington Fishery (0676) 22754. There are three old established lakes of twenty eight, eighteen and six acres which are reserved for members, and three former gravel pits totalling forty four acres on which day tickets are available. The lakes are stocked with the fisheries own reared browns and rainbows and the minimum size is 12oz. The fishery has a best rainbow of 10lb 6oz and a brown 5lb 8oz. The fishery also has two miles on the River **Blythe**. A day ticket costs £16.50 and that will give you a bag limit of 15 fish! The Blythe has rightly been called a 'sparkling gem' for the entire river is a site of Special Scientific Interest (SSI). The reason for this is that, botanically, the river is one of the richest in lowland England, with some sections containing as many species as the very richest chalk streams. The SSI system is similar to the way buildings are listed and can be a bit of a headache for river managers and riparian owners, as any improvements they wish to make must first be agreed by English Nature.

At Coleshill, in the West Midlands, is Shustoke Reservoir, the home of Shustoke Fly Fishers Limited (0675) 81702. The fishery consists of a main reservoir of 92 acres and a settling pool which can only be fished by members. Visitors can fish the main water where a five-fish day ticket costs £12. An added attraction is the rather good pub within a hundred yards of the main gate. Patshull Hall at Burnhill Green, near Wolverhampton, was once the seat of the Earl of Dartmouth, but now stands empty. Patshull Great Lake, (0902) 700774, is occupied by many splendid hard fighting brownies and rainbows. The Great Lake covers some seventy-five acres and was designed by 'Capability' Brown in the 1740's, the result being one of the most picturesque fisheries in the country. The fishery is particularly keen to support the disabled angler and boats have been specially adapted to take wheelchairs. There is easy access to the bank and there is a very popular annual fishing competition for the disabled. A six-fish day ticket costs £7 and a further £1.80 per fish caught. West of here and some four miles north of Kidderminster on the A442 are Shatterford Lakes (02997) 403. There are four lakes here ranging from half an acre to two acres, and a ten-fish day ticket costs £6 with a further £1.65 per fish caught. The fishery is set in a delightful location on a hillside on the edge of the beautiful Severn Valley and has fine

views over the Shropshire Countryside. There are herds of Red, Fallow and Sika deer and a number of peacocks. There is a wealth of bird life including Pied Flycatchers and wild flowers such as Spotted Orchids.

The River Teme rises near Newton in Powys and its winding course takes it over the Welsh border into Hereford until it flows south to join the Severn at Worcester. There is an unusual way to fish the upper reaches of this charming little stream - all you have to do is stay in one of the houses in the Knighton area that do bed and breakfast and your fishing is free. Knighton stands half way down Offa's Dyke and was described in A. E. Housman's 'Shropshire Lad' as one of the 'quietest places under the sun'. G. H. Medlicott and Son, Solicitors, of Station Road, Knighton, Powys can provide more details about the fishing. The river and its feeders here are pretty small and you won't need anything bigger than an eight foot rod. Suggested flies include Black Gnat, Black Pennell, Zulu, Red Spinner, Blue Dun, Coachman and Alder. At Lindridge, Mr Ken Powell (058470) 208, has one and a half miles of single and double bank fishing near Tenbury Wells. This delightful gentleman has been fishing the river for over sixty years and welcomes day visitors to his water. The water was stocked with several thousand trout which have now reached a fair size. There are salmon here too and this beat has several pools including one of particular merit. A day in this delightful area can be had for the very modest amount of £2.

The headwaters of the **Severn** are also in Wales and, having a course of over 180 miles on its journey to the Bristol Channel, it is the longest river in England and Wales. The upper reaches offer good trouting and although, in common with most other rivers, the salmon run is not what it was, the Severn is still not bad and produces some good sized fish. The best part for salmon fishing is the middle reaches since the lower ones are mainly noted for their excellent coarse fishing. If you want to fish the headwaters, the Poachers Pocket Pub at Llanidloes (0686) 688233 issue day tickets which cost £4 for the Dinas Estuary Fishing which is two and a half miles of well-stocked, double-bank trout water. Llanidloes Angling Association have approximately twelve miles of fishing on the Severn and its tributaries. Salmon are hardly ever seen this far up, except occasionally in a very wet season and afforestation schemes have caused drainage problems here. For a good days trouting, Mr Davis of the Association recommends a visit to Clywedog Reservoir, permits for which can be had from Mrs Gough at the Travellers Rest Restaurant (05512) 2329. Downstream at Caersws, the Maesmawr Hotel (0686) 688255 has one and a half miles of double bank fishing which is free to residents, while visitors can buy a day ticket for £4.50. This is a beautiful part of the country and there is one particularly good pool on this water. Mike's Tackle Shop at Newtown (0686) 624388 is run by Mike and Carol Barber who can give you comprehensive advice on salmon fishing in the area. This friendly couple are both experienced anglers who welcome phone calls and visitors to the shop and can also introduce you to local fishermen who will be pleased to show you their favourite waters.

With its medieval church spires, Norman castle, and beautiful Georgian and Tudor black and white houses, Shrewsbury must have one of the richest visible histories of any English town. It also has some good fishing, especially at the Weir and at Monkmoor. Further details can be had from the Council offices (0743) 231456. A must for any fisherman is a visit to Chris

THE MIDDLE SHIRES

Partington's Vintage Tackle shop at 103 Longden Coleham in Shrewsbury (0743) 369373. Chris deals in tackle that spans four centuries and has also set up Britain's Angling Heritage Trust. He is a very experienced fisherman and generous with his advice on tackling the Severn and the area generally.

Another interesting town lies about fifteen miles downstream, for here is Ironbridge which witnessed the birth of the Industrial Revolution, and the iron bridge that gave the town its name still spans the Severn. A great deal of restoration has been done to the old buildings and factories in the last twenty years and the town now has a wealth of interesting exhibitions. Further downstream, at Stourport on Severn, day tickets can be had from John Whites's Tackle Shop (02993) 71735. Although salmon are caught here it is predominantly a coarse fishery and the game fisherman would probably prefer to cast his fly elsewhere.

Returning north to Cheshire, Chester, with its half timbered buildings and old shopping area called 'the Rows', is another attractive town while a short distance away is Mickle Trafford and Meadow Fishery (0244) 300236. This fishery has two lakes of five and two of three quarter acres which are stocked with both brown and rainbow. A four-fish day ticket costs £15 and June 1991 saw a splendid 10lb rainbow, and a bag of 22 fish - someone must have been feeling rich! - caught in five hours with a best fish of 5lb 8oz. East of here at Mobberley, which is located between Knutsford and Wilmslow, is the Clay Lane Farm Fishery (056587) 3337. This is a one and a half acre spring fed water where a four-fish day ticket costs £16. Clay Lane has produced a brown of 9lb and a rainbow of 12lb. I am delighted to see that this is a fishery which states that barbless hooks must be used. Other Cheshire stillwaters include Brookside at Crewe (0270) 820528, Marton Heath at Macclesfield (0260) 224221, and Wall Pool Lodge (0260) 223442, also near Macclesfield.

Across the county border at Meerbrook, near Leek in Staffordshire is Tittesworth Trout Fishery (0538) 34389. We are on the edge of the Peak District here, and the reservoir has been called 'the Loch of the Peaks', indeed loch style drifts in a boat with a team of small wet flies are very successful. There are five miles of interesting bank fishing here. Lure specialists will enjoy the deep marks at Badger and Scar Hole, while nymph fishermen will have good sport in the shallower waters such as Fosters and Troutsdale. There is also fishing on the Churnet which is one of the few rivers in the country where rainbow breed naturally. A six-fish day ticket costs £7. Other Staffordshire stillwaters include Gailey Fishery at Penkridge (0785) 715848 and Donkhill Fisheries near Burton-on-Trent (0827) 383296. Also near Burton is Severn Trent Water's Foremark Reservoir, (0283) 701709. A day on this well stocked water can be had for £8.50.

North of here is Derbyshire's Peak District with its heather-clad moss moors and dry stone walls. The source of the River **Derwent** is High Peak in the north of the county from where it flows some sixty miles to join the Trent, below Derby. Its lower reaches are monopolised by coarse fish but the upper reaches of the river and its tributary, the Wye, are first class trout and grayling water. The Peacock hotel at Rowsley (0629) 733518 has a small stretch on the Haddon Hall water which holds two rods. Downstream at Matlock Bath, the Midland Hotel (0629) 582630 has a mile of trout and grayling water which can be fished for £5 a day. The Derwent Hotel (0773)

856616 currently has half a mile of single bank fishing but the proprietors are hoping to extend the fishing by two miles in 1992. This lovely virginia-creeper clad hotel is beside the bridge at Whatstandwell. Fishing is free for guests while visitors pay £1.50 a day. A party of three rods from a well known angling journal recently had 24 trout in a day and I am glad to say returned most of them. The Duke of Rutland's Haddon Hall Estate has six miles of double bank fishing on the **Wye** which is let through the Peacock Hotel at £20.50. The water is extremely well managed by two keepers who look after approximately twenty two miles of river. The Head Keeper is committed to restoring the river to as close to a naturally re-generating river as possible, so that 'fishermen will pay for the good fishing and not for the limit of fish,' which sounds highly commendable. Many fish are around 1lb 8oz but five pounders have been caught in the Mayfly season. There is a rather unique stock of natural rainbows. You can't mistake them - full finned, streamlined bodies and beautiful, vivid markings - hence their name! There is of course, a fair number of wild browns and a limited restocking program. At this stage, the Wye can be likened to 'an old fashioned wild river,' meandering through open meadowland and coppice of alder and willow. The Duke of Devonshire's Chatsworth Estate owns six miles of which one mile is available to visitors. Tickets can be had from the Head River Keeper (0629) 87484. The Cavendish Hotel (0246) 582311 has access to the syndicated water owned by the Chatsworth Estate which is three rods on the Wye and three on the Derwent. Darley Dale Fly Fishing Club (Secretary; Brian Jones (0457) 872967) has four and a half miles of the Derwent, downstream from Chatsworth Park. Residents at The Grouse and Claret can fish it for £16 a day, but if you are staying at the Peacock it will cost you four pounds more. Darley Dale is a most attractive spot and both the Derwent and the Wye have good natural fly life, such as Olives, Mayfly and Cranefly.

For a large part of its course the River **Dove** forms the boundary line between Staffordshire and Derbyshire. It is also rightly associated with Izaak Walton, but I wonder how many people realise it was his friend Charles Cotton who wrote the part about trout fishing? Among its many fine and interesting possessions the Flyfishers Club in London has got Walton's creel and his casting hand. Leek Fishing Association stock and control the whole of the river. The Izaak Walton Hotel (033 529) 555 has a three mile stretch which holds four rods. Another hotel steeped in angling history is the Charles Cotton hotel at Hartington (0298) 84229 which has quarter of a mile, let out for £10 a day. Doveridge Sporting Club (0889) 565986 has one mile of excellent single bank fishing and also has a well stocked lake. It is set in 70 acres and has a variety of clay pigeon traps. Callow Hall Country Club at Ashbourne (0335) 43164 has a mile of double bank fishing for guests. The River **Manifold** is a tributary of the Dove but the only fishing available is a stretch which is owned by the National Trust, who lease it to Mr Grindey of Wetton Mill Farm, of Wetton near Ashbourne (0298) 84341. He allows four rods on his water and the cost of a day is £1.25.

On the Staffordshire border, near the delightfully named village of Wincle, are Danebridge Fisheries (0260) 227293. The fishery has a two and a half acre lake in the pretty Dane Valley. You may think the lake small but it holds trout of 16lb and is regularly featured in the angling press. At the other end of the county in North Sheffield, is Ladybower Reservoir (0433) 51254. The cost of a six-fish day ticket ranges from £8 - £30, and this year Severn Trent Water plan to introduce 30,000 stockies on

THE MIDDLE SHIRES

this 504 acre water. Residents of the city of Nottingham are fortunate to have Colwick Country Park (0602) 870785. There is a twenty five acre lake for wind surfing, but the fishing lake is some sixty five acres and is just for fishing, and at the end of a successful day you can have a pleasant drink in the Georgian designed Colwick Hall which now acts partly as a restaurant and bar.

East of Nottinghamshire is the flat rich arable land of Lincolnshire. There is not much in the way of trout streams here but there are some nice stillwaters. The River Witham here is good coarse fishing water while above Grantham it provides decent trouting. However, most of this is in private hands and the one or two clubs who have game fishing also have long membership lists. Among the stillwaters are Toft Newton at Market Rasen (0603) 7453. The fishery is a privately run reservoir that has been leased from NRA and I am pleased to see it has given up the salmon experiment and now puts brookies in. This 40 acre water is right next door to RAF Scampton. The aeroplanes are not too intrusive but you do get a free Red Arrow display every now and again. The fishery can sell you tackle and gut or smoke your catch. A six-fish day here costs £11 and I am pleased to see that you can buy a catch-and-release ticket for £2 providing you use a barbless hook. Hill View Trout Lake (0754) 72979 is at Hogs Thorpe near Skegness. This two acre lake is in an attractive woodland setting with lovely views over the Lincolnshire Wolds and is only two miles from the sea. It's mainly stocked with rainbows but there are some browns; the best brown so far has been 6lb 8oz and Hill View has produced a great 12lb 8oz rainbow. Pheasant Tail and Montana Mymphs do well, as do Invictas, Hawthorns and Black and Peacock

Spiders. A four-fish day ticket can be had for £10.50. Stemborough Mill Fishery (0455) 209624 is an attractive three and a half acre lake, set in open countryside two miles north of the Roman Centre of England near Lutterworth, and £10 buys you a four-fish day ticket. Other good Lincolnshire stillwaters include, Hatton (0673) 858682, Syston Park (0400) 50000, Red House Farm (052 277) 224 and Lakeside Farm (0400 72758).

I trust we have converted any of you who thought of this area as the Black Country. Whether you are planning a day out or a week's holiday, you can be assured of finding good fishing in pleasant surroundings.

FISHING FAYRE

The Midlands of England may not have been the Mecca for game fishing but its huge city populations house many an enthusiast who delights in a day away from the metropolis. The scenery contrasts hugely; the delightful border country of Hereford and Worcester, the dales of Derbyshire and the more sedate fens and broads of Lincolnshire and East Anglia all make up a rich, varied picture. There are numerous stillwaters on the territory and if you are planning a day's fishing we hope the following suggestions will be of interest. They include several pubs, some with bedrooms, and a number of hotels - some of which are outstanding establishments. The type of place you go for a real treat, perhaps to keep the other half sweet!

Suffolk is a beautiful county with thatched villages and many a country tavern. Bury St. Edmunds is a marvellous town to visit and The Angel (0284) 753926 is an historic vine-covered inn

Lady Bower Reservoir   (Severn Trent Plc)

THE MIDDLE SHIRES

which has welcomed visitors since the mid 18th century. It is a fine place to stay and boasts a very good restaurant. Visitors to Mendham Mill should consider the 17th century Scole Inn (0379) 740481 in Scole which provides a warm welcome. North of here, travellers to Lewade might consider the King's Head, East Dereham (0362) 693842 or The Buckinghamshire Arms, Blicking (0263) 732133 - a really splendid pub with excellent food and ale as well as a number of cosy bedrooms. If you are fishing on the Bure or the Nar then the Boar Inn at Great Ryburgh (032 878) 212 is a really welcoming and characterful place to stay.

The Peterborough area has a number of good stillwaters and an inn of considerable charm is The Haycock at Wansford (0780) 782223. The hotel has a gorgeous riverside setting and its restaurant and bedrooms are of an excellent standard. Alternatively, The Bell at Stilton (0733) 241066, an historic inn which has been well renovated, has great character. These establishments are also well placed for Grafham, Eyebrook and Rutland Water.

If you are visiting this celebrated fishery then how about an equally splendid hotel or inn. Well there are a good number of choices: The George of Stamford (0780) 55171 is one of the finest inns in Britain. It dates from the 16th century and combines historic charm with all the modern comforts of today - an outstanding restaurant makes the hotel yet more appealing. A similar summary can be applied to Hambleton Hall in Hambleton (0572) 756991. The house enjoys wonderful views from its grounds over Rutland Water. The hotel exudes quality and the restaurant is one of the finest in the country. The Whipper In (0572) 756971 is also first class and has a fine setting in Oakham's Market Place, once again, the restaurant is excellent. Other splendid establishments to add to this list include Barnsdale Lodge (0572) 724678 and Normanton Park (0780) 720315. The former is a coachhouse which has been sympathetically restored. The latter, a former country farmhouse which offers every comfort and a high standard of cuisine. These hotels are all excellent but are also in the more expensive end of the range. Less pricey are the Rutland Angler (0572) 755839 in Oakham and the White Horse Inn (0780) 86221, they provide a good standard of accommodation and some excellent bar meals. Good food can also be enjoyed at a number of nearby pubs, including the Berwicke Arms at Hallaton (085 889) 217. Visitors to nearby Eyebrook should visit Lydington, where there are a brace of hostelries, and those who are planning to stay overnight should consider The Marquess of Exeter (0572) 822477 a 16th century coaching inn with a lot of charm. There are a number of hotels in the Oundle area and the Ship (0832) 273918 is good value and extremely comfortable. The Chequered Skipper at Ashton is also a fun pub to visit, while the Falcon at Fotheringay (08326) 254 serves excellent bar food. Those anglers visiting Pitsford or Ravensthorpe should also note the Fawn (060129) 200 at Castle Ashby, a pleasant hotel in a picturesque village or the Red Lion (0604) 770223 at East Haddon.

Bishop's Bowl Lakes has a number of pubs in its environs. The Old Mint at Fouthern is particularly good as is The Falcon at Prior's Manor (0327) 605620. A friendly hotel to consider is the Easthorpe Park (0926) 632245 in nearby Easthorpe. Or south of here, at Charlecote, The Charlecote Pheasant (0789) 470333. Less grand but still a great place for a 'swiftie' is The Plough at Warrington which is handy for the recently opened M40. In addition to these fine establishments, The Dunn Cow (0788)

810233 at Dunchurch is a delightful old inn - the building boasts a bundle of character and is a fine port of call. In Meriden, The Manor Hotel (0676) 22735 is a good place to stay for the Packington Fishery, and The Bear at Berkswell is a pub to note. Visitors to Shustoke should consider The Griffin, a fine pub in which to discuss the day's exploits. Patshull visitors may well be out for a day in the country but people who want to have a sporting break should make a note of the Patshull Park Hotel (0902) 700100, west of Pattington, there is a fine golf course here as well. Shatterford is a lovely spot and The Black Boy at Bewdley (0299) 402119 is a cosy inn in the centre of the town in which to stay. Alternatively, The Little Pack Horse is a splendid pub to partake in a little liquid refreshment. Other lovely places to stay are The Crown at Hopton Wafers (0299) 270372 or The Talbot at Cleobury Mortimer (0299) 270036.

There are numerous streams and rivers flowing through Herefordshire, Shropshire and Worcestershire, and the Teme runs through gorgeous countryside and Hopton Wafers. There are numerous places to stay along its banks and in Knighton, the Milebrook House Hotel (0547) 528632 is a tremendous place with fly fishing thrown in. Ludlow is a delightful town. The Angel Hotel (0584) 872581, and the marvellous Feathers at Ludlow (0584) 875261 are places to consider here. Those who happen to want an excellent spot for dinner should try Poppies at the Roebuck Inn (058472) 230 in Brimfield - it is outstanding. There are some comfortable bedrooms here as well. In Tenbury Wells, The Ship is well worth visiting for good food and some comfortable accommodation. If you are looking for a superb hotel in which to stay then The Elms (0299) 896666 at Averley enjoys superb views of the Teme Valley and is an outstanding edifice in every way. The Manor Arms at Abberley (0299) 896507 is also welcoming though a little less grand.

Returning westwards to the Severn, we travel through some delightful border country before encroaching again on Welsh soil. The game fishing, although improving, is not tremendous and talk of a barrage on the water puts the fear of God into those that still enjoy fishing it and its abundant tributaries. Those who wish to fish the Severn should consider staying at the friendly and comfortable Red Lion (05512) 2270, not grand but most convenient, or the equally welcoming Elephant and Cracke (0686) 626271, a Severn side hotel and the birthplace of Robert Owen. Upstream, The Lion at Berriew (0686) 640452 is an extremely comfortable hotel and is well worth considering.

Chester is another delightful town and its surrounding countryside, though dotted with urban life, also offers some fine scenery and some delightful pubs. Stillwater trout fishing can also be found and for those anglers who enjoy nothing more than a fireside chinwag at the end of a day the following ideas may be of interest. The Bells of Peover in Lower Peover (0565) 722269 is an elegant, wisteria-clad pub with excellent bar food. The Golden Pheasant in Plumley is also pleasant and has some accommodation, while The Dun Cow at Ollerton is another welcoming pub which is ideal for your fireside chat. There are many other splendid pubs in the vacinity, ensuring a wonderfully complete day.

The Peak District offers some of the most delightful scenery in England and there are a number of hotels here that fair take the breath away - several of which also have fishing. The Peacock Hotel (0629) 733518 offers an excellent restaurant and some good accommodation. Fishermen should note the aptly named

THE MIDDLE SHIRES

Derwent Hotel (0773) 856616 where they will be thoroughly well looked after. Some outstanding accommodation and culinary delights can be found at the Cavendish Hotel (0246) 582311 which has a glorious setting overlooking the Chatsworth Estate. The fishing it offers is a bonus and the hotel is thoroughly recommended. Those of you who are less inclined to stay around should consider at least one of the excellent pubs in the area. The Chequers at Froggatt Edge (0433) 30231 or the Bulls Head at Wardlow (0298) 871431 both have simple accommodation, or alternatively the splendidly named Lazy Landlord at Foolow (0433) 30873 provides excellent bar food.

The Dove is another sporting river on which to cast the old fly. Callow Hall is a wonderful hotel with excellent bedrooms as well as game fishing for guests. Dovedale reveals a celebrated fishing hotel, The Izaac Walton (033529) 559. The hotel enjoys splendid views up the Dove Valley and it was here that Walton penned much of the material for his celebrated fishing work. His great friend and co-author Charles Cotton also has a hotel named after him, The Charles Cotton (0298) 84229 in Hartington has a Peak District location and offers simple but comfortable

accommodation. The popular Jug and Glass (0298) 84224 is a fine ale pub to consider. Visitors to Ladybower, east of Sheffield will find some fine scenery and a pub or two to sample. The Derwent at Bomford (0433) 51395 is convenient and a pleasant place for a leisurely drink. Bedrooms are also available. Lovers of the historic pub will enjoy the Strines Inn, handy for the reservoirs and offering tremendous views, this pub also has modest bedrooms.

Much of Lincolnshire is given over to agriculture and its fishing opportunities are somewhat restricted. Pubs are also fairly thin on the ground. The Priory at Louth (0507) 602930 is a welcoming comfortable hotel in which to stay and The Leagate at Coningsby (0526) 42370 is a pub that is well worth a visit. There may not be the abundant game fishing opportunities offered to those who live in the middle of England or northern Scotland, but there are a number of waters that provide satisfactory sport and, in many cases, there are pubs and hotels aplenty where one can enjoy a relaxing day or two, free from the pressures of modern day living.

The Peak District (*Staffordshire Moorlands District Council*)

CARVED SALMON REPRODUCTIONS

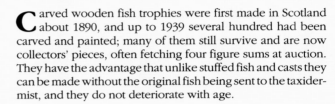

Carved wooden fish trophies were first made in Scotland about 1890, and up to 1939 several hundred had been carved and painted; many of them still survive and are now collectors' pieces, often fetching four figure sums at auction. They have the advantage that unlike stuffed fish and casts they can be made without the original fish being sent to the taxidermist, and they do not deteriorate with age.

Now it is again possible to commission a carved trophy of a salmon caught recently or many years ago. I have been a keen fisherman since boyhood, and have a special interest in making life-size salmon models. I think I am uniquely qualified for this work, being good with my hands and something of a perfectionist, and having been trained as an anatomy student to observe the fine details of body shape and physiognomy.

Like the old trophies mine are relief carvings: they are made from seasoned lime with the fins, gills, eye, mouth etc. carved in fine detail, and meticulously painted in acrylics. All I need to know to produce a trophy is the weight, length and sex of the fish, but for greater accuracy it helps to have good colour close-up photographs and if possible a carefully drawn profile on brown paper.

Illustrations alone cannot capture the beauty of the finished trophy, but examples of my work can be seen in various parts of the U.K., especially at the following hotels mentioned in this book:

Inver Lodge, Lochinver
Seafield Lodge, Grantown on Spey
Gleneagles, Auchterarder
Ballathie House, Stanley
Dryburgh Abbey, St. Boswells
Sunlaws House, Kelso
Tillmouth Park, Cornhill on Tweed
Bishop Field, Allandale

A trophy made now will provide you with a permanent record of a special fish, and your grand-children with a valuable reminder of the fisherman!

To discuss
a commission
please telephone

Dr Peter Lyne
Rinteln
Barrowfield Close
Hove
Sussex BN36TP
☎ (0273) 507328

SOUTH OF ENGLAND

Artist: **Don Vaughan**   *PEACEFUL MOMENTS*   *Courtesy of:* **Rosenstiels'**

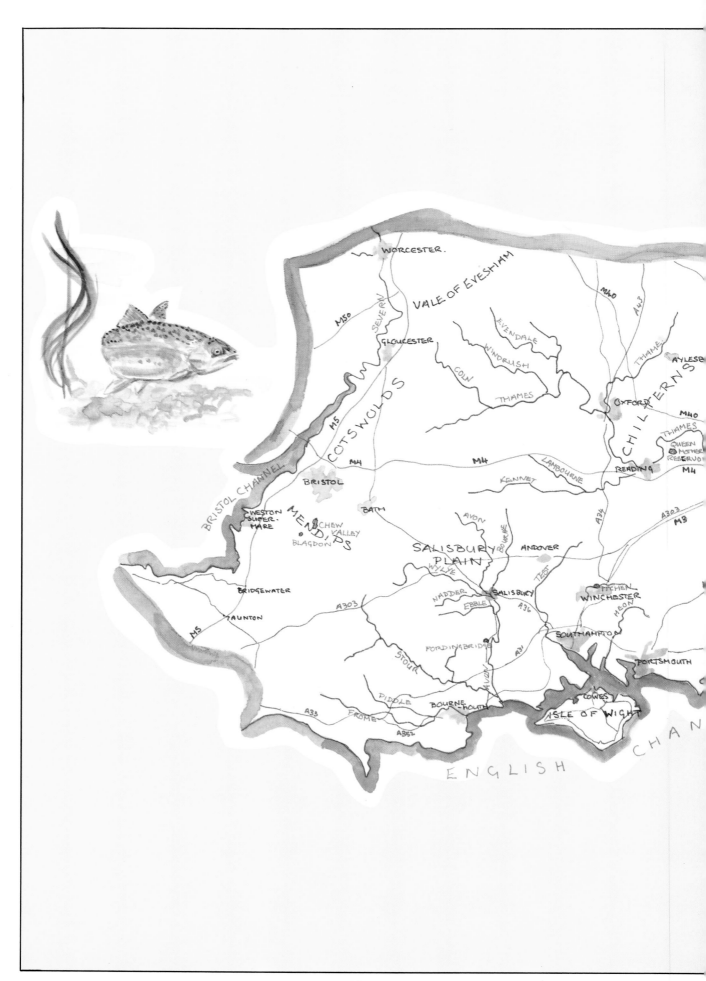

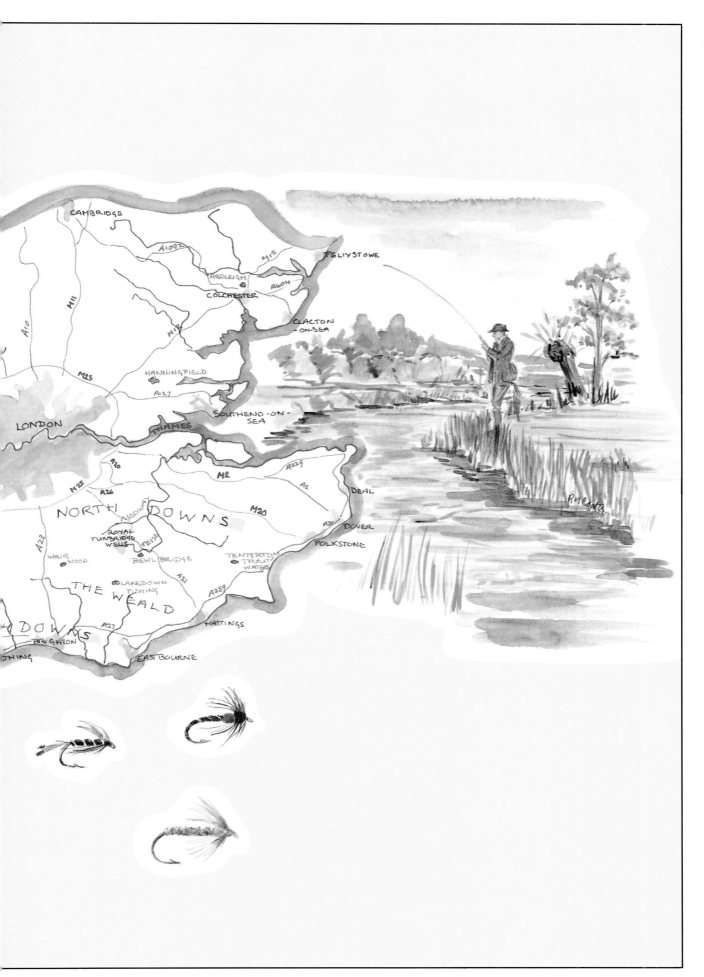

CAMBRIDGE

A1092

M12

FELIXSTOWE

ARDLEIGH

COLCHESTER

A604

M11

A10

CLACTON
- ON-SEA

M12

M25

HANNINGFIELD

A127

LONDON

THAMES

SOUTHEND-ON-
SEA

A229

A20

A2

M2

DEAL

M25

A26

NORTH

MEDWAY

DOWNS

M20

A20

DOVER

A23

ROYAL
TUNBRIDGE
WELLS

TEISE

FOLKSTONE

WEIR
WOOD

BEWL
BRIDGE

A21

TENTERTON
TROUT
WATERS

LAKEDOWN
FISHING

THE WEALD

A259

DOWNS

A27

HASTINGS

BRIGHTON

JTHING

EASTBOURNE

R.HEGATE.

PENNYHILL PARK

Just 50 minutes from central London in the full splendour of the English countryside lies the little village of Bagshot and Pennyhill Park.

At the end of the winding driveway the stone-fronted, creeper-clad house stands surrounded by 112 acres of parkland and lake. This is Pennyhill Park, built in 1849 by the pioneering Canadian bridge-builder, James Hodge. The building has been altered several times to suit the individual tastes and requirements of its various owners.

The total commitment to service at Pennyhill complement the traditions of its historic past. On entering the main hallway and with the stately sweep of the period staircase a warm welcome awaits you from attentive staff. Trained to Edwardian standards of courtesy they provide impeccable and discreet service.

Peace and tranquillity surround this house which, though old, provides every modern amenity.

You can watch polo at Smiths' Lawn Windsor; Sunningdale and Wentworth are just two of the nearby prestigious golf courses. Pennyhill Park also has its own nine-hole golf course and other sporting facilities including tennis courts, a Roman-styled swimming pool, clay pigeon shooting and horse riding stables with professional coaching. The sauna and solarium are housed in the Pennyhill Park orangery, and the three-acre lake is annually stocked with brown and rainbow trout for those in search of more tranquil pursuits.

The award winning Latymer restaurant provides all the elegance amd quiet dignity expected of its surroundings. The food, of mainly British produce, is served in the traditional way; and the service, known to many, is complemented by an outstanding selection of fine wines.

There are 76 bedrooms and suites in this fine example of the English country house, all individually designed and beautifully furnished. Each room is named after a shrub or flower, save for the most luxurious Hayward suite, the namesake of the last permanent occupant of this English country manor house. Every room at Pennyhill Park is furnished and decorated using soft, elegant fabrics and comforting themes such as walnut and oak.

Pennyhill Park Hotel and Country Club,
London Road,
Bagshot,
Surrey. GU19 5ET
Tel: (0276) 71774

SOUTHERN ENGLAND

This area includes such legendary chalk streams as the Test, the Itchen and the Kennet and still waters from Bewl Water in Kent to Blagdon and Chew in the west. As well as the big reservoirs, there are many private fisheries which range in size from small single lake concerns to those which have several large lakes and are run on a bigger commercial basis. The result of all this is that while a day on a famous chalk stream may be too far away or too expensive, there is a good variety of trout fishing available to all within a short distance of any town. There is even fishing to be had within London for one can spend a pleasant and relaxing evening after the cares and stresses of office life at the Nine Elms Reservoir in Barnes. There is also a limited amount of salmon fishing to be had in the area on rivers such as the Hampshire, Avon and the Frome in Dorset.

The chalk streams of southern England have long been famous and their praises have been sung by many generations of fishermen. A day on these gin clear and beautifully maintained waters is a unique experience. Before the improvements to the A303 I always used to take the A30 for not far from the M3 motorway the road winds down a hill to the small town of Stockbridge. At the Grosvenor Hotel here, is that most exclusive of fishing clubs, the Houghton, which has been so ably served by three generations of the Lunn family. Looking over the bridge to the far end of the town, one can see the clear water with its inviting patches of weedy shelter and the trout swimming lazily against the current. Several of the houses have little feeder streams running past their gardens and here, where only two or three feet separate the banks, there can be trout of up to 2lb, fat on tit-bits from their human neighbours.

Another good place for trout watching is Hungerford which is not far beyond Newbury and is a few miles away from the M4. This small town is the antiques capital of the area; there is a large range of shops from an indoor antique market to the most exclusive dealing in top quality Georgian furniture. At the bottom of the town there is a bridge under which flows that delightful stream, the Kennet and closeby is the recently restored Kennet and Avon canal. Walking though the meadows alongside the river one can see trout lying in wait for those appetising morsels that the river brings to their larder. You can fish the Kennet for free as some of the old buildings have fishing rights and shooting rights on the common.

One of the delights of fishing a chalk stream is the abundance of fly life. Many fisherman's favourite natural fly is the mayfly for this is the trout's favourite delicacy to which he rises without thought or care. The Mayfly hatch which is around the first two weeks in May and is often referred to as 'duffers delight' because the trout rise so freely that beginners will strike lucky. Old fishing books are full of stories about the excitement the news of a hatch bought.

The Mayfly, or Ephemera Danica to give it its proper name, is a remarkable creature. This beautiful insect is Britain's largest aquatic insect. It is also unusual for its punctuality and the size of hatches. Perhaps its most remarkable characteristic is that the adult Mayfly can neither eat nor drink. This is why its life is so short and within a few hours of the hatch the water can look like a greyish soup of trembling bodies, twisted wings and nymphal shucks broken only by the rings of rising trout. It is a matter of grave concern to all fishermen that the mayfly is on the decline and has disappeared in parts of Wiltshire, Dorset, Kent, Sussex and even Hampshire. The culprit is modern farm-

ing with its insecticides which get into the water and fertilisers which result in huge growths of algae and land drainage schemes which cause unatural rises and falls in water levels. As well as affecting the mayfly, they affect the whole character of the river just as hydro-electric and afforestation schemes have done in Scotland. With so much talk of conservation and potecting the environment is it not time that something was done?

Dorset is a sportsman's paradise. While the hunting may not be as good as Leicestershire, the shooting as good as Norfolk or the fishing as good as Hampshire, few other counties can boast such a good standard of all these sports.

The best known river in Dorset is the **Frome** whose source is near Evershot. This river has been described as a miniature Test with chalk hills on either side and rich meadows in between which the river meanders over its gravel bed on its way through Dorchester to Wareham and Poole Harbour. The upper reaches are good for trouting while below Dorchester it used to be regarded as one of the best little salmon rivers in the south of England and at the turn of the century regularly used to produce 40 pounders! I have heard of salmon as far up as Maiden Newton where the river is no more than a few feet across but it holds some nice wild trout.

Downstream at Frampton, there used to be marvellous trout fishing in the days of the Great Edwardian sportsman, Squire Brinsley Sheridan, a descendant of the famous playwright. In 1907, the Vicar the Rev. Filleul hooked a notable trout just above Dorchester. Having played his fish he eventually bought it to the bank but it was too big for his net. Luckily a servant was passing on her way to the Manor and she was asked to bring him a washing basket! The fish was successfully landed in the basket and found to weigh 12¾ lb. The Frome holds the record for a sea-trout caught in the British Isles at 24lb. The salmon fishing suffered a setback about thirty years ago when the army dumped a large quantity of lead based paint in the river. However, the Frome has recovered well and has produced a 42 pounder in the last decade while fish of between 15lb and 18lb are not uncommon.

The other main river is the **Piddle** which is mentioned in he Domesday Book and whose name is of Saxon origin. From its source near Alton Pancras to its mouth at Poole Harbour near that of the Frome, the river is some twenty two miles long. The names of some of the villages through which it flows were bowdlerised by the Victorians who felt that Piddle offended their sensibilities for after flowing through Piddletrentide and Piddlehinton the prefix changes to puddle and the river reaches Puddletown and then on to Tolpuddle of 'martyr' and trade union fame. The river is smaller than the Frome and produces the occasional salmon and sea-trout, but these can be big fish. A salmon of 34lb and a sea-trout of 14lb have been caught within the last fifteen years. The Piddle and its feeders offer good trout fishing with fish weighing up to 3lb.

Nearly all the fishing on the rivers is privately owned and difficult to get on, but help is at hand from Richard Slocock's Wessex Fly Fishing at Tolpuddle (0305) 848460. First class tuition is available here as is bed and breakfast at £19.50 a night or alternatively you can rent one of the cottages. There is a comprehensive tackle shop and a wide range of courses from one hour casting lessons to four day courses. Fishing for guests can be arranged on both the Frome and the Piddle and the cost varies between £20 and £40 according to the beat. The fishing on the Piddle is on a catch and release basis with barbless hooks and a maximum of ten fish may be caught in a day. Wessex also has lakes stocked with brownies and rainbows up to 10lb where a four fish day ticket will cost you £18.50. Mr Harry Maddox of Wool Bridge Manor (0929) 462313 has one and a quarter miles of single bank fishing below East Burton on the Frome. Salmon here are around 16lb and the grilse run between July and September and are between 7lb and 10lb. 1990 saw 28 fish caught on this water and in 1991, eleven had been caught by July. This beat has two rods and a day permit costs £25.

Another good still water fishery is Flowers Farm (0300) 341351. This fishery is not far from the village of Cerne Abbas with its famous pre historic giant cut into the chalk hillside and is situated on the edge of Batcombe Down with views over Blackmore Vale. There are five spring-fed lakes here, all of a smallish size and a ticket will cost £16 per day. Half day and evening tickets are available too. Day tickets start at 5.30am. Completely different in character is Wessex's waters 142 acre reservoir at Sutton Bingham. This is just off the A37 Dorchester to Yeovil road on the Dorset Somerset border. It is a very attractive situation and much work has been done recently to remove the silt from the southern arm of the reservoir which should also improve the fishing both in that area and generally. The lodge is designed to cater for the disabled fisherman and boats can be hired from the Ranger, Ivan Tinsley (0935) 872389. 1990 saw a rainbow weighing in at 8lb 8oz and a brown trout of 7lb 15oz.

Any county would consider itself fortunate to have one river as famous as the Test, or the Itchen or the Avon but Hampshire has all three! The **Avon** rises near Devizes in the Vale of Pewsey and its course runs close to Stonehenge. At Salisbury it is greatly enlarged by its tributaries of which the Wylye and the Nadder offer the best trout fishing. From Salisbury the river runs due south to enter the sea at Christchurch in Dorset. The Avon used to be one of the most famous mixed fisheries in England; the Upper Avon is a typical chalk stream and offers first class trouting for those lucky enough to fish it. The middle Avon has salmon, trout and course fish, while its lower reaches offer salmon, trout and superb sea-trout fishing. The river has good weed growth throughout its length which makes for good insect life and while it may not be a prolific salmon river, its deep pools are renowned for producing heavy fish. Salisbury and District Angling Club has some excellent varied chalk stream fishing.

Their twelve miles of the Avon is prime trout and grayling water and some of the lower stretches offer the chance of salmon. The Club's fishing stretches from Durnford, north of Salisbury down to Burgate and also includes some fishing on the Bourne and two miles of the Nadder and two stretches of the Wylye. The Club has a relatively open membership and your first year will cost £83 for a seasons fishing (1991 price). Further details are available from John Eadies, 20 Catherine Street, Salisbury (0722) 328535.

Downstream at Braemore the Bat and Ball (0725) 22252 has approximately one mile of double bank fishing which is free to guests and day tickets are available to non-residents. Bisterne is some three miles south of Ringwood and the Bisterne Fishery comprises just under three miles of double bank fishing divided into three beats which hold two rods. This is a very pretty spot, with its wildflower meadows and great variety of

wildlife it is a Site of Special Scientific Interest. The water is usually booked well ahead but there is a chance of getting a day here. A few miles south on the B3347 is the village of Winkton and the Winkton Fishery whose two and a half miles of double bank fishing is divided into two beats. In the old days this used to be a spring fishery but the season now extends until the end of July. Day rods are occasionally available and if you are interested in fishing either this water or the Bisterne Fishery you should write to Major J. M. Mills of Bisterne Manor, Ringwood, Hampshire. Alternatively, for Bisterne you could try the Tyrrells Ford Hotel (0425) 72646 or the Fisherman's Haunt (0202) 484071 for Winkton. This used to be a favourite pub for fishermen but in the opinion of the keeper now caters more for yuppies!

At Christchurch, is the famous Royalty Fishery which has two miles of water. Bridge Pool is particularly good for sea-trout and June 1991 saw a fine fish of 14lb caught here. Fishing starts at 6.00am and most rods start the day with a fly before changing to bait during the day and returning to fly in the evening. Only two rods are allowed and the price for two rods, including a punt varies between £64 and £80 according to the season. Rather less expensive is the stretch of river above Bridge Pool where a day's salmon fishing costs £24 and sea-trout between £6.50 and £11. The 'Compound' at the top weir tends to only fish well in good water levels while the holding pool, Parlour, does well in low water conditions. Two rods can fish the pool for between £46 and £64 a day. Further details may be had from Major D. E. Ransley of West Hampshire Water Company, Water Mill Road, Christchurch, who own the fishery. Day tickets are also available from Davis Tackle Shop (0202) 485169 at 75, Bargate which is almost opposite the Royalty Inn (used to be the Red Lion), known locally by some as the 'spud pub' for its large variety of baked potatoes.

The **Wylye** and the **Nadder** are both first class chalk streams. The Marquess of Bath's Estate at Longleat has the uppermost two and a half miles of the Wylye dry fly water. Season tickets only are available at a cost of £450 plus VAT and can be obtained from T. R. W. Moore Esq. of the Longleat Estate (0985) 844324. Day tickets can, however, be bought for the Sutton Veny Estate's water (0985) 40682 which is the next main fishery downstream, at a cost £25 per week day or £30 at weekends. Tuition and tackle can be arranged for guests but prior notice is required. The estate has three and a half miles of double bank fishing and the average brownie on this stocked water is 1¾ lb. The Hunter's Moon Sporting and Country Club in Warminster (0895) 219977 has a mile of single bank fishing on the outskirts of the town. Membership costs £5 per annum which allows you to fish one of the two beats for £7.50. This is for one of the sessions which the day is divided up into and the limit is a brace. Roxton Sporting Agency (0488) 683222 can arrange a day or a season for parties of up to eight people. Both the Wylye and the Nadder flow through Wilton Park. Wilton House is famous for its cube and double cube rooms designed by Inigo Jones and there is a delightful Palladian Bridge over the Nadder. Tisbury Angling Club has a good stretch of approximately four miles on the Nadder. This water has a good stock of wild brown trout who average around 1¼ lb. The Club is keen on its grayling fishing and has many imports from other clubs anxious to limit their numbers of this prolific breeding fish. Membership costs £20 a year with a small joining fee and further details are available from the Secretary, Mr H. J. Marshall of The Forge, Fovant, Nr Salisbury (0722) 70203. The Rod Box

SOUTHERN ENGLAND

in Winchester (0962) 883600 have one beat available on a day basis on the Compton Chamberlayne water. This an excellent, well managed fishery and is well stocked with good size brownies and rainbows.

The **Test** is probably the most famous chalkstream in the world. Talk to fishermen as far apart as the Shores of Lake Taupo in New Zealand or on the banks of a trout stream in Montana and the Test is 'The' English trout stream. Although fishing books have spread its fame, its glories have been known to fishermen for hundreds of years. Many famous fishermen have stalked its banks and peered into a pool or a likely lie. At Longparish, here is that veteran of Wellington's Peninsular Campaigns, Colonel Peter Hawker who killed forty trout in three hours and over 12,000 trout in fifty years. I purposely used the word 'killed' as this great sportsman only killed fish of over 3¾ lb and returned far more than he took. In Stockbridge is the Grosvenor and, above its portico, is the Houghton Club, founded in 1822 and the most famous fishing club in the world. Here is Compton, the home of the late Sir Thomas Sopwith, the designer of the pioneer fighter plane, the Sopwith Camel, who would not allow his guests to fish in the evening and who, with his wife, killed twenty one salmon in a day in 1954. Broadlands used to belong to Lord Mount Temple and here is Lady Mount Temple fishing, the special place where monster trout lurk. In the morning, she has seen a large fish and determines to try for him in the evening. She hooks him and brings him safely to the net but he is not the one she spotted earlier on so he is returned although he weighed 11lb. The pool is rested and she tries again with a 'special lure' for these trout are more accustomed to dining on exotic morsels such as liver rather than flies! There is a fierce tug, it is the fish, and after a gallant fight he is landed

and found to weigh 13lb. Many famous fly tiers have walked these banks and observed the hatches and the trouts' ensuing banquets. Here are Francis Halford and George Marryat of the Houghton Club who helped to pioneer dry fly fishing and G.E.M. Skues who tied many a fly but is probably best known for his pheasant-tail nymph which also works so well in still waters.

The twenty five mile course of the **Itchen** which Skues knew so well, offers superb trout fishing along its length from its source near New Alresford down to Southampton. Like the Test, it has an abundant weed growth and hence a wide and varied insect life with prolific hatches of mayflies, olives, hawthorn, damselfly and sedges. Similar to its famous sister, salmon and sea-trout are caught on its lower reaches. The Test may be better known but I know several friends who would prefer to fish the Itchen. Just as the many excellent small streams like the **Meon** are overshadowed by the better known waters. Fishing on the Test and the Itchen is very sought after to say the least! As a result, they are difficult to get on and very expensive when you do! Mrs Howlett of the Rod Box in Winchester (0962) 883600 may be able to help you as the company rents, or acts as agent, for approximately forty miles of fishing on the two rivers. The fishing is let on a seasonal basis on a named day of the week either as a full or half rod. Prices start at £61 per day and the water is always booked years ahead for the mayfly season.

The Greyhound Hotel at Stockbridge (0264) 81033 has a third of a mile single bank fishing which is adjacent to the hotel and just downstream from the Houghton Club's Grosvenor Hotel. This beat holds two rods and although hotel guests have priority, day tickets are sometimes available and cost between £40 and £50.

Broadlands   (Broadlands Estate)

LEE PARK LODGE

Lee Park Lodge is a converted farm house on the famous Broadlands Estate situated at the Southern end of the Test Valley close to the River Test. It has been luxuriously and very tastefully refurbished to provide comfortable reception rooms and eight twin bedded bedrooms, all with bathroom en suite and direct dial telephones.

Food at the Lodge is of Cordon Bleu standard and we can adapt our menus to accommodate any particular dietary requirements specified by our guests. The meals are accompanied by fine wines, many of which have been carefully selected from the Broadland's cellars.

The Lodge is ideally situated for a great many sporting activities, fishing being one of the favourites. During the April - October season it is possible to fish on the waters that Prince Charles has known and loved ever since he was a young boy, whilst staying in first class accommodation close by. Lee Park Lodge offers superb fly fishing for trout for up to six rods on its own beats on the world famous River Test - full outfits of rods, flies and nets are available for an extra charge.

A residential fishing package at the Lodge includes accommodation, all meals, fishing with a ghillie service available and use of a hospitality marquee on the river bank for relaxation and weather protection. A picnic lunch will be prepared each morning and brought over to you wherever you are fishing so the only thing you have to think about is the sport.

It is not necessary to stay at the Lodge in order to 'sample its many delights', a day fishing package can also be arranged, consisting of three course lunch and a buffet supper at the Lodge, fishing with ghillie service and use of the hospitality marquee.

For a relaxing break filled with all the comforts of home yet the service of a first class hotel, Lee Park Lodge has successfully combined the two to provide the perfect holiday for the keen fisherman.

Lee Park Lodge
Broadlands
Romsey
Hampshire SO51 9ZD
Tel: (0794) 517888
Fax: (0794) 516878

FIFEHEAD MANOR

The foundations of this lovely Manor house date from the 11th century when it was part of the estates of Saxon Earl Godwin. Together with its barns and stables, it stands in several acres of lovely gardens. The 'Wallops' are known for their quaint thatched cottages and beautiful Saxon church, and the Wallop brook meanders peacefully through the villages.

Fifehead Manor is ideally situated for visiting Salisbury and its lovely cathedral. Winchester cathedral is equally beautiful and breathtaking. Romsey Abbey and Broadlands, the home of the late Earl Mountbatten, can be seen on the same day and every visitor to this part of the world should, of course, gaze in wonder at Stonehenge which is only 15 minutes drive from Fifehead Manor.

For the fishing enthusiast, excellent fishing is to be had on the nearby Rivers Test and Itchin. After a day's excursion, be it sight-seeing or fishing, our guests can at all times expect a warm and friendly welcome.

Our dining-room was the main hall of the medieval Manor of Fifehead where one can still see the remains of the minstrels' gallery used in the Middle Ages. Here, you can delight in the inventiveness and culinary skills of our chef who uses only the freshest of ingredients.

Fifehead Manor has 15 very attractive bedrooms each charmingly and individually decorated. They are well equipped with the latest amenities and have pleasant bathrooms attached. They are rooms in which to feel relaxed and at peace.

Fifehead Manor
Middle Wallop
Stockbridge
Hampshire S020 8EG
Tel: (0264) 781 565
Fax: (0264) 781400

To take a day for fishing on a famous chalkstream, in pursuit of the native brown trout, amongst unspoilt countryside, has a powerful appeal. So much so, that fishing men & women are drawn from across Britain and around the world to sample the delights of fishing such rivers as the Test & Itchen.

The Test & Itchen are the undisputed kings of a region that abounds with top-class fishing, with other rivers, the Alre, Dever, Kennet, Nadder & Wylye proving worthy courtiers. They share in common the benefit of water drawn from the chalk hills, flowing with crystal clear water, in which the hard-fighting, brown trout thrive.

Fishing Breaks offer an exclusive service that gives the opportunity to fish some of the finest beats on the Test, Itchen & other rivers in southern England. As an independent company, not tied to any particular river, beat or agency, they are able to select the fishing best suited to the requirements of their clients.

Fishing Breaks have a range of services for clients, in addition to simply providing the fishing. Perhaps you would like a Guide? The Guide will acquaint you with the beat, local rules and best methods to employ. He'll remain with you throughout the day to 'gillie' and generally look after your needs. The Guide also carries a supply of tackle, clothing & footwear. So, if you don't

have all that's necessary, or simply prefer to travel light, he'll be able to kit you out.

Skilled tuition is provided at all levels; from those who have never picked up a rod before, to those who simply want old skills revived.

Fishing Breaks offer daily fishing throughout the trout fishing season which runs from early April until the end of October. The coveted Mayfly period usually falls during the last two weeks of May & the first week of June. Clients are welcomed from home & abroad, including business groups & parties.

So, if you'd rather be fishing, why not call Fishing Breaks. They offer a complete range of services to the fishermen who wish to try some of the best chalkstream fishing that England, and perhaps the world, has to offer.

Fishing Breaks Ltd
16 Bickerton Road
London
N19 5JR
Tel: 071 281 6737
Fax: 071 281 8151

SOUTHERN ENGLAND

Mr Robin Gow of Orvis at Nether Wallop (0264) 781212 can arrange a day for you on the Itchen near Abbots Worthy. This half mile beat is mainly stocked and dry fly and upstream nymphing are the permitted methods. The trout average 2 1/2lb and the cost of a day is £300 for three rods and includes a ghillie. Mr Gow also has access to beats on the Test such as Timsbury 5 and 6 which are below Kimbridge and the famous Ginger Beer Beat at Kimbridge. This is four miles upstream from Romsey and this prime beat comprises half a mile of shallow pools and deep runs. It has four rods and costs £375 per day. At Broadlands, the home of the late Lord Mountbatten, there is over two miles of the Test which is divided into three beats. A season's salmon fishing for two rods on a named day costs £780 while half a rod is one day a fortnight and costs £395. The comparative costs for trout fishing are £950 for a full rod and £500 for a half. Day tickets are available at between £55 and £75 per day and further information can be obtained from the Estate Office (0794) 517888. Roxton Sporting Agency (0488) 683222 have recently been instructed to let days on the Compton Manor Estate water which comprises some six miles of prime fishing on the Test divided into ten beats. Two of these beats will be let by the day at a cost of just under £1200 or £1400 during the mayfly season (May 15th to June 10th). This price includes fishing for four rods, lunch and a ghillie.

For those of us with more modest means, there is an excellent still water fishing to be had in Hampshire. Avington Trout Fishing (0962) 78312 is near Itchen Abbas and offers fishing on three lakes and a chalk stream feeder of the Itchen which are stocked on a daily basis. The fishery is open all year, including Christmas Day and New Year's Day, and is renowned for its big rainbows. Several 14lb to 20lb fish have been caught here and in 1986 saw a superb fish of 20lb 7oz. A day here costs £30. At Sandleheath, near Fordingbridge, there is the Rockbourne Trout Fishery (0725) 3603. The fishery has six spring fed lakes which have good hatches of fly and three beats on the Sweatford water which is a tributary of the Avon. The lakes are stocked on a daily basis with rainbows which average 2lb 8oz and a five fish day ticket costs £24.50. A comprehensive range of flies and tackle is available from the fishery office. In 1990, 10% of the fish caught here were over 4lb, the best rainbow was 13lb 12oz and best brownie 6lb 14oz. An added attraction is that the fishery has a licensed bar with meals and snacks.

There are two good stillwaters in the Andover area. Rooksbury Mill and Dever Springs, Rooksbury Mill (0264) 35292 is set in sixteen acres on the outskirts of Andover and has two lakes of six and a half acres and two and a half acres and one mile on the river Anton which is a tributary of the Test. The fishery shop has a comprehensive range of tackle including their own range of carbon rods. Expert tuition is available as is a smoking service. The fishery can also organise corporate days for parties of more than twenty rods and will prepare breakfast and lunch. A five fish day ticket costs £25. If its big fish you're after then I suggest you visit Dever Springs (0264) 72592 at Barton Stacey which is just off the A303 some six mile east of Andover. The fishery has two lakes totalling six acres and a half mile stretch of the Dever, a tributary of the Test. The minimum stocking size is 3lb and the average is 4lb 8oz . Double figure fish are taken most days on this water which has excellent fly life including an abundant Mayfly hatch. Casts with a breaking strain of under 6lb are prohibited which is not surprising since the Dever

River Itchen   (Winchester Tourism)

THE ROYALTY FISHERY

Set at the lower end of the Hampshire Avon which then runs on into Christchurch Harbour and to the sea, lies one of the South of England's most famous fisheries. Granted into private ownership by the Crown prior to Magna Carta, this part of the river is noted for its combination of coarse and game fishing. Spring and summer salmon run regularly and sea trout are prolific in the revered Bridge Pool in the centre of the town.

Anglers also find a wide choice of coarse species including barbel, chub, carp, roach, bream, pike and perch. The easy access to the banks makes it a favourite with visitors from all over the country. Juvenile anglers are also encouraged and there are one or two areas which offer anyone who may be disabled a chance to fish.

Permits are readily available from both Davis Fishing Tackle Shop at 75 Bargates, about a hundred yards from the main fishery car park, where there is ample parking space; and from the Bailiffs Office at the Fishery House, 2 Avon Buildings. The price of a permit includes the National Rivers Authority rod licence because the Fishery has a General Licence. The quoted price of the permit also includes VAT.

For those who enjoy fly-fishing, there is a stocked Rainbow trout lake of about one acre available for a limited number of rods each day.

Christchurch itself is very handy for shopping, restaurants, pubs and entertainment. There are a number of hotels in the area, including The Kings Arms which is conveniently adjacent to the Bridge Pool, as well as guest houses only a few minutes from the fishery, catering specifically for the needs of fishermen. Bournemouth is a ten minute car drive away if the rest of the family is not addicted to the piscatorial skills. Caravan and camping sites abound in the area.

Details of permit prices can be obtained in a brochure
available from:
The Manager, Recreation Services
West Hampshire Water Company
Mill Road
Christchurch
Dorset BH23 2LU
Tel: (0202) 499000
Fax: (0202) 499100

SOUTHERN ENGLAND

has produced a rainbow of 22lb 15oz and a brown trout of 18lb 2oz. The chance of catching one of these big fish on a four fish day ticket costs £40.

Among other good stillwater fisheries in Wiltshire is Arrow Springs (0980) 53557. This fishery is at Durrington on the A345 and just a few miles north of Amesbury. There are two spring fed lakes of two acres and five acres which have excellent mayfly, sedge and olive hatches. The water is stocked on a daily basis with fish from 2lb upwards. The fishery also has a stretch of the Avon which is dry fly and upstream nymphing water and only barbless hooks are permitted. A four fish day ticket on the lakes costs £24. 1990 saw a best bag of 24lb 10oz and a best fish of 12lb 3oz. Perhaps more significant is the high average weight of 3lb 4oz and the rod average was 3.2 fish. Some ten miles further west on the A303 is the junction with the A36 and less than two miles south on this road is the village of Steeple Langford and Langford Fisheries (0722) 790770. There are two lakes of seven and fifteen acres here. The lakes have excellent insect life and in particular have spectacular evening rises to hatching buzzers. The average fish is around 2lb 4oz while the record rainbow is 17lb and brownie is 8lb 5oz. A five fish day ticket will cost you £23. The fishery can also arrange corporate days when tuition by well known experts can be arranged. It is in the beautiful Wylye Valley and is unique in that it is also an officially recognised nature reserve. Zeals is the most westerly Wiltshire village on the A303 and here, Zeals Fish Farm (0747) 840573 has a two acre lake stocked with rainbows of up to 14lb. The record is 14lb 4oz. A day ticket costs £18 for four fish and it is nice to see that barbless hooks are preferred.

West of here are the well known Bristol Waters Fisheries of **Chew, Blagdon** and **Barrow.** Blagdon was the first reservoir to be opened to the public for trout fishing. In 1904 this was regarded as a daring venture but it soon gained popularity and the precedent has been followed by many other reservoirs. Over the years, the fishery has mellowed and now has all the appearance of a natural lake with varied marsh vegetation, wild-flowers, rich meadows and mixed conifer and broadleafed woodlands. Twelve rowing boats, including one adapted for the disabled, are available on this 440 acre water. Chew is nearly three times the size of Blagdon and is surrounded by unspoiled meadows and woods. There are some seven miles of bank fishing and twenty six motorboats are available. Barrow consists of three small reservoirs of 60, 40 and 25 acres and the average fish is around 1lb 10oz, slightly less than Blagdon and Chew where the average is 2lb. The total yearly catch on these waters is over 50,000 and there are many better fish of 4lb and over. The company is actively concerned with conservation. There is a nature reserve at Herriotts Pool on Chew where a number of islands have been created to encourage nesting ducks and in the 20 acres of parkland which are managed by the Nature Conservancy Council there is a number of green winged orchids. A day costs £10 and permits can be obtained from the lodges which also sell tackle and flies. There is a wide range of help on offer to beginners. There are free casting lessons or you can pay for more comprehensive tuition given by NAC qualified instructors. For under 18s, there is a special £1 permit for the first five visits is accompanied by an experienced fisherman. Also on offer are special beginner's days when experienced local anglers will help you to have a go at trout or bank fishing. Further details can be had from the company's Woodford Lodge Office (0272) 332339.

There are several stillwater fisheries in the disused gravel pits around Cirencester in Gloucestershire. They tend to be quite deep and having only recently been converted, lack the maturity of Blagdon and Chew. North of here at Upper Swell near Stow-on-the-Wold is Donnington Fish Farm (0451) 30873.

The lake is stocked with browns and rainbows and an unusual feature is that two fish are guaranteed on a day ticket. The shop sells both hot and cold smoked trout and a very good smoked trout paté.

The River **Coln** is a typical Cotswold chalk stream and has long been prized for the availability of its trout fishing. The Bull Hotel at Fairford (0285) 712535 has one and a half miles of single bank fishing which takes six rods. Hotel residents pay £9.50 for two fish day ticket and the charge for non-residents is £17.50. The water is stocked with browns and rainbows which average around 1½ lb which is slightly more than the browns. At picturesque Bibury, the Bibury Court Hotel (0285) 740337 has got just under a quarter of a mile of river which is available to guests only and costs £10 per day. Also at Bibury is the recently refurbished Swan Hotel (0285) 74204 whose six hundred yards hold three rods. There is a three fish limit and in 1988 an 11lb fish was taken here. This part of the river is a popular tourist attraction and although requested not to, people often throw bread for the trout. However, they will take a fly and early morning and evening are the best times.

East of here are the **Lambourn** and the **Kennet.** The Lambourn is a delightful little chalkstream with a good stock of brownies and a two pounder on this small water is a good fish. All the fishing is syndicated out but Field and Stream Tackle Shop (0635) 43186 in Lambourn may be able to arrange a day for you. The course of the Kennet covers some 44 miles from its source near Marlbrough Downs to where it joins the Thames above Reading. The lower reaches are a combination of river and canal and are not of interest to us, but the stretch from above Marlbrough to the Hungerford area has long been famous as some of the finest chalk stream fishing in the country. The Town and Manor of Hungerford bought their fishing from King James I in 1617 and, as a result, enjoy fishing on two miles of the Kennet, half a mile of one of the carries and a mile on the Dunn. A full time keeper is employed on the water which has both brownies and rainbows. Two pounders are caught regularly and there are fish of up to 5lb. Season tickets only are available and cost £890. Further details may be obtained from Colonel Macey (0488) 682770.

Some of the best small stream fishing you could wish for can be found at the Denford Fisheries (0488) 684179 which has two and a half miles of carriers and a short stretch on the Kennet itself. 1990 saw 1100 rainbows and 125 brownies caught here and of the rainbows, eighty were over 2lb, thirty over 3lb and three topped the 4lb mark. Dry fly only is the rule until the end of June after which upstream nymphing is permitted. The water holds six rods and a day's fishing costs £30, except in June when it is £32.50. The reason for this is that early June sees a fine Mayfly hatch. The owner, Mr Wilson, reckons his keeper Fred Taylor, who is 82, is the oldest keeper in the country!

At Kintbury, is Mr Edward Hill's Barton Court Fishery (0488) 58226 which has three miles of double bank fishing on the three main streams and some carriers. This area of the Kennet used to be marshland until it was drained by French prisoners

FINE FISHING IN AVON'S LAKELAND

Blagdon Lake, Bristol Water Co. Mention Blagdon and Chew Valley Lakes to any trout fisherman ---and his eyes will light up!

For these two beautiful lakes, set in fine Mendip countryside near Bristol, are renowned for the quality of the fishing and their superb surroundings.

Blagdon, in fact, was the first reservoir in England to be opened to the public for trout fishing...way back in 1904. Since then, the reputation of the Bristol Water fisheries has spread world-wide.

Both Lakes offer high quality bank and boat fishing in idyllic surroundings. Blagdon (440 acres of water) nestles close to the hills; while Chew (1,200 acres of water) lies a few miles away in the heart of the Chew Valley, surrounded by unspoilt meadows and woodland.

Bristol Water hatches and grows all its own trout and aims to produce the best quality Browns and Rainbows for restocking. The total catch at all the company's fisheries in 1990 was 53,781, with an average weight of 2lbs at Chew. A brown trout weighing in at 11lbs 7oz was caught at Chew this year, establishing a new record.

The Company offers comfortable, well-equipped Lodges at Chew and Blagdon where permits, tackle and advice can be obtained. For more information, contact:

Bristol Water Fisheries,
Woodford Lodge,
Chew Stoke,
Bristol BS18 8XH.
Tel: 0272 332339

WESTBURY FISHERY

Westbury Fishery is now one of the older venues in the country and is accepted as one of the very best. The lakes are situated in a beautiful part of the Thames Valley, surrounded by the Tudor farm and buildings and the vineyard. The lakes have great charm, which is preserved by limiting the number of daily rods and the fish are all very high quality, good fighters, good eaters and plenty of them; the stocking rate is high to ensure first-class sport all the time and it is one of the few fisheries that does not close during the winter.

The constant aim of the owner and all his staff is to provide conditions which will give the rods a happy day and their comfort, convenience and pleasure is paramount.

Westbury Fishery
Westbury Lane
Purley-On-Thames
Reading
Berkshire RG8 8QL
Tel: (0734) 843123

SOUTHERN ENGLAND

of war in Napoleonic times and now offers many types of water. A four fish day ticket on this brown trout water costs £25. It is regularly stocked and the stocking size is 1lb to 1lb 8oz. The best fish here was 7lb and July 1991 produced one of 5lb 10oz. Downstream at Newbury, the Millwaters Hotel (0635) 528838 has half a mile of fishing and a stocked lake which is available to residents only. This though, is on the Lambourn which like the Kennet flows through the hotel's gardens.

North of here, at Abingdon, near Oxford is Millet's Farm Trout Fishery (0865) 391394. The fishery has two spring fed lakes on limestone which total seven acres. There is an abundance of natural water life such as nymphs, shrimp and corixa. Tackle and flies can be obtained from the lodge and professional tuition is available. The water is stocked with the powerful fighting Shastra strain of rainbows which average 1½ lb. A five fish day ticket costs £20 to £50 and half days and evening tickets are also available. At Purley-on-Thames near Reading, is the seven acre Westbury Trout Fishery (0734) 843123. A four fish day ticket here costs £20 and an added attraction is the adjoining vineyard where a conducted tour and tasting of six English wines can be enjoyed.

There is a wealth of trout fishing within easy reach of London. Church Hill Farm (0296) 720524 at Mursley, near Winslow in Buckinghamshire is only fifty miles away. The two spring fed lakes total ten acres and both are alkaline and very productive of natural lifeforms. The water is regularly stocked with brownies and rainbows of between 1½ lb and 12lb. The fishery has a particularly fine clubhouse which is a converted 18th century barn. Nymphs such as Damsel, Mayfly and Montana are particularly successful and the best fish caught here was 17lb 1½ oz. The price for a four fish day ticket is £20.

Also in Buckinghamshire are the Latimer Park Lakes (0494)

762396 which are sited in the Chess Valley on the south eastern side of the Chilterns. The lakes, which are eight acres and four acres, are well over two hundred years old and the fishery can also offer chalk stream fishing on the river **Chess**. The lakes are chalk stream fed which ensures a prolific food supply and are restocked on a daily basis with rainbow and brown trout that are reared on the premises. Around 10,000 fish are caught here every season and over half of them are larger than 2lb. A four fish day ticket will set you back £21. At Slough, is the Queen Mother Fly Fishery (0753) 683605. A day ticket on this 475 acre water costs £10. There have recently been improvements here, including thirty-three new boats and ninety-six casting platforms and the water is now stocked with brookies as well as browns and rainbows.

If you live in East London or Essex, a wide range of stillwater fishing is available. Near Chelmsford, is the Essex Water Company's Hanningfield Reservoir (0268) 710101. Boats are available on this six hundred acre water which is stocked with the company's home-reared rainbows. A six fish day ticket costs £12 and the average fish is just over 1½ lb. The catch for 1990 was 55,729 fish and saw a best rainbow of 10lb 5oz and brown trout of 4lb 12oz. The whole area of the reservoir is a wild bird sanctuary which adds to the tranquility of an excellent days' fishing. Near Colchester is the well known Ardleigh Reservoir (0206) 230642 which in 1991 hosted the European International Trout Fishing Competition. The average weight is just under 1 ¼ lb and the record is 4lb while the best brown is 9lb 12oz. An eight fish day ticket is priced at £13. Expert tuition is available as are locally tied flies and bed and breakfast can be arranged. Among the good, privately owned waters are Aveley Trout Lakes (0708) 868245, Chelmer's Fisheries at Thaxted (0371) 3595, Chigboro at Maldon (0621) 57368 and Cooks Farm at

Artist: **Roger Desoutter** *SEPTEMBER MORNING* *Courtesy of:* **Rosenstiels'**

SOUTHERN ENGLAND

Brentwood (0277) 72265.

South of the Thames, there is the excellent still water and river fishing in Surrey, Kent and Sussex. In the Tillingbourne Valley, near Guildford in Surrey are the Duke of Northumberland's Albury Estate Fisheries (0486) 412323. They are set in a 3,000 acre estate which has pleasure grounds and terraces laid out by the 17th century diarist John Evelyn and offer a wide range of fishing. The Park Fishery has two lakes and three beats on the river Tillingbourne which is predominantly chalk water, and can be fished on a season ticket basis only. The Powder Mills Fishery is a lake of nearly four acres and is designed to appeal to the experienced fisherman. The water provides excellent buzzer fishing and is stocked with rainbows. A less experienced fisherman might prefer the Weston Fishery which has wide banks and easy casting. The main lake is some four acres and there is a smaller one which is ideal for dry fly. A four fish day ticket for either Weston or Powder Mills costs £20. One of my favourite fisheries is Willinghurst (0483) 275048 which is just off the A281 Guildford to Horsham Road. There are two main lakes and four smaller ones which are set in woodland. It is a delightful country setting with not a house in sight. Other good Surrey stillwaters include Crosswater Mill at Churt (0251) 254321, Enton Lakes at Godalming (0428) 792620, and Gatton Manor at Dorking (0306) 79555.

At Lamberhurst, Kent, is **Bewl Water** Reservoir (0892) 890352 which attracts over 20,000 fishermen a year. Six fish day tickets here will cost you £10.50. Boats are available, as are a range of courses which are designed to cater for the beginner as well as the more experienced fisherman. Nearby, is the excellent sixteen acre Bayham Lake Trout Fishery (0892) 890276. This lake is one of the most prolific trout fisheries in the country; it is stocked with rainbows averaging 2 1⁄2 lb and running up to 12lb and more. The fishery includes double bank fishing on the River Teise which has a series of beautiful and very prolific waterfalls and pools downstream from the lake. Instructors are on hand to help and advise if required and you can also try your hand at clay pigeon shooting in the nearby woodland. Bayham can also provide superb lunches which are served in the former boathouse which has a promenade deck overlooking the lake. A six fish day ticket costs £26. The River **Teise** rises near Tunbridge Wells and covers some twenty miles on its journey to join the Medway near Yalding. The upper reaches are well stocked with brown and rainbow trout and offer good dry fly fishing. Just below Bayham's water, is the Hoathly Fishery which has 1 1⁄2 miles of the Teise and a similar amount on Bartley Mill. A day here is priced at a modest £3 and tickets are available from Bassett's Garage in the village. Other stillwaters include Chequertree at Ashford (0233) 820383 and Tenterden Trout Waters at Tenterden (05806) 3201. Tenterden has three lakes totalling five acres of water and is situated at Coombe Farm which is about a mile outside the town. One lake is for dry fly and nymphing only and the water is regularly stocked with brownies and rainbows of between 1 1⁄2 lb and 10lb. The fishery has a unique basket system which allows continuous fishing with no restriction on the number of fish caught though fish not required must be returned at the end of the day. A three fish day tickets costs £15.

The Rivers of Sussex are best known for their course fishing but the lower reaches of the Arun, Western and Eastern Rother, Ouse and Adur all have runs of sea-trout which are generally larger than in Hampshire. There are a number of good stillwaters

in the county too. At Burwash, near Heathfield is Lakedown Trout Fishery (0435) 883449. This is owned by Roger Daltrey of 'The Who' fame; game fishing is popular in the music business and Eric Clapton is also a very keen fisherman. The fishery is set in a delightful valley and has four lakes and a well equipped lodge. North of here, just off the A267, is the Yew Tree Trout Fishery at Rotherfield (0892) 852529. The fishery consists of three beautiful lakes surrounded by fields and woodland. The price of a four fish day ticket is £16 and tuition is available. At Flimwell, on the A2115, the Spring Wood Trout Farm (0580) 87525 consists of three lakes totalling more than five acres and is set on the peak of a hill overlooking Bewl Water. Two lakes are dry fly and nymph only and the water is stocked with brownies and rainbows. Bed and Breakfast is available at the farm house and a four fish day ticket costs £18.

West of here, on the A24 London to Worthing Road some ten miles south of Horsham, at Ashington is Ashington Trout Farm (0903) 893066. This is a new fishery set under the famous Chactonbury Ring at the base of the South Downs. The water is fed by chalk streams and stocked with rainbows and consequently has some double figure fish. Overnight accommodation is available and a four fish day ticket costs £16. Further west at Arundel, on the Duke of Norfolk's Estate, is the delightful Chalk Springs Fishery (0903) 883742. The four spring fed lakes total five acres and a four fish ticket costs £22.50. The water is very clear and gives you the opportunity to stalk rainbows and brown trout which run into double figures in weight.

The Hasting's Flyfishers Club (0580) 880407 was formed as a limited company in 1932. The club has the fishing on two reservoirs; Darwell which is 165 acres and Powdermill at 54 acres. Rowing boats are available on both waters which are very attractive and well established. Powdermill is so named because it used to drive the waterwheel of a gunpowder works which blew up! The waters are well stocked, mainly with rainbows, but there are some natural and stocked browns. A six fish day ticket costs £12.50 and the average size is around 1 1⁄4 lb but fish of up to 6lb and more can be expected.

FISHING FAYRE

With such a wealth of good fishing on offer, the only choice you have to make is whether to extend your day trip and make a weekend break, or even a week of it!

The south of England has a number of celebrated rivers and although demand invariably exceeds supply there are still opportunities for the fishing enthusiast. Fishing such waters as the Test and the Itchen can be quite expensive but the fishing is often excellent and there a many establishments in which to celebrate after a good day on the river! The following suggestions give you just an inkling of the vast choice of establishment on offer in this part of the world and we have tried to include all manner of different hostelries, ranging from pubs and inn with inglenook fireplaces and friendly bars to the super deluxe country house hotels which are to be found here.

Just as your fishing in this part of the world most often needs to have been planned well in advance, if you are to stand a chance of getting on to your favourite stretch, so it is usually essential to book accommodation - fishermen are not the only ones who are out and about in this very popular tourist area. Not to be overlooked, are the companies who can organise

ALBURY ESTATE FISHERIES

The River Tillingbourne, fed by spring water originating from deep below the greensand and chalk of the Surrey Downs, rises near Friday Street, and meanders through Surrey's most beautiful countryside.

Five miles from its source the Tillingbourne enters the Albury Estate, and it is here you will find chalk stream and lake fishing which, for over a century has been the preserve of the Dukes of Northumberland.

Albury Estate Fisheries offer brown and rainbow trout fishing in this unique private parkland setting, with spring fed lakes, tumbling pools and a wealth of natural fly life, particularly the Mayfly.

The clear waters of the Tillingbourne support an abundance of native brown trout together with larger browns stocked by Albury Estate Fisheries.

In an age of 'put and take' waters, it is a privilege to fish a classic chalk stream or spring fed lake overlooked by formal gardens and natural woodland.

Albury Park Fishery is run primarily as a private members syndicate, with numbers strictly controlled, but a number of days are set aside each year for private parties. On such days, guests are also allowed access to the extensive terraced gardens surrounding Albury Park mansion.

The lake fisheries, Weston and Powdermills, are bounded by the river Tillingbourne and are famous for their catches of sizeable rainbows.

They gained a reputation as two of the premier day ticket locations in the south of England and are regularly stocked with trout from the Fisheries' own Trout Farm.

Albury Estate Fisheries is situated approximately four miles to the south east of Guildford.

For further information and full colour brochure call the Estate Office on Shere (048641) 2323.

CHELWOOD HOUSE HOTEL

Just minutes from beautiful Chew Valley Lake, Chelwood House enjoys an enviable location between Bristol, Bath and Wells - all cities of exceptional historic and cultural interest. A former dower house dating from 1681, the upper rooms of the hotel enable visitors to take in far-reaching views over the meadows and rolling Mendip Hills. An impressive staircase leads up to the distinctively designed guest rooms; three have four-poster beds of different national styles - French, Victorian and Chinese. Antique furniture, ornaments and paintings from the personal collection of owners, Rudi and Jill Birk, enhance the relaxed ambience of the two lounges. Rudi Birk's Bavarian origins are a key influence on his first-class cuisine - in addition to an English a la carte menu a selection of traditional Bavarian dishes can be prepared. In 1990 the hotel's 'Restaurant in a Garden' opened, consisting of a conservatory dining room with plants, fountain, gazebo and hand-painted murals, creating a lush setting for dinner. The hosts take credit for inspiring a convivial family atmosphere at this professionally run hotel which represents good value for money. The hotel is ideally situated for a variety of leisure pursuits and there are many places of natural, historic and sporting interest close at hand.

One of the best fishing lakes in Britain, Chew Valley Lake, is just 10 minutes away and Blagdon Lake is also closeby.

There are approximately 15 Golf Courses within a radius of 20 miles and, for the racing enthusiast, Bath Races can be reached in 20 minutes and Chepstow and Wincanton within an hour.

Chelwood House
Chelwood
Avon BS18 4NH
Tel: (0761) 490730

SOUTHERN ENGLAND

package breaks for you. UK Field and Stream (0527) 66344 and Fishing Breaks 071-281 6737 are two examples, but for those wishing to organise their own 'get away', here are a few good suggestions.

The rivers Frome and Piddle weave their intricate pattern through much of Hardy's Wessex. This is a delightful part of England and, whilst much has changed since Thomas penned his first epistle, it remains very picturesque with sleepy villages nestling in the English countryside. Near the source of the Frome we find an hotel of outstanding quality; Swanner Lodge (0935) 83424 in Evershott. It is small but well kept with superb grounds and a first rate restaurant. Dorchester offers the King's Arms (0305) 65353 which has its roots in the 18th century and is a popular spot for fishermen. More outstanding value and character can be found at Cerne Abbas. Here, The New Inn (03003) 274 dates from the 11th century (it was refurbished in the 17th!) and is a tremendous place to stay, full of character. This fine establishment is very conveniently situated for the Flowers Farm Fishery.

Both the Piddle and the Frome arrive at Poole Harbour in the vicinity of Wareham, and here we find The Priory (0929) 552772. Beautifully maintained gardens reach down to the River Frome and the hotel has a number of contacts who can arrange some excellent fishing for guests. If you want to spoil yourself, this is an excellent place in which to do it.

The Piddle is responsible for some of the most delightfully named villages; Affpuddle, Puddletown, Tolpuddle and even Piddletrenthide to name but a few. The latter is home to The Old Bakehouse (03004) 305 - a very comfortable hotel. Those considering a trip to Sutton Bingham Reservoir, which is only a short distance from Evershott, will be pleased to hear that they are surrounded by pleasant pubs. One such beauty is the Rose and Crown (0935) 850776. There is no accommodation here but the food is good. People wishing to stay in the area should try The Four Acres at West Cocker (093586) 2555 or the 16th century King's Arms (093582) 2513, a former coaching inn. While the majority of the River Avon runs through Hampshire territory, the folk in Wiltshire and Dorset can also lay claim to its sparkling waters. The upper reaches, which boast such fine trouting offer relatively few hotels, largely because it flows through the remote expanses of Salisbury Plain. However, Salisbury does have a number of hotels and the Red Lion (0722) 23334 is an historic inn in which to stay, as is the Rose and Crown (0722) 27908 in Harnham. The Conservatory here enjoys a fine view to the River Avon. Although some of the Wylie is the reserved water of the historic Wilton Fly Fishing Club there remain opportunities available on parts of the river. Two selections, both near Warminster, are The Dove at Corton (0985) 50378 which offers superb fayre and secondly, the Bishopstow House (0985) 212312. This is a majestic hotel in which to stay where guests can enjoy some free fishing on the hotel water or alternatively may fish the nearby estate water for £35 per day. Those prepared to travel a little further should consider the Longleat Arms (09853) 308 which is a pleasant village pub with good food and accommodation. For those fishing the Nadder, Fovant reveals a brace of pubs with more modest, but essentially very comfortable accommodation. The Cross Keys (072270) 284 and The Pembroke Arms (072270) 201 which was formerly the shooting lodge of the Earl of Pembroke. Alternatively, the Lamb at Hindon (074789) 573, formerly a smugglers' haunt, is a good place to take shelter and

the food here is very good.

Returning to the Salisbury area, we can recommend another outstanding food pub; the Silver Plough (0722) 72266 at Pitton, a really superb establishment but unfortunately with no accommodation. A less elaborate, but still a welcoming pub, is The Radnor Arms (0722) 29722. Fordingbridge offers the Ashburn Hotel (0425) 652060, a quiet but no less characterful abode which is well worth considering. South of here, at Stackton, lovers of fine cuisine should earmark the Three Lions (0425) 652489 - an extremely sophisticated and very good restaurant. Journeying through the Ringwood Forest we have two suggestions to make. Firstly, the Moortown Lodge (0425) 471404, and secondly, the Struan Hotel (0425) 473553 in Ashley Heath. A little way south is Tyrells Ford Country House (0425) 72646. The hotel is situated on the edge of the New Forest and is an excellent base for those who are fortunate enough to be fishing in the area. It is extremely comfortable and has a choice of menu as well as good bar food. The Fisherman's Haunt (0202) 484071 may be a popular haunt with the upwardly mobile but it remains well worth a visit. The Avon runs alongside the grounds and trophied fish add to the character. There are a number of bedrooms here which are spotless and very comfortable.

The Test and Itchen are truly celebrated chalk streams. For much of their length they run parallel and are only a few miles apart. As a result, there are a few hotels that will serve both waters.

However, let us start with the Test. Hurstbourne Tarrant is conveniently situated for the upper reaches of the Test and lovers of style should try Esseborne Manor (0264) 76444. Charm happily blends here with comfort and luxury; accommodation and cuisine are both of a high standard. Journey towards Stockbridge and you find the Pleasant Mayfly pub in Testcombe (026474) 283. The Test flows through its garden making it a delightful spot for lunch. Further down the valley we arrive at a hotel which is a mecca for serious fishermen; the Grosvenor Hotel (0264) 810606 in Stockbridge, the home of the Houghton Fishing Club. The hotel is now owned by Whitbread Brewery but in keeping with tradition, fly fishing tackle adorns the walls. However, you should note that the hotel is well equipped, comfortable and offers good food. The White Hart Inn (0264) 810475 and the Greyhound (0264) 81033 are also worth considering. A short distance west of Stockbridge we find the charming Wallops, that is to say Nether Wallop and Middle Wallop. The latter houses the Fifehead Manor (0264) 781565 which is very comfortable and dates back to the Middle Ages. The welcome here is warm and a visit is highly recommended.

Venturing through the villages of Houghton, Horsebridge and Timsbury, we trace the Test to Romsey where the White Horse (0794) 512431 is an historic hotel to try. Alternatively, lovers of outstanding cuisine should sample the Old Manor House (0794) 517353 in Palmerston Street. Our final port of call is the excellent Lee Park (0794) 517888 which is, by virtue of its Broadlands associations, able to provide good fishing as well as outstanding hospitality. The Test may be tricky to fish but it is not impossible as many visitors to Lee Park can testify. Midway between the Test and the Itchen stands the village of Crawley. The Fox and Hounds (096272) 285 is a splendid red-brick built pub which is very cosy. This pub has good food and a few rooms should you wish to stay in the area. Sparsholt is similarly sandwiched between the two rivers and handy for Lainston

House (0962) 63588 - a really outstanding hotel to try. It is lavishly decorated and furthermore has its own fishing on the Test for guests. As you can imagine, this is an extremely popular place so conatct the hotel well in advance of your proposed trip.

A little south of Eastleigh is the village of Hedge End. Here we find a hotel that will please the fisherman. It's not set on the Itchen but it is a well run, beautifully situated hotel and convenient for the lower reaches. In Winchester, an historic town, we find a number of excellent hotels; The Wykeham Arms (0962) 52834 has a fine restaurant. The Bush Inn, on the Itchen at Ovington (0962) 732764 is a delightful pub and a superb place to stop for some liquid refreshment. Alternatively, try the Tichborne Arms (096273) 3760 in Tichborne, further up the Itchen Valley - a pub with a good atmosphere and excellent bar food.

Although the fishing on the Test and the Itchen is often excellent, if expensive, Hampshire also provides a number of still waters. Those of us who enjoy a weekend away at such a venue will hopefully find the following thoughts of interest. Avington Trout Fishery is well served by the pubs recommended for the upper waters of the Itchen. Some distance away is The Wheatsheaf (0256) 398282 in North Waltham which offers good weekend breaks. Visitors to the Rockbourne Trout Fishery will find a number of opportunities neighbouring the Avon and slightly further upfield, The Horton Inn at Horton (0258) 840252 and the Langton Arms at Tarrant Monkton (025889) 225 provide excellent pub accommodation and a friendly atmosphere. A similar summary can be applied to The King's Arms at Fonthill Bishop (074789) 523 where you will find good food and accommodation.

If you are venturing further westwards to Zeals, The Old Ship, Mere (0747) 860258 is an historic inn with comfortable bedrooms. This is a friendly and informal establishment. The Barrows Fishery, Blagdon Lake and the Chew Valley Lake are all within a few miles of Bristol and should you wish to stay in this area the Carpenters Arms (07618) 202 at Wick is worth a try. The Penscot Farmhouse, Shipham (093484) 2659 is very welcoming and provides good value accommodation. Grander accommodation in Shipham can be found at Daneswood House (093484) 3145, an Edwardian house with a wooded setting in the Mendip Hills. Our final thought is Chelwood House (0761) 490730 which is the perfect base if you are fishing the nearby Avon.

Although the still waters of Gloucestershire lack the maturity of their Southern cousins, the Cotswolds provide some of the most spectacular scenery and charming hostelries in England. Visitors to the Donnington Fish Farm at Upper Swell are positively spoilt for choice. A splendid place at which to stay is Lords of The Manor Hotel (0451) 20243 - a delightful hotel with a well stocked trout lake in the grounds. In Lower Swell, The Old Farmhouse (0451) 30232 is a convivial place to stay and is particularly good value. The Grapevine Hotel (0451) 30344 is another to note - a thoroughly well maintained and welcoming hotel. If you prefer a pub-type environment then two gems to try are the Horse and Groom at Boulton On The Hill (0386) 700413, a splendid village inn and the Black Horse at Naunton (04515) 378; more wonderful countryside, modest accommodation and excellent bar meals. Not so very far away, the clear waters of the Coln flow by and fishing here is tremendous fun.

In Fossebridge, we find the Fossebridge Inn, an ivy-clad building standing on the Fosse Way where it crosses the River Coln. The Bridge Bar dates back to the 18th century and is delightful whilst the rooms are comfortable. This is a good value hotel with much charm. More excellent hotels from which to organise your fishing trip can be found in Bibery. Bibery Court (028574) 337 is a fine place with a beautiful setting and a well recommended restaurant. The Swan Hotel (028574) 204 has its own spring which feeds into the River Coln. It is another lovely setting to inspire all fishermen. Moving on to Fairford, we come across The Bull (0285) 712535 with a cosy beamed bar, log fires and friendly atmosphere.

Lambourn Downs offers the Lambourn River, much of which is preserved. However, if you are lucky enough to arrange a day's fishing here then a pub which might interest you is The Pheasant (0488) 39284 - a characterful boozer and a good place for some bar snacks. In Kintbury, The Blue Boar (0635) 248236 has some comfortable rooms. Those who prefer more luxury should head for the Royal Oak, Yattendon (0635) 201325 nearby, a delightful mix of pub and inn with an outstanding restaurant. Many of these establishments will also be convenient for those who are fishing the Kennet, as is the Millwaters Hotel (0635) 528838 which has the benefit of fishing as well as over 30 rooms. Elcot Park (0488) 58100 has recently been refurbished and is very appealing. In Hungerford itself, there are several hotels and pubs . The Bear (0488) 682512 is the best known and is very popular with visitors and locals alike. The John O'Gaunt (0488) 683535 is a pleasant pub with good bedrooms and excellent bar snacks. The Bell (0672) 20230 at Ramsbury is a good friendly free house to visit and reflect on your day. Marlborough is another delightful town and hotels to try here include the Ivy House (0672) 515333 and The Castle and Ball (0672) 515201 on the High Street.

There are a number of excellent trout fisheries in the London area and the neighbouring home counties and small hotels and pubs may appeal to the fisherman who is seeking an early start, or anticipating a late night. The tremendously named Dog House (0865) 390830 in Frilford Heath is certainly one for the notebook. Accommodation alongside the Thames can always be found. Jerome K. Jerome mentioned the historic Barley Mow at Clifton Hampton (086730) 7847 which remains a welcoming hostelry. In Abingdon itself, another hotel which boasts an historic waterside setting is the Upper Reaches (0235) 5223 1. If you are visiting the Welling Trout Fishery then The Swan Diplomat at Streatley is outstanding and once again has a marvellous Thameside setting. Similarly, the Beetle and Wedge in Moulsford (0491) 651381 is a delightful hotel and restaurant, whilst those seeking a first rate hotel should try Pennyhill Park (0276) 71774 in Bagshot. This has a very good restaurant too. Visitors to Church Hill Farm should consider the Bell at Windslow (029671) 2741, a delightful bar and some very cosy bedrooms make these an ideal stopping place. The Bricklayers Arms at Flaunden is a pleasant place for a pint and The Greyhound at Chalfont St Peter (0753) 883404 is also popular and has some satisfactory accommodation. In Chenies the Bedford Arms (09278) 3301 is a fine hotel for those who are seeking good value accommodation.

Essex has a number of well stocked waters and Hanningfield Water which is situated due south of Chelmsford is surrounded by some good pubs. The Hoop in Stock is renowned for its good value bar food and well kept real ales and The Gardeners

SOUTHERN ENGLAND

Arms in Loghton is also popular. Good value accommodation is less easy to find but the Haybridge Mont House in Ingatestone (0277) 355355 is extremely well run and has a pleasant atmosphere. Better value perhaps is Ye Old White House at Burnham-on-Crouch (0621) 782106. Visitors to Ardleigh should visit the Marlborough Head (0206) 323124 in Dedham, an outstanding hotel, or for real sophistication try Le Maison Talbooth (0206) 322367 - an outstanding hotel and restaurant. Alternatively, The Angel Inn in Stoke by Nayland (0206) 263245 is a beautifully restored village inn with pleasant bedrooms and excellent bar food. Visitors to Chelmes should consider The Swan at Thaxted (0371) 830321 while visitors to Cooks Farm should note The Oak House, Axbridge (0934) 732444.

Surrey also has a number of good fishing opportunities for the resident members of the 'stockbroker shire' and the capital. Although many consider Surrey to be a suburb of London, it does have some beautiful countryside. It also has numerous good pubs. The Crown at Chidingfold (042879) 2255 offers some pleasant bed and breakfast accommodation, as does The King's Arms, Ockley (0306) 711224. Another good base for the numerous still waters is Lybble Hill Hotel (0428) 51251 in Haslemere which is a superb, former farmhouse converted to a welcoming hotel.

The Lamberhurst area is something of a meeca to many fishermen and there are many good pubs in the area with rooms too.

Two excellent ones to note are The Rose and Crown, Mayfield (0435) 872200 and The Bell Inn at Burwash (0435) 882304. Good food can be enjoyed at the appropriately named Brown Trout in Lamberhurst (0892) 890312 or The Bull at Ticehurst (0580) 200586. People looking for rather more style and some excellent cuisine should note the Spindlewood Country House Hotel (0580) 200430, an altogether grander affair.

South-east of here, is Tenterten, a pretty Kentish village, where all lovers of good food should try the Three Chimneys at Biddenden (0580) 291472 or The Bell at Smarden (023377) 283 which also has pleasant rooms. Finally, The White Dog Inn at Eashurst Green (058083) 264 is an extremely pleasant place to stay when in this area.

If you are heading for the Arundel area, once again you have a good choice of establishment but The Spread Eagle (0730) 816911 in Midhurst or The Norfolk Arms at Arundel (0903) 882101 are both excellent.

There are an infinite number of pubs and inns to recommend in this beautiful part of Britain and the above could only ever be a guide line for visitors to the south. However, those establishments we have recommended are certain to meet your requirements and can only add to what must certainly be a very enjoyable trip.

Small Lake Solitude (Chalk Springs Fishery)

LAKEDOWN TROUT FISHERY

Lakedown is a premier still water trout fishery. Situated in a secluded Wealden valley with scenic views and no visible habitation, the fishery consists of four picturesque lakes covering an area in excess of 20 acres specifically designed for fly fishing. Each lake is well stocked with rainbow and brown trout with sizes ranging from 1½ lbs to 20 lbs. Fishing is from 8.00am to sunset with day, half day and evening tickets available. Catch limit 5 fish on a day ticket. All fish to be killed. No fish to be returned to the water once caught.

Also available for self catering fishing trips and vacations:-

A four double bedroomed Scandia Hus. Lounge, kitchen, util-ity room, bathroom, shower, etc. Sleeps eight persons. Situated within 50 yards of the lakes, overlooking the fishery and set within woodland.

Minimum hire period 3 nights and 4 anglers. Anglers £65 per night (which includes a 5 fish day ticket). All non angling wives free. Lakedown is within easy driving distance of Brighton (30 miles), Eastbourne (20 miles), Hastings (18 miles). One hour 15 minutes from central London. Available for hire all year round.

All bookings for fishing or accommodation please contact Alan Bristow or Nigel Eyres.

Lakedown Trout Fishery
Swife Lane
Burwash Common
East Sussex TN21 8UR
Tel: (0435) 883449

SOUTH WEST PENINSULA

Artist: **D.F. Dane** PATIENCE *Courtesy of:* **Rosenstiels'**

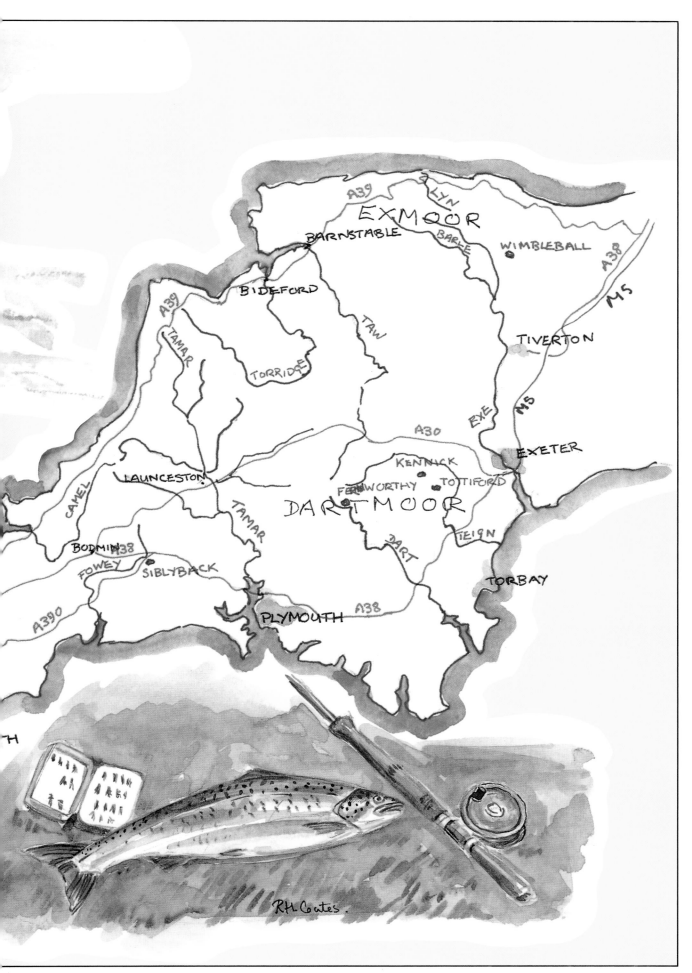

R.H. Coates.

SOUTH WEST WATER

Scattered throughout the beautiful landscape of the South West peninsula are a wide range of reservoirs and water parks, ranging from Argal near Falmouth, set among rolling hills near the coast, to the wild moorland setting of Fernworthy on Dartmoor and Wimbleball on Exmoor.

These varied and beautiful waters offer a wide choice of top quality fishing.

The company's Ranger Service manages these waters to ensure that you get the most from your visit.

Fishing from boat or bank is available at lakes such as Kennick, Fernworthy, Wimbleball and Siblyback, while boat fishing only is available at Argal between 1 June and 14 September inclusive.

Our aim is to offer a wide choice of trout fishing across the region.

Stocked rainbow trout provide lake fly fishing at affordable prices. Fish are trickle stocked throughout the year from top quality fish farms to ensure fish are in tip top condition at all times.

Sizes of fish stocked average 1lb plus, with occasional stocking of larger fish up to 4lbs plus.

Budget trout waters provide a challenging day's sport at low prices. Fish stocking takes place to enhance and improve natural stocks.

A 'catch and release' scheme gives anglers greater flexibility enabling smaller fish to be returned, and the whole day is used to reach the bag limit.

Our premier brown trout fishing is stocked brown trout at Fernworthy, where loch style fishing is offered in the grand surroundings of Dartmoor.

A leaflet is available giving further information.
South West Water
Peninsula House
Rydon Lane
Exeter EX2 7HR
Tel: (0392) 219666

THE SOUTH WEST PENINSULA

Much as we all dislike motorway driving it has to be said that it makes getting to places like the South West much easier, providing of course there are no road works to hold things up! It is perfectly possible for anyone living in London or the Midlands to be on Exmoor in three and a half hours or less. After leaving the M5 at Junction 27 one can afford to drive at a more leisurely pace and take the A396 which follows the course of the Exe and then north of Bampton a left turn on to the B3222 will take you to Dulverton and on to the heart of Exmoor.

Exmoor is immortalised in R.D. Blackmoore's classic novel, 'Lorna Doone', with Old Carver Doone and his family living their lawless life in a hidden valley. The character of Exmoor is still much the same. This is an undulating landscape of gentle rolling moorland with little villages tucked away in the fields of the valleys. There is some cultivated land in the valleys, but this soon gives way to grazing pasture enclosed by dry stone walls and then to moorland. There are hills which offer delightful panoramic views but their gradients are gentle like the Yorkshire Dales. The only steep hill is where the landscape falls away sharply at the coast down to Porlock with its one in four hill.

My first visit to Exmoor was nearly forty years ago. My family had taken a farmhouse for the school holidays and after a long journey in our Morris Minor we reached Exford. The farm was a mile or two outside the village and we slowly made our way up the farm track. Although this was the early 1950s mains electricity had not reached this spot. There was gas lighting with paraffin lamps for reading and having a hot bath was quite a performance. First the water had to be pumped up by hand from the well in the garden and then kettles had to be boiled on the range and taken to the bath which was one of those Victorian cast iron affairs. For a schoolboy it was great fun and a wonderful sense of adventure. There was always plenty to do, pumping water, chopping wood for the fires and watching the cows being milked by hand.

I also remember it well because it was here that I caught my first trout. The Exe flows through the village but at Exford it is in its infancy and no more than a few feet across. I was lent a rod and some flies and after a ten minute lesson on casting left to get on with it. On my first attempts at casting I caught a fair number of daisies, buttercups and trees. The fly seemed to have a mind of its own and went everywhere except on the water! After a while I managed to land it success in a clumsy fashion which would have frightened any fish away. I was beginning to give up hope when there was a tug on the line. Luckily the fish was kind enough to stay hooked and after a short tussle I had him in the net. He was only about 4oz and I can remember my disappointment when being told to release him. However, a few days later I was lucky enough to catch a monster of just over half a pound!

The best way to see the countryside is on horseback when you can go where you please and riding on Exmoor gives one a special sense of freedom. However you need a horse or pony as it was in my case, who is used to the moors. This terrain is not for the shire hunter used to galloping across open fields and jumping manmade fences. There used to be a livery stable in Exford run by a marvellous old man called Frank Mullins. The first time I was taken into his yard he talked to me for a few minutes and then called to one of his grooms. My mother looked at the very shaggy pony that was led from a box and asked to

see another but Frank would stand no nonsense, that was the pony for me. He was right, the pony gave me a super ride and I returned tired but wreathed in smiles and happiness. Frank had a unique gift of being able to match people and horses. Although he had quite a big yard only one horse was ever led out for you but he was always right and I had many memorable days on his ponies and later horses.

Serious fishing on the **Exe** begins at Dulverton. The Carnarvon fishing is reserved for guests and trouting costs £8.40 a day or £42 a week, while salmon fishing ranges from £8.40 to £15.75 a day or £84 to £105 a week. In recent times it has become rather a summer and autumn river with September being the best month. The Exe has become predominantly a spate river and summer fishing especially this far up depends on rain but can be very good with grilse averaging around 5lb and salmon between 8lb and 12lb. Flies such as the Black Great, Tupps, Greenwells Clergy and Blue Nun are popular choices.

The Carnarvon Arms Hotel (0398) 23302 has five miles of fishing on the Exe and its main tributary, the **Barle**. It has been a sporting hotel for many years and looking at an advertisement in the 'Anglers Diary' for 1928, little seems to have changed apart from the telephone number which in those days was Dulverton 2! It still has a billiard room and livery stables as it had then. These days it can also offer guests a day's shooting and the re-formed West Somerset Polo Club plays on the hotel meadows. The trout here are not very big and average around the half a pound mark but take freely and offer good sport.

Just the other side of the A396 from Dulverton is **Wimbleball Lake**. This is the third largest reservoir in the area and is administered by South West Water whose dedicated team of rangers do a great job running all the company's fisheries. They have a busy life as several of their waters have over 100,000 visitors a year, are drawn by the nature reserves and sailing as well as fishing. Wimbleball is fairly new, having opened for fishing in 1980, but has built up an impressive reputation and the Benson and Hedges competition heats are held here. Near the dam wall it is 160 feet deep, but the best fishing is to be held at the shallower northern end and Cow Moor is a favourite spot. Boats are available and there is one which is specially equipped for handicapped anglers. The lake's 374 acres have a natural stock of brownies which run up to 4lb and are regularly stocked with rainbows, for which the current record is 10lb 4oz. Before setting out it is worth calling Bob Lunk, the ranger, to ensure that it is not a competition day. Nearby is the Exe Valley Fisheries (0398) 23328 which has been a trout hatchery and rearing farm since 1885. This is a put and take water which is just the place for a beginner. The cost is £5 a day and £1.30 per lb of fish caught and they will clean, smoke and freeze your fish if you want.

The village of Oakford is not far from Bampton and is just off the main road to Barnstaple and here you will find Bellbrook Valley Trout Fishery (03985) 292. Peter Swaby's fishery is as pleasant a stillwater as you could wish to find. Its three lakes and two pools are in a beautiful valley and the old Iron Mill Stream and adjacent woodland supply an abundance of natural feed for the fish. Professional tuition is available as is bed and breakfast accommodation at the fishery farmhouse. The cost of a day on this noted Troutmaster Water is £20 with a 4 fish limit. Half day tickets are available or you can pay less and then pay £1.50 per lb of fish caught. One lake is for large fish only,

THE SOUTH WEST PENINSULA

the minimum weight is 3lb and you can have a half day for £17 with a two fish limit, or a full 3 fish day for £25 or a 4 fish limit day for £30. These big fish are fine fighters and not like the underweight submarines found on some fisheries. To give you some idea of what may be in store, Bellbrook holds the South West record with a superb 17lb 12oz fish taken in 1988.

The Barle is the most important tributary of the Exe and flows through the heart of Exmoor Forest. The Exmoor Forest Hotel at Simonsbath (064383) 341 can offer guests fishing on eight and a half miles of the Barle and a small stretch of the Bray. Trout fishing costs £8 a day and salmon £15 but these are maximum prices as the hotel realises the importance of water levels and prices are revised accordingly. Some of the fishing takes some getting to and it is rather rocky in places so good boots or stout shoes are essential. However, like all things that require an effort, it is well worthwhile.

Downstream just above Hawkridge are the picturesque Tarr Steps which appear on so many calendars and boxes of chocolates, but this is not surprising for they capture the spirit of English countryside at its best. The Tarr Steps Hotel at Hawkridge (0643) 85293 has three miles of fishing, most of which is double banked and free to guests. It is good to hear that salmon catches are on the increase and 1988 the best recent year, saw 76 fish grassed from this water. The proprietor, Mr D. Keane, can also arrange fishing on the Exe and shooting for guests. The Fishing Tackle shop in Dulverton's high street can steer the under 16s towards some free water exclusively for them. An NRA licence is required but no grown-ups is the rule and that includes Peter Pans! John Sharpe of J.S. Sporting has seven miles of fishing on the Exe and the **Haddeo** and a nice one and three quarter acre lake stocked with rainbows. The Haddeo is the small river that drains Wimbleball Reservoir and compensation flows help to keep a reasonable water level. The cost of fishing on this stretch of the Middle Exe is £10 for trout and between £18 and £25 for salmon according to season and tuition is also available.

By the time the Exe reaches Tiverton the valley has widened out and from here to the sea the river, which is the longest in the area, strolls through rich and fertile parkland until it flows into the estuary near Exeter and finally into the sea between Exmouth and Dawlish Warren. The Tiverton Fly Fishing Club owns half a mile of the Exe and leases a further half mile from the NRA where the cost is £3.30 a day, with August being the best month for salmon. The club also has three and a half miles of fly only trout fishing on the Knightshayes Estate Water. This concession was granted by the late Sir John Amory to residents within Tiverton Borough, the estate however retains the salmon rights.

Five miles or so south of Tiverton is the village of Bickleigh where the Fisherman's Cot (0884) 855289 has a quarter of a mile for guests. The NRA own three miles of the Exe and the Exeter Angling Centre (0392) 436404 will be able to give you further information about this water. Exeter City Council also own some water but it has to be said that it is not that good, besides with so much fishing in lovely countryside being readily available, I would rather fish there than near a town.

The **Teign** begins its life as the North and South Teign high up on Dartmoor. These small streams join forces just west of Chagford and between there and Steps Bridge the river tumbles through a wooded gorge. Fingle Bridge is a popular beauty

spot and vantage point from which to see the river. Down to just south Mortonhampstead the river is referred to as the Upper Teign and from there down to Newton Abbot is the Lower Teign. It is not a big river and so easy to cover and is also one which will delight the spring fisherman for at that time of the year the banks are thick with daffodils particularly around Clifford Bridge. There is good brown trout, sea trout and salmon fishing to be had here. Permits for the Upper Teign Fishing Associations water may be had from the Anglers Rest at Finglebridge (0647) 21287 or James Bowden and Son of Chagford (0647) 433271. Chagford Weir provides a good holding pool and it is essential to book as only two permits a day are issued. A combined salmon and sea trout ticket costs £12 and a sea trout only is £5. Sea trout offer particularly good sport here and many fishermen mark the fish in daylight and return to stalk them at night.

The Mill End Hotel at Chagford (0647) 432282 has just under half a mile, which is free to guests and fishing can also be arranged on six miles of the Upper Teign Fishing Association's Water. In winter the hotel can arrange a days shooting , either walked-up game or driven birds and there is even a limited amount of deer stalking in the wooded valleys near the hotel. Mrs C. Thatcher (0647) 52805 issues permits for the Ryecroft Fishery at £17 which is for 24 hours and so covers sea trout. This one mile stretch of double bank fishing is first class and it is advisable to book as it is very popular. A day's permit for the Lower Teign Fishing Association's water can be had for £10 from the secretary, Mr P. Knibbs of Sheldon (0626) 873612.

A fifteen minute drive south west of Chagford will take you into the heart of Dartmoor and **Fernworthy** Reservoir. This is a beautiful away from it all spot where you will only meet fellow fishermen or ramblers. The 76 acre water is very established, having been created fifty years ago and with its moorland setting will remind many of a Scottish loch. It is stocked on a regular basis with brown trout which go up to 4lb and may succumb to the allure of a Hawthorne early in the season, while Daddies, Black Marilous and Sedge Patterns work well later on. The cost of a day with a four fish limit is £12.50 and if you want to book a boat it is advisable to ring the ranger, Mr David Long (0647) 432440, in advance.

Approximately ten miles east of Fernworthy and a quarter of an hours drive north of Bovey Tracey, are **Kennick** and **Tottiford Reservoirs** where £10-15 buys you a 6 fish day ticket. This is another beautiful but remote water and is regularly stocked with rainbows and has a stock of native brownies. The best rainbow to date is 5lb 14oz and there are rumours of brown trout of just under double figures. Hawthorns and Daddies do well here as do Montanas and Vivas. This water is only 23 foot at its deepest/widest point so it is possible to fish all of it.

If you prefer big fish on a smaller and more private water you should try John Hern's Watercress Farm Trout Fishery at Chudleigh (0626) 852168 which is about seven miles north of Newton Abbot. The three gin clear lakes are fed by springs and stocked on a daily basis with rainbows of between 1 1/4 and 12lb. Day tickets are available but booking is essential as the number of rods is limited.

MILL END HOTEL

The River Teign flows through some of the most beautiful and unspoilt countryside in Devon. The fishing the Teign has to offer is varied. Between Chagford bridge and Steppes Bridge the angler can fish for moorland trout. Salmon and Sea trout begin to appear in the Upper Teign waters from about April, with greater numbers becoming available from the middle of June until the end of the season on 30th September. The hotel can arrange fishing for its guests on about fourteen miles of brown trout water and six miles of salmon and sea trout water.

The Mill End Hotel is a superb base for fishing. Immediately adjacent to the hotel are 600 yards of private bank and four pools for salmon and sea trout. Fernworthy and Hennock reservoirs, stocked with rainbow trout, are within easy driving distance. Mr Roddie Rae, a local expert and Upper Teign water bailiff, is available to tutor the inexperienced or act as a ghillie to skilled fishermen.

The Mill End hotel was formally a flour mill and its wheel still turns in the peaceful courtyard. Converted in 1929 the hotel has an atmosphere of a comfortable private house. All rooms have a private bathroom, telephone, colour television, hairdryer and other practical comforts.

To complete your day a superb dinner with fresh ingredients, carefully prepared on the premises the day you eat them - is the Mill End promise. An award winning cheese selection includes several local favourites as well as many from France. There are over a hundred wines listed and an interesting selection of Cognacs and Malt Whiskys.

For the non-fisherman Mill End is ideally situated for exploring Dartmoor. There is an excellent 18 hole golf course near by and opportunities to ride and shoot. There are many delightful walks on Dartmoor and National Trust properties to explore.

Mill End Hotel
Sandy Park
Chagford
Tel: (0647) 432282

THE SOUTH WEST PENINSULA

The **West Dart**'s source is on the moor above the famous prison at Princetown. It joins the **East Dart** at Dartmoor and much of the river is owned by the Duchy of Cornwall. Below Dartmoor the river tumbles down a wooded valley and leaves the moor at Buckfastleigh to flow to its estuary at Totnes and the sea at Dartmouth under the guard of the famous naval academy. This is good fly water and its tributaries also fish well. There is a delightful reach on the Blackbrook, a tributary of the West Dart which can produce pre-life hatches of duns where you can have the fun of fishing to rising trout, though success, of course, depends on whether you can match the hatch. The Prince Hall Hotel (0822) 89403 issues permits for the West Dart as does the Two Bridges Hotel (0822) 89581 where the river runs through the hotel grounds.

Below Dartmeet at Holne, the Church House Inn (03643) 208 issue NRA licences and Duchy permits and make a point of putting visitors in touch with experienced locals. This is particularly helpful as there is a lot of water and advice on likely spots and flies will save you a long walk and a boring day. Just downstream at Ashburton the Holne Chase Hotel (0364) 3471 has a nice stretch of just over a mile of single bank fishing upstream from Holne Bridge, which has five pools and is free to hotel guests. This is fast flowing water which fishes best on the fall after a spate. This fishing is in a wooded valley and the ability to spey or roll cast will save you a lot of time from trying to retrieve flies from trees.

There are many, especially those who live in the area, who consider the **Dart** to be the most beautiful river in the South West. It is a spate river whose occasional floods can scour the banks of vegetation, but this of course is on the upper reaches and below Dartington Hall the river is much more sedate. This is another river which alas suffered the ravages of UDN and the spring run is sadly now almost non-existent and July onwards is the best time. It is particularly good sea trout water with 1990 producing a 12 pounder, while several 11 pound plus fish had been caught by June 1991. The Dart Angling Association has five and a half miles which is good sea-trout water. A day's salmon fishing costs £12 and sea-trout £10 while the charge for a week's fishing is £40 and £30 respectively. Weir Pool is a local favourite and in 1991 permits were available from C Harris of 'Prismatic' in Totnes (0803) 867154, though it is worth checking with the Totnes Information Centre (0803) 863168 as permit issuers do change. From a family point of view, there is the added attraction of a ride on a steam train for the Dart Valley Railway runs close to the river between Totnes and Buckfastleigh.

West of here, entering the sea at Thurlestone is the Avon, one of the better, what I would term 'minor league', rivers in the area. It is the sort of water that produces fifty or more salmon and around two hundred sea-trout a year. The Erme produces a handful of migrating fish but the Plym and Tavy are another matter. The Tavy rises in Cranmere Pool, that strange spot which also sees the start of the Dart and that good tributary of the Torridge, the Okement. The Plym produces under fifty salmon a year but it averages over 300 sea-trout a season and some years have yielded double this amount. The Tavy is slightly better averaging around 400 sea-trout and over a hundred salmon. All these rivers are very good dry fly waters.

Fishing for sea-trout on these rivers is great fun. The water is crystal clear and requires a very careful approach as it is very easy to put them down. A thorough reconnaissance during the day is essential and with polaroids and a stealthy approach you can see the fish and mark the lies. It also gives you the opportunity to work out how you are going to fish the water at night. Casting at night confuses many a fisherman as it is impossible to see what is going on! There is a natural tendency to bring the tip of the rod back too far which can lead to lost flies to cast too quickly will cause the line to land in a heap and make for wind knots in the cast. Night fishing is no different from day fishing in that to be successful the fly has got to be presented in the right manner and the best thing to do is to practice away from where you will be fishing. Once you have mastered the art, the memory of a successful night's sea-trout or peal fishing as they are locally known will cheer many a winter's evening. Numerous tacklists in the area can be of help and supply day permits for the Tavy, for example, Barkells in Tavistock (082261) 2198. The cost for the fisherman is £10 per day or £15 a week and trout fishing is £3 per day or £10 per week.

Among other stillwaters in this area are the **Avon Dam** and **Meldon** reservoirs, where fishing is free to NRA licence holders-although I can't help feeling that this reflects the quality of the fishing. If you enjoy reservoir fishing the 150 acre **Burrator Reservoir** near Yelverton is likely to be more productive, and a day ticket costs a modest £3.

On the north coast of Devon is a small river of just some six miles in length that fishes very well and is inexpensive whilst set in beautiful countryside. What more could you want apart from knowing its name! It is the **East Lyn** and until recently seems to have been a well kept local secret. The river is formed by several small Exmoor streams. Weir Water and Chalk Water continue to form Oare water which is joined by Badgworthy Water at Malmsmead and this is the start of the East Lyn. It is very much a spate river which drops and clears very rapidly after rain and as with any river of a similar character it is all a matter of hitting it at the right time. From Brendon Bridge down to Rockford through a deep wooded gorge, which, though a local beauty spot, is no place to wander about at night and for sea-trout it is advisable to pick a good pool before the light goes and stay there. This part is the Glenthorne Fishery while below Rockford down to Lynmouth is the Watersmeet Fishery which has the best salmon fishing. This belongs to the National Trust and like Glenthorne is administered by the NRA. This white water tumbles from pool to pool, some of which are quite large and others 'pocket handkerchief' size. The spinner and worm are the most successful methods and the fly only really works on the large slower pools. There is a daily limit of two salmon and six sea-trout and permits can be had from the Brendon House Hotel at Brendon (05987) 206.

Driving south west from Lynmouth on the A39, is the road to Barnstaple and the much better known **Taw**. This river which rises on Dartmoor is, at 50 miles, one of the longer ones in the region. It and the neighbouring Torridge, have long been regarded as the most important Devon salmon rivers. Indeed they are recorded in the Domesday Book where they were valued at 25 shillings a year. In the 1950s, rods were accustomed to taking 2000 salmon a year while a further 3000 were netted. Sadly, catches have declined since then but they are both good salmon and sea-trout waters as is the Taw's main tributary, the Mole at Eggesford near Chumleigh. The Fox and Hounds (0769) 80345 has seven miles of fishing on the Taw and also has some water on the Little Dart. The cost of a day's

THE SOUTH WEST PENINSULA

salmon and sea-trout fishing is £18.50 or a half day costs £10, while a day's trouting can be had for £10. To help get beginners started the hotel has a three quarter of an acre novice pond which is well stocked.

Downstream at Umberleigh there is the well known Rising Sun (0769) 60447 which has been looking after fishermen for many a year. Its three and a half miles are divided into seven beats which produce good numbers of summer sea-trout and autumn salmon and a fair few fish in spring, although the spring run is not what it was. Lower down is the Barnstaple and District Angling Association's water which extends to some two miles and it also has trout fishing on the **Yeo**. Four permits are issued a day but not for weekends or Bank Holidays and they can be obtained from the Secretary, Mr A .J. Penny (0271) 73241 or the Devon Angling Centre in Barnstaple (0271) 45191.

The source of the **Torridge** is not far from the picturesque seaside town of Clovelly near the border with Cornwall. After a tortuous course, full of bends and loops, the river doubles back on itself and flows into the Taw estuary at Bideford. Throughout its length it flows through rock rolling farmland and in spring its banks abound with daffodils and primroses. This river also has a famous sporting hotel at Sheepwash, the Half Moon Inn (040923) 376, which has twelve miles of very good fishing. Spinning is allowed in spring - which has seen fish of up to 19lb but fly only is the rule after May 1st. It is not a large river and an 11 foot rod will enable you to cover the water. Popular salmon flies are the Yellow Torrisch, Silver Doctor and Thunder and Lightening while the Silver Butcher, Peter Ross and Connemara Black are favourite choices for sea-trout. The fishing is easy to get at as the banks have been cleared on all beats. It also offers excellent trout fishing and its waters are stocked with good brownies of around the 1 lb mark.

Group Captain P. Norten-Smith (08053) 317 owns the Little Warham Fishery at Beaford. This one and a half mile stretch of single bank fishing is divided into four beats and there are four named pools on each beat: This, like the Half Moon's stretch, is prime water, however, for those wishing to fish the upper reaches both the Devil's Stone Inn at Shebbear (040928) 210 and the Woodford Bridge Hotel at Milton Damerel (040926) 481 have their own water. A few miles south of Beaford on the B3220, is Winkleigh and the Stafford Moor Fishery (08054) 360. This well known stillwater consists of two lakes of fourteen acres and eight acres and produces some very big rainbows. A stillwater of a larger size at 41 acres is **Wistlandpound Reservoir** which is north east of Barnstaple, and a day costs £7.50.

The A30 is the main road to Cornwall and its sandy beaches and sailing creeks. Just east of Launceston this road passes through the village of Lifton. To the casual driver there is nothing remarkable about it, houses line the road on both sides and on one side is a pleasant looking hotel. This ivy-clad building is the Arundell Arms (0566) 84666 which is known to fishermen around the world as a hotel for fishermen run by fishermen. Anne Voss Bark has fished the hotel's waters for many years. Expert tuition is on hand and the hotel runs many courses. There are courses for beginners, advanced salmon and trout casting, fly fishing and 'refreshers' to brush up your technique. In winter, the hotel can arrange a day's shooting, including driven snipe. The Arundell Arms has twenty miles of fishing on the **Tamar**, its tributaries, the Lyd, Carey, Wolf and Thrushel. The salmon that run up the hotel's water on the Tamar and the

Lyd average 10lb but there is always the chance of a 20 pounder, while the average sea-trout is between 3/4lb and 1lb 8oz, but there are a number of larger fish up to 6lb. There is very good trout fishing to be had here and dry fly works particularly well. The trout average two or three to the pound but are genuinely wild and are prime fighters. When the rivers are in spate, excellent sport can be had on the hotel's Twynhay Lake. This three acre water is just down the road from the hotel and is stocked with rainbows and some browns up to 9lb. The water is clear and quite deep and nymphing with a long leader is often a productive method.

The beautiful Endsleigh House at Milton Abbot (0822) 87248 is set in seventy acres and is owned by a syndicate; the Endsleigh Fishing Club. For most of the year it is run as a hotel and guests can fish the hotel's nine miles of double bank on the Lower Tamar. The cost of a day varies between £20 and £38 and fly is the most successful method. The seven year average for this water is 228 fish. Launceston Anglers Association has fishing on the Tamar, Ottery and some other waters. It is good to hear that there was an encouraging spring run in 1991. Flies such as the Stoats Tail or Torrish, or spinning with a Mepps are particular successful on the Association's six miles where the average is 9lb. Permits for salmon and sea-trout cost £30 a day or £190 a week, while trouting costs £4 a day or £15 a week and can be obtained from the Association's Secretary, Mr Mike Summers of Launceston (0566) 776532.

The Lamerhooe Lodge Fishings on the Lower Tamar have recently been bought by the River Beauly Fishings Company Ltd. (0463) 782215. This delightful beat is set in a beautiful wooded valley and consists of one and three quarter miles of double bank fishing with 18 named pools. It has been in private hands with only three owners since the 16th century and the fishing has always been retained for these and their guests. The Beauly team have made substantial improvements to the river and the pools and fly only is the rule. The fishing is now available to let to four rods who can stay at the company's Lammerhooe Lodge

Last of the Light   (South West Water Plc)

RAINBOW TROUT STUFFED WITH FENNEL AND SMOKED HAM

SERVES 4

INGREDIENTS

4 Rainbow Trout approx 12oz each (cleaned and filleted)

2oz (50g) Butter

Lemon Juice

2 Shallots (chopped)

1 Small, Fennel Bulb (finely chopped)

4oz (115g) Cooked Smoked Ham (chopped)

Touch of Garlic

Parsley (chopped)

2 Egg Yolks

Salt and Pepper

4oz (115g) Fresh, White Breadcrumbs

2oz (50g) Butter

Lemon Rind (grated)

METHOD

FOR THE STUFFING

Cook the shallots, fennel and garlic in the butter until soft. Remove from the heat, stir in the parsley, breadcrumbs, and chopped ham, a touch of lemon rind, the lightly-beaten egg yolks, and salt and pepper.

Put the stuffing between the trout fillets and re-form as a whole trout.

Place the stuffed trout in a large buttered baking pan with knobs of butter and a squeeze of lemon juice. Cover with foil and bake in a fairly hot oven, 190 C (375 F, gas mark 5) for 20 to 30 minutes.

TO SERVE

Serve hot with new potatoes and tossed green salad.

A FAVOURITE OF THE ARUNDELL ARMS

THE ARUNDELL ARMS

A charming, ivy-clad old coaching-inn is the home-from-home for the visitor to the Arundell Arms. On a site that dates back to Saxon times the hotel nestles in a valley of five rivers, close to the uplands of Dartmoor and not far from the North Cornish coast and the ruins of Tintagel Castle.

The hotel holds the enviable postion as one of England's premier fishing hotels and has done for over a century. It has its own three-acre lake well-stocked with rainbow trout, but more importantly twenty miles of its own water on the Tamar and four of its tributaries. These are spate rivers, flowing from the moors through farm and woodland down to the valleys, gradually widening and deepening to provide an infinite variety of water, from long slow pools to fast shallows and open glides. The hotel can teach fishing, providing courses for the beginner, or for the more experienced it can sell tackle, give advice, provide maps and then leave you alone to fish a mile of beautiful river for wild brown trout and salmon. Considering the owner is herself a keen fly fisher and is married to the fishing correspondent of the 'Times', the experience and enthusiasm is here right across the board.

From the warmth of the sitting-room you can look out over the peaceful garden and 250-year old cockpit, one of the few remaining in England. The bedrooms all have private bathrooms, colour television, direct-dial telephones and fresh flowers.

The young chef here has been praised by the Daily Telegraph as 'excellent' and adds an imaginative flair to his traditional French and English dishes.

The pleasures of countryside such as this are not confined solely to the rippling rivers. Four hundred square miles of moors provide horse-riding and hill-walking through the mysterious menhirs and stone circles of Gidleigh and Challacombe; explore du Mauriier country and the original Jamaica Inn. In autumn the shooting parties begin to arrive and fireside conversations begin to change to talk of high birds and driven snipe. Some things don't change for centuries though, and the natural splendour and warmth of Devon is here to be enjoyed by all, whatever your pursuit.

The Arundell Arms
Lifton
Devon
PL16 0AA
Tel: (0566) 84666
Fax: (0566) 84494

ENDSLEIGH HOUSE

Endsleigh House, 5 miles west of Tavistock, is set high on the bank of the River Tamar amongst some of the most breathtaking scenery in Devon. Seventy acres of garden, grounds and arboretum give it total seclusion. Endsleigh was built in 1811 for the sixth Duke of Bedford from the designs of the architect Jeffry Wyattville and the landscape gardener Humphrey Repton. The House, which is Listed Grade 1, is an outstanding example of what is properly called a Cottage Ornee and has been lovingly restored by Endsleigh Fishing Club who acquired the property in 1961.

Because it has more accommodation than the Members of the Syndicate require for themselves it is run as a Country House Hotel at which fishermen and non-fishermen are equally welcome. The friendly relaxed atmosphere is in fact more reminiscent of a house party rather than a hotel. There are 23 bedrooms, most with private bathrooms, and the house is full of period furniture. The cooking is of the first-class English variety

and there is an excellent wine list. The House is open late March to early October.

For the fishermen there are 9 miles of double bank salmon fishing on the Tamar. The number of rods is strictly limited. The average annual salmon catch is 228 and over 90% of the fish are caught on fly. Cars can be driven to most pools along riverside tracks. Some of the fishing is done from the bank or croys and some wading. There are boats on 2 pools.

For the non-fisher there are endless walks in the grounds or along the river. Expeditions can be made to Dartmoor about 5 miles away and to famous gardens and Historic houses within easy driving distance.

A stay at Endsleigh is an unique and memorable experience and most guests are drawn back year after year, so early booking is desirable.

Endsleigh House
Milton Abbot
Nr. Tavistock
Devon PL19 OPQ
Tel: (082287) 248

which has five double bedrooms and is set in 60 acres. A ghillie is on hand to help guests.

The Bude Angling Association has trout fishing on the upper reaches of the Tamar and the River Claw. Permits cost £1 a day or £3 a week and can be had from Bude Sports (0288) 352943. The Tamar is a small river this far up as it runs through rolling farmland and produces fine trout of about 10 or 11oz and the odd grayling in winter. Nearby, for those who enjoy stillwater fishing, is Upper Tamar lake. This water which was flooded in 1975 is very productive and has plenty of fly life. Nymphs and dry fly work well and a local favourite is a Black and Peacock Spider.

Heading west from Launceston the A30 takes you through the heart of Bodmin Moor. Just before you reach Bolventor there is a small turning on the left which will take you to Liskeard. This minor road follows the upper reaches of the Fowey over Smallacombe Downs and **Sibleyback Reservoir** is close at hand. This 140 acre water is widely considered the second best of South West Water's first class stocked rainbow fisheries. Every year sees some good trout caught here and the current record is 13lb 2oz. There is a natural head of brownies and permits can be had from the Ranger, Reg England (0579) 42366, who can also advise you on flies and where the fish are! Reg also looks after neighbouring **Colliford** which is brown trout only and has many pleasant bays.

To the east of here are several good small rivers. The Lynher rises on Bodmin Moor and joins the Tamar estuary opposite Plymouth. The twin rivers, East and West Looe, have their sources near Liskeard and join shortly before reaching the sea at Looe. Still small is the Tiddy which enters the sea near Devonport. These rivers produce the occasional salmon and good brownies, but their main claim to fame is that they are excellent sea-trout fisheries so don't ignore them! The Tavy is one of the several rivers that have their source in Cranmere Pool on Dartmoor and flows through Tavistock on its way to Plymouth where in the estuary it meets up with the Tamar. It is an excellent salmon and sea-trout water.

The best sea-trout water in the area, and indeed in the south west, is the **Fowey**. Although like every river, the last year or so has been disappointing, in the past it has yielded between 1500 and 2000 or more fish in a good year including around 300 salmon. On this small river, which has few pools and tumbles down wooded valleys, fly fishing can be difficult, though a flashy fly which resembles a small fish such as the Silver Invicta may be very successful. Most rods however, will be spinning and Rapallas are a popular choice. The river flows through the ground of the National Trust's beautiful property, Lanhydrock House and permits for here cost £5 a day or £15 a week and can be had from the Trust's regional office or Lanhydrock (0208) 74281. Slightly more expensive at £7 a day or £25 a week is the water belonging to the Liskeard and District Angling Association, but they do have six miles of it. Indeed, the Association has some twenty five miles of fishing in all, including stretches of the Camel, Lynhea, Inny, Looe and Seaton. Permits for here and the two miles controlled by the Lostwithiel Fishing Association can be had from Ken Raymond's Fishing Tackle in Liskeard (0579) 47324. The Fowey produces big sea-trout that can be up to 8lb, while its average salmon is between 8lb and 12lb, although in 1990 a 38 pounder was found dead, beached on a bank.

Lamerhooe Fishings   (River Beauly Fishing Co)

LAMERHOOE FISHINGS-RIVER TAMAR

The Lamerhooe Lodge Fishings on the Lower Tamar was recently purchased by The River Beauly Fishings Company Limited.

This simply delightful beat set in a beautiful wooded valley, consists of one and three quarter miles of double bank fishing with 18 named pools.

The beat has been in private hands, with only three owners since the 16th Century, with the fishings always having been retained for the owners and their friends.

We have however made substantial improvements to the river and pools and the beat is now available to let to parties of 4 rods. Fishing will be **FLY ONLY** and the season runs from

March until mid October. The excellent Ghillie will look after all the guests.

LAMERHOOE LODGE - RIVER TAMAR

The Lodge, set in fifty five acres with stunning views over the Tamar Valley, offers luxury accommodation for guests fishing the Lamerhooe beat on the River Tamar.

This well designed modern Lodge has accommodation on two floors and comprises five double bedrooms and four bathrooms as well as a comfortable lounge and dining room. A drying room and rod room are also provided.

Full details of the above fishings are available from:

Mr P Spence
The River Beauly Fishings Company Limited
The Kiln House
Kiln House Yard
Royston
Herts SG8 5AY

FISH YOUR OWN STRETCH OF THE TAW

The River Taw is one of Devon's longest and most prolific rivers.

Rising in Mid-Devon, it flows through wooded valleys and farmland, with an abundant population of wild animals, birds and butterflies, bordered by Sporting Hotels and Private fishing beats nurtured over many years. The river has been managed by the Riparian owners to ensure maximum protection for its salmon, sea trout and brown trout.

As a result, trouble from pollution has been less than that experienced by other rivers in the South West. With a long-term restocking policy, and careful husbandry, fish returns have been extremely consistent and have produced exciting sport for many fishermen.

The Fractional Share Scheme: A total of six 25 year fractional shares are being offered on an attractive and challenging three mile stretch of the River Taw (Single Bank) in a beautiful part of North Devon. The stretch includes the first Resting Pool on the river and 17 other main pools.

It is possible to purchase one or more shares, or all shares may be purchased by one owner. An owner may join with other names to share a rod if he wishes.

The imaginative scheme has been designed to enable all owners to share the best fishing weeks, each having a rod throughout the Spring and Autumn runs. During the Summer months, owners may, from time-to-time, have the whole river to themselves. It will always be possible to rent various weeks throughout the season when available.

For further details of this and other schemes please contact:

English Country Lodges
Lower Moorhayne Farm
Yarcombe
Near Honiton
Devon EX14 9BE
Tel: (040486) 284

THE SOUTH WEST PENINSULA

At Bolventor is the 'Jamaica Inn' of Du Maurier fame and from Fowey West we are in the romantic hidden creeks of Cornwall, which the author also immortalised. It is an area which abounds in picturesque place names like St Just in Roseland, Praze-an-beeble, Nancegollan, Mevagissey and Indian Queens, so called because the tragic Red Indian, Princess Pocahontas, stayed there. On the north coast, is the River Camel which hit the headlines after aluminium sulphate was inadvertently released into the domestic water system and then flushed out into the river. As a result, a large proportion, 60,000 was the estimated figure, of the young fish stock were killed. Time will tell how badly this has affected the river. Accidents by their nature are chance happenings, but like the 1991 spillage of 25,000 gallons of slurry into the Tamar, a very short time can undo many years work. In 1990, the level of rod caught salmon was relatively normal and saw three fish of over 20lb. This river is the converse of the Fowey for it is a better salmon water than it is sea-trout, though those that are caught are large fish.

The Camel rises near the Fowey and this clear, fast flowing river has a course of some 25 miles before reaching the estuary at Padstow. The best fishing is from Trecarne down to the tide and there are about 150 pools in this stretch. This is a river for winter fishing with a good salmon run from October through to December. Wadebridge and District Angling Association has four and a half miles which is best suited to spinning. Mepps always do well, as do a local creation called Muppets. Permits can be had from North Cornwall Angling Centre in Wadebridge. Bodmin Angling Association has 11 miles of the Camel and a short stretch of the Fowey. From 1st April to the end of October a day costs £6 and a week £20, after which time a day costs £10 and no weekly permits are issued. However, no visitor's permits are issued for the last two weeks of the season. Permits are available from the Bodmin Trading Co. (0208) 72557. The scenic 'Camel Trail' runs beside the river for several miles from Padstow to Wenford. This smooth sanded path is the track of the former Bodmin to Adebridge railway line. Further down the coast at St Mawgan, which is just above Newquay, trout fishing can be had on the River Menalhyl.

There is good stillwater fishing to be had in the area. Porth is a 38 acre stocked lake near Newquay. Not far off the A394, south of Penryn, is **Stithians Reservoir**. Permits cost £5 and can be had from the Golden Lion which is right on the north west shore and serves a lethal local brew called 'wreckers'! This water is also a water sports centre and though it does yield some big browns you might prefer the peace and quiet of the neighbouring **Argal Reservoir**. This 65 acre water holds double figure rainbows and boats are available. An unusual feature is that no bank fishing is allowed between June 1st and September 14th. Permits can be obtained from the Ranger, Bob Evans (0326) 72544.

FISHING FAYRE

The south west is an ideal area for a family to enjoy a whole range of activities such as sailing, surfing, riding and walking, allowing you to go off and enjoy some of the excellent fishing opportunities which abound in the area.

The craggy coastline of Cornwall has little in common with the moorland scenery of inland Devon, but both counties have stunning countryside. The fishing found here is both accessible and often excellent, and for the fishing fraternity who have not yet discovered this area, with its remote beauty, you are urged to visit. Some of the finest fishing hotels are situated within the compass of the south west, so let us consider these fine establishments and a few others besides that will offer a friendly welcome after a day on the moors. The Exe, which rises in Exmoor, flows through some stunning moorland and we start our journey with one of its well known tributary's, the Barle. Simonsbath reveals the Simonsbath House Hotel (064383) 259 a tranquil spot and extremely comfortable. The Royal Oak Inn, Withypool (064383) 506 is also on the shortlist. It is a cosy hotel and a delight in which to stay. Log fires and a good restaurant all add to the ambience of this friendly establishment. The inn does not have its own water but can arrange fishing through contacts.

North of Dulverton, we find another gem, The Royal Oak (064385) 455, a delightful inn which dates back to the 12th century and sits in one of the most beautiful of Exmoor's many pretty villages. There is a great atmosphere here and, although fishing takes a back seat, the vast Wimbleball Lake is not far away and makes for an excellent day trip.

At Exbridge, the Anchor Inn (0398) 23433 only has a small stretch of the Exe but should not be forgotten. It is a very comfortable hotel with a friendly welcome and marvellous views of the river. It was tremendous to hear of some good salmon running in 1991 in these flowing waters. The hotel is also well situated for the Bellbrook Trout Fishery. South of Tiverton, a welcoming pub to put in the equation is The Trout at Bickleigh which has some accommodation.

The Teign also enjoys an immensely beautiful journey and once again a number of good opportunities arise for fishing. In its upper reaches, the river tumbles through the grounds of Gidleigh Park (0647) 432367, surely one of our finest hotels and restaurants. Fishing can be arranged by the hotel and if you are prepared to part with considerable amounts of hard earned cash you will enjoy a really wonderful stay. Chagford has a number of pleasant hotels and the Mill End Hotel (0647) 432282 has delightful gardens which lead down to the Teign. This is a fine place to stay and thoroughly recommended. It is also convenient for Fernworthy Reservoir as is the Ring of Bells (0647) 40375 in North Bovey, a 13th century inn with great character and some good value accommodation from which to explore the delights of Dartmoor. It is also very convenient for a visit to Kennick and Tottiford as is the Riverside Inn (0626) 832293 in Bovey Tracey, a welcoming and unpretentious establishment. In Kingsteignton, two fine establishments can be found; The Passage House (0626) 55515 which overlooks the Teign Valley and the Old Rydon Inn (0626) 54626 which are both splendid.

The Dart is another delightful water. It flows through breath-taking scenery and travels through tree-bound territory and the wilder terrain of the upland moors. Here, amidst the bleak landscape of Dartmoor, we find The Prince Hotel (082289) 403 and The Two Bridges Hotel (082289) 581. Both hotels are comfortable and command breathtaking views of this marvellous scenery. Near to Holne, thee are two further possibilities. Firstly, the Church House, Holne (03643) 208 - a listed medieval building with a truly beautiful setting. This is a superb place to stay when fishing the upper reaches of the Dart. The Holne Chase Hotel (03643) 471 is an attractive house with another superb setting. Some good fishing can be arranged here and the hotel is well worth visiting. Less grand but equally welcoming, is the

GREAT TREE HOTEL

Set on a south facing hillside 700 feet up in the Dartmoor foot-hills in 18 acres of its own grounds and gardens, the Great Tree Hotel enjoys a delightfully sheltered and secluded location. There are spectacular views from the lounge and most bed-rooms which look out across the gardens and surrounding woods and hills to Dartmoor beyond.

The building itself was once a hunting lodge and it retains much of the character of the old colonial era. A wide ornately carved staircase leads from the reception down to the large and com-fortable lounge with log fire and adjoining cosy cocktail bar. The elegant restaurant serves a five course table d'hote dinner each evening. The menu, which changes daily, uses much home grown produce from the hotel's own gardens and is comple-mented by an extensive wine list, very much the personal choice of Bev and Nigel Eaton-Gray, the owners, whose informal and relaxed style makes this a splendid hotel in which to unwind.

Located as it is, right in the centre of Devon, the hotel is ideally placed as a base to visit most of Devon's best fishing venues. Salmon, trout and sea trout are all to be found in nearby waters. The river Teign is less than a mile away and the Dart and the Exe

can be reached with a short drive. Fernworthy and Hennock reservoirs and the Stafford fishery are all close by while the North and South coasts are both within easy reach. Permission to fish at any of the venues can be arranged by the hotel prior to your arrival or during your stay if you wish to make your plans later. Expert assistance is available for those embarking on their first tentative foray into the pleasures of sport fishing and also for the more experienced fisherman wishing to add polish to his techniques or seeking information and advice on local fishing conditions.

In addition to fishing, there are several excellent golf courses nearby, riding and pony trekking and of course, walking either on the moor or in the hotel's own grounds. Should the weather gods fail to co-operate on the day you choose for your outdoor activities, then there are drying facilities available at the hotel.

Modern roads have made the Great Tree Hotel easy and quick to reach by car. Motorway and dual carriageway via the M5 and A30 lead to the Whiddon Down roundabout where a left turn onto the A382 leads to the entrance drive of the Hotel just two miles to the south.

Great Tree Hotel
Sandypark
Chagford
Devon
TQ13 8JS
Tel: (0647) 432491
Telex: 9312132116

THE SOUTH WEST PENINSULA

excellent Sea Trout (080426) 274. Fishing on the Dart can be organised from here and the lounge bar will delight fishing enthusiasts. The bedrooms are also very cosy making this a lovely spot to stay. If you are planning a fishing trip in south west Devon, the Bedford Hotel in Tavistock (0822) 613221 is welcoming and a real pleasure to visit.

North of Tavistock, we find a whole host of waters and the Tamar is just one celebrated example. Endsleigh House is also a good place to stay for those who are fishing the Tamar. The river cuts its way north through some beautiful scenery on the way to Launceston and nearby Lifton, visit the Royal at Horsebridge, a thoroughly unspoiled pub. The bridge, from which the river takes its name, was the first built over the Tamar and dates from 1437, a fascinating spot for a swiftie or two.

There are several celebrated fishing hotels in the country but there are very few that have the reputation and renown of the Arundell Arms, Lifton (0566) 84666. Rivers seem to congregate at its very door step and a splendid selection of fishing opportunities can be found here. The hotel has an excellent facilities for the fisherman and inside, flagstones and rugs add to the friendly but unfussy atmosphere. This is an hotel that all fishermen should visit - it is a real treat. Not a 'fishing' hotel as such, but another tremendous place to stay or to dine is the Lewtrenchard Manor (056683) 256, situated midway between the Thrushel and the Lyd.

The Taw and the Torridge are yet two further rivers for the angler to inspect. The Taw volunteers the Fox and Hound's Hotel (0769) 80345 which offers a great welcome to those planning many fishing forays. The Rising Sun at Umberleigh (0769) 60447 is a comfortable inn catering for the fisherman. Highbullen (0769) 540561 at Chittleham Holt is a sporting hotel which offers all manner of excellent sporting opportunities in addition to 1,000 yards of fishing on the River Mole. The fishing is free to guests staying at the hotel.

River Torridge   (Woodford Bridge Hotel)

THE SOUTH WEST PENINSULA

The Black Horse at Torrington (0805) 22121 is an ancient public house and it is allegedly haunted. The Half Moon Inn at Sheepwash (040923) 376 not only has excellent fishing opportunities but also a delightful atmosphere and great character. Our final thought for Torridge is the Woodford Bridge Hotel, Milton Damerel (0409) 26481. Tuition and expert advice are available from the hotel, which has some fishing rights on the Torridge. The hotel has recently been upgraded, which has added to its charm whilst retaining its character. Assuming you feel, as we do, that a fishing foray on the Fowey is a good idea, you may be seeking a place or two in which to stay. The following ideas may be of help. The Punch Bowl Inn at Lanreath (0503) 20218 is a cosy place to stay, while lovers of history and intrigue will no doubt make a beeline for Jamaica Inn, a popular inn and tourist attraction. They should also consider the Royal Oak at Lostwithiel (0208) 872552, which has smugglers associations as well as good food and bedrooms. The Cormorant Hotel (072683) 3426 is a welcoming place and the bar has splendid views overlooking the river - an ideal base for any trip to this part of England.

The Camel, despite its pollution problems, runs through some delightful scenery and if you are wishing to stay nearby, The Cornish Arms (0208) 880263 with the 'Pendogget' restaurant is a charming location. The Malster's Arms (020881) 2473 is also recommended for its good bar food. There are numerous hotels to be found in and around Newquay and if you are journeying this far down the country, perhaps for a family holiday, you should contact the local Tourist Board. Indeed, it is worth emphasising that the tourist boards are generally extremely helpful and a mine of useful local information.

The South West of England is a busy but very beautiful place. In the spring and autumn, when fishing is often at its best, the area will be less crowded, but on the moors, no matter when you go, you will find for yourself some splendid isolation.

BELLBROOK VALLEY TROUT FISHERY

Bellbrook Valley Trout Fishery is one of the South West's premier big Trout Waters with excellent and challenging sport available to the discerning angler.

Bellbrook aims to provide a select and rewarding fly fishery in the natural unspoiled surroundings of some of Devon's most glorious countryside. The fishery is comprised of three lakes and two large pools which are fed by the former Iron Mill Stream. This waterway is renowned for it's remarkable fertility and this, combined with the adjacent verdant woodland ensures an abundant supply of natural feed for the fish. One lake is devoted to large fish with the minimum stocking size a generous 3lb. The lakes are stocked daily with rainbow trout reared on site, either Triploid or Mono-sex female. A small quantity of wild brown trout are also present, ensuring a constant supply of varied sport. The largest rainbow caught to date at Bellbrook was in December 1988, when a monster of 17lb 12oz came in. This remains a South West record to this day. Such a feat does not indicate that fish do not have to be earned, for Bellbrook fish are renowned for their condition, fighting qualities and flavour.

The facilities at Bellbrook match the quality of the fish. Within the fishery is a lodge where anglers and their families may rest and shelter. Tackles, flies and tackle hire are all available, as are refreshments and tea and coffee making facilities. Additional facilities include professional tuition, barbecue, toilets, picnic area and freezer service. Bed, breakfast and evening meals are available nearby at the fishery's 17th century farmhouse. Corporate and Private parties can also be catered for. For superb all-year fishing in a setting of beauty and tranquillity, Bellbrook Valley is hard to beat. Contact Peter Swaby at:-

Bellbrook Valley Trout Fishery
Bellbrook Farm,
Oakford
Tiverton, Devon
Tel:-(03985) 292

ROYAL BEACON HOTEL

Situated in Exmouth, the oldest seaside resort in Devon, the Royal Beacon has long been established as a premier hotel. An elegant building, it was originally a Georgian posting house. The early traditions of hospitality, good fare and comfort have continued throughout the years, adapting, evolving and modernising to meet the expectations of today's sophisticated guests.

The quiet location is magnificent, facing south and looking down across our own gardens immediately to the beach, the sea and the Devon coastline.

Beautiful surroundings and comfortable furnishings are not everything - our staff create the real atmosphere. Courtesy, friendliness and professionalism are a matter of pride for them all.

The lounge and bar are spacious and there is a superb snooker room for the enthusiast ... and outside there's Devon! The perfect place for windsurfing, bird-watching, fishing, walking, visiting the theatre or playing a round of golf. Exmouth is an

ideal centre from which to explore an area rich in natural and man-made beauty from the estuary's flocks of sea birds and the beautiful flower and tree displays at Bicton Gardens to the colour and excitement of Exeter Maritime Museum or the splendour of Exeter Cathedral.

End the day at the hotel's exceptional Fennels Restaurant which reflects the Victorian period in its charm and elegance. Traditional Devon cream teas are served in the afternoon and in the evening you are invited to choose from our thoughtfully planned table d'hotel or extensive a la carte menu complemented by fine wines.

Retire for the night to one of the Royal Beacon's superbly appointed, spacious rooms, many of which enjoy sea views. All have en suite facilities and colour television, radio, direct line telephone, tea and coffee making facilities, hair drier and trouser press. Each room has its own distinctive style and individuality.

Royal Beacon Hotel
The Beacon
Exmouth
Devon
EX8 2AF
Tel: (0395) 264886/265269
Fax: (0395) 268890

THE FOX AND HOUNDS, EGGESFORD HOUSE HOTEL

The family owned and run Fox and Hounds, Eggesford House Hotel has been a rendezvous for salmon sea and brown trout fishermen since Victorian times. The tumbling spate River Taw runs through the hotel grounds on its way from Dartmoor to the sea at Barnstaple. There are some seven miles of private prime fishing with about two dozen named pools owned by the hotel with a short stretch on the Little Dart tributary where the famous junction and Millers Pools may be found on beat 9. All our beats are readily accessible from the road, long hikes across fields and fences are not required. Our resident fisheries manager is at your service as a ghillie on the river, in our accessories shop, tying flies or giving help with casting on our stocked practice pool.

Nestling in the sheltered and picturesque Taw Valley just off the A377 at Eggesford the hotel is mid way between the University City of Exeter with its magnificent cathedral and busy shopping centre and the coastal town of Barnstaple famed for its ancient pannier markets.

This famous old coaching inn has been tastefully restored with 20 en-suite bedrooms, some with four poster beds, offering fine modern facilities in an old tradition of country hospitality. The dining room is both elegant and comfortable serving the widest choice of the finest traditional English food with speci-

ality dishes from our chefs. Tables overlook our landscaped gardens with the wide variety of specimen trees of Eggesford forest as a delightful backdrop.

Forest and river walks provide the careful observer with seemingly endless wildlife experiences, kingfishers, otters, badgers, salmon leaping and brown trout rising to the fly, Truly a painters paradise.

The hotel residents have exclusive use of our 9 hole approach golf course in the grounds. Clay pigeon shooting is available in our woodlands on request and in the season driven pheasant shooting parties are organised on shoots.

Interesting floristry work and demonstrations for the ladies by Sarah, our resident National Diploma Florist are often combined with practical hands-on cookery exploits with our chefs.

There is a full size billiards/snooker match play table and we have conference facilities for up to 200 people and can arrange corporate fun days.

Come to the Fox and Hounds Eggesford House Hotel which is but only half an hours drive from the M5 Tiverton junction, and let us spoil you!

The Fox and Hounds House Hotel
Eggesford
Nr. Chulmleigh
Mid Devon EX18 7JZ
Tel: (0769) 80345

THE EXMOOR FOREST HOTEL

Set amidst the incomparable beauty of the Exmoor National Park, this splendid hotel basks in its place as a leader in the local field. The rugged scenery of the Barle Valley and River gives way to vast coombes that unfold into a naturally untamed splendour.

For the avid fisherman, the location of this enviable hotel is ideal. Over eight miles of peaceful waters, including many named pools are there to be enjoyed. Starting at the the source of the river they include Pinkworthy Pond which is roughly three acres, and stretch to a point near Sherdon hatch. Fishing is available from either bank and the numerous wild trout are good fighters and provide a worthy competition. There is a fine selection of salmon beats at Dulverton, and being only a few easy minutes from the town centre the less enthusiatic fisherman's partner has plenty of exploring (and shopping!) to do. If the sportsman himself feels the urge to accompany, then all is not lost, since the town contains one of the best stocked angling shops in the area. The hotel is more than happy to provide packed lunches for the variety of fishing that is available, from sea trout and salmon on the Lyn to reservoir fishing at the Wimbleball, Wistlandpound and Clatworthy. Peace and solitude are almost guaranteed to be your companions, only interrupted by the sport of the wilder inhabitants of Exmoor.

For a change from fishing, being in the heart of stunning Exmoor leaves one with many options. Historic sites abound, the Tarr steps have been dated back to the Bronze Age, and on a clear day from the top of Dunkery Beacon, you can catch a sight of sixteen different counties. For the horse-lover, all types of riding can be arranged through the hotel. Or if you prefer the independence of walking, Exmoor is perfect, full of fascinating trails and ever-changing scenery. Rough and clay shooting can be arranged by the hotel as can gun hire and tuition if required. Of course, the charm of the hotel itself may mean you feel like doing nothing more than relaxing by an open fire with a delicious cream tea.

The Exmoor Forest hotel has gained a quite a reputation over the years as one of the areas leading restaurants. Tempted by an ever-changing menu, the discerning diner has the difficult choice of a variety of local produce, Exmoor being famous for its salmon, venison and pheasant, all complemented by a well-stocked cellar. Retire afterwards to the homely bar with its massive log fire, selection of real ales, fine ports and a quite astonishing display of over seventy different blended and malt whiskies. The perfect West Country hospitality at the end of a perfect West Country day.

The Exmoor Forest Hotel
Simonsbath
Nr Minehead
Somerset
Tel: (064-383) 341
Fax: (064-383) 277

THE WOODFORD BRIDGE HOTEL

Situated on the banks of the River Torridge, this charming fifteenth century thatched coaching inn is the perfect hotel for anglers and non-anglers alike. Based at this hotel is the Simon Gawesworth School of Fly Fishing, famous for the quality of the instruction offered and providing the opportunity for either the novice to learn the basic skills of fly fishing or the more experienced angler to have a quick brush-up on the more tricky casts, such as the Spey's or the double haul. Also on site is a well stocked tackle shop, drying room, freezing facilities and rod room. Tackle or waders are available for hire.

The hotel has approximately 18 miles of fishing rights on the rivers Taw, Torridge and Bray, all famous for the Sea Trout and Salmon fishing, as well as the wild Devon Brown Trout. The best time to come is late March, April and May for Salmon, and late June, July and August for Sea-Trout whilst the month of September generally provides an excellent end to the season. The Brown Trout fishing is probably best from mid May onwards. All the beats are 'fly only' from May 1st though spinning is allowed between March and the end of April. For the stillwater angler the hotel is an ideal base as it is within an hour's drive of some twenty lakes and reservoirs.

For the non-angler there is a large range of leisure facilities at the hotel which include an indoor heated swimming pool, squash courts, a fully euipped gym, spa bath, solarium and sauna. Indoors, the Egon Ronay listed restaurant offers a delicious choice of a la carte and table d'hote menus, with a good selection of wines in the cellar.

For more details of a wonderful holiday contact: Simon Gawesworth.

Woodford Bridge Hotel
Milton Damerel
Near Holsworthy
Devon EX22 7LL
Tel: (040926) 481
Fax: (040926) 585

ENGLAND : FURTHER FORAYS

CORNWALL

AVIARY COURT,
Mary's Well, Redruth, Tel: (0209) 842256
This popular guesthouse stands on the edge of Illogen woods in its own extensive grounds. Some of the comfortable bedrooms are ensuite and guests can also enjoy a bar and real fire in an agreeable lounge.

BEACH DUNES HOTEL,
Ramoth Way, Perranporth, Tel: (0872) 572263
This family hotel is an ideal base for exploration of the fabulous Cornish coastline. Food served here is nutritious and imaginative, and vegetarians can also be catered for.

CARNSON HOUSE HOTEL,
East Terrace, Tel: (0736) 65589
Conveniently situated for the town centre and local amenites, Carnson House offers eight well-appointed bedrooms, all of which have central heating and tea/coffee makers. Many local attractions, including St Michaels Mount, are within easy reach.

EAST CORNWALL FARMHOUSE,
Fullaford Road, Cornwall, Tel: (0579) 50018
A former Count House set in the beautiful Silver Valley, East Cornwall Farmhouse is particularly popular for imaginative cooking prepared using local and home-grown produce. All bedrooms have colour TV and tea/coffee making facilities and two are ensuite. Cotehele House is only two miles away, whilst for golfers the tremendous St Mellion complex is only ten minutes drive.

HIGH MASSETTS,
Cadgwith, Helston, Tel: (0326) 290571
This extremely comfortable establishment offers fabulous views over a sandy cove which offers safe bathing, fishing and skin-diving. Accommodation is equally impressive and all bedrooms have modern amenities and tea/coffee makers.

MANOR FARM,
Crackington, Nr. Bude, Tel: (08403) 304
This manor house is steeped in history. Built in the eleventh century, it belonged at one time to The Earl of Mortain, half brother to William the Conqueror. Today's accommodation is highly acclaimed and guests also have the benefit of attractive gardens.

OLD SCHOOLHOUSE,
St. ErvanPadston, Wadebridge, Tel: (0841) 540811
Hidden away in a historic country lane, the Old Schoolhouse retains both its original character and the old school bell! Furnishings and rooms are both of a very high standard.

PERRAN HOUSE,
Fore Street, Tel: (0726) 882066
This well appointed guesthouse is extremely convenient for local amenities and places of interest for Cornwall's many tourists. Cream teas in summer are an added and tempting inducement.

RASHLEIGH ARMS,
Quay Road, Tel: (0726) 73635
Excellent value is always worth seeking out and this attractive inn will not fail to please. Rooms are modern and well-kept and real ale is always on tap (not in the bedrooms though!).

ROSEBUD COTTAGE,
Bossiney, Tel: (00840) 770861
Accommodation and food are both highly recommended at this attractive Cornish cottage guesthouse. Three comfortable bedrooms are equipped with modern facilities and tea/coffee makers.

TREVISPIAN-VEAN FARM HOUSE,
Trevispean-Vean, Erme, Truro, Tel: (0872) 79514
Twelve comfortable bedrooms, most of them ensuite, are provided for the benefit of guests at this highly recommended and picturesque farmhouse. Trevispean-Vean is perfectly situated for excursions to both coast and countryside.

DEVON

BUCKLEIGH LODGE,
135 Bayview Road, Westward Ho, Tel: (0237) 475988
Golfers are often in evidence at this popular guesthouse which stands on the outskirts of the attractive village of Westward Ho. However, less active visitors will find the accommodation on offer just as stylish.

CHERRYBROOK HOTEL,
Tavistock, Tel: (0822) 88260
An agreeably furnished lounge bar provides the opportunity for viewing the changing moods of the moors from a position of lazy comfort. The warm and attentive service will not increase any desire to depart.

CRESTA,
26 Sticklepath Hill, Barnstaple, Tel: (0271) 74022
An accommodating and welcoming guesthouse, Cresta is only one mile from the centre of Barnstaple. Features include a colourful lounge and ample parking.

DOCTORS,
Halberton Road, Willand, Tel: (0884) 820525
An intriguingly named property, Doctors is in fact a character-rich farmhouse and visitors should not be deterred by the name. Ninety acres of grounds should provide for plenty of active pursuits.

HEASLEY HOUSE,
Heasley Mill, Devon, Tel: (05984) 213
Overlooking a babbling mill stream, Heasley House is a charming edifice from the outside, and the antique filled interior is equally appealing. Accommodation is clean and well-kept.

HUGHSLADE,
Oakhampton, Tel: (0837) 52883
The glories of Dartmoor and the A30 road have little in common but both are located close to this attractive farmhouse. In the event of anybody tiring of the former, snooker provides indoor recreation.

HUXTABLE FARM,
West Buckland, Barnstaple, North Devon, Tel: (05986) 254
Huxtable Farm is a listed medieval longhouse and features a barn furnished with antiques. It is ideally situated for Saunton, Royal North Devon and other golf courses, and various Stately Homes and gardens can be explored by non-playing escorts.

KENWITH CASTLE HOTEL,
Abbotsham, Bideford, North Devon, Tel: (0237) 473712
An idyllic spot to stop and rest awhile, Kenwith is a totally secluded country house fronted by one of Devon's most exclusive Trout Lakes, lying in a fold of picturesque Devon countryside. Excellent cuisine is also on offer, served in the magnificent Wedgewood room restaurant.

LODGE HILL,
Ashley, Tiverton, Tel: (0884) 252907
The town of Tiverton is easily reached from this spacious farmhouse that sits astride a hilltop in The Eve Valley. Nine rooms are available.

MERTON HOUSE,
Beaford, Tel: (08053) 364
This charming Georgian residence offers unobtrusive comfort from April to October, although prospective guests may be advised to visit during the summer months when the grass tennis court is most likely to be in use.

ROWDEN BARTON,
Roundswell, Barnstaple, Tel: (0271) 44365
Friendliness and genuine attention to every detail make this farmhouse a tourist's favourite. Good food and splendid bedrooms confirm the opinion.

SUNNYMEDE,
24 New North Road, Exeter, Tel: (0392) 73844
Yet another Georgian property, this one with the advantage of being located in the neighbourhood of extensive shopping facilities. Exeter offers an abundance of other amenities.

ENGLAND : FURTHER FORAYS

THATCHED COTTAGE,
9 Crossley Moor Road, Kingsteigntnon, Newton Abbot, Tel: (0626) 65650
A host of modern comforts, including ensuite bedrooms, make this sixteenth century cottage an engaging mix of the new and the old. The cuisine is imaginative and often quite adventurous.

THE BLENHEIM HOTEL,
Bovey Tracey, South Devon, Tel: (0626) 832422
This is a family run hotel on the edge of the Dartmoor National Park. Local attractions are many-The Manor House Morehampstead is six miles away, Stover is only one mile away and Teignmouth, Chelston and Torquay golf courses are within ten miles.

WATERCRESS FARM TROUT FISHERY,
Kerswell Springs, Chudleigh, Newton Abbot Tel: (0626) 852168
The fishery consists of 3 lakes which provide superb fly fishing in crystal clear spring fed water. The lakes are stocked daily with trout from 1 1/4 lbs-14lbs. Day tickets and rod hire are available but booking is essential.

WIGHAM,
Morchard Bishop, Tel: (03637) 350
Extensive and sympathetic restoration has made this one of the county's most acclaimed guesthouses. Patrons will not be disappointed; staying in a four poster bed in a sixteenth century thatched longhouse would be somewhere near most people's idea of fun!

WOOLSGROVE,
Sandford, Crediton, Tel: (0363) 84246
The majority of moderately-priced accommodation in Devon seems to be in farmhouses and no-one should bemoan that fact. This is yet another fine example with yet more spectacular views.

SOMERSET

BINCOMBE HOUSE,
Bincombe, Overstowey, Tel: (0278) 732386
Set in secluded woodland at the foot of the Quantock Hills, this a picturesque farmhouse that really is a scenic delight. The interior is no less engaging and the bedrooms are unsurprisingly comfortable.

MANOR FARM,
Chiselborough, Stoke-sub-Hamdon, Tel: (093588) 203
In addition to accommodation that will never provoke the slightest disatisfaction, the food at Manor Farm is quite something to behold. Home baked rolls and jugs of cider all make for a cheery stay.

OLD STOWEY FARM,
Wheddon Cross, Minehead, Tel: (064384) 268
A delightful sixteenth century farmhouse, imposingly set in eighty acres of land within the boundaries of Exmoor National Park. Log fires and woodburning stoves all make for a most congenial atmosphere.

WARREN GUESTHOUSE,
29 Berrow Road, Burnham-on-Sea, Tel: (0278) 786726
This an ideal centre for both family and activity-based holidays. Within a short distance of this pleasant guesthouse can be found the town centre, swimming pool and championship golf course.

AVON

EASTCOTE COTTAGE,
Crossways Knapp Road, Thornbury, Bristol, Tel: (0454) 413106
Three comfortable bedrooms with modern ameneties are offered by this charming, unpretentious guesthouse. The M4/M3 interchange is conveniently near, although thankfully not too near!

FOUNTAIN HOUSE,
9/11 Fountain Buildings, Lansdown Road, Bath, Tel: (0225) 338622
Fountain House is Bath's first all-suite hotel, offering a combination of the comfort of a conventional hotel with the independence and privacy of one's own home. A central situation gives quick and easy access to the city's array of historical attractions.

HIGHWAYS HOUSE,
143 Wells Road, Bath, Tel: (0225) 21238
Bath is a holiday centre that thousands of tourists make for annually, and it is a safe bet that Highways House has received a good few of them. A guest lounge and nicely decorated breakfast room are doubtless part of the attraction.

OAKLEIGH GUESTHOUSE,
19 Upper Oldfield Park, Bath, Tel: (0225) 339193
Only ten miles from the city centre, Oakleigh is a comfortable distance from the majority of Bath's architectural glories. All rooms have TV and tea/coffee making facilities and most have private bathrooms.

DORSET

CRANSTON COTTAGE,
25 Church Street, Bridport, Tel: (0308) 56240
The sandy beaches and ice-cream sellers of West Bay are only a stroll away from Cranston Cottage. In case more secluded sunbathing is preferred, a patio complete with sun loungers awaits all lazy guests!

OLD RECTORY,
St John's Hill, St James, Shaftsbury, Tel: (0747) 2003
The most succulent Cordon Bleu cuisine is a feature of this highly recommended guesthouse. Elegant furnishings and a friendly ambiance simply make the food taste even better.

PARKLANDS HOTEL,
4 Rushton Crescent, Bournemouth, Tel: (0202) 552529
Parklands Hotel is situated on the edge of lovely Meyrick Park with it's fine golf course and facilities for tennis, bowls and squash. Bournemouth, with it's shops, woods and golden sands is only minutes away. Parklands also specialises in arranging tailored golfing packages.

VARTREES HOUSE,
Moreton, Crossways, Dorchester, Tel: (0305) 852704
The burial place of Lawrence of Arabia is contained within the pretty village of Moreton. The surrounding countryside is just as scenic and nobody will regret a visit to Vartrees House.

WILTSHIRE

BAYLYS ALE HOUSE,
High Street, Box, Tel: (0225) 743622
As befits its name, Baylys is celebrated for a mouth-watering range of beers and spirits. However three bedrooms are also available, all are ensuite and have colour TV.

OXFORD HOTEL,
32/36 Langley Road, Chippenham, Tel: (0249) 652542
For travellers passing through and for those wishing to stay awhile, the Oxford offers a refreshing combination of modern amenities and traditional standards of service.

RATHLIN,
Wick Lane, Devizes, Tel: (0380) 721999
A number of tasteful antiques adorn this comfortable guesthouse and make for a dignified and elegant atmosphere. The accommodation is immaculate and comfortable.

ENGLAND : FURTHER FORAYS

WIDBROOK GRANGE,
Trowbridge Road, Bradford-on-Avon, Tel: (02216) 31
Only a short drive away from the glories of Bath, Widbrook is a Georgian listed house and provides a warm and sincere welcome to all guests. Bedrooms are all ensuite.

HAMPSHIRE

CEDAR LODGE,
100 Cedar Road, Portswood, Tel: (0703) 226761
Cedar Lodge is the perfect base for either a shopping trip to Southampton or a picnic in the New Forest. The bedrooms at this popular guesthouse are spacious and the service uncommonly attentive.

CHURCH FARM HOUSE,
Barton Stacey, Winchester, Tel: (0962) 760268
Winchester is one of England's most celebrated towns, with its medieval cathedral as a crowning glory. Lucky guests have the choice between staying in the main house and an adjacent coach house.

COCKLE WARREN GUESTHOUSE,
36 Seafront, Hayling Island, Tel: (0705) 464961
Such a picturesque name risks being slightly over-ambitious but in this case the reality does not disappoint. Ensuite bedrooms look out onto hens and ducks, enclosed by a white picket fence, and the sea beyond.

KINGS HEAD HOTEL,
Hursley, Tel: (0962) 75208
An excellent place for a roadside drink, the Kings Head also offers a number of spacious bedrooms and some extremely tasty food.

NIRVANA HOTEL,
384-386 Winchester Road, Bassett, Southampton, Tel: (0703) 760474
Personally run by the proprietors Douglas and Eileen Dawson, guests are assured of a warm and friendly welcome at this comfortable hotel. As well as the extensive facilities, one recent addition is a superb conference room.

PLUM TREE COTTAGE,
Sandleheath, Fordingbridge, Tel: (0425) 53032
Only a few minutes from the new forest, Plum Tree is a fairytale thatched cottage that offers such charming features as an inglenook fireplace and a wood stove. The cottage may be rented for self catering holidays.

WHEATSHEAF HOUSE,
25 Gosport Street, Lymington, Tel: (0590) 79208
Once a seventeenth century tavern, Wheatsheaf House is now a twentieth century guesthouse of some distinction. The market town of Lymington is most attractive and is obviously convenient for The New Forest.

YEW TREE COTTAGE,
Lower Baybridge Lane, Baybridge, Owslebury, Tel: (096274) 254
A secluded setting some six miles out of Winchester are the tempting credentials of Yew Tree Cottage. Antique furniture and oak beams add an air of authenticity, and are almost as impressive as the home cooking.

JERSEY

ALMORAH HOTEL,
Lower Kings Cliff, St Helier, Tel: (0534) 21648
Virtually every bedroom at the Almorah has ensuite facilities and the furnishings are well chosen and stylish. A Breton-style dining room adds further flavour to some delicious cuisine.

CLIFF COURT HOTEL,
St Andrews Road, First Tower, Tel: (0534) 34919
An enviable position overlooking St Aubin's Bay makes this quiet property a favourite with discerning holidaymakers. A lounge, bar and dining rooms will all contribute to a comfortable stay.

LAVENDER VILLA HOTEL,
Rue A Don, Grouville, Tel: (0534) 54937
The Lavender Villa is a popular venue for both locals and visitors; both are no doubt drawn by a pleasant setting, friendly atmosphere and wide selection of food and drink.

PANORAMA,
St Aubin, Tel: (0534) 45940
A highly acclaimed establishment with stunning sea views, the Panorama is in the capable hands of owners John and Jill Squinks. Guests are particularly appreciative of afternoon tea served in a silver pot on a silver tray.

GUERNSEY

ANN-DAWN PRIVATE HOTEL,
Route des Capelles, St Sampson, Tel: (0481) 725606
This hotel will find approval with guests who are seeking traditional comforts and a dignified atmosphere. Elegant accommodation gives way to splendid lawned and landscaped gardens.

LA GIROUETTE COUNTRY HOTEL,
Perelle, Tel: (0481) 63269
Perrelle Bay is only minutes away from this comfortable and accommodating guesthouse. Both bedrooms and public rooms are spacious and well-appointed.

LES OZOUETS LODGE,
Ozouets Road, St Peters Port, Tel: (0481) 21288
Outstanding cuisine is prepared and served by the chef patron, complemented by an extensive wine list. Impressive gardens feature putting and bowling greens, and a tennis court.

MIDHURST HOUSE,
Candie Road, St Peter Port, Tel: (0481) 724391
It is difficult to know what to highlight most in this attractive cottage - all round excellence is the order of the day. Bedrooms, cooking, surroundings and service are all of the highest order.

SUSSEX

BOLEBROKE MILL,
Perry Hill, Edenbridge Road, Hartfield, Tel: (089277) 425
An entry in the Doomsday book is only one of the claims to fame of this excellent hostelry. Originally a watermill, Bolebrook has been caringly converted and provides a scenic retreat for those in search of relaxing escapism.

CHALK FARM FISHERY,
Arundel, Tel: (0903) 883742
Situated on the Duke of Norfolk's Estate in Arundel, Chalk Springs possesses four clear lakes in beautiful surroundings, covering a total of five acres. Anglers will be delighted to learn that Rainbow and Brown Trout are not an uncommon occurrence. Open seven days a week, day tickets and fishing tuition are available.

CLEAVERS LYNG,
Church Road, Herstmonceux, Tel: (0323) 833131
Situated beside Herstmonceux Castle, Cleavers Lyng itself has the aura of times past, with inglenook fireplaces and exposed oak beams giving an air of solidity and dependability. The high standard of care will more than bear this out.

ENGLAND : FURTHER FORAYS

CROUCHERS BOTTOM,
Birdham Road, Appledram, Chichester, Tel: (0243) 784995
A converted farmhouse, set in extensive grounds, the imaginatively named Crouchers Bottom possesses four ensuite bedrooms and an attractive guests lounge. Chichester Cathedral and the South Downs are distantly visible.

GLEBE END,
Church Street, Warnham, Horsham, Tel: (0403) 61711
Visitors are spoilt for choice at this agreeable guesthouse. On one hand, guests may be tempted to take advantage of nearby opportunities for golf and tennis. Alternatively, with mediaeval architecture, log-burning stove, Tudor dining room and a beautiful walled garden, there are good grounds for staying put!

HATPINS,
Bosham Lane, Old Bosham, Tel: (0243) 572644
The weary traveller in search of a soft pillow for the night would do a lot worse than to seek out Hatpins. All rooms are ensuite and beds can even be made up with French linen.

HOOKE HALL,
250 High Street, Uckfield, Tel: (0825) 61578
The attractive and bustling market town of Uckfield is the setting for Hooke Hall, an elegant and popular guesthouse. Leeds and Hever Castles are easily accessible and Glyndebourne is only fifteen minutes distant by car.

JEAKES HOUSE,
Mermaid Street, Rye, Tel: (0797) 222828
Jeakes is a listed building, dating from the seventeenth century and guests will enjoy a tranquil and dignified atmosphere. All bedrooms are either ensuite or have private facilities.

LITTLE ORCHARD HOUSE,
West Street, Rye, East Sussex, Tel: (0797) 223831
This Georgian townhouse and garden stands at the very heart of the unique Conservation Area that is ancient Rye. Although recently renovated to provide central heating and bathrooms, the house retains an inherently Georgian character.

OLD RECTORY,
Cot Lane, Chidham, Nr. Chichester, Tel: (0243) 572088
This is an old, period house that proudly stands in the village of Chidham. Bedrooms are more than adequate and a large garden and swimming pool provide outdoor amusement.

OLD STORE GUEST HOUSE,
Stane Street, Halnaker, Chichester, Tel: (0243) 531977
The twin delights of Goodwood and Fontwell racecourses are each only three miles from this popular resting place. A range of accommodation is available, and all rooms are comfortable and well-appointed.

POWDERMILL HOUSE,
Powdermill Lane, Battle, Tel: (04246) 2035
As far as sportsmen's paradises go, this must rank highly. In addition to well-appointed accommodation, also available are walks, fishing, swimming, croquet, golf and riding.

RACECOURSE COTTAGE,
Nepcote, Findon, Tel: (090671) 3783
Both the accommodation and the welcome are to be applauded here. If that does not suffice, then a wealth of nearby attractions and amenities surely will.

TAPLOW COTTAGE,
81 Nyewood Lane, Bognor Regis, Tel: (0243) 821398
Racing and Stately Home enthusiasts will find this a convenient and pleasant base for Arundel Castle and Goodwood racecourse. For really hardy souls, the sea is almost within touching distance.

WESTERN HOUSE,
113 Winchelsea Road, Rye, Tel: (0797) 223419
An insight into the past is on offer for guests at Western House, with the owner's propensity for antiques everywhere apparent. The town of Rye and the Brede valley provide further historical interest. All rooms are ensuite.

WESTLANDS,
Brighton Road, Monks Gate, Nr Horsham, Tel: (0403) 76383
Three large bedrooms with modern amenities are the important feature of this large, conveniently situated guesthouse. Gatwick, Brighton, Horsham and the Sussex coast are all easily reached, and with the exception of Gatwick, are all worth a visit.

WILLOWAYE,
60 Manor Road, Selsey, Chichester, Tel: (0243) 602472
Water abounds everywhere at Willowaye. Set in the fishing village of Selsey, a walk of only a few hundred yards takes one to the shimmering (occasionally) sea. Fishbourne Roman Palace is another local attraction.

KENT

CARVAL HOTEL,
56/58 London Road, Maidstone, Tel: (0622) 762100
A garden and car park are among the amenities at the Carval, a pleasant and welcoming hotel, in a quiet residential setting. A well stocked bar also contains useful tourist information.

CHEQUERS INN,
Smarden, Nr. Ashford, Tel: (023377) 217
Chequers dates back to 1450 and has been inhabited since that time by a resident ghost. Walking, golf and fishing are among a multitude of local pursuits on offer.

CROMER,
194 Parrock Street, Gravesend, Tel: (0474) 361935
Gravesend appears unusually well blessed with guesthouses of fine quality, and this is a particularly notable example. All rooms are well appointed and well equipped and public rooms are tasteful and relaxing.

DELL GUESTHOUSE,
233 Folkstone Road, Dover, Tel: (0304) 202422
Dover is a splendid place and the Dell Guesthouse is an ideal base. Rooms and service can not be faulted and breakfast is even served from 6.00am for the benefit of those wishing to catch the early morning cross-channel ferries.

DOLPHINS HOTEL AND RESTAURANT,
Dymchurch Road, New Romney, Tel: (0679) 63224
The glorious coastline of Kent can be absorbed at your own pace by staying at this popular establishment. The surrounding countryside is equally appealing and is dotted with opportunities for golf, walking and fishing.

FRITH FARM HOUSE,
Otterden, Faversham, Tel: (079589) 701
An immaculately restored Georgian farmhouse, Frith farm is pleasantly set in an area of outstanding natural beauty. The whole of magnificent Kent awaits the avid explorer.

GREYSWOLDE HOTEL,
20 Surrey Road, Cliftonville, Margate, Tel: (0843) 223956
Only yards form the promenade, Greyswolde is an imposing Victorian Hotel whose appearance has remained largely unaltered over the last hundred years. Many of the admirable bedrooms are ensuite.

ENGLAND : FURTHER FORAYS

NUMBER ONE GUESTHOUSE,
1 Castle Street, Dover, Tel: (0304) 212007
Looking out onto the majestic castle, Number One guesthouse actually dates back to 1800. Six bedrooms all possess modern amenities and tea/coffee making facilities.

OVERCLIFFE HOTEL,
15-16 The Overcliffe, Gravesend, Tel: (0474) 322131
Both bedrooms and public rooms are of a uniformly excellent standard and the level of service is no less outstanding. Amenities and facilities are within easy reach.

PORTFIELD LODGE,
33 Church Road, Chichester, Tel: (0243) 780883
Close to Goodwood racecourse, several golf courses and the Festival theatre, Portfield Lodge should suit tourists of all tastes. The city centre is also within striking distance.

SUTHERLAND HOUSE,
186 London Road, Deal, Tel: (0304) 362853
This is a guesthouse of unusually high quality, offering a level of comfort and cuisine on a par with hotels of much higher aspiration. Royal St Georges, Royal Cinque Ports and Princes will entertain and test all golfing enthusiasts.

WALLETS COURT MANOR,
West Cliffe, St. Margarets, Dover, Tel: (0304) 852424
Once a home of William Pitt the Younger, this 17th century manor house enjoys a spectacular setting, looking down proudly over the White Cliffs of Dover. Oak beams and inglenook fireplaces add further charm.

WALNUT TREE FARM,
Lynsore Bottom, Upper Hardes, Nr. Canterbury, Tel: (022787)
Walnut Tree excels in all the things for which farmhouses are renowned- breakfast, fresh eggs, home-made bread and comfortable accommodation.

WINDYRIDGE GUESTHOUSE,
Wraik Hill, Whitstable, Tel: (0227) 263506
The benefits of a family-run guesthouse are only too obvious here:- attentive and friendly service, home cooking, clean and comfortable rooms. Vegetarians are also catered for.

YORKE LODGE GUESTHOUSE,
50 London Road, Canterbury, Tel: (0227) 451243
Six nicely furnished bedrooms are at this disposal of guests at this agreeable guesthouse. A library with extensive tourist information is a thoughtful and invaluable extra.

LONDON

ABER HOTEL,
89 Crouch Hill, Hornsey, Tel: 081-340 2847
A medium-sized, family-run hotel, the Aber offers a peaceful night's sleep within easy reach of the bright lights and loud noises of central London.

BELGRAVE HOUSE HOTEL,
28-32 Belgrave Road, Tel: 071-828 1563
The Belgrave House is centrally located with easy access to Victoria stations, Buckingham Palace and the West End. All bedrooms are centrally heated and some have private facilities.

BYRON HOTEL,
36-38 Queensborough Terrace, Tel: 071-243 0987
Opposite Kensington Gardens, this acclaimed hotel aims to recapture some of the charm and elegance of Victorian England. Whatever the objectives, the results are excellent, with the interior decor particularly fine.

CHASE LODGE,
10 Park Road, Hampton Wick, Kingston-upon-Thames, Tel: 081-943 1862
This excellent and high-quality establishment, close to Kempton and Sandown racecourses, is a perfect base for avid tourists. A multitude of places of interest are within easy travelling distance, including Syon Park, Kew Gardens, Wisley, Hampton Court Palace, Windsor Castle, Osterley House and Royal Bushy Park.

CHESHAM HOUSE HOTEL,
64-66 Ebury Street, Tel: 071-730 8513
The Chesham has undergone recent and extensive refurbishment, and looks set to reap immense benefits. Service, too, is consistently courteous and helps to create an atmosphere of well-being.

CLEARVIEW HOUSE,
161 Fordwych Road, Cricklewood, Tel: 081-452 9773
Guesthouses in the capital set in quiet residential areas are not always over-easy to find, but this example is well worth seeking out. Accommodation is both modern and tasteful.

CRANBROOK HOTEL,
24 Coventry Road, Ilford, Essex, Tel: 081-554 6544
The occasion to pamper oneself without spending a small fortune does not arise frequently. However, this extremely comfortable suburban hotel offers some rooms with ensuite facilities and jacuzzi, and most importantly is not excessively priced.

KNIGHTSBRIDGE HOTEL,
10 Beaufort Gardens, Knightsbridge, Tel: 071-589 9271
The first time visitor to the Knightsbridge will immediately be impressed by its elegant facade. Entering the hotel will most definitely not prove a letdown, with stylish and appropriate furnishings the order of the day.

STONEHALL HOUSE,
35-37 Westcombe Park, Blackheath, Tel: 081-858 8706
Stonehall is a traditional guesthouse that will make its visitors more than welcome. A TV lounge and garden are both well used and well thought of.

WIMBLEDON HOTEL,
78 Worple Road, Wimbledon, Tel: 081-946 9265
Cosy and family run, this popular hotel is always highly praised by previous residents. Local amenities are within walking distance.

WINCHESTER HOTEL,
12 Belgravia Road, Westminster, Tel: 071-8282972
The elegance of the area is matched by this well-appointed and furnished hotel. Rooms are of a uniformly high standard and guests will leave feeling refreshed and invigorated.

SURREY

BULMER FARM,
Holmbury St. Mary, Dorking, Tel: (0306) 730210
Convenient for the varied and interesting scenery of Sussex and Surrey, Bulmer Farm offers a taste of authentic countryside. The farm produce is overwhelmingly delicious.

CRANLEIGH HOTEL,
41 West Street, Reigate, Tel: (0737) 223417
An outdoor heated swimming pool will provide summer relaxation for residents. In the colder months, the interior of this hotel is just as appealing.

ENGLAND : FURTHER FORAYS

DEERFELL,
Blackdown Park, Fernden Lane, Haslemere, Tel: (0428) 53409
Sussex, rather than Surrey is the county in focus here, as Deerfell offers splendid views of the Sussex hills. Walking, riding, fishing and golfing can all be easily found.

IELD HOUSE,
Babylon Lane, Lower Kingswood, Tadworth, Tel: (0737) 221745
Strange though it may seem, this guesthouse is only fifteen minutes from Gatwick Airport yet occupies a secluded and attractive setting. A guests' lounge and gym provide different types of indoor relaxation.

GLENCOURT,
St Johns Hill Road, Woking, Tel: (04862) 64154
This hotel can be recommended without reservation. The reasons? One is tempted to say, go and find out:- however surroundings, service and food are all top-notch.

QUINNS HOTEL,
78 Epsom Road, Guildford, Tel: (0483) 60422
Guildford is near enough London to be convenient and far away to be relatively relaxing. Quinns Hotel is proud of its location and equally so of its service and style.

HERTFORDSHIRE

ARDMORE HOUSE,
54 Lesford Road, St. Albans, Tel: (0727) 59313
This is a large, detached house that dates from the Edwardian era and has retained much of the tradition and elegance from that age. Both Clarence Park and the city-centre are within walking distance.

BRIGGENS HOUSE HOTEL,
Stanstead Abbots, Nr. Ware, Tel: (027 979) 2416
Briggens House is an extremely comfortable and cultivated country house hotel. Set in its own beautiful grounds, golf, tennis and swimming can all be enjoyed by guests.

VENUS HILL FARM,
Venus Hill, Bovingdon, Tel: (0442) 833396
Three bedrooms all offer modern amenities at this three hundred year old converted farmhouse. An outdoor swimming pool provides the perfect early-morning prelude to a short drive to Heathrow.

VINTAGE CORNER HOTEL,
Old Cambridge Road, Puckeridge, Tel: (0920) 822722
A modern hotel in the pretty village of Puckeridge may seem an incongruous idea; however the Vintage Corner sits easily into its environment and provides more than adequate accommodation.

BEDFORDSHIRE

CHURCH,
41 High Street, Roxton, Tel: (0234) 870234
Moderate prices do not conceal moderate standard accommodation in this particular instance and Church can be thoroughly recommended in all respects.

CLARENDON HOUSE HOTEL,
25/27 Ampthill Road, Bedford, Tel: (0234) 266054
For travellers requiring a restful bed for the night and a sensible, unpretentious meal, this hotel should fit most peoples bill.

HERTFORD HOUSE HOTEL,
57 De Parys Avenue, Bedford, Tel: (0234) 50007
Mouth-watering breakfasts served on the first floor dining room are a feature of this clean, comfortable hotel. The atmosphere is invariably friendly and relaxed.

LAWS HOTEL,
Turvey, Bedford, Tel: (023 064) 213
A popular restaurant and splendid gardens are particularly notable characteristics of the Laws Hotel. It is also ideally situated for all central amenities.

ESSEX

BOVILLS HALL,
Ardleigh, Colchester, Tel: (0206) 230217
Accommodation at this splendid manor house is both well appointed and equipped to a high standard. The proprietor obviously takes a great pride in her establishment, and equally so in her guests.

NEWHOUSE FARM,
Radwinter, Saffron Walden, Tel: (079987)211
This grade II listed farmhouse is truly a pleasure to behold, with Georgian and Tudor features blending serenely into gardens, lake and moat. Renowned local fare will not take long to seek out.

SWAN HOTEL,
Maldon High Street, Maldon, Tel: (0621) 53170
This hotel is far from opulent, but it does offer clean accommodation in a friendly atmosphere, and food that will satisfy the most ravenous of diners.

WHITE HART,
Bocking End, Braintree, Tel: (0376) 21401
For those wishing a high-standard, bustling hotel close to the city-centre, the White Hart may prove an irresistible choice. Architecture-for the enthusiasts-is part Tudor and part Georgian.

BERKSHIRE

AERON PRIVATE HOTEL,
191 Kentwood Hill, Tilehurst, Tel: (0734) 424119
This well-run guesthouse is conveniently situated for the town centre and provides clean, tidy rooms all of which have colour television, direct-dial telephones and tea/coffee making facilities.

BRIDGE COTTAGE,
Station Road, Woolhampton, Reading, Tel: (0734) 713138
This picturesque riverside cottage contains exposed oak beams and an olde-worlde atmosphere gives added charm. Disabled guests are welcome.

GREEN MEADOWS,
Bucklebury, Reading, Tel: (0734) 713353
A warm welcome is guaranteed at this pleasant country manor that is set in its own substantial grounds. Bedrooms are relaxing and comfortable, and Heathrow is within easy travelling distance.

GREENWAYS,
Garden Close Lane, Newbury, Tel: (0635) 40496
Conveniently located for London-bound travellers, this well-appointed country house will make every guest feel quite at home. Excellent facilities include an outdoor swimming pool and relaxing guests lounge.

LYNDRICK HOUSE,
The Avenue, Ascot, Tel: (0344) 883520
Set in a peaceful residential area, this pleasant, five bedroomed house is only ten minutes drive form Wentworth Golf Club. Meals are served in an elegant conservatory and bedrooms have colour TV and tea/coffee making facilities.

PILGRIMS REST GUEST HOUSE,
Oxford Road, Newbury, Tel: (0635) 40694
This medium-sized guesthouse provides comfortable accommodation in a convenient location, only minutes from the town centre. All rooms are tastefully furnished and ensuite accommodation is available.

ENGLAND : FURTHER FORAYS

ST MARY'S HOUSE,
Church Steet, Kintbury, Tel: (0488) 58551
Originally a Victorian schoolhouse, this splendid establishment offers seven comfortable rooms including some that are ensuite. A TV lounge and drinks licence ensure a relaxing stay for every visitor.

SUNDIAL HOUSE,
Buccleuch Road, Datchet, Nr Windsor, Tel: (0753) 47090
Sundial House was once the coach house of the Duchess of Buccleuch. Built in the eighteenth century, it is now a tasteful and elegant guesthouse, offering four bedrooms, all with ensuite facilities. Windsor Castle is within one mile.

BUCKINGHAMSHIRE

CLIFTON LODGE HOTEL,
210 West Wycombe Road, Tel: (0494) 440095,
Recently refurbished and modernised, this small hotel offers a highstandard of accommodation and food. A friendly welcome and attentive staff are other excellent features.

ELMS COUNTRY HOUSE,
The Elms, Radnage, Nr. Stokenchurch, Tel: (024026) 2175
This elegant and well appointed guesthouse offers accommodation of an uncommonly high standard. Set in an area of Outstanding Natural Beauty, the Elms contains the reflects the atmosphere of a bygone age.

FOXHILL,
Kingsey, Tel: (0844) 291650
A farmhouse dating back to the seventeenth century, Foxhill provides elegant bedrooms and a splendid garden, complete with ornamental pond. Guests will be made most welcome.

POLETREES FARM,
Brill, Nr Aylesbury, Tel: (0844) 238276
The charm and elegance of a 500 year-old farmhouse are immediately apparent in this popular guesthouse. Accommodation is spruce and thoughtful and the farmhouse meals are worth a visit in themselves.

OXON

COURTFIELD PRIVATE HOTEL,
367 Iffley Road, Oxford, Tel: (00865) 242991
Conveniently and pleasantly located in a central residential area, the Courtfield is within easy reach of the city centre and it's many attractions. Excellent service is constantly provided.

CRAVEN,
Fernham Road, Uffington, Tel: (036782) 449
Half-way between Oxford and Swindon, this seventeenth century thatched and beamed house offers an extremely relaxed atmosphere. Choose between open log fires in the winter and an attractive terrace and gardens in the summer.

FALLOWFIELDS,
Southmoor with Kingston Bagpuize, Abingdon, Tel: (0865) 820416
Only ten miles from Oxford, this lovely country house is set in twelve acres and offers an outdoor pool, croquet and tennis. Golfers are spoilt for choice with various courses in the proximity including a splendid 36 holes at Frilford Heath.

FELDON HOUSE,
Lower Brailes, Nr. Banbury, Tel: (0060885) 580
Set in beautiful grounds, this imposing house dates back to the seventeenth century and has retained much of its original charm. Rooms are spacious and tidy and the food prepared by the owners is quite superb.

FULFORD HOUSE,
The Green, Culworth, Nr. Banbury, Tel: (029576) 355
Personal attention and service are the hallmarks of this highly recommended guesthouse. Guests will be made to feel quite 'at home' and should find time to explore the delightful gardens.

THREE PIGEONS,
Great Milton, Tel: (0844) 279247
This country inn makes a friendly and enjoyable stopping place for travellers. Three comfortable bedrooms are all well equipped and home cooking is also worth sampling.

WEST AND EAST MIDLANDS

ASHLEIGH HOUSE
Whitley Hill, Henley-in-Arden, Tel: (05642) 2315
The Cotswold Hills provide some memorable scenery and this elegant guesthouse provides splendid views of the said range. Most bedrooms are ensuite and all have colour TV and tea/coffee making facilities.

AVONDALE,
16 Elsee Road, Rugby, Tel: (0788) 578639
Close to the town centre and Rugby School, Avondale is popular with business and holiday guests. All appreciate the personal touches that are given a high priority by the attentive and conscientious proprietors.

BEARWOOD COURT HOTEL,
360-366 Bearwood Road, Bearwood, Warley, Tel: 021-429 9731
This medium sized hotel can offer guests all that they require in terms of a restful night and attentive service. The benefits of a family-run hotel are clearly demonstrated.

CAPE RACE HOTEL,
929 Chester Road, Erdington, Birmingham, 021-373 3085
Cape Race is a popular stopover for business travellers. However those with a little more time to spare will no doubt appreciate the outdoor swimming pool and tennis courts.

CHURCH FARM,
Tysoe, Tel: (029588) 385
If the world isn't exactly your oyster when saying at this popular farm, then a sizable part of Warwickshire certainly is. The Cotswolds, Oxford, Warwick Castle and Stratford all make for exhilarating exploration.

CRAIG HOUSE,
67/69 Shipston Road, Stratford-upon-Avon, Tel: (0789) 293313
As well as the well-documented historical attractions and associations, Stratford-and more especially Craig House-also makes a practical base for the walking, angling and golfing communities.

CRANDON HOUSE,
Avon Dassett, Leamington Spa, Tel: (029577) 652
Set in twenty acres of picturesque ground, Crandon House is actually a working farm and the fresh produce is used to prepare some excellent dishes.

HALFORD BRIDGE INN,
Fosse Way, Stratford on Avon, Tel: (0789) 740382
Halford Bridge happily specialises in excellent value, immaculate bedrooms and helpful service. The food is good too!

HEATH LODGE HOTEL,
Coleshill Road, Marston Green, Tel: 021-779 2218
What the rooms may lack in size at this highly recommended hotel they certainly make up for in comfort and style. A bar and television lounge provide further relaxation.

HIGHFIELD HOUSE,
Holly Road, Rowley Regis, Tel: 021-559 1066
Comfort and convenience contribute to a happy, friendly atmosphere at this family run hotel. Although mainly populated by commercial visitors, local amenities and golf courses can be found in the locality.

ENGLAND : FURTHER FORAYS

KAWARTHA GUESTHOUSE,
39 Grove Road, Stratford-upon-Avon, Tel: (0789) 204469
Stratford is one of the country's most 'visited' places, and the Kawartha guesthouse constitutes a convenient headquarters for a thorough exploration. Guests are likely to leave later rather than sooner.

LYNDHURST HOTEL,
135 Kingsbury Road, Erdington, Birmingham, Tel: 021-373 5695
This is a perennial favourite with the business community, due partly to the unobtrusive comfort and service and partly to its proximity to the motorway network.

MALT HOUSE,
Broad Campden, Chipping Campden, Tel: (0386) 840295
An unusually striking property, the Malthouse has been converted from Cotswold stone cottages and little expense has been spared either outside or inside. A combination of French and English cuisine can contribute to a memorable stay.

MELITA PRIVATE HOTEL,
37 Shipston Road, Stratford-upon-Avon, Tel: (0789) 292432
As well as the delights of Stratford, the Melita is within relatively quick access of Warwick, Coventry and the Cotswolds. Attentive staff are only too pleased to offer advice and assistance.

STANDBRIDGE HOTEL,
138 Birmingham Road, Sutton Coldfield, Tel: 021-354 3007
Accommodation here is simple but perfectly acceptable. Particularly in the Standbridge's favour is its location - convenient for The Belfry, Birmingham and the Midlands motorway network.

WILLOW TREE HOTEL,
759 Chester Road, Erdington, Birmingham, Tel: 021-373 6388
The majority of rooms at the Willow Tree Hotel have ensuite facilities and all are fitted out with direct dial telephone, colour television, video channel, hostess trays and radio. A quiet, residential setting should make for a restful stay.

GLOUCESTERSHIRE

HILL FARM GUESTHOUSE,
Bishops Norton, Nr. Gloucester, Tel: (0452) 730351
Cream teas on a sun terrace is an idyllic situation for most holidaymakers. Add to this a thatched, oak timbered farmhouse dating back to the fifteenth century and you have Hill Farm-an excellent guesthouse.

SEVERN BANK,
Minsterworth, Tel: (0452) 750357
Severn Bank enjoys a picturesque location some four miles west of Gloucester. A fine country house set in six acres of grounds on the banks of the Seven, the Forest of Dean, the Wye Valley and the Cotswolds are easily reachable. This is bed and breakfast at its best.

MILTON HOUSE HOTEL,
12 Royal Parade, Bayshill Road, Cheltenham, Tel: (0242) 582601
Set in a quiet residential area, Milton House is close to both golf courses and racecourses, as well as a wide range of local amenities.

NORTHFIELD,
Cirencester Road, Northleach, Cheltenham, Tel: (0451) 60427
The small market town of Northleach is an attractive and convenient backdrop for this well-established guesthouse. Three comfortable bedrooms guarantee a restful night's sleep.

WOODLEYS,
Toddington, Nr. Winchcombe, Tel: (024269) 313
A ideal centre for touring the Cotswolds and surrounding areas, the Woodleys has undergone extensive refurbishment and is one of the area's most distinguished guesthouses. Moderate prices make it too good to miss!

HEREFORDSHIRE

LEIGH COURT,
Leigh Sinton, Tel: (0886) 32275
Superb countryside makes this an ideal base for active-minded tourists, whilst those in search of more tranquility will be equally impressed by a billiards room, tithe barn and library.

LION,
Clifton upon Teme, Tel: (08865) 617
One of the county's oldest coaching inns, the Lion offers traditional and well maintained bedrooms and a menu of some style.

PARK LODGE,
Eye, Leominster, Tel: (0568) 5711
A popular retreat with visitors who appreciate simple, clean accommodation and friendly service, Park Lodge enjoys a quiet location yet is within easy reach of civilisation, for those who wish it.

THE RED LION,
The Red Lion, Herefordshire, Tel: (09817) 303
This is one of the leading fishing hotels on the Wye, controlling its own water and offering one of the longest privately owned stretches in the country. Accommodation is pleasant and the food delicious.

WORCESTERSHIRE

BARBOURNE,
Worcester, Tel: (0905) 27507
A frequent and much appreciated resting place with the commercial community, the Barbourne is unpretentious but extremely comfortable. Bedrooms all have colour TV.

COTTAGE IN THE WOOD HOTEL,
Holywell Road, Malvern Wells, Worcestershire, Tel:(0684) 573487
Following recent refurbishment, The Cottage in the Wood, a three star country House Hotel, offers a high level of comfort and service. Perched high in the Malvern Hills and with a truly spectacular view, the hotel offers 20 ensuite luxury bedrooms. Extremely convenient for Cheltenham Races.

OLD PARSONAGE FARM,
Hanley Swan, Tel: (0684) 310124
This is a truly excellent establishment where the standard of accommodation is matched only by the warmth of the welcome. A copious range of wines and foods are certain to cap an extremely enjoyable stay.

PHEPSON,
Himbleton, Tel: (090569) 205
This is a seventeenth century farmhouse, whose decor and furnishings are of a tasteful simplicity. An annexe provides bedrooms that are spacious and relaxing.

SUFFOLK

BEDFORD LODGE HOTEL,
Bury Road, Newmarket, Suffolk, Tel: (0638) 663175
Renowned among the horseracing fraternity for it's hospitality, this listed Georgian House is set in four acres of grounds, surrounded by mature trees. With it's restaurant, bar and conference facilities, guests find the relaxing atmosphere of a bygone era.

LIMES FARMHOUSE,
Saxtead Green, Framlingham, Suffolk, Tel: (0728) 685303
The Limes Farmhouse, a listed Grade 2 building, dates from the fifteenth century and is situated opposite Saxtead Mill. Historic places nearby include Framlingham Castle and Church, Otley Hall, Orford Castle and Dunwich museum.

ENGLAND : FURTHER FORAYS

OTLEY HOUSE,
Otley, Ipswich, Tel: (047339) 253
Golf, sailing and riding are all passtimes that can easily be enjoyed from this splendid guesthouse. Other local places of interest include Woodbridge, Oxford and Dunwich.

TUDOR HOUSE,
34 Guildhall Street, Bury St. Edmunds, Tel: (0284) 703677
Bed & Breakfast of an agreeable nature are provided at this pleasant, sixteenth century dwelling. Rooms are thoughtfully furnished and the food is wholesome and imaginative.

NORFOLK

ABBEY HOTEL,
Church street, Wymondham, Tel: (0953) 602148
Overlooking an ancient abbey, this hotel has a reputation of providing yesterdays charm with today's comforts. For the business community there is an excellent Conference Suite and three syndicate rooms.

AMBERLEY HOUSE,
24 Eaton Road, Norwich, Tel: (0603) 57115
Although pleasantly located in a quiet residential area, Amberley House is within easy reach of the town centre, university and a challenging 18-hole golf course. All rooms have radio, TV and tea/coffee making facilities.

BARNHAM BROOM HOTEL,
Barnham Broom, Norwich, Tel: (060545) 393
Set in the beautiful valley of the river Yare, this modern hotel and sports complex has 52 luxury bedrooms plus a host of leisure facilities including two 18 hole golf courses, squash, tennis, sauna, fitness centre and indoor swimming pool.

FIELDSEND HOUSE,
Homefields Road, Hunstanton, Tel: (04853) 2593
Golf and fishing are only two of the attractions of Hunstanton, and both can be found within a short distance of this highly-recommended guesthouse. Sea views from every bedroom are certainly partly responsible for it's perennial popularity.

STAITHEWAY HOUSE,
Staitheway Road, Wroxham, Tel: (06053) 3347
Welcome, bedrooms, cooking and general ambiance are all consistently high at this popular guesthouse. Needless to say, this part of the country is ideal for boat lovers and walkers.

CAMBRIDGESHIRE

CHISWICK HOUSE,
Chiswick End, Meldreth, Royston, Tel: (0763) 60242
This impressive black and white timbered house dates as far back as the fourteenth century. It is even believed that King James I used the house as a hunting lodge. Nowadays, the emphasis has shifted to comfortable accommodation and friendly service.

DYKELANDS GUESTHOUSE,
157 Mowbray Road, Cambridge, Tel: (0223) 244300
Both the city of Cambridge and the surrounding countryside are reached with ease from this well-appointed guesthouse. The majority of rooms are ensuite and all are equipped with radio, TV and tea/coffee making facilities.

HARTFORD COTTAGE,
Longstaff Way, Hartford, Huntingdon, Tel: (0480) 54116
Splendid gardens form an engaging backdrop to this spacious homely guesthouse. The surrounding countryside is justifiably well documented and London is little more than an hour away.

KIRKWOOD HOUSE,
172 Chesterton Road, Cambridge, Tel: (0223) 313874
The charms of Cambridge are enough to warrant a book in itself. Suffice to say that the visitor staying at Kirkwood House is highly unlikely to suffer from boredom. The city centre is a mere ten minutes walk.

MILLSIDE COTTAGE,
9 Mill Street, Houghton, Tel: (0480) 64456
Service and cleanliness are everywhere in evidence at Millside Cottage, a tribute to the conscientious and welcoming propietors. Houghton itself is a extremely picturesque and is surrounded by villages of equal charm.

DERBYSHIRE

DALES AND PEAKS HOTEL,
Old Road, Darley Dale, Tel: (0629) 733775
Set in the Derwent valley, the Dales and Peaks is unsurprisingly a great favourite for walkers and riders. Accommodation is both thoughtfully conceived and moderately priced.

DANNAH,
Bowmans Lane, Shottle, Tel: (077 389) 273
If character, atmosphere and quite superb home cooking are your requirements for a suitable abode to stay, then there is absolutely no danger of Dannah failing to live up to your expectations.

LE CHEVALIER BISTRO RESTAURANT,
2 Borough Street, Derby, Tel: (0332) 812005
Although rarely uncomfortably overcrowded, this city centre bistro is sufficiently busy to create an animated and friendly atmosphere. A number of bedrooms are available for those who wish to extend their socialising.

PACKHORSE,
Tansely, Tel: (0629) 582781
A feeling of splendid isolation can be the happy consequence of a stay at this comfortable, secluded farmhouse. Meticulously maintained gardens add a further agreeable dimension.

PEVERIL OF THE PEAK,
Dovedale, Thorpe, Ashbourne, Tel: (033 529) 333
This is a striking country hotel set in eleven acres of grounds below The Thorpe Cloud hill at the gateway to Dovedale. Rooms are spacious and contain every modern amenity.

NOTTINGHAMSHIRE

BALMORAL HOTEL,
55-57 Loughborough Street, West Bridgeford, Tel: (0602) 455020
Ardent cricket and football followers will find that this modern, efficient hotel has much to recommend it. Both The Nottingham Forest football ground and Trent Bridge cricket ground are within walking distance and the city centre is also in the close vicinity.

PARK HOTEL,
7 Waverley Street, Nottingham, Tel: (0602) 786229
A Georgian period house that still exudes an air of elegance, this city centre hotel has much to commend it, including a high proportion of ensuite bedrooms.

ENGLAND : FURTHER FORAYS

TITCHFIELD GUESTHOUSE,
300/302 Chesterfield Road North, Mansfield, Notts, Tel: (0623) 810356
Two large houses converted into one, Titchfield is a family run guest-house offering eight bedrooms, a T.V. lounge and drinks facilities. A warm and friendly welcome is extended to all guests.

UPTON FIELDS HOTEL,
Southwell, Tel: (0636) 812303
Conveniently located for visitors to both Southwell and Upton, the Upton Fields Hotel comes highly recommended for a number of reasons, not least excellent bedrooms and highly-edible food.

LINCOLNSHIRE

BOURNE EAU HOUSE,
30 South Street, Bourne, Tel: (0778) 423621
Bourne Eau is an handsome country home that dates back to Georgian/Elizabethan times. The friendly welcome is matched only by the superb standard of accommodation which would put many aspiring hotels to shame.

DUNS,
The Broadway, Woodhall Spa, Tel: (0526) 52969
The nearby championship golf course provides this hotel with a fair proportion of it's custom although businessmen and tourists find it equally congenial. Service is particularly attentive.

DUNSTON MANOR,
Dunston, Lincoln, Tel: (0526) 20463
The small village of Dunston has ceded little to modern civilisation and Dunston Manor retains an elegant atmosphere that has little to do with urban hotels. Bedrooms are quaint and splendidly furnished but should be temporaily abandoned to taste the admirable home cooking.

MANOR HOUSE,
Nocton Road, Potterhanworth, Tel: (0522) 791288
Proudly standing in some ten acres of gardens, this elegant nineteenth century manor house contains four agreeably furnished rooms, each with radio, TV and tea/coffee making facilities. An outdoor swimming pool and summer house distinguish this establishment from the crowd.

STAFFORDSHIRE

HILLCREST,
3 Leighton Road, Uttoxeter, Tel: (0889) 564627
A hilltop location provides guests with extensive and impressive views of the surrounding countryside. Most rooms are ensuite and all are comfortably furnished.

LARKSFIELD COUNTRY ACCOMMODATION,
Stoniford Lane, Aston, Tel: (063081) 7069
This will prove an ideal base for visitors envisaging golfing, fishing, walking or simply sightseeing. Expert gun tuition is even available for the really ambitious.

LEONARDS CROFT HOTEL,
80 Lichfield Road, Stafford, Tel: (0785) 223676
Set pleasantly on the outskirts of Stafford, Leonards Croft Hotel is a well-appointed, impressive detached house. First appearances are not at all deceiving.

MARSH,
Abbots Bromley, Tel: (0283) 840323
Hospitality that always aims-and invariably succeeds-to please is the hallmark of this friendly and well run farmhouse accommodation. The surrounding farmland makes impressive viewing.

WHITE GABLES HOTEL,
Trentham Road, Blurton, Stoke-on-Trent, Tel: (0782) 324882
The White Gables has earned a formidable reputation among battle-hardened travellers, with a relaxing and friendly atmosphere making for an enjoyable stay.

SHROPSHIRE

BELDEVERE GUESTHOUSE,
Burway Road, Church Stretton, Tel: (0694) 722232
Church Stretton is a delightful village and Beldevere is an integral and much admired part of it. Guests risk spending little time there, however, as Shropshire has much to offer.

NEW FARM,
Muckleton, Nr. Shawbury, Telford, Tel: (0939) 250358
The tranquility and beauty of the Shropshire-Welsh border-not that it has always been so peaceful-is the setting for this splendid farmhouse. Hawkstone Park is close by and the historic towns of Chester and Ludlow are equally convenient.

OLD POST OFFICE RESTAURANT,
9 The Square, Clun, Nr. Craven Arms, Tel: (05884) 687
Careful restoration has resulted in an imaginative and attractive restaurant whose fare is quite delicious. Accommodation is provided for those who really over-indulge.

SANDFORD HOUSE HOTEL,
St Julians Friars, Shrewsbury, Tel: (0743) 343829
Only a short distance from the town centre, Sandford House occupies a quiet setting and has many pleasant country walks within easy reach. Bedrooms are tastefully decorated and the public rooms no less agreeable.

TANKERVILLE LODGE,
Stiperstones, Nr. Minsterley, Shrewsbury, Tel: (0743) 791401
This is surely one of the area's most friendly and welcoming establishments. Guests are made to feel totally at home and are provided plenty of sustenance with which to tackle the nearby Stiperstone Ridge and Devils Chair.

CHESHIRE

AMBASSADOR PRIVATE HOTEL,
13 Bath Street, Southport, Tel: (0704) 543998
Selecting a hotel in Southport can be a daunting experience, but all those confused tourists can rest assured that the Ambassador will not prove an erroneous choice. All rooms are ensuite and the elegant town centre only minutes away.

SHIRE COTTAGE,
Benches Lane, Chisworth, Hyde, Cheshire, Tel: 061-427 2377 (daytime) (04578) 66536 (after 4 pm)
This modern bungalow affords magnificent views over Etherow Country Park. An ideal location makes it convenient for Manchester Airport, city centre, the Peak District, Kinder Scout and various Stately Homes. Early breakfasts can be arranged.

SUNNINGDALE HOTEL,
85 Leyland Road, Southport, Tel: (0704) 538673
Weary golfers will find that returning from the local clubhouse to this guesthouse involves minimal effort. For lovers of less energetic pursuits, the guesthouse offers a pool table, dartboard and spacious lounge bar.

ENGLAND : FURTHER FORAYS

LANCASHIRE

CULLERNE HOTEL,
55 Lightburne Avenue, St. Annes on Sea, Tel: (0253) 721753
Close to the town centre and every facility that a visitor could wish, the Cullerne is a typically good Lancastrian guesthouse and will undoubtedly receive many return visits from satisfied guests.

FALICON FARM,
Fleet Street Lane, Hothersall, Longridge, Preston, Tel: (025484) 583
A sandstone farmhouse in an enviable setting, Falicon Farm offers modern conveniences in a traditional ambiance. All three bedrooms are ensuite and have an array of other, thoughtful facilities.

HOTEL PROSPECT,
363 Marine Road East, Morecambe, Tel: (0524) 417876
Ensuite bedrooms and a seafront location make this a favourite haunt for visitors to the region. No doubt a fair proportion of them are golfers, enticed by the area's wealth of championship courses.

HOTEL WARWICK,
394 Marine Road East, Morecombe, Tel: (0524) 418151
Morecombe still has much to offer in the way of family holidays and all guests will find that this pleasant guesthouse makes a good and practical headquarters. Added pluses are the friendly atmosphere and attentive service.

LYNSTEAD PRIVATE HOTEL,
40 King Edward Avenue, Blackpool, Tel: (0253) 51050
The challenging Blackpool North Shore Golf Club is almost within putting distance of this quiet, relaxing establishment. Away from the bright lights of town, guests appreciate the peaceful, friendly atmosphere.

MAINS HALL,
Mains Lane, Little Singleton, Blackpool, Lancashire, Tel: (0253) 885130
This elegant country house hotel is a sixteenth century manor house and is steeped in history. Situated on the banks of the river Wyre, Mains Hall retains many of it's original antique fittings and is convenient for golfers and many Stately Homes.

NEW CAPERNWRAY FARM,
Capernwray, Carnforth, Tel: (0524) 734 284
This is a remote location that is well worth searching for. An imposing, stone built house, New Capernwray Farm provides award-winning accommodation at reasonable prices. The food on offer has to be seen to be believed.

NORTH EUSTON HOTEL,
Esplanade, Fleetwood, Tel: (039 17) 6525
Travellers wishing to treat themselves without spending their entire holiday budget should seriously consider this fine hotel. The Lakeland Hills are distantly visible, although golfers and anglers will probably not have time to enjoy the spectacle!

ROSENEATH,
Preston road, Charnock Richard, Nr. Chorley, Tel: (0257) 791772
Roseneath can virtually guarantee a good nights sleep-unless visitors are distracted by striking views of The Pennines. Extensive grounds allow the opportunity for walking and jogging.

STRATHMORE,
305 Clifton Drive South, Lytham St Annes, Tel: (0253) 725478'
Conscientous owners ensure that this guesthouse moves from strength to strength, with its central location a particular advantage. Bedrooms are spacious and well-furnished.

WYTHA FARM,
Rimington, Clitheroe, Lancaster, Tel: (0200) 445295
Panoramic views over the Ribble Valley give added appeal to this well-established and welcoming farm. Walkers would do worse than to start their journey here.

ISLE OF MAN

EDELWEISS,
Queens Promenade, Douglas, Tel: (0624) 675115
Set just behind the main promenade, Edelweiss makes a relaxing and agreeable base. All bedrooms are ensuite and the lounge is equally well-appointed.

MALLMORE PRIVATE HOTEL,
The Promenade, Port St Mary, Tel: (0624) 833179
This hotel does certainly not fall into the luxurious category, but gains its fine reputation from simple clean bedrooms and some splendid home cooking.

REGENT HOUSE,
The Promenade, Port Erin, Tel: (0624) 833454
This well-established hotel is a firm favourite with discerning visitors who appreciate home comforts and imaginative cooking. The hotel affords fine views of the bay.

ROSSLYN GUESTHOUSE,
3 Empire Terrace, Central Promenade, Douglas, Tel: (0624) 676056
In case the many and varied attractions of the Isle of Man become too much for the travel-weary, Rosslyn Guesthouses offers a relaxing bar and first floor television lounge.

RUTLAND HOTEL,
Queen's Promenade, Douglas, Tel: (0624) 621218
The owners of this hotel have a great deal of pride in their establishment and this is reflected in a smooth running hostelry where every guest is almost made to feel one of the family.

YORKSHIRE

ALEXA HOUSE HOTEL,
26 Ripon Road, Harrogate, Tel: (0423) 501988
This splendid hotel is a previous award winner, and standards have not been allowed to slip. Originally built in 1830 for Baron de Ferrier, Alexa is now in the capable hands of Marilyn and Peter Bateson. Twelve bedrooms are all ensuite.

CARLTON HOTEL,
Albert Street, Hebden Bridge, West Yorkshire, Tel: (0422) 844400
Visitors will find a warm and friendly atmosphere at this splendid hotel, typical of the town and of Yorkshire. Guests will find the perfect setting to relax and recover, be it from the rigours of business or country pursuits.

ELMFIELD HOUSE,
Arrathorne, Bedale, North Yorkshire, Tel: (0677) 50558
Nestled in the heart of 'Herriot Country', Elmfield House sits in it's own secluded grounds with uninterrupted views. Golf, riding, fishing, hang gliding are all within easy reach, as are York and Rippon racecourses.

GRASMEAD HOUSE HOTEL,
1 Scarcroft Hill, The Mount, Tel: (0904) 629996
The splendours of York ensure that time spent indoors is usually minimal but this hotel will do it's best to change your mind. The standard of every aspect-rooms, service, food and character-is absolutely and consistently first-rate.

ENGLAND : FURTHER FORAYS

HEATHER COTTAGE
12 Chapel Street, Flamborough, Tel: (0262) 851036
This homely cottage is set in the midst of a typically picturesque Yorkshire village and is within comfortable striking distance of Danes Dyke, Bempton Bird Reserve and the Heritage Coast.

INGLEWOOD GUESTHOUSE,
7 Clifton Green, York, Tel: (0904) 653523
A charming Victorian House, guests will instantly feel at home at Inglenook. Some bedrooms are ensuite and all have colour TV and amenities.

KNOX MILL HOUSE,
Knox Mill Lane, Harrogate, Tel: (0423) 560650
The centre of Harrogate lies only a few minutes drive from this beautiful old millhouse. The bedrooms are all equipped with modern amenities but retain an olde-worlde graciousness that captivate the visitor of today.

MANOR HOUSE,
Corner of Tower Street and Lighthouse Road, Flamborough, Nr. Bridlington, Tel: (0262) 850943
A handsome Georgian House, the Manor House offers superior accommodation. Situated on the Heritage Coast, interesting walks, golf courses and other scenic attractions abound. Of particular interest are Castle Howard and the RSPB reserve.

MANOR HOUSE FARM,
Ingleby Greenhow, Great Ayton, Tel: (0642) 722384
This is truly a farm well worth visiting, both for the quality of accommodation and it's splendid setting. Horse riding, fishing and golf are among a wide variety of pursuits that can be locally enjoyed.

PARAGON HOTEL,
123 Queens Parade, Scarborough, Tel: (0723) 372676
Splendidly located overlooking the North Bay, the Paragon offers good old-fashioned value and good old-fashioned service. Scarborough has something to please everyone.

RUSKIN HOTEL AND RESTAURANT,
1 Swan Road, Harrogate, Tel: (0423) 66630
The dales and stately homes of Yorkshire do not involve an inordinate amount of travelling using Ruskins as a base. For those more interested in home comforts, the hotel is attractively laid out and takes good care of its guests.

WHITE HORSE,
Farm Hotel, Rosedale Abbey, Nr. Pickering, Tel: (07515) 312
Seclusion and splendid isolation are two words used frequently to describe the North Yorkshire Moors, and the White Horse is set right in their midst. Riding and Golf can be practised nearby, in addition to the innumerable places of interest in the locality.

HUMBERSIDE

BARMBY MOOR,
Hull Road, Barmby Moor, Tel: (0759) 302700
Accommodation and cuisine vie for this casting vote in this immensely popular hotel. Bedrooms contain every conceivable convenience and the elegant Honeysuckle restaurant overlooks a courtyard containing a heated swimming pool.

LANGDON HOTEL,
Pembroke Terrace, Bridlington, Tel: (0262) 673065
Bridlington is mostly about the sea and there is certainly plenty of it on view from the Langdon Hotel. The public rooms are particularly alluring.

PARKWOOD HOTEL,
113 Princes' Avenue, Hull, Tel: (0482) 445610
Hull city centre is only a short bus or car journey from this well-appointed guesthouse. Rooms are well furnished and the cuisine carefully prepared.

SOUTHDOWNE HOTEL,
South Marine Drive, Bridlington, Tel: (0262) 673270
Twelve comfortable bedrooms are of a standard that will satisfy the most uncompromising of guests. The sea is constantly in view, always an important consideration in seaside resorts!

TRITON INN,
Sledmere, Tel: (0377) 86644,
Sledmere is an engaging and attractive village that proves an excellent base for a touring holiday. Food and bedrooms are both worth sampling.

CUMBRIA

BESSIESTOWN FARM,
Penton, Carlisle, Tel: (022877) 218
A friendly Northern welcome paves the way for an enjoyable stay at this beef and sheep rearing farm that overlooks the nearby Scottish borders. All seven rooms are ensuite and are furnished with taste and care.

LYNWOOD GUESTHOUSE,
Broad Street, Windermere, Tel: (09662) 2550
Six nicely furnished bedrooms make this Victorian house popular with discerning Lakeland visitors. A pleasant TV lounge provides entertainment for the weary and weather-beaten.

OXENHOLME FARM,
Oxenholme Road, Kendal, Tel: (0539) 27226
New arrivals at this painstakingly renovated sixteenth century farmhouse are greeted with genuine warmth and welcome refreshments. Accommodation is equally pleasing with modern amenities.

THE OLD RECTORY,
Bolton Gate, Tel: (09657) 647
Dating back all the way to the fifteenth century, the Old Rectory can be found in the village of Bolton Gate, midway between Carlisle and Cockermouth. Fabulous views and a garden orchard will provide glorious memories.

NORTHUMBERLAND

BILTON BARNS,
Alnmouth, Tel: (0665) 830427
Set in the glorious Northumbrian countryside, this well-furnished and spacious farmhouse is only minutes away from the picturesque fishing village of Alnwick. The farmhouse food is truly excellent.

CLIVE COTTAGE,
Appletree Lane, Corbridge, Tel: (0434) 632617
A warm welcome is accompanied by pleasant accommodation and personal attention at this charming period cottage. Two bedrooms feature 4-poster beds and all rooms have tea/coffee facilities, hair dryers, and electric blankets.

HOLMHEAD GUESTHOUSE,
Hadrians Wall, Greenhead, Carlisle, Tel: (06972) 402
This a truly excellent guesthouse and is immensely popular with visitors to Hadrians Wall, venue of some Britain's bloodiest history. Fabulous walks and opportunities for sightseeing abound.

ENGLAND : FURTHER FORAYS

KITTY FRISK FARM,
Corbridge Road, Hexham, Tel: (0434) 606850
The bustling and attractive market town of Hexham is only a few miles from this pleasant and welcoming establishment. Acres of stylish gardens and woodland offer the opportunity for some relaxing escapism.

DURHAM

BURNBRAE,
Leazes Villas, Burnopfield, Tel: (0207) 70432
Burnbrae is pleasantly situated in the heart of Burnopfield village and is surrounded by country parks, bowling greens, tennis courts and golf courses. Newcastle and Hexham racecourses are within striking distance, as are Durham, Beamish Museum and Hadrians Wall.

COURT PRIVATE HOTEL,
Yarm Road, Stockton-on-Tees, Tel: (0642) 604483
This impressive edifice is conveniently located for the busy town centre and provides spotless accommodation at reasonable prices. A pleasant dining room serves up ample and tasty fare.

CROXDALE,
Spennymoor, Tel: (0388) 815727
A roadside inn with an agreeable lounge bar, the Croxdale also possesses a number of pleasantly furnished bedrooms which make for a refreshing stopover.

DUN COW,
High Street, Sedgefield, Tel: (0740) 20894
Excellent cuisine and a warm welcome are the trademarks of this popular and well-established inn. Bedrooms lack for nothing and Sedgewick racecourse is a notable nearby attraction.

GABLES,
Front Street, Haswell Plough, Tel: 091-526 2982
The cathedral city of Durham provides a wealth of things to do and see, and The Gables makes a pleasant headquarters for all types of stay. Rooms are well appointed and a dining room of real character adds extra ambiance.

TYNE AND WEAR

CHIRTON HOUSE HOTEL,
46 Clifton Road, Newcastle-upon-Tyne, Tel: 091-273 0407
The pleasant and cosmopolitan suburb of Jesmond houses the equally pleasant Chirton House Hotel. Bedrooms and public rooms are decorated with style and panache.

DENE HOTEL,
40-42 Grovenor Road, Newcastle-upon-Tyen, Tel: 091-281 1502
This is a well-established and conscientiously run hotel that makes a point of ensuring the well-being of its guests. Nearby Jesmond offers tranquility, a taste of the countryside and even a children's zoo.

LINDISFARNE HOTEL,
11 Holly Avenue, Whitley Bay, Tel: 091-2513628
A family run hotel with the accent on care and friendliness, the Lindisfarne hotel is the perfect base for the seaside resort of Whitley Bay. The wider delights of the region provide endless opportunities for all ages and persuasions.

PARKHOLME GUESTHOUSE,
8 Ocean View, Whitley Bay, Tel: 091-253 0370
Only one hundred yards separate this attractively proportioned Edwardian house and the shimmering (sometimes!) North Sea. Bedrooms include central heating and colour TV.

Fishing in the North   (Tufton Arms Hotel)

WALES

Artist: **Wendy Reeves**   ***MORNING GLOW***   *Courtesy of:* ***Rosenstiels'***

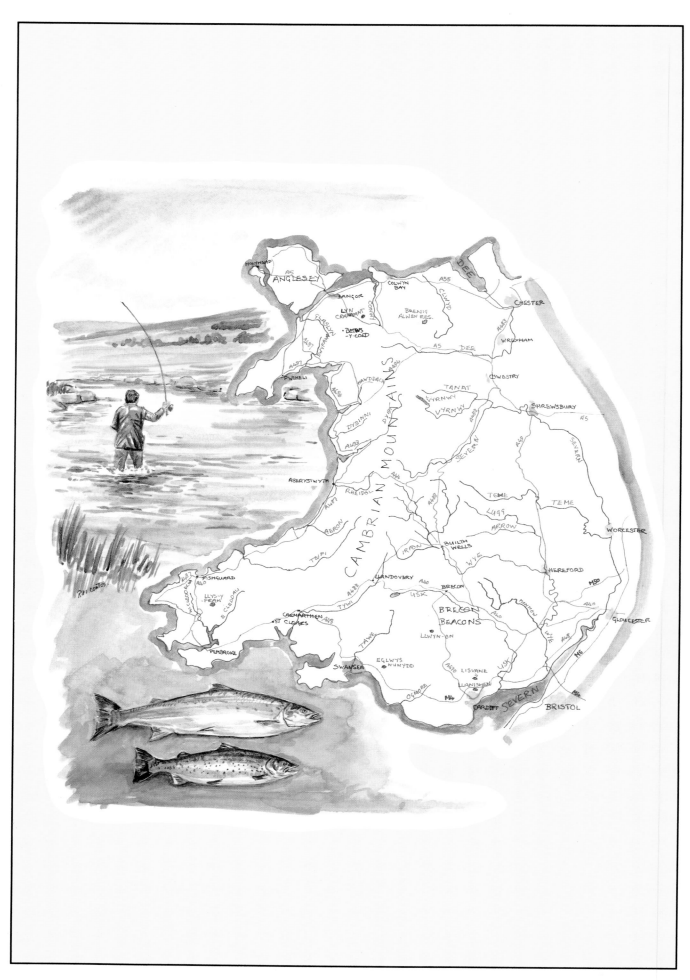

WALES

MONMOUTHSHIRE TO PEMBROKESHIRE

Wales is a land of spectacular scenery and rich history. It is also a country which boasts several fine rivers weaving intricately through unspoiled mountainside and wooded countryside. It may not be game fishing's mecca but it has a number of excellent salmon rivers as well as some delightful streams where the brown trout fight like demons.

Sewin fishing, Welsh for 'sea-trout', like rugby, is a passion amongst the Welsh. Sea-trout are prolific here and tend to move in pairs or threes, often reaching 8lb to 10lb. Sewin fishing is a real game fisherman's delight and only starts properly at twilight when the world around is quiet. Make no mistake, these fish fight and good judgement and planning are essential if you are to be successful. Unlike brown trout, the sewin will journey within the river system and the visiting angler must therefore endeavour to track them down before embarking on an evening that will rank alongside any game fishing you can find. One tip here, it is always worth visiting the local boozer where you will pick up some essential tips for the battle ahead. The locals will tell you that colour and depth of presentation are two major keys to your success. Fishing a good pool will achieve little if you are unable to offer your fly on a plate, so to speak. Mind you, when you feel that monumental tug, prepare for chaos. The sewin plunges to the depths and occasionally, unbowed, he will leap skyward. This is a celebrated fish and pound for pound, it will give you a fight equal to the wildest salmon.

As in many places, the salmon fishing is not as good as it once was. However, salmon fishing is still available in all rivers although the runs do vary radically from year to year. The River Wye is particularly excellent. Autumn runs tend to be more productive than those in the spring when the salmon dart up the river in good numbers. This is the sport at its best. Brown trout fishing is also good in Wales and this crafty fish will test all your skills.

Whether you are fishing at nightfall or early in the morning in hopeful anticipation of your lunch, you will find a wealth of good sport in Wales. In this age of pollution, grinding mechanisation and awesome technology you will find places where seemingly time has stood still. These are charming villages in idyllic surroundings, providing a perfect excuse for a timely excursion into some of Britain's most remote and unspoiled reaches. Here, you can pause from fishing as otters plunder the waters. Here, you are accompanied by birds of prey and many wildfowl. The Welsh Water Authorities are doing a tremendous job of promoting these waters without ruining their intrinsic charms. If you are keen on fly fishing then a journey to all corners of Wales must be high on your list of forays.

The River **Wye** is probably the best known river in Wales and one of the most famous of Britain's salmon rivers. It crosses the border between England and Wales and is often referred to as England's best salmon river! The Wye rises on the south side of Plynlimon and rushes, as a boulder strewn stream down river - a delight for brown trout. As the river grows, so the trout gain stature. Around Rhayader a number of important tributaries join the Wye, including the Irfon of which we will have more anon. Through careful conservation and control of nets the salmon catch is impressive. Although much of the river is privately owned there are several hotels and associations with rights to the water.

Many people who fish the Wye will take advantage of some of the splendid opportunities afforded by Harris and Stokes (0432) 354455 who have reminded me of a Scottish fishing custom. On the first day of the season, a half bottle of whisky should be poured into the water to bless, and hopefully intoxicate the fish. You must be sure to keep a half bottle nearby, not only to celebrate your catch but also to keep you warm. It can be very cold on the Wye as the 1991 season proved. Demand remains high for the prime beats and lettings are far from cheap, but some lesser known beats are good value and the fishing is still very good.

Another point that Roger Stokes makes is that the economic recession is effecting the take up of certain beats and if you haven't been too badly effected yourself then you might just be able to acquire some rods here. Harris and Stokes have in excess of 400 salmon rods to let each year, principally on the Wye and the Usk but can also arrange fishing in the smaller rivers.

The Wye from Chepstow to Builth Wells is made up of large bends and loops and the water glides leisurely, in striking contrast to its infant pace. There is some one and three quarter miles of fishing, some double bank, such as at Lydbrook five miles below Ross-On-Wye, with season tickets still available. The price of a day ticket in 1991 was £20 and the man to contact is Mr Philips (0594) 60048 for further information. Ross itself has some town water available to visiting anglers and G. & R. Sports (0989) 63723 will provide you with all the details. It is also worth mentioning that trout streams abound here; the Monnow, Lugg and Garron are particularly good and landowners sometimes do consent to fishing them. The Birmingham Anglers Association have a number of excellent opportunities here as well as on other waters in Wales.

Hattons (0432) 272317, who are based at St Owen Street in Hereford also issue day licences and permits. Although the visiting fisherman may often be referred to the splendid Red Lion Hotel (09817) 3030 at Bredwardine who own eight miles of the Wye and, assuming the water is good, provide excellent fishing. The water is made up of nine beats which run consecutively and hold two rods per beat. The fishing has been much improved in recent years and the brown trout have been particularly prolific. The hotel sell and lend tackle to residents and day tickets can be purchased for £28, or £35 for non-residents. Weekly tickets cost £155 and a season ticket which covers one day per week is priced at £350. Permits and tackle, along with some good fishing, can be obtained from H. R. Grant (0497) 820309 in Castle Street, Hay-On-Wye. As well as issuing permits for town waters they have one mile of their own single bank fishing. The Swan Hotel (0497) 821188 also offers some good water. The Swan is a member of a syndicate which owns a four and a half mile stretch of single bank fishing on the Wye which is excellent salmon fishing. The Old Black Lion in Hay (0497) 820841 does not have its own water but has good local contacts who can provide fishing on one and a half miles of single bank and about eight good pools. This water is understandably available to residents only, who must bring their own tackle. Two weeks notice is also required. This is a very friendly place to stay and if you are seeking a bit of local advice then a ghillie can be hired at a cost of £25 per day.

The Wye has numerous tributaries and one of the most celebrated is the River **Irfon** in which good trout and salmon fishing can be enjoyed. The Grove Park and Irfon Angling Club

THE CAMMARCH HOTEL

The Cammarch is a privately owned, typical Welsh Victorian Hotel/Inn nestling under the Myndd Eppynt range of hills and surrounded by rivers Irfon and Cammarch. It offers 8 miles of river fishing on the Irfon, Cammarch, Dulais and Wye.

The river Irfon starts its journey in the picturesque Abergwesyn Valley it twists and winds its way down through heavy woodland and the small town of Llanwrtyd Wells. It then starts to open out into softer pastures passing the Cammarch Hotel at Llangammarch Wells. It is in this area, that some of the finest Brown Trout fly fishing in Wales is to be had, Jon Beer referred to it in an article in Trout & Salmon as a 'little corker'. The river at this junction is very varied, slow glides, fast runs over a slate bottom and deep pools where very healthy big browns lurk.

In addition to the wild brown trout, the hotel also stocks with 11" - 13" brownies 3 times a year, add to this the large head of grayling up to and above 2lb, also the mid to late Salmon run. This river truly has a lot to offer the discerning angler.

The Cammarch and Dulais are much smaller streams, running at times through thick riverside vegetation and the angler has to use different tactics in stalking these fish.

The bird life is very varied and interesting giving the watcher many species including snipe, kingfisher, dippers, curlews, buzzard, peregrine falcons and the very rare red kite.

The Cammarch traditionally offers a warm welcome to its fisherman. The dinner in the evening is a traditional Roast, consisting of 5 courses, using fresh vegetables whenever possible and there is always an additional fish menu. The soups and sweets are invariably home made.

There are 2 small log fired bars which the locals also use and a very comfortable residents lounge on the first floor where one can relax those aching bones. Alternatively you could just take afternoon tea and sun yourself in the secluded lawned gardens. The whole feel about the Cammarch is relaxing.

The Cammarch Hotel
Llangammarch Wells
Powys
Wales LD4 4EE
Tel: (05912) 205
Fax: (05912) 396

have water available on both the Wye and the Irfon as well as Caer Beris Stillwater Fishery. Tickets are available from Mrs Morgan (0982) 552759. Caer Berris Manor (0982) 552601 at Builth Wells have some 1000 yards of the Irfon with access to some excellent fishing on the Wye and some lake fishing at Caer Beris. The brown trout on the Irfon are fighting fit and provide tremendous sport. They usually weigh in at under 1lb but there are a few wily fish who are considerably larger. The salmon fishing can also be good and 38lb 8oz record fish is a testimony to this. The hotel offers a day package for £87 per person which includes dinner, bed and breakfast and free fishing - excellent stuff!

The Lake Country House Hotel (05912) 202 also has private fishing on the Irfon available to guests. This spans four and a half miles of single bank fishing. The hotel is situated at Llangammarch Wells and you have to inspect your map closely to find it at all. The river is a typical Welsh stream which runs over a hard stone bed of layered rock resulting in some delightful pools. In other locations the river is wide and shallow but always take care when wading as it is easy to slip over here. The wild trout are supplemented by the Lake Hotel (05912) 202 and its charming companion the Cammarch Arms Hotel (05912) 205, also in Llangammarch Wells. The proprietor of this establishment, Mr Alan Tansley has made a considerable effort to keep these waters and his care has most definitely reaped dividends. Incidentally, in the vicinity lies the only barium spring in Britain, considered to be a cure for gout, heart disease and rheumatism. Any afflicted anglers will therefore have a second good reason to make a trip here.

The Cammarch Arm's water is divided into three sections spanning three and a half miles of single bank fishing, available to non-residents as well as guests. The hotel also has a mile of the

Wye and three and a half miles of the Cammarch and Upper Dulas. Further upstream, we find real 'trout country'. In Rhayander, you will find the newsagents have excellent value day tickets and licences, sold on behalf of the Elan Angling Club who own a one mile stretch of double bank fishing. This is the place where a 10lb trout was caught - that should give you food for thought.

There have been a number of efforts made to stock this part of the river but the fishing is likely to take some time to regenerate itself, despite all efforts made. Indeed, the water bailiffs believe it may be as long as five years before the likes of Llangurig see fish of any consequence again.

The River **Usk** is regarded as one of the finest fisheries in the United Kingdom and it is certainly one of the finest trout rivers in the Principality. It is also a fine salmon water. The river affords some spectacular scenery and the wild native brownies offer a challenging duel. The best fishing is in April and May, during the prolific fly hatches.

The water starts its journey some 2400 feet above sea level from Carmarthen Fan and travels through limestone and sandstone outcrops. Much of this water is preserved but the visitor can still fish on the town water and Jean Williams at Sweets Fishing Tackle (02913) 2552 is perhaps the best person to talk to. Tickets are £7 a day and a licence can also be obtained here. The Bridge Inn (0873) 853045 is situated on the river and on occasion when the river floods and breaks its banks the hotel is in the river! The water is particularly good and comprises calm stretches which break into rapids and changes again into deep pools. Trout tickets are available from The Bridge at a price of £5 per day or £12 per week. Salmon fishing will cost you £9 per day and £27 per week. One of the best spots from

Pontsticill Reservoir   (Welsh Water Plc)

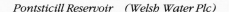

SALMON MOUSSELINE WITH DOVER SOLE, SMOKED SALMON AND PISTACHIO NUTS ON A LOVAGE AND SHALLOT SAUCE

SERVES 4

INGREDIENTS

8 oz (225g) Salmon

4 Small Dover Sole fillets (boned and skinned)

2 oz (50g) Sliced Smoked Salmon

l oz (25g) Pistachio Nuts (chopped)

3-4 oz (75-115g) Whipping Cream

l Egg White

Salt and Pepper

½ Glass White Wine

3 teaspoon Chopped Lovage

¼ Pint (115ml) Double Cream

Lovage Leaves and Parsley to decorate

2 tablespoon Shallots (chopped)

METHOD

FOR THE SALMON MOUSSELINE

To start with the salmon and cream must be well chilled. Place the salmon in a food processor and blend until smooth. Add the egg white and incorporate, then blend in the cream slowly while the machine is still running to make a smooth paste. Season (to check if enough seasoning, poach a little of the mousse in a saucepan of boiling water and taste).

Put the mousse in a bowl and mix through the pistachio nuts and one teaspoon of lovage.

Place the Dover sole on a chopping board, skin side up and spread a little of the mousse to cover the sole, then lay on the sliced smoked salmon to cover the mousse. Roll the Dover sole up and press any of the mousse which has squashed out back into the fish roll. Repeat with the remaining ingredients and put the fish into an oven proof dish. Add the white wine and ¼ pint water, cover with foil and bake in an oven at 180 C (350 F,gas mark 6) for 20 minutes or until firm to touch.

FOR THE SAUCE

Gently fry the shallots in butter until soft. Pour the cooking liquid off into the saucepan and reduce by half. Add the double cream and reduce again to a sauce. Add the remaining lovage and simmer for 2 minutes. Season.

TO SERVE

Slice the sole with a very sharp knife along the roll and arrange on a plate with lovage and parsley to decorate - pour the sauce around the fish.

A FAVOURITE FROM THE LAKE COUNTRY HOUSE

THE LAKE COUNTRY HOUSE

The Lake is a riverside country house set in 50 acres of beautiful grounds with sweeping lawns, woods, riverside walks and a large well stocked lake.

The hotel offers spacious and luxurious accommodation, enhanced by log fires and antiques. Excellent imaginative food, prepared from fresh local produce, is served in the elegant dining room, accompanied by one of the finest wine lists in Wales. The Lake has been awarded the 'Restaurant of the Year' by Johansens for 1991 and has also received a Rosette for food from the AA for the last two years. The Lake offers all that is best in country house hospitality and satisfied guests return again and again.

It is a fisherman's paradise with a lake covering 2½ acres, within the grounds and a 4½ mile stretch of the River Irfon running through the extensive parkland of the hotel. The trout in the river are mostly wild fish and run up to 5lb, with some larger. Our water is divided into six beats, a maximum of two rods being allowed on each. **The Wye** provides good trout fishing, specimens up to and over 1lb are not uncommon. The number of rods per beat is restricted. **The Irfon** is likely to produce salmon almost anytime in the season, but really comes into its own in the latter part. There are also a number of Welsh Water Authorities Reservoirs within easy reach. Our gillie is on hand to give fishing instruction at a very reasonable charge.

The region is well known to birdwatchers and is an ideal centre for walkers and also a haven for wildlife, including badgers and red kite. There are spectacular drives in all directions. Nearby are three full-size golf courses. Clay pigeon shooting and horse riding are available. AA and RAC 3 Stars and Merit Award. Children welcome. Dogs by arrangement.

The Lake Country House
Llangammarch Wells
Powys
Wales LD4 4BS
Tel: (05912) 202/474
Fax: (05912) 457

GLIFFAES COUNTRY HOUSE

A thoroughly charming Victorian country house hotel, Gliffaes boasts fine gardens and parkland, situated in the National Park yet only one mile off the main A40 road. It offers peace and tranquillity as well as being easily accessible.

The house, which faces due south, stands in its own 29 acres in the beautiful valley of the River Usk, midway between the Brecon Beacons and the Black Mountains. Built in 1885 as a private residence, it has been ideally adapted to provide spacious comfort in the country house tradition. There are 22 bedrooms with private bathrooms or showers and all are individual in decor and furnishings, including three in the converted lodge.

The downstairs rooms include a large, comfortable, panelled sitting-room which leads into an elegant regency style drawing-room. From here, french windows open into a large conservatory with double doors on to the terrace. The dining-room and comfortable bar also open on to the terrace, with the glorious views of the surrounding hills and River Usk one hundred and fifty feet below. The billiard room has a full sized table and provides an additional sitting-room with something of a club atmosphere.

Breakfast is served from a sideboard, lunch is a cold buffet with soup and a hot dish. Dinner is either table d'hote or a la carte. In fact, country house standards of the old order are carefully maintained by the resident owners; the Brabner family have held sway here since 1948.

External facilities include fishing for salmon and trout in the part of the Usk which the hotel overlooks, tennis, bowls, putting and croquet. There is an extensive range of short walks in the vicinity and a nearby riding and pony trekking establishment where horses and ponies can be hired.

The hotel is justly proud of its in-house cooking and remains open from the middle of March to the end of the year.

Gliffaes Country House Hotel
Crickhowell
Powys
Wales NP8 1RH
Tel: (0874) 730371 Fax: (0874) 730463

which to enjoy the Usk is from Gliffaes Country House Hotel (0874) 730371 who hold two attractive stretches. Gliffaes owns a mile of water and has two thirds of a mile double bank fishing a few miles upstream. The Usk is extremely susceptible to changes in the water level and 1991 did not start well, however, when the waters are up the river is a delight to fish. The Usk is renowned for its early start and fine sport can be had in March and April. The hatches tend to occur in the morning during March and the rise gradually occurs later through April and May until the evening hatch in June. Traditional wet flies work well and this is also good dry fly water.

Naturally, each individual has their own preferred methods and the Gliffaes offers local advice on the most successful methods and flies. The water is divided into beats which are rotated each day. In recent years salmon catches have dwindled significantly due to a number of factors. There is some reason for optimism as sea nets are being restricted in Ireland and the estuary nets are also been more stringently controlled. The average size of the salmon tends to be about 10lb to 12lb but there are some bigger fish to be taken and the largest caught at Gliffaes was 35lb. Gliffaes offer trout fishing at £10 per day and salmon at £15 per day. Non-residents are welcome but guests do have preference.

The Vine Tree Inn (0873) 810514 at Llangattock issues tickets on behalf of the Crickhowell and District Anglers Association waters which comprise three separate stretches. One is a mere 100 yards from the inn which is great value at £2 per day. The other stretches are a little further away and consist of three quarters of a mile of double bank water and one and a half miles of single bank fishing. Trout fishing is priced at £5 per day and salmon fishing at £10. The fishing is good provided the water is not too low and although the summers have been dry in recent years, 1991 has provided us with a fair old soaking. Returning downstream, The Bell Hotel (0873) 810247 at Glangrwyney has a few hundred yards of single bank, predominately trout water which is priced at £3.50 per day.

Talybont on the Usk offers a variety of waters and one of the most accessible to the visiting angler is the three quarters of a mile stretch of single bank fishing available at the Usk Hotel (0874) 87251. This water includes four good salmon pools and is also some of the best brown trout fishing in the vicinity. The hotel has a number of shooting opportunities available too, including; grouse, pheasant, partridge and duck.

There are a large number of still waters in south east Wales and the fishermen who crosses the Severn in the hope of a good catch will surely not be disappointed. Lladegfedd (04957) 55122 covers a huge area and is located in the lowlands among wooded, rolling hills between the Usk and the valleys of South Wales. The water is restricted to fly only and there are numerous opportunities available to the visiting angler. Day tickets are priced at around £7.50 and season tickets £260. The season runs from mid March to mid October. The fishery opens at 10.00am and boats may be rented from 8.00am onwards. Closing times vary from month to month in accordance with the daylight hours. There is a six fish limit per day and if you wish to explore the water to its full extent, then a motor boat will set you back £15 and a rowing boat £6. They can be reserved in advance by telephoning the fishery (04957) 55122. In the closed season, the water is a haven for wintering wildfowl. Llwyn-On (0874) 3181 is another water, stocked and managed by Welsh

Water. Day tickets only are available here at a price of £6. Tickets are obtained from machines so take plenty of change with you. Visitors may fish with fly, spinner or bait and the record brown trout is weighed in at 5lb and the rainbow at 13lb. Llwyn-On is near Merthyr Tydfil, and is bordered by mature conifers amidst the heart of the Brecon Beacons National Park - ample excuse for the journey itself. Two fisheries to the south of here are Llanishen and Lisvane (0874) 623181 which are joined by a central embankment and cover some 80 acres in total. They are situated a short distance outside Cardiff on the southern tip of the Welsh Hills in attractively wooded and open countryside. Lisvane is another reservoir which is popular with wintering wildfowl as well as local fishermen. There are two boats available which can be hired for £12 per day and the reservoir is stocked with rainbows and browns. Day tickets are priced at £7 and the waters are open from sunrise to an hour after sunset.

There is some fine sewin fishing in south and west Wales. The still waters are also useful when other waters are out of condition. Before we examine the delights of the major rivers a glance at one or two less well known ones is well worth while. The River **Ogmore** has fishing opportunities for trout, sewin and salmon and the Ogmore Angler's Association which has just celebrated its centenary year, owns eighteen miles of double bank fishing of this good water. Weekly tickets are available at £25 which represents good value for money. The Association bye-laws stipulate that you may only fish if you are introduced by a member of the club. In reality, the extremely friendly Mr Protheroe, Secretary, (0656) 861139 will merely sound you out on the telephone.

The River **Tawe** flows through some superb scenery in its upper reaches and the sewin and salmon fishing is very much improved although some parts of the river still suffer from pollution. Mainwaring's in Dillwyn Road, Sketty (0792) 202245 sell licences and permits for the Pontardawe Angling Club who own eight miles of double bank fishing between Pontardawe and Morriston. Assuming conditions are in our favour, the fishermen can enjoy some fine sport and day tickets can be purchased for £6.

The River **Towy** (or Tywi) rises in the Cambrian Mountains and flows thence from the Brianne Reservoir to Carmarthen and the Bristol Channel. Although the reservoir has been blamed for many ills in the water it does act as a potential 'safety fuse' for surges of water and consequent flooding. This generally ensures some good, easy fishing. It is excellent sewin water and the fish generally run from the first day of the season in March. The association waters are available but some of the water is understandably retained for private use. However, the Land and Leisure Group (0874) 623181, a subsidiary of Welsh Water, have a large amount of opportunities for sewin and to a lesser extent salmon. Prices vary here from £100 to £250 for a seven day rod. The Group also have some water on the River **Cothi**, a rocky stream which can prove quite difficult to fish. This tributary of the Towy has some excellent sewin fishing from June onwards. Prices are available on application. The Forest Arms (0267) 202339 in Brechta also have a mile on the Cothi. The locals are generally delighted to share their expertise and permits are available for £8 and £4. The Forest Arms also doubles as a good value bed and breakfast for people who wish to stay a day or two. The Tackle Shop at Felingwm Uchaf (0267) 290207 sells permits and can also arrange fishing on the

SANNAN COURT
AND THE ABERCOTHI & GOLDEN GROVE FISHERIES

The Afon Tywi (River Towy) is not only a good salmon river by English or Welsh standards it is also "The Best in Britain" for sea trout (Trout & Salmon Magazine 1990). Tywi sea trout run early, run large and run in quantity.

We own, or otherwise control, two of the finest sections of fishing on this famous Welsh River. Our Abercothi and Golden Grove Estate Fisheries comprise some 10 miles of double bank and 4 miles of adjoining single bank fishing on the main river Tywi and its principal tributary the Afon Cothi. We·have ten beats available to anglers on a day/week/season or exclusive syndication basis (for parties of up to 5 rods). Wales has few fishing hotels of any note (unlike Scotland or Ireland) and since there were none within the scenic Tywi Valley, we acquired Sannan Court in 1991 to provide our fishing guests with self-catering accommodation of a high standard convenient to the fishing.

Sannan Court is a converted former Victorian vicarage and barn in the quiet village of Llanfynydd some 4 miles off the A40, midway between Llandeilo and Carmarthen and central to all beats. It contains six self-contained flats which can accommodate either the lone angler or parties of 2,4,6 or 10 anglers. Most bedrooms have twin beds and a private or en-suite shower or bathroom. All flats have a fully-fitted kitchen with a fridge freezer and microwave, lounge and dining area with colour TV.

In addition to the accommodation, there is a generous rod room with rod-racks, chest freezers, drying cabinets, sink, tackle lockers, 'tackle shop', fly-tying bench and tackle hire facility. We can also arrange ghillies and instruction.

We are anglers catering for other anglers. Sannan Court is, perhaps, a response to our experience of fishing hotels elsewhere. We have tried to provide the same level of comfort with the freedom to come and go as your please and to eat, sleep and relax whenever the fishing permits!

There is much to do and see within the general area. You do not have to be angler to enjoy your stay at Sannan Court. We are open all year and cater for spring, autumn and winter breaks for non-anglers.

Sannan Court
Abercothi Estate Fishery
c/o Hamdden Ltd
Cambrian Way
Brecon
Powys LD3 7HP
Tel: (0874) 623181
Fax: (0874) 624167
Telex: 497 429

WALES

Treflyn Estate some distance away near Tregaron. This comprises some six and a half miles of double and single bank fishing on what is delightful water. The Estate also rents cottages by the week which may appeal to the many fishermen who enjoy the freedom of self-catering.

Returning southwards we arrive at Llandovery. Mrs Thomas at Tonn Farm has a short half a mile stretch which is good for trout fishing enthusiasts. Mrs Barbara Leech, who runs the antique shop (0550) 20602 sells tackle as well as licences for LLandovery Anglers Association who have a good stretch on the Towy. Permits cost £7.50 for a day and £20 per week. The proprietor is most helpful and will be delighted to assist you. LLandovery AA also have three miles of the River Bran, an excellent trout stream. Although much of the water is in the hands of Land and Leisure, The Golden Grove Arms Hotel (0558) 668551 has a three quarter mile stretch of single bank which is excellent for sewin and salmon. The hotel bar is well frequented by locals who are happy to offer good advice on the area, especially if you are buying.

Carmarthen and District Anglers Club (0267) 231945 is currently in the care of Mr Evans. The Club has six miles of mixed bank fishing on the Towy as well as a stretch of the Cothi. Permits on most waters are £12 a day though some fishing is available at £5 per day. Lyric Sports, King Street in Carmarthen (0267) 237166, will supply tickets for these waters and also for the Carmarthen Anglers Association waters. These comprise some six and a half miles of predominately double bank fishing on the Towy and two and a half miles on the Cothi. The Club Secretary (0267) 237362 is also extremely helpful and you should note that a £32 weekly permit will allow you to fish any of the Club's waters, which also includes stretches on the Gwili and Taf.

The better salmon fishing tends to take place toward the end of the season and the sewin will provide some thrilling sport earlier in the year. There will be few fishermen who will not delight in the varied opportunities that are afforded by the River Towy.

The River **Cleddau** has two limbs one which stretches to the east and the other west. Both then journey north through parts of unspoiled Wales. The Pembrokeshire Anglers Association have fifteen miles of fishing, much of which is double bank. Salmon tend to run from March to the end of June and sewin from mid June onwards. In league with the NRA, the Association have also an extensive cleaning operation underway to improve the banks and habitat of the Western Cleddau, creating some five or six new pools to add to the many already existing. Country Sports in Haverfordwest (0437) 763740 issue permits and licences at £6 per day or £34 a week, together with an extensive range of tackle. Maps are issued with the permits which is often the case in Wales - just as well as some of the pools are in remarkably remote settings. The Membership Secretary, Mr Tony Summers (0437) 763216 is extremely helpful and is happy to advise you on currently favoured flies and the better times to fish. This is a common trait amongst the Welsh fishing fraternity who could not be kinder but obviously, visitors should be respectful of privacy.

The Eastern Cleddau is mostly taken up by private syndicates but the Slebech Estates (0834) 860905 have one and a half miles of double bank fishing which offers good opportunities for salmon, sewin and trout fishing. The water is restricted to fly only and a 24 hour permit will cost you £17, and a day pass in the order of £12. The Estate also rents riverside cottages to visiting anglers which sounds very promising. Try and contact Jim Brown around meal times!

River Towy   (Glanrannell Park Hotel)

WALES

Those anglers fishing in south west waters should make a note of Llys-y-Fran (0437) 532273 which is an attractive reservoir on the edge of the Preseli Hills and provides bank and boat fishing. Fishing takes place from 8.00am to half an hour after sunset. The reservoir which is situated near to Haverfordwest, has good quality fishing for rainbow and brown trout. If you are looking for a family day out this is a good place as there are picnic tables, walks and nature trails. The price of a day ticket is £7 and there is a six fish bag limit. Boats may be hired for £15 per day and a superb wheelie boat is available for disabled anglers free of charge. Another fishery which also provides additional activities is located at Mynyddcerrig near Pontyberem. The Garnffrwd Trout Fishery (0269) 870539 provides riding and shooting as well as some fine fishing. Day tickets are in the region of £12 and the fishery enjoys a wonderful setting just nine miles from Camarthen.

TEIFI TO THE DEE

The River **Teifi** rises in Lyn Teifi near Strata Florida in the Cambrian Hills not far from the source of the Towy. The river is often titled the Queen of Welsh Rivers and this is hardly surprising when one reflects on the sport available. The river flows south west and then westwards, entering Cardigan Bay south of the town. There are a number of opportunities for the visiting fisherman and fishing is at a premium for sewin in July and August, particularly from dusk until dawn. The Cenarth area holds good salmon and at Cilgerran one can see historic Coracles The river runs through enchanting scenery including the Caron Bog, a renowned nature reserve. Salmon and sewin tend to dominate in the lower reaches while trout naturally tend to predominate in the upper reaches and the tributaries.

The Teifi concludes its journey a little south of Cardigan where M. & A. Williams (0239) 612038, the tackleists sell permits on behalf of the Teifi Trout Association. Permits are in the region of £15 per day or £55 per week. Mr Cliff Jones (0239) 710405 is Secretary of the Teifi Trout Association and is something of a Welsh wizard on the area when it comes to fishing. The association have some fifteen miles of the Lower Teifi. One bank offers continuous fishing, the other has four beats in and around Newcastle Emlyn and permits can be obtained from Andrew Sports in the town (0239) 710349. Cenarth Falls is the last site of historical coracle fishing for salmon. The Castle Malgwyn Hotel (023987) 644 in Llechryd have a mile of fishing which is available to guests as do the Llwyndywys Mansion Hotel (023987) 263. These waters both have trout, salmon and sewin fishing.

The Llandysul Anglers Association has some 22 miles of the middle waters of the Teifi and this is an extremely popular stretch of the river. Salmon run in the spring months and again from August through September while sewin are prolific from July onwards. Mr Artie Jones (0559) 362317 is the secretary and permits are available from Alma Stores in Llandysul (0559) 363322, just beyond Barclays Bank.

The Llanbydder Anglers Association has some five miles on the Teifi and Bill Wilkins (0570) 480038 is the man at the reel, so to speak. Tickets are available direct from him or David Morgan, Siop-y-Bont, Llanybdder (0570) 480980. Incidentally, the water which includes some excellent beats was formerly in the hands of the Black Lion Hotel, Llanybydder (0570) 480212. The proprietor, Mr Morris, can arrange temporary membership and issues permits at £12 per day or £40 per week.

River Cothi   (Glanrannell Park Hotel)

LLANDEGFEDD RESERVOIR

Enclosed within gently rolling hills and meadows yet easily accessible from the M4 motorway, Llandegfedd Reservoir near Pontypool in Gwent is considered by many to be amongst the finest stillwater trout fisheries in Wales. Anglers travel from far afield to fly fish from the wooded banks or to enjoy the comfort and convenience of our fleet of 40 modern fishing boats each equipped with a quiet and reliable outboard motor.

A recently acquired 'Wheely' boat provides an opportunity for disabled anglers to fish safely and in comfort.

In addition to the range of morning, evening and full day and season permits special concessions and discounts are available subject to eligibility. Special discounts are available for Competitions and Corporate Days.

A programme of regular trickle stocking ensures that the reservoir is well stocked throughout the season, principally with Rainbow Trout, and this productive water has produced a Rainbow Trout of 12lbs 2ozs and a Brown Trout of 8lbs 12ozs.

Llandegfedd is a popular venue for Club, National and International fishing competitions and in recent years has hosted the Welsh heats of the Benson and Hedges Fly Fishing Championships and the first Youth International Fly Fishing Championship.

At Glascoed a small cedarwood chalet is available for use by angling groups and planning permission has recently been granted for the construction of a reception lodge and waterside

centre which will enable our friendly and knowledgeable staff to further extend the range of services and facilities available to our customers.

Hamdden Ltd
Welsh Water Plc
Pentwyn Road
Nelson
Treharris
Mid Glamorgan CF46 6LY
Tel: (0443) 450577

LLYS-Y-FRAN RESERVOIR

Llys-y-Fran Reservoir is set in the heart of Pembrokeshire, West Wales. At an altitude of 310 feet, the reservoir of 187 acres is surrounded by mature deciduous woodlands and permanent pasture land.

The reservoir is well stocked annually with quality rainbow trout, many in excess of 5lbs; the use of cages in the reservoir being a primary factor in both the quality of fish and regularity of stocking. In April of this year, the reservoir record was smashed with a magnificent fish of 14lbs. There is a large population of wild brown trout and each season fish are caught in excess of 2lbs.

The reservoir has developed as a premier fly fishery for boat anglers; twenty five 15 foot Loch Sheelin fishing boats with silent electric outboards are available for hire, and in 1990 the new boathouse was opened, which further improves the facilities at Llys-y-fran for boat anglers. Being by far the largest body of water in the region, there is ample room to fish from nearly 4 miles of bank.

Early season fishing requires sinking lines and dark bodied lures or weighted nymphs. From late April onwards, intermediate and floating lines predominate for the rest of the season with small traditional flies and imitative nymph patterns coming into their own.

A special area of bank, with easy access is set aside for disabled anglers; a purpose built boat for disabled anglers is also available from the boathouse - free of charge - although the disabled

angler must purchase a fishing permit. A new Visitor Centre opened in 1990 with Cafe/Restaurant and Tackle Shop.

Hamdden Limited
Llys-y-Fran Centre
Llys-y-Fran
Clarbeston Road
Haverfordwest
Dyfed SA63 4RR
Tel: (0437) 532273

GLANRANNELL PARK

Glanrannell Park lies in the valley of the river Cothi, the largest tributary of the Towy which flows six miles east of the hotel. Eight miles west runs the river Teifi which rises in the hills north of Tregarvon and meets the sea at Cardigan. These three rivers and numerous feeder streams are the basis of the sport available to the resident angler at Glanrannell.

Glanrannell Park Country house hotel, surrounded by lawns and overlooking a small private lake is set in twenty-three acres of parkland bounded on one side by the Annell, a trout stream from which the hotel gets its name. Arriving at Glanrannell Park you will be captivated by the setting of the hotel and the calm and serenity of the surrounding countryside.

The hotel has eight comfortable bedrooms with views over the lawns and paddocks of the estate, whilst the dining room overlooks the lake and adjoins a modern well-equipped kitchen. Local produce is used and our menu and service are in the best traditions of the country house.

Glanrannell Park provides an excellent base from which to explore this lovely part of Wales. Nearby are the Dolaucothi Roman gold mines at Pumpsaint, the 12th century Talley Abbey and Felin Newydd, a water mill still producing stone ground flour. The Brecon Beacons National Park is a short distance to the east and to the west are the sea cliffs, rocky coves and sandy beaches of Cardigan Bay and the Pembrokeshire Coast National Park. To the South is the expanse of Carmarthen Bay, sheltered by the Gower Peninsula, Britain's first designated area of outstanding natural beauty.

West Wales has an abundance of castles, woollen and flour mills, craft workshops, museums and many other places of interest besides its excellent fishing so there is always something for you to do and see.

At Glanrannell Park we take personal care of our guests and great pride in the relaxed, happy hotel that we run. The Welsh for 'welcome' is Croeso - which is what we provide.

Glanrannell Park
Country House Hotel
Crugybar
Llanwrda
Dyfed SA19 8SA
Tel: (0558) 685230
Fax: (0558) 685784

WALES

The Tregaron Anglers Association controls several miles of the Upper Teifi and Mr D.L. Evans (0974) 298304 is the Association's Honourary Secretary. There is some fine brown trout fishing available on these stretches. Wet fly fishing tends to be the most favoured in March and April with dry fly coming into its own in early May. Salmon will run up this far if the water conditions are favourable, particularly later in the season. Permits can be purchased from the newsagents in Tregaron or from the Post Office in Pontrhydfendigaid and (try asking for directions to this village!) There are also good value day tickets available here for trout fishing only. The Talbot Hotel (0974) 298208 have good contacts with the local Association and are delighted to arrange fishing for their guests. The Water Bailiff is also a helpful chap as are so many of the association officials. This may be a queen of rivers but it is one of the most accessible as well as one of the most beautiful in the area.

Finally, if you are endeavouring to fish the seven mile stretch of Llyn Gynon you will find the Visitors Centre in Glan Village (0597) 810880 a mine of useful information. Permits are also available from the centre. Access to this water is difficult but well worth making an effort for. The wild brown trout fight like tigers. Day tickets are priced at a reasonable £3. If you happen to be sitting at home with little to do, reflect on the River Teifi. Imagine, if you will, the morning quiet or the evening solace, the flow and he ripple. Life is too short, they say. It certainly is a too brief if you haven't yet enjoyed the Teifi.

There are many reasons for going fishing; the solitude, the scenery and the challenge. The River **Aeron** is a relatively small but still attractive river with an excellent run of sewin from June onwards. The lower reaches are generally the most productive and are controlled by the Aberaeron Angling Club. Permits are available from Cei Lee Sports in Bridge Street, Arberaeron (0545) 571123. Local residents are given priority and pensioners and juniors even better treatment. Visitors who live two or more miles away from Aberaeron are required to pay £60 for a year's fishing. Please contact Geoff Parry, West Winds, Wellington Street, Aberaeron for further details. Night fishing for sewin in this area is often excellent. Upriver the water flows through farmland but the waters are still often fishable by virtue of the local farmers who allow fisherman onto their land. The Post Office in Aberaeron generally has a list of farmers who are welcoming. The banks are often overgrown here, but in the later weeks of the season the sewin fishing is phenomenal. The Butcher and the Silver March Brown are two popular flies used locally. There are numerous streams in Dyfed and the **Rheidol** is one that is well worth your attention. The sewin that run upriver in May are of top quality and the middle reaches, which has long glides suits wet fly fishing for sewin. The level of water often fluctuates dramatically by virtue of the fact that the Nant-y-Moch and Dinas Reservoirs are used for hydro-electric power generation. Although the increased levels may aid fishing, the changes in water temperature make it doubly difficult to tempt the devious sewin which are so prolific in these waters. The Aberystwyth Anglers Association own all the water and some eight lakes in the district. Permits can be obtained from the Aberystwyth Tackle Shop (0970) 611200 and prices are in the region of £12 par day or £44 per week. There are some excellent sewin lurking which will give you some great sport should you be lucky enough to catch one. It is a good idea to use both floating and a sinking line to counteract the changes in temperature that follow any fluctuation in the water level. Equipped with wet fly you should be fortunate to have a lot of fun amid the pools and deep glides of the River Rheidol.

The River **Ystwyth** is much improved and has some large sewin in the summer months. It is a fairly fast running river with long runs and relatively few large pools. Consequently, a wet fly is favoured. The LLanilar Angling Association (0970) 623073 have weekly and daily tickets for sale at £25 and £8 respectively.

The **Dovey** is one of the finest waters in Britain and its sewin fishing is outstanding. The 30 or so miles of water starts amidst mountainous terrain and hereafter the waters wind their way in a south westerly direction to Aberdovey. This spate river also has some 350 miles of feeder tributaries which offer some fine trout fishing. The New Aberdovey Fishery Association (0654) 702721 controls 28 miles of river and, as you may imagine, rods are somewhat hard to come by. Indeed, no day tickets are available to visitors although weekly permits at £80 are available. The lower beats are almost impossible to get on and you must book well in advance to stand any chance here. The upper beats are less popular and you may well be able to purchase a weekly ticket from the Post Office in Cemmaes. The sea-trout tend to range from 2lb to 8lb and salmon from 8lb to 10lb. In June 1991, a 30lb fish was taken - the largest since 1930. There are numerous pools of note; Rhiwlas, Tank, Glandwr and Cottage are some of the most celebrated. Equally notable is the 'Haslan' Fly which has made a reputation for itself on this water. The Brigands Inn (0650) 531208 is an historic establishment in which to stay. It dates from the 18th century and has welcomed anglers to the area for a hundred years. The inn owns two miles of predominantly double bank fishing on the Dovey which is almost entirely reserved for residents. Eight rods are allowed per day and these are priced at £14. The hotel arranges special fishing breaks and you should contact them for further details. We have received very positive reports on the sea-trout fishing in this stretch and in 1990 a 24lb fish topped the scales here. Salmon are also reported to be on the increase. This is a first class river and if you are able to fish it you are extremely fortunate.

The River **Vyrnwy** runs from the lake of the same name to the north of Powys and offers some fine trout and salmon fishing as well as some good course fishing. The Vyrnwy is a tributary of the Severn and whilst it is not a classic salmon river, it has given up some 30lb fish in recent seasons and is well located for the many anglers of the Midlands who are not so spoilt in their choice of good game fishing rivers. The sport has been restricted of late by low water levels here but when the river rises the clear waters are a delight to fish. A mere £8 covers the cost of a season ticket here - tremendous value. 1991 saw a 38lb salmon caught in these waters - food for thought indeed! Tickets are available from Sundore Fishing Tackle and Leisure in Shrewsbury (0743) 361804 or direct from Oswestry and District Angling Society (0691) 772045. This is a wonderfully unspoiled area and awaits your attention.

The River **Tanat** is a tributary of the Vyrnwy and is a good trout river which will appeal to those living on the border. Much of the water is owned by syndicates but two inns offer good value fishing and provide an excellent base for exploring this delightful countryside. Llan-y-Blodwel finds the Horseshoe Inn (0691) 828227 which has three rods available per day for fly fishing only. The Green Inn in Llangedwyn (0691) 828234 has three quarters of a mile of single bank fishing, again with three rods available (the other bank is too steep to fish from).

GLANRHYD-Y-PYSGOD

Glanrhyd-y-pysgod is set in beautiful woodland surroundings situated in unspoilt countryside in the lovely Teifi Valley, midway between Newcastle Emlyn, Lampeter and Carmarthen. This alone makes Glanrhyd-y-pysgod an ideal place for a fishing holiday or even just a relaxing break away from it all.

For those who wish to explore the beautiful countryside, Glanrhyd-y-pysgod is an ideal touring centre for Cardigan Bay and the Gower peninsula with Cenarth Falls only 16 miles away. Wildlife enthusiasts will find the area a particularly rich source of interest.

Accommodation consists of four attractive one and two bedroom cottages which sleep anything from two to six people.

These tastefully furnished stone-built cottages are self-catering and fitted to a very high standard, amenities include barbecue facilities and televisions.

Glanrhyd-y-pysgod has its own mile long stretch of private salmon and sewin fishing, incorporating 8 holding pools on the river Teifi. Access to the river, which is only a hundred yards from the cottages, could not be easier and once there, fly, spinning and worm fishing can all be enjoyed.

Also running alongside the cottages is Glanrhyd-y-pysgod's own trout lake covering an area of approximately three acres and stocked with rainbow trout, giving excellent fishing for the beginner as much as the enthusiast.

Glanrhyd-y-pysgod Farm
Maesycrugiau
Pencader
Dyfed SA39 9LX
Tel: (055 935) 253

DOLMELYNLLYN HALL HOTEL

Dolmelynllyn Hall, or 'Dolly' as it is affectionately known, began its life back in the 16th century, it was enlarged in the 18th, rebuilt and enlarged again in the 19th and finally taken over in the last decade and turned into an hotel. Since then, it has been re-decorated, re-carpeted and re-furnished. It has retained the friendly atmosphere of a family home from a bygone age, an atmosphere which begins to penetrate even as one begins the trip up the gently winding, quarter mile, beech-lined drive to the house itself. There are 11 guest rooms, each with a different decorative theme and all well equipped. Each has an en-suite bathroom, colour TV and direct dial telephone.

The Dining Room is the centre of the house where five course dinners are served in an 'highly imaginative, traditional British' style. The menu changes daily and is complemented by a comprehensive wine list.

The Conservatory Bar, adjoining the Dining Room is tastefully well-stocked with bottles and flowering plants fighting for space. The elegant yet comfortable sitting room offers superb views down the valley through three large windows, there is also a library cum writing room.

Surrounding the hotel are three acres of terraced formal gardens, bounded by a swiftly running stream flowing into a small lake - part of the 1,200 acres of mountains, meadow and the Coed y Brenin Forest, all in the care of the National Trust. One can walk all day without seeing a car or crossing a road. Nearby there are castles, stately homes and all manner of other diversions.

Fishing here is excellent and the hotel offers twin bank fishing for salmon and sea trout over a stretch of some 12 miles on the Rivers Mawddach and Wnion. There is also lake fishing for wild brown and reared rainbow trout on the twin Creggenan Lakes and Lake Cynwch.

Dolmelynllyn Hall Hotel
Ganllwyd
Dolgellau
Gwynedd
Tel: (034) 140 273

The River **Mawddach** rises on a remote hillside between Bala and Trawsfyndd Lake, holds salmon, trout and to a lesser extent, sea-trout. Although much of the water is preserved, there are two excellent hotels from which to enjoy the fishing. The Tyn y Groes Hotel, Granllwyd (034140) 275 has a mile and a half of single bank fishing available for guests. This is predominately salmon water and licences can be obtained from the nearby Post Office. Permits are available at the hotel and are priced at £9 per day. The proprietor, Barry Rithwell, is himself a sporting enthusiast and has access to other rivers as well as a splendid knowledge of the Mawddach. The delightful Dolmelynllyn Hall (034140) 273 is a true haven and the hotel can provide guests with some twelve miles of fishing on the Mawddach and its best known tributary the River Wnion. This is a tumbling, often turbulent water which gives some fine fishing. Permits are available to residents and non-residents, although the latter should always enquire in advance as to availability. Guests are asked to pay £5 per day, non-residents, £20. Licences can be purchased in the local village.

Further information is also obtainable from Dolgellau Angling Club (0341) 422906 who control much of the association waters. They are particularly well organised and have in the region of twelve miles of salmon and sea-trout fishing on the Mawddach and Wnion at Dolgellau in addition to the recently acquired Storehouse waters. Both rivers are stocked with salmon and sea-trout from the Mawddach Hatchery. Weekly permits are well priced at £24 and day permits are £9. Tickets can be purchased from the newsagents, Siop y Bont in Dolgellau (0341) 422891 or the Seafarer (0341) 280978, a tackle shop in Barmouth.

Journeying westwards, we find the River **Dysynni** which rises in Llyn Cau on the towering Cader Idris. The water falls rapidly via Dol-y-Cau and into the picturesque Tal-y-Llyn. Emerging from the lake it flows westwards as a small upland river but grows ever deeper as it carves its way through the valley to enter the sea at Cardigan Bay, a mile or so to the north of Tywyn. The river offers interesting trout and sewin fishing and in the late summer the occasional salmon will be encountered. The Estimaner Angling Association owns three miles of the lower river and seven miles of its upper reaches and the Peniarth Estate has a further four miles. This is one of the most picturesque rivers you are ever likely to fish and permits are available from Abergynolwyn Post Office (0654) 782635 in the Square, opposite the Railway Hotel. Day tickets cost £5, weekly tickets, £10. The Sports Shop in Tywyn (0654) 710772 also has permits for sale. If you are looking for an escape in superb scenery then this fishing is first rate.

Central Wales reveals some interesting lake fishing, all of which offers good daily forays for brown trout and rainbows. Bag limits are usually around six fish per day and tickets start at £6 for a full day's fishing. Dinas and Nant-y-Moch Reservoirs are both under the ownership of Powergen (097084) 667 and are part of the Rheidol Hydro-Electric Power Scheme. They are both very popular and the fisherman landing the largest fish wins a season ticket for the following year. East of this area and south of Newtown we find Lake Machdre (Nettesheim Fishery) (0686) 625623, formerly Newtown Reservoir. There are only eight rods permitted here each day and a day ticket for the lake costs £15 or £8 for a half day. The lake has a resident rainbow trout called Trevor who was introduced to the water three years ago when he weighed 12lb. He has been hooked on several occasions but at the time of writing Trevor is still at

large. The reservoir has a picturesque setting cut into a dammed valley. Two brooks create waterfalls adding to the scene. Wildlife abounds and Merlin can be seen from time to time (no, not the Welsh wizard of folklore). The water holds brook trout, brown trout, Loch Leven trout, rainbows and Trevor! The fish have a reputation for being fighters and if you are looking for a tussle then this water fits the bill. If you happen to be fishing the Rhayader, then surely a visit to Elan Valley Fisheries is in order. In fact, it is a good idea even if you're not in the area. The interlinked reservoirs of Caban Coch, Garreg Ddu, Graig Goch and Pen-y-Garreg are controlled by Elan Trout Fisheries and provide 850 acres of excellent trout fishing in a beautiful setting. Permits can be bought from the Elan Valley Visitors Centre (0597) 810898, take the B4518 from Rhayader.

One of the most renowned still water lakes in Britain is **Lake Vyrnwy**. It spans 1100 acres and is 800 feet above sea level. The rights to this water are owned by the Lake Vyrnwy Hotel (069173) 692, a delightful place to stay. The lake is surrounded by moorland, meadow, mountain and forest which all provide a stunning backdrop for the casting fisherman. The lake is restricted to fly fishing only from the hotel's boats which are available with, or without engines. Tackle can be hired and licences can also be purchased from the hotel. Late in the season when the water level drops, bank fishing is also possible. The lake is well stocked throughout the season with brown, rainbow and American brook trout to complement the indigenous population of brownies. For groups, tuition is available and the services of a ghillie can be arranged. The price of day tickets varies during the season from £6 to £8.50. There are a whole host of other permits obtainable from the hotel and this is an ideal place to stay and enjoy some good fishing in a superb natural environment.

Gwynedd offers a number of fishing opportunities. The Lakes of **Blaenau Ffestiniog** number twenty and offer some first class fishing for wild trout. Here, the fishing is managed by the local angling association and if you like being well away from the crowds then these lakes are for you. The Dolgellau Angling Association (0341) 422706 control the waters of **Llyn Cynwch** as well as first class river fishing. The lake is situated near the renowned Precipice Walk and all around are stunning views of Cader Idris and the Mawddach Estuary. The lake is stocked every three weeks with brown and rainbow trout and has natural brown trout too. The record fish is an impressive 10lb. The northern section of the lake is fly-only but the remainder is open fishing. Tickets for the lake are priced at £7 and for the views that come with it, that seems like good value!

South of Dolgellau we find another hotel which provides superb lakeside fishing. The Tynycornel at Talyllyn (0654) 782282 provides fishing on one of the most beautiful waters in the principality. The management also control the fishing on Bugeilyn, a truly remarkable setting in the hills above Llanbrynmair where boat fishing for the wild brown trout will provide a feast of memories.

Snowdonia not only has wonderful scenery but some delightfully unspoiled mountain lakes too, gouged out by glaciers many thousands of years ago. One such lake is **Llyn Crafnant** (0492) 640818. Formerly the exclusive territory of the wild brown trout these wild fish now share their home with rainbows which are stocked weekly, including a former record fish of some 17lb. The lake is signposted from Trefriw on the B5106 which is in the Conway Valley some five miles north of Betws-y-Coed. Day tickets are priced at £9 with a six fish limit and boats are available at £9 per day. All tickets can be purchased from the Lakeside Office. There is also some cottage accommodation available.

Venturing ever northwards, one has a choice between the wilds of Snowdonia or the coastline, dotted with small fishing villages and larger resort towns. There are numerous streams in Gwynedd and the Dwyfawr, Glaslyn and Erch are three which flow from the Lleyn Peninsula and attract quality fish. The locals love their fishing here and when the sewin are running everyone knows! However, in recent years numbers have been substantially reduced. This is an area of quite stunning scenery, much of which can be enjoyed with fishing rod in hand. Most of the **Dwyfawr** is in the hands of Criccieth, Llanystumdwy and District Anglers Association and permits, licences and tackle can be purchased from Pritchards (0766) 522116. Mr Goodman Jones is a member of the Club and is very helpful. Permits are priced at £70 for a season or £25 for a week. A days fishing will cost you £10. It is desperately sad to hear of the decline in sea-trout here in recent years. Welsh Water and the NRA are endeavouring to collate information in order that they might redress the situation but only time will tell. However, although the sewin are not so numerous, salmon have increased in number. The **Glaslyn** which rises in Llyn Conwy and runs along the valley floor to Portmadog is another sewin river although the Glaslyn Anglers Association owns much of the river. Monday to Friday tickets are £5 and are available from the Angling and Gun Centre (0766) 512464. If you wish to fish at the weekend you must hold a season ticket which is priced at £30. Once again, the surroundings are perfect and the river is well known for its early run of Sewin.

The River **Conway** (Conwy) rises in Migneint and flows through the Carnarvonshire countryside through Betws-y-Coed and Llanrwst and into Conway Bay. The upper part of the Conway Valley takes in some celebrated unspoiled countryside and much of the land is in the care of the National Trust. Permits are available for a number of stretches of the river between Conway Falls Bridge and Rhydlanfair. In total, the National Trust (0492) 860123 handle four beats and weekly tickets are available at £7 or £2 per day. Although the trout are small, they fight well and the scenery is quite breathtaking. It is also worth considering the National Trust on a number of other fishing opportunities.

It is difficult to consider such beauty and at the same time pay sufficient attention to the worries over pollution and acid rain, but the Conway is susceptible to both these problems, and as a result trout fishing is not what it used to be here. Sea-trout, for which the river was once renowned, have also depreciated dramatically. Salmon still run the river and average between 9lb and 12lb. The Betws-y-Coed Angling Association (0690) 710618 has some four and a half miles of mixed bank fishing as well as three lakes on the river. The Committee have recently passed a ruling that no day or weekly tickets are to be issued after August each year but prior to that, day fishing is available at £15 and weekly tickets at £40. A season ticket is priced at £100. Mr Melvin Hughes, the Membership Secretary is happy to hear from prospective members. Permits and maps are obtainable from Tan Lan Restaurant, Betws-y-Coed (0690) 710232.

Those wishing to fish later in the season might be advised to

stay at one of the nearby hotels. The Maenen Abbey (049269) 230 have one mile of single bank fishing available to guests and there are a number of locals who frequent the bar with useful knowledge and advice! The Gwydyr Hotel (0690) 710777, Betws-y-Coed has about six miles of double bank fishing. Tackle is also available for hire but only guests can fish for salmon at £60 per day or £130 per week between March and May, and £220 per week for the latter part of the season. Night-fishing for sea-trout has suffered of late but is still possible at a price of £16. Let us hope that the NRA in league with Welsh Water can address this tragic situation .

The **Clwyd** which meets the sea at Rhyl is predominantly controlled by clubs and associations which restrict the waters to members only, however, the St Asaph Angling Association have two beats available to day visitors from Monday to Friday. The fishing which includes salmon in the summer and autumn is priced at £5 per day. The Club also has two miles of excellent trout fishing on the River Elwy. Permits are £3 per day - great value indeed! Foxon's Tackle (0745) 583583 in St Asaphs sells permits for the waters and will help with any information. The water is good below Ruthin and the Ruthin Castle Hotel (08242) 2664 has rights to the water which is free to guests. It is fly-only and guests may fish for salmon, brown and sea-trout.

Unlike the Clwyd, the River **Dee** is far easier to fish and the visitor will not only find good value but also a delightful setting. In an age when the price of a beat is extremely high and fish harder to find, the Dee is a real treat. It is well cared for by the associations that own much of this water. The nature of the valley is varied, sometimes deep, and on other sections bordered by meadows. As you will appreciate, access is not always possible. The River Dee rises in the Cambrian Mountains and threads its way to Chester, flowing through Bala, Corwen, Llangollen and Overton. The river holds trout, salmon, sewin and grayling. The grayling in particular are top quality and offer good sport when other game fish are out of season. The insect life is staggering and your fly box will have to be well filled to compete. Membership of the principal clubs such as the Corwen and Llangollen is excellent value. The Llangollen Angling Association has some six and a half miles of double bank fly fishing and recently hosted the 10th World Fly Fishing Championships. D. M. Southern in Chapel Street, (0978) 860155 Llangollen sells permits at £3 a day for trout and £10 for salmon. Weekly permits are priced at £15 and £30 respectively. Mr Southern can also sell permits for Midland Fly Fishers Syndicate who have three miles of double bank fly only water, priced at £4 for trout and grayling fishing.

The Bryn Howel Hotel (0978) 860331 have access to the Llnagollen Anglers Association waters and issue permits at £5 per day. As we head towards the Corwen Anglers Association waters we should pencil in a visit to the Berwyn Arms Hotel at Glyndyfrdwy (0490) 83210 which has two miles of single bank fishing. There is a tackle shop at the hotel and the owner, Mr Gallagher, fishes regularly. Permits for trout and grayling cost £4 and salmon is priced at £10 per day. There are special weekly rates if you wish to stay a little longer. Corwen and District Angling Club controls most of the trout and grayling fishing on the Rhug Estate, permits are available from local tackleists and a visit is thoroughly recommended. Pale Hall at Llandderfel (06783) 285 have bought some 10 rods on the Dee, using Bala Association water and covering several sections of the Dee, Towyn and a mountain lake. There is some good salmon fish-

WALES

ing here and tackle is available should you wish it. Fishing is reserved for guests only and is free. A licence can also be purchased at the hotel should this be required. In Bala itself, Siop Yr Eryr, Sports and Tackle (0678) 520370 has an excellent range of tackle and the proprietor, Mr Evans, is a member of the local association and as something of an expert he is also generous with his advice. Mr Evans is a specialist in fly tying and has some good examples of old 18th and 19th century Welsh patterns.

North Wales has a number of still waters rich in fish. **Llyn Brenig** (049082) 463 is situated high on Denbigh Moors and offers fly fishing for rainbow and brown trout. It is particularly notable as a boat fishery and hosted the World Championship in 1990. Day Permits are £8 and boats can be hired for £15. Fishing takes place from mid-March to the end of October and between 8.00am until an hour after sunset. The water is located off the B4501 and is well worth a visit. Other waters to note include Felin-y-Gors (0745) 584044 which offers ten acres of fly fishing and four spring fed lakes in secluded surroundings. The fishery which opens from 9.00am to 10.00pm hires out tackle and also has some pleasant self-catering accommodation for people wishing to stay in the area. The cost of fishing varies with the duration of your stay and the longer you are here the more fish you may keep. Four hours will cost £8 and two fish, whilst a day ticket costs £22 with a six fish limit.

Journeying to the Moelfre Hills, we find the Tan-y-Mynydd Trout Lake (0745) 823691 on the B5381, St Asaph to Conway Road just three miles outside Abergele and three and a half miles from the coast. There are ten self-catering cottages on site and a licenced bar and restaurant too. The tariffs and bag limits vary according to the number of hours you wish to spend here.

There are a total of five small lakes which cover three and a half acres and each lake is stocked with rainbows, American brook trout and brown trout.

FISHING FAYRE

MONMOUTHSHIRE TO PEMBROKESHIRE

There are numerous hotels in Wales and many offer a warm welcome and some splendid fishing too. Visitors to Wales are seldom very far from beautiful countryside and if you have not yet considered a trip here then we would advise you to do so. There are several places in Wales where time has seemingly stood still.

Firstly, we consider the waters of the Wye which manage to sneak into England too. Around Chepstow, there are several superb hotels to consider. The St Pierre Hotel (0291) 625261 has outstanding leisure facilities, including a championship golf course, whilst lovers of tradition will enjoy the Castle View Inn (02912) 70349. This timber clad hotel stands directly opposite the historic fortress.

History continues in Tintern where we find the Beaufort Hotel (0291) 689777 which has marvellous views over the ruined abbey. The Royal George (0291) 689205 dates from the 17th century and has delightful gardens through which a trout stream cascades into the River Wye. Another good value establishment on the Wye is Parva Farmhouse (0291) 689411. The Crown at Whitebrook (0600) 860254 is to be recommended for its fine restaurant and cosy bedrooms whilst Clearwell Castle (0594) 32320 is an impressive neo-Gothic castle and the proprietor is happy to arrange some fishing for his guests.

River Dee   (Tyddyn Llan Hotel)

LLYN BRENIG

Set high in the Denbigh Moors in magnificent scenery, Llyn Brenig (999 acres) offers some of the finest fishing in North East Wales for brown trout, rainbow trout and book charr. Selected as a venue in 1990 for the World Fly Fishing Championship, Brenig has also hosted many other prestigious events. Readily accessible from the Midlands via the A5 and from the North West via the new A55 Expressway, the fishery has a good head of wild brown trout and is stocked annually with some 25,000 rainbow trout and charr. There are 42 boats with engines and a specially adapted boat with winch for disabled anglers. Special rates are available for Competitions and Corporate Days. The Lakeside Cafe enjoys panoramic views and provides hot meals, light snacks and beverages. Fishing is fly only. Season 15 March - 25 October. Limit 6 fish.

Hamdden Ltd
Llyn Brenig Visitor Centre
Cerrigydrudion
Corwen
Clwyd LL21 9TT
Tel: (049 082) 463

Artist: **T.M.Richardson** *FISHING*   Courtesy of: **Rosenstiels'**

THE GRIFFIN INN

Dating back to the fifteenth century, The Griffin Inn is believed to be one of the oldest sporting inns in Wales. That tradition endures and today, under the ownership and management of the Stockton family. The Griffin lays claim to being one of the finest sporting inns in the principality.

Undoubtedly a superb mile-long beat on the upper reaches of the River Wye contributes much to that reputation. A keen fisherman himself, Richard Stockton aims to ensure that visitors to The Griffin are able to enjoy a rewarding variety of game fishing. In addition to the excellent salmon beat on the Wye, including the noted Llangoed Pool, the inn is able to offer exciting sport on a nearby mile-long stretch of trout stream, where purists have a rare opportunity to fish for wild 'brownies'. Good local lake fishing is yet another option.

The Griffin exudes all the warmth and welcome to be expected of a hostelry where enthusiasm for country pursuits is shared by all - the Stockton family, regulars and visitors alike. Three generations of Stocktons contribute to the smooth running, comfort and friendly atmosphere of The Griffin - Richard and Di Stockton have succeeded in creating a delightfully relaxed and informal ambience. Their son James is both ghillie and keeper, an accomplished country-sportsman, he discreetly ensures sporting guests are able to make the most of their stay in Llyswen.

Game fishing is very much a theme of The Griffin - the attractive cottage-style bedrooms are all named after famous fishing flies,

while the bar features a fascinating collection of cased flies, fish and maps of the River Wye.

The unspoilt Fisherman's Bar of The Griffin deserves special mention. Dominated by a huge inglenook fireplace and decorated with traditional simplicity, it has a timeless charm - a haven in which to enjoy good ale, good food and good company. While conversation naturally tends to turn to country matters - in particular, game fishing and shooting - the Stockton family always welcomes those just seeking a quiet, 'get away from it all' break, in one of Britain's loveliest river valleys.

The Griffin has a well-established and far-reaching reputation for serving outstanding meals - country-style cooking at its best, always prepared from fresh local produce. The inn's sporting interests are, not surprisingly, reflected in the menu - depending on the season - it will generally include fresh salmon, river trout or game, invariably well prepared and attractively presented in either the restaurant or bar.

There is residential accommodation for sixteen guests, a comfortable residents' lounge with separate TV room and an attractive dining room.

A free house, with fully licensed bars, The Griffin Inn is on the A470 Builth Wells road, 9 miles from Brecon and 7 miles from Hay-on-Wye.

Further details are available from: Richard & Di Stockton:

The Griffin Inn
Llyswen
Brecon
Powys LD3 0UR
Tel: (0874) 754241

WALES

In the Monmouth area, the King's Head (0600) 712177 is a good place to stay and at Symonds Yat, where the Wye is fast and furious, is the Royal Hotel (0600) 890238 on the banks of the river. In nearby Goodrich, the well named Ye Hostelrie (0600) 890241 is situated in a quiet rural setting, ideally placed for the Wye and a fishing foray!

Like Monmouth, Ross-On-Wye and its environs offer up many good hotels, inns and bed & breakfasts. A small selection for you to ponder would include; Pengethley Manor (098987) 211, four miles north of the town and with impressive views over Herefordshire. Similarly impressive is the Wharton Lodge (098981) 795; a Georgian property which stands in 15 acres of parkland in Weston-Under-Penyard. This is another outstanding establishment. The Bridge House (0989) 62655 is worth a visit as is our final selection here, the King's Head (0989) 763174, a 14th century inn and a delightful place to stay. The whole area is particularly well endowed with old inns and The Green Man (0432) 860243 at Fownhope dates from the 15th century and is quite splendid with open fires, beams and that sort of thing.

The Wye spans many miles and Hereford reveals yet more delights. Netherwood Country House Hotel, Tupsley (0432) 272388 is a charming Victorian house which once belonged to the Baskerville family of hound fame. Travelling towards Hay-On-Wye, the visitor may chance upon another fascinating establishment; The Ancient Camp Hotel (0981) 250449, built on the site of an Iron Age fort which has panoramic views of the river. This is a characterful and comfortable hotel. Hay-On-Wye also reveals a number of hotels to use as a base for your fishing holiday. These include the Old Black Lion (0497) 820841 and the Kilvert Court Hotel (0497) 821042 another friendly establishment. The Swan Hotel (0497) 821188 has good fishing and offers superb fishing breaks.

As the Wye gently meanders its way through the valley it has carved so majestically, we chance upon some delightful villages with pubs a plenty and numerous inns too. The Three Cocks (04974) 215 stands in the village from which it takes its name and here you can enjoy some pleasant bedrooms and an outstanding restaurant. Naturally, prices vary throughout the region but those with deeper pockets could consider a visit to Llyswen and the Llangoed Hall (0874) 754525. Sir Bernard Ashley has restored this superb building and if you enjoy gracious living then this is one for you. The restaurant here is also first class. Those with less loot should not be unduly worried as the Griffin Inn (0874) 754241 is a lovely establishment offering good value for your money.

Heading relentlessly upstream, following the A470 northwards, we arrive at Builth Wells where we find several good hotels and inns. The fisherman will be well aware that in addition to the Wye there are numerous other waters in the vicinity and Caer Beris Manor (0982) 552601, an attractively restored country house hotel in peaceful grounds, takes advantage of such a position close to these waters. In the market town of Builth Wells and near the Wye we find a hotel in the traditional sense with plenty of character; The Lion (0982) 553670. Shortly after Builth Wells the Wye is joined by two tributaries; the Ithen and Irfon. Those journeying north eastward should perhaps earmark Penybont, here an historic inn, the Severn Arms (059787) 224, will fit the bill, while those journeying further on, following the course of the Wye, should earmark Newbridge-On-Wye and the extremely popular New Inn (059789) 211, a comfortable village inn which is thoroughly recommended.

Many fishermen will, however, be heading for the Irfon and in particular the delightful fishing village of Llangammarch Wells. This is an ideal location to use as a base to enjoy the spectacular surrounding scenery. The visitor faces a difficult choice between The Cammarch (05912) 205 or The Lake Country House Hotel (05912) 202. Both have contributed enormously to the excellence of the fishing here. The former is an unpretentious fishing hotel providing excellent value for money and great character. The Lake however, is for those who prefer a little more style.

The Wye runs through some outstanding areas of natural beauty yet not to be out done, the Usk reveals its own delights. If you are seeking an hotel of great style and excellent leisure facilities then The Cwrt Bleddyn Hotel (063349) 521 is one to try. Less grand, but no less worthy of a mention, is the Glen-yr-Afon (02913) 2302 situated on the very edge of the Usk - a pleasant and convenient place to stay. Abergavenny is one of the principle towns on the Usk and the Llanwenarth Arms (0873) 810550 nestles on the riverbank to the west of the town enjoying stunning views across the valley. Those who enjoy fine eating should consider the Walnut Tree Inn (0873) 852797 in nearby Llandewi Skirrid. Although the first impression is that of a country pub, this is a renowned restaurant and one of the finest in the country.

Crickhowell is another notable town and here we find The Bear (0873) 810408; an inn of real class and character which has some lovely rooms and a marvellous bar. A little outside the town we find a celebrated fishing hotel, Gliffaes (0874) 730371. The grounds here are magnificent and this is an elegant but friendly hotel in which to stay. More good fishing can be found at Talybont at the Usk Hotel (0874) 87251 which offers excellent value. The Aberclydach House (087487) 361, some two miles south west, is set in a wooded valley within the Brecon National Park and is also a charming place to stay.

Hotels of character are not as plentiful in the industrial areas of Wales and we shall therefore skip hurriedly down the M4 corridor towards Dyfed which has some wonderful scenery and fine fishing. The Tywi reveals some suitable contenders; The Plough Inn (0267) 290220 in Felingwm-Uchaf, is a splendid restaurant which also has some good bedrooms and is well placed for those wishing to fish the Twyi or the Cothi, its principle tributary. A similarly well located hotel is Ty Mawr (0267) 202332, a charming establishment. The Forest Arms Hotel (0267) 202339 is a friendly hotel too.

Returning to the main stream, there are some fine watering holes well worth inspecting when fishing the Tywi. The Golden Grove Arms at Llanarthney (0558) 668551 is a popular spot and has good value accommodation too. Further upstream, we find The Cawdor Arms in Llandeilo (0558) 823500, an elegant place to stay. Crugybar is another location to head for where we find the Glanrannell Park (0558) 685230, nestling in the hills between the Brecon Beacons and the Cambrian Mountains. This is a small country house hotel and a popular place for those wishing to find a rural retreat away from it all.

The waters of Eastern and Western Cleddau can not only be justified in fishing terms but also for those who delight in the

WALES

beautiful scenery which can be found in the Gower Peninsula. In Haverfordwest, the Hotel Mariners (0437) 763353 is an ideal base from which to explore Pembrokeshire, while in nearby Wolfescastle, the Wolfscastle Country House Hotel (043787) 225 is an extremely pleasing place to stay.

FISHING FAYRE

TEIFI TO THE DEE

The Teifi will surely be the destination of many a fisherman eager to catch a sewin or two and there are some excellent opportunities to enjoy some good hospitality too. The Castle Malgwyn Hotel (023987) 644 has some good value breaks available. The Black Lion Hotel in Llanybydder (0570) 480212 is also well worth considering - more good value and a friendly Welsh welcome.

Heading further upstream, we arrive at Lampeter and the Falcondale Country House (0570) 422910, a charming mansion set in fourteen acres of parkland. Our final thought here is the Talbot near Tregaron (0974) 298208 a cheap and very cheerful establishment.

Should you be touring the country, then waters you might perchance also be considering are the Aeron, the Rheidol and the Dyfi. There are several hotels to consider en route north, however, and these include the Gwesty Ffern Penbontbren Farm (0239) 810248, a delightful hotel predictably set on a farm. The restaurant here is one to note. The Conrah Country Hotel (0970) 617941 in Chancery, a few miles from Aberystwyth, is a distinguished hotel for those who are venturing to Rheidol and its waters. Hotels which don't have specific rights on the river but still provide a worthy establishment in which to stay include the Ynyshir Hall (0654) 781209 at Eglwysfach. This hotel will appeal still more to lovers of bird life as the

RSPB's Ynyshir Reserve neighbours the hotel. If you are fishing the Dovey then you might consider Dolguog Hall (0654) 702244 in Machynlleth. The Hall dates from the 17th century and is the focal point for a small holiday centre. Meanwhile, in the centre of this market town, The Wynnstay Arms (0654) 702941 is a popular meeting place. Beside the river lies Llugwy Hall (0654) 791228, a mile or so outside Pennal which offers charming accommodation.

An hotel which combines both fishing and a good welcome is the 15th century Brigand's Inn (06504) 208 in Mallwyd. This is a very popular hotel amongst the fishing fraternity. The bar snacks, warming fires and pleasant bedrooms all add to the charming atmosphere. Another hotel with a picturesque setting is Buckley Pines (06504) 261 - a fine place to stay and enjoy the delights of the local sewin fishing.

Journeying ever northwards, progressing around the coast and through the stunning inland scenery, we find Tal-y-Llyn and the Tyn-y-Cornel Hotel (0654) 782282 which has welcomed anglers for over 150 years. This is a delightfully comfortable abode and, in addition to some superb fishing, you will enjoy fine cuisine and views that will last long in your memory.

While we are on the subject of hotels with lake fishing we should consider Lake Vyrnwy Hotel (069173) 692 which is another excellent establishment. If you enjoy fine food, good fishing and marvellous countryside then this is the place for you. The Minffordd Hotel (0654) 761665 may not perch alongside a lake but it boasts impressive views as it lies in the shadows of the mighty Cader Idris. Dolgellau fronts the Mawddach Estuary and has a number of good hotels in which to stay. Abergwynant Hall (0341) 422238, formerly part of a large sporting estate, has marvellous views of the estuary and similarly, Borthwnog Hall (034149) 271, a splendid Regency house dating from the 1670s, looks out over the estuary. These three

River Irfon   (The Cammarch Hotel)

TYDDYN LLAN

Smooth lawns surround this Georgian House of stone, setting up the resonance of a quiet oasis among mountains, rivers and the great outdoors. Inside all is light and elegance.

A cosy bar, often the centre of fishing exploits, looks into our much acclaimed Restaurant. The food, prepared with skill and imagination from fresh ingredients of the highest quality, will add to your feeling of satisfaction and physical well being at the end of an exhilarating day. Run as a very high quality country house, the Hotel is friendly, informal and always ready to help with any of your plans or requests. We take pleasure in providing a haven for guests wanting a peaceful holiday in style and comfort.

We have 4 miles of private fishing on the River Dee. This beautiful stretch of water has many named holding pools, where some excellent salmon have been caught, either on lure or fly.

The river is also known for its trout, but mostly as superb grayling water, with an enormous head of this wonderful fish. The grayling, caught on wet or dry fly, is a great fighter and very good to eat. Average weight is 1lb to 2lb.

As a natural unspoilt river, surrounded by the most breathtaking scenery, the fisherman will encounter a large variety of indigenous wildlife that will add greatly to the pleasure of the day.

Fly fishing lessons can be arranged by the Hotel with experienced Ghillies, whose expert tuition and personal knowledge of the local waters is invaluable. They will also give lessons in the art of tying your own fly or act as Ghillie to Hotel guests requiring their special knowledge.

Rod licences can be obtained at the Hotel.

Tyddyn Llan
Country House Hotel & Restaurant
Llandrillo
Near Corwen
Clwyd
Tel: (049 084) 264
Fax: (049 084) 264

TYN-Y-CORNEL HOTEL

Set beneath the southern slopes of Cadair Idris (2,957 feet) amidst some of the finest mountain scenery in the Snowdonia National Park and located on the banks of Llyn Mwngil, its own 220 acre natural lake, the Tyn-y-Cornel Hotel at Tal-y-Llyn has been welcoming anglers for over 150 years. Indeed, it is one of the oldest fishing hotels in the British Isles.

Llyn Mwngil ('the Lake of the Pleasant Retreat' in English) was Mecca for trout anglers during the Victorian era. It is still one of the finest brown trout fisheries in Wales. Over 2,500 fish were caught by our guests in 1990 with an average weight of 1lb 8oz. The best brown weighed 8lbs 4oz and the best bag (six fish) weighed 16lbs. The 220 acre lake is shallow and productive and famous for its prolific hatches of 'Olives' throughout the season. Dry-fly fishing and dapping can be more productive than the wet-fly when the 'swallows are down'.

Llyn Mwngil is also one of the few lakes in England and Wales with a natural run of salmon and sea trout. Catches are not large but fish up to 14lbs have been taken in recent years.

Fishing is fly-only from a drifting boat and the 'classic-style'. The six fully equipped boats have engines. There is a fully fitted rod-room with freezer, personal lockers and drying facility and a small Tackle Shop. Our Fishery Manager can arrange instruction and Tackle hire.

The Tyn-y-Cornel Hotel at Tal-y-Llyn also controls the fishing for wild brown trout at Llyn Bugeilyn (45 acres) in the magnificent Plynlimon mountains and for salmon and sea trout on the middle section of the Afon Dysynni below Llyn Mwngil. We also have access to 4 boats for guests at Llyn Brenig (1000 acres) on the Denbigh Moors for rainbow and brown trout and brook charr and have two rods on a private section of the Upper Dee near Bala for autumn salmon and grayling. (Brenig and the Upper Dee were both venues for the World Fly Fishing Championships in 1990).

The Tyn-y-Cornel hotel also has an attractive portfolio of shooting over some 20,000 acres of ground for Pheasant, Grouse, Duck, Snipe and, especially, Woodcock.

Recently refurbished to a high standard of comfort. All 18 bedrooms have en-suite shower or bathrooms, TV and tea/coffee making facilities. We offer a free use of the heated outdoor pool (May to September), sauna and solarium.

Tyn-y-Cornel Hotel
Tal-y-Llyn
Tywyn
Gwynedd
LL36 9AJ
Tel: 0654 782282
Fax: 0654 782679

WALES

hotels are part of a select group of establishments called Welsh Rarebits (0686) 668030 who have a marvellous selection of country house hotels throughout Wales.

The Coed-y-Brenin Forest reveals another fine place to visit; Dolmelynllyn Hall (034140) 273 in Ganllwyd. This is a delightful Victorian house restored to all its former glory set amidst some breathtaking scenery. Fishing can also be arranged by the hotel for their guests.

Although the sea-trout fishing may have declined somewhat recently it is still worthwhile, especially in North Wales. The River Dwyfawr and its environs offer a number of good establishments. Plas Bodegroes (0758) 612363 is one such example. A delightful restaurant with rooms await. A little north of busy Criccieth one finds Llanystumdwy, famous for its Lloyd George connections. Here, the Gwyndy (0766) 522720 is a place for you to consider when trekking through these parts. There are numerous lakes and sreams that one can fish and a charming hotel to shortlist is the Royal Goat Hotel at Beddgelert (076686) 224. A welcoming hotel amidst spectacular scenery in the heart of Snowdonia National Park. In addition to the views, the hotel is an ideal base from which to fish or enjoy all manner of other attractions. In Llanrug, midway between Caernarfon and Llanberis, we find yet another outstanding hotel, Seiont Manor (0286) 673366 in Snowdonia and with fishing in the grounds - a veritable haven for keen fishermen.

Although the Conwy (Conway) is not an easy river to fish it does offer several opportunities. Conwy itself is a busy resort with numerous hotels. However, it may be preferable to journey south through the majestic scenery of the Conwy Valley to find some fine brown trout waters and good hotels. A small establishment with first class catering is located in Trefriw. The Hafod House (0492) 640029 is a wonderfully rustic place to stay. Llanrwst also reveals a number of good hotels which overlook the valley. The Plas Maenan (049269) 232 is one such example while the Maenan Abbey (049269) 247 is an impressive hotel with pleasant gardens and some fishing rights on the Conwy.

In Betws-y-Coed, the Gwydyr (0690) 710777 has some excellent fishing and some good value mini-breaks can also be ar-

ranged. The centre of the village also reveals the Royal Oak Hotel (06907) 710219, a former coaching inn which stands on the River Llugwy. There is some good eating to be enjoyed here and comfortable accommodation.

Another riverside setting, on the Lledr this time, reveals Plas Hall (0690) 710206 - a really delightful place to stay. The Clwyd and Welsh Dee are other first rate rivers to visit, more gorgeous countryside and a number of pleasing dwellings in which to find accommodation. In St Asaphs, The Plas Elwy (0745) 582263 is a busy and popular hotel full of character, with a respected restaurant. In Ruthin, The Ruthin Castle (08242) 2664 has some 12 miles of fishing available and also boasts some fine grounds and facilities.

The Dee has some excellent fishing in the Llangollen area and there are some equally good hotels in which to stay. We would urge you to try Bodidris Hall (09788) 434, a really delightful place which has a trout lake and some first class shooting. Bryn Howel (0978) 860331 enjoys panoramic views of the Dee Valley and is a hotel which is thoroughly recommended to the game fisherman. Upstream in Glyndyfrdwy, one finds another fishing hotel of note; The Berwyn Arms (049083) 210 - good value and exceptionally welcoming. The Dee is a fine river and the Tyddyn Llan Country House Hotel (049084) 264 is a majestic place to make the most of it. The bedrooms are pleasant and the cuisine mouth-wateringly good - a perfect place to stay. At Pale Hall (06783) 285, in Llanderfel, near Bala, there are good fishing opportunities and some public rooms full of character at this baronial mansion.

These last two hotels and the spectacular waters of the Dee are a fitting way to conclude our brief journey through Wales. When you consider Wales, do not think of mines or rugby (both are really in the doldrums in the valleys). Instead, consider some superb fishing, marvellous scenery and a Welsh welcome to remember. Our recommended hotels are often outstanding in every way and therefore fairly pricey but there are numerous less expensive establishments not mentioned and the local tourist boards, as ever, will provide lists of bed and breakfast, guest house and self-catering accommodation, so always get in touch before you make up your mind. Whatever you decide, we wish you good sport in a delightful and relatively unspoilt country, a rarity in this day and age.

Tal-y-LLyn   (Tyn-y-Cornel Hotel)

WALES : FURTHER FORAYS

SOUTH AND MID WALES

ANGEL HOTEL ,
Castle Street, Cardiff, Tel: (0222) 232633
Few hotels can boast of such a location-in the heart of the Welsh Capital between the world famous Cardiff Arms Park and Cardiff Castle, minutes from the business centre and St. David's Hall. Restored with care, the Angel is again in it's place as Cardiff's premier hotel.

AUSTINS,
11 Coldstream Terrace, Cardiff, Tel: (0222) 377148
Austins is a small, friendly hotel situated in the centre of Cardiff, 200 yards from the castle. Most rooms are ensuite and the reasonable rates include a full English breakfast. A generous discount for readers is available.

BIKEREHYD FARM,
Pennant, Llanon Dyfed, Tel: (0974) 272365
This highly recommended guesthouse is peacefully set in its own farmland. Guests are comfortably housed in either the main house or in three adjacent cottages. A beautiful restaurant offers first-class food, and paves the way for a visit to one of many places of scenic and historical interest.

CASTLE VIEW HOTEL,
16 Bridge Street, Chepstow, Tel: (0291) 270349
Golf and racing enthusiasts staying at this hotel are really spoilt for choice. Chepstow racecourse is a mere stones throw away and the championship links of St Pierre only three miles distant. The Castle View is open all year round.

COURT HOTEL,
Lamphey, Pembroke, Tel: (0646) 672273
A huge range of sporting and leisure opportunities are offered at this excellent hotel. As well as special golfing breaks, guests can enjoy swimming, yachting, sauna, solarium and gym. Conference and wedding facilities are also available.

CROWN AT WHITERBROOK,
Whiterbrook, Monmouth, Gwent, Tel: (0600) 860254
Award winning cuisine is one feature of this comfortable hotel. Accommodation is also of a high standard and guests are always assured of a warm welcome. Racing and golf are among the many local attractions.

DRAGON HOTEL,
Montgomery, Powys, Tel: (0686) 668359
This popular hotel can provide both active and relaxing holidays to suit every taste. A wide range of facilities are available, including swimming, tennis and a well-equipped gym, whilst the surrounding countryside offers many scenic and historic attractions.

FLEECE HOUSE,
Market Street, Knighton, Powys, Tel: (0547) 520168
Originally an eighteenth century coaching inn, Fleece offers a genuine 'olde worlde' atmosphere that has been maintained despite extensive modernisation. Weekly and weekend golfing breaks can be arranged.

FOUNTAIN INN,
Trellech Grange, Chepstow, Gwent. Tel: (0291) 689303
The Fountain is a lovely old inn situated just off the Wye Valley in a designated Area of Outstanding Natural Beauty. Simple but comfortable accommodation is available, as well as excellent food and a fine selection of wines and beers.

GLASFRYN HOUSE,
Church Street, Llanfaes, Brecon, Powys, Tel: (0874) 623014
Guests are always welcome at this small, clean and friendly hotel that provides excellent value and personal attention. Set in the heart of The Brecon Beacons National Park, the surroundings are unforgettable.

HAMMONDS PARK HOTEL,
Narberth Road, Tenby, Dyfed, Tel: (0834) 2696
This family run hotel provides accommodation and service of a high standard. All rooms have TV and hospitality trays, and parking is available within the hotel grounds. A readers discount is available in winter for groups of eight or more.

HIGH HOUSE FARM,
Bryngwyn, Raglan, Gwent, Tel: (0291) 690529
Comfortable accommodation is available on this working farm. A convenient location makes it easy to reach and the surrounding countryside is quite delightful. Golf and fishing can be found nearby.

HIGH NOON GUESTHOUSE,
Lower Lamphey Road, Pembroke, Dyfed, Tel: (0646) 683736
This modern guesthouse is highly recommended and can offer several ensuite rooms. Golf are fishing are available nearby, as is the magnificent Pembrokeshire coastal path and beaches. A restaurant provides excellent fare.

HILDERBRAND HOTEL,
Victoria Street, Tenby, Dyfed, Tel: (0834) 2403
Tenby's championship golf course is only a short distance from this friendly hotel. Most bedrooms have private bathrooms and a dining room and lounge make for a comfortable and relaxing stay.

PARC LE BREOS HOUSE,
Parkmill, Gower, Swansea, Tel: (0792)-371636
A secluded and picturesque nineteenth century farmhouse, Parc le Breos offers an opportunity to enjoy local riding, ponytrekking, walking, golf, and the many facilities of nearby Swansea. A lounge and gamesroom are at the disposal of residents.

PENBONTBREN HOTEL,
Glynarthen, Cardigan, Dyfed, Tel: (0239) 810248
This comfortable hotel provides a range of comfortable accommodation and a high level of service. Disabled guests are welcome and the hotel can also be hired for weddings and conferences.

ROYAL OAK HOTEL,
The Cross, Welshpool, Powys , Tel: (0938) 552217
Accommodation is well-appointed and extremely comfortable at this highly recommended medium-size hotel. A restaurant serves fine cuisine and can also cater for weddings and conferences. A readers discount is available.

ST-Y-NYLL HOUSE,
St Brides, Super Ely, South Glamorgan, Tel: (0446) 760209
The comfort and elegance of a country house combine with first-rate service at St-Y-Nyll. Set in the vale of Glamorgan, it is surrounded by many places of interest, including its own extensive grounds. A beauty clinic is located on the premises.

STARCROSS GUESTHOUSE
Starcross Guesthouse 1 Archer Road Penarth Nr Cardiff Tel: (0222) 702718
The Starcross is an attractive Victorian house located in a quiet residential area. Excellent food includes the availability of vegetarian meals and home made bread. The atmosphere is always friendly and welcoming.

TY HEN FARM HOTEL AND COTTAGES
Ty Hen Farm Hotel and Cottages Llwyndafydd Near New Quay Tel: 0545 (560346)
A wealth of facilities are provided at this working sheep farm. Ensuite bedrooms are provided in the farm, together with luxury cottages, superb leisure centre, heated pool and restaurant and bar.

WALES : FURTHER FORAYS

NORTH WALES

BRYN DERWEN HOTEL,
34 Abbey Road, Llandudno, Tel: (0492) 76804
This highly recommended hotel will provide visitors with an uncommonly high level of service and care. Accommodation is comfortable and reasonably priced, with the food prepared by acclaimed chef S. Langfield consistently excellent.

DEUCOCH HOTEL,
Abersoch, Pwllheli, Gwynedd, Tel: (075) 881 2680
This highly recommended hotel features panoramic views, an excellent restaurant and a fine collection of malt whiskies. Golfing breaks can be arranged, including DBB and green fees at various local courses.

DOLMELYNLLYN HALL,
Ganllwyd, Dolgellar, Gwynedd, Tel: (034) 140273
Golf, fishing and Stately Hall fans are well catered for at this elegant Country House Hotel. Of particular local note are the castles of Erdigg and Powis, whilst the rivers Mawddach and Wnion are sure to keep eager anglers occupied.

EDELWEISS HOTEL,
Off Lawson Road, Colwyn Bay, Tel: (0492) 532314
A multitude of facilities are provided to suit all tastes at this well-established hotel. Features include swimming, tennis, sauna, solarium and squash. Disabled guests are also welcomed.

ELENS CASTLE HOTEL,
Dolwyddelan, Gwynedd, Tel: (0690) 6207
Elen's Castle Hotel dates back to the eighteenth century and has been transformed in recent years into an elegant private hotel. This is also an Angler's dream with fishing possible on river frontage owned by the hotel and a nearby lake leased for residents.

HAFOTY,
Rhostryfan, Caernarfon, Gwynedd, Tel: (0286) 830144
Hafoty is a comfortable farmhouse set in seventeen acres, overlooking Caernarfon with the nearest golf course only ten minutes drive. An oak-beamed lounge with an open fire provide a warm welcome and are complemented by excellent food.

LLYS LLYWELYN,
Trefriw, Nr Llanrwst, Gwynedd
Relax and enjoy an idyllic break in this comfortable old house, nestling in a pretty, village location at the foot of the Carneddau Mountains. The food here is renowned and is prepared using many local ingredients.

PLAS COCH HOTEL,
Bala, Gwynedd, Tel: (0678) 520
This hotel is popular with both locals and holidaymakers, offering as it does comfortable accommodation and a convivial atmosphere. An added enticement is free golf at the nearby Bala Club.

ST TUDNO HOTEL,
Promenade, Llandudno, Gwynedd, Tel: (0492) 874411
This award-winning hotel provides accommodation of the very highest calibre and is equally renowned for it's fine cuisine. Golf, fishing and various castles and homes are all within easy travelling distance.

STANTON HOUSE HOTEL,
Whitehall Road, Rhos-on-Sea, Tel: (0492) 44363
Colwyn Bay is an ideal centre for touring the wonderful scenery of North Wales and The Stanton House Hotel makes the ideal base. Facilities are agreeable and only a short walk away from the Promenade, shops, squash club and other amenities.

THE FAIRBOURNE HOTEL,
Fairbourne, Gwynedd, Tel: (0341) 250203
Good food is the order of the day at this popular hotel. Thoughtful service and a friendly atmosphere are always present, leaving ample time for golf, fishing, pony-trekking, climbing and canoeing. Pets are welcome.

THE OLD RECTORY,
Llanrwst Road, Llansnffraid, Glan Conwy, Tel: (0492) 580611
Tourists wishing an enjoyable holiday in a relaxing atmosphere will find this the perfect solution. The Georgian Country House offers panoramic vistas and a host of local facilities. Penrhyn Castle is a particular local favourite.

TYDDN PERTHI FARM,
Porftdinorwic, Gwynedd, Tel: (0248) 670336
Tyddyn Perthi is a family-run, working dairy farm situated between the historic town of Caernarfon and the University City of Bangor. There is much to see and do in this beautiful part of North Wales and guests will be made extremely welcome.

UNIVERSITY COLLEGE OF NORTH WALES,
Conference Office, Bangor, Gwynedd, Tel: (0248) 351151 Ex. 2561
Clean and comfortable accommodation is available from July to September in these Halls of residence. Each residence has a dining room and a multitude of university facilities are at the disposal of guests.

Llangammargh   (The Lake Country House)

THE SOUTH OF IRELAND

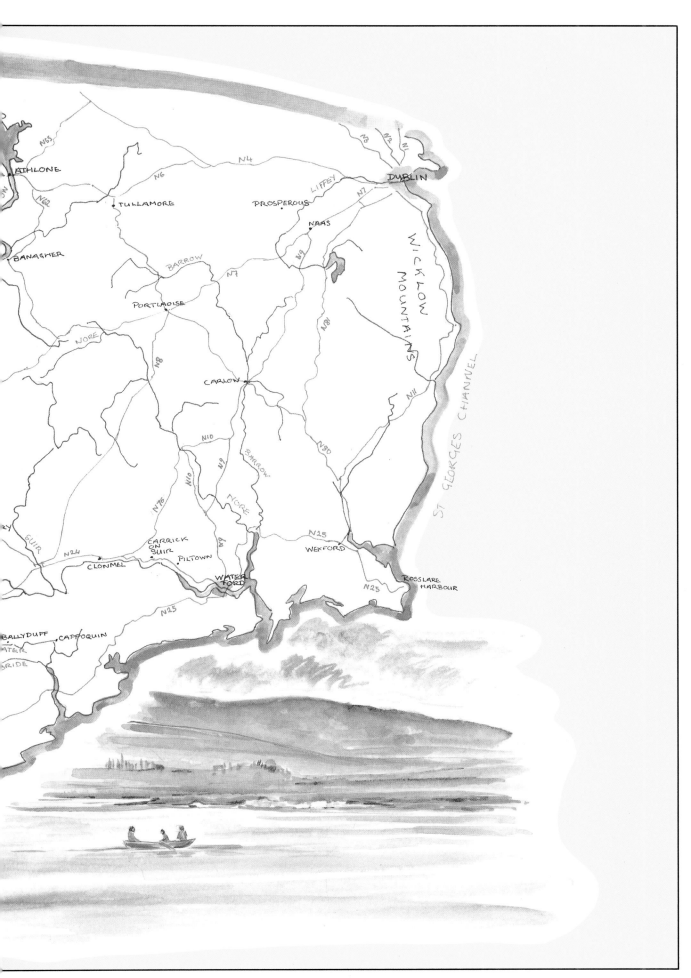

ATHLONE

N55

N6

N61

TULLAMORE

BANAGHER

BARROW

PORTLAOISE

NORE

N8

N8

CARLOW

N10

N9

N76

N10

N9

CARRICK ON SUIR

PILTOWN

N24

CLONMEL

SUIR

N25

BALLYDUFF

CAPPOQUIN

ATER

BRIDE

N4

N7

PROSPEROUS

NAAS

N9

N7

LIFFEY

N7

DUBLIN

N3

N2

N1

WICKLOW MOUNTAINS

N81

N11

BARROW

NORE

N80

N25

WEXFORD

WATER FORD

N25

ROSSLARE HARBOUR

ST GEORGES CHANNEL

233

IRELAND - AN INTRODUCTION

With 3,500 miles of coastline, 610,000 acres of lakes and 9,000 miles of fish-bearing rivers, it is not surprising that Ireland is regarded by many as an angler's paradise. The very high ratio of water to land (1 acre water: 35 acres land) is due to the structure of the country and the unusual nature of its surface. Broadly speaking it consists of a central plain of carboniferous limestone ringed almost completely by a coastal belt of highlands of varying geological structure. The streams which rise on the seaward slopes of the mountains are short and rapid offering ideal spawning ground for the migratory fish, namely the salmon and sea trout. The rivers whose sources lie on the inland side of the mountains have mostly long and devious courses and these waters hold mainly coarse fish.

The clean and unpolluted waters of Ireland have established it as a haven for the angler and the game fishing in particular is steeped in tradition. Within a narrow compass many areas can offer a variety of stillwater and river fishing at a cost that is always reasonable, and often remarkably so. Salmon, sea trout and brown trout are the most widespread species and rainbow and char are available in certain waters.

For the salmon angler there are opportunities to catch from New Year's Day to September 30th. The spring run brings in the larger fish of 10 to 20 pounds into the majority of the coastal rivers. With low temperatures and high water levels opportunities to fish with the fly can be restricted and spinning is the most productive method. It is generally April before the conditions become favourable for the fly angler. Towards the end of May the grilse, fish of around six pounds, enter the systems and what they lack in size, they certainly make up for in number. These fish predominate for the rest of the season and their willingness to rise to the fly makes them a firm favourite. Many anglers' first experience of hooking a salmon on fly has come from these hardy fighters. Salmon angling in Ireland is by no means restricted to the rivers and a large number of fish are taken every year from the loughs. Drifting from a boat with a cast of three flies is the most popular method but trolling is also employed.

The sea trout, or white trout as it is so often called in Ireland, can be found in most of the shorter coastal streams and their lakes, in particular along the west and south coasts. Some Kerry waters, especially the Waterville fisheries, offer the earliest opportunity with large sea trout up to nine pounds being taken as early as March. Most of these fish are taken on the troll with the fish starting to respond to the fly from May. Sport here can be as exciting as anywhere the angler is likely to have fished and each rise to the fly must be treated with respect as it can be a sea trout of one to eight pounds or even a salmon. The angler never knows until the last moment.

In the myriad of waters in Galway, Mayo and Donegal it is July before the fisheries come to life as the fish start to run into the many streams and rivers and into the loughs where the majority are caught. These fish average around the pound mark but two and three pounders are always a possibility. Sea trout fishing

Fishing in Ireland

IRELAND - AN INTRODUCTION

in the Connemara region has been suffering from reduced numbers of fish during the 1989/90 period but it is hopeful that things are now starting to improve although it is worth checking before making any final plans.

For the brown trout angler there is literally a fishery to suit his every need and requirement. The mighty loughs of the West coast such as Corrib, Mask and Conn offer a challenge that no committed angler can resist. The most popular method is traditional wet fly casting from a broadside drifting boat and fish of up to six pounds are taken every year with the average over a pound and a half. For the really big fish trolling is the best method. These are the ferox trout which live about 30 feet down and are primarily flesh eating. The Irish record stands at a staggering 26 pounds 2 ounces and although this record has stood for many years there are many double figure fish taken every season. Many anglers associate trout fishing in Ireland with the May Fly and the last week in May and first in June, labelled by some as 'Duffers Fortnight' can offer great fishing to even the most inexperienced. Before this, on offer is some early season sport with the Duck Fly, which hatches in most Irish lakes in early April and can certainly at times rival even the mighty May Fly sport.

As a change from lake fishing, Ireland's limestone rivers and streams are a joy to behold. These waters are very similar in character to the chalk streams of the south of England, producing trout between half a pound to three pounds in the main and larger fish on occasions.

For the angler who wishes the ultimate challenge, shark fishing is carried out along both the south and west coasts. The well equipped boats and helpful skippers can make a day afloat a memorable one. Most of the shark caught in Ireland are Blue shark, averaging about 60 pounds, but fish to over 100 pounds are a real possibility. Catches of ten or more fish a day are recorded throughout the summer months and the warmer and calmer the sea, the better the fishing becomes. In the interests of conservation, most fish caught are tagged and released. It is also possible to catch the larger Porbeagle shark and this can weigh up to 300 pounds.

There is one thing certain, however, that no matter where you fish or for what species, the Irish hospitality and the 'crack' in the evenings around the bar will ensure a memorable and enjoyable holiday.

For further information, contact The Irish Tourist Board, 151 New Bond Street, London W1Y OAQ, or their Angling Adviser - Paul Harris, Loveitts Farm, Brinklow, Near Rugby, Warwickshire CV23 OLG. Telephone: (0788) 833203

Licences. No licences are required for sea, coarse or brown trout fishing. A yearly State Rod licence is required for salmon and sea trout and this costs IR £25 for the entire country or IR £12 for one region.

River Blackwater   (Blackwater Lodge)

235

PARK HOTEL KENMARE

Welcome to a hotel of unrivalled charm, elegance and splendour. Welcome to the Park Hotel Kenmare. Step over the threshold and take a step back in time. Surrender to the gracious living of a forgotten age. Allow us to attend to your every need, let your senses succumb to the allure of our hospitality, commitment and dedication to service. From the moment you arrive we are ever-mindful of your individual desires and are unwavering in our resolve to fulfil them to your satisfaction.

Treat your eye to antiques from all over Ireland and Europe which create the magnificent furnishings in our guests bedrooms and the classical elegance of our dining room. Treat your palate to our innovative culinary delights from a cuisine judged among the highest in the land.

Spend your nights at the Park Hotel Kenmare, in comfort and splendour. Spend the day in outdoor pursuits of croquet, walking, tennis, golf or fishing - so rich and varied is the terrain of the Emerald Isle.

Based at Park Hotel Kenmare, you can choose to play golf at

Killarney's 36 holes - it's famous courses of Mahony's Point and the newer Killeen sited on the shore of the Lakes of Killarney -or at Waterville - one of the largest courses in Europe and one of the greatest golfing tests.

A little further afield is Ballybunion, a glorious links course on the Atlantic shore regarded as one of the world's best. Closer to home, adjacent to the hotel is an executive 9 hole course, ideal for our guests.

If fishing is more your line you are spoilt for choice. In the Rivers Waterville and Comeragh and lakes Currane and Caragh you can fish for trout and salmon in one of Ireland's most beautiful regions. In the stretch of water around Bearon Island, an angler can catch ray, conger, flatfish and dogfish. As this could entail boat-fishing the Park Hotel Kenmare would prepare your packed lunch.

The Park Hotel Kenmare bids you an eternal welcome.

Park Hotel Kenmare
Kenmare
Co Kerry
Ireland
Tel: (010 353 64) 41200
Fax: (010 353 64) 41402

THE EMERALD ISLE

Only the fifty miles of St George's Channel separate Ireland from mainland Britain, but it is a totally different country. Ireland has three great assets; its countryside, the Irish themselves and the fishing! Everyone has heard of the description 'The Emerald Isle'. Indeed, so often does the phrase crop up in advertisements and tourist brochures that you probably begin to wonder what the fuss is all about. Naturally, the only way to find out is to go there!

I well remember my first visit which was to stay with friends in Tipperary. My friends met me at Dublin and in a very short time we had passed the Curragh and were heading west. Fields of lush, emerald green pasture succeeded each other, broken only now and then by cornfields. The green really is of a much deeper and richer hue than that of its English counterpart. One of the big surprises is the lack of traffic. Even on the main roads it is a fraction of what we have to put up with and if you turn off onto one of the country roads you can drive for miles without seeing another car. Motoring is a real pleasure and you have ample opportunity to admire the magnificent scenery.

Villages and towns are on a smaller scale than in Britain, the cities too are comparatively smaller. The Irish have been conservation minded for a long time and the city of Dublin is a fine example of this. Many fine Georgian terraces had, by the 1950s, fallen into decay. Instead of pulling them down and erecting monstrous high-rise blocks, the Government has restored them and the modern buildings, such as they are, have been designed to fit in with their surroundings.

The Irish are justly renowned for their charm and hospitality. They are also famous for their love of sport. Horse racing is a passion for the Irish and everyone seems to know of a 'likely' horse. 'Likely' is a much used word and capable of many interpretations, as punters will know. Fishing is another sport which has a national following and the Irish are always keen to offer help and advice to the visiting angler.

I remember on one occasion being asked if I had fished Lough Corrib, some sixty miles away. Answering in the negative, I was assured that it would be a shame to return without having fished such a grand water. I thought no more about it and stumbled up to bed. However, at breakfast the next morning, my host announced that he had organised two days for me on the Corrib and would be coming too. We had a great two days during which I was introduced to the art of dapping and was lucky enough to return with some fine sea-trout.

I have received the same hospitality and friendship whenever I have gone fishing on my own. On one holiday, I stopped at a garage to fill up with petrol. When the proprietor noticed the rods in the back of the car he asked if I was there for the fishing. We got talking and he asked me if I could spare a day as he knew of a small lough which held some fine trout. The following day his son was left in charge of the garage and we set off. The lough was miles from anywhere and I would never have found it on my own. My new-found friend gave me some flies he had tied the previous evening which resembled no pattern I had come across - but did they work! Within an hour and a half we both had two brace of fine brownies, the best being over 4lb.

If this all sounds too good to be true, I know of many others with similar tales and urge you to go and try for yourself! If you

Delphi Fisheries   (Delphi Estate)

THE EMERALD ISLE

would prefer to explore Ireland on a more organised basis there are several excellent operators who can organise fabulous holidays: Gillaroo Angles (0232) 862419 and Rod and Stream plc. (0704) 501450; to name but two.

Please note that telephone numbers quoted for Northern Ireland are national and those quoted for Eire are international. To call a number in the south from the British Isles it is necessary to drop the '0' from the code and use the prefix: 010 353.

THE SOUTH OF IRELAND

DUBLIN AND THE EASTERN SEABOARD

Dublin City, its environs and the Counties Wicklow, Meath, Kildare and Louth make up the naturally beautiful Eastern Seaboard which leads down to the Irish Sea. Dublin Bay makes a glorious sweep northwards to Howth Head Peninsula, where there are spectacular views across the bay from the cliff walks, and southwards to the picturesque Dalkey, and its island with Benedictine ruins, then on to Killiney where it is said that the view south compares with that over Naples. The Georgian city of Dublin was the European City of Culture in 1991 and its heritage trail around the old medieval parts of the city allows the visitor an insight into the nature of the Irish and also gives them the opportunity to sample some of Ireland's more modern culture - in the pub! The Irish are world renowned for their hospitality and in Dublin you will not be disappointed. There is no such thing as a quiet pint in Ireland as you will inevitably be drawn into conversation by the entertaining locals.

With early Christian monuments scattered around the Boyne Valley to the north, the Newgrange burial chamber dating from 3000 BC, some fine stately homes and gardens at Kilruddery and Mount Usher to the south, there is much to see and do. To the west of the city is the 'mecca' for Ireland's other great passion - horseracing. Here, on the flat open plains of County Kildare, some of the best racehorses in the world are bred, trained and indeed, raced at the nearby Curragh.

The two principle rivers in the area are the Boyne to the north and the famous Liffey which flows through Dublin.

The River **Boyne** rises near Edenderry and flows for about seventy miles through County Meath to enter the sea near Drogheda, north of Dublin. Leave Dublin to the north-west, on the N2, where the imposing Slane Castle dates from 1785; the road from Dublin to the castle was supposedly straightened to hasten George IV's visits to his mistress! Here, we find the fine limestone fishery with good runs and some deep pools. Unfortunately, due to low water levels in 1990, few fish were taken but some large salmon were caught and this fishery really deserves a better reputation than it has. Once a river of note for salmon, the arterial drainage scheme has lowered the water table and this has effected the runs up river. Brown trout are prolific in certain areas and come to wet and dry flies as well as spinners and worms. However, the river does tend to 'weed up' from late July onwards. Sea-trout on the lower reaches are good in the autumn but generally the river is better known for its brownies. Local knowledge is absolutely essential and can be gleaned from any of the fourteen angling clubs or landowners who control the water.

In recent years, some of the best fishing has been between

Navan and Drogheda, with the lower stretches having good runs of grilse and sea-trout. The Kells Blackwater and Lough Ramor have also produced some good trout, averaging 2lb, especially during the mayfly hatch and in the evenings. The season runs from 1st February to 1st September for salmon and 1st March to 14th September for trout with permits priced at around IR£10 per day.

The Navan Anglers' Association, Abbey Road, Navan, has fourteen miles of mixed bank fishing with excellent wild brown trout, and both wet and dry fly fishing is permitted. Michael Connor is the man to contact for information on (046) 29007. Permits for the Navan Club Waters only are available from the Sports Den (046) 21130 in Tringate Street, Navan.

Drogheda and District Anglers control one mile of the tidal section near the town which is good for sea-trout, and three miles up river which is particularly good for brownies around mayfly time. Salmon can be caught here too depending on the height of the river. In addition, the Club controls the rights to two reservoirs at Killineer, fly-only fishing, and Bernattin, where you can use any method. Both are 'put and take' reservoirs and are stocked with brownies and rainbows. The club also have the rights for the nine mile long River Nanny nearby, well stocked with brown trout.

Sean Keenan, The Military Connections (army surplus and tackle shop) (041) 34371, 8 Lawrence Street, Drogheda, sells permits for the Drogheda Angling Waters and Shane and Rosslin Anglers' Association who have stretches of mixed bank fishing on the Boyne totalling two miles. These adjacent waters have a good mixture of deep pools and fast flowing waters with a couple of weirs. Sean Keenan will be happy to advise you as he fishes these waters himself.

The source of the River **Liffey** is around thirteen miles southwest of Dublin in the Wicklow mountains but it winds its way through Poulaphouca, Golden Falls and Leixlip Reservoirs before reaching the sea eighty miles away at Islandbridge. It is essential to check the river before beginning to fish as artificial floods do affect fly fishing and there are few salmon above Leixlip Bridge, while the lower stretches are much better.

The Liffey is controlled by the Federation of Liffey Angling Clubs, which co-ordinates all the club's fishing. The river is either club or privately owned with no free fishing anywhere on the eighty mile stretch. The season here runs from February to September with the best salmon fishing from February to April, and sea-trout and grilse from July to September. The first hatches of dark olives begin in late March, the hawthorn and iron blue dun in early May, mayfly in May and June and various sedges throughout the summer. The Clubs welcome visitors and the cost of a day's fishing is IR£4. The public relations officer of the Federation, Alistair McDonald (01) 6242179 reckons that Clane Anglers have a truly exceptional six mile stretch of mixed bank water as far as wild browns are concerned. All the clubs re-stock as necessary but overfishing is a problem and some restrictions now operate so it is best to check beforehand.

Dublin and District Angler's Association; Pat O'Molloy (01) 558594 at 16 Whitehall Crescent, Terenure, controls fisheries at St Raphaels, Celbridge, Avondale and Islandbridge. Rory at Rory's Tackle Shop (01) 772351, 17a Temple Bar, Dublin 2,

WATERFORD CASTLE

Built around the time of the Norman Invasion, Waterford Castle Hotel stands in splendid isolation on its own island off the south-east coast of Ireland.

The Island's private ferry provides the only access to the Hotel. Once there, guests will find rooms of supreme elegance and luxury and enjoy exceptional cuisine in the oak-panelled majesty of the Great Dining Room.

Keen anglers will find excellent fresh water fishing at the Knocktoffer Lake, where trout and various flatfish provide regular catches. Deep sea fishing 'off the hook' is also available less than five miles from the Island.

The Castle boasts its own leisure club which offers tennis, an indoor heated swimming pool, gymnasium and sauna, while horse riding and clay pigeon shooting can also be arranged.

In April, Waterford Castle Golf Course will be ready for play. Designers Des Smyth and Declan Branigan have used the natural undulations to fashion Ireland's first island course.

The Castle may be private, but it is not remote. Ryanair fly direct from Stansted to Waterford Airport, itself only ten minutes' drive from the Castle.

For tranquility and luxury coupled with a range of sporting activities, there is nothing quite as perfect as the Isle of Waterford Castle.

Waterford Castle - the Isle of the Castle
For further information and bookings, contact:
Geraldine Fitzgerald
Tel: (010 353 517) 8203
Fax: (010 353 517) 9316

KILCORAN LODGE

Set in 20 acres of beautifully lanscaped gardens, Kilcoran Lodge overlooks one of the most delightful parts of the River Suir Valley with the Distant peaks of the Knockmealdown mountains rising in the background. Originally built as the hunting lodge for the Earl of Glengal in the last century, Kilcoran now enjoys an enviable reputation as an impressive and welcoming hotel. The restaurant is particularly attractive, with spectacular views over the Knockmealdown mountains. The a la carte menu features a wealth of freshly caught local produce, and the chef is more than happy to look after any special wishes of his guests. Table d'Hote is also available for lunch and dinner.

For the serious fisherman, Kilcoran Lodge is perfect, being one of the renowned venues for trout and salmon fishing in County Tipperary and indeed in the whole of Ireland. The hotel has nine miles of fishing on the River Suir and eight on the Aherlow, both only a short drive away. The famous Blackwater can be fished by arrangement.

For a fascinating break from fishing, Kilcoran is ideally placed to enjoy some of the most stunning scenery in the country. Beautiful walks will carry the visitor to the medieval castle at nearby Cahir, or to Cashel and its ancient Priory, or to spectacular views at the Mitchelstown caves, all only minutes away. There are three attractive golf courses close by and pony trekking is also well worth organising for it provides a visit to the slopes of the Galty Mountains.

If you are feeling in need of a rest after the great outdoors, the hotel has an indoor heated swimming pool, jacuzzi, sauna and solarium in its newly completed Leisure Centre.

There are 25 rooms in Kilcoran, all have ensuite bathrooms, colour television with video channel, radio, direct-dial telephone, tea/coffee making facilities, trouser press and hair dryer.

Kilcoran Lodge
Cahir
Co. Tipperary
Eire
Tel: (010) 35352 41288
Fax: (010) 35352 41994

fishes all over Ireland and is also a member of the North Kildare Trout and Salmon Association. He is happy to advise on the Liffey and elsewhere. The North Kildare Association have around thirty miles of mainly double bank fishing stretching from Millicent Bridge to Kilcullen with good salmon in September and an excellent stretch for trout near Millicent Bridge. Tom Walshe, also a member of North Kildare, can be contacted at John Cahill & Sons (045) 79655, and is happy to offer advice on all matters.

Dublin Trout Anglers' Association have fisheries at Clane and Straffan and contact should be made with Mr J. R. Miley (01) 902163. Also, Dan O'Brien, New Road, Blackhall and Sye Gallagher, Reeves, Straffan, both County Kildare, can provide you with day permits. Tom Deegan (01) 980222 of the Ballymore Estate Anglers' Association also controls some stretches in this area. Leixlip Angler's have a good salmon pool but it tends to be very heavily fished. Garnetts and Keegans in Dublin can supply you with all the necessary tackle.

THE SUNNY SOUTH EAST

The River **Suir** runs through one of four picturesque river valleys that wind their way to the sea; the Suir, the Barrow and the Nore at Waterford and the Slaney at Wexford. This is the sunny south east corner of Ireland with long stretches of sandy beaches along the south coast. It is the home of the world famous Waterford crystal and is one of the most beautiful areas of the country. Of great historical importance, the National Heritage Park at Wexford traces the history of man and here we find the medieval Kilkenny with the imposing castle on the bank of the Nore.

The Suir has some of the finest trout fishing in the country for virtually its entire 130 mile length, from its source on Devils Bit Mountain near the border of County Tipperary and County Offally to Carrick on Suir where it meets tidal waters. A 57lb salmon was taken here in 1874 but unfortunately, today the average weight for fish taken here is around 7lb and trout are far more abundant than salmon. The season runs from March to September with fine fly fishing in May, June and September. The Suir is a rich limestone river with several shallow and deep glides, only occasionally interspersed with shallow riffles. At Templemore, where the river is about fifteen feet wide, many trout are taken at around the 2lb mark.

Downstream from Thurles, the River Drish joins the Suir near Turtulla Bridge where Michael Mockler (0504) 22493 is Secretary of the Thurles, Holycross and Ballycamas Anglers' Association. There is some free fishing on this stretch where good trout are taken and further information on the best water can be gleaned from the locals here who are only too happy to offer help and advice. Further downstream, Ardmayle House (0504) 42399 is four miles west of Cashel on the L185 and has one mile of double bank fishing which is free to guests staying at this comfortable hotel. The water is quite slow in parts here and deep, but good for brownies. The owners can also organise fishing on other stretches both up and downstream.

At Camas Bridge, the river becomes wide and shallow with some spring salmon. The grilse run is in July and August. The Cashel Golden and Tipperary Anglers' Club control both banks up to the delightful Suir Castle and share the west bank to New Bridge with the Cahir and District Anglers' Association. Permits

are available to fish this peaceful and secluded stretch set in beautiful rolling green countryside from Breeda Morissey at Morissey's Bar (052) 41516. Permits can also be obtained from Breeda for the Ara and Aherlow tributaries. The bar is a favourite haunt for many fishermen and is an excellent place to pick up good local tips as well as to hear some very entertaining stories.

Downstream from Cahir, fly fishing only is the rule. The waters here are shallow and free flowing as they glide under the walls of the beautiful Cahir Castle standing on the banks of the River Suir. Good stocks of trout are found in this pretty stretch of water. Kilcoran Lodge (052) 41288, set in twenty acres of landscaped gardens on the slopes of the Galtee Mountains, has a nine mile stretch of the Suir and eight miles on the Aherlow.

In the beautiful Knockmealdown Mountains, the Shanbally and Duag join forces to form the River Tar with good sized trout found in the deeper pools. The Tar enters the Suir upstream from Newcastle, but for much of its length the fishing is free and also readily accessible as the river runs close to the main road to the west of Newcastle. The Ardfinnan Anglers' Club do control some of the Suir around this area and contact should be made with John Maher (052) 66242, the Club Secretary, Green View, Ardfinnan (the corner house beside Maher's Foodstore).

The bubbling, fast flowing River Nire winds its way from the Nire lakes through treelined glens and enters the Suir downstream from the town of Newcastle. The river varies in width from between fifteen to fifty feet and contains a good stock of brown trout. All legitimate methods of fishing are allowed here. As the Nire enters the Suir it widens to forty yards and comprises fast flowing shallows interspersed with long glides. Frans Beckers (052) 36433 and Eileen Ryan (052) 36141 control a four mile stretch of water on the Suir and seven miles on the Nire. Fishing here is fly only and the cost for a day ticket is IR£5 for brown trout and IR£10 for salmon. As if proof were needed that this glorious part of Ireland was attractive to overseas visitors, Jean Loup Trautner of the Marlfield Fisheries (052) 25234 has an answering message in French!

Downstream from Clonmel, the Rivers Anner, Clashawley and Moyle meander peacefully through the Tipperary countryside past Anner Castle, to enter the Suir upstream from Kilsheelin. The Glencastle Fishery's water (052) 33287 is one and a half miles long and is very well stocked to provide some of the best fishing on the Suir with deep pools and gentle glides, although it is barely two miles upstream from tidal waters. Fly fishing only is the rule and day tickets can be purchased for IR£5. Mrs Long organises self-catering accommodation right on the river - perfect for a fishing holiday.

At Carrick-on-Suir, in a spectacular setting lodged between the Slievenamon Hills and the rolling slopes of the Comeraghs with their small mountain loughs, there is good salmon and trouting on what has become a splendid stretch from the Devils Bit Mountain.

From its source in the Killarney Mountains near the Cork border with County Kerry, the **Munster Blackwater**, sometimes referred to as the 'Irish Rhine', meanders slowly eastwards through the scenic Blackwater Valley before turning sharply south at Cappoquin to enter the sea at Youghal Bay through an estuary which stretches for fifteen miles. This is probably the

THE EMERALD ISLE

most famous salmon river in Ireland and consistently provides fishermen with excellent sport and excitement. (This great river has to be fished - even if it is the last thing you do.)

The salmon and sea-trout season begins on 1st February and brown trout on the 15th February and runs until the 18th September. Sea-trout tend not to go up the main river but rather swim up the River North Bride, although they may occasionally be caught in the tidal section of the Blackwater River. The river runs through some twenty five miles of the most beautiful countryside from its source, to be joined by the Rivers Dalau and Allow at Kanturk. Salmon predominate these waters with good brown trout in the tributaries and permits are available from John O'Sullivan (029)50257 at the Tackle Shop in Kanturk. The Assolas Country House (029) 50015 is an elegant manor house set on the banks of the river . This family run establishment, near to Kanturk, has a well known restaurant where the Bourkes use freshly prepared local produce. The hotel can organise fishing for their guests on the nearby Blackwater and you should contact Mr Bourke for further information. Downstream, there are more good stretches of salmon fishing, some of which is free, but details on the waters are available from Dick Willis (022) 21057 at the Bridge House Bar in Mallow. Day tickets for this six mile stretch are priced at IR£7 for brown trout and IR£10 for salmon if the water level is high enough.

Blackwater Castle (022) 26333 is an imposing 12th century fort, built to protect the Holy St Patrick's Well which stands high above the Awbeg River at Castletownroche in County Cork. It provides excellent accommodation and has a fine gourmet restaurant. The Castle can also offer guests fishing on the Awbeg in one of the most scenic parts of the Blackwater Valley.

The Careysville Fishery, three miles downstream from Fermoy, consists of two miles of double bank fishing with good pools and provides some of the most productive beats in Ireland. There is an excellent run at the start of the season below the Weir, with good salmon fishing throughout the fishery until May. June sees the grilse run, with good catches taken downstream peaking in July. The fishing remains good throughout the latter part of the season. The average weight in recent years for salmon has been 10lb with some rare fish weighing as much as 50lb. Details for the fishery can be obtained from the Estate Office, Lismore Castle, County Waterford (058) 544244, who also sell sea-trout and brown trout permits. The Ballymaquirk Fishery run by Julie O'Conner at Greybrook House, Waterfall, County Cork, has a good stretch of water upstream from Mallow. Peter Dempster Ltd. (058) 56248 in Conna has approximately nine miles of fishing for clients and prices vary between IR£20-27 per rod per day. Tackle and tuition are also available. The Blackwater Lodge Fishery (058) 60235 at Upper Ballyduff is a high yielding stretch with over thirty miles in total downstream from Ballygarrett near Mallow. Again, there is a good spring run of salmon in February and March and the grilse run starts in May and peaks in July. The autumn run in late August and September generally sees some heavier fish. In recent years 1,500 fish have been taken in a season, up to 25lb in weight. The most popular methods have proved to be spinning and worms. Permits are available at a cost of IR£15 to IR£25 per day and ghillies can also be arranged through the Lodge. The Blackwater Lodge is owned and run by Ian Powell who is happy to advise all his guests on one topic - fishing! The Lodge stands on the south bank of the Blackwater in an ideal location for the fisherman.

GLENCASTLE FISHERY

Legend says that Cuchalain raced suitors to the summit of a mountain to win his wife's hand. The Glencastle Fishery rests by the slopes of this myth enshrouded Mount Slievenamon, meaning 'Mountain of Women', surrounded by the beautiful scenery of the Tipperary plains and backed by the foothills of Coneragh. The fishery is one and a half miles long and boasts some of the most exciting and varied fishing available on the famous River Suir. An angler's paradise it still holds those fast eddies, and deep pools where the watching fish can lurk unknown.

The fishery is only a short drive from two major airports and within five miles of a number of graded hotels and many approved bed-and-breakfast establishments. Self-catering accommodation is available on the river and the fishery owner is more than happy to help travelling anglers arrange somewhere to stay.

The waterfalls and weirs that the river travels through tend to oxygenate the water, breaking it into exciting pools and ripples, ideal habitat for the atlantic salmon and native brown trout, just waiting for the keen and skilful angler. Many areas of the fishery can be waded and the usual array of fishing tackle is applicable. Spinning for salmon is particularly good throughout the season and fly can produce some applaudable results.

Glencastle Fishery
Glencastle House
Kilsheelan
Clonmel
Co Tipperary
Ireland
Tel: (010 351 52) 33287

SHEEN FALLS LODGE

Discover the charming village of Kenmare along the coastal peninsula of Ireland's South West and you will come upon the luxurious Sheen Falls Lodge.

The Lodge nestles against a background of hazy mountain panoramas and overlooks the Falls of the Sheen River as they tumble dramatically into the Kenmare Estuary.

Sheen Falls Lodge is all you could possibly dream of in a gracious country hotel as it stands amid 300 acres of lawn, semi tropical gardens restored to their 17th century glory, green pastures and forests. We invite you to golf on any of six golf courses within a 40 mile radius of Kenmare.

Sheen Falls Lodge exclusively owns the fishing rights on a 15 mile stretch of the Sheen River, which is famed for its salmon and sea trout.

Guests of the hotel fish the river free of charge. Rods are available on request. Ghillies can also be arranged on a daily basis.

Other facilites include a conference centre, health and fitness centre, horseback riding along wooded trails, tennis and croquet.

Sheen Falls Lodge
Kenmare
Co. Kerry
Ireland
Tel: (010 353 64) 41600
Fax: (010 353 64) 41386

CRUTCH'S COUNTRY HOUSE HOTEL

Crutch's Country House Hotel has become renowned both in Ireland and further afield as a haven of tranquillity, situated among some of the most glorious scenery imaginary.

Originally a titled gentleman's hunting lodge, with Captain Padget, Le Marchant and Lord Harrington among its former owners, Crutch's has been transformed into a friendly, modern hotel without sacrificing its atmosphere of charm and elegance. Under the caring and astute management of Ron and Sandra MacDonnell, the hotel offers its many visitors a tempting combination of genuinely warm hospitality and every single convenience that could be expected of a modern hotel.

Located near Fermoyle Beach on the Dingle Peninsula, Crutch's has twenty four bedrooms complete with private bathrooms and a fully licensed bar/lounge and restaurant. For those seeking a greater degree of independence, two self catering cottages are available on the hotel grounds. Each cottage has two bedrooms, bathroom with toilet, bath and shower, lounge with open fireplace and a fully equipped kitchen.

One of the undoubted highlights of a stay at Crutch's is the home cooking prepared by Sandra MacDonnell. Locally grown produce-free of additives-is used wherever possible and the results are truly to be savoured. Main courses range from fresh grilled salmon steaks to delicious sea trout with Irish coffee ice cream providing a fitting finale.

The surrounding coast and countryside provide a wealth of things to see and do. Anglers will find the Owenmore river less than a fifteen minute drive from the hotel. This is a natural salmon and sea trout river, and fish of ten and fifteen pounds are not uncommon. Fishing permits and deep sea fishing can all be arranged through the hotel.

For golf enthusiasts, the Kerry coast has few equals. The Championship links of Ballybunion and Killarney are less than an hour away whilst nearby Tralee offers a challenging course with wondrous views. The newly developed Castlegregory golf and fishing club, meanwhile, is just five minutes from the hotel. Other leisure opportunities that can be enjoyed whilst at Crutch's include day trips, walking, boat trips, windsurfing and riding. Such variety, combined with the comforts of a well-established hotel and some wonderful cooking make a visit to Crutch's an experience not to miss.

Crutch's Country House Hotel
Fermoyle Beach,
Dingle Peninsula
Co. Kerry,
Ireland
Tel: (010 353) 66 38118
Fax: (010 353) 66 38159

GLENCAR HOTEL

For two hundred years now the Glencar Hotel has been providing its own brand of warmth and open hospitality. Framed by 3000 feet of Macgillycuddy's Reeks - Ireland's highest peaks - it rests in the heart of Co Kerry, probably the most charming and delightful of Irish landscapes.

Near the banks of the River Caragh, the hotel is perfect for the ardent salmon angler. As one of Ireland's best salmon rivers it is not surprising that it yields up hundreds of them every year for guests who fish the twelve and a half miles of running water and three loughs that the hotel owns sole rights to. All the pools have easily accessible banks, and cabins for rest and shelter. For an interesting variation, seven rowing boats with outboard motors are always ready. Drying rooms and workshop are maintained by the hotel, complete with scales and deep-freezing facilities. A ghillie, expert with fish flies, is always on hand to help and offer advice, and ladies with a guest angler can fish free of charge.

The beauty of the surrounding countryside offers stunning beauty enriched by the natural serenity. Hill walking and climbing, golfing and pony-trekking all offer themselves to the guest in search of quiet relaxation.

The hotel itself is ready to meet the expectations of the discerning traveller and angler. Most of its bedrooms have their own bathroom and the comfort continues down into the lounge and dining-room, where the excellent kitchen serves superb cuisine. Afterwards, why not retire to the bar and have a Guinness or a whisky by the open fire, with the possibility of live Irish music.

With this degree of welcome, everything arranged by the management, and only a short drive from a couple of major airports, it's hard to imagine a better place for the visitor to really make his time his own.

Glencar Hotel
Glencar
Co. Kerry
Ireland
Tel: (010 353 66) 60102
Fax: (010 353 66) 60167

THE EMERALD ISLE

THE GULF STREAM COAST

Counties Cork, Limerick and Kerry, with their warm gulf breezes provide a conducive climate for exotic and sub-tropical species of plants and vegetation. To the west of the area lie picturesque river valleys contrasting with the mountain ranges, deep loughs and rugged coastline.

In Cork itself, lies the famous Blarney Castle and Stone. One kiss and you're immediately bestowed with the Irish gift of the gab!

The River **Lee** drains Gouganebarra Lake and flows fifty three miles to Cork Harbour through rugged mountains and rolling moorland, through two large dams used to create hydro-electric power. There is a feeling amongst the locals that the introduction of the dams has had a detrimental effect on the fishing here, but not everyone shares this view. However, game fishing on the Lee now seems to be concentrated on the seven miles or so between the dams and the city of Cork. The salmon season runs from February to the end of September. Mid-March is the best time for spring fish and September fishing is also good, if the water levels are right. The trout season runs from 15th February to 12th October and licences are not required. Although more noted for its salmon, the Lee is also a first class trout stream. Anglers should contact the local angling clubs as there are voluntary restrictions operating with regard to the minimum length (seven inches) and size of catch.

The South Western Regional Fisheries Board (026) 41221 in County Cork can advise you on where to fish and will also issue you with some useful local maps. Immediately below the dam is the Inniscarra Fishery, controlled by the Board, which consists of three quarters of a mile of double bank fishing, noted for its spring fishing and grilse run in June and July. Both spinning (Yellow Belly or Toby) and fly fishing (Hairy Mary or Shrimp) have proved very successful in recent years. The Board's fisheries are manned by keepers and bailiffs and permits can be obtained from the fishery. However, advance booking is strongly advised. The Lee Salmon Anglers (021) 342511 (Brendon O'Flaherty) have about three miles of the lower River Lee, below the dam, and sell daily and weekly tickets at IR£10 and IR£40 respectively. The Cork Salmon Anglers (021) 872137 (John Buckley) also have about three miles of mixed bank fishing here, with several salmon pools on their stretch. Day tickets cost IR£10 and can be obtained from the very helpful Mr Buckley at T.W. Murray and Co. (021) 271089 in Cork. There is also free fishing from the footpaths along the river above Waterwork's Weir.

Downstream, the Lower Lee Fishery at Thomas Davis Bridge (also a Fisheries Board stretch) is one and a half miles of water with a fine, deep pool which is best fished around high tide with shrimp or prawn. The Tackle Shop, Lavitts Quay (021) 272842 will take bookings and give advice on all other matters regarding the fishing here.

Rising some fifty miles to the west, the River **Bandon** flows through this beautiful part of County Cork to enter the sea at Kinsale. The season for salmon and trout on the Bandon runs from the 15th February to 30th September and a permit here costs IR£10 per day. February through to May are considered the best months for salmon, especially if it rains, and there are reasonable runs in August and September. Sea-trout and grilse

run in June and brown trout fishing is good all season.

From just below Cork, down to the coast, the river becomes tidal and so the fishing is largely free. However, it is advisable to check locally beforehand. Mr Lee (023) 41178 at the Saddlers and Tacklelists in Cork regularly fishes the river and is very happy to advise you on the appropriate flies to use. Michael O'Regan (023) 41674 of Bandon Anglers' Association controls eight miles of double bank fishing on the Lee. Contact him directly for further information.

David Lamb (023) 47279 at Kilcoleman Fishery in Enniskeane can arrange self-catering accommodation in a lodge or part of a larger house, with one rod included in the accommodation fee. The brownies here are excellent. Accommodation is also available at Blandfield House (021) 885167 which has access to a mile of single bank fishing on the Bandon with good salmon in February and August.

Peter Wolstenholme (023) 46239 is a member of Bandon Anglers and part of a group known as the Argideen Anglers Ltd. who control the rights on the Argideen river, a fourteen mile long tributary of the Bandon. The Argideen is rated in the top three rivers in the country for sea-trout. The river's best periods are when the water is low, so if the Bandon is low and salmon not forthcoming, switch to the Argideen.

Mr Wolstenholme has a Tourist Board approved cottage for just IR£30 per week which sleeps four or five people. He is also buiding a lodge on the banks of the river which should be ready for the 1992 season.

The Innishannon Hotel (021) 775121 owns eight miles of the tidal Bandon and fishing is free for guests and within the hotel's own grounds. The hotel also has access to five miles of water controlled by Bandon Anglers' Club. Trout is fly-only and fishing here is best from June to the end of the season. Any legal method is permitted for salmon.

Several small salmon rivers, principally the Roughty and the Sheen, discharge into the Kenmare river and its deep lough where the spectacular coastline and picturesque valleys are a delight. March is the best time for spring salmon with grilse starting their run in July and August.

The Sheen Falls Lodge (064) 41600 in Kenmare is situated on the River **Sheen** and the hotel enjoys seventeen and a half miles of water which is reserved for residents only and the fishing is free. The fishing is limited to fifteen rods per day with ghillies also available from the hotel. The two mile stretch immediately adjacent to the hotel is the best stretch for salmon. Mr Jan O'Hare (064) 41499 runs an electrical shop in Kenmare's Main Street but he is more than willing to give interested parties a guided tour of the local fishing - by phone! He also sells tackle, licences and permits for a one and a half mile stretch of the River **Roughty** belonging to Artully Castle Salmon Fishery (064) 41447 run by Michael Harrington, just five miles outside Kenmare on the Code Road. The river is about fourteen miles long and the stretch owned by the Artully Club have some fabulous holding pools. Much of the river runs through open farmland and permission must be obtained from the local farmer or landowner. There is also some good sea-trout here but few brown trout in the Roughty or the Sheen.

THE EMERALD ISLE

Lough Currane in County Kerry, often referred to as Waterville Lake, is linked to the sea by the short Waterville river. The lake is generally considered to be one of the best game fishing loughs in the country. Near to the village of Waterville, it yields more sea-trout than any other fishery in the country, usually over 3000 each year with some of the fish weighing over 10lb. A few years ago sea-trout numbers were down. The Waterville Anglers' Association began some extensive work cleaning up spawning grounds, putting new gravel down and with the new salmon hatchery up and running, there is much less pressure on the sea-trout for spawning beds. Hence, whilst the west of Ireland and most of the British Isles are experiencing a catastrophic reduction in numbers of sea-trout, Currane was having an excellent season in 1991. The best fishing is from May to the end of the season in mid October. In addition to the sea-trout, however, there is excellent spring salmon from January through until June and the average weight is 10lb. The grilse run in the lough is best in July and August. It is an excellent water for the beginner and expert alike and the fishing is free except for the cost of your State Licence. Boats may be hired through the Waterville Anglers' Association. Michael O'Sullivan (0667) 4255 is more than happy to offer advice on the waters in the area and he can be found at The Lobster Bar and Restaurant in the centre of Waterville. There is also a Waterville Hotel (0667) 4310, now owned by Club Med which testifies to the area's popularity with European visitors. Possibly one of the best known hotels in Ireland, the Butler Arms Hotel (0667) 4156 looks out over the Atlantic. The Huggards provide a warm welcome to all guests and keen anglers are able to make use of the hotel's four privately owned lakes set high in the mountains where boats and fishing are free to guests. The hotel will also arrange ghillies on request. Non-residents are charged IR£20 per day for fishing which includes a boat. The hotel will also be happy to arrange a day's salmon fishing on the River Inny at a cost of IR£10.

Lough Namona, connected to the Currane by the Cummeragh River, it holds a good stock of brownies but is fished for the large sea-trout, as is Cloonaghlin Lough. Also part of this system, is Derriana Lough set high amidst the most spectacular scenery and fishes well for salmon, sea-trout and brown trout which are taken from the bank. Towards the end of the season, you must try the Coppal Lough which drains into the Currane at the east shore via the Coppal river. If you are not staying at the Butler Arms permission will be required for these four loughs.

Driving north-east across country from Waterville will bring the intrepid fisherman to another great Irish lough - **Caragh**. Set at the mouth of the magnificent Glencar Valley, Caragh is often called 'Glencar Lake' and is noted for its spring salmon and grilse. For some unexplained reason the fly is not a method often used and most salmon are caught towards the southern end of the lough on the troll or by spinning. Sea-trout are caught from July and, historically, the best area has been around the mouth of the outflowing Lower Caragh. Brownies are small but on light tackle the sport is very thrilling. Fishing is free and for boats and boatmen contact the Glencar Hotel (066) 60102 which owns Loughs Acoose, Cloon and Reagh. Acoose will provide a great day for the trout fisherman who might find himself battling it out with a small salmon. The trout are small but quite free rising and many a local lad has been 'broken-in' on this water.

The River **Caragh** completes the system flowing north into

Dingle Bay. Mr Pat O'Grady (066) 68228 has been fishing this corner of Ireland for years and is very happy to advise newcomers to the area. He also issues permits for two miles of double bank fishing on the Lower River Caragh; some private boats on the nearby River Laune; and day tickets for some rainbow stocked lakes. Mr O'Grady lives 600 yards outside Glenbeigh on the Killarney road. His house is called 'Ferndale Heights'. The Glencar Hotel (066) 60102 has a good seven miles of double bank fishing on the Upper Caragh costing between IR£160-260 per week. After July 1st, day tickets are available for IR£22. The hotel is owned by a Swiss-German partnership and bookings made during the season are handled by Mrs Doppler in Küssnacht, Switzerland (01- 910) 3662. Bookings made out of peak season are done directly through the hotel. Salmon are from 1st February to mid-July.

Wild brown trout, sea-trout and Atlantic salmon lie in the rivers and lakes of the Shannon region, which comprises the Counties of Clare, Tipperary, West and South-west Offaly, Limerick and North Kerry.

The River **Shannon** is the largest, longest river in Ireland and Great Britain. It stretches from its source three miles south of Blacklion, running for two hundred and twenty miles through central Ireland to enter the Atlantic via a very long estuary.

Mainly a slow running, limestone river with an abundance of weed and insect life, the active fishery management have, to a large degree, rescued the river from the devastating effects of an hydro-electric scheme introduced in the 1940s.

South of the Shannon estuary and Limerick lies County Limerick and North Kerry. Numerous rivers and loughs enter the estuary with the productive River Feale often yielding over 3,000 fish each season. The Loobagh and Camogue join the River Maigue which enters the estuary west of Limerick, with good stocks of brown trout.

Bunratty Castle stands on the banks of the Bunratty River at the river's estuary and there is some easy fishing from the river banks with sea- trout best in June and July.

Chris Meehan (061) 361555 at Shannon Development, Shannon Town Centre, County Clare, controls the fishing in the Shannon region and is very helpful with up to the minute information about the state of the river and the best stretches to fish.

At 22 miles long, **Lough Dergh** is the largest lake on the Shannon with the best trout fishing during the mayfly season which can start as early as the end of April. Dapping is popular here. Artificial flies such as the Spent Gnat and Grey Wolff are popular, with trout averaging 2lb although much larger fish are regularly caught. Historically, Derg was one of the great trout fisheries but has not lived up to its reputation of late. However, many anglers still make the pilgrimage during the mayfly season. This is a large lough and a boat is something of a necessity. There are boats available from points all around the lough and Chris Meehan will be able to give you a contact for wherever you wish to fish.

South Offaly and North Tipperary stretches from the River Brosna, with its small run of spring salmon and good grilse in early July, to Limerick in the south. Contact Jim Robinson (061)

THE EMERALD ISLE

414900/377666 at his shop in Limerick or Castleconnell for licences, permits, ghillies and boat hire. The best salmon fishing is on the Lower Shannon at Plassy where a day's fishing will cost IR£10. You will also find good salmon on the Mulcair, a twenty mile spate tributary at Castleconnell where the 'salmon are fabulous' and the season extends from March 1st to the end of September.

Elsewhere on the Shannon, the season starts on February 1st for salmon and February 15th for trout, ending on September 30th. Jim Robinson can also arrange private beats at Castleconnell and boats on his own trout fishery - stocked with browns and rainbows at the 55 acre Lough Bleach.

The Fisheries Office, E.S.B. Hydro Group, Ardnacrusha, near Limerick (061) 345588 and The Limerick Sports Store, 10 William Street (061) 345647 can make all the necessary arrangements for anglers around Parteen, Plassey, Castleconnell and the Mulcair.

Good trout fishing is possible at Killaloe, especially during May and in the autumn. This is where Lough Derg drains into the Shannon and the people to contact are McKeogh's in Ballina (061) 376249.

Shannon Region Fisheries re-stock Pallas lake, eighteen miles east of the river, with rainbow and brown trout. Here, the season starts late on the 1st May and runs until the 12th October with good bank fishing. Further information is available from Jim Robinson.

Lough Ree, 25,000 acres, at Athlone, is stocked with trout by the local angling association and good trout fishing is available here in June. Through County Roscommon, Longford and Leitrim is Lough Allen, the most northerly lake on the Shannon where large trout and pike are often taken. This is, in fact, a reservoir supplying Limerick's power station and the water levels rise and fall to leave dangerous rocks exposed.

The Shannon Regional Fisheries Angling Centre (049) 36144 overlooks Chambers Bay on **Lough Sheelin**. Reached by heading north east from Granard on the M55 and following the small signpost. Take the turning off to the right towards the lake shore which serves Mullaghboy Guest House, Kilnahard Boat Quay and the angling information centre. Sheelin is one of the great Irish limestone loughs with a high-pH ensuring a rich stock of natural food for the sizeable and excellent quality trout. In fact, fishery scientists have estimated that the lake has the greatest trout carrying capacity in Ireland and supports approximately 100,000 trout! Crover House (049) 40206 sits on the northern shore providing fine views down the lough and has excellent accommodation. This 200 year old manor house is run by the friendly O'Reilly family. Set in 90 acres, this hotel has its own airstrip and a boat pier with fifteen boats and ghillies available. A permit costs just IR£5 for a season from the angling information centre and the fishery officers can give you all sorts of useful advice. Please ring first before you go.

BUTLER ARMS HOTEL

Butler Arms Hotel, overlooking the Atlantic Ocean on the Beautiful South West Coast of Ireland, is one of Ireland's best known family hotels and the holiday retreat for Charlie Chaplin and his family for many years. It has been owned by the Huggard family for over 70 years and offers guests an intimate homely atmosphere. There are 26 bedrooms all en suite, many with seaviews overlooking beautiful Ballinskelligs Bay. The recently renovated fishermen's restaurant is renowned for locally caught seafood as well as succulent steaks and Kerry Lamb. You won't find a better atmosphere than in the Olde Worlde Fishermens' Bar with many stories of the day's catch or the 'ones that got away'. Salmon and sea-trout fishing and Waterville have been synonymous for generations and the free fishing on Lough Currane is considered by many anglers to be the best in western Europe. The season extends from 17th January, to 30th September, while seatrout only carries on until 12th October. Guests can also avail of the hotel's privately owned Loughs Namona, Coppal, Cloonaughlin or Derrianna as well as beats on the nearby River Inny. Local experienced ghillies who are happy to advise on tackle, flies etc, can be arranged through the hotel. Deep sea angling is also available nearby.

If golf is your sport, you need go no further than the famous Waterville golf links, one of Ireland's longest courses and rated among the top 50 resort courses of the world. Over the years, it has hosted many of the world's top golfers such as Tom Watson, Gary Player, Nick Faldo, Ray Floyd, Sam Snead as well as Ireland's own Christy O'Connor, just to mention a few.

Waterville is also an ideal centre for hill walking with scenery that is difficult to equal. Staigue Fort, Church Island on Lugh Currane or the famous Skelligs Monastic settlement, 16 miles offshore. The area boasts many fine safe sandy beaches. The hotel has its own hard tennis court as well as full size snooker table. Excellent Woodcock and Snipe shooting can be arrange during November, December and January.

Butler Arms Hotel
Waterville,
Co. Kerry,
Ireland
Tel: (010 353 667) 4144
Fax: (010 353 667) 4520

INNISHANNON HOUSE HOTEL

One of the most exclusive hotels in the country, the Innishannon effortlessly lives up to its reputation as "the most romantic hotel in Ireland". Dating back to 1720 when it began its varied life as a substantial farmer's residence, it grew up beside an ancient ford, the first point at which the Bandon River could be crossed, and an important commercial centre in medieval times.

Conal O'Sullivan, the owner and manager likes to see his hotel as a "restaurant with rooms", and has gone to quite enormous efforts to ensure that the food is of a superlative quality. Only fresh herbs and vegetables from surrounding farms are used, along with local meat and game. Seafood such as brill, turbot, salmon and Dublin Bay prawns are served on the same day as they are landed in nearby Kinsale. An excellent selection of carefully chosen wines complements superb cuisine, served in a dining-room as elegant as the food itself.

The hotel also boasts a lounge bar, cosy snug, and ballroom catering for special occasions such as weddings, thoughtfully self-contained for privacy.

All of the bedrooms offer the modern amenities of colour television, direct-dial telephone cum clock/radio with extension in the bathroom. All bedrooms are, of course, ensuite and have been individually decorated and furnished with traditional woods, chintzes and a selection from the O'Sullivan's exten-sive collection of original paintings and prints, which also brighten the walls of the public rooms.

For the avid angler, the Innishannon offers a tremendous opportunity to fish for salmon and sea trout from the hotel lawns, comprising both banks of the river, or on the quarter-mile stretch of the Brinny River where the hotel holds exclusive rights. Permits can also be obtained for fishing other stretches. Deep sea angling can be arranged by the hotel for those with an interest in those waters.

It would be presumptious of me to try to describe the beauty of the surrounding countryside, when poets such as Edmund Spenser have already done so, but perhaps a small poem by local girl Alice Taylor, "Return to Innishannon", best captures visitors' sentiments:

"I have lived my life
far from here
But I have taken
This little place
In the walled garden
Of my heart
To rekindle
My tranquillity."

Innishannon House Hotel
Innishannon
Ireland
Tel: (010 353 21) 775121
Fax: (010 353 21) 775609

LONGUEVILLE HOUSE

Longueville is set in the centre of a 500 acre private wooded estate, overlooking one of the most beautiful river valleys in Ireland, the Blackwater - itself forming the Estate's southern boundary, famous as one of Ireland's foremost salmon and trout rivers.

Longueville is three miles on the Killarney road ex Mallow; Killarney itself in the heart of scenic Kerry being less than one hour away. Cork airport is 24 miles distant and Shannon airport is 54 miles away. Guests can make day trips to the Dingle and Beara Peninsulas. Blarney, Kinsale and the Vee Gap are all less than one hour's drive. For stay-at-homes, Longueville offers three miles of game fishing on the famous Blackwater river. There is horse-riding at nearby stables and golf at a dozen courses closeby including Premier Championship courses at Killarney, Ballybunion and Tralee.

A games room with full sized billiard table is in the basement. The estate is quiet and peaceful for walking or jogging with idyllic paths through wooded ways and water meadows.

Built in 1720, Longueville is the ancestral home of your hosts. Their aim is to maintain the friendly atmosphere of a home rather than a hotel. The centre block and two wings were added in 1800 and the Turner Curvilinear Conservatory was added in 1862.

Inside, Longueville offers many beautiful ceilings, doors and items of antique furniture in the public rooms and bedrooms - but in the latter, whether it be antique or otherwise, the acme of comfort is the bed. All bedrooms have en suite bathroom, colour television, radio and direct dial telephone.

The aim of Longueville's hosts is to have guests relax and feel completely at home in the comfort of their beautiful house, a classic Georgian country house. Central to all this is the kitchen, the heart of Longueville, over which the O'Callaghans' son William, a French-trained chef, presides. In here three lovingly prepared meals a day are made, using only the fresh produce of the estate's river, farm and gardens.

To match the superb food, Longueville's cellar includes over 150 wines, both from the Old and New World. The family's interest in wine has led them to plant their own three acre vineyard - unique in Ireland - produced in years of favourable climate.

Longueville House & Presidents' Restaurant
Mallow
Co Cork
Republic of Ireland
Tel: (010 353 22) 47156/47306
Fax: (010 353 22) 47459

BLACKWATER LODGE HOTEL

Blackwater Lodge is a world-renowned retreat for anglers, nestling in a picturesque location overlooking the Munster Blackwater from the south bank. It caters especially for angling parties, with all requirements catered for including a tackle shop, drying room and facilities for in-house smoking, freezing or marinading of your catch, together with all the information and friendly advice you might need from the expert staff here.

The theme at Blackwater Lodge is definitely 'fishy' with the emphasis on catching salmon. There are information folders available on your allocated beat, how to get there and how to fish it, as well as angling videos to view in the lounge bar. You will fish on private beats which are rotated daily and average about three quarters of a mile in length. The Blackwater is considered to be Ireland's premier salmon river with the best fishing between Lismore and Mallow, of which some fourteen miles are preserved exclusively for your own use when you are fishing at Blackwater Lodge.

If you feel you need a diversion from all that salmon fishing, the Lodge is ideally situated for a variety of activities the beautiful, scenic drives through Blackwater Valley and the Knockmealdown and Galtree Mountains. The Blackwater estuary and Youghal's long sandy beaches are nearby too. Other facilities in the area include tennis, swimming and golf at Lismore and Fermoy. Riding and pony trekking can also be arranged at various locations in the surrounding area.

The Lodge has 21 bedrooms. Ten are in the main building the rest in annexes, ideal for small parties . There is a cosy A La Carte Restaurant and a spacious Fishermans Lounge Bar. The Lodge can also organise self-catering accommodation in cottages closeby, combined with rod reservations, ferry tickets and car hire if required.

Whether you are an experienced fisherman or just here with 'fishy' friends, you are assured a special break in this beautiful part of Ireland.

Blackwater Lodge Hotel
'The Complete Angler Centre'
Upper Ballyduff
Co Waterford
Ireland
Tel: (010 353 58) 60235
Fax: (010 353 58) 60162

THE NORTH
OF IRELAND

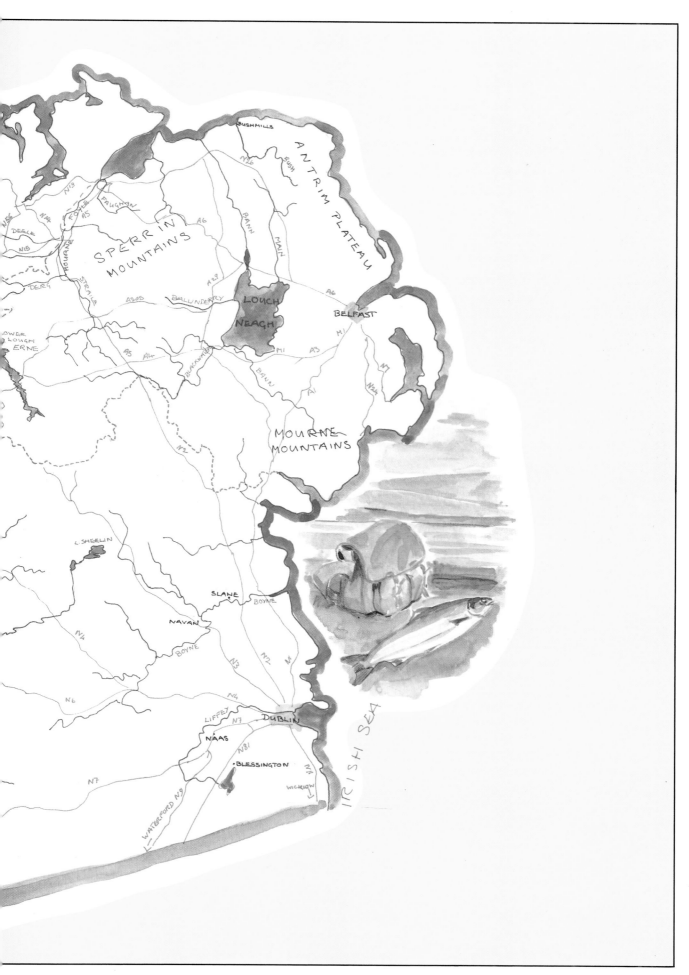

GILLAROO ANGLES

Fermanagh Lough Melvin (Northern Ireland Tourist Board)

Imagine drifting across a beautiful lough in the search for truly wild trout or perhaps using the double handed rod and wading deep for salmon; alternatively, stalking your fish, be it trout, sea-trout or salmon, in a small river in splendid isolation. If this is your idea of game fishing, then Gillaroo Angles can help you to enjoy your angling in a certain degree of piscatorial elegance.

From Sligo and Donegal in the West, to the Antrim coast in the East, there is a wide variety of game angling to choose from, not to mention varied and beautiful scenery. Included are the big loughs such as Arrow, Melvin and Erne, famous for their May-fly fishing but which can also fish well at other times of the year. There are many smaller loughs holding either salmon, sea-trout or small but lively brown trout. Numerous spate rivers from the hills in Donegal to the Lough Neagh Rivers in the East contain either salmon or sea-trout or the big Lough Neagh trout known as dollaghan (lake trout of up to 12lbs). The Bann, Bush and Mourne are some of the better known rivers, with the Bann being one of the most prolific rivers in Ireland.

Salmon fishing begins on the 1st January on some of the rivers in Donegal with March-May being the peak of the spring fishing. June-August brings in the grilse and there is always the chance of a big late fish in September/October. Mid-late July sees the arrival of the sea-trout and by August the brown trout fishing picks up again.

Whichever facet of the sport you enjoy, we will endeavour to place you on 'principle water' and provide a package to suit you or your party's particular requirements.

Excellent accommodation in a choice of country houses, hotels or self-catering cottages is widely available throughout the area with Ghillies or Ghillie/driver services also possible - (no one can guarantee you can catch all the fish you want, but a little local knowledge can be a great help).

Why not indulge yourself in a fishing foray, and give us a call.

Gillaroo Angles
7 Cooleen Park
Jordanstown
Co Antrim BT37 ORR
Tel: (0232) 862419
Fax: (08494) 67159

THE EMERALD ISLE

THE NORTH OF IRELAND

WESTERN REGION

The Western Fishery Region comprises almost all of County Galway and part of County Mayo, stretching from Hog's Head in Galway Bay to Pidgeon Point in Westport Bay and taking in the great limestone loughs of Corrib, Mask and Cara.

The short River **Corrib,** only four and a half miles long and 150 yards wide, runs through the city of Galway into Galway Bay and draining the vast 41,000 acre Lough Corrib, the Republic's largest lough. About two and a half miles of the river is suitable for salmon and sea-trout fishing, depending on the time of year. Don't forget your state licence as no local permits are required. Licences, tackle and advice are all available from Freeney's in Galway's High Street (091) 68794. It is the only tackle shop I know of that has a bar right next door, (of the same name and owner!) providing a ready made audience for those tall fishing tales!

Lough Corrib, or 'The Corrib' as it is generally known, stretches some thirty miles north from Galway to Maum Bridge. Like Loch Maree in Scotland, Corrib was world famous for sea-trout. Sadly, the last few years have seen a sharp decline here, as has happened all over Britain. With its numerous tiny islands, bays and inlets it is perfectly suited for good brown trout - the larger fish tend to be taken in the southern part of the lough, although salmon have also been taken here. The 15th February signals the start of the salmon season with trolling particularly popular at this time of year. Flies are also quite successful even this early in the season. Mid-March sees hatches of chironomids, whilst olive hatches are best in April, May and September. From around the second or third week in May, the mayfly season allows you to fish for trout by dapping the natural Mayfly using both wet and dry flies. Some 5000 trout are usually caught in this period which lasts for approximately four weeks. Right up to the end of the season, daddy-longlegs and grasshoppers can de dapped and wet fly fishing is also successful. As no permit is required, fishing is free on this vast expanse of water. Recently, good catches have been taken in the Cornamona, Greenfields and Cong areas generally using dapped mayfly or wet flies, the best being Hackled and Winged Mayflies, Green Peter, Olives and Bibio.

Detailed maps and information on fishing, boats, accommodation and other necessities are available from the Angling Officer of the Western Regional Fisheries Board at Weir Lodge, Earl's Island, Galway (091) 63118 for the southern end of the lough. For information on the northern end, contact the office at Cushlough (092) 41562. Currarevagh House, Oughterard (091) 82313 is a splendid Victorian manor set in 150 acres of park and woodland overlooking Lough Corrib and will provide boats, gillies and tackle for hire at around IR£30 per day.

The mysterious **Lough Mask** has several underground outflows where you can hear the water leaving. There is also a canal which has been constructed connecting Loughs Mask and Corrib which only flows in times of high water in the winter months. The water levels between summer and winter can vary here between seven or eight feet. This 20,000 acre limestone lake holds large brown trout, with the larger fish normally caught by trolling. 'Rapallas' were last year's favourites but there are many excellent lures to use and if you have suc-

cess with one - the advice is to stick to it! Traditional wet flies that do well are Connemara Black, Invicta and Olives.

The Mask has a similar season to the Corrib and anglers are free to use their own boats although it is possible to fish from the lough shore. The annual World Cup Wet Fly Angling Competition is held here. Open to everyone, it normally attracts around 400 entrants, including some of the sport's more famous names. Sponsored by Guinness, the first prize is a boat and outboard motor. Further information on the competition is available from the Western Regional Fisheries Board Information Centre, Cushlough, Ballinrobe (092) 41562 and the Fishery Board Officer, Joe Cusack (092) 41180, will also be willing to help. The information centre is a new bungalow-type building on Lough Mask's shore in Cushlough which can be reached from a tiny, dead-end track from Ballinrobe. The centre is open from 8.30am until 5.00pm but it is best to try to get there between 8.30am and 9.30am. There are numerous public access areas but anglers are asked to be cautious due to the dangerous shallows.

Lough Carra lies in the shadow of Lough Mask (it shares the same information centre) and covers an area of over 4,000 acres. Tiny in comparison to Lough Mask, this limestone lake is one of the most picturesque in the country, with perfectly clear water over a white marl bottom the trout are easily seen when rising to take the fly. The season here lasts from March to September and the lough is stocked with brownies each year by the Fisheries Board in order to supplement the native wild brown trout. An 18lb trout has been taken in the past but the average is nearer 1¼ lb. The mayfly season can produce good catches by dry fly, wet fly and dapping. Although standard patterns, including Green Drakes, are popular it is the Spent Gnat dry fly that produces the best results at all times of the day. In the summer and autumn, lake olives, murroughs and small sedges are the main fly hatches with artificial flies such as Claret, Murrough, Invicta and Bibio being the most popular. A boat is essential for fishing Lough Carra and hire can be arranged through the Western Regional Fisheries Board at Cushlough (092) 41562 and other local outlets.

The **Lough Inagh Fishery** is set in a beautiful valley between the Twelve Bens to the west and the Maumturk Mountains to the east. Lough Inagh and Derryclare Lake combine to make up the Lough Inagh Fishery. The N59 and N344 run along the east side of the fishery and enquiries should be made to the Fishery Manager (095) 34670 at the Lough Inagh Fishery, County Galway. At four miles long and up to three quarters of a mile wide, Lough Inagh offers quite splendid fishing. Fine sea-trout fishing is available at Corloo, where the outflow from the Inagh tumbles through the Trout Pool. There is excellent fishing for sea-trout at night at the Derryclare Butts, where the river enters the lake. Glendollogh Butts on the south east of Derryclare Lake provides good fishing with the well known Pine Island a favourite spot for salmon and sea-trout. At the outfall from the lake, the angler can take both salmon and sea-trout from an area known as Green Point.

April and May are the best months for salmon here, with fish averaging 10lb. June and September are generally the most productive times for grilse whilst sea-trout are traditionally summer sport. However, last year saw a very slow start to the sea-trout season. Wet fly and dapping are both successful with Blue Badger, the Shrimp and Red Daddy flies best for salmon;

THE EMERALD ISLE

Bibio, Delphi, Silver and Green Peter recommended for sea-trout. Boats and tackle are available at the fishery office with ghillies normally required to be booked in advance. The clarity of the waters and the clean crisp air, together with the number and size of fish make this a veritable haven for the fisherman.

The **Delphi Fishery** is situated in south County Mayo, off the R335 Leenane to Louisburgh road. The Delphi Estate is idyllic, set in a lovely green valley with a magnificent mountain backdrop. In the distance, the Partry Mountains rise from the shore of Lough Mask to the east and the Maumturk Mountains rise, equally daunting, to the south. The crystal clear waters afford the most perfect and tranquil setting for the fishing. The two and a half mile long Bundorragha River drains four main loughs and four main rivers to the sea at Killary Harbour.

From high in the beautiful hills at Lough Cunnel, where brown trout thrive, the Glencullin River tumbles into the lough of the same name, one of the most peaceful in the country with steep mountains rising from the shore. Here at Glencullin Lough, there are two boats to cover the half mile of lough with good sea-trout taken on the fly from July onwards. With five boats, and fishing allowed from all shores, nearby Doolough is well known for large salmon and trout. Generally, fly only fishing is allowed although some trolling for salmon may be possible in the early part of the season. The Delphi Lodge and cottages overlook Finlough where two boats cover the shallow picturesqe

water with its fine stock of salmon, grilse and sea-trout. Just a couple of miles south of the Delphi system is Tawnyard lough, the beautiful principle lough on the Errif System, famous for salmon and sea-trout taken on the fly. However, possibly the best river in the west of the country, with plenty of white water and nineteen pools, is the Bundorragha River, which is semi-spate and is most productive after heavy rain. Again, fly fishing only is the rule here, with salmon taken throughout the season and sea-trout from June to August. All enquiries regarding accommodation, boats, ghillies and even State licences should be made to Peter Mantle (095) 42213.

Recommended flies here include the Delphi Silver and Badger, Green Peter and Hairy Mary but again, it is worth spending some time chatting to Mr Mantle who is full of useful tips on the local waters. The long season, the variety of fishing, the perfect setting and the water's excellent record, averaging 100 salmon and 1000 sea-trout annually, make the Delphi Estate the ideal location for the keen fisherman. It must be said that this average does not include 1990's disastrous sea-trout figures. Delphi, like most of Ireland and the British Isles, has experienced the depressing disappearance of the sea-trout. In fact, the renowned Zetland Fishery closed in 1991, but the lovely Zetland House Hotel (095) 31111 is still thriving as there is much to do in this part of Connemara. Fishermen in the area could, of course, cast a fly on nearby Lough Shannaghcloontippen (19 letters, to save you counting!).

GILLIE ANGLING

GAME FISHING IN THE WEST OF IRELAND

Gillie Angling is a service catering specifically for the needs of the game angler in Western Ireland. The service is run by Roy and Sorcha Peirce from their home at Grasshopper Cottage on the shores of Lough Corrib. Being anglers themselves, they are totally familiar with the needs of the game fisherman.

The West of Ireland has a vast and varied amount of water available to the fisherman. It would be easy if all waters fished equally well but, of course, they do not - each water fishing better at different times under different conditions. As Gillie Angling does not have a specific base, it is our sole objective to place you, the angler, in the most appropriate place at the most appropriate time to suit your requirements. It is the personal attention and on-the-spot information combined with the arrangement of travel, accommodation, boats and engines, pre-booking of private fisheries and the indication of where and when to fish that makes Gillie Angling one of the most comprehensive game angling services in Ireland.

We can offer you the full range of travel options - ferry or fly/drive. Ideally, we will try to place you in accommodation as close to your fishing as possible. We can offer a wide selection, ranging from top class hotels, country houses and guest-houses to cottages. Information on coarse and sea angling, golf, horse riding and hill walking is also available.

Gillie Angling
Grasshopper Cottage
Cornamona
Claremorris
Co. Galway
Tel/Fax: (010 353 92) 48165

'Mayfly at the Grasshopper Cottage 1991'

THE DELPHI ESTATE

Delphi lodge is one of the finest sporting lodges in Ireland. A magnificent 1830's country house which exudes a rich history and tradition. With fine antique furniture, beautiful decor, roaring fires, the Lodge is elegant yet totally relaxing.

Four charming country cottages surrounded by a network of traditional dry stone walls, tumbling streams and rich vegetation, form part of the famous Delphi sporting estate. Beautifully restored in recent years, the cottages are comfortable and full of character. Antique country pine furniture, large open fireplaces, traditional stone floors downstairs and rich carpeting upstairs, all combine to give a wonderfully cosy atmosphere to these ancient cottages. The perfect setting for a relaxing country break.

The historic Delphi Fishery is a gem of Connemara. Set in a wild, unspoilt and stunningly beautiful valley, it offers gin-clear water, towering mountains, abundant wild life and total peace. It's the perfect haven for the discerning salmon and sea trout angler.

Delphi's sensational setting and prolific sporting fish have attracted generations of anglers from all over the world. With spring salmon, summer grilse and sea trout, it has long been recognised as a fly fisherman's paradise.

Delphi offers a wide variety of fly fishing over an unusually long and interesting season. Three fascinatingly different lakes, one and a half miles of tumbling river and the ideal fishing climate - all combine to offer relaxation, challenge and opportunity for expert and novice alike.

For centuries the sporting estate of the Marquis of Sligo, Delphi was acquired in 1986 by a young fisherman, Peter Mantle, who has ensured that the fishery and its facilities - from experienced ghillies to top quality flies, from helpful fishing maps to excellent drying facilities - are second to none. A unique fishery, managed superbly for the future.

The Delphi Estate
County Galway
Ireland
Tel: (010 353 95) 42213
Fax: (010 353 95) 42212

NEWPORT HOUSE

Adjoining the town of Newport and overlooking the tidal river and quay the impressive country mansion of Newport House stands guard over the centuries of history that form the backbone to its grounds and the surrounding countryside. Once the home of a branch of the O'Donel family, descended from the famous fighting Earls of Tir Connell and cousins to 'Red Hugh' of Irish history, it is now a superb example of a lovingly maintained Georgian Mansion House.

Encircled by mountains, lakes and streams, Newport is within easy reach of some of Ireland's most beautiful rivers. Renowned as an angling centre, it holds private salmon and sea-trout fishing rights to 8 miles of the Newport River; and the prolific waters of the stunning Lough Beltra West are close by. Less than twenty minutes drive from the hotel are Lakes Mask and Corrib, while the nearby Loughs Feeagh and Furnace are the site of the Salmon Research Trust of Ireland.

The discerning golfer has the pleasure of the 18-hole championship course at Westport as well as the more relaxed 9-hole course near Mulrany.

Outdoor activities are numerous amidst the breath-taking scenery of County Mayo. Riding is easily arranged or try swimming and diving on wide and often empty beaches, while hang-gliding is a relatively new sport gaining popularity from the local Achill Cliffs. One of the best recreations though is simply walking across the ever changing panorama of mountain, forest and sea.

Warmth and friendliness fill this beautiful hotel in a country already famed for its hospitality. The house is furnished with a tasteful collection of fine antiques and paintings and the elegant bedrooms are individually decorated. Food is taken seriously, with much of the produce collected fresh from the fishery, gardens and farm. Home-smoked salmon and fresh sea-food are specialites, and all the dishes are complemented by a carefully chosen and extensive wine list.

Many of the staff have been long in the service of the estate, up to forty years in one case. Combine this with the solid background of the house and there is a rare feeling of continuity and maturity so rare in modern hotels today.

Newport House
Co. Mayo
Ireland
Tel: (010 353 98) 41222
Fax: (010 353 98) 41613

THE EMERALD ISLE

The North Western Fisheries Region is made up of the majority of County Mayo and parts of County Sligo, County Leitrim and County Roscommon. From Pidgeon Point, County Mayo around the coastline to Mullaghnmore Head, County Sligo, the area encompasses all the rivers and loughs which flow into the sea between these two points.

Without a doubt, the best known water is the River Moy with its principal lake, Lough Conn, forming a link at Pontoon to Lough Cullin. In addition, good runs of salmon and sea-trout are to be enjoyed at the Newport River and Lough Beltra system and at the Owenmore and Owenduff Rivers together with the Burrishoole Fishery. Lough Cull, off the Mulraney to Achill road and Loughaun, set in picturesque Achill Island, may just surprise the dedicated angler, not only with the delightful setting but also the quality of the water.

Lough Beltra and the **Newport** River can be found in south County Mayo, south west of Castlebar off the R311/R312. Lough Beltra is three miles long and one mile wide and is drained by the Newport river running into Clew Bay at Newport. Over seventeen miles long, with seventeen good holding pools, streams and glides, both the river and lough get a good run of spring salmon from the end of March (opening day is 20th March), grilse in June and sea-trout from mid-June. Unfortunately, there is no real brown trout fishing here.

Newport House in Newport (098) 41222 overlooks the river's estuary with the hotel gates facing you as you come into Newport from Castlebar. The house is set between Achill Island and the mountains of Mayo and the wild unspoiled splendour of Erris and Connemara. The house owns the westside of the lough with five boats and five ghillies available for hire. The boats fish one side of an invisible line, although they can cross with permission, and generally the boats for hotel guests have priority. In addition, guests also have priority on an eight mile stretch of the river which completes the Newport House fishery and there is a boat for use on Lough Furnace. Newport House can also arrange fishing on the Moy system should you wish to test those waters.

The eastside of the Beltra is owned by Glenisland Co-op (094) 21302 where fishing costs around IR£7 per day, plus IR£15 per boat with an outboard motor. Five boats are available for hire here and the salmon fishing is good but due to lack of numbers, any sea-trout caught must be returned to the water. Late March, April and May tend to be the best fishing but this depends on the water level and weather conditions. An average of eighty to ninety salmon are caught on this side during the season, some up to 20lb in weight.

BURRISHOOLE FISHERY

The Burrishoole Fishery is owned and managed by the Salmon Research Agency of Ireland. It offers some of the most productive lough fishing for salmon in the west of Ireland. Fishing is strictly limited to 6 boats (with engines) on each lough and fly only is the rule. Experienced ghillies are available and fully serviced luncheon huts are located on each lough. No estuarine netting takes place and a major smolt enhancement programme has been operated for over 20 years. Fishing starts in mid-June and closes on September 30. Naturally, sport varies, but generally the quality of fish caught is best in July when all are fresh run, but larger bags may be made in the September, when only some of the fish are straight in from the sea. The Fishery has successfully operated package holidays offering fishing with accommodation at local Bord Failte (Tourist Board) approved guesthouses. Alternatively, approved hotel or self-catering accommodation can be organised for clients. When salmon fishing is difficult clients may fish Ballinlough; an extremely rich, spring fed, limestone lough of 55 acres. It is only stocked with fry and yearling brown trout and rainbow trout and grows fish from 4oz to 4lb in just two years! Both boat and shore fishing are available, free of charge, to our guests. Alternatively sea angling trips may be arranged locally.

The Manager
Burrishoole Fishery
Farran Laboratory
Furnace
Newport
Co. Mayo
Ireland
Tel: (010 353 98) 41107/41705

THE EMERALD ISLE

Burrishoole Fishery is now owned and managed by the Salmon Research Agency of Ireland and comprises the tidal Lough Furnace and the freshwater Lough Feeagh.

One of Ireland's few productive tidal loughs **Lough Furnace** rises and falls two feet each day. Both loughs are often referred to as 'spate loughs' as they have a catchment area of approximately 100 square miles and after heavy rain the levels can rise very sharply. During hot, dry spells Furnace can become quite brackish and fish have to adjust to fluctuating salinity levels of between eight and twenty parts per thousand. Furnace has two separate stocks of fish; a natural stock and a supplement from the agency's ocean ranched salmon. The season runs from 10th June to 30th September, with July being the best month when all the fish are fresh. However, September may give larger bags with the autumn run. Salmon are to be found at both the Salmon Leap and the Millrace, and also at Long Shore, Duffy's Point and Fahy's Bay. For sea-trout, try Black Stone and Blacksod Bay, although they are currently subject to a restrictive byelaw and any caught have to be returned. Furnace also has excellent mullet fishing - so don't be surprised if you land a mullet or a bass for that matter!

Lying in a deep valley, **Lough Feeagh**, although best known for salmon, holds good stocks of sea-trout and brown trout and the agency records the number of fish passing up into the lough through the counter. Again, June and July are the best months for salmon particularly around the mouth of the Black River and Glenamong River. The best water for sea-trout is the area towards the lower lough, around Schoolhouse Bay.

Furnace and Feeagh are set in the beautiful countryside of Nephin Beg, easily accessible from Newport. Permits are available from the Manager's Office at the Burrishoole Fishery (098) 41107 at Farran Laboratory, Furnace, Newport, some two miles outside Newport on the south shore. Bank fishing is not allowed here and only five boats (with engines) are allowed on each lough. Fly-only is the rule, with Green Peter, Daddy, Bibio, Black Pennell, Fiery Brown and Delphi recommended. The average weight for salmon from this water is around 9lb and for sea-trout 3/4 lb.

Bunarella Lough, managed and partially owned by the agency, is a good brown trout lough just ten miles north of Newport and enjoys a lovely tranquil setting. Trout are small, averaging about 8oz but provide great fun on light tackle as they are quite free rising, especially during the summer hatch of sedges. In addition to the standard lough patterns, try Greenwell's Spider and Glory and Connemara Black on the east and north shores.

The agency has recently opened up a new fishery at Ballinlough, two or three miles north of Westport on the N59. Generally speaking, this is the only lough run by the agency to allow bank fishing. It is very rich in limestone and well stocked with rainbows and browns with 4oz fish growing to 4lb in two years.

Visitors are advised to book well in advance for the whole fishery, especially for June, July and September and a ghillie is recommended. Fishing rates are from IR£50 per day for two rods plus a boat and boatman, rising to IR£250 per week. Permits are obtained from the office situated on the southern shore of Furnace, approximately two miles outside Newport. It's a signposted turning off to the right.

Situated twenty-eight miles west of Ballina and two miles northwest of Bangor Erris in County Mayo is **Carrowmore Lake**. Four miles long and approximately three miles wide it is primarily a brown trout fishery with occasional salmon and sea-trout. This is probably the last of the truly wild lakes as it has never been stocked. Owned by a syndicate in Dublin and controlled by Bangor Erris Angling Club, permits can be obtained from Seamus Henry at The Post Office in Bangor Erris (097) 83487 at a cost of IR£10 per day. There are twenty-five boats available and these are recommended, as bank fishing is not very productive. The Post Office is adjacent to the 'West End Bar' - surely a recipe for disaster with regards to writing postcards! Mr Henry will also issue permits for the club's stretches on the River Owenmore and is happy to advise on both fishing and accommodation. Cloonamoyne Fishery (096) 31112, attached to the Enniscoe Hotel at Lough Conn, can also arrange fishing at Carrowmore.

The Oweniny river flows into the Owenmore and then enters Carrowmore Lake before reaching the Atlantic at Blackrod Bay. On Carrowmore, the traditional fly patterns at Herrity's and Derreen's Islands on the north shore and the mouth of Glencullin River are the ones to use.

The River **Moy** is one of the top salmon producing rivers in Ireland, flowing from the Ox Mountains to Killala Bay at Ballina. Its tributaries drain an area of some eight hundred square miles over its full sixty three mile length and there are over thirty miles of double bank fishing. Around 8000 fish are taken from its waters every season, with stretches to suit fly fishing and spinning.

The season starts on the 1st February but it is more usual for serious fishing to start towards the end of the month. The main grilse run starts in May and peaks in June with an unbelievable number of fish in the river. Angling on the Moy is reasonably priced and available in spring and summer through to the autumn. Sea-trout can be taken from boats in the seven mile long estuary from Ballina to Killala Bay.

The Moy Fishery Office (096) 21332 at Ridge Pool Road, Ballina controls some of the best beats on the river, including the famous Ridge Pool where sixteen fish were taken in two days in June 1991. Prices range from IR£8 to IR£60 for two rods, boat hire and a ghillie in high season for the Ridge Pool. Advance booking is essential.

The Ballina Angling Centre (096) 21850 at Dillon Terrace, Ballina is run by Michael Swartz who claims to be able to organise everything. Certainly permits, tuition, ghillies and general information are available here pertaining to the fishery which stretches out on both banks, from the Weir to the confluence with the Corroy river.

The Downhill Hotel, Ballina is set in beautiful landscaped gardens overlooking the River Brosna, a tributary of the Moy. Mount Falcon Castle Fishery, between the Corroy and Foxford, controls seven and a half miles of double bank fishing with good fly and spinning stretches. The Mount Falcon (096) 21172 is four miles from Ballina on the Foxford Road, set in 100 acres of beautiful parkland. The Alpine Hotel (096) 36144 overlooks Killala Bay some fifteen miles away, where guests have priority over one mile of left bank fishing, just upstream from the junction of the Rivers Yellow and Moy.

THE EMERALD ISLE

The Armstrong Family are one of the few Irish families that own a piece of the Moy. The cost to fish here is about IR£10 per day and you are advised to book in advance for this one and a half mile stretch. The Armstrongs (094) 56580 live almost on the river, down a track off the Ballina to Foxford Road and you can't miss the 'Armstrong Fishery' sign.

Beal Easa is a one and a quarter mile stretch on the left bank owned by the Gannon family who run a guest house and takeaway, in addition to the Post Office (094) 56101. Permits for the Leckee Fishery to the south of the town can be obtained here for around IR£12 per day. Foxford Salmon Anglers control both banks immediately to the south of Foxford and anglers should contact Jack Wallace (094) 56238 at Swinford Road, Foxford.

Cloongee Fishery permits can be purchased from Michael Ruane (094) 56634 in Cloongee for fishing on both banks where Lough Cullin enters the Moy.

The East Mayo Anglers' Association control the Moy from around Cloongee House by the Ballylahan Bridge, to beyond the point where the Gweestion river joins the Moy. Permits cost IR£10 per day and are available from Mrs Wills at Ballylahan Bridge (094) 56221 and Boland's Lounge, Bridge Street, Swinford (094) 51149. In addition, a short stretch downstream of Foxford Bridge offers free fishing.

A few miles west of the Moy is the infamous **Lough Conn**. At around 13,000 acres, this beautiful lake provides the fisherman with an excellent challenge in stunning surroundings. Nephin, rising to almost two and a half thousand feet dominates the western horizon. A limestone water of about 9 miles long and 2-4 miles wide, it has vast areas of relatively shallow water that sustain a huge population of wild trout. During fly hatches, trouting is excellent and with the many attractive bays and islands, Conn remains a firm favourite with all fishermen. The angling season begins in March with traditional wetfly fishing over shallow water. Brownies average just over the pound mark but three pounders are not uncommon. The chronomids hatch throughout the first half of the season but the fun really begins when the Mayfly starts to hatch in mid-May. The latter is extensive and lasts until the end of June with the lesser hatch extending until mid-August. Sedges hatch towards the end of the season and so do not forget your sedge patterns at this time of year. Salmon are also present in fair numbers and are mainly taken by trolling from the end of March to July. Historically, the best areas have been at the northern end - try Masebrook, Cornakillew and Castlehill Bay. Access is not difficult and all your needs can be organised through the Pontoon Bridge Hotel, Foxford, (094) 56120. There are several people who have boats to hire and it is recommended that even if you do not wish a boatman to accompany you, a guide of some sort would make a difference to the size of your bag. At the very least, on a blank day, you can exchange jokes! Michael Schwartz in the Angling Centre, Ballina (open 7.00am to midnight) (096) 21850 can also help you here. On the northern shore Enniscoe House (096) 31112 stands alone amongst its gardens and parkland. Just off the N59 Crossmolina to Ballina road, this lovely Georgian house is the place to stay for all that is splendid. Barry Segrave is the fishery manager and can organise an impressive fishing package. You might prefer to speak to Healy's Hotel, Pontoon (094) 56443.

Lough Cullin is connected to the southern tip of Lough Conn at Pontoon. This 2000 acre lake holds a good stock of brown trout up to about 4lb and also has a good run of salmon. In fact, all the fish must pass through Cullin to get to Lough Conn and its feeder rivers. The narrow inlet that joins the two lakes is a favourite haunt of the salmon fisherman. Salmon are often caught by anglers flyfishing for trout. So if it is trout you are after, use a slightly heavier leader than normal. In addition to the contacts for Lough Conn, You might prefer to speak to Healy's Hotel, Pontoon (094) 56443.

Lough Arrow is drained by the river of the same name. Only fifteen miles in length, the River Arrow is not widely fished. Access is awkward with many overhanging trees and after June ends the weed growth becomes too thick to cast a fly. There are, however, large trout in this river but they are not often seen as they feed deep down. Guests of Coopershill, Riverstown, County Sligo (071) 65108 are welcome to fish it but the O'Haras would prefer to organise fishing for you on Lough Arrow. This fine Irish water is one of the best mayfly fisheries in the country and is situated close to the border of County Sligo and Roscommon. At just over 3000 acres this rich limestone lough is small by comparison to some but brownies are here in good numbers and fish to 6lb and 7lb are caught on the fly every year. There are significant hatches of duckfly, olives, murroughs and even Green Peter. The season runs from March to September and all fishing is free. Before you start though ring or pop into the N.W. Fisheries Board Information Centre (079) 66033 in Ballinafad, beside the cemetary, for a fishing report and advice. First thing in the morning is the best time to catch a fishery officer; or contact Tim McGrath at the Rock View Hotel (079) 66073.

River Brosna   (Downhill Hotel)

ENNISCOE HOUSE

Enniscoe House is a fine Georgian home on the shores of Lough Conn which has recently been described as the 'last great house of North Mayo'. Declared a 'Heritage House of Ireland', it is owned and managed by Susan Kellet, a descendant of the original family who settled on the lands in the 1660s.

The house, which is lovingly and carefully maintained, retains its family portraits, antique furniture and welcoming open fires. In this setting, good food and wine contribute to a pleasant and relaxed atmosphere. The main bedrooms which have a canopy or four poster beds and private bathrooms, have attractive views of parkland trees and the lake.

The 150 acres estate, which has its own farm and gardens, presents a tranquil setting for the house in mature woodlands through which paths run to the lake.

There are attractively renovated self-catering units in the stable yard and some old farm buildings have been taken over by the local Historical Society where a heritage centre for North Mayo is being developed.

Enniscoe House, which has a long fishing tradition is the ideal base for the keen fisherman. Situated on the shores of Lough Conn, it has a private landing stage, boats and engines together with a rod and drying room on its own shore and within easy walking distance from the house. The Fishery Manager provides advice, tackle and tuition as well as arranging boats, engines and ghillies for the guests.

Lough Conn is renowned for its wild brown trout and spring salmon fishing. For a varied fishing holiday, the Fishery Manager can also arrange fishing on other local lakes and rivers including the River Moy as well as estuary and sea fishing.

In addition to its fishing attractions, North Mayo is a fascinating though little known area. The nearby North Coast has unspoilt and clean beaches at Ballycastle and Lacken, while further along the coast there are great cliffs overlooking the Atlantic where stone age settlements at Ceide Fields are being excavated.

Nephin Mountain, which overlooks the area, presents a challenge to the hill climber and at the base has a range of relatively unexplored small lakes, forests and boglands. There is also Achill Island to the south and Sligo Yeats Country to the north, both within easy driving distance of Enniscoe. Golf is readily available, as is horse riding and bicycle hire.

You will find Enniscoe House an ideal base for an enjoyable and varied angling holiday.

Enniscoe House
Castle Hill
Near Crossmolina
Ballina
Co Mayo
Tel: (010 353 96) 31112
Fax: (010 353 96) 31773

COOPERSHILL

Coopershill is a fine example of a Georgian family mansion. Home to seven generations of the O'Hara family since it was built in 1774, it combines the spaciousness and elegance of an earlier age with the comfort and amenities of today. Five of the seven bedrooms have four-poster or canopy beds and all have their own private bathrooms. The rooms retain their original regal dimensions and much of the furniture dates from the time that the house was built.

Guests can relax in front of a log fire in the large and comfortable drawing room. Dinner by candle light with family silverware and crystal glass, a wide choice of wines and the personal attention of the hosts all add to the special Coopershill atmosphere.

Standing in the centre of a 500 acre estate of farm and woodland, separation from the outside world seems complete. There are many delightful walks and wildlife is abundant and undisturbed.

One of Ireland's finest limestone lakes, Lough Arrow, is five miles away. Best known for the Mayfly hatch, the lough fishes almost as well at other times of the year. Large indigenous brown trout are caught during the late evenings of summer and autumn. Boats and ghillies are available.

The river from the lake flows through the property. It contains large brown trout which are mainly bottom feeders and a real challenge to the fly fisherman.

Long uncrowded beaches, spectacular mountains and hills for walking, lakes and megalithic monuments all add to make Sligo, which is Yeats' country, an ideal place to visit.

Coopershill is two miles from the village of Riverstown and 13 miles from Sligo town, signposted clearly from the Sligo to Dublin route N4.

We are served by two airports; Sligo Airport is 15 miles away with daily flights to Dublin; Knock Airport is 30 miles away with daily flights to Luton, North of London. Car hire is available at both Sligo and Knock.

Coopershill
Riverstown
Co. Sligo
Ireland
Tel: (010 353 71) 65108
Fax: (010 353 71) 65466

THE EMERALD ISLE

THE NORTH

Fermanagh's loughs and rivers, treelined glens and islands, stately mansions and ruined castles form the perfect accompaniment to the spectacular fishing to be found in Loughs Erne and Melvin. Here, in the south west corner are two of the best trout loughs in the land. The Upper and Lower Lough Erne is over fifty miles long with the medieval·town of Enniskillen dividing the lough; and Lough Melvin, straddling Fermanagh's Republican Border.

Lough Melvin is approximately 5000 acres, eight miles long by nearly 2 miles wide, and unique. It is scientifically accepted that there are four genetically distinct trout in this lough - brown, ferox, gillaroo and sonaghan. This rare salmonid displays the normal attributes of sea-trout - powerful tails and hard fighters although much darker in colouring than sea-trout. They only grow to about 1½lb and are typically mid-water feeders of daphnia and emerging insects. The gillaroo is very similar to a brown trout but with more spots and a yellow belly. They feed a lot on the bottom in shallow water but do come up for the dry fly in the evening. Ferox are usually caught by trolling the deeper sections of the lake and char are caught at even greater depths. Brownies are best caught fishing a team; with a dark pattern on the point, a traditional wet fly, such an Invicta, on the dropper and a local favourite, like a Gosling or Dabbler, on the bob. These latter two are based on patterns from two hundred years of fly-tying experience passed down through the years. Local fly-tyers still tie in the traditional way - hooks held in the hand without help from a vice! One word of caution, Lough Melvin is scenic but can sometimes cut up rough and dangerous as it is very exposed to the prevailing westerlies. A good man to speak to for local advice is Terence Bradley (072) 54029 whose house, Eden Point, is situated on the east shore, the first house on the left as you leave Rossinver on the R282. Mr Bradley has ten boats for hire at IR£25 per day which includes two rods. Gillaroo Angles (0232) 862419, based in Newtownabbey, are also able to organise fishing forays throughout this area and the man to contact here is John Todd.

The River **Drowse** drains Lough Melvin and provides some spectacular sport when the salmon are running in the spring. Thomas Gallagher (072) 41208 owns the fishing rights on this short six mile river. There are fifty two named pools that yielded eight hundred fish in the first seven months of 1991. March produced over one hundred and fifty fish alone, with half caught on the fly. A tip here - use size 8 to 10 doubles for spring salmon which have an average weight of 10lb, and size 10 to 12 for the grilse which average 5lb. Mr Gallagher charges a very reasonable IR£6 per day or IR£25 per week operating from the Kinlough end and also hires boats for the lough. February to July is best for salmon here. Also in this area, the National Trust properties at Florence Court and Gardens and the Palladian Castle Coole are well worth a visit.

Picturesque **Lower Lough Erne** is a huge expanse of water (37,000 acres), twenty six miles long, running north west from Enniskillen to Rosscar viaduct where the River Erne enters the ocean at Ballyshannon. The whole Erne system provides superb brown trout fishing in clean unpolluted waters containing plenty of fish. Trout up to 20lb in weight are caught every season, usually on the troll in spring whilst duckfly fishing begins in earnest in April. The numerous islands, rocky outlets and secluded coves and bays make for an idyllic setting for the

fisherman to enjoy whilst pursuing his sport.

Near Enniskillen, try St Catherine's and Rabbit Island where Mayfly sport is particularly good for the trout when fish of 6lb can be taken. Trout fishing naturally tends to die away in late June and early July but returns with a vengeance in August with the arrival of the daddy-longlegs and sedges and you may even pick up a salmon which are now returning in larger numbers. The season generally runs from 1st March to 30th September with some minor extensions and details of permits and State licences can be obtained from John Richardson (0365) 322608, 9 East Bridge Street, Enniskillen who also has holiday cottages to let on Lusty Island. For those anglers keen to try their luck with the salmon, the stretch from Rosscor viaduct to Belleek has been good in August and September in recent years and Michael McGrath (0365) 658181 at Carlton Cottages, Belleek is an excellent source of local knowledge. The scenic Ballinamallard and Colebrooke, which are feeder rivers for the lough, get a run of large brown trout during August and September which provide great sport.

The **Foyle System** is managed by The Foyle Fisheries Commission and is unique in that it extends into Donegal in the Republic, as well as Londonderry and Tyrone. It was once the best salmon fishery in Western Europe but the ravages of UDN and overfishing, both legally and illegally, took their toll, although there are signs that things are improving. Consisting of Lough Foyle and the Rivers Finn, Strule, Derg, Mourne, Glenelly, Owenkilliew, Carnowen and Drumragh, the Foyle System has some superb fishing in this area on private, semi-private and association waters. Mr Ronnie Kerrigan at the Commission (0504) 42100 is very helpful and will give you advice on all areas to fish.

Classic fly fishing is available on the Mourne which like the Tay and Spey fishes best in low to medium water. Good spring fishing can often be found on the Finn, but it is usually mid June before there is any consistancy. Most of the other rivers are of a 'spatey' nature and therefore require a good deal of rain. Not usually a problem as Ulster's lush countryside testifies! Patrick Bonner (06487) 65920 is a very helpful water bailiff who fishes all over Northern Ireland and he can be contacted after 11.00a m. (He is out fishing until midnight!)

The Rivers Roe and Faughan are part of the Foyle System and often yield first class salmon and sea-trout, with stretches on the Roe controlled by Roe Anglers' Association and Dungiven Anglers' Association. Sea-trout of up to 4lb are not uncommon and grilse between 4lb and 10lb are regularly caught here. Salmon from these waters tend to weigh around 8lb to 10lb.

For further information on fishing in Northern Ireland contact the Department of Agriculture which is responsible for the public waters and can give advice on angling permits, stocking and other matters. They can be contacted at The Department Of Agriculture, Fisheries Division, Hut 5, Castle Grounds, Storemont, Belfast. Telephone (0232) 63939. Licences are available from either the Fisheries Board or the Foyle Fisheries Commission.

Lough Neagh is the biggest lake in the British Isles and its main rivers are the Upper Bann and Blackwater to the south and Moyola to the west and the Maine and its tributaries to the north. The system drains a vast area of central Ulster. The Lower

THE EMERALD ISLE

Bann drains the lough to the north, through Lough Beg to the Atlantic near Coleraine. All these rivers enjoy a reasonable run of salmon from July to October and produce an indigenous population of brown trout from 1/4lb to 1 1/4lb. Dollaghan, a big lough trout sometimes over 10lb can be taken during the autumn. Similar to sea-trout in colour and size, they are best caught at dusk but, unfortunately, do not put up the entertaining resistance of the sea-trout.

The River **Blackwater** is the largest of the rivers but, according to the locals, is virtually unfishable due to the Department of Agriculture's arterial drainage scheme. The last seven or eight miles of the upper part of the river in the Benburb area has some reasonable trout fishing and a few salmon. Permits are available from Hamiltons (06487) 63682. Around Black-watertown there is a one and a half mile stretch of right bank fishing with good trout fishing here run by the Department of Agriculture. Permits should be purchased from Cahoon, 2 Irish Street, Dungannon (0867) 22754. The **Upper Bann** rises in the Mourne Mountains and meanders and tumbles through the delightful County Down countryside to Lough Neagh. Between Banbridge and Hilltown, the Department has two, ten mile stretches of water. Brown trout and some late season salmon are taken from the banks between March and October.

The **Ballinderry** river is about thirty miles long and flows east to enter the lough near Ardhoe Cross. About two thirds of its length yields good brown trout and some dolaghan. Permits are obtainable from Cookstown Angling Club.

From the Sperrin Mountains in South Derry, the **Moyola** river twists and winds its way to the north west corner of the lough, yielding some brown trout and a few salmon in the latter part of the season. This is private land and anglers must seek the landowner's permission to fish these waters. Principally a brown trout river with some big lough dolaghan, the **Maine** flows south from Glarryford Bogs. Several angling clubs and the Department of Agriculture own stretches on the river. Cullybackey has two and a half miles of the best trout waters with day tickets obtained from local newsagents in Cullybackey. In recent years there have been some very good runs of salmon in the Maine and its tributaries, the Braid and Glenwhiry providing the angler with excellent sport. The **Lower Bann**, which is the largest river in the British Isles in terms of water volume, is a slow running river which drains Lough Neagh. The water is 'owned' by Bann Systems but most of the river can be fished without day permits although there are several private stretches fished by syndicates on Monday to Thursday and only available to day visitors at weekends. Although expensive, up to IR£160 per day, the salmon fishing can be fantastic below the weirs and lockgates where fast running waters can produce many salmon. Portna and Culiff rock are good stretches. Possibly the best, however, is Camroe where the number of fish taken is quite phenomenal, although this is a restricted stretch. There are several small rivers feeding into the Lower Bann which can yield some good salmon in their own right. From Coleraine to the river mouth there is some very good sea-trout fishing, especially from boats. Contact Bann Systems Ltd at Coleraine (02657) 31215.

Wholly owned by Bann Systems Ltd., the thirty mile River **Bush** flows from the Tievebulliagh through Bushmills village and distillery - one of the oldest in the world - to the Atlantic near the Giant's Causeway. The owner of Bann Systems, Sir Patrick

McNaughton, sells day tickets on two miles of the river at the mouth where the fishing is mainly restricted to salmon, although there are some trout to be had. The remainder of the river is leased by the internationally renowned Research Station of the Department of Agriculture who allow fishing only on the strict understanding that anglers co-operate with the research project's progress by returning day tickets with details of the catch and whenever possible, submitting salmon for examination. It is particularly important to recover fin-clipped fish (those from which the adipose fin has been removed) as these individuals may contain minute tags which can only be detected using specialised equipment at the hatchery. All fish will be returned to anglers immediately and a reward is currently payable for each salmon submitted. Anyone catching a fin-clipped fish outside office hours or at the weekend is asked to retain the fish's head and report the catch on a returned day ticket or by telephone at their earliest convenience.

Angling on the river has been deliberately divided up so as to give the best sport to as many people as possible and to cater for varying desires, but the river is of a 'flashy' nature and does not remain in top class order for extended periods. When in form, however, it can be excellent. At present the season lasts from 1st March until 30th September. Advance booking is essential for these waters and contact should be made with the Department. Ask for form ARB1 and bear in mind applications are dealt with on a first come first served basis. Rods for spring and September go in a day as it is reputed to be bursting with salmon. If you can track down Sean Fleming (02657) 32422 at the Tackle Shop in Bushmills he will be happy to advise you on all waters in the area. Permits are also available from Barry Jones (02657) 31435 at the Hatchery Office in Bushmills.

The fishing in Ireland is without doubt outstanding and this is in spite of a dramatic decline in sea-trout catches and the continued netting of huge numbers of salmon. You see, when we say 'fishing in Ireland' it is not just catching fish that matters to the Irish, it is the sport combined with the company, the stories and the hospitality enjoyed in the many riverside pubs. A wicked sense of humour blends with informality and a welcome that is renowned throughout the world.

FISHING FAYRE

THE SOUTH OF IRELAND

Many fishermen are drawn like magnets to the same stretch of water each year and to some this may seem odd. However, familiarity and fond memories are a draw for the angler herever they fish. Stick with your week in Devon or Scotland in the area you know, but do also consider fishing in Ireland. Once you've experienced it, I for one will be surprised if you do not return time and time again.

The Shannon Fishery Region is particularly well organised and this is just as well due to size of the water, not to mention the many tributaries. Its significance as a coarse fishing water should not be underestimated but we intend to isolate several locations where the game fishing comes to the fore. The area is well served by Shannon Airport and the Shannon International (061) 61122 is extremely handy for those flying in and out of the area. County Clare reveals a number of superb hotels but before we embark on these, spare a quick thought for Limerick and County Kerry. The Listowel Arms (068) 21500 is a well equipped and

265

THE EMERALD ISLE

convenient for the River Feale while the modest but welcoming Leen's (068) 31121 is an outstanding hotel in which to stay. It is pricey but excellent in every way. The Dunraven Arms (061) 396209 is less expensive but is still a very comfortable hotel.

Incidentally, it is worth emphasising that The Irish Tourist Board are extremely helpful and will provide lists of self-catering accommodation and bed and breakfast establishments.

Bunratty Castle is a beautiful example of Ireland's heritage and its situation, overlooking the River Bunratty, is quite stunning. The Fitzpatrick's Shannon Shamrock (061) 361177 is by contrast a more modern edifice but a comfortable hotel nonetheless. Wending our way northwards up the Shannon, we find Castleconnell. The Castle Oaks House (061) 377666 is well thought of here. The Lakeside (061) 376122 at Killaloe is also well worth a visit. Further north still, and we arrive at Athlone County Westmeath. The Royal (0902) 72924 is a very friendly hotel in which to stay when in this vicinity.

Visitors to Lough Sheelin will be well catered for and the splendid views from the northern shore of Lough Sheelin are best appreciated from the two hundred year old Crover House (049) 40206 run by the friendly O'Reilly family. In this idyllic setting, every need of the fisherman is catered for with twelve comfortable bedrooms, its own airstrip, a boat pier with fifteen boats and ghillies if required. There is a fine restaurant too and the chef will cook your own catch!

The capital and its surroundings boast a combination of culture and wild scenery which will fascinate the visitor. Those who are planning to stay in the city for the night are spoilt for choice. The Berkeley Court (01) 601711 is an hotel of international acclaim but there are, however, numerous establishments, all extremely good, from which to choose. For help and advice, the Dublin City Tourist Office (01) 747733 is always a good place to start. Outside the city, in Navan, the Ardboyne Hotel (046) 23119 is modern and comfortable. A more traditional and cosy establishment is Bearpark (041) 24207 near Slane. The Conyngham Arms (041) 24155 is also a relaxing hotel from which you can enjoy the Boyne Valley. Another jewel of an hotel which offers fishing too is the Red House in Ardee (041) 53523. You should definitely book in advance for this establishment and expect a very high standard. It is a wonderful place for the sportsman.

While in Kells, The Headfort Arms (046) 40063 is a friendly establishment in which to stay. Our final thought for the area is the Boyne Valley Hotel in Drogheda (041) 37737, a handy place from which to enjoy the fishing on the lower reaches of the Boyne

The Liffey flows through the Wicklow mountains and Kildare before it reaches Dublin. Tulfarris Hotel (045) 64574 overlooks Poulaphouca Lake and is lovingly sheltered by the Wicklow Mountians which rise at the rear of the hotel. Ringwood (01) 6288220 is a splendid Georgian house in 65 acres of farmland and is another good place to stay whilst visiting this area. The Springfield in Leixlip (01) 6244925 should also be considered when planning your trip as should the Setanta House (01) 6271111 in Celbridge which is convenient for the river.

Leaping Salmon (Burrishoole Fishery)

ROD & STREAM (TOURS) PLC

Ireland is the finest game angling holiday resort in Europe, and if you wish to take advantage of some of the best fishing then who better to approach than Rod & Stream (Tours) Plc. They are specialists in game fishing holidays and have brought together an excellent selection of hotels and locations offering the fisherman every type of fishing to suit everyone's preferences and because of this, you can enjoy a wealth of fishing in the cleanest waters in Europe with a climate to match. Long hours of uninterrupted angling, because of the Gulf Stream influence, means an open angling season longer than anywhere else in Europe. Go salmon fishing on the famous Munster Blackwater or sea-trout fishing in Connemara and brown-trout fishing on a number of loughs. By going with Rod & Stream (Tours) Plc you are guaranteed a comfortable stay - exactly what you need after fishing all day. Most of the hotels have drying rooms, storage rooms and of course, freezing facilities if you wish to keep one or two of your catches and all have been selected for the standard and availablity of fishing. All are Irish Tourist Board approved so that you are guaranteed to find the standard of comfort and fishing that you want. All of the hard work of choosing a venue has been already carried out on your behalf. The extra benefit of a company like Rod & Stream (Tours) Plc is that it is not linked financially to the hotels, so the information you get is totally unbiased - each hotel is included purely on its merits.

Rod & Stream (Tours) Plc
24 Wright Street
Southport PR9 OTL
Tel: (0704) 501450
Fax: (0704) 501452

JACKSON'S HOTEL

On the banks of the River Finn, overlooking the beautiful woods of Drumboe and its own charming garden, is this delightful hotel, ideally situated for touring the beautiful countryside of Donegal and only a few minutes drive from Glenveagh National Park and the Glebe Gallery.

All of the hotel's forty bedrooms have ensuite facilities, direct-dial telephone, television and video, and many boast splendid views of the gardens and off into the Finn and Drumboe woods beyond. Family suites are available, as is the delightful honeymoon suite.

The restaurant also commands views of the gardens. Its relaxed atmosphere is ideal for enjoying the excellent menu on offer, fresh local produce and a wealth of sea-food being one of the hotel's many specialities, with a comprehensive wine list to perfectly complement your meal. Or if the attractions of the surrounding countryside leave you with a little less time to eat, try a tempting meal from the delicious array available from the popular Bally Buffet. Relax afterwards in the luxurious bar lounge. Soak up its Old World atmosphere and sample a world-famous Irish Coffee in the hotel where it originated, back in 1952.

For a larger meeting, the hotel has a choice of suites, able to accomodate anything from the smallest seminar to a conference of a 1000 people. The larger Pyramid Suite has played host to a variety of functions, ranging from weddings to concerts and fashion shows.

In its unique location underground, the Pharoahs Niteclub, with its distinctive decor and lighting systems, promises an exciting experience for those who want it, while not disturbing the peace of those who do not.

The town of Ballybofey has long been known as 'The friendliest little market town in Europe', and in a country renowned for its welcoming hospitality, that is saying quite a lot. Nearby there is something for everyone, excellent fishing is available, in particular with the renowned Salmon Leap nearby; an 18-hole golf course waits to be tested by the sportsman, while squash and tennis compete with the joys of outdoor pursuits such as canoeing, horse-riding, shooting and of course walking, for attention from the visitor to this hotel in the beautiful north-west.

Jackson's Hotel
Ballybofey
Co Donegal
Ireland
Tel: (010 353 74) 31021

THE EMERALD ISLE

Cork is a friendly city and well worth a visit. It is also easily accessible and has both a ferry terminal and airport. The River Lee is one of the better local rivers and there are numerous hotels to choose from while staying in the area. The Arbutus Lodge (021) 501237 dates from the 18th century and has some superb grounds which run down to the Lee. The restaurant is first rate and very popular.

Fishing the River Bandon can prove tremendous fun and the Innishannon Hotel (021) 775121 is a superb base from which to conduct your fishing foray. The hotel has a parkland setting with riverside gardens. It boasts a friendly atmosphere and a fine cellar. In Bandon itself, lies the Manster Arms (023) 41562 which offers some good value accommodation.

County Kerry has some of the most beautiful scenery in Europe. Here you will find a range of scenery lovingly crafted by nature and a delight to behold. There are a number of small but worthy salmon waters in the area and no further excuse should be needed for planning a trip here. In Kenmare, there are hotels to suit all budgets and the fisherman is again spoilt for choice. The Sheen Falls (064) 41600 has more glorious fishing opportunities and is obviously high on the list but there are several other options. The Park Hotel (064) 41200 is a palatial establishment with an excellent restaurant. More modest, is the Lansdowne Arms (064) 41368, a welcoming hotel in which to stay. Many will seek to fish Lough Currane and the sport here is good. The Butler's Arms (0667) 4144 has an idyllic setting on the Ring of Kerry overlooking the Atlantic. The Fisherman's Bar is a fine place to reminise on the day's sport.

North of Waterville, we find Caragh Lake where a number of good hotels are to be found. Ard-Na-Sidhe (066) 69105 is an attractive creeper-clad house set in delightful gardens on the lakeside. This is an ideal place to stay and enjoy the surrounding countryside. Caragh Lodge (066) 69115 has a pretty run down to the lake too, and this well kept Victorian hotel offers a friendly welcome to its guests. Glendalough House (066) 69156 also enjoys panoramic views of the lake, albeit from a greater distance.

Fermanagh and Donegal reveal some wild and rugged land, almost beyond compare. Trout fishermen will be in their element. The Kilyreagh Hotel (036587) 221 is a good spot from which to explore the many local waters and the Kilyhevlin Hotel (0365) 323481 has a superb setting on the shores of Lough Erne amidst the lakeland scenery of Fermanagh. The Hilton Park (047) 56007 in Scotshouse, near Clones, is a first class hotel. The many visitors wishing to fish Lough Melvin should contact Gillaroo Angles (0232) 862419 who have excellent local contacts. Once again, bed and breakfast accommodation is available throughout the area but one recommendation is Lake House (072) 41808 in Cloghan or Mountain View (072) 41525 in Gurteendarragh. Both are well situated for the fishing.

If you are looking to fish the vast waters of the Foyle System then you should find some excellent sport in this northerly corner of the country. Rathmullan House (074) 58188 has a glorious setting above Lough Swilly in the wilds of Donegal. The cuisine which is based on local game is also first class. In Kilmacrennan, the Angler's Haven (074) 39015 should also be noted. The Haw Lodge (074) 41397 near Lifford is well positioned, close to the border.

In Northern Ireland itself, an excellent hotel is Blackheath House - a former rectory and an ideal place from which to tour the area. All types of fishing; salmon, trout and sea fishing are possible in the vicinity.

County Down offers yet more sensational scenery and a golf course to delight followers of the fairways. Lovers of fishing will also find some good opportunities here and the Tourist Board for Northern Ireland (0232) 231221 is very helpful. If you are fishing the River Bann then the Downhill Inn in Castlerock (0265) 848090 offers good value accommodation. The Bann System produces some outstanding fishing and the River Bush is also well worth trying, especially in the early autumn. Last, but certainly not least, the Bushmills Inn (02657) 32339 is a friendly and informal inn with a charming atmosphere.

FISHING FAYRE

THE NORTH OF IRELAND

People who are visiting County Galway will once again be rewarded with some superb countryside and a variety of inns, hotels and manor houses. A fine place to start one's trip is the splendid Moycullen House (091) 85566 which overlooks Lough Corrib. The proprietors can organise fishing for guests and for those who love traditional Irish hospitality, this is a must. Incidentally, it is worth noting a really outstanding restaurant nearby; Drimcong House (091) 85115 which enjoys a similarly stunning setting. Further round the lake we find a country house hotel of distiction at Oughterard, Currarevagh House (091) 82312. The house dates back to the mid 19th century and is a mere 100 yards from Lough Corrib. It is a delightful hotel in which to stay and is thoroughly recommended, especially if you enjoy fishing. Surely an hotel with one of the world's most stunning settings must be Ashford Castle (092) 46003, overlooking Lough Corrib. The hotel is part 13th century castle, part French-style chateau and is one of the most delightful places to stay.

North of Lough Corrib, we find Lough Mask. Hotels are not so prolific in this area but the scenery of the Partry Mountains is quite majestic. The Park View House Hotel (092) 41263 is an hotel with pleasant rooms and Cushlough House (092) 41180 offers an intimate and friendly atmosphere. Another modest, but equally comfortable establishment in the area is Alder House (092) 41148.

Lough Carra is another delightful water to fish and is quite remote. Good value bed and breakfast accommodation can be enjoyed at Loughbawn (092) 43046 in Partry. This idyllic and unspoiled countryside offers many opportunities for the fisherman and just driving through this beautiful part of the country is quite an experience. Those anglers who are seeking to fish in the south west of County Mayo on Western Galway will surely find some good sport. One hotel to note here is Cashel House (095) 310001 standing at the head of Cashel Bay and is an idyllic house with a superb restaurant. The Ballynahinch Castle Hotel (095) 310006 is a superb hotel in which to stay with some good shooting and fishing. There is a delightful atmosphere here and it is a fine base from which to explore the surrounding countryside. The Rosleague Manor Hotel (095) 41101 overlooks Bertraghboy Bay to the Connemara National Park and is one to recommend for all lovers of good hotels. Our final thought for the area is the Delphi Lodge (095) 42213 which

THE EMERALD ISLE

stands within the Delphi Estate, making it one of the finest sporting lodges in Ireland.

The north west of Ireland is scattered with numerous loughs and rivers and encompasses some of the most renowned fishing in Ireland. Although some of the waters are well known in fishing circles others remain relatively undiscovered. While every enthusiast will seek to explore the best known waters, large rewards lie in store in the less celebrated waters and a beat off the better trodden tracks will often offer up some exciting fishing. However, we start our journey at one famous fishing hotel; The Newport House Hotel (098) 41222. The hotel lawns reach down to the estuary and this Georgian mansion boasts a civilised and friendly atmosphere - the ideal base for a fishing foray. The hotel offers a number of fishing opportunities while home smoked salmon and fresh seafood feature heavily in the splendid restaurant. In short, Newport House Hotel provides a perfect place to holiday, surrounded as it is by breathtaking scenery and excellent fishing.

Crossmolina also offers some first class fishing opportunities and a superb hotel here is Enniscoe House, Castlehill (096) 31112. This is another splendid Georgian house with a grand but welcoming atmosphere. Fine food and lovely views add to its charms. Lough Conn offers brown trout and spring salmon fishing in season. River salmon are also available as well as a whole range of other leisure pursuits. If you are feeling somewhat exhausted, then fear not, this a place to relax and unwind.

Alternatively, those who are journeying to the wilds of Bangor Erris should consider The Hillcrest (097) 83494, a good value and out of the way establishment with much appeal. If you are staying in Ballina then there are a number of hotels to choose from. The Downhill Hotel (096) 21033 has another fine setting with gardens overlooking the River Brosna. Open fires combine with a lively cosmopolitan atmosphere in this friendly establishment. There is an extensive range of leisure facilities which will keep even the most sports mad family occupied. Another outstanding hotel keen to organise game fishing for you is the Mount Falcon Castle (096) 21172. This is a place to catch salmon, to explore deserted beaches and generally relax and enjoy yourself in luxurious surroundings. Mount Falcon Castle has fishing on the River Moy and salmon and trout fishing in Lough Conn is free to guests. The hotel is efficiently run by Constance Aldridge and she ensures that all guests are are completely pampered during their stay. Other pursuits on offer include horse riding and shooting. The Alpine Hotel (096) 36144 also offers a warm welcome and offers some good value fishing.

Someway south of here we come to Pontoon and the Pontoon Bridge Hotel (094) 56120. This is a good hotel which also provides some fishing. The restaurant here also enjoys a good reputation. Healys Hotel (094) 56443 is another friendly hotel of note in the area. Visitors should also remember that there are numerous bed and breakfasts in places such as Foxford and Swinford which are excellent value. Equally abundant are the many smaller loughs in the surrounding countryside which offer some compelling fishing.

Those of you who enjoy brown trout fishing will no doubt head for Lough Arrow. Here, you find the splendid Coopershill (071) 65018 in Riverstown. The hotel has been in the O'Hara family since 1974 and stands proudly, surrounded by a five hundred

acre estate providing the ideal base from which to explore the surrounding countryside, commonly referred to as 'Yeats Country'. This is a country house hotel of distinction and a perfect place for a short stay. The Cromleach Lodge (071) 65153 is another first class hotel in the region which offers good fishing and another excellent restaurant. The Rock View (079) 66073 on Lough Arrow is smaller and less expensive but still has much charm and is ideal for the fisherman.

Although it might seem some distance away when on the map, we should not overlook Rosses Point. There are a number of delightful loughs here and some superb golf too. A restaurant of character is Reveries (071) 77371. Magnificent views of Sligo Bay are complemented by some first class Irish cooking and this is well worth a special trip. A fine hotel nearby is the Ballincar House (071) 45361, an extremely elegant hotel.

The south east of Ireland is very 'reachable' from England, with flights into Cork and Waterford and the ferry docking at Rosslare. The River Suir reveals a number of first rate fishing opportunities as well as several first class hotels. In Thurles, one finds numerous guest houses and The Anner Hotel (0504) 21799 is a good place to stay in town. Many of Ireland's more significant hotels are located near here. These often tend to enjoy remote settings as they were formerly the homes of wealthy merchant families. Ardnayle House (0504) 42399 is excellent value and an obvious choice for anglers. The Cashel Palace Hotel (062) 61411 is a Palladian mansion with stylish interiors and very comfortable bedrooms. In Dundrum, The Dundrum House Hotel (062) 71116 has a fine situation in acres of parkland through which the river flows, ensuring every game fisherman can be kept fully occupied. Bansha House (062) 54194 is also well worth considering, as is Aherlow House (062) 56147 in Aherlow. Midway between Cahir and Tipperary we find the delightful Lismacue House (062) 54106. The house has been in the family for over 180 years and is a classically beautiful dwelling, boasting all the tradition of Ireland. Trout fishing is available on the estate's own river and salmon and trout fishing are available on the Suir some four miles away.

A fine fishing hotel, near Cahir is Kilcoran Lodge (052) 41288, a former hunting lodge which overlooks the Suir Valley. Twenty or so bedrooms with all modern facilities are found here and the hotel has its own pub too. Nearer to Clonmel, Knocklofty offers the Knocklofty House (052) 38222 which once again enjoys a superb setting overlooking the River Suir. The interior is elegant and the hotel offers numerous leisure facilities. The Hotel Minella (052) 22388 also stands on the banks of the river and is worth noting.

Waterford Castle (051) 78203 is often referred to as Ireland's most outstanding hotel. It is certainly a luxurious establishment with sumptuous bedroooms and elegant public rooms. The cuisine here is also first class.

South of the Suir, we find another river of great repute, the Blackwater River. At Kenturk, The Assolas Country House (025) 50015 has an extremely friendly atmosphere with cosy log fires in winter and some very comfortable bedrooms complete the picture. Fishing is also available, organised by the hotel. This is a peaceful, elegant establishment and a visit is highly recommended. Another fine hotel is Blackwater Castle (022) 26333 at Castletownroche. This is a tremendous hotel for the fisherman and enjoys a delightful setting. Longueville House (022) 47156

THE EMERALD ISLE

is a Georgian house and an ideal base for touring the countryside. It is a first class hotel and one of Ireland's best. The Blackwater runs through the 500 acre estate and both salmon and trout fishing are available to guests. The President's Restaurant here is renowned and is adorned with - you guessed it - paintings of past Presidents.

A small hotel of great charm enjoying a marvellous setting overlooking a wooded gorge cut by the River Arweg, is Creagh Castle (022) 24105. This is an hotel with tradition and is highly recommended. Similarly popular, is Ballyvolane (025) 36349, surrounded by farmland and woods. Guests here can enjoy fishing on eight miles of the River Blackwater. Our final thought for this area is The Blackwater Lodge (058) 60235 - an angler's dream hotel. The enthusiasm for fishing here is almost on a par with the service and this hotel is a charming place to stay.

HEALY'S HOTEL- PONTOON

This ten bedroomed hotel, recently refurbished under new ownership - was originally established in the 1880's by the Healy family.

The premises was originally a Bianconi halting stop, and was developed and opened as a hotel in 1887 by Patrick Healy. The Hotel remained in the Healy family until 1990 when Mr Brendan McGeever, a native of Co. Mayo, returned from Australia to take over ownership of the establishment.

The Hotel is ideally situated in the heart of Mayo's lakeland district, between Lough Conn and Lough Cullen.

The Hotel, nestling in enchanting surroundings amid colourful woodlands and picturesque islands, has all the comforts of a modern hotel, while still retaining its original charm and character.

It is noted for its home-cooking cuisine and friendly atmosphere in the hotel's lounge and bar.

The Hotel is a Bord Failte (Irish Tourist Board) Approved Grade B.

The Hotel is one hours drive from Sligo, Galway, Connemara and Achill Sound.

There is excellent trout and salmon fishing on the lakes and reasonably priced salmon fishing in the River Moy.

Boat hire and ghillie service is available while other facilities for fishermen include a drying room and freezer facilities, and packed lunches prepared on request.

Healy's Hotel Pontoon
Pontoon
Co. Mayo
Ireland
Tel: (010 553 94) 56443
Fax: (010 553 94) 56572

DOWNHILL HOTEL

Far away from polluted air and water is the Downhill Hotel adjacent to the River Moy which is famous for its salmon fishing, attached to Lough Conn and flowing into Killala Bay provides an area rich in fresh and sea water fishing, course angling also available. We are in a position to organise a boat for your day trip be it on the lake, estuary or river (advance booking necessary). For that perfect game angling holiday come to the Moy and stay at the Downhill Hotel in the West of Ireland.

This Grade A hotel offers excellent cuisine, personal and friendly service and fine facilities. Bedrooms are luxurious with TV/video, radio, telephone and tea/coffee making facilities. The

Downhill is situated in beautiful grounds and offers Frogs Pavilion Piano Bar, split level restaurant with extensive menu, swimming pool, sauna, jacuzzi, gymnasium, squash, snooker room, sunbed and craft shop. If you are unable to escape from work the Downhill offers excellent conference facilities and is equipped to meet the most exact requirements.

The Downhill Hotel is conveniently located from Knock Airport and Sligo Airport both 35 miles away. In addition to excellent game angling guests may enjoy golf, walking on the many beautiful sandy beaches and scenic touring.

Downhill Hotel Limited
Ballina, Co Mayo
Ireland
Tel: (010 353 96) 21033
Telex: 40796

MOUNT FALCON CASTLE

Resting in its one hundred acre estate, is the historic country mansion of Mount Falcon. Originally built in 1876 by John Fredrick Knox, it overlooks the Moy Valley towards the changing hues of the heathery slopes of the Ox mountains in the distance.

The owner, Constance Aldridge, plays the part of hostess to her visitors who quickly realise that, in keeping with the tradition of the house, they will experience the friendliness and attention given to a personal guest rather than simply another booking. Here, you can relax beside a log fire in the tranquillity of gracious rooms filled with antique furniture and fresh flowers picked from the gardens.

The superb menu is traditional country house cuisine. Frequently acclaimed in international good food guides, it includes local ingredients, fresh produce from the estate as well as fresh rod-caught salmon from the Mount Falcon Fishery on the River Moy. The delicious food is accompanied by a comprehensive selection of fine wines. After dinner, coffee and drinks are served in the Drawing Room where guests can engage in conversation or make plans for the following day.

There are ten bedrooms all enjoying views of the estate. All the bedrooms have private bathrooms as well as all the amenities you would expect of a good hotel.

Mount Falcon is the ideal base from which to explore the magnificent countryside of County Mayo. Beautiful beaches, rugged coastline, lakes and mountains are all on the doorstep as are fascinating sites of ancient Celtic history.

For the golfer, the first class 18 hole course of Enniscrone is only ten miles away and Ballina has a good 9 hole course. Horse riding is available in the area and the lively old fashioned town of Ballina is worth a visit.

For the serious fisherman, Mount Falcon has excellent facilities having catered for generations of county sportsmen. The River Moy is Ireland's most prolific salmon river and 3 miles away the large limestone loughs, Conn and Cullen provide some of the finest fishing for wild brown trout in Europe.

In the winter months, the castle can arrange excellent rough shooting for woodcock and snipe.

Mount Falcon Castle
Ballina
Co. Mayo
Ireland
Tel: (096) 21172
Fax: (096) 21172

BALLYMAQUIRKE LODGE

Fish Ireland's famed Munster Blackwater and live in complete comfort at Ballymaquirke Lodge.

The Blackwater is arguably the best salmon river in Ireland and Ballymaquirke Lodge and Fishery offers the dedicated angler the opportunity to explore a very private and not usually fished section of it. The fishing comprises a full mile of the Blackwater with 24 named pools and about a quarter of a mile of its tributary, the Allow, both ideal for fly fishing. In addition to salmon and grilse, you will find spirited brown trout in abundance. The season is 1st February to 30th September and wading is not necessary.

Ballymaquirke Lodge is a converted farm cottage completely redesigned and rebuilt by its architect owner. It is pine panelled throughout with a log fireplace, central heating, three bedrooms and two bathrooms and is fully equipped for self-catering. Fishing is just 50 yards from the front door.

The Lodge and fishing are 30 miles north of Cork on the Cork/Killarney road; just two miles from Kanturk and five from Mallow which both offer extensive shopping facilities. Besides the fishing, guests find themselves in one of the most beautiful parts of the Blackwater Valley and about 30 miles from Killarney and its lakes. There is also golf locally, hill-walking and bird-watching, even hunting with the Dunhallow (Hunt) if you like. There are several excellent luxury restaurants within easy reach and a host of pubs and hostelries to welcome you.

The Ballymaquirke Lodge and fishings may be let by the week. The water will accommodate three rods and the Lodge will take five people in considerable comfort. Bookings may be made through the owner, Brian Murphy-O'Connor, by telephone on Cork (010 353 21) 502555 during office hours or by fax (010 353 21) 502376 at anytime.

NORTHERN IRELAND : FURTHER FORAYS

LE MON HOUSE HOTEL,
41 Gransha Road, Castlereagh, Tel: (0232) 448631
Enjoying a countrified location only five miles from Belfast City Centre, Le Mon offers a host of modern comforts. Bedrooms are ensuite and are equipped with TV and telephone, whilst for the insatiably active, a health spa will prove invigorating and refreshing.

WINDERMERE HOUSE,
60 Wellington Park, Belfast, Tel: (0232) 662693
Belfast city centre offers a surprising amount, and this comfortable guesthouse is convenient for shops, theatres, cinemas and restaurants. In addition, the Ulster Museum and Botanic Gardens are only a ten minute walk away.

THE BEECHES,
10 Dunadry Road, Muckamore, Tel: (084 94) 33161
Situated near to the airport, this secluded detached guesthouse provides quiet rural accommodation in the peaceful locality of Dunadry. Local attractions include golf, fishing, bowling and Lough Neagh.

CARRICK-DHU GUESTHOUSE,
6 Ballyreagh Road, Portrush, Tel: (0265) 823666
Portrush is one of Northern Ireland's most vibrant resorts and all types of visitor will enjoy its animated atmosphere. Carrick-Dhu is pleasantly situated in a residential area and is particularly notable for it's cuisine.

GLEN HOUSE,
212 Crawfordsburn Road, Crawfordsjohn, Tel: (0247) 852610
Built in 1710, Glen House can be found in the picturesque village of Crawfordsburn. The friendly proprietor provides attentive and friendly service and will direct guests to the private entrance to Crawfordsburn Country Park.

TRANNER COTTAGE,
5 Main Street, Groomsport, Tel: (0247) 464534
The visitors book is all that is needed to describe the calibre of Tanner Cottage. Comments include:- 'The perfect place to spend a wedding night', 'A home away from home' and 'You've made our visit extra special'.

ARDSHANE COUNTRY HOUSE,
5 Bangor Road, Holywood, Tel: (023 17) 2044
Extensive restoration has transformed this former Edwardian gentleman's residence into an elegant hotel that has not lost touch with yesterday's values. An impressive restaurant offers à la carte and table d'hote menus.

ENNISKEEN HOUSE HOTEL,
98 Bryansford Road, Newcastle, Tel: (039 67) 22392
Splendid views across the Shimna Valley to the Mourne Mountains make this country house hotel an idyllic retreat. All bedrooms have ensuite facilities, colour TV and telephones.

TULLYHONA HOUSE,
Marble Arch Road, Florencecourt, Enniskillen, Tel: (036 582) 452
This acclaimed beef and sheep farm guesthouse is situated beside Florencecourt National Trust House and Marble Arch Caves. Game shooting, golf, fishing and lambing tours offer plenty to keep everyone occupied.

DOWNHILL INN,
5 Mussenden Road, Castlerock, Tel: (0265) 848090
Impressively located overlooking the beach at Downhill, recent refurbishment has made this hotel even more tempting. The busy resort of Portrush is just four miles away.

GREENMOUNT LODGE,
58 Greenmount Road, Gortaclare, Omagh, Tel: (0662) 841325
Greenmount is a particularly popular establishment with touring holidaymakers, partly due to an enviable location. The varied attractions of Fermanagh Lakeland, Gortin Forest Park and Ulster History Park can all be reached with ease.

HALL CRAIG,
Springfield, Enniskillen, Tel: (036589) 330
Hall Craig enjoys an enviable location and is convenient for Belmore Forest, Lough Navar Forest, Lower Lough Erne and National Trust properties. Enniskillen is six miles away and Derrygonnelly some four miles.

MADDYBENNY FARM,
Logestown, Portrush, Tel: (0265) 823394
This award winning guesthouse is justifiably the pride and joy of its friendly proprietor. Bedrooms are beautifully furnished but the real piece de résistance are the sumptuous breakfasts that often eliminate the need for lunch and tea!

TWENTY ACRES,
46 Torr road, Ballyvoy, Ballycastle, Tel: (02657) 62629
This farm bungalow is pleasingly located on the scenic coast road to Murlough Bay, Torr Head and Cushendun. Two double rooms and two ground floor rooms are available from April to October.

WELLINGTON PARK HOTEL,
Belfast, Tel: (0232) 381111
One of the popular weekend spots for local revellers, the Wellington Park also offers fairly reasonably-priced accommodations and more than edible cuisine.

Fishing   (Sheen Falls Hotel)

IRELAND : FURTHER FORAYS

CO CARLOW

BELMONT HOTEL,
Kilkenny Road, Carlow, Co. Carlow, Tel: (010 0353) 503 42002
Only three miles from Carlow, the Belmont is a popular establishment and possesses ten comfortable, ensuite bedrooms. The cuisine is worth a visit in its own right.

GARRYHILL,
Bagenalstown, Co. Carlow, Tel: (010 353) 503 57652
A quaint farmhouse occupying a peaceful woodland setting, Garryhill is available for self-catering holidays. Mountain views provide many exhilarating walks.

CO DONEGAL

DERRYBEG HOTEL,
Cotteen, Derrybeg, Co. Donegal, Tel: (010 353) 75 31005
This is a family-run hotel and the difference is revealed in friendly service, warm hospitality and home cooking that will surely bring you back for a second visit (and helping!).

MANOR HOUSE,
Rosnowlagh, Co. Donegal, Tel: (010 353) 72 51477
Romantically situated between Swan Lake and the Atlantic, Manor House is an immaculate and engaging guesthouse. Bedrooms are spotlessly clean and all have ensuite facilities.

CO CLARE

GREENBRIER INN,
Lahinch, Co. Clare, Tel: (010 353) 65 81242
The world-famous links of Lahinch is within a driver distance of the Greenbrier. Rooms with ensuite facilities will be very welcome after a day on the punishing links.

HALPINS HOTEL,
2 Erin Street, Kilkee, Co. Clare, Tel: (010 353) 65 56032
A family-run seaside hotel, Halpin's is constantly seeking to promote personal attention, combined with a relaxing ambiance. Entertainment is regularly provided.

SHEEDYS SPA VIEW HOTEL,
Lisdoonvarna, Co. Clare, Tel: (010 353) 65 74026
This superb hotel offers sterling accommodation at moderate prices. Both hotel and restaurant are award winning and highly recommended, ensuring the regular return of many guests. For the more energetic, a tennis court is provided.

BUNRATTY LODGE,
Bunratty, Tel: (010 353) 61 72402
Bunratty Lodge is an elegant neo-Georgian house that can be reached by the road that cuts between Bunratty Castle and Durty Nelly's. All six rooms have private facilities, orthopaedic beds and colour TV.

SANCTA MARIA HOTEL,
Lahinch, Co. Clare, Tel: (010 353) 65 81041
The Sancta Maria possesses an enviable reputation for cuisine that is prepared using only the finest and freshest foods. That is only half the story however, and accommodation is of an equally high calibre.

CO CORK

ARBUTUS LODGE,
Montenotte, Cork, Co. Cork, Tel: (010 353) 21 501237
This highly-recommended hotel occupies a splendid setting, overlooking the city of Cork. The hotel is enhanced by an acclaimed restaurant.

CRAIGIES HOTEL,
Camentringane House, Castleownbere, Co. Cork, Tel: (027) 70379
A warm welcome awaits at Craigies Hotel on the beautiful Beara Peninsula. The hotel itself is extremely well appointed and the restaurant enjoys glorious views of Bere Island and the picturesque harbour. The hotel has fishing rights on Glanmore river and lake system, and excellent sport is available.

MOUNT CARMEL,
Ballyvergan, Cork Road, Co. Cork, Tel: (010 353) 24 92542
Seaside and countryside can both be explored in abundance from this popular retreat. Bedrooms are spacious and even include electric blankets, just in case the climate does not live up to its warm reputation.

HILLSIDE,
Cahirkeem, Eyeries, Bantry, Tel: (010 353) 27 74005
Hillside is a thirty acre working farm, and visitors are more than welcome to join in with milking and walking cattle etc. Disabled guests can be specially catered for.

KILLEENLEIGH,
Glandore, Co. Cork, Tel: (010 353) 28 33103
Killeenleigh is an eighteenth century farmhouse that has been converted into a friendly country home. The picturesque and bustling harbour of Glandore is close by and birdwatchers and artists will also find plenty to keep them occupied.

CO GALWAY

ARD EINNE,
Cill Einne, Aran Islands, Inishmore, Co. Galway,
Tel: (010 353) 99 61126
Some of Ireland's wildest and most spectacular scenery can be absorbed from this relaxing guesthouse. Bicycle and walking tours can all be arranged for those who wish to take advantage of this glorious countryside.

ROCKLAND HOTEL,
The Promenade, Salthill, Co. Galway, Tel: (010 353) 91 22111
Fourteen sumptuous bedrooms feature ensuite facilities, direct dial telephone, satellite TV and coffee/tea making facilities. As if all that wasn't sufficient, the beach is only a few hundred yards away.

ERRISEASK HOUSE HOTEL,
Ballyconneely, Connemara, Co. Galway, Tel: (010 353) 95 23553
Breathtaking scenery and private beaches prove sufficeient to attract discerning holidaymakers to a beautiful corner of Ireland. The renowned Connemara golf course is but a few miles away.

CO KERRY

LINDEN HOUSE,
New Road, Killarney, Co. Kerry, Tel: (010 353) 64 31379
Set in a residential area away from the thronging town centre, Linden House is a family run guesthouse, renowned for it's excellent and nutritious cuisine prepared by the owner/chef.

ST MARTINS,
Oakpark Road, Tralee, Co. Kerry, Tel: (010 353) 66 25004
As well as offering comfortable accommodation, St Martin's is conveniently situated for the bus/rail station and sports centre. The Championship golf course is also within easy reach.

EAGLE LODGE,
Ballybunion, Tel: (010 353) 68 27224
Eagle Lodge offers a great deal more than the average guesthouse. All bedrooms have private bathrooms and are centrally heated. The restaurant is renowned for it's cuisine with a range of Table d'Hote and A la carte menus.

IRELAND : FURTHER FORAYS

HILLCREST,
Mountway, Ballyheigue, Tel: (010 353) 66 33306
Ballyheigue is a renowned family resort, whose shoreline and country-side provide walks and exploration for the energetic visitor. Hillcrest is a spacious bungalow that is convenient for all local amenities.

DOYLE'S SEAFOOD BAR AND TOWNHOUSE,
John Street, Dingle, Tel: (010 353) 660 51174
Eight generously sized bedrooms await the lucky visitor at this popular townhouse. Moreover, every bedroom comes complete with private bathroom, direct dial telephone and television.

CO MAYO

MASK VIEW,
Treen, Tourmakeady, Co. Mayo, Tel: (010 353) 92 44021
With Lough Mask as an imposing and spectacular backdrop, Mask View provides modest, tasteful bedrooms and typically warm Irish hospitality.

SEASIDE HOUSE,
Dooega, Achill Island, Co. Mayo, Tel: (010 353) 98 45116
Only a short walk from the beach, this popular guesthouse is also convenient for sea angling and a nearby Art Gallery. Family holidays are a particular speciality.

TRAVELLERS FRIEND HOTEL,
Westport Road, Castlebar, Co. Mayo, Tel: (010 353) 94 23111
The name of this hotel is quite indicative of the atmosphere that prevails inside. Excellent restaurants and bars complement the historic John Moore Lounge and open fire foyer.

CO ROSCOMMON

ROYAL HOTEL,
Bridge Street, Boyle, Co. Roscommon, Tel: (010 353) 79 62016
This busy, friendly town offers a number of opportunities for activities and places of interest. Anglers will also find the river Boyle a particular attraction.

CO SLIGO

TARA,
Ballina Road, Inniscrone, Co. Sligo, Tel: (010 353) 96 36398
The acclaimed championship golf course of Innescrone ensures that this guesthouse receives its own share of attention. Organic produce and wonderful home cooking are two other reasons for recommending it.

DUBLIN

ELEGANT IRELAND,
15 Harcourt Street, Dublin 2, Tel: (010 353) 1 751632/751665
Elegant Ireland are an incoming Tour Operator that can offer a wide range of services to interested clients. In addition to securing all travel and accommodation arrangements, possibilities include Garden Tours, Stately Home Tours, Art Tours and Golf Tours-a comprehensive service indeed.

LANSDOWNE HOTEL,
27 Pembroke Road, Dublin 4, Tel: (010 353) 1 682522
Georgian Dublin is a splendid sight and the Lansdowne Hotel is set right in its heart. A wealth of amenities are within easy reach including the Royal Dublin Society, Lansdowne Rugby Club and a multiplicity of shops.

MOUNT CLARE HOTEL,
Merrion Square, Dublin 2, Tel: (010 353) 1 616799
Close to Trinity College, in the very heart of Dublin City, Mount Castle Hotel is within walking distance of Grafton Street, DART, Dail Eireann Art Gallery and Museum. Needless to say, there are plenty of distinguished bars also in the vicinity.

IONA HOUSE,
Glasnevin, Tel: (010 353) 1 306855
The hospitality that is liberally offered by the Iona has made it renowned with lovers of Ireland the world over. Pleasantly located in Galsnevin, the city centre is only a fifteen minute walk.

CO DUBLIN

THE DUNES HOTEL,
Donabate, Co. Dublin, Tel: (010 353) 436111
Only six miles from Dublin Airport, the Dunes is a haven for golf enthusiasts with four courses-the Island, Beaverstown, Donabate and Corballis-all ready to welcome visitors

SEA VIEW GUESTHOUSE,
Strand Road, Portmarnock, Co. Dublin, Tel: (010 353) 1 462242
Overlooking Dublin Bay, this warm, friendly guesthouse is an ideal base for Dublin Airport, Malahide Castle and the Dublin Mountains. A hair salon and sun bed in the hotel mean that good weather is not even a necessity!

CO. KILKENNY

NEWPARK HOTEL,
Castlecomer Road, Kilkenny, Co. Kilkenny, Tel: (010 353) 56 22122
The new and majestic Mt. Juliet complex is only a short drive from this popular hotel. The Newpark itself has more than enough to keep visitors happy, including an impressive leisure centre.

THE QUAY,
St Mullin's, Graiguenamanagh, Co. Kilkenny, Tel: (010 353) 51 24665
This picturesque and well-maintained house is located on the River Barrow in historic St. Mullin's village. Angling is available locally.

CO MEATH

HAMWOOD,
Dunboyne, Co. Meath, Tel (01) 255210
Hamwood was built in 1760 and has been lived in by the Hamilton family ever since. It is a very pleasant and comfortable house for guests and possesses beautiful gardens. Racing, golf and fishing are all nearby attractions.

CO LIMERICK

TUOGH-VILLA,
Askeaton Road, Adare, Tel: (010 353) 61 396432
This pleasant bungalow enjoys a peaceful setting, only a mile from the beautiful village of Adare. Golf, fishing and Curraghchase Forest Park figure among the nearby attractions.

FOUR SEASONS,
Ballyneety, Limerick, Tel: (010 353) 61 351365
This friendly, family run guesthouse will find favour with all the family-features include a children's playground, tea/coffee making facilities, board games and a free baby-sitting service. Lough Gur, the Hunt Museum and Bunratty Folk Park will provide endless hours of amusement.

IRELAND : FURTHER FORAYS

WOODFIELD HOUSE HOTEL,
Ennis Road, Limerick, Tel: (010 353) 61 53023
Only a mile from Limerick City, Woodfield House Hotel is a family run establishment that has recently undergone extensive refurbishment. An excellent Steak House, lounge bars, sun lounges and a beer garden all ensure ample refreshment.

CO OFFALY

HIGHFIELD FARMHOUSE,
Rosfaraghan, Ferbane, Tel: (010 353) 902 54387
Highfield is a working dairy farm, some two miles from Ferbane on the main Clara Road. Nature enthusiasts will delight in the many boglands whilst anglers will find comfort in the rivers Brosna and Shannon.

ASHBROOK,
Shannonbridge, Athlone, Tel: (010 353) 905 74166
Located in the heart of one of Ireland's premium fishing areas, Ashbrook provides immaculate accommodation in a beguiling setting. Clonmacnois, one of Ireland's most historic sites and a former great Christian University, is only five miles away.

CO KILDARE

HARBOUR VIEW,
The Harbour, Naas, Co. Kildare, Tel: (010 353) 45 79145
Service with a genuine smile are impressive trademarks of this family run guesthouse. Punchestown, the Curragh and Mondello are within easy reach.

CO LAOIS

PARK HOUSE,
Stradbally, Portlaoise, Co. Laois, Tel: (010 353) 502 25147
This award winning farmhouse accommodation, only an hours drive from Dublin is actually a working tillage farm. Fresh farm produce is used to prepare meals that have to be seen to be believed.

CO LEITRIM

GORTMOR,
Lismakeegan, Carrick-on-Shannon, Co. Leitrim, Tel: (010 353) 78 20489
Only two miles from the main Dublin road, Gortmor House makes a convenient base for the many pleasures of Co. Leitrim. The standard of cooking is unlikely to hasten your departure!

RIVERSDALE,
Ballinamore, Co. Leitrim, Tel: (010 353) 78 44122
A glance at a reasonable tariff does not anticipate quite excellent facilities, including squash and sauna. The surrounding countryside is worthy of exploring and exploring.

CO LOUTH

ORLEY HOUSE,
25 Brayanstown, Drogheda, Co. Louth, Tel: (010 353) 41 36019
A wide variety of local amenities can be found close to this splendid guesthouse. The bus/rail station, beach, golf, fishing and horse riding among many other attractions are sure to keep everyone happy.

CO TIPPERARY

BALLYCORMAC HOUSE,
Aglish, Borrisokane, Co. Tipperary, Tel: (010 353) 67 21129
Mouth watering Cordon Bleu food is served here using home-grown organic vegetables. All of the well-appointed bedrooms are ensuite.

BANSHA CASTLE,
Bansha, Co. Tipperary, Tel: (010 353) 62 54187
Dating from the nineteenth century and with a secluded woodland setting, Bansha House provides excellent accommodation at reasonable rates. Golf, fishing and walking are popular pursuits available in the locality.

CURRAGHBAWN HOUSE,
Lake Drive, Newtown, Nenagh, Tel: (010 353) 67 23226
A spacious residence set in a rural location, Curraghbawn House can provide visitors with a whole array of facilities and amenities. Fishing, golf, windsurfing, shooting and clay pigeon shooting can all be arranged with the minimum of fuss.

CO WATERFORD

BYRON LODGE,
Ardmore, Co. Waterford, Tel: (010 353) 24 94157
Overlooking an immaculate beach, Byron Lodge offers open fires and superb seafood. Local places of interest include the fishing village of Ardmore and a Monastic Settlement Round Tower.

HANORAS COTTAGE,
Nire Valley, Ballymacarberry, Co. Waterford, Tel: (010 353) 52 36134
This converted ancestral cottage is beautifully set among woods and mountain splendour. Golf, walking, riding and fishing are all available locally.

CO WEXFORD

WOODLANDS HOUSE,
Killinierin, Gorey, Co. Wexford, Tel: (010 353) 402 37125
Accommodation and cuisine can both be highly recommended at this pleasant farmhouse. A resident pony will keep the children amused; if not, the beach is only ten minutes away.

CRANE FARM,
Ferns, Tel: (010 353) 54 33476
All the facilities that guests expect of high calibre farmhouse accommodation are present at Crane Farm. In addition, Co. Wexford is absolutely steeped in history, not least of which is Crane Farm itself, landing site of the first plane to cross the Irish sea, in 1912.

DEVEREUX HOTEL,
Wexford Road, Rosslare Harbour, Co. Wexford, Tel: (010 353) 53 33216
The proximity of this hotel to Rosslare Ferry Port makes it an ideal first or last stop in Ireland. The steak and seafood delights of the Le Coquille Restaurant will make it all the more difficult to leave.

CO WICKLOW

ABHAINN MOR HOUSE,
Corballis, Rathdrum, Co. Wicklow, Tel: (0404) 46330
This acclaimed and highly popular establishment provides ensuite bedrooms and extensive conveniences. A tennis court offers an outdoor alternative to the local beaches.

BALLYKNOCKEN HOUSE,
Glenealy, Ashford, Co. Wicklow, Tel: (0404) 44627
Ballyknocken House offers bedrooms that are tastefully and elegantly furnished. Mount Usher Gardens, providing a wealth of colour, are only three miles distant.

KILCORAN SEA FLOWERS

SERVES 4

INGREDIENTS

4 Fillets of Trout

1 Small Carrot (Sliced)

½ Stick of Celery (Sliced)

½ Small Onion (Sliced)

4 Courgettes

8 Courgette Blossoms

3 fl.oz (75ml) White Wine

1 Dessertspoon Coriander Seeds

2 Dessertspoon Orange Juice

4oz (115g) Butter.

METHOD

Skin the fish fillets and place the skins in a saucepan with the carrot, celery and onion and pour in ¾ pint of water. Bring it slowly to the boil and then simmer for 10 minutes, strain and keep the stock.

Cut one courgette into thin petal like strips, blanch the strips for 30 seconds in boiling water and drain on paper towels. Chop the other courgettes finely and sprinkle with salt and pepper. Wash the courgette blossoms, open out and stuff with chopped courgettes. Put the stuffed courgettes on a steamer rack and set above simmering water, cover tightly and steam for 6 minutes.

Cut fillets into thin petal-like slices and place into a frying pan, cover with the reserved stock. Poach for 15 minutes.

FOR THE SAUCE

Keep the fish warm and strain the stock into a saucepan. Add wine and the coriander seeds to the stock and boil rapidly. Reduce by one half, then add the orange juice and begin beating butter into the sauce bit by bit. Please note do not allow it all to boil when adding the butter.

TO SERVE

Strain the sauce onto a serving plate and arrange the fish petals on the sauce. Place the courgettes petals on top of the fish and add two stuffed courgette blossoms to each serving.

A FAVOURITE FROM THE KILCORAN LODGE HOTEL

ABERCROMBIE AND KENT'S
WORLD OF FISHING

Abercrombie and Kent's 'World of Fishing' brochure is entering its fourth year of operation and is now well established as an international fishing brochure with a strong reputation in Great Britain offering the greatest variety of some of the best game fishing available in both hemispheres.

The 16 page colour brochure offers a comprehensive range of fresh and saltwater fly fishing as well as big game fishing holidays throughout the world in some of the most famous and unique fishing destinations.

These include some excellent Atlantic Salmon fishing in Norway and the Soviet Union, Pacific Salmon fishing in Alaska, and Trout fishing in Montana, Chile, New Zealand, the Falklands and South Africa.

For those who prefer a tussle with larger quarry there is some excellent and reasonably priced big game fishing in Madeira as well as the superb sport to be had off Malindi in Kenya and off the South West coast of Mauritius.

For those who like to try their hand at something different, the saltwater fly fishing destinations of Christmas Island, Deep Water Cay, Boca Paila and Andros Island will all put people in dramatic touch with Bonefish, Tarpon and Permit.

Flexibility is one of Abercrombie and Kent's bywords and, where possible, fixed itineraries are avoided and an attempt is made to accommodate all requirements in a tailor made itinerary suitable for both the serious fisherman, the family holiday or even business trip.

Abercrombie and Kent has facilities for coping with most travel problems; flights can be arranged, extensions made and reservations booked all under one roof thus offering a complete travel service. The company also has a selection of other travel brochures, which are available on request, all with the same attention to detail, service and style.

For further information on Abercrombie and Kent's World of Fishing programme or a copy of the brochure please contact Sara Eley or Andrew Wallace at the following address:

Abercrombie and Kent
Sloane Square House
Holbein Place
London SW1W 8NS
Tel: 071 730 9600
Fax: 071 730 9376

FOREIGN FORAYS

This final section is not designed to go into great detail about the fishing available worldwide, but to give you a taste and to whet your appetite for the delights that can be discovered, ranging from the vast expanses of Canada to some fine sea trout fishing in Chile or fishing in the spectacular surroundings of New Zealand. Fishing trips worldwide are not inexpensive but for the fishing experience of a lifetime, some of the fishing contained within these pages cannot be surpassed, either for the quality or quantity of the catch, or for the magnificent locations in which the fisherman will find. As you can probably imagine, if we tried to give a detailed account of the fishing just in Canada you would now be the proud owner of a 600 page book. So what we have tried to do here is to describe some of the best fishing along with giving some useful numbers so that you can either arrange your own package or to use one of the experienced fishing tour operators who offer a number of very tempting tours, each with different itineraries.

CANADA

What can be said about **Canada**? There are literally thousands and thousands of rivers and lakes, some of which have probably never seen a hand crafted fly before; each Province has a speciality, whether it be fishing for salmon (Atlantic and Pacific), 30lb lake trout or Arctic grayling. Well, I suppose it's only to be expected from a country which has probably a third of the freshwater available worldwide. We will not attempt here to classify the fishing or list them in a table of merit, but allow the readers to judge for himself, from the descriptions and from the words of those who have had the privilege to have fished these waters which fishing or which country suits each individual's requirements.

It's hard to choose which province to start with. For ease of reading we will start in the east and head west.

So we begin the journey in Newfoundland and Labrador. Fishing in Labrador, it is impossible to practically define the difference between good and great fishing, for it has world class salmon and trout fishing.

You will be fishing in surroundings where the day's activities will often be interrupted by the sighting of moose, black bear, caribou and countless other species of wildlife. You can fish for Atlantic salmon averaging 15-20lb, though fish over 20lb are regularly hooked (the Eagle River is world famous) and if you are unfortunate enough to fail to bag one of these beauties then there are plentiful grilse of up to 8lb.

Another marvellous test of your fishing skill is the hard fighting Brook (speckled) Trout with trophy size fish of 5-6lb being caught. Labrador holds 4 world records (IGFA) for brook trout in different categories but all were taken using fly rods, and were caught on Minipi lake and Minipi river. Don't let their size fool you into a false sense of security, they'll fight you all the way in. Marvellous sport.

If Labrador sounds like the place for you, it is probably best to know that, like a lot of fishing in Canada, it is not for the weak willed or faint hearted. A lot of the best fishing is off the beaten track, so the accommodation is comfortable but basic, but by the time you're hooked into one of the many fish to be had, your few worries about comfort will have evaporated. The salmon season runs from the 1st July to the 15th September, while Brook trout can be fished between the 2nd June to 15th

Labrador   (Go Fishing Canada)

FOREIGN FORAYS

September, with a few local differences.

To get there, a number of UK based operators have several packages available. Choose between Abercrombie & Kent 071-730-9600, Ker & Downey 071-629-2044, Go Fishing-Canada (0371) 876785, Sport Elite Ltd. (093589) 477, Newfoundland and Labrador Tourism (0101-709) 576 2830.

In Nova Scotia, which is renowned for its wildlife, such as numerous species of birds including a vast colony of puffins which act as a superb backdrop to the fishing, you will be drawn again by the prospect of some excellent Atlantic Salmon fishing. One of the beauties of Canada is that unlike a lot of the great fishing in Europe, nearly all the waters are accessible, so enjoy salmon and trout fishing on nearly all of the rivers and lakes of Nova Scotia.

Traditional methods of fly fishing work perfectly here, in fact, probably better than you're used to. The catches here can be so prolific that limits on the numbers of fish you are allowed to keep are strictly enforced and, indeed, as elsewhere in Canada, the use of barbless hooks is enthusiastically encouraged. When you buy your licence each fisherman is issued with 10 tags, each which will have the number of your permit on them, which must remain on the fish you keep up until the moment you cook them; this in no way will ruin your enjoyment of the sport. As long as you return the fish immediately, you can catch as many fish as you want, so the main enjoyment, the thrill of the chase, is still there.

Although the season varies throughout the province, most of June through to September is open season, but remember Nova Scotia is a strict fly fishing only province.

If any of this apparent red tape has dampened any of your enthusiasm then think again Nova Scotia has some of the best, and most prolific Atlantic Salmon fishing, dare we say, in the world. The most bountiful rivers are Medway and Lehave in the south, Stewiacke and St Mary's in mid-province and Margeree in the north.

Having said that, there are a number of rivers with substantial but smaller salmon runs throughout the province, so keep your ears open for any titbits imparted by the locals.

We don't want to give the impression that Nova Scotia has nothing but Atlantic salmon, if that wasn't enough it has some marvellous fishing, whatever your particular favourite happens to be. It might be fishing for landlocked salmon, slightly smaller than its saltwater brethren, known locally as Sebago salmon, found primarily in Shubenacadie Grand Lake, although smaller numbers can be fished in countless other lakes.

If you get bored with landing salmon after salmon, or you feel you want to give your arms a rest, brook trout offer a challenge but need slightly lighter tackle. As the sport of landing one of these fighting beauties is much sought after, the best fishing can be had off the beaten track. Take yourself off to the following counties: Cape Breton, Cumberland, Halifax, Guysborough and Lunenburg.

The brook trout that manage to avoid the unwelcome attention of the fisherman migrate to the open sea and after a couple of years return as sea-trout. These provide truly exceptional sport

Miramichi (Go Fishing Canada)

on many of the rivers more famous for their salmon catches. If you think travelling to Nova Scotia to fish for rainbow trout is odd, don't worry. The rainbows you will encounter in North America bear little relation to their European counterparts. They are ferocious fighters and their added benefit is that they make delicious eating.

The best lakes are Levers, Rumsey and Clearwater. The brown trout introduced from Europe in 1923 can be found in numerous lakes, although if you want to fish for large trout, the lake trout growing upwards of 20lb can be fished in Sherbrooke lake although it must be said in lesser numbers.

Go Fishing-Canada (0371) 876785, Fresh Adventures Ltd. (0462) 816424 and Sport Elite Ltd. (093589) 477 have a number of packages including trips to the Margeree river, one of the most famous salmon rivers in Canada. If you feel you would prefer to organise your own trip then the Nova Scotia Tourist Office (071)-930-6864 will be more than happy to help.

Off the coast of Nova Scotia can be found Prince Edward Island which although it cannot boast the vast array of fishing that other provinces can, the fishing is good enough to make a trip well worth while with Atlantic salmon on the Morel river and rainbow and Brook trout on most of the rivers and lakes. The best people to speak to, before you arrange your trip here are the Department of Tourism on (0101-902) 892-3420.

New Brunswick again shares the jewels that its sister provinces boast both in terms of the fishing and the scenery. 88% of New Brunswick is covered in forest so wherever you find yourself fishing it is guaranteed to be in splendid surroundings.

The country is dissected by three major river systems, and not surprisingly for Canada they are very good salmon rivers, the Restigouche, the Saint John and the mighty Miramichi. The Miramichi with its many tributaries literally drains the entire centre of the province by itself, providing salmon in huge numbers so much so that the Miramichi is responsible for half the Atlantic salmon caught in North America. Again, the true sports fisherman is rewarded as only fly fishing is allowed for sea run salmon. They are quite strict on the size of fish that can be retained, which, in the interest of keeping a good stock of trophy fish, and has to be applauded. Any fish under 63 centimetres must be released; salmon steal the show again with salmon caught on the Miramichi weighing up to 40lb (10-12lb being the average). With your thoughts being on catching salmon after salmon, many being trophy size, your departure date will come all too soon, but less of these depressing thoughts. New Brunswick can also boast an alternative if you should so desire in the form of Brook trout and landlocked salmon, known locally as 'ovananiche.'

Go Fishing-Canada (0371) 876785 will be introducing New Brunswick into their programme next year; Fresh Adventures Ltd. (0462) 816424 and Escape Activities (0754) 23812 already operate to New Brunswick. For those who prefer the 'Do-it-Yourself' trip, New Brunswick Tourist office (0101-506) 453-2444 will be happy to assist.

If someone asked you if a land the size of Texas, covered by forest with thousands of lakes and rivers whose neighbours boasted marvellous fishing, had anything to offer the serious game fisherman, then you would probably hazard the guess

'Yes'. Well, you'd be right: Quebec is twice the size of Texas, with just over half its area the ideal location for game fishing of all varieties, including what many consider to be the ultimate game fish, the Arctic char.

With over a million lakes, rivers and streams you will not have difficulty in fishing for one or two if not all of your favourites.

In the west of Quebec are the renowned Moisie and Chaloupe rivers which are famed for the abundance of, and the fighting spirit, of the Atlantic Salmon. The rivers here are not large, so for those of you who enjoy your fishing in waders, Quebec offers a reasonable alternative to the Miramichi. There are other fine but less prolific rivers to accompany the Chaloupe and the Moisie. The problem of overcrowding does not exist in Canada, with only 10 rods per 60 miles of river in many cases.

In the north there are two rivers which offer excellent sport, the Delay and Melezes, which both flow into the Koksoak. There are over 120 miles of fishing here on these two rivers, where trophy salmon of over 30lb can be caught although the average is more around the 12lb mark. The Moisie holds one of the world records (IGFA) for an Atlantic salmon caught in freshwater by fly with a fish weighing 44lb 12oz.

The Gaspe Peninsula has two very good rivers, the Bonaventure and the Cascapedia but, unfortunately, a lot of the fishing is private. This is not surprising as the Cascapedia holds the all time world record (IGFA), for a salmon caught in freshwater using a fly, weighing in at 47lb. Another premier salmon river is the George which runs through the Ungava territory in the north into the Ungava Bay. One of the reasons for the superb fishing is quite simply the inaccessibility of the locations.

Quebec   (Quebec Tourist Board)

FOREIGN FORAYS

As I mentioned earlier, one reason for travelling to Quebec is to fish for Arctic char, found in large numbers in the estuary of the Tuksukatuk River. These fish, which can be caught up to weights of 25lb, are greatly admired for the formidable fight they put up, worthy of a salmon of one and a half times its weight; once fished you will understand why they are so highly regarded by the serious sports fisherman..The lake from which this river flows, the Tuksukatuk, is the venue for some excellent lake trout fishing. They can be caught up to weights of 30lb and as the waters are so cold they do at least swim relatively close to the surface.

For some light relief, but if you still wish to enjoy a spirited scrap the brook trout (some weigh up to 8lb), will prove to be an admirable opponent and can be found in the rivers or in many of the coves and inlets of the lakes, one of the best being the Assinica Broadback River. Bag limits have been imposed, but most of you will be happy to release them satisfied completely with the combination of the idyllic surroundings and the thrill of combat. The Quebec experience is heightened by the different culture; the majority of Quebec enjoying a French influence. Look out also for the largest caribou herd in the world.

A company who has already recognised the potential of Quebec is Fresh Adventures (0462) 816424; Go Fishing-Canada (0371) 876785 will be introducing it as part of their 1991/1992 season.

Quebec's Tourist Office (071)-930-8314 can (if you should so desire) give you full details on all the rivers and lakes but I would imagine the details here although brief would satisfy the appetite of the most voracious fisherman.

We move sedately onto Ontario. It has both the capital Ottawa and the commercial centre Toronto. If you've come to Ontario to fish for salmon, then, unfortunately, you've come to the wrong place, apart from a little titbit that we will impart slightly later. There is fishing and it is good fishing. It's all in the North and the majority of the best sport is to be had at the fly-in fishing camps - you really are fishing out in the wilderness. Due to this it has some of the best conditions in the world for brook trout, it boasts the all time world record (IGFA) of 14lb 8oz and so if these glorious fighting fish are your particular cup of tea, then you will find little better. The price you pay for fishing two of the best rivers, the Nettogami and the Sutton is that you have to pay for it in sweat and toil. You will have some exhilarating sport but you will feel as though you've earnt it.

Now, as promised, that little titbit. There is salmon fishing in Ontario, well there's one salmon, and it will be in lake Ontario from May 1st onwards. The Toronto Star, the local newspaper, organises what is known surprisingly enough as the Toronto Star Salmon Hunt. Now this may not appeal to the purists of you out there, because traditional fly techniques are unlikely to prove successful, although you may well be tempted to push your morals to one side for the day, for the lucky fisherman who bags this tagged salmon will receive $1,000,000. Go Fishing-Canada (0371) 876785 specialise here or alternatively contact the Ontario Tourist Board on (071)-245-1222 if you are tempted by either the brook trout or early retirement.

If you're looking for somewhere in the world to fish, matching the thrill of salmon fishing, but fishing for what can only be described as monster trout, then you've found one in Manitoba where the lake trout, the native of North American waters, can reach upwards of 50lb, although they average out between 15

Manitoba   (Anglers World Today)

FOREIGN FORAYS

and 25lb. The official record is 62lb and if you can't imagine a trout that size, then you'll just have to go out there and experience one yourself. These fish can match and probably beat the Atlantic salmon pound for pound for the length and toughness of the battle. They only inhabit lakes that are clear, cold and highly oxygenated. In the spring when the surface water is cold, they can be caught using light tackle or spinning gear. During the summer months as they prefer the cold, you will find them in the deeper parts of the lake, although fly fishing techniques can be used all season in the northern parts of the lakes due to the surface water remaining cold.

The big two, where the majority of the big catches have been taken, are Nueltin and Nejanilini lakes. Big catches have been recorded in numerous others but not in such prolific numbers.

The trout family continues to entertain in Manitoba with Brook trout and the rainbow. For the purist who is primarily interested in quality rather than quantity, then again, fly fishing for Brookies because of their zesty fighting qualities is hard to match. The best places to find the Brook are the South Knife River, God's River and East Blue; Bower Deep and Barbe lakes for the rainbow, although, as usual, there are plenty of marvellous alternatives, producing good catches but again, not in the same quantities. You may also come across the European brownie when fishing for rainbow on East Blue lake or on Williams lake.

Finally the Arctic grayling: I say finally, but purely because it is the last fish to be mentioned and not a true game fish by right, but it is a superb fish for the traditional fly fisherman. It has few rivals for its beauty, being known as the 'Sailfish of the North' because of its high sail - like dorsal fin. It is a small fish by comparison but it more than makes up for it with its spectacular show, often leaping clear out of the water; it is found only in extreme northern streams, preferring cold clear flowing waters. The best of Manitoba's Arctic grayling fishing is to be found around and on Munroe and Kanapakaksis lakes as well as Nueltin and Nejanilini.

Again, you can leave all the worries of organisation to the experienced, Anglers World Holidays (0246) 221717 who offer a package with a nice extra, that you can extend your holiday if you haven't had enough fishing after 7 days, which is very unlikely. There is a rumour that one gentleman is still there after two and a half years! Manitoba's Tourist Office can be reached on (0101-204) 945-3777. Northwest Territories' name in itself gives you a fairly good idea of what to expect. Although it takes up almost a third of all Canada, it is home to only 55,000 people, the population of a small English town like Warwick. It has ocean coastline, countless fresh water lakes, mountains, glaciers, Precambrian Shield, Tundra and Polar desert all on an unbelievable scale; it includes two of the world's largest lakes, the Great Bear and Great Slave, the enormous Mackenzie river and Virginia falls, (twice the height of Niagara). The sport here tends to be exceptional, due primarily to the shortness of the season. It lasts only 8-12 weeks, the rest of the time, it's frozen over. Like Manitoba you are here to fish for lake trout and Arctic grayling. They encourage a catch and release policy, a practise which would greatly improve the fishing everywhere if more fishermen were sympathetic to it, which means that there is a good chance that some of the fish or maybe even all the fish that you will catch will be of a good size. North-west Territories hold the world record (IGFA) for a lake trout at 65lb, but also

the freshwater fly record (IGFA) of 21 lb, both being taken on the Great Bear and the world records (IGFA) for Artic grayling, freshwater fly as well as the all time world record (IGFA) of 5lb 15oz. There are countless lakes in Northwest Territories. Three of the best for quality and accessibility are Fergeson, Drum and the Great Bear itself. Although you can never guarantee catching a big fish on whatever water you fish, Northwest Territories is one place where you get pretty close. Anglers World Holidays (0246) 221717 who specialise in fishing for trophy size lake trout will be happy to advise you what is on offer. Go Fishing-Canada (0371) 876 785 are introducing this area for 1992. The tourist office of Northwest Territories can be reached on (0101-403) 873-7200.

We've told you about two locations for trophy size lake trout and Arctic grayling. Due to the sheer size of Canada, there are three more: Saskatchewan, the Yukon and Alberta. Anglers World Holidays (0246) 221717 are including Alberta next year, to continue their itinerary of lake trout fishing and also the marvellous fishing offered on the Bow river. The tourist offices to be contacted are: Saskatchewan (0101-306) 787-2300, Yukon (0101-403) 667-5340 and Alberta (071)-491-3430. With a choice like this it may be easier to toss a coin; they all have exceptional fishing in unsurpassed settings.

BRITISH COLUMBIA

British Columbia is further to fly to from Britain, but the one thing that will get you on that plane without a second thought is that this quite simply is the Pacific Salmon capital of the world. Nowhere else can you fish for five types of salmon, each one possessing a different characteristic, making catching each

British Columbia   (Go Fishing Canada)

FOREIGN FORAYS

type a unique experience. If that doesn't stir the emotions, then how about the prospect of catching a 70lb plus salmon, the king of all salmon, the 'Chinook' as it is known by the Indians, or simply as the King salmon. However you refer to it, there can be no experience like it. With reports of 4 to 5 hour battles, the thrill of landing one of these beautiful specimens will cap even the most travelled and experienced of fisherman's careers. It should be said that a lot of the fishing in British Columbia for salmon is run on a highly commercial basis, where you go out on trawler-like boats, and almost dredge the waters for salmon using three rigs of many lures, known as trolling, for the salmon to hang themselves on, rather like hanging coats on a coatstand. If all you want to do is to say 'I've caught a 70lb salmon' then that's fine, the Campbell river will suit your requirements perfectly. If you don't, then don't despair, the sports fisherman is still offered an abundance of fishing, the whole enjoyment and just as important the pride of catching a fish using the more traditional methods. The five species of salmon to be found in British Columbia are the Chinook, the Chum, the Coho, the Pink and the Sockeye. Each one offers a different and exciting challenge. The Chinook after taking the line will dive to the depths of the river or lake in an effort to shake you off. It can be a long and tiring struggle, but I'm sure you'll agree it is well worth it for the chance of landing a 70 pounder. The Coho will put up a fight, no less ferocious, but certainly more spectacular with many often leaping and dancing clear of the water, a spectacle to behold.

British Columbia also offers some 22,000 lakes with rainbow trout predominating, boasting the freshwater fly world record (IGFA) of 28 lb, taken on the Skeena River, these waters also have Brook trout and wild cut-throat trout, which, if caught,

you are particularly asked to release unharmed. You can also find some marvellous Steelhead fishing rainbows who have migrated to the sea and returned, so as you can imagine, a Rainbow with 2 years' ocean experience on top of its natural fighting instincts is a formidable foe. In the north you can fish for Arctic grayling in the colder clearer waters; look out also for the Dolly Varden trout, a local good quality fish.

It does sound like a fishing paradise and it comes very close to being one. There are few, if any, places that can offer sport of this stature anywhere in the world and if you wish to fish here, you have a good choice of specialist tour operators who will try and make your daydreams become reality. Abercrombie & Kent (071)-730-9600; Ker & Downey (071)-629-2044; Anglers World Holidays (0246) 221717; Go Fishing-Canada (0371) 876785; Fresh Adventures Ltd (0462) 816424; British Columbia House (071)-930-6857.

Canada, as you have read, has an abundance of fishing to suit every enthusiast from, the relative beginner up to the veteran of many waters. It's hard for us to put into words exactly what the whole experience is like, so to really appreciate its waters, you will have to travel there yourself.

If after reading about Canada you have the impression that it has all the world's best fishing, you'd be mistaken for although it does have a wealth of marvellous fishing, it certainly doesn't have a monopoly. Chile, the next country we take a look at, has every reason to stake its claim as having some of the world's best fishing as do all of the countries the rest of the section is devoted to.

River Frio   (S.S. Valdes-Scott)

FOREIGN FORAYS

'Manitoba - Northwest Territories - quite simply it is the most exciting, underfished trout fishing in the world, fishing for the worlds biggest trout.'

John Wilson, 'Go Fishing' Television programme

'Sport fishing visitors to the Yukon will not only remember the exceptional fishing for native Lake trout, Dolly Varden trout, rainbow trout, Arctic grayling, pike and four salmon species. They will marvel at the natural beauty of the midnight sun. They will also experience the legends of the Klondike gold rush days nearly a century ago and take with them some of the friendly independent spirit which lives on in Yukon's 25,000 residents.'

Don Toews, Fisheries Department - Yukon Government.

'The Bow River (Alberta) provides the finest dry fly fishing for rising rainbow that I have experienced anywhere in the world.'

Leigh Perkins, CEP of Orvis, Fishing Tackle Manufacturer.

'Anglers agree the Bow River in Alberta offers the finest fly-fishing in North America. Fly-in fishing in remote northern Alberta fishing lodges provides the ultimate in trophy fishing.'

L. Dowling, Director of Tourism.

'Quebec, with 18% of the world's fresh water supply and over a million lakes, is a land of fishing thrills second to none. With almost all of the most sought after species with trout, salmon and Arctic char found in abundance there.'

Michel Leblanc, Official of Marcel Gignac, the Government of Quebec.

'Saskatchewan has some of the finest fresh water fishing in North America. Here you can catch trophy size Lake trout, Northern pike, pickerel and Arctic grayling.
With its many fishing lodges and wilderness campgrounds Saskatchewan allows you to return to nature in its grandest setting, without giving up the comforts of civilization.'

Ted Hornung, Official of the Government of Saskatchewan.

A life-time experience:-grandeur, challenge, limitless excitement-primeval wilderness, soaring eagles, massive whales, towering forests -and the marvellous harvest of the North Pacific is yours to seek
There's nothing like it!'

Garde B. Gardom Q.C., Agent General of British Columbia.

The world records mentioned here are recorded by the IGFA (The International Game Fish Association) using their methods of verification; and the records are either for fly fishing only with the occasional record being for the all time weight which does not specify technique used. The Association was formed in 1939 and only records catches that they could personally verify are mentioned, so it explains why Mrs Ballantine's salmon is not included in their records. We can only hope that one day your name and catch will be included in their number.

Labrador   (Go Fishing Canada)

EXPERIENCE CANADA
WITH ANGLERS WORLD HOLIDAYS

The Northwest Territories and North Manitoba, situated in Canada's far north, are home to huge Lake Trout and beautiful Arctic Grayling. A number of angling lodges have been carefully selected by Anglers World Holidays each offering some of the world's finest freshwater game fishing in an exclusive environment. A catch and release policy is applied to ensure the finest game fishing is continued. The exception is shore lunch, when an occasional trout and few grayling are taken for a delicious shore lunch cook-out -- a welcome midday break from arm aching sport.

Nueltin Lake Lodge. North Manitoba. Lake Nueltin. A delightful series of rustic individual log cabins surrounding the main lodge of modern timber construction which houses a fine restaurant and lounge. Facilities include private showers, all meals, bar, library, tackle shop, guide service, boats and unlimited fishing. Nueltin Lake and surrounding waters amount to 14,000 square miles of prime fishing, shared by only 40 anglers per week over a ten week season, exclusive fishing by any comparison.

Ferguson Lake Lodge. NWT. Ferguson Lake and River. A rustic old mining camp tastefully converted into a fine and exclusive angling lodge. You are close to the Arctic Circle and above the treeline at Ferguson. Here huge herds of Caribou and occasional musk ox and grizzley bear roam the arctic tundra. Accommodation comprises of twin rooms with ensuite facilities and the main lodge houses a relaxing lounge with bar and "Prospectors" dining room. Boats, guides, all meals and unlimited fishing are included. The Ferguson River which links innumerable lakes, has streamy glides and deep crystal pools literally teaming with Grayling and Lake Trout.

Lake Trout are ferocious and aggressive feeders, taking advantage of the short but warm summer months. Sport is virtually guaranteed with fish averaging 18lb but many are caught (and released) in the twenty, thirty and forty pound class. The biggest Lake Trout recorded weighed 109lbs. Lake Trout will take large flies and brightly coloured spoons with equal enthusiasm. Fly rods should be strong (8/9/10 class) and leaders of 10lb strength.

Arctic Grayling are most energetic fighters of immense beauty. With a large sail-like dorsal fin, edged with red, silver and blue flanks with black "freckles" these graceful fish take wet and dry flies with great zest. They are to be found both in the shallow crystal clear bays and the north's cold clear rivers - in great abundance. To catch 40-60 grayling in a day is not exceptional. They average 1-2lbs with occasional fish from 3-4lbs. Dry and wet flies work well throughout the season, and in late summer a small mepps also works well.

These lodges are accessed by private charter plane from Winnipeg and Rankin Inlet (the only means of access). AWH also offer coach tours, city stop-overs and self drive cars and campers for clients wishing to extend their stay and explore more of Canada.

Anglers World Holidays
46 Knifesmithgate
Chesterfield
Derbyshire S40 1RQ
Tel: (0246) 221717
Fax: (0246) 824515

GO FISHING CANADA

Go Fishing - Canada specialises in fly-fishing holidays to Canada as the name indicates. The company offers a wide range of fishing packages. There are fishing holidays that will appeal to the fly fishing experts as well as the less experienced angler, fishing families and fishermen accompanied by non fishing companions.

Canada has been described as a fishing paradise. Those visiting the eastern Canada venues of Labrador, Newfoundland, Nova Scotia and New Brunswick can expect to enjoy large runs of Atlantic Salmon and Sea Trout. In Labrador there are also huge Arctic Char and Northern Pike to catch. If you choose the superb fishing in the wilderness of Northern Labrador you have to fly in by float-plane to your fishing lodge, an experience in itself.

Alternatively, there are the more gentle and enticing attractions of the other two eastern seaboard provinces. Here one will find the world famous rivers of Nova Scotia; the Margaree and the Stewiacke and the superb Miramichi river in New Brunswick. All offer equally exciting prospects for the salmon and trout fisherman: south eastern Canada provides a leisure experience that can be enjoyed by those who fly-fish and their non-fishing companions.

Fishermen visiting British Columbia on the western seaboard of Canada will enjoy lifetime-lasting memories of fishing some of the most prolific Pacific Salmon rivers in the world. In addition, Go Fishing-Canada features holidays to the Babine River where Trophy Steelhead have the reputation of being the world's best fighting game fish.

Some splendidly exciting, specimen trout fishing is also to be found in the beautiful rivers of Ontario; the Albany and the Sutton.

For the truly dedicated fly-fishing expert the Moisie river in Quebec, the home of the famous Seize-Vingt Club were 20lbs salmon are fished for with flies tied on size 16 hooks, will be an inescapable challenge.

Go Fishing-Canada will be happy to tailor a fishing package designed to fit your individual requirements. In the first instance, please contact one of our staff on the telephone number given below.

Go Fishing - Canada
Paddon House
12 Stortford Road
Great Dunmow
Essex CM6 1DA
Tel: (0371) 876785
Fax: (0371) 873899

FOREIGN FORAYS

CHILE

The trout you will fish for in Chile were introduced at the turn of the century, they took to the perfect conditions that Chile has to offer, clean unpolluted waters and now rainbow and brown trout thrive in these lakes and rivers. If this, in itself, does not tempt, many of the fish are now migratory and return as Steelhead and sea-trout and it is more for these fish that Chile is famed. Those of you who have fished for either will appreciate the magnificent sport that they both offer.

The best rivers in the Lake District are the San Pedro, the Pretrohue and the Golgol. The beauty of fishing in Chile is that not only is the sport superb, the scenery unforgettable, but the summers in Chile are perfect for enjoying your favourite pastime. Patagonia, the fjord country of Chile, also offers some marvellous fishing. The lake district is heavily fished, although in no way am I suggesting that it is fished out. The rivers to head for in Patagonia for Steelhead and sea-trout are the Simpson, the Cisnes, the Plaena, the Baker and its tributary, the Cocherin, whilst the Nirehuao is famous for brown trout. You may be surprised to learn that you can also fish for King and Coho salmon. They were first introduced in the late seventies to early eighties and there have been a few reported sightings of the salmon returning to their spawning grounds, with the experiment repeated three years ago, but only time will tell whether they will have taken to these waters. You may, of course, raise a few eyebrows when you return home purporting to have fished for salmon in Chile, but at the moment it is a little known secret. Who knows, it may become the warm alternative to British Columbia. It seems odd that, with the rivers teeming with some exceptional sport already, the locals would bother trying to introduce new species, although financially salmon have always been a lucrative lure to fishermen. There are two specialist tour operators who offer great packages to Chile, Abercrombie & Kent (071)-730-9600 and Sport Elite Ltd. (0935) 891477.

River Warrah (Falkland Island Tourism)

THE FALKLAND ISLANDS

The Falkland Islands will, of course, be known to all of you as a place of conflict in 1982, but perhaps what you are less aware of, is that it is a marvellous venue for the serious game fisherman. If you're a bit concerned about your fishing break being marred by the military presence, although there are still 2000 active troops on the Islands and you will see the occasional military vehicle on the roads, the vast majority of the Falklands goes on as though nothing ever happened.

The brown trout were introduced to the Falkland Islands almost 40 years ago, as the only trout nature endowed the Islands with was the Falkland trout, which isn't technically a trout or even a char. The brown trout quickly adapted and a fast growing migratory strain soon established itself and very soon populated most of the Islands' rivers. These give us today some of the world's best sea trout fishing, the record to date taken on a fly was caught on the Malo and weighed in at over 20lb. A larger fish was taken of 23lb but it was caught using a spinner.

The rivers to look out for are the Chartres (subject to availability of accommodation), the Warrah on West Falkland, and the San Carlos on East Falkland.

Most of the rivers are fishable for Brown trout, but they tend to be small, a symptom of the acidity of the rivers.

You may be thinking that although the fishing sounds very tempting it's a long way to go to what many think to be a barren, cold and inhospitable place to fish for large sea trout.

Success (Falkland Islands Tourism)

Goose Green (Falkland Islands Tourism)

FOREIGN FORAYS

Well, you will be surprised to learn that the summers are remarkably temperate with weather very similar to that of eastern England, and is still warmer during winter, as the Falklands lie on the same latitude south as London is north. On top of this, you will be surrounded by what is literally a conservation park, full of elephant seals, dolphins and numerous species of birds.

The lodges you'll be staying in operate honesty bars, where you settle up at the end of your stay, but drink is remarkably cheap due to the different taxation laws. Port Stanley does have 5 pubs, so it's worth popping in to meet the locals.

The only way to get to the Falklands at the moment is by RAF Tristar, but if that panics you Abercrombie and Kent (071)-730-9600 and Sport Elite Tours (093589) 477 have complete packages for fishing the Falklands.

FINLAND

Like Canada, Finland offers the fisherman the complete choice of game fishing. Being so long the landscape changes gradually along its entire length from gently rolling hills in the south to the mountainous regions of the north with elevation of over 1000 feet. It is known as the land of 10,000 lakes, but after an exhaustive study the true count is just a little under 188,000. Finland also offers a wide selection of wild animals, with 65 species, bears, wolves, 120,000 elk and the Finnish equivalent of the cow, the reindeer!

Back to the form of wildlife you are primarily interested in, the fish. Atlantic salmon can be found in good numbers in the Teno, Tornio Naatamo, Simo and Kiiminkl rivers, in fact, Finland's record salmon caught in the Tornio was just over 94lb. Information on how it was landed is not available, but may I suggest - with a little help from his friends! The restrictions they impose is that the salmon must be over 60cm to be retained, and, thankfully, due to an active stocking programme, the numbers of salmon are increasing.

Sea-trout, which have improved once again due to heavy stocking, thrive even in the waters around Helsinki, with the record being 41lb but the average being more around the 6-10lb mark. Again the named salmon rivers are where you'll find the sea trout.

In the big lakes, primarily of southern Finland, and the rivers and lakes of Lapland, you'll find a good number of brown trout. Lapland boasts the record, with a brown trout weighing close to 34lb being caught from Lake Inari. Father Christmas was not involved in the catch!

In many of the areas where you'll find brown trout you will also find the brook trout, especially in the north of Finland, and because of this you are asked to return all trout under the length of 32 centimetres, as the brook trout is almost indistinguishable from the young brown trout. In this way the brown trout will be allowed, hopefully, to grow to spawning size and help continue its presence in these waters.

You may be lucky to catch an Artic char, although they are quite rare, if you're fishing on the lakes in Lapland or very occasionally in Lake Saimaa, Finland's largest water system.

Grayling are again found in suitably large numbers primarily in

the north and east of Finland, and they are a favourite of a number of fly fisherman because of their intense fighting spirit. A grayling of 15lb which is rare, was caught at Lake Konnevesi in central Finland. They are also a very tasty fish when grilled.

When fishing in Finland the best people to contact are Lapland Travel (010 358) 6016052.

ICELAND

There are some countries in this world where you could be forgiven for thinking that they were specifically designed with the fisherman in mind. Iceland is one of them. It is a land of cold fast flowing rivers, enormous glaciers and countless lakes.

It is also volcanic, the 'zone' as it's referred to is approximately 25,000 square kilometres, with 10% of the country being glacier while 50% is covered with trees like birch and willows together with alpine sub-artic Flora.

So once again you can enjoy your favourite sport in some splendid surroundings. There are numerous species of birds, puffins, guillemots, gannets, a large colony of seals, with over 7 species of whales in the territorial waters.

Although the climate of Iceland is milder than you might expect due to the Gulf Stream, it is still affected by quick changes in the weather and high winds.

Another feature of Iceland is 24 hours of daylight during the summer months (21st June through to August) so if you are into long stints then Iceland will accommodate you.

Due to the esteem in which Iceland's salmon rivers are held worldwide, there are 60 salmon rivers, over half being classified as first class, they are difficult to get on and obviously are quite expensive but if you can afford it they offer some of the best Atlantic salmon fishing in the world. Iceland is very keen to promote alternative fishing as the salmon fishing is always booked well in advance of the season opening. There are 1500 trout rivers and lakes so you can keep the expense of a fishing trip to Iceland reasonable by mixing two or three days salmon fishing with some very good trout fishing, with the occasional surprise of a salmon in most of the lakes.

The best areas for brown trout, char and sea-trout are Lake Medalfellsvatn near Mount Esja, 3 lakes north of Hvalfjorour, Geitabergsvatn, Porisstaoavatn and Eyrarvatn, and some other superb sport can be found on six small lakes on Snaefellsnes peninsula, the Vatnsholtsa lakes. If you prefer river fishing, the Bruara east of Rejykjavik and Varma and Thorleifslaekur near Reykjavik offer some good char fishing.

The best people to contact for fishing in Iceland are Icelandair (071)-388-5599 and Artic Experience Limited (0737) 362321.

There is one point that fisherman should be aware of. To prevent the spreading of infectious diseases of freshwater fish to Iceland from other countries, the wearing of waders, rubbers boots and other equipment that has been used in other waters is prohibited unless it has been disinfected for 10 minutes in a solution of 2% formaldehyde and a valid certificate from a authorised veterinary officer is acceptable if presented on entering Iceland.

FOREIGN FORAYS

NEW ZEALAND

Having travelled to one side of the earth visiting Canada we now travel to the other side, New Zealand. It is renowned for some of the finest trout fishing in some of the most spectacular scenery you will find anywhere in the world, a formidable partnership to beat.

There are dozens of rivers that run from the mountains into the sea, where you will find good fishing for rainbows and brownies and their migratory cousins, steelhead and sea-trout. Although the fishing here can often be excellent, it is not this fishing that New Zealand is famed for. The best and most prolific fishing is enjoyed in the lake systems where most of the fishing is reserved for fly only; so it is again the venue for the purist. It is fair to say that two distinct categories describe New Zealand's fishing: Rotorua and Taupo for rainbow and steelhead fishing. This is primarily winter fishing, the best lakes being Taupo and Tarawera, with the Tongariro River offering some rugged sport. The winter season runs April to September/October, the summer fishing runs from October to April.

Travelling to the South Island, you will find some good salmon fishing in the Rakaia, Wainmakariri, Rangitata, Ashburton and Waitaki rivers, the season in the south is from October to April with the months of January, February and March being the prime months, but be prepared to get up early as that's when you'll experience the best that's on offer. Although spinning is the primary method of fishing, slowly but surely the pursuits are educating the locals and fly fishing is becoming more and more popular. Take the time to explore the culture of New Zealand, the Maori's are well known for their friendliness as long as you are not frightened off by the Haka, although I am assured that it is kept now only for ceremonial and public events, and of course for the All Blacks.

To organise your fishing trip to New Zealand, Abercrombie & Kent 071-730-9600 will be happy to advise and organise tailor made packages.

NORWAY

As our final country to be featured we look towards Norway, last but in no way least, as many keen fisherman will know of Norway's reputation; for many the mecca for salmon and sea-trout fishing in Europe and possibly the world. Norway is the home of the fjord, where a superb vista of mountains and trees awaits you. Anglers are fortunate that in all the places we have featured, and Norway is no exception, they can enjoy some of the world's best fishing in some of the worlds most memorable scenery.

Although we are not awarding marks for different rivers, it is important that you are aware that the Vosso ranks in the top five salmon rivers in the world, although most of the fishing is done by spinning. It isn't as good as it used to be but still the average catch, since records began 100 years ago, maintains at a remarkable 25lb. Unlike the great Icelandic rivers, it is not horrendously expensive to fish the Vosso but the waiting list can be long.

Other beats in Norway are much sought after, particularly on such renowned waters as the Tana and the Alta, which, boasts a number of world records (IGFA) using fly fishing techniques

with a fish of 38 lb 8 oz being caught in 1983. Laerdal, the Driva (Once a very good river, has suffered recently due to a virus gyro-dactilus which unfortunately kills the smolts) Eira, Orkla, Gaula, Aaro, Aa and Surna are also good, but they do command some high prices.

Some relatively inexpensive fishing can be had by staying at the hotels who own private stretches, this is especially true in the North. The best salmon fishing is in June and July, although the season is longer extending from May to September 5th, with the best sea-trout fishing being in August, it offers the perfect way of finishing off the season.

If the cost of salmon fishing proves prohibitive there are some marvellous alternatives, in brown trout and char fishing. Around Oslo there are numerous well stocked lakes and streams, if you don't mind travelling further a field, 25 pound trout have been caught on the Randselvern, the Drammen and on Norway's largest lake the Mjosa.

In the deep cold mountain lakes Artic chars prefer, you will be rewarded with the thrilling sport the char are famed for, although as many will know, it is a difficult art, many years in the learning. To fish in Norway may we suggest Abercrombie & Kent (071)-730-9600, Ker and Downey (071)-629-2044 and Fresh Adventures (0462) 8164224.

We've hopefully stirred your emotions in looking outside of the confines of the British Isles for your next fishing foray or the trip of a lifetime, the culmination, if you like, of all those days that went unrewarded. I think that most of you will agree that if you have spent twenty years fishing or more, contenting yourself with the occasional 12lb fish, you deserve to fish for the big fish, at least once. All of the fishing described here is without equal so choosing which country will be difficult, but I am sure most will warm to the prospect of knowing the only decision you really face is in what surroundings you want to find yourselves.

As a final note; to allow all fisherman, now and in the future, the chance of enjoying fishing for trophy sized fish, everywhere in the world, if you are not going to eat it, release it. They are beautiful creatures to watch when they are left in their natural surroundings, they loose all their beauty when surrounded by wood and glass, so enjoy the sport for now and the future. The thought of great rivers like the Miramichi or the Margaree being fishless is one of the saddest things I can think of.

THE GAME ANGLING CODE

A guide to good practice prepared by the Salmon & Trout Association, in conjunction with leading conservation and angling bodies with support from Laphroaig.

THE PRINCIPLES OF THE CODE

Environment

All anglers should be actively concerned in protecting the environment.

Conservation

Fishing and the management of fisheries, should be conducted so that healthy fish populations are maintained.

Behaviour

Moderation, courtesy and consideration for others are the marks of a sporting angler.

The Sport

There is more to fishing than catching fish.

INTRODUCTION

Rod fishing is a traditional and pleasurable pastime. As more people take up the sport of game fishing there is increasing pressure on wild fish stocks and more demand is put on the limited space on rivers, lakes and lochs; at the same time there is an increasing public concern for the environment and for wildlife.

The purpose of this Code is to encourage proper standards of sportsmanship among game anglers and those who manage and regulate game fishing and help them show regard for the environment, the sport, their quarry and for each other. All involved with game angling are expected to obey the relevant laws and fishery regulations and to avoid any behaviour which might bring the sport into disrepute. In this Code, Game Angling covers fishing for salmon, sea-trout, grayling and char.

LAPHROAIG®

SINGLE ISLAY MALT
SCOTCH WHISKY

FISHERY OWNERS AND MANAGERS

Standards

The Code expects that all owners, managers, associations and clubs will set and maintain high standards of sportsmanship and encourage mutual courtesy among rods fishing their own and adjacent waters.

Conservation

Wherever there are wild fish, angling pressure should be regulated to ensure that the natural stock can regenerate and be preserved. Where there is any danger of over-fishing, owners and managers of fisheries should control catches by adopting some of the following measures;

By limiting the use of certain baits or methods of fishing

By voluntary alteration of the number of days fished

By introducing catch limits daily, weekly or annually

By discouraging the sale of rod caught fish by anglers

By limiting the number of rods or fishing effort.

Fishing Methods

This general Code cannot attempt to define the proper use of all legal fishing methods in every locality and in varying water and weather conditions. Appropriate fishing methods are established by regulation and often by tradition. Where particular baits or methods of fishing are reasonably damaging to fishing stocks or to the interest of other anglers, or are seen locally to be unsporting, they should be prohibited.

Stocked Fisheries

Many fisheries, both stillwater and river, depend on regular stocking. Stocking should take account of the ability of the water to support, in a healthy condition, the number of fish introduced.

Natural populations of wild fish need to be preserved. Stocking policies should take account of the risk involved by the introduction of conflicting species. To avoid genetic change through inter-breeding, local broodstock should be used wherever possible.

Fishery Managers should set catch limits (in size and numbers) and have a clearly understandable policy on fish to be returned. They should keep, and are encouraged to publish, accurate records of numbers and weights of fish stocked and caught.

Competitive Game Fishing

Rules for fishing competitions should comply with the principles of this code.

THE GAME ANGLING CODE

RESPONSIBILITIES

Owners and managers are encouraged to:

Draw up and publish fishery rules based on this Code

Provide adequate supervision to ensure compliance

Co-operate with adjacent fisheries in implementing this Code

Make provision for local anglers

Owners and fishery managers should call for the introduction of bye-laws or regulations by the relevant authority wherever this is necessary to ensure that the principles of this Code are applied.

THE GAME ANGLER

The Environment

Good anglers are the watch-dogs of the water and its environment. Any sign of deterioration must be reported immediately to the fishery manager and the appropriate authority in the area. The report should include:

'What' has been noted

'Where' the occurrence was spotted

'When' the event was noticed

'The extent' of any pollution

Anglers should take great care to avoid damage to the waterside or disturbance to wildlife. No tackle or litter must be discarded and particular regard should be paid to the hazards to wild life from monofilament nylon.

The Fish

Fish retained for food should be promptly and efficiently despatched. All other fish should be released as quickly as possible. Fish should only be handled with wetted hands; they should never be thrown back into the water, but held facing upstream in running water until they swim free. Where 'Catch and release' is practised, barbless hooks are recommended.

Fishing Conduct

Angling as a sport and recreation is a fragile and personal experience which can so easily be disrupted by external interference. However, water space is in great demand both from anglers and other activities and therefore its enjoyment has to be shared. The following points should be observed by every angler:

Ensure you have permission to fish and a rod licence where appropriate

Observe the bounds of any beat to which you have been assigned

Be prepared to give way after you have fished a drift or pool and never fish too long in one place

Never crowd or obstruct an angler near to you on the bank or in a boat

Do not walk into or cut across another person's fishing and avoid unnecessary wading

Give consideration to anglers on the opposite bank

Make sure you can distinguish between takeable and non takeable fish

Where there are no bag limits, exercise restraint in the number of fish taken, particularly when fish are easily caught

Accept that the 'blank days' are part of the experience of fishing

Acknowledge considerate behaviour by other legitimate water users

Follow the Country Code, particularly in relation to the control of dogs, the risk of fires and fastening gates

Wear unobtrusive clothing and respect the peace of the countryside

Do not park vehicles so that they obstruct gateways or cause a hazard on the road

Support the organisations which safeguard your sport

Safety

All anglers should be aware of the inherent dangers of fishing, not only to themselves but to others. They should:

Wear head and eye protection, particularly when casting in windy conditions

Look behind before casting

Keep rods and lines away from overhead electric power lines

In an electric storm cease fishing put the rod down and move well away from it

When wading in difficult conditions, use a wading stick and always have one foot firmly on the river bed before moving the other

Wear personal buoyancy aids wherever appropriate and be familiar with the location and use of any other buoyancy or life saving equipment provided by fishery owners

Be prepared to help anyone in difficulty.

SUGGESTIONS FOR INCLUSION

Our constant aim is to provide an accurate, up-to-date and valuable guide to the best places to eat and stay throughout the country. An exhaustive guide is an ambitious objective and can only be achieved with the assistance of our readers. We would therefore be grateful for any recommendations of hostelries of distinction that have not been included in our publications, together with your comments on just what makes them worthy of inclusion. Equally as important are those establishments which for whatever reason fail to reach the high standards for which we originally included them.

The reasons for your proposal are naturally subjective and you may or may not wish to list them. However obvious qualities necessary for a hotel to be considered include the standard of accommodation (with cleanliness and value just as important as luxury), the quality and variety of the food on offer, the service and the atmosphere. We can't promise to include every suggestion but we will try, even if it means a jaunt there ourselves, just to double-check!

The form below details the information that we need, although you may wish to send your comments on a separate sheet of paper. All correspondence received will be treated with the utmost confidentiality and the sender will also be entered into a prize draw with three complete sets of the Kensington West Collection (Following the Fairways, Holiday Golf Guide, Fishing Forays, Excursions into Britain's Heritage and Travelling the Turf) to be won.

NAME OF ESTABLISHMENT:

ADDRESS:

YES SHOULD BE INCLUDED:

NO SHOULD NOT BE INCLUDED:

REASONS (optional!):

THE KENSINGTON WEST COLLECTION

Kensington West publish a range of fine sporting and leisure publications, designed to suit the interest and pocket of every leisure enthusiast. Each book is lavishly illustrated and contains extensive and up-to-date information on a range of leisure activities, together with invaluable advice on nearby places of repute (and occasionally of ill-repute!) to eat and stay.

If you have enjoyed this guide, why not acquire one of its distinguished companions. Each edition makes a beautiful addition to any library and will provide endless informative pleasure as both a guidebook and an enjoyable reading experience. Make your selection from the following eminent titles.

Travelling the Turf (seventh edition).

The complete guide to the racecourses of Great Britain and Ireland. TTT incorporates colour maps, extensive illustrations, many previously unpublished racing scenes with illuminating and witty analysis of every aspect of the racing scene. Comprehensive features on hotels, restaurants, pubs and B & B's are backed up with points and places of interest for the non-racegoer. A powerful resume of the world's most stylish sport.

Following the Fairways (fifth edition)

The complete guide to the golf courses of Great Britain and Ireland. FTF contains an exhaustive directory of over 2,000 golf courses and in-depth features on seventy five of the nation's most celebrated tests. The guide is superbly illustrated throughout with many rare examples of golfing art and contemporary golfing landscapes. Some 2,000 practical ideas for places to stay and entertainment off the course make FTF a priceless guide for every golfer. An authoritative guide to the world's fastest growing leisure pursuit.

Fishing Forays

This latest addition to the Kensington collection embraces in-depth appraisals of famous beats, maps of lochs, lakes and rivers with helpful tips for beginners to the sport on where to fish. The usual comprehensive guide to where to stay and eat out combines to make Fishing Forays a treasured addition to any fisherman's library. An engaging summary of one of the world's most exclusive sports.

Excursions into Britain's Heritage

The cream of Britain and Ireland's Stately Homes, gardens, castles and country houses make this a lavish and not to be missed publication. Over one hundred of our most regal buildings are described in an informative, graphic and lively style, complemented by illustrations and photographs of a variety of paintings and memorabilia from the houses themselves. Additional coverage is given to over 1000 alternative historical sites, with essential recommendations of where to stay and eat out nearby. A beautifully illustrated and practical guide to one of the world's most enviable historical collections.

The Holiday Golf Guide

Of the plethora of books offering advice on where to golf throughout the world, the HGG is undoubtedly the most authoritative and the most colourfully presented. An almost unbelievable amount of information is packed into this comprehensive handbook, and lavish photography is sure to make many of the destinations an irresistible attraction. Golfing information is backed up with all manner of enticements for non-golfing companions.

'The best guide to the best courses all over the world.'

Please send me the following books at **£13.95** each or **£59.95** for all five titles:-

	Quantity	Value
Travelling The Turf 1992		
Following the Fairways 1992		
Fishing Forays 1992		
Excursions into Britain's Heritage 1992		
Holiday Golf Guide 1991/92		
1. I enclose a cheque/postal order for £_____		
2. Please debit my visa/mastercard for £_____		

Cheque (payable to KWP Ltd.) / Access / Visa

Card no._____

Expiry date_____

Name: _

Address: _

_ _